P9-APT-204

Economic development, the family, and income distribution

STUDIES IN ECONOMIC HISTORY AND POLICY
THE UNITED STATES IN THE TWENTIETH CENTURY

Edited by
Louis Galambos and Robert Gallman

Other books in the series:

Peter D. McClelland and Alan L. Magdovitz: *Crisis in the making: the political economy of New York State since 1945*
Hugh Rockoff: *Drastic measures: a history of wage and price controls in the United States*
William N. Parker: *Europe, America, and the wider world: essays on the economic history of Western capitalism*
Richard H. K. Vietor: *Energy policy in America since 1945: a study of business–government relations*
Christopher L. Tomlins: *The state and the unions: labor relations, law, and the organized labor movement in America, 1880–1960*
Leonard S. Reich: *The making of American industrial research: science and business at GE and Bell, 1876–1926*
Margaret B. W. Graham: *RCA and the VideoDisc: the business of research*
Michael A. Bernstein: *The great depression: delayed recovery and economic change in America, 1929–1939*
Michael J. Hogan: *The Marshall Plan: America, Britain, and the reconstruction of Western Europe, 1947–1952*
David A. Hounshell and John Kenly Smith, Jr.: *Science and corporate strategy: Du Pont R&D, 1902–1980*
Moses Abramovitz: *Thinking about growth and other essays on economic growth and welfare*

Simon Kuznets

Economic development, the family, and income distribution

Selected essays

SIMON KUZNETS

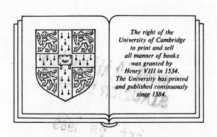

The right of the
University of Cambridge
to print and sell
all manner of books
was granted by
Henry VIII in 1534.
The University has printed
and published continuously
since 1584.

Cambridge University Press

Cambridge

New York   New Rochelle   Melbourne   Sydney

HD
75
K88
1989

Published by the Press Syndicate of the University of Cambridge
The Pitt Building, Trumpington Street, Cambridge CB2 1RP
32 East 57th Street, New York, NY 10022, USA
10 Stamford Road, Oakleigh, Melbourne 3166, Australia

© Cambridge University Press 1989

First published 1989

Printed in the United States of America

Library of Congress Cataloging-in-Publication Data
Kuznets, Simon Smith, 1901–1985.
Economic development, the family, and income distribution:
selected essays / Simon Kuznets.
p. cm. – (Studies in economic history and policy)
"Bibliography of Simon Kuznets": p.
Includes index.
ISBN 0-521-34384-4
1. Economic development. 2. Income distribution. 3. Developing
countries – Economic conditions. I. Title.
III. Series.
HD75.K88 1989   88-20244
338.9–dc19   CIP

British Library Cataloguing in Publication Data
Kuznets, Simon, 1901–1985
Economic development, the family, and
income distribution: selected essays.
– (Studies in economic history and
policy: the United States in the twentieth
century)
1. Economic development 2. United States.
Income. Distribution inequalities
I. Title II. Series
330.9

ISBN 0-521-34384-4

ROBERT MANNING
STROZIER LIBRARY

SEP 28 1989

Tallahassee, Florida

Contents

Preface

In the late spring of 1985 Simon Kuznets selected a set of his recent essays that he thought would make a useful book. He died (July 9, 1985) before he was able to arrange for their publication. We subsequently learned of his plans through Moses Abramovitz, read the manuscript, decided that the project should certainly be completed, and prevailed upon Professor Kuznets's widow, Edith, to allow us to bring the book out in this series. Two of Professor Kuznets's former students, Richard Easterlin and Robert Fogel, agreed to provide us with a Foreword and an Afterword, while Edith Kuznets took on the difficult task of editing Simon Kuznets's bibliography for the volume. We thank Professors Abramovitz, Easterlin, and Fogel, and particularly, Mrs. Kuznets for their cooperation.

Simon Kuznets was born in Russia in 1901 and came to the United States in 1922. He studied at Columbia with Wesley Mitchell, whose influence on him was profound. In 1926 he received the Ph.D. and shortly thereafter joined the National Bureau of Economic Research, where he met his future wife, Edith Handler. He was made director of the Bureau's national income project, in which capacity he designed the national accounts and supervised their construction. Subsequently he organized and carried out research on various aspects of economic change, most notably long swings (often called Kuznets cycles, in honor of his work on them), changes in the size distribution of income, and the processes of economic growth and economic development. It was his work on economic development that won him the Nobel Prize in Economics in 1971. He had previously been honored with election to the offices of president of the American Statistical Association (1949) and president of the American Economic Association (1954).

From 1930 until his retirement from teaching (he never retired from research), Kuznets regularly divided his time between research and the classroom. At various times he held academic appointments at the University of Pennsylvania, Johns Hopkins, and Harvard. He was a brilliant teacher, although it is doubtful that he ever gave a moment's thought to the *techniques* of teaching. His success came from his immense interest in and clear commitment to scholarly work, from the sense he conveyed that the work bore on large social issues and could have important results, and from his analytical brilliance, creativity, and erudition. The students in his classes came to believe that scholarly work is cumulative and that each of them could have a part in the advance of knowledge. His classes were pervaded by the excitement of discovery and were absolutely unforgettable.

In teaching and research, Kuznets was dedicated to work that would have social consequences. His research was explicitly connected with policy questions during his time as associate director of the Bureau of Planning and Statistics of the U.S. War Production Board from 1942 to 1944. But throughout the rest of his career his purpose was not so much to settle specific policy issues as it was to build an empirical account of the economy resting on a firm theoretical structure. This account, he believed, would provide a basis for sensible policy positions. His design and construction of the national accounts figured crucially in the development of modern fiscal policy and in the study of modern economic growth.

The essays in this collection are vintage Kuznets. Since Richard Easterlin devotes much of his Foreword to an analysis of them, we need say no more here than to remark that they are concerned with the process of economic growth, and that about two-thirds of the book is devoted to the topic that had been engaging Kuznets for virtually the last decade of his life: the relationships among population structure, the family, economic growth, and the size distribution of income and wealth. We are delighted to have this book in the series *Studies in Economic History and Policy: The United States in the Twentieth Century*.

Louis Galambos
Professor of History
Johns Hopkins University
Robert Gallman
Kenan Professor of Economics and History
University of North Carolina

Foreword

Simon Kuznets's scholarly work spans over half a century and includes over twenty books and several hundred articles. In terms of sheer volume it is a prodigious individual record; by any quality-adjusted measure, it is awe-inspiring. The present collection of essays and research articles, done by Kuznets when he was in his seventies and now assembled and published posthumously, helps round out the record of this remarkable scholar and individual. The volume is not a "capstone," for Kuznets's systematic search for new knowledge was never-ending. It represents, rather, the concerns at the top of his research agenda at a late phase of his career, plus several articles expounding on themes from earlier work.

I.

The first four chapters fall in the category of expounding on earlier themes. They deal with the economic epoch that Kuznets, more than any other individual, has identified and analyzed, "modern economic growth." It was for his empirically founded cross-national study of this epoch that Kuznets was awarded the 1971 Nobel prize in economics. In the first four chapters of this volume he returns to the subject, developing new insights and elaborating old. Chapters 1 and 4 deal in somewhat different fashion with what Kuznets calls the "driving forces" of economic growth. In these two chapters Kuznets departs from his usual insistence on measurement – the reader will note the absence of the usual statistical tables – to speculate on causation. Such speculation was not lacking in Kuznets's prior work, but it was infrequent, and it is good to have a sample of it here. The two essays are complementary – that in chapter 1 asks "what can we learn from history?"; that in chapter 4 is directed to today's less developed countries and speculates on the obstacles to their growth and the circumstances that may foster breakthroughs to sustained growth.

1

Chapters 2 and 3 return to questions of repeated interest to Kuznets, how production structure affects the rate of economic growth and the degree of income inequality. Production structure means here the changing allocation of resources between agriculture, industry, and services. The statistical evidence examined relates to the decade or two before 1970, and the special concern is with the effects of production structure on current comparisons between more and less developed economies.

Chapters 5 and 6 turn to the main theme of the remainder of the volume – interrelations between demographic change and income inequality. These two chapters deal with the implications of changing vital rates for inequality – in chapter 5, for a developed country, the United States, in chapter 6, for today's developing countries. The basic question is how the demographic transition – from initially high to eventually low mortality and fertility rates with associated differences by economic and social class – affects income distribution between rich and poor. Does the demographic transition increase the concentration of the population in lower income families and thus complicate the achievement of a broad-based advance in per capita income? Kuznets also notes the rising share of the elderly in the population of a developed country like the United States, and asks what this bodes for the trend in income inequality in more advanced phases of modern economic growth.

The first six chapters, one suspects, were not so much self-motivated, as responses by Kuznets to pressures from others to participate in conferences or special-purpose volumes, although chapters 5 and 6 clearly draw on some of the concurrent research reported in the subsequent chapters. With chapter 7 one turns to the issues that were the primary focus of Kuznets's research interests at the time. This chapter is a key one, from which the ensuing chapters flow. The general nature of the problems under study is readily outlined. Most studies of income inequality examine the distribution of income among families or households. But families differ in the number of their members, and if, for example, family size were typically greater in higher income families, then the distribution of income among families would not correctly reflect the distribution among persons. Moreover, because the "needs" of children are less than those of adults, systematic differences between rich and poor families in the age composition of families might undermine the pertinence of the income distribution among families, even if the number of family members were the same for all families. This consideration suggests that income inequality is better measured in terms of consumer equivalents. Finally, the magnitude of income inequality at any given time, whether among families, persons, or consumer equivalents, is sensitive to the distribution of households by age of head. A larger proportion of younger households in time 1 than time 2 would lead by the usual measures to higher point-of-time income inequality in the first situation, even if lifetime income inequality were the same in the two situations.

Anyone familiar with the demographic history of the United States since World War II is aware of the dramatic shifts in size and age composition of families, and in age of head; hence the pertinence of Kuznets's concerns to inferences regarding recent trends in American income inequality. Clearly when one turns to international comparisons among countries with widely different income levels and institutional structures, such concerns become even more pressing. For Kuznets, with his ever-present interest in long-term economic growth, such comparisons are at the forefront of his interests.

In chapter 7 Kuznets lays out this set of problems and explores their empirical significance, chiefly with American data, although some use is made of data for several other countries available at the time he was writing, in the early 1970s. Chapters 8 through 10, written subsequently, draw on a wider set of data to explore the bearing of several of the questions raised in chapter 7 on comparisons of income inequality among societies at widely different levels of development. The primary function of chapter 8 is to formulate a technique for determining to what extent international differences in average household size reflect, on the one hand, differences in the presence of children, and, on the other, differences in the proportion of adults living jointly or separately. Chapter 9 pursues the implications of this analysis for cross-sectional comparisons of income inequality for the limited number of countries for which the necessary income data are available. Chapter 10 drops the constraint imposed by the availability of income data to look specifically at the implications of household size. The motivating concern is this: if income inequality is at least partly due to inequality in the size distribution of households, then what do trends and cross-sectional differences in the size distribution of households imply for corresponding differences in income equality? Chapter 11 returns to data for the United States to develop more fully the importance of differing childbearing patterns for income inequality. Because of a strong negative association between family size and income per person, greater childbearing implies, other things constant, greater inequality. Put more starkly, some couples choose to have more children despite the depressing effect of this on per person income. What does this imply for welfare and for the long-term prospects of economic growth? With the posing of this tantalizing issue, the volume ends.

II.

In a number of ways the work here is typical of Kuznets's research more generally, and demonstrates how different was his approach to research from that in which today's economists are indoctrinated. First and foremost is Kuznets's interest in measurement. The overriding objective throughout chapters 7 through 11 is to establish the facts on income inequality. This insistence on establishing facts goes back to Kuznets's very first studies of economic time series, continues through his work on national income, and persists into his comparative studies of economic growth.

Second is the notion that measurement should not be a blind collection of numbers, but a search for theoretically meaningful measures based at least in part on the concepts of economic theory. Kuznets's aim in chapters 7 through 11 is to go beyond simple measures of income inequality to measures that provide a better indication of differences within the population in economic welfare, at a minimum by moving to a per person or per consumer equivalent basis and assessing life-cycle implications, potentially by exploring more radical notions, such as income distributions among economic and social classes (see his provocative remarks at the end of chapter 7). This emphasis on economic welfare as an object of measurement typified his earlier national income studies. It was, in fact, the neglect of this objective by governmental estimators of national income that led Kuznets to break with the "official" social accounting approach that emerged in the 1940s.

A third distinctive feature of Kuznets's approach, exemplified throughout the volume, is the comparative study of populations differing widely in levels of economic development, via international cross-sectional comparisons of developed and developing countries and through time series comparisons of the historical experience of developed countries. As was mentioned, such systematic comparisons provided the basis for Kuznets's generalizations about the nature of modern economic growth that led to his Nobel prize. But Kuznets's interest in comparative study went beyond identifying features of modern economic growth as such. It also provided a breadth of perspective, rooted in the experience of societies differing widely in time and space, that ensured one against overgeneralizing the current experience of contemporary developed market economies, as Kuznets felt was so frequently the case in much economic research.

Fourth is the logical progression of Kuznets's research, illustrated here in the manner in which the topics examined in chapters 8 through 11 unfold systematically from the initial statement in chapter 7. So, too, did Kuznets's research generally. In time series study, he proceeded from cyclical to seasonal to secular movements; in national income, from factor payments to industry-of-origin to final product estimates; in analyzing modern economic growth, from aggregate output and inputs to the allocation of resources, distribution of income, and external relations. It is this characteristic that explains the never-ending quality of Kuznets's search for knowledge.

Fifth is the reliance on simple statistical methods – chiefly, measures of central tendency, dispersion, and frequency distributions. One will not find in this volume, or in Kuznets's earlier work, the regression techniques so common in economics today, let alone more "sophisticated" methods. Why did Kuznets, whose first faculty appointment was as professor of statistics at the University of Pennsylvania, and who was elected president of the American Statistical Association in 1949, shun more elaborate methods? The answer lies in two concerns of Kuznets – first, the importance of establishing facts, and, second, the need for awareness of the *variety* of experience. Especially in his use of frequency distributions Kuznets was seeking to convey a caution against simplistic linear generalizations of the type common in regression analysis.

III.

Kuznets's approach to research, with its strong empirical emphasis, may be contrasted with that dominant in economics today. Currently the focus is wholly on hypothesis testing – statement of a formal model routed in economic theory followed by empirical testing using the latest econometric methods. Could a doctoral student today present for a dissertation topic a purely measurement thesis? Consider a topic at the heart of chapter 11 here and the focus of a lively debate currently in the United States – the economic welfare of children. Would a dissertation devoted purely to establishing the facts on this question be acceptable in a graduate economics program? One suspects not. And yet, how much of the work of Simon Kuznets is precisely of this nature? It has become common in economics to sneer at descriptive studies as "measurement without theory" (though it is doubtful that the author of this term, Tjalling Koopmans,

6   Economic development, family, and income distribution

intended it in this way). But where would economic science be today if Kuznets and all those he influenced had been discouraged from the pursuit of quantitative facts?

As several of the chapters here attest, Kuznets was not opposed to theoretical speculation, and the importance that Kuznets attached to theory as a guide to measurement has already been noted. What sets Kuznets apart from today's methodological precepts is not an absence of theory, but a view of how theory and fact are best blended. Today's methodology starts with a model deduced from economic theory and ends with testing against the "facts." In contrast, Kuznets starts with establishing facts, with careful attention to the reliability of the data and variety of experience, and uses theory (and not only economic theory) as a guide to a tentative interpretation of a specific real-world situation. For Kuznets, the real world, not economic theory, dictated the problems to be studied. One can only feel that economics today is poorer for its lack of tolerance of approaches more like Kuznets's.

As the foregoing demonstrates, in the discipline of economics Kuznets was an intellectual maverick, steadfast in his pursuit of a scholarly vision. The general nature of this vision reflects his intellectual heritage. In the history of economic thought, Kuznets stands in a line of descent tracing back through the American institutional school to the German historical school and thence to Karl Marx. The common thread is a search for laws or generalizations about long-term economic development based on comparative study of historical experience. What is unique about Kuznets's work and endows it with the prospect of more enduring success, is its foundation in quantitative measurement. In using national income as the key organizing principle of his comparative studies, Kuznets made possible the replication and extension of his work by others and thus the cumulation of a body of systematic knowledge about economic development forming the basis for tested generalizations.

The intensity of Kuznets's vision is witnessed by the fact that he pursued it relentlessly at a time when the discipline generally was moving in other directions, especially methodologically. He was a rare individual with passionate convictions about the needs for knowledge and the courage to pursue them independently, and economic science is richer because of him.

Richard A. Easterlin
University of Southern California

1. Driving forces of economic growth: what can we learn from history?

I. Introduction

In defining the scope of this paper, we had to answer several questions. First, if one necessarily deals with a limited period in the long history of mankind from the hunting-gathering tribes to the industrial societies of 1980, what should the reference period be? Second, in reflecting on economic growth, what classes and groups of societies, in the wide range of units among which mankind is divided, should we emphasize? Third, while we cannot pursue quantitative analysis here, we should be clear as to the quantitative and related criteria of economic growth. Different criteria will result in focusing our attention on different aspects of economic growth, and on different groups of driving forces. Finally, how do we deal with "driving forces," a concept for which it is difficult to establish *ex ante* empirically observable counterparts?

However carefully considered, the answers to these questions were bound to leave us with a theme so wide as to warrant only selected reflections, rather than tested and documented conclusions. We reflect on the historical record of the last two centuries, viewing it as a distinct epoch of economic growth. Yet the period is too short, in excluding important antecedents in the earlier history, particularly of what are now economically developed countries; and too long, in encompassing changes in growth trends that cannot be adequately noted here. We emphasize the record of the currently developed countries, especially of the earlier entrants, all of which were market economies; and hence neglect the totalitarian developed countries, with their distinctive mechanism and

Remark: This paper was presented at the Kiel Conference "Towards Explaining Economic Growth" which was held at the Institut für Weltwirtschaft on June 25–28, 1980. It is also to be published in the forthcoming conference volume. Weltwirtschaftliches Archiv, Band 116, Heft 3, 1980, pp. 409–431.

drives. We gauge economic growth by the long-term rise in the volume and diversity of final goods, per capita, with some attention to sectoral structure and shifts; but exclude cases where such rise was due largely to natural resources made valuable by advanced technology elsewhere, or was attained in good part by intensified efforts of workers mobilized to involve a rising proportion of the population. Finally, we comment on selected aspects of the ways by which economic growth had been attained for the range of developed market economies just indicated, in the hope that they will at least suggest the identity and characteristics of the driving forces. The relevance of the latter to economic growth, or lack of it, in countries excluded from direct discussion here, may then be considered; but this cannot be done within the limits of this paper.

The records of growth of the currently developed market economies indicate that, despite a substantial rise in the growth rate of their population, the rate of rise in per capita income was substantially higher than in the centuries preceding their entry into modern economic growth – the entry occurring over the historical span from the last quarter of the 18th century to the recent decades. This acceleration of economic growth was associated with a number of other economic and social processes; and we select a few that seem illuminating of the driving forces involved. The impression which suggests the first topic is that modern economic growth, as exemplified by the group of countries defined above, was accompanied by, and based upon, a high rate of accumulation of useful knowledge and of technological innovations derived from it. The second important associated process was that of shifts in the production structure of the economy, in the shares of different production sectors in output, labor, and capital, with a close relation between the high rate of growth of per capita product and a high rate of shift among the various production sectors. The third major strand in the unfolding of modern economic growth was the complex of functions and influences associated with the national sovereign state.

II. Technological innovations and capital formation

By a technological innovation we mean a new way of producing old goods, or a necessarily original way of producing new goods. Since we deal here with technological innovations that have materialized, the results of unsuccessful attempts having long vanished, we assume that the new ways, the new methods of production, were better than the old, and thus should have contributed to growing productivity, and hence to economic growth. Note that technology here is confined to control over nature (including man only in his physiological, not social aspects) for human purposes, economic purposes among them; hence the association between technological innovation and rising productivity. In the present connection, the high rate of technological innovations and their large cumulative impact on economic growth is reflected in the known succession of major innovations in a variety of fields; in the pervasiveness of new technology in extending to even the oldest production sectors (like agriculture); and in the large proportion of new goods, and of old goods produced by new methods, in the total product of developed countries.

We emphasize major technological innovations, major in that they affect large components of final consumption and of intermediate demand for reproducible capital, and thus contribute substantially to growth of product and productivity. A familiar illustration is provided by the innovations in the production of light and washable fabrics like cotton cloth, of a new industrial material like iron and eventually steel, and of a new source of industrial power like steam, the three major innovations of the "first" industrial revolution; and more illustrations could be easily provided. This emphasis focuses our attention on the long periods over which the unfolding of such innovations takes place, from the pioneering demonstrations of their technical feasibility and of their great potential as a framework for a host of subsidiary innovations and improvements; to the complementary changes that are called for in the institutional structure of the economic enterprises and in conditions of work and life of the actively engaged workers, to channel the innovation into efficient uses; to the retardation phase that follows maturity of the given innovation in the pioneer country, once its lesser potential for further cost reduction, lower price elasticity of demand, and the competitive pressures of either emerging foreign followers or of more recent innovations, make for slower growth and lessened impact on the country's advance in product per worker. These long sequences of interplay between the growth-promoting effects of the extending application of a major technological innovation, with increasingly effective institutional and human response, and the eventual exhaustion of these effects because of both internal and external pressures, represent slices of a long and complex growth process. They should be illuminating and suggestive of both the driving forces of economic growth and of those that limit the latter, when confined to one sector of a country's economy, or even to one country, as compared with others.

The key feature of an innovation is that it is *new* – and thus a peculiar combination of new *knowledge* sufficiently useful and promising to warrant the attempt to apply it; and of *ignorance* of the full range of possibilities and improvements that can be learned only in extended application. A major invention is a crude framework, major in the sense that it is a new base to which a wide variety of subinventions and improvements can be applied – but that are yet unknown, and rarely foreseen. Clearly, one of the requirements of a high rate of technological innovation is a society (or a related group of them) that encourages the continuous production of a variety of new knowledge relevant, directly or indirectly, to problems of economic production; that contains an entrepreneurial group perceptive of such new knowledge, and capable of venturing attempts to apply it on a scale sufficient to reveal its potentials; and a capacity to generate, without costly breakdowns, institutional changes and group adjustments that may be needed to channel efficiently the new technology – with its distinctive constraints. The driving forces or permissive factors are those involved in man's search for new knowledge of nature and of the universe within which we live, including the inventive links between it and production; and the capacity of societies both to encourage technological innovations, and to accommodate them, despite the disruptive unevenness of their impact on different social groups.

The major role of rapidly advancing observational and experimental science, i.e., systematic study of the universe, in creating increasing opportunities for invention and technological innovation, is a distinctive characteristic of modern economic growth, and is directly relevant here. Whatever science discovers about the properties of the physical world is of possible application in technology, which deals with rearrangement of the physical world for human ends. Hence, the advance in the stock of useful knowledge contributes to an explanation of the continuous *succession* of major innovations and of the rising power of technology. The aspect of most interest here is the reinforcing relation between technological innovation and additions to useful knowledge, observational and experimental science among it. Once technological innovations embody new, yet incomplete knowledge, they imply an important learning process, dispelling ignorance of hitherto unknown, yet relevant, aspects of nature. This adds to the data and puzzles of science and thus stimulates further observation and search. In addition, mass application of major inventions may generate new observational tools hitherto not available for scientific use. And, of course, the addition to economic resources made by a successful innovation may provide the wherewithal and stimulus for the search for further useful knowledge. One should stress that the contribution of a technological innovation to *learning* is most directly a function of the "ignorance" component: were the innovation based on complete knowledge of the process or material in question, no learning would have occurred and the contribution to new knowledge would have been limited to effects of cost reduction and of greater potential availability of economic resources.

A notable aspect of technological innovations associated with modern economic growth was the large volume of fixed, reproducible capital required. The demand for the latter, revealed by the capital intensity of the production of new types of industrial power and of the use of this power in the mechanization of a wide variety of formerly labor-intensive processes, was due to distinctive features of the new technology. To illustrate, if steam expansion could deliver large charges of concentrated power, with a reliability, economy, and flexibility of location hitherto unknown, the very large magnitude of physical power made available required a durable and costly envelope for controlling and channeling this power into beneficial rather than destructive uses. Also, the application of stationary steam engines to say manufacturing operations required tools of a material that could withstand continuity and high velocity of turn, again a new industrial material with a high capital intensity of output. What was true of stationary steam power was even more applicable to its use in land transport – with large fixed capital embodied not only in rolling stock but also in the roadbeds and associated facilities. But large amounts of fixed capital meant a large scale of plant and economic enterprise, with increasing economies of scale continuously pushing upwards the optimum scale involved. There was thus a direct line of connection between the greater productivity available in the new technology, the greater volume of physical nonhuman power that the latter employed in the mechanization of a variety of productive processes, the increasing demand for fixed capital that embodied and controlled the new power, and the rising scale of plant and of the economic firm unit. Somewhat different, yet essentially similar connections between the technological features of the new and changing technology, and economic implications in the way of demand for fixed reproducible capital and scale of plant and enterprise, can be suggested for more recent clusters of technological innovations, e.g., those associated with electric power or with the internal combustion engine.

The large demand for fixed capital exercised a restraining influence on the rate of application of new technology, alongside with the limited supply of technological talent capable of exploiting the potential of major inventions through the generation of subinventions and improvements, and with scarcity of entrepreneurial talent capable of innovative organizational tasks in the mobilization of capital, labor skills, and administrative capacity. These several constraints serve to explain why over given intervals of economic growth, long enough to reveal the extent of the latter but short enough to permit observing secular changes, major technological innovations were limited to a few sectors in the economy – the identity of which changed from one period to the next. This concentration on foci of growth did not mean absence of technological advance elsewhere in the economy: it only meant a higher growth rate in the favored industries and sectors and a lower growth rate, but still increasing productivity, in the preponderant majority of others.

One should note here the changes in economic and social institutions that were required to respond to the capital demands and other corollaries of the distinctive features of the new technology. If large volumes of durable, reproducible capital and large-scale plants and hence firms were involved, new devices for mobilizing savings and of channeling them into the new uses, and legal innovations for the proper organization of investors, entrepreneurs, and workers in effective economic enterprise were called for. There was, consequently, a connection between say the emergence of steam railroads, on the one hand, and major changes in financial institutions engaged in mobilization and channeling of savings and the emergence of the modern corporation as the increasingly dominant form of organization of private economic enterprise, on the other hand. Furthermore, if the fixed capital structure of private enterprise in some sectors resulted in a kind of competition that ended up in monopoly and in spreading of the latter to other sectors, new forms of government intervention had to be devised to mitigate the undesirable effects of such a development. Thus, the unfolding of major technological innovations or of clusters of them, with their large demand for fixed capital and associated changes in size, structure, and behavior of plants and enterprises, involved a sequence of technological and institutional changes. The latter responded to the former, as an effective way of channeling the innovations; but also generated trends of their own, some of which may have facilitated and others may have impeded further growth in product per capita or per worker.

This brings us to another related aspect of major technological innovations, the unpredictability of their long-term consequences. It applies particularly to *clusters* of related innovations, many of the latter major – such clusters representing innovations in the several steps of a given industry's production process from the raw material to the finished product, or the several innovations that emerge from the widening application of a new industrial material or of a new source of industrial power. It is these clusters that are important, because a technical breakthrough in one step of a production process or in one use of a new source of power is bound to stimulate related innovations in the sequence or in the range. But when we consider the long-term cumulative consequences of the unfolding of such a cluster, we find a long, interrelated chain of changes in technology and changes in institutional and social adjustments, spread over decades and occurring in a complex and changing national and international environment. It is difficult to assume that anyone at the end of the 18th century could have predicted the magnitude and character of the contributions of steam power to economic growth and structure of the advanced economies in the 19th century; or that anyone at the end of the 19th century could have foreseen the contribution, the widespread positive, and some problematical, effects of the internal combustion engine. This is not to deny the descriptive prescience of some early advocates of the great merits of science, and of science-fiction writers of the 19th and 20th centuries. It is only to emphasize that predictability of the more sober type, one that would yield acceptably firm expectations of direction and magnitude, was not possible, because the chain of connections began with a technological innovation that contained a substantial component of unknown and hence of ignorance, to be overcome only with extended application; and continued to generate a long chain of interweaving links of technological and social change in a sequence of uncertain speed and mixture of successes and temporary failures.

Given such unpredictability, the opportunity for taking steps in good time to maximize the positive contributions of a major innovation and to forestall or minimize the negative, was narrowly limited. This meant that there was little automatic about growth based on the cumulative contributions of technological innovations: the latter could generate pressures and bottlenecks, which could be resolved, but which could also mean delays and breaks in the resulting growth. A record of a high rate of sustained economic growth, powered largely by technological innovation, implies that the society has sufficient capacity to overcome either technological or institutional bottlenecks without incurring such heavy costs as to reduce the advance of net product per worker.

In the discussion so far I chose to emphasize the sustaining elements in technological innovation in their feedback relation with the advance of systematic observational and experimental knowledge; the interplay of technological change with social changes and innovations; the elements of unpredictability and hence of occurrence of bottlenecks and delays; and the pattern of exhaustion of growth opportunities within a sector or a country that once benefited from a cluster of major technological innovations. This is a selective view, and the discussion fails to touch upon a variety of important related aspects. Some of these can be listed as illustrations of unanswered questions.

The discussion above failed to deal with the possibility of a trend – from empirically derived innovations, with inventive response to pressing bottlenecks suggesting necessity as the mother of invention, to invention and innovation that were applications of new knowledge to the production of new goods where invention was the mother of what eventually became a deeply integrated necessity. The discussion also neglected the difference between the mixture of new knowledge and ignorance associated with a major innovation in a *pioneer* country, from that faced in a *follower* country, which can profit from greater knowledge attained by the pioneer but must make up for its greater backwardness in attempting to exploit the already known but still new technology. Above all, the discussion failed to deal directly with the old, and still persisting, issue of the limits imposed by scarcity of natural resources relative to the growth of world population and its needs. The issue could be posed at least in the sense that, advanced economic growth having so far been limited to not more than a quarter of world population, modern technology could afford to be generous in its use of natural resources. Such use might not be feasible with the widening spread of economic growth to rising proportions of mankind, with resulting challenges that perhaps could not be met easily. The omission of the first two topics was due largely to difficulties of summarizing diverse and incomplete evidence; while the last topic involved long-term projections, requiring venturesome assumptions concerning feasible advance of science and technology.

III. Structural shifts

The high rate of increase of product per worker or per capita, characteristic of modern economic growth, was inevitably associated with a high rate of structural shifts. These were changes in the shares of production sectors in the country's output, capital, and labor force, with implicit changes in shares of various labor-status groups among the gainfully engaged and in the conditions of their work and life; of different types of capital and forms of economic enterprise; and in the structure of the country's trade and other economic interchanges with the rest of the world. The implications of such structural shifts for the changing position of the several socioeconomic groups were particularly important, because the responses of these groups to the impacts of advancing technology shaped modern society.

The shifts in the proportions of population actively engaged in the several production sectors, the latter distinguished by different types of product, of production process, and, particularly important here, of conditions of work and hence life of the actively engaged, were due to several complexes of factors. One was the differential impact of technological innovations, which, over any limited secular period, tended to be concentrated in a few industries, old or new. Another was the differing income elasticity of domestic demand, in response to the cost-reducing effects of advancing technology in the old goods and to the availability of new goods. A third was provided by the shifts in comparative advantage in international trade in tradable goods. In the long run, technological advance was all-pervasive, affecting old as well as new sectors; so that, e.g., the decline of the share of labor force in agriculture was due to a combination of low income elasticity of domestic demand for its product, the advance of labor productivity within the sector, and the adverse shifts in comparative advantage in trade with less developed countries.

The consequences of rapid shifts in the distribution of the economically active population (and their dependents) among the several production sectors were numerous, and crucial in the transformation and modernization of developed countries. One major consequence was the discontinuity, the disjunction between the sectoral attachment of successive generations – of a magnitude that could not be accommodated by differences in rates of natural increase or by differing changes in labor force participation proportions. If, to illustrate, the share of total labor force attached to agriculture declined, over a two decade period, from 50 to 43 percent, a not unusual drop, and total labor force grew over the period by 30 percent, the result was that the agricultural labor force grew from 50 to 55.9 or less than 12 percent, while the nonagricultural labor force grew from 50 to 74.1, or over 48 percent. Such differences in growth rates of what we take to be employment opportunities in the two sectors could not be accommodated by lower rates of natural increase or by a more rapid drop in labor force participation proportions in the agricultural sector. In fact, as the rates of natural increase and labor force participation proportions declined (with the spread of lower birth rates and lower labor force participation proportions among the young and the old), they declined less among the agricultural, rural population than among the nonagricultural, urban population. Even if we assume the same growth rate of 30 percent over the two decades for the initial agricultural and nonagricultural labor force, the indicated migration of labor force between the two sectors would amount to 65.0 minus 55.9, or 9 percent of total labor force at the start of the period. But this is only part of the process: change of attachment and intergenerational migration would be amplified by the higher rate of natural increase and slower decline in labor force participation proportions among the slowly growing, more traditional sectors and occupations; a more detailed sectoring would increase the calculated migration streams; and the latter would have occurred *within* sectors, between the smaller scale, more traditional units and the larger scale, more modern firms.

Associated with this large volume of internal migration and mobility, both spatial and inter- and intrasectoral, was the rise in requirements in education and skill for the succeeding generations of workers. This trend was largely powered by the demand of advancing technology for a greater capacity on the part of the economically active population to deal with the application of new knowledge to production problems. But it was also partly a response to the increase of the migratory component within the additions to labor force supply: migrants had to be evaluated in terms of their potential capacities in the performance of their production tasks, and such evaluation had to be based on objective criteria, if only for lack of information concerning their personal "roots." Yet the shift to overt criteria of capacity to perform, away from criteria of social status and origin, was essentially due to the doubt that the status and social affiliation of the parental generation conveyed adequate assurance as to the performance capacity of the younger generation.

The decline in the importance of status and the rise in the weight of objectively tested criteria of capacity and skill of the person was, like many other modern trends, qualified by exceptions and discrimination that represented survival of earlier and more traditional views. Yet the significance of this trend, and its connection with the increasing contribution of new knowledge and technological innovation to economic growth, and with the disjunction between the sectoral attachments of the older and the younger generations, cannot be denied. It was manifested in, and strengthened by, the demographic transition, the shift from the more traditional to modern patterns of population growth. In this transition, reduction in mortality, due either to higher income levels or to scientific advance in medical arts or to both, was a crucial step, particularly in that it most affected mortality in the infant and the younger ages. It was combined, after some lag, with reduced birth rates, the latter reflecting the growing need for greater human capital investment in the younger generation. This involved the parental generation in greater input for the benefit of children, reversing the earlier traditional views of the children being for the benefit of family and older generation. This also meant that it was the younger generation that was the carrier of the new knowledge, acquired by formal education and by learning on the job – neither of which was secured from the blood-related parental generation.

One could argue that there was, partly in consequence of the trends mentioned, a deauthorization of the traditions carried by the older generation. If so, structural shifts under discussion were an important strand in the whole process of modernization, in the movement away from the premodern and hence to us traditional views – as was the case with the effects of science on traditional religion, or with the emphasis on man as the master of his destiny on traditional views concerning sources of political and social authority.

The suggested connection between new-knowledge originated technological innovations and rapid structural shifts, on the one hand, and changing views on the role of man within society, on the other, is particularly relevant because the shifts among the socioeconomic groups were not without breakdowns and conflicts. If a technological innovation rendered a major group of older handicraft firms obsolete, or if a combination of advancing labor productivity and low income elasticity of demand for products of agriculture displaced large groups of agricultural workers, the rate of impact could easily have resulted in prolonged and costly technological unemployment. If established groups, attached to large economic sectors, suffered, or foresaw, contraction in the share and role of their base in economic society, with the possibility of shift problematic and costly, they were likely to resist by using political pressure to slow down the process. If the classes that were in power in premodern society observed reduction in the economic base of their power because of the emergence of new foci of growth, the natural reaction was to resist the change, unless promised assurance of retention of some part of former power by enforceable action of accepted social authority. Historical illustrations abound of such conflicts, engendered by the unequal impact of modern economic growth on the several socioeconomic groups, and of resulting resistance by some of these groups to modernization and growth. If these conflicts were to be resolved so as to preserve a sufficient consensus for growth and change, and yet not at a cost that would retard it unduly, some resolution mechanism was needed – acceptable to, and consistent with, the modern view on man and society.

This mechanism was the national sovereign state, a form of social organization that relies on a sense of community, of belonging together, of common interest, among its individual and group members, in order to serve as overriding arbiter of intranational group conflicts; as authoritative referee among new institutional devices needed to channel advancing technology into efficient use, or to mitigate the negative effects of economic change in order to reduce resistance to growth. The secularization and strengthening of the national sovereign state played a strategic part in modern economic growth. It proved to be so far, with some qualifications, the one form of organization of society that, while discarding the status-bound discriminations of traditional authority of religious and religiously anointed royalty (and aristocracy, or castes, etc.), preserved a unity and centralization of decisions compatible with the modern view on man as the basic source of social authority. Considering that the modern state was meant to formulate and advance the short- and long-term interests of the society over which it was sovereign, its major role in setting the rules and monitoring the conditions for economic growth is hardly surprising. We shall return to this topic in the next section.

There is another series of implications of the changes in conditions of work and life of the various socioeconomic groups in modern economic growth – bearing partly on comparative valuation of different types of final goods that comprise net product, partly on the distinction between intermediate and final goods in defining net product under changing conditions. These implications reveal some aspects of the driving force in economic growth, and some difficulties in measuring its full costs and benefits for guidance in generating an adequate social response.

If we think of final product as the sum of consumer outlays by individual and group consumers and of capital formation, and of the weights of physical units of these components as prices reflective of social valuation, the common finding is that weighting the final goods by initial-year prices yields greater aggregate growth than the weighting of the physical units by end-year prices. The reason for this difference, between the Paasche and Laspeyres indexes, is the negative correlation between temporal change in quantity and temporal change in price: those goods that decline in unit price relative to other prices tend to reflect greater cost-reducing effects of technological innovation – and the expected response of demand (domestic or foreign) warrants greater growth. This difference may also be expressed by saying that the earlier generation, looking *forward* to growth, values it more highly than the later generation, looking *back* at growth that has occurred. This contrast suggests one aspect of the driving force in economic growth – the tendency to value the new more highly than the old, and to treat the already established as a low cost necessity. Of course, if anything happens to affect the latter adversely, without adequate substitution, the driving pressure of the resulting bottleneck is all the greater.

The implication of changed conditions of work and life for the distinction between intermediate goods, i.e., those used to produce the final goods, and final product, results in more intricate problems. If the changed requirement for active participation in economic production is more education, should it be viewed as a capital asset – as has been argued in much of the recent literature; and if so, how does one distinguish the consumption from the capital component of educational outlay? If the requirement for modern jobs is living in urban communities, or serving as an employee rather than as a self-employed worker, should one try to estimate comparative costs of living in the countryside and in the cities, taking into account some of the positive and negative externalities in both? And how does one evaluate the net human cost (or benefit) of shifting from self-employed to employee status?

One should note that the economic accounts of even the advanced countries, from which we derive the parameters of modern economic growth, neglect every one of the questions just raised. All we have so far are experimental analyses by individual scholars. But the important point is not statistical lacunae: it is the inevitable presence, in a society within which social groups shift from one set of conditions of work and life to another, of a mixture of gains and losses for which the market does not provide an agreed-upon social valuation. The scope of these unreflected gains and losses would only widen, were we to add other noneconomic concomitants and conditions of economic growth that are of obvious bearing upon its quality.

IV. National and international aspects

While modern science and technology are truly *transnational,* in that their findings and procedures are valid and applicable worldwide, the observations and analyses of economic growth deal preponderantly with *national* sovereign units – the decision units that set the conditions and monitor the ground rules for the application of science and technology to human purposes, economic goals among them. These national units have evolved through a long historical process of building a strong feeling of community allegiance and of common interest; and in the case of the presently developed countries, emerged long before the late 18th century which ushered the period of modern economic growth. This growth contributed to strengthening the combination of nationalism with sovereignty in a secular national state, first among the presently developed countries and later spreading to much of the rest of the world.

Our interest here is in suggesting the effects of the presence in the world, two centuries ago, of a group of national states, largely in Western Europe and in some of its offshoots overseas, that were already in substantial advance of the rest of the world; and that are now in the economically developed group and dominate the latter. It was only recently that Japan, the only developed country of non-European origin, joined the ranks; and the same is true of Russia, which, however, combined European components with a long non-European past. Going back to the late 18th century, one is struck by the wide difference already existing between the more developed Western Europe and the rest of the world; as well as by the differences among the Western European countries proper in the level of their economic performance and in related aspects of their political and social organization.

Diversity means also differences in capacity to generate major technological innovations and associated social changes, which constitute the substance of modern economic growth. It is the more advanced among the existing nation states, not the ones far behind, that have the resource to pioneer and may be induced in that direction by pressures of bottlenecks generated by current technology and by pulls of new technology for new goods. This is not to overlook the competitive emulation by follower countries, starting from an inferior position and, utilizing the advantages of backwardness, closing the gap – after some delay. But even so the backwardness must be limited, to make effective emulation feasible. While it may sound like a simplistic *post hoc, ergo propter hoc*, one is tempted to argue that the two major types of diversity observed in the late 18th century explain much of what happened over the last two centuries – the dominant pioneering role of Great Britain; the relatively slow spread of a high level of economic attainment, sufficiently high to qualify to the rank of an economically developed country, limited largely to the Western European countries and their offshoots overseas; and the persistence of low levels of economic performance in most of the rest of the world, with the gap between the developed and less developed regions widening.

In the present context, the important emphasis is on the connection between economic and social diversity among established national units; and on the presence of relatively high levels of attainment, which can provide the base for a substantial further advance, of a revolutionary and epoch-setting character. If by a feat of imagination we were to think of the world's human community as a single unit, at what necessarily would be a low average level of performance, the absence of diversity and of inequality would make revolutionary departures difficult to the point of improbability. If so, the divisive organization of the world, and particularly of the European community and its overseas offshoots, in national sovereign units, permitted the kind of diversity that enhanced the possibility of revolutionary breakthroughs in technology and in needed social change. In this sense, the combination of diversity and separateness was a permissive condition of modern economic growth.

One should also note that even among the limited group of Western European countries, their offshoots overseas, and Japan and Russia, the competitive effective emulation was a delayed and lengthy process – despite the relatively advanced standing of most of these followers. The delay in the initial shift toward the higher rate of economic growth by the follower country, combined with the catching-up time, once modern growth started, made for a long period before the follower country approximated the level of per worker or per capita product of the pioneer.

It is the delay span, rather than the catching-up period, that is of interest here. Three groups of factors appear to have been involved in this time-gap between the beginning of modern economic growth of the pioneer and of successive followers. The first was the time required in the unfolding of the new basis of economic growth in the pioneering country – sufficient to demonstrate the nature and potentials of the advance, and thus permit judgment by would-be followers of the value of the new technology to them. The second was the time and effort required by the follower to make the institutional and other changes needed to channel the new technology into effective use – whether this involved technological adjustments to the specific factor endowments of the follower, responses to new insights into sources of modern economic growth not available to the pioneer, or social and political modifications of traditional organization. In the latter connection, one should note the long search for an adequate political structure, in the course of unification of the type involved in Germany and Italy, or of separation like that between Netherlands and Belgium, or of independence of overseas offshoots from their mother country. Finally, the delay, at least in the case of Japan, was that of access by the Western developed countries to this long-isolated, traditional country – confronting it with the need to modernize as the only way of restoring its independence. This combination of the demonstration effect of modern technology, with capacity to change the institutional framework in order to channel modern technology into effective use, and the security pressure against falling far behind in economic power, is, with some modifications, still operative in the international diffusion of economic growth.

The spread of modern economic growth among an increasing number of developed nations was accompanied by expansion of peaceful flows among them – the widening spread of ideas and knowledge, and flows of goods and people in international trade, migration, and capital movements. Indeed, these flows across boundaries were an indispensable mechanism in the diffusion of growth from the pioneer to the follower nations. Likewise, the reaching out of the more developed countries for trade and other peaceful contacts with the rest of the world involved flows of benefit, if unequal benefit, to all. Thus, the separateness of nations was combined with rapidly growing flows across boundaries that represented effective cooperation, even if with some elements of competition and friction.

But other distinctive features of the national state suggest a propensity to warlike forms of international competition. The sovereignty of the national state is supreme and hence exclusive, except in so far as it has been limited by effective international agreement – a process that has not gone far as yet. Hence, in absence of overriding authority, conflicts of interest among nations may lead to a resolution by recourse to war.

Our concern here is with warlike aspects of international competition for they suggest another major driving force in modern economic growth – that for national power, alongside the drive for the application of useful knowledge for greater material welfare. These warlike aspects include use of power by developed nations to impose contact, and subordinate status, on much of the rest of the world – a topic of direct bearing on the recent growth experience and problems of the less developed countries. More directly relevant to the major question here, the driving forces of economic growth, is the continuing propensity toward armed conflict among the developed countries proper. It was certainly endemic in the recurrence of limited wars; and explosive in the "world" wars, the latter involving the extended engagement of the larger developed nations, and exemplified by the series of French-Napoleonic wars of late 18th and early 19th centuries, and the two World Wars of the 20th century.

It is beyond my competence to deal with the mixture of forces involved in the persistence of bellicosity among the developed countries, despite the enormous advantages of the growing peaceful flows among them and of the corresponding extension of effective cooperation. There was the view that saw economic and related advantages in exercise of military power in relations even among the developed countries; there was the historically long-established practice of recourse to war as the last resort, for attaining national goals not attainable by peaceful means; there was the defensive reaction when war preparations were initiated elsewhere; and there was a mixture of accident and error leading to war, as revealed by the wide discrepancy between the results and the expectations of the participants, both winners and losers, especially in major conflicts. All I can do here is to suggest some implications of the continuing propensity to war conflicts, particularly among the larger developed countries.

First, the technology of peacetype production is relevant to that of warfare: the latter involves transportation, communication, an extensive use of nonhuman power, and an organized employment of a large body of people, similar to that involved in large-scale transport and manufacturing production. Given the propensity to warfare, defensive or offensive, the effective search for new knowledge and for its exploitation in the production of goods for peacetype uses, served, in good part, also war purposes – because of the technological affinity between the two. Reciprocally, some of the search for new knowledge and for its exploitation specifically for war purposes was of use for peacetype production. Thus the large overlap between peacetype and war-directed technology amplified both the stimulating effects on economic growth and resulted in a rise in the volume of resources committed to war at rates as high as, or higher than, those of consumption and capital formation representing the peacetype components.

Yet the overlap is far from complete, and technological innovations in response to specific, war-oriented demand, were significantly biased – in emphasizing transportation, communication, and delivery of controlled destructive power over increasingly long distances. One may venture the suggestion that these particular fields of technology have advanced at a greater rate than peacetype production of goods and services, not so closely related to needs of international warfare. It would be interesting to speculate on the alternative patterns of technological innovation and a different structure of national product that might have evolved, would international warfare have been avoidable with minor inputs of economic and technological resources; but this involves an imaginative reconstruction of history not feasible here.

Second, one must note the implications of the obvious differences between peacetype and wartype consumption – the destructive impacts of the latter on human life and material wealth, and the wide uncertainty of the magnitude and outcome of such destruction for the participants, an uncertainty far greater than that involved in the use of knowledge for peacetype consumption and capital formation. The implication then is of a strong inducement and drive toward a national consensus that accepts such dangerous and uncertain ventures. One may argue that the driving forces involved here are significantly different from those that affect the use of knowledge for greater material provision for peacetype needs – considering the difference in the nature of the task and the character of the arguments and incentives as overtly expressed. If so, one might ask whether the warlike forms of international competition, driven by forces different from those involved in the peacetype competition and cooperation, have made a net contribution to economic growth. It seems obvious that they made a *gross* contribution, if we adhere to the conventional concept of net national product which includes consumption of real resources by government for war purposes also, as a final product component. And, given the overlap between peacetype and war-directed technology, there might have been a gross contribution even to product limited to consumption by households and peacetype capital formation. But whether there was a net contribution, in the sense of the addition to product under discussion outweighing the lost potential contribution, lost because of absorption of resources in war-oriented uses, is a moot question – moot in terms of the comparison as formulated. There is little doubt of a negative answer in terms broader than economic.

The third comment refers to the potentially greater incidence of war conflicts, with the increase in the number of large developed countries – because their multiplication increases the number of potential points of major conflict, and because the latecomers may have historical roots and hence institutional responses to the challenge of economic growth that widen the possibility of conflict. The relatively peaceful period between the 1820s and 1914 in Western Europe may have been due to the dominance, at least until the 1870s, of Great Britain as the one major developed country. The strengthening of divisive elements among the developed nations from the 1870s onwards, culminating in World War I; and the exacerbation of these elements in recent decades by the emergence of a major totalitarian developed country, the USSR, can be viewed as relevant illustrations of this association.

Finally, what does the discussion above of the role of the national sovereign state in modern economic growth imply for the definition of net product per capita or per worker, the rise of which we use as a rough gauge of the growth attained? The discussion in this paper was largely in terms of the conventional definition of net product, as it has been used in the economic accounts of the developed market economies. This meant including all of the government consumption of real resources, whether for peacetype or war-oriented purposes; and neglecting the political and related changes associated with economic growth, which could be viewed either as gains or as costs. Yet alternative treatments would be warranted. One could view government activities involved in setting the conditions and monitoring the rules that govern, in a given nation, the application of knowledge to economic production, as intermediate product, as an input of resources for the purpose of facilitating output of consumer goods and consumer goods oriented capital. Likewise, production of goods and services for defensive purposes could be viewed as that of intermediate product needed for maintenance of desired political and related conditions of the nation – so that the measure of final product should reflect both its quantity and the quality of the conditions under which it was turned out. These comments imply that the conventional measures of net product as currently defined include intermediate inputs by government that should be excluded; and fail to include costs and benefits of political and related change associated with the nation's economic growth, its non-economic determinants and corollaries.

These notes on alternative views of net product are made not in assurance of feasibility, and easy acceptability, of such alternatives; but rather to suggest the limitations of the present paper. We had to use the conventional definitions and structures to make it possible for us to take for granted the results of a large volume of quantitative description and analysis based on them, a familiar background against which to suggest a variety of reflections on the driving forces of economic growth. We could not try to learn from the historical record of economic growth, and, at the same time, try to revise it by exploring, in adequate fashion, the alternative ways of defining and measuring net product, and thus provide a different base for our reflections. But these alternatives indicate the limitations of our discussion; and suggest the questions that remain for a more systematic examination and experimentation outside the framework of this paper.

V. Concluding comments

The force that drives economic growth, i.e., the sustained rise in economic product per capita or per worker, must, at the basic level, be the desire of man for greater supply of economic goods – for welfare or for power. But in absence of socially acceptable means to satisfy this desire, it could hardly be a driving force of consequence. Hence, the availability of such means, their characteristics, their capacity to enhance productivity and thus to stimulate economic growth become crucial – as permissive yet in themselves not compelling, as necessary yet not sufficient, factors. It is for this reason that we stressed, in the first substantive section of the paper, the role of science in the search for useful knowledge and of new-knowledge related technological innovations in modern economic growth over the last two centuries, as suggested by the experience of the currently developed market economies. Whether the underlying desire for more goods was stronger in these countries over the last two centuries than, say, over the preceding two or three centuries, is a question not easily answered. But as long as this basic desire remained in some strength, rather than be replaced by rigid asceticism, the immensely greater power to implement it because of the contributions of new knowledge and technology, is what counted.

Economic growth is a socially bound process, which is one reason for our referring above to socially acceptable means of pursuing growth. It is also the reason why two of the three substantive sections of this paper were largely devoted to reflections on the ways society and its component socio-economic groups responded to the challenge of modern economic growth. It was a challenge because while the new knowledge and technological innovations meant a potentially revolutionary expansion in productive power, they also had a variety of disruptive effects. There was disruption in that large proportions of the economically active population had to shift to the rapidly growing sectors, with their new requirements and conditions of employment; in that the relations between the older and younger generations were affected by the disjunction in their occupational and sectoral attachment structures; in that some earlier established socio-economic groups saw their economic base within the economy narrowed and their relative power diminished. Such changes, attractive as they may have been to those ready and capable to exploit the new growth opportunities, were disruptive to those who lost relatively. And one must add that the very widening spread of new knowledge and the growing effects of its great productive power resulted in changes in the traditional views on man's position in the universe and in society – again, like everything new, having both an expansive and disturbing impact on the dominant range of views in society. It follows that another permissive, necessary but not sufficient, factor, was the capacity of the society undergoing modern economic growth to contain the disruption and the resistance, without such great costs as to reduce sharply the rate of advance.

This maintenance of sufficient consensus, while channeling economic growth into efficient uses, is one of the major functions of the modern, national, sovereign state. It utilizes the historically derived feeling of communal belonging and common interest to formulate the major common goals, to serve as a referee among alternative views on new rules, and to monitor the agreed-upon rules and conditions within which the nation's economic growth is to take place. Our brief comments touched not only upon the internal functions of the national state, but also on its exclusivist tendency, and the nationalistic competition with other nations that it stimulates. In most extreme form, this competition involves war conflicts, and suggests the drive for power as distinct from the drive for material welfare.

This paper presents one man's impressions, derived from the modern economic growth record of currently developed market economies, of the major combinations of drive and resistance that generated and shaped the growth. However, the emphasis here has been on economic growth defined as sustained rise in net product per capita, with some associated aspects of structural shifts; and the discussion relied on a familiar background of findings relating to characteristics of this growth as revealed in conventional economic accounts. The limitations of this approach, some suggested in the paper and others that would emerge were we to consider additional criteria of economic growth, are recognized.

A final brief reference to a puzzling contrast between the prevalence of critical reflections on various inadequacies of modern economic growth, even in the developed market economies, and their long record of impressive advance in the capacity to supply man with economic goods, for welfare or for power. This contrast may seem particularly puzzling in that the criticism often refers to high *costs* of economic growth; whereas the measure of economic growth is supposed to be that of *net* product, and thus net of all identifiable costs. Hence, if there are such costs – in the way of lower quality of goods, or of greater pollution, or of wider inequity in the distribution, and the like – the proper measure of economic growth should reflect additions to product *net* of all such costs and limitations. In theory, there can be no "costs" in a net product properly defined as a gauge of economic growth.

But, as indicated at several points in the paper, the widely used national economic accounts, and the conventional measures of net product based on them, do not reflect such newly emphasized economic "costs"; and the emphasis on the latter may serve the useful purpose of calling our attention to them – so that we are urged to include them in our measures, for possible guidance in our interpretations and in policy implications. To be sure, such overemphasis on currently neglected costs, or on other questionable aspects of our measures, combined with lack of attention to the enormous positive result of past economic growth accepted as a matter of course, yields an extremely unbalanced picture of the sum total of modern economic growth. Yet, so long as the imbalance and the bias are recognized, the critical overemphasis may be viewed as a positive spur.

A similar comment applies not only to possibly neglected *economic* costs, omitted from conventional measures of net product, but also to what may be referred to as *social* costs of economic growth. The links between economic growth and the accompanying changes in the non-economic institutions and in other aspects of society are not easily established; and it is particularly difficult to distinguish between the elements of necessity and choice within them. It would be even more difficult to assign economic or other weights to the noneconomic inputs into, or the noneconomic returns from, economic growth. Yet, any critical reflections on what may seem to be undesirable social costs of economic growth must be formulated and viewed within a wider balance of what clearly are the large social returns from the economic growth process. It is plausible to argue that a major driving force in modern economic growth was the promise not only of greater material welfare but also of a more desirable organization of society that growth would, and does, make possible.

A bibliographical note

Most comments in this paper are too broad to permit specific documentation and references. Still, it may be helpful to list here some of my publications, which present a more detailed discussion of several of the topics touched upon here, and which also contain some relevant references. These publications are:

Modern Economic Growth: Rate, Structure, and Spread. Studies in Comparative Economics, 7, New Haven, 1966.
Economic Growth of Nations: Total Output and Production Structure. Cambridge, Mass., 1971, particularly pp. 303–354.
"Innovations and Adjustments in Economic Growth." In: *Population, Capital, and Growth. Selected Essays.* New York, 1973, pp. 185–211.
"Modern Economic Growth: Findings and Reflections." In: *Ibid.,* pp. 165–184.
"Technological Innovations and Economic Growth." In: *Growth, Population, and Income Distribution. Selected Essays.* New York, 1979, pp. 56–99.

2. A note on production structure and aggregate growth

I. Introduction

The initial hypothesis that led to this chapter concerns the effects on aggregate growth of differences among production sectors in the potential rise in their productivity (per worker, or per unit of total input). Assume production sector I, which, for a variety of reasons (e.g., lesser role of recent technological innovations or greater institutional resistance to them), is assigned an expected lower rise in productivity over the next decade than production sector II. Then, if two economies differ in the proportions of sectors I and II in their product and inputs, economy 1, with a larger proportion of sector I and lower proportion of sector II, would tend to show a lower rise per worker (or per unit of total input) than economy 2; and this, under usual conditions, would also mean a lower rate of increase in per capital product (i.e., aggregate growth) in economy 1.

The general statement above can be made more meaningful by referring to identifiable major production sectors – A, agriculture and related activities, and the rest, $(I + S)$, or the sum of industry and services. We can also use the familiar ratios for the less developed (LDC) and developed (DC) market economies. The simple example presented in Table 2.1, using labor force as the only productive factor (our data on others are still quite scarce), and thus dealing with changes in product per worker, illustrates the initial hypothesis.

The illustration is unrealistic in several respects. It sets the absolute magnitudes of labor force, total product, and per worker product at the same levels for the less and more developed countries – a simplification that permits concentration on the rates of *relative* increase in sectoral or

Reprinted in the United States of America from *Economic Welfare and the Economics of Soviet Socialism: Essays in Honor of Abram Bergson*, edited by Steven Rosefielde © Cambridge University Press 1981.

Table 2.1. *Effects of different rates of rise in sectoral product per worker on aggregate growth (of total product per worker)*

	(1)	(2)	(3)	(4)	(5)	(6)	(7)
	Labor force		Product per worker		GDP		Growth in product per worker (%)
	A	$(I+S)$	A	$(I+S)$	A	$(I+S)$	
Initial structure							
1. LDC	70	30	0.714	1.667	50	50	—
2. DC	14	86	0.714	1.047	10	90	—
Case 1. Rise in product per worker of 20% in A sector and of 40% in (I+S) sector							
3. LDC	70	30	0.857	2.334	60	70	30
4. DC	14	86	0.857	1.466	12	126	38
Case 2. Rise in product per worker of 20% in A sector and of 40% in the (I+S) sector in LDCs; rise in product per worker of 40% in both sectors in DCs							
5. LDC	70	30	0.857	2.334	60	70	30
6. DC	14	86	1.000	2.334	14	126	40

total product per worker. Furthermore, whereas we allow for growth in product per worker in the two cases, the share of the A and $(I + S)$ in the labor force are kept constant. Changes in these shares, reflecting structural shifts, are, of course, important in the growth process of an economy. So are adjustments in the process of growth to differing changes in productivity in the several sectors. But we are concerned here, and throughout the paper, with the effects of differences in potential growth in product per worker among the several sectors on the growth of total product per worker – differences that prevail over a period long enough to affect substantial growth rates (say, a decade or two), but not so long as to merge different phases of long-term growth in which the differential constraints are likely to be modified.

The conclusions suggested by Table 2.1 are obvious. First, if we assume (case 1) a lower growth rate of per worker product in the A sector, in both LDCs and DCs, and equal growth rates in sectoral product per worker in both sets of economies, the aggregate growth rate in per worker product in LDCs will fall short of that in the DCs.

Second, if we were to assume (case 2) that no such differential in sectoral growth in product per worker is found in the DCs, whereas it is characteristic of LDCs, the addition to the disparities in aggregate growth in per worker product is small. This is clearly due to the low weight of the A sector in the DCs. In other words, it is the initial assumption of lesser capacity of per worker product in the A sector to grow in the LDCs that yields the wide disparity in aggregate growth per worker.

Third, if there is a close relation between growth of labor force and growth of population, differences in aggregate growth of product per worker will be translated into similar differences in growth of product per capita, aggregate growth.

Thus, the crucial question in the initial hypothesis is whether it is plausible to expect, in the LDCs, a lower growth rate in per worker product in the A sector than in the $(I + S)$ sector. This expectation would, presumably, be affected by the rate of increase in the sectoral labor force and the absence or presence of a shift in labor force away from the A sector. All of this also disregards capital, human and material, as a complementary factor in production, in addition to labor force measured in numbers and without regard to quality differentials. This is not the place, nor is it fully within my competence, to deal with what is clearly a complex and variable set of production relations.[1] I can only suggest some factors that would lead to the expectation just stated.

These factors lie in the difference between the A and the $(I + S)$ sectors, taken broadly, in the ease with which the diffusion of modern technology from the DCs to the LDCs can be expected to occur. If it can be assumed that in the wide difference in per worker product between the A and the $(I + S)$ sectors in the LDCs, suggested in the illustration and confirmed by empirical evidence, a major source lies in the greater weight of "modern" technology in the $(I + S)$ sector (in manufacturing, public utilities, mining, transport and communication, and some professional services), it can be argued that the importation and implantation of such modern technology in the LDCs is far easier in the $(I + S)$ than in the A sector. The reason may lie partly in the wider difference in natural conditions that affect the A sector in the LDCs as compared with those in DCs; the lesser control over the environmental factors in the A sector

---

1 See, however, a brief discussion of the factors underlying intersectoral inequality in product per worker, largely between A and $(I + S)$ sectors, in my *Economic Growth of Nations: Total Output and Production Structure* (Cambridge, Mass.: Harvard University Press, Belnap Press, 1971), pp. 236–48. The general bearing of that discussion was "to emphasize various aspects of duality of structure in the less developed countries, and suggest that such duality, if present in the developed countries, plays a much less important role" (p. 247). In this emphasis the earlier discussion supports the argument in the text relating to factors that might result in a lowered growth rate in product per worker in the A than in the $(I + S)$ sectors in the less developed market economies.

even in the DCs, relative to their weather and other conditions – let alone in the LDCs, in which the A sector operates in soil and climate conditions relatively unfamiliar to modern agricultural technology in the DCs. One may also stress that in market economies, the A sector in the LDCs (much more so than in DCs) is dominated by a large number of small-scale firms in conditions which, because of high-risk, limited reserves, and a wide degree of dispersion, would not encourage rapid diffusion of modern technology, even if it were as fully available and as suitable as is the modern production technology in much of the $(I + S)$ sector.

This argument can be elaborated further by reference to the limited transport and communication framework in the countryside of LDCs, inhibiting rapid diffusion of new elements in technology; the greater concentration of political power and government in the urban centers of the LDCs, so that government policy directed at economic growth is likely to favor the $(I + S)$ sector more than the A sector; and the conditions of pressure on natural resources so much greater in the A sector of the LDCs. But the comments already advanced are, perhaps, sufficient to explain why the initial hypothesis was framed in terms of growth propensities of per worker product in the A and other sectors, particularly in the less developed market economies. This naturally determined the direction of whatever statistical probing was feasible, and we turn to the latter.

II. Statistical findings

To secure broad coverage of the production structure and growth rates of product (GDP, at constant prices), we exploited the UN estimates for market economies in several broad regions, developed and less developed; and to these we matched the ILO estimates of labor force, total and by three broad sectors (see the UN and ILO sources cited in the notes to Table 2.2). In a more intensive analysis, not feasible here, it would have been more illuminating to deal with single countries rather than congeries of them for wide regions. But the main limitation of the data, even for a simple task of relating output to labor force, lies in the brevity of the period covered. The UN indexes of GDP, total and by sector, are available only back to 1950, and for some regions only back to 1960; the ILO estimates of labor force, total and by sector, are given only for 1950, 1960, and 1970. We have therefore concentrated on the decade from 1960 to 1970, using GDP and LF estimates that distinguish three major sectors:

Table 2.2. *Gross domestic product (GDP) and labor force (LF), market economies in six major regions, 1960 and 1970*

	(1) East and Southeast Asia, excluding Japan	(2) Africa excluding South Africa	(3) Asia– Middle East	(4) Latin America	(5) Europe	(6) North America
GDP, 1970 market prices, $US billion						
1. 1960	78.5	35.9	22.1	91.6	494	712
2. 1970	123.5	58.4	46.7	159.6	758	1,064
3. % change	57.4	62.8	111.1	74.2	53.5	49.5
Population, millions						
4. 1960	804	256	79.7	216	328	199
5. 1970	1,031	327	105	283	356	226
6. % change	28.2	27.7	31.7	31.0	8.5	13.6
GDP per capita, $US, 1970 market prices						
7. 1960	97.6	140	277	424	1,506	3,578
8. 1970	120	179	445	564	2,129	4,708
9. % change	23.0	27.9	60.6	33.0	41.4	31.6
LF, excluding women in A sector, millions						
10. 1960	251	75.5	23.3	67.6	132.0	79.3
11. 1970	305	94.8	29.7	86.2	140.9	95.3
12. % change	21.4	25.5	27.5	27.6	6.8	20.2
% LF, excluding women in A sector, to population						
13. 1960	31.2	29.5	29.2	31.3	40.2	39.8
14. 1970	29.6	29.0	28.3	30.5	39.6	42.2
GDP per worker, $US, 1970 market prices						
15. 1960	313	475	948	1,355	3,742	8,979
16. 1970	405	616	1,572	1,852	5,380	11,165
17. % change	29.7	29.7	65.8	36.6	43.6	24.4

Notes: Lines 1 and 2: The data on GDP in 1970 are from United Nations, *Yearbook of National Accounts Statistics 1976,* vol. 2, *International Tables* (New York, 1977), Table 1A, pp. 3–9. The totals for 1960 were calculated by applying to the 1970 totals the growth rates for the decade 1960–2 to 1970–2 (shown in line 3). The latter were computed from *ibid.,* Table 6B, pp. 255–63. This table shows annual index numbers, for 1960 to 1975, of GDP in 1970 market prices, originating in six production subsectors, and the 1970 weights (shares in total GDP) for each. This permitted us to calculate the weighted indexes for the three major sectors (*A, I,* and *S*) and combine them to total GDP; and to compute the growth rates for 1960–2 to 1970–2 for GDP, and for the *A, I,* and *S* sectors (the latter used in Tables 2.3 and 2.4).

Lines 4 and 5 and 10 and 11: The data on population and on labor force (the latter excluding women in the A sector) are directly from International Labour Office, *Labour Force Estimates 1950–1970 and Projections 1975–2000,* vol. 5, *World Summary* (Geneva, 1977), Table 2 (on population and total labor force), pp. 6–39, and Table 3 (on labor force by sex and sector), pp. 40–8; and vol. 1, *Asia* (Geneva, 1977), analogous Table 2 (pp. 7–50) and 3 (pp. 51–61).

A – agriculture and related activities; I – mining, manufacturing, power, light and fuel utilities, and construction; S – transport and communication, trade, other services. We secured these estimates for the market economies grouped into six major regions – four in the less developed group and two in the developed.

Table 2.2 presents the major absolute magnitudes, in the aggregate, without distinguishing the production sectors, for 1960 and 1970. The technical comments, not only on the sources but also on the procedures and some tests of the results, are in the notes to the tables so as not to encumber the text. Here the only point to be noted is the exclusion of female labor force in the A sector from the LF totals and sectoral shares. This is done largely because of the highly variable treatment of this component in the several regions, with obvious effects in unlikely discrepancies of the resulting ratios.[2]

Table 2.2 summarizes a wide variety of data; and we comment briefly on aspects that are of interest.

First, the six regions distinguished include most of the less developed and developed market economies of the world, and reveal relatively fully the international disparities in the distribution of population and in their per capita product. Since the UN estimates involve conversion to com-

2 Thus, the ILO source shows for Latin America a ratio of female to total workers in the A sector of less than 10 percent in both 1960 and 1970. A similar ratio of Africa (total) was over 30 percent in both years; and somewhat higher for eastern South Asia and middle South Asia. (See Table 3 in the World Summary volume of the ILO source cited in the note to Table 2.1.) There are also differences among Moslem and non-Moslem subregions in the reporting of female labor in agriculture.

Notes to Table 2.2 *(cont.)*

The more detailed data on population and labor force available in the ILO source were used to fit them into regions comparable to those used for the GDP indexes and sectors in the UN source. For East and Southeast Asia, excluding Japan, we combined East South Asia and Middle South Asia, excluding Iran, with the data on South Korea and Hong Kong. For Africa, excluding South Africa, we combined the data on North, East, and Middle Africa. For Asia–Middle East we took the sum of Western South Asia and Iran. The totals for Latin America were of the same coverage in the two sources. For Europe we took the sum of Northern, Western, and Southern Europe (the latter without adjustment for inclusion of Albania). For North America, largely Canada and the United States, the coverage of the two regions is the same.

The closeness of the adjustment can be checked by comparing the population totals for 1970 from the ILO sources (line 5) with those derivable from Table 1A in the UN source used for line 2. The latter, for the regions in successive columns 1–6 are, in millions 1,029; 324; 104; 271; 334; 225. The agreement is close.

Lines 3, 6, 9, 12–14 and 17: By calculation from entries in the other lines.

parable dollars by use of "prevailing dollar exchange rates," the wide ranges in per capita product in lines 7 and 8 exaggerate purchasing power differentials; but the adjustment to approximate the latter would still leave a wide spread in the range between say Asia and North America; and leave the rough sequence in comparative levels relatively unaffected for regions as broad as these.[3]

Second, the ratios of labor force (excluding women in the A sector) to total population, although roughly similar, at about 30 percent, for the four less developed regions, are distinctly below those for the two developed regions (see lines 13 and 14). The difference is associated with that in the rate of natural increase of population, which largely determines the rate of population growth in line 6 and also the structure of population by age. A high rate of natural increase means a high proportion in the population of age groups under 15, for whom the labor force participation rates are naturally low. Hence, growth rates in population over the decade of close to 30 percent (line 6, columns 1–4) are associated with low ratios of labor force to population in line 14, columns 1–4; whereas the low rates of growth of population in the two developed regions are associated with high ratios of labor force in total population (columns 5 and 6, lines 6 and 14). There is also evidence of the wide swing in the rates of natural increase in North America, where high rates of increase peaking in the late 1950s produced a larger upswing in the labor force proportions by the end of the 1960s (see column 6, lines 6, 12, and 14).

Third, despite significant differences among the regions in proportions of labor force to population, and in the movements of labor force relative to population, the differences among regions in product per worker (lines

3 On this topic, see Irving B. Kravis, Zoltan Kenessey, Alan Heston, and Robert Summers, *A System of International Comparisons of Gross Product and Purchasing Power* (Baltimore, Md.: Johns Hopkins University Press, 1975); and by three of the four authors (excluding Zoltan Kenessey), *International Comparisons of Real Product and Purchasing Power* (Baltimore, Md.: Johns Hopkins University Press, 1978), and "Real GDP *per Capita* for More than One Hundred Countries," *Economic Journal*, 88 (June 1978), 215–41.

The exchange rate deviation index (i.e., relative disparity between dollar exchange and purchasing power rates) ranges from somewhat over 3 for the low-income LDCs, such as India, to over 2 for the upper ranges of the LDCs (such as Brazil) to somewhat over 1.3 for the DCs in Europe. With these ratios for 1970, their application to per capita GDP in line 8 would reduce the range between columns 1 and 6, from almost 40:1 to 13:1; and that between columns 4 and 6 from somewhat over 8:1 to about 4:1. The adjustment applies also to the differences in GDP per worker in line 16.

15 and 16) are similar to those in product per capita (lines 7 and 8); and differences in changes over the decade in product per worker (line 17) are similar to those in the decadal change in product per capita (line 9). One can assume, therefore, that over long periods, differences in growth of product per worker among regions will be associated with differences in growth in product per capita; and whatever effect production structure will have on the former will be translated into effects on the latter (i.e., on aggregate growth as reflected in per capita product).

Finally, one should note the marked differences among the regions in the decade's growth of product per capita or product per worker. Some elements in these differences may be associated with factors specific to the rather short period covered; others may be due to longer term factors. Thus, the high growth rate in the Asia–Middle East region is probably associated with the petroleum boom that occurred even before the recent sharp rise in oil prices; whereas the high rate of growth in Europe was probably in compensation for the preceding decades of stagnation and war destruction that reached back to the late 1920s and that would find an even more striking illustration in the case of Japan. Elements of the oil boom may have affected the African region, as well as Latin America, but to a much lesser degree; and in the case of the latter there may have also been the recovery from the recession of the 1930s and the slowdown during the World War II years. Were our record to cover a longer historical span, some of these transitory elements would have been reduced; and the longer term differences in growth rates would have emerged more clearly.

We turn now to the data that reveal the sectoral structure of both GDP and LF for 1960 and 1970, data needed to derive our measures of levels and growth of sectoral product per worker (Table 2.3). The regions are the same as in Table 2.1; and because of the nature of the ILO data, the sectoral division must be limited to three sectors. One should also note that the exclusion from GDP of the output in two subsectors of the S sector, banking, insurance, and real estate and income from ownership of dwellings, which involve directly little of the total labor force, could not be carried out. Consequently, there is an exaggeration of the product per worker in the S (and hence also $I + S$) sector; but it is not likely to invalidate the major findings.

Of the variety of differentials, changes over time, and associations, summarized in Table 2.3, the most conspicuous general, and most relevant to our discussion, is the low product per worker in agriculture com-

Table 2.3. *Sectoral structure of GDP and LF, market economies, six major regions, 1960 and 1970*

	(1) East and Southeast Asia, excluding Japan	(2) Africa excluding South Africa	(3) Asia– Middle East	(4) Latin America	(5) Europe	(6) North America
% shares of sectors in GDP						
1960						
1. A sector	49.3	42.3	25.0	16.7	7.8	3.9
2. I sector	17.7	20.7	35.1	32.0	42.6	34.6
3. S sector	33.0	37.0	39.9	51.3	49.6	61.5
1970						
4. A sector	40.9	32.1	16.9	13.7	6.1	2.9
5. I sector	22.8	28.0	40.7	35.0	45.6	34.9
6. S sector	36.3	39.9	42.4	51.3	48.3	62.2
% shares of sectors in LF (excluding women in A sector)						
1970						
7. A sector	65.7	70.9	57.8	45.2	18.0	6.5
8. I sector	13.6	10.7	19.3	21.0	43.3	36.5
9. S sector	20.7	18.4	22.9	33.8	38.7	57.0
1970						
10. A sector	59.2	65.0	48.6	38.7	11.3	3.7
11. I sector	16.1	13.7	22.0	22.6	43.7	34.3
12. S sector	24.7	21.3	29.4	38.7	45.0	62.0
Relative product per worker, by sector (regionwide relative = 1.00)						
1960						
13. A sector	0.75	0.62	0.43	0.37	0.43	0.60
14. (I+S) sector	1.48	1.98	1.78	1.52	1.12	1.03
15. I sector	1.30	1.93	1.82	1.52	0.98	0.95
16. S sector	1.59	2.01	1.74	1.52	1.28	1.08
1970						
17. A sector	0.69	0.49	0.35	0.35	0.54	0.78
18. (I+S) sector	1.45	1.94	1.62	1.41	1.06	1.01
19. I sector	1.42	2.04	1.85	1.55	1.05	1.02
20. S sector	1.47	1.87	1.44	1.33	1.07	1.00
Intersectoral ratio in product per worker, (I+S)/A						
21. 1960	2.0	3.2	4.1	4.1	2.6	1.7
22. 1970	2.1	4.0	4.6	4.0	2.0	1.3
Total disparity between sectoral shares in GDP and in LF (TDM)						
23. 1960	32.8	57.2	65.6	57.0	21.8	9.0
24. 1970	36.6	65.8	63.4	50.0	10.4	1.6

pared with the product per worker in the $(I + S)$ sector. The former, in the less developed regions, is between a half and a fourth of the latter, even with exclusion of women workers from the A sector. To be sure, the A to non-A gap in product per worker may be partly due to inadequate adjustment for factor price differentials between the two groups and for the greater extent to which A workers may engage part of their time in non-A pursuits than would be the case of $(I + S)$ workers in their part-time engagement in the A sector. But one may doubt that adjustment would reduce materially the range of the gap.

Next, one should note that the relative disparity between per worker product in the $(I + S)$ and the A sectors differs significantly among the regions, either in 1960 or 1970 (see particularly lines 21 and 22). It ranges from a low of about 2 in the lowest income ESE Asia region to a high of over 4 in the Asia–Middle East, and more significantly the Latin American region; then drops back to between 2.6 and 1.3 in the two developed regions, Europe and North America. Insofar as the $A - (I + S)$ differential in product per worker is an element in the inequality of income

Notes to Table 2.3 *(cont.)*

Notes: The A sector covers agriculture and related industries (fisheries, forestry, and hunting). The I sector includes mining, manufacturing, power and light utilities, and construction. The S sector covers transport and communication, wholesale and retail trade, and other services. This division is governed by that followed in the ILO data on labor force.

Lines 1–6: The sectoral structure of GDP in 1970 is directly from the UN source, Table 6B, cited in the notes to lines 1–2 of Table 2.2. The sectoral shares in GDP for 1960 were obtained by calculating them for 1960–2 and 1970–2, and applying the differences to the shares in 1970.

For four of the six regions (excluding Africa and Asia–Middle East), an alternative procedure was feasible, using the annual indexes for total GDP and subsectors (in 1963 factor costs) reaching back from 1968 to 1950 as well as the sectoral shares in 1963 [see United Nations, *Yearbook of National Accounts Statistics, 1969,* vol. 2, *International Tables* (New York 1970), Table 6B, pp. 159–65]. These data made it possible to extend the annual indices of GDP total and by sectors, in 1970 market prices, to cover 1958–9; and, instead of 1960–2 and 1970–2 use quinquennial averages, 1958–62 and 1968–72, centered on 1960 and 1970, respectively. The sectoral shares in GDP yielded by these calculations differed only slightly from those shown in lines 1–6; and the same is true of the alternative percent changes in sectoral product per worker, when we compared them with those now shown in Table 2.4. The differences would affect the major findings but little; and there was no need to show the results of alternative sets of calculations.

Lines 7–12: Calculated from Table 3 of the ILO source cited for lines 10–11 of Table 2.2.

Lines 13–20: Obtained by division of the given sector's share in GDP by the same sector's share in LF. This yields the ratio of product per worker in the given sector to the aggregate product per worker in the region.

Lines 21 and 22: By division of the relative product for the $(I+S)$ sector by that for the A sector.

Lines 23 and 24: Obtained by subtracting the three sectoral shares in GDP from the shares of the corresponding three sectoral shares in LF, and adding the deviations regardless of sign. This may be shown to equal the sum of deviations of the relative product of each sector from 1.00 (the regionwide average), each weighted by the shares of the sectors in LF – the deviations being taken regardless of sign.

Table 2.4. *Growth from 1960 to 1970 (%), GDP, LF, and product per worker, total and by sector, market economies in six major regions*

	(1) East and Southeast Asia, excluding Japan	(2) Africa, excluding South Africa	(3) Asia– Middle East	(4) Latin America	(5) Europe	(6) North America
A. Growth from 1960 to 1970 (%)						
Gross domestic product						
1. Total	57.4	62.8	111.1	74.2	53.5	49.5
2. *A* sector	29.7	22.9	42.9	41.5	19.5	10.7
3. (*I+S*) sector	82.6	91.1	133.8	80.6	56.4	51.1
4. *I* sector	100.6	119.8	144.6	90.2	64.5	50.9
5. *S* sector	72.9	75.3	124.2	74.6	49.4	54.2
Labor force (excluding women in A sector)						
6. Total	21.4	25.5	27.5	27.6	6.8	20.2
7. *A* sector	9.2	15.0	7.4	9.3	−32.7	−32.0
8. (*I+S*) sector	44.7	51.1	55.5	42.6	15.4	23.8
9. *I* sector	44.4	60.8	45.1	36.9	7.6	13.0
10. *S* sector	44.8	45.5	64.3	46.2	24.2	30.7
Product per worker						
11. Total	29.7	29.7	65.8	36.6	43.8	24.4
12. *A* sector	18.8	6.9	33.1	29.5	77.5	62.8
13. (*I+S*) sector	26.2	26.5	50.4	26.7	35.5	22.0
14. *I* sector	38.9	36.7	68.6	36.9	53.0	33.5
15. *S* sector	19.4	20.6	36.5	19.4	20.3	15.7
B. Decomposition of growth in total product per worker (line 11)						
Growth in sectoral product per worker, weighted						
16. *A* sector	9.3	2.9	8.3	4.9	6.0	2.4
17. (*I+S*) sector	13.3	15.2	37.8	22.2	32.7	21.1
18. Weighted total (lines 16 + 17)	22.6	18.1	46.1	27.1	38.7	23.5
19. Residual (due to sectoral shift)	5.8	9.8	13.5	7.5	3.7	0.73
20. Total shift (% points)	6.5	5.9	9.2	6.5	6.7	2.8
21. First factor	0.73	1.36	1.35	1.15	0.69	0.43
22. Second factor	1.062	1.183	1.130	0.978	0.764	0.749
23. Combined factors (line 21 × line 22)	0.775	1.609	1.526	1.125	0.527	0.322
24. Contribution to growth, % points (line 20 × line 23)	5.0	9.5	14.0	7.3	3.5	0.90

Notes: Lines 1–15: The percentage changes from 1960 to 1970, for GDP, LF, and product per worker, total and by sector, were calculated from the two sources used for Tables 2.2

measured or conjectured in the distribution of total product among the relevant recipients units, the differential must have made greater contribution in the higher income less developed regions (such as Latin America) than either in such low-income less developed regions as ESE Asia or in the developed regions.

Finally, it is clear from lines 21 and 22 that the intersectoral ratio in product per worker, $(I + S)/A$, changed significantly between 1960 and 1970. In three of the regions, the ratio rose over the decade, indicating that in them – Asia, Africa, and Asia–Middle East – the growth in per worker product in the A sector must have been lower over the decade than the total growth in per worker product in the $(I + S)$ sector. In Latin America but more conspicuously in the two developed regions, Europe and North America, the intersectoral ratio declined, indicating that the product per worker in the A sector must have grown over the decade more than the product per worker in the $(I + S)$ sector. And these results are shown explicitly in the top panel of Table 2.4. The *weighted* measures of intersectoral disparities in product per worker, calculated for three rather than two sectors, show the same pattern and changes, but qualified by the decline in the total share of the A sector (see lines 23 and 24).

Before turning to Table 2.4, one may note that the disparities in per worker product between the I and S sectors, although significant, are far narrower than those between the A sector and either $(I + S)$ sector, or the I and S sectors taken separately. Hence, given the conventional classification of production sectors, large differentials will be observed

Notes to Table 2.4 *(cont.)*

and 2.3. Indeed, for the totals (lines 1, 6, and 11) the percentage changes are identical with those in lines 3, 12, and 15 for the corresponding regions in Table 2.2.
Lines 16 and 17: The growth in sectoral product per worker (in lines 12 and 13) was weighted by the shares of the two sectors in total GDP in 1960 (since the proper weights are the initial share in LF, weighted by the comparative level of product per worker at that date).
Line 19: The difference between line 18 and line 11, related to the entry in line 18 (the latter treated as a fraction and added to 1.0). For example, the 5.8 in column 1, line 19, is $29.7 - 22.6 = 7.1$, the latter divided by 1.226. The residual multiplied by the weighted total (in line 18), used as a fraction and added to 1, yields the relative that, minus 1.0 and converted to percentages, would yield the entry in line 11.
Line 20: The shift from the A to the $(I+S)$ sectors in their share in the labor force (derived by subtracting the percent share of the A sector in total labor force in 1970 from that in 1960; see lines 7 and 10 of Table 2.3).
Line 21: The first factor is the difference between the relative product in the $(I+S)$ sector and that in the A sector, in 1960 (derivable from lines 13 and 14 of Table 2.3).
Line 22: The second factor is the relative difference between the growth per worker product in the $(I+S)$ sector and in growth of per worker product in the A sector. These are shown in lines 12 and 13 of this table; and the factor is derived by using the percentages as fractions, adding them to 1.0, and then dividing the result for the $(I+S)$ sector by that for the A sector.

only in the A to non-A division, even in the developed countries; and in the latter, the sharp drop in the share of the A sector reduces the weight of the disparity to quantitatively insignificant dimension. One may argue that the sectoral classification of the non-A division should focus more than it does now on the subsectors that are distinctive in the level of their per worker product and the propensity in their growth.

As already indicated, the top panel of Table 2.4 reveals a variety of implications of the sectoral shares in GDP and LF shown in Table 2.3. The commonly observed declines in Table 2.3 of the shares of the A sector in GDP are translated in lines 2 and 3 of Table 2.4 into the commonly observed lower growth of GDP in the A sector than in the $(I + S)$ sector; the commonly observed declines in Table 2.3 of the share of the A sector in total LF are translated in lines 7 and 8 of Table 2.4 into a much lower growth (or actual decline) of labor force in the A sector than of labor force in the $(I + S)$ sector. Finally, the different movements of the intersectoral ratio in per worker product $(I + S)/A$ observed in Table 2.3 are translated here in lower growth rates of per worker product in the A than in the $(I + S)$ sector in ESE Asia, Africa, and Asia–Middle East, and in higher growth rates in per worker product in the A sector in Latin America, Europe, and North America (lines 12 and 13). One should note particularly the very high rates of growth in per worker product in the A sector in the two developed regions, in which the estimates of labor force in that sector show a marked relative decline. This may reflect an almost revolutionary change in the technology of the A sector in the developed market economies following World War II, and induced by rapid spread to this sector of technological innovations that may have been held in abeyance over the preceding decades of depression and war, reaching perhaps as far back as the 1930s.

The distinction between the I and S sectors (lines 4 and 5, 9 and 10, and 14 and 15) reveals interesting differences in growth within the combined non-A division. Except in North America, GDP originating in the I sector grew more than that in the S sector; but in most regions, labor force in the I sector grew less than in the S sector. In consequence, growth in product per worker in the I sector was strikingly greater than that per worker product in the S sector, in all regions. Indeed, if we except the untypical case of the Asia–Middle East region, the rise in per worker product in the S sector was about the same in the remaining five regions, ranging from 16 to 21 percent (see line 15). There is a suggestion here of a limit on the growth rate of productivity for this sector, but for reasons unlike those suggested for the A sector. They may lie partly in the difficulty of measuring productivity levels and changes for several important subsectors within the S sector, partly in the substantial in-migration of labor into the low-productivity subsectors.

In panel B we decompose the growth in aggregate product per worker in each region (line 11) into the contribution of growth in product per worker in the sectors, properly weighted; and the contribution of the shift of the labor force from the lower-product-per-worker sector, such as A, to sectors with higher product per worker. To simplify calculation and presentation, the analysis is carried through for two sectors, A and $(I + S)$, although it could have been done for three (and, in general, can be carried through for several sectors).

Lines 16–20 reveal that the weighted growth of the two sectors account for only a part of the aggregate growth of product per worker in line 11 – and this was to be expected as long as there was a shift in the structure of the labor force from lower- to higher-product-per-worker sectors. But the significant aspect of this finding is that the shortfall of the weighted growth of sector relative to aggregate growth in per worker product is significantly greater for the less developed regions than for the developed regions. Even excluding the untypical Asia–Middle East region, we find that the shortfall (observable by comparing lines 18 and 11) is about one-fourth of the aggregate growth rate in ESE Asia, about four-tenths in Africa, and over one-fourth in Latin America – compared with somewhat over one-tenth in Europe and insignificant in North America. In consequence, the weighted contribution of sectoral growth in product per worker in the LDC regions, if it were to have been observed with the sectoral structure of the labor force constant, would have yielded distinctly lower aggregate growth rates and their level relative to those in the DC regions would have been lower (compare the range in line 18 with that in line 11). To the extent that the lower growth rates in per worker product in the A sector in the LDC regions contributed to a lower level of the total in line 18, there was partial compensation in the intersectoral shift in the labor force of a magnitude that could not be easily matched in the DC regions.

Lines 20–2 attempt to approximate the contribution of the shift in labor force from the A to the $(I + S)$ sectors to the growth in aggregate product per worker in the region. The total shift, in percentage points of the shares of the sectors in total LF from 1960 to 1970, is weighted first by the initial difference in relative product per worker between the two sectors (line 21) and then by the relative difference in growth rates between the per worker product in the two sectors (line 22). The first factor ranges from a low in the lower income LDCs to higher levels in the higher income LDCs and then declines sharply for the DC regions; and a somewhat similar pattern is observed for the second factor, in line 22. The resulting approximations in line 24 differ somewhat from the residuals in line 19, owing partly to errors of rounding and partly to intercorrelation between the two sets of variables; but the differences are minor, within 1.0 percentage point.

III. Concluding comments

The findings, relating to the decade 1960–70 and the market economies in several major regions, can be briefly stated.

First, excepting the unusual case of the Asia–Middle East region, the major lower income regions, ESE Asia and Africa (excluding South Africa) showed a lower growth of per worker product in the A than in the $(I + S)$ sectors; the higher income LDC region of Latin America showed a rise in per worker product in the A sector about the same as in the $(I + S)$ sector; whereas in the two developed regions, the rise in per worker product in the A sector far exceeded that in per worker product in the $(I + S)$ sector.

Second, the growth per worker in the A sector in the three LDC regions, ranging between 30 and less than 10 percent for the decade, was clearly below the growth in the A sector in the two developed regions. The growth rates per worker in the $(I + S)$ sector in the three LDC regions were about the same at about 27 percent for the decade, distinctly below that for Europe but somewhat higher than that for the North American region.

Third, weighted sectoral growth in per worker product in the LDC regions was substantially below the growth in aggregate product per worker, the difference contributed by the shift in labor force away from the A to the $(I + S)$ sectors. The contribution of this intersectoral shift in labor force to the level of growth in aggregate product per worker was relatively greater in the three LDC regions than in the two developed regions.

There is thus a clear suggestion in the data of limiting constraints on growth of per worker productivity in the A sector in the low-income LDCs, in which the share of the A sector in total labor force and product are still high – as compared with the higher income LDCs, in which these proportions of the A sector have declined to moderate levels and as compared with the developed regions. There is also a suggestion of low-level constraints on the growth in per worker product in the S sector, in both LDC and DC regions, in all of which (again excepting the Asia–Middle East region) growth over the 1960–70 decade was between 16 and 21 percent.

Although the statistical data here relate to a short period and to broad regions, two brief comments can be made to suggest broader empirical relevance and wider general significance of the findings.

One may reasonably surmise that occurrence of lower growth rates in product per worker in the A sector than in the $(I + S)$ sector was fairly widespread. To illustrate (a full demonstration would require summary of a large literature on the subject), one may refer to the discussion of long-term trends in sectoral product per worker for a number of countries in the monograph cited in note 1 (pp. 289–302). This discussion, carried on largely in terms of the basic intersectoral ratio in product per worker, $(I + S)/A$, reveals that for the majority among the 13 currently developed countries, this ratio tended to rise over the decades, until World War II, thus indicating a lower growth rate in per worker product in sector A, with the decline in this ratio emerging largely after World War II. The discussion also suggests, although on the basis of a limited number of countries for 1950 to 1960, that "the basic sectoral inequality in product per worker did not respond to rising per capita (and presumably per worker) product in the less developed countries, but did so in the developed countries" (p. 301). Nor would it be difficult to suggest plausible factors that would account for lower growth rates in per worker product in the A than in the $(I + S)$ sector even for developed countries in the earlier phases of their modern economic growth experience.

The more general comment is to reiterate the emphasis in the brief discussion here on the supply side of output and productivity – as distinct from the demand side, which may be more important in understanding differences in growth rates of sectoral output (rather than of productivity). The differences among production sectors in availability of innovational sources for increase in productivity, sources lying either in technological innovations, or in institutional innovations or resistance, are clearly important in that they are prevalent among production sectors, in different ways in countries at different levels of economic development and change over time. It is, therefore, likely that such differences in potential growth of productivity, due to supply side factors, influence the levels of aggregate growth rates, per worker or per capita, that can be attained. And their influence, combined with conditions that facilitate or impede the shift of resources from sectors of lower to those of higher product per worker (or per unit of total inputs), must be considered in explaining differences in aggregate growth rates among countries at different levels of economic development, and hence with different sectoral structure of production.

3. The pattern of shift of labor force from agriculture, 1950–70

I. Introduction

The comprehensive estimates by the International Labor Office of the industrial structure of the labor force distinguish three major sectors: agriculture, including forestry, fisheries and hunting; industry, including mining, manufacturing, construction, water, power and light utilities; and services, comprising all the other branches, ranging from transport, storage and communication to trade, finance, business services, personal services and government services.

Our interest here is in the *pattern* of the decline in the share of labor force in agriculture, a decline that was widespread from 1950 to 1970 – the two decades covered so far by the ILO estimates. Because the treatment of the female labor force varies widely among regions and countries, particularly for female workers in agriculture, we use the estimates for the share of the male labor force alone. While parallel calculations show that the patterns derived from the share of the *total* labor force in agriculture would differ only in detail, we thought it best to limit the statistical evidence here. It is not feasible to appraise critically the validity of the ILO estimates. We accept them as referring to approximate orders of magnitude, acceptance implying that the findings suggested by the estimates merit discussion and probing.

In *The Theory and Experience of Economic Development: Essays in Honor of Sir W. Arthur Lewis*, edited by Mark Gersovitz, Carlos F. Diaz-Alejandro, Gustav Ranis, and Mark R. Rosenzweig. London: George Allen and Unwin, 1982, pp. 43–59.

II. Pattern of the decline in the share of male labor force in agriculture, in relation to the initial share

The pattern of the declines in the share of the male labor force in agriculture during 1950–70 in relation to the initial share in 1950, is clearly conveyed in Table 3.1. As we move from countries in which the initial share of the agricultural sector is high to those with appreciably lower shares, the absolute decline in the share (let alone the relative drop) widens. In the decade 1950–60, the decline was less than 3 percentage points for countries with an initial share in agriculture of over 90 percent, and reached a peak of 8.8 points for the group with an initial level of the share in agriculture of about 46 percent. And if we continue with the group formed by the 1950 rankings, the decline from 1960 to 1970, which amounts to 3.3 percentage points for the highly agricultural countries in line 1, reaches a peak of 9.3 percentage points for the group with the initial share in agriculture at the 46 percent level. The absolute magnitude of the decline then diminishes as we move to countries in which the initial share of agriculture is lower. The pattern suggests a parabolic curve, the latter describing the movement of the absolute declines on the y-axis, as we shift on the x-axis from the high to the low initial shares of male labor force in agriculture, the peak point being reached in the neighborhood of 50 to 40 percent.

This pattern is derived from a cross-section comparison for a large group of countries, including subgroups that, for our analytical purposes, should be excluded. One such subgroup comprises the communist countries, in which the distinctive character of the economic-growth policies may yield sharp declines in the share of labor in agriculture, regardless of how high or low the initial share may be – within the relevant range from 90 to 40 or 30 percent. Another subgroup are those less developed countries (LDCs) that may benefit from oil (or similarly valuable natural resources exploitable for the benefit of the host nation) – and for many of these, declines in the share of labor in agriculture were dramatically different from those shown by the other LDCs. Also, national units that are tiny, and there has been an increasing number of them in recent years, may be subject to erratic behavior. For all of these reasons, we decided to check the pattern so clearly indicated in Table 3.1, by selecting countries with 1 million or more population in 1950, excluding communist units and those appreciably affected by oil export possibilities. We arrayed these countries separately within each of three major less developed regions,

Table 3.1. *Proportions of male labor force in agriculture (1950) and changes over 1950–70: selected sequences of eleven country moving averages, 1950 ranking*

Sequence	%age proportion (1950) (1)	Decline, %age points (1950–60) (2)	%age proportion (1960) (3)	Decline, %age points (1960–70) (4)	Decline, %age points (1950–70) (5)	%age proportion (1970) (6)
1. 5–15	92.9	2.8	90.1	3.3	6.1	86.8
2. 25–35	84.3	3.8	80.5	3.8	7.6	76.7
3. 45–55	76.3	5.0	71.3	6.0	11.0	65.3
4. 65–75	66.8	5.1	61.7	7.0	12.1	54.7
5. 85–95	55.4	6.5	48.9	8.6	15.1	40.3
6. 95–105	46.1	8.8	37.3	9.3	18.1	28.0
7. 105–15	33.2	5.8	27.4	7.0	12.7	20.4
8. 115–25	23.2	5.6	17.6	5.6	11.2	12.0
9. 121–31	16.7	4.7	12.0	3.9	8.7	8.0

Notes: The entries in the vertical stub are the order numbers of the countries included in each of the selected eleven country averages – taken from an array of all 131 countries in declining order of the share of male labor force in agriculture in 1950.
The averages are unweighted arithmetic means. The totals may show slight discrepancies because of rounding.
The total number of countries, including residual groups in some regions, was 131 – covering both less and more developed countries, market economies and communist units, in short, world coverage.
Source: The table is based on Table 28, p. 62 of *Labour Force, 1950–2000: Estimates and Projections*, Vol. VI, 2nd ed. (Geneva: International Labour Office, 1977), Methodological Supplement. It was supplemented to cover a wider selection, using appendix table C, pp. 118–20 in the same source.

and added the more developed region that would provide, within the re-gional array, countries at the lower ranges of initial shares in agriculture (Table 3.2).

Table 3.2 includes, in the three less developed regions, groups of coun-tries in which the initial, 1950, share of labor force in agriculture ranges from 96 to about 64 percent – with the odd small group in Temperate South America (line 13) with an initial share of only 33 percent. The sig-nificant finding is that the arrays, within each of the three less developed regions, show a rise in the magnitude of the decline – as we move down from the initially high shares of labor in agriculture. We fail to observe here the drop that follows the rise, because with the single exception of Latin America, we miss the groups with an initial, 1950, share level that would be past the peak of the parabolic pattern referred to in connection with Table 3.1. In other words, lines 1–12 of Table 3.2 confirm the pres-

Table 3.2. *Decline in percentage share of male labor force in agriculture: selected countries in one developed and three less developed regions, 1950–70 (1950 ranking)*

	%age proportion (1950) (1)	Decline (1950–60) (2)	%age proportion (1960) (3)	Decline (1960–70) (4)	(1950–70) (5)	%age proportion (1970) (6)
			Less developed regions			
East and Southeast Asia						
1. 1–5	85.2	2.3	82.9	2.9	5.2	80.0
2. 6–10	66.0	4.1	61.9	4.7	8.9	57.2
Africa, excluding South Africa						
3. 1–5	95.8	2.5	93.3	3.6	6.1	89.7
4. 6–10	92.1	3.5	88.6	3.9	7.4	84.7
5. 11–15	89.6	3.8	85.8	3.6	7.4	82.2
6. 16–20	86.0	3.8	82.2	4.2	8.0	78.0
7. 21–25	79.5	5.0	74.5	4.6	9.6	69.9
8. 26–30	71.4	5.3	66.1	5.5	10.8	60.6
Latin America						
9. 1–4	80.6	2.5	78.1	5.4	7.9	72.7
10. 5–8	72.0	2.8	69.1	7.4	10.2	61.7
11. 9–12	65.1	4.4	60.7	5.9	10.3	54.8
12. 13–16	63.7	5.1	58.6	7.8	12.9	50.8
13. 17–19	33.1	4.1	29.0	6.2	10.3	22.8
		Developed region (noncommunist Europe and overseas offshoots)				
14. 1–4	52.3	6.1	46.2	14.3	20.4	31.9
15. 5–8	38.3	8.0	30.2	10.6	18.6	19.6
16. 9–12	26.6	7.4	19.2	7.3	14.8	11.9
17. 13–16	20.5	5.6	14.9	4.0	9.6	10.9
18. 17–20	13.0	4.7	8.3	3.2	7.9	5.2

Notes: Only countries with about 1 million or more of population in 1950 were included. Communist countries were excluded, limiting the group to the market economies. Units affected by being major (in terms of their economy) oil exporters were also excluded. So were units like Hong Kong and Singapore, being essentially urban enclaves within a larger economic sphere.

Within each of the four regions, the countries were arrayed in descending order of the share of male labor force in agriculture in 1950. The numbers in the vertical stub are the order numbers of the countries within each of the four arrays. Then, for the successive groups within each region, unweighted arithmetic means of the 1950 percentage shares of male labor force in agriculture, the 1960 and the 1970 shares (columns 1, 3 and 6) were computed – as well as unweighted means of the declines in columns 2, 4, and 5. The averages will not fully check because of rounding.

The identity of the individual countries included (in declining order of the share in column 1 within each of the four regions) is as follows:

line 1:   Nepal; Bangladesh; Afghanistan; Thailand; Burma
line 2:   India; Philippines; Pakistan; Malaysia; Sri Lanka

ence, among those countries that are less developed market economies, of the rising phase of the pattern revealed for a far more heterogeneous population of countries in Table 3.1.

The confirmation of the declining phase of the pattern of Table 3.1 is provided by the countries covered in lines 14–18 – the dominant majority of which would be classified as more developed countries.[1] These countries cover, at least in the 1950 rankings, the range of initial shares of male labor in agriculture that extends over the declining phase of the parabolic pattern. A glance at the movement of the declines in the shares in lines 14–18 shows the large magnitude of the average declines in line 14 (with an initial share of over 50 percent) and the sharp drop in these declines as we move to the low initial levels of the share in line 18.

Table 3.2 relates to eighty-nine countries, rather than the 131 countries covered in Table 3.1. But at least thirty countries, and possibly a few more, in the larger total would be classified as either communist (centrally planned), or oil export units. Table 3.2 omits some important and relevant units, particularly Japan among the industrial countries, some of the closely associated rapidly growing LDCs such as South Korea and Taiwan, South Africa, and the like. But for our purposes, it is sufficient to show that the parabolic pattern so clearly indicated in Table 3.1 would

---

1 The World Bank (1979, table 1, pp. 126–7) classifies seventeen out of the twenty countries used in lines 14–18 as industrial countries. Only Spain, Portugal and Greece (included by us in the group in line 14) are classified as the upper range of the 'middle-income' group within nonindustrial countries.

Notes to Table 3.2 *(cont.)*

line 3:	Niger; Chad; Rwanda; Mali; Upper Volta
line 4:	Madagascar; Malawi; CAR; Ethiopia; Ivory Coast
line 5:	Uganda; Sudan; Tanzania; Somalia; Burundi
line 6:	Togo; Guinea; Benin; Kenya; Cameroon
line 7:	Zambia; Senegal; Liberia; Zaire; Angola
line 8:	Sierra Leone; Ghana; Tunisia; Morocco; Egypt
line 9:	Haiti; Honduras; Nicaragua; Dominican Republic
line 10:	Guatemala; El Salvador; Bolivia; Colombia
line 11:	Panama; Brazil; Paraguay; Mexico
line 12:	Costa Rica; Ecuador; Jamaica; Peru
line 13:	Chile; Uruguay; Argentina
line 14:	Spain; Portugal; Greece; Finland
line 15:	Ireland; Italy; Norway; France
line 16:	Denmark; Austria; Sweden; Canada
line 17:	New Zealand; Switzerland; Australia; The Netherlands
line 18:	Germany (FR); USA; Belgium; United Kingdom

Source: The basic source for the data on individual countries used here is the same as that used for Table 3.1: see Vol. I, for Asia; Vol. II, for Africa; Vol. III, for Latin America; and Vol. IV, for the developed region.

hold even if we were to limit our universe to market economies, less and more developed. We can then retain the general features of the pattern in Table 3.1, while discussing the behavior of market economies at different levels of industrialization – as revealed by shares of male (and most likely also total) labor force in agriculture.

III. Findings and implications

Let us return now to Table 3.1 and, using its parameters as rough approximations to those in the group of market economies, consider aspects of the findings that were not discussed so far. The first impression that deserves noting is the enormously wide range in the share of labor force in agriculture – from well above 90 percent in the least industrialized countries to well below 10 percent in the industrial countries. It leads one to wonder whether the agricultural sector, while bearing the same title in all these countries, is at all comparable as between countries at extreme positions in the range. Still, we should assume that there are sufficient elements of comparability to warrant the comparison, if only to make it possible to discover the important differences that may still be found.

Secondly, given the two phases of the pattern in Table 3.1, it will be noted that for the less developed countries, in the range of shares of the labor force in agriculture from 93 down to 46 percent (lines 1–6 of Table 3.1), the declines over the period 1950–70 *widened* the differences among the less and more industrialized countries. The range was 46.8 percentage points in 1950; 52.8 points in 1960; and 58.8 points in 1970 (see columns 1, 3, and 6). By contrast, for the more developed countries, associated with the declining phase of the pattern in Table 3.1, that is, in the range from 46 percent of the labor force in agriculture down to less than 10 percent (lines 6–9), the declines over 1950–70 *narrowed* the differences: the range was 29.4 percentage points in 1950; 25.3 points in 1960; and 20.0 points in 1970. Of course, such a comparison implies that the countries do not shift from the less developed to the more developed category, despite the decline in the share of labor force in agriculture – an assumption tenable only for the shorter run.

Thirdly, recent cross-section comparisons of share of labor force in agriculture and per capita product all indicate close and markedly negative association between the two. A comparison (Kuznets, 1971, table 28, p. 200) including some fifty-nine countries, with per capita GDP for 1958 and the share of labor force in agriculture about 1960, shows a decline in the latter from 80 percent in the lowest income group (of about $72 per capita) to 12 percent in the top income group (with about $1,500 per capita). A more elaborate analysis, based on a larger number of countries (over ninety-three) utilizing time-series data for them within the span 1950–70, and fitting a variety of regression equations, estimates the 'predicted' values of the share of labor in *primary* production (agriculture and mining, but most predominantly agriculture) for a range of income levels (per capita GNP, US dollar 1964) from $70 to about $1,500, the share of the labor force declining consistently from 71.2 to 15.9 percent (Chenery and Syrquin, 1975, table 3, pp. 20–21).

Given the close negative association between the share of labor force and per capita product of the country or group of countries, it seems reasonable to argue that a more *moderate* decline in the labor share in the *A* sector characterizing the groups with the initially high shares implies a *smaller* rise in per capita product than that for the less developed market economies with initially lower share of the labor force in agriculture. In other words, the finding of the *widening* over 1950–60 and 1960–70 in the differences among the less developed economies in the share of labor force in agriculture, discussed above, is translated into a *widening* of per worker (or per capita) income differentials among the groups of less developed countries in the array associated with the rising phase of the pattern found in Table 3.1. The higher share of labor in agriculture groups which are initially also the lower per capita product groups, showing moderate declines in the labor force shares, would presumably show also the lower rates of increase in per capita product.

Partial, yet significant, support for this inference is provided in Table 3.3. Here, we have again a group of seventy-two less developed market economies, omitting the oil exporters, purely urban enclaves (such as Hong Kong and Singapore), and a few countries for which national product data were not available. These countries are grouped throughout by the share of male labor force in agriculture in 1960; and one should first note that the negative association between the magnitude of declines in the share during 1960–70 and the level of the initial share is quite similar to that observable for the much larger and more heterogeneous group in Table 3.1 (see columns 3 and 4, lines 1–6 of that table, in comparison with columns 1 and 2, lines 9–13 of Table 3.3). In Table 3.1 the declines associated with 1960 shares ranging down from 90 to about 37 percent

Table 3.3. *Grouping of less developed market economies by share of male labor force in agriculture (MLFA), for comparison with level and growth rate of GNP per capital (1976 US dollar)*

	%age proportion, MLFA (1960) (1)	Decline in column 1 (1960–70) (2)	Growth rate, per year, GNP per capita (1960–76) (3)	GNP per capita (1976 US dollar) (1960) (4)	(1976) (5)
Successive sequences, nine countries each					
1. 1–9	92.7	3.0	0.94	124	144
2. 10–18	87.7	3.7	1.52	191	243
3. 19–27	83.8	3.8	1.37	159	198
4. 28–36	76.5	5.0	2.22	352	500
5. 37–45	70.6	6.1	2.12	220	308
6. 46–54	64.3	8.8	3.26	469	783
7. 55–63	57.3	4.7	3.07	422	684
8. 64–72	39.9	9.2	3.17	881	1,452
Sequences above, averaged					
9. 1–9	92.7	3.0	0.94	124	144
10. 10–27	85.8	3.6	1.44	175	221
11. 28–45	73.6	5.6	2.17	286	404
12. 46–63	60.8	6.8	3.16	456	733
13. 64–72	39.9	9.2	3.17	881	1,452

Note: The GNP data used for columns 3–5 were taken from table 1, pp. 76–7, *World Development Report*, 1978 (Washington, DC: World Bank, 1978). This table presents data on GNP per capita in 1976 US dollars, and on the growth rate, percentage per year, for 1960–76, in GNP per capita in 1976 US dollars, for ninety-two less developed (low-and middle-income) countries. We selected seventy-two countries, omitting the communist economies, the oil exporters, the city enclave units (such as Hong Kong and Singapore) and the few units for which data were incomplete. In terms of 1976 per capita GNP, the seventy-two countries ranged from $70 for Bhutan, to $2,920 for Spain.

For these seventy-two countries we used the shares of male labor force in agriculture in 1960 and 1970, provided in the source used for Table 3.1, above (table A, pp. 105–7, for 1960; and pp. 111–13, for 1970). The countries were arrayed by decreasing share of male labor force in agriculture in 1960, and grouped into eight sequential groups of nine countries each. The entries in columns 1–2, lines 1–8 are unweighted arithmetic means of the shares in 1960 and of the declines (percentage points) from 1960 to 1970.

The growth rates in column 3 are similarly unweighted arithmetic means of those for the individual countries included in each of the eight sequential groups; and so are the unweighted means of 1976 GNP per capita in column 5. Those in column 4 were extrapolated from the eight means in column 5 by applying the average growth rates in column 3, cumulated over sixteen years and carried backwards from 1976 to 1960.

The entries in lines 9 and 13 are identical with those in lines 1 and 8, respectively. Those in lines 10–12 are unweighted means of the entries in lines 2–3, 4–5, and 6–7, respectively. The calculations for the MLFA shares used shares to two decimal places, and the averages were rounded off.

move from 3 percentage points to roughly 4, 6, 7, 8.6, and 9; in Table 3.3 the analogous declines move from 3 to 3.6, to 5.6, to 6.8 and, finally, to 9.2.

It is with this array of MLFA shares and declines that we associate, in columns 3 and 4 of Table 3.3, the growth rates of GNP per capita, and the roughly estimated initial levels of GNP per capita in 1960. The growth rates are for 1960–76, a sixteen-year span, while the changes in MLFA shares are over a decade; but one may doubt that the broad association shown would be much changed with recalculation of growth rates in per capita GNP to relate to a shorter span. The entries given now in columns 2 and 3, lines 9–13 show a significant positive correlation between magnitude of decline in the MLFA share over 1960–70 and the growth rate in per capita GNP over 1960–76. Also there is the expected negative association between the levels of the MLFA shares in 1960, in column 1, and the approximate levels of GNP per capita in 1960, in column 4.

To be sure, the association is subject to a few exceptions when we deal with the more detailed groups in lines 1–8; and, more important, association is not causation. It would be impermissible to argue that the declines of the MLFA share were small *because* the initial MLFA shares were high, among the poorer LDCs; and that the *small* declines in the MLFA shares *caused* low rates of growth in per capita GNP. A more realistic and plausible approach would be to argue that the economic and social characteristics of less developed market economies at high levels of the MLFA share were such as to make it difficult to attain a high growth rate in per capita or per worker product, and the latter being the consequence, it also impeded a substantial decline in the share of labor in agriculture. Yet the association noted is of both interest and value, because it draws our attention to the character of the socioeconomic structures within which the pattern of movement of labor from agriculture indicated by Tables 3.1, 3.2, and 3.3 is embedded.

Fourthly, we turn to the last aspect of the pattern to be noted explicitly – its possible effects on inequality in product per worker between agriculture (*A*) and the other (*I + S*) sectors, and hence possibly, at further remove, on inequality in income per worker or per capita. The effects to be considered are specifically of the conspicuous rise and fall in the magnitude of the changes in the shares of male labor force in the two sectors, as we move from the high initial shares of the *A* sectors to about 37 percent (in 1960) and down to 12 percent (see Table 3.1, columns 3 and

4). To illustrate these possible effects we are forced to use assumptions, with whatever loss of realism they imply. But stating these assumptions and considering their possible limitations could, in itself, be useful in suggesting the significant connections.

The first step is to view the decline in the share of MLF in the A sector, and the corresponding rise in the share in the $I + S$ sector, as 'migration' – a change in the sectoral attachment either of workers within their working lifespan, or in the new generation of workers compared with the older, or in both. The change may or may not involve migration in space, although the likelihood of such migration would be substantial, considering the dominance of rural locus for the A sector and the dominance of the urban locus for the $I + S$ sector.[2] But it is a change that means a group of *new*comers in the $I + S$ sector, whereas such new migrants would be absent or scarce in the labor force of the A sector.

Identifying the net change in the share of MLF in the A and $I + S$ sectors as the migration component, as we do in Table 3.4 (see columns 3 and 5 of panel I), implies an assumption. It is to the effect that the rates of increase (natural increase combined with the change in male specific labor force participation rates) are, say, over the decade 1960–70, the same for the 1960 male labor in the A and the $I + S$ sectors. If these rates of increase are *unequal*, for instance, if the rate is higher for the 1960 labor force attached to the A sector, the migration or shift segment, of newcomers to the $I + S$ sector, would be larger than now stated in Table 3.1 (and hence in Table 3.4). No firm evidence is available for recent years on this point, particularly if we recognize that the data would be needed separately for the groups of countries at different levels of socioeconomic development associated with the different initial levels of the share of MLF in the A or $I + S$ sectors. We decided not to illustrate the effects of variant assumptions on this aspect of sectoral shift in labor force, to avoid complicating unduly the presentation in Table 3.4.[3]

The next set of assumptions refers to differentials in per worker product

2 See in this connection, United Nations (1980, ch. V, pp. 68–71).
3 For the pre–First World War decades in the currently developed countries, the rates of natural increase of the urban population were so much lower than those in the countryside that the implicit migration component in the rural–urban distribution of the labor force must have been appreciably greater than that obtained as net change in the percentage shares. But it is not clear that similar differential rates of natural increase between the cities and countryside are true of the LDCs in the post–Second World War decades. And such urban–rural differentials are not a fully relevant guide here.

Table 3.4. *Effects of decline in share of MLF in agriculture (1960–70) on inter-sectoral inequality in product (P_1 and P_2) per worker in 1970 (data from Table 3.1)*

Panel I. *%age shares in MLF and in product (P_1P_2), Total MLF and MLF in the (I+S) Sector, 1970*

Successive sequences from Table 3.1	%age shares in total MLF				%age shares in (I+S)	
	(A)	(I+S)			Recent migrants	Old-timers
		Total	Recent migrants	Old-timers		
	(1)	(2)	(3)	(4)	(5)	(6)
5–15						
1. MLF	86.8	13.2	3.3	9.9	25.0	75.0
2. P_1 (113.2)	76.7	23.3	2.9	20.4	12.4	87.6
3. P_2 (126.4)	68.7	31.3	2.6	28.7	8.3	91.7
25–35						
4. MLF	76.7	23.3	3.8	19.5	16.3	83.7
5. P_1 (123.3)	62.2	37.8	3.1	34.7	8.2	91.8
6. P_2 (146.6)	52.3	47.7	2.6	45.0	5.45	94.55
45–55						
7. MLF	65.3	34.7	6.0	28.7	17.3	82.7
8. P_1 (134.7)	48.5	51.5	4.5	47.0	8.7	91.3
9. P_2 (169.4)	38.55−	61.45+	3.5	57.95	5.7	94.3
65–75						
10. MLF	54.7	45.3	7.0	38.3	15.45	84.55
11. P_1 (145.3)	37.6	62.4	4.8	57.6	7.7	92.3
12. P_2 (190.6)	28.7	71.3	3.7	67.6	5.2	94.8
85–95						
13. MLF	40.3	59.7	8.6	51.1	14.4	85.6
14. P_1 (159.7)	25.2	74.8	5.4	69.4	7.2	92.8
15. P_2 (219.4)	18.4	81.6	3.9	77.7	4.8	95.2
95–105						
16. MLF	28.0	72.0	9.3	62.7	12.9	87.1
17. P_1 (172.0)	16.3	83.7	5.4	78.3	6.45	93.55
18. P_2 (244.0)	11.5	88.5	3.8	84.7	4.3	95.7
105–115						
19. MLF	20.4	79.6	7.0	72.6	8.8	91.2
20. P_1 (179.6)	11.4	88.6	3.9	84.7	4.4	95.6
21. P_2 (259.2)	7.9	92.1	2.7	89.4	2.9	97.1
115–125						
22. MLF	12.0	88.0	5.6	82.4	6.4	93.6
23. P_1 (188.0)	6.4	93.6	3.0	90.6	3.2	96.8
24. P_2 (276.0)	4.35	95.65	2.0	93.65	2.1	97.9

Table 3.4 (cont.)

	%age shares in total MLF (A)	(I+S)			%age shares in (I+S)	
Successive sequences from Table 3.1	(1)	Total (2)	Recent migrants (3)	Old-timers (4)	Recent migrants (5)	Old-timers (6)
121–131						
25. MLF	8.0	92.0	4.0	88.0	4.35	95.65
26. P_1 (192.0)	4.2	95.8	2.1	93.7	2.2	97.8
27. P_2 (284.0)	2.8	97.2	1.4	95.8	1.4	98.6

Panel II. *Measures of disparity (TDM), product per worker*

	For total MLF and P				For MLF and P in (I+S)		
Successive sequences	TDM (A)– (I+S) (1)	Ratio RM to MLF in (A) (2)	Col. 1 × Col. 2 (3)	TDM (A)– RM–OT directly (4)	TDM RM– OT (5)	Weight (I+S) in total (6)	Col. 5 × Col. 6 (7)
			For P_1				
28. 5–15	20.2	0.038	0.8	21.0	25.2	0.132	3.3
29. 25–35	29.0	0.050	1.4	30.4	18.2	0.233	3.8
30. 45–55	33.6	0.092	3.1–	36.6	17.2	0.347	6.0
31. 65–75	34.2	0.128	4.4	38.6	15.5	0.453	7.0
32. 85–95	30.2	0.213	6.4	36.6	14.4	0.697	8.6
33. 95–105	23.4	0.332	7.8	31.2	12.9	0.720	9.3
34. 105–15	18.0	0.343	6.2	24.2	8.8	0.796	7.0
35. 115–25	11.2	0.467	5.2	16.4	6.4	0.880	5.6
36. 121–31	7.6	0.500	3.8	11.4	4.3	0.920	4.0
			For P_2				
37. 5–15	36.2	0.038	1.4	37.6	33.4	0.132	4.4
38. 25–35	48.8	0.050	2.4	51.2	21.7	0.233	5.1
39. 45–55	53.5	0.092	4.9+	58.5	23.2	0.347	8.1
40. 65–75	52.0	0.128	6.6	58.6	20.5	0.453	9.3
41. 85–95	43.8	0.213	9.3+	53.2	19.2	0.597	11.5
42. 95–105	33.0	0.332	11.0	44.0	17.2	0.720	12.4
43. 105–15	25.0	0.343	8.6	33.6	11.8	0.796	9.4
44. 115–25	15.3	0.467	7.1+	22.5	8.6	0.880	7.6
45. 121–31	10.4	0.500	5.2	15.6	5.9	0.920	5.5

Notes: *Panel I, lines 1, 4, 7, 10, 13, 16, 19, 22 and 25:* taken directly, or computed from Table 3.1, columns 6 and 4. No assumptions are involved except in viewing the decline in the share of MLF in agriculture in 1960–70 as net migration (change) over the decade from the *A* to the *I+S* sectors (see discussion in text).
Panel I, lines 2, 5, 8, 11, 14, 17, 20, 23 and 26: calculated on the assumption that the ratio of product per male worker in the *I+S* sector to product per male worker in the *A* sector

between the two major sectors. In Table 3.4 we used two variants, with differences in product per worker of 2 to 1 and 3 to 1, both in favor of the $I + S$ sector. And most importantly, we assumed that either of these ratios, once adopted, was the same for the nine groups of countries that we distinguished, and that differed so much with respect to the share of labor force in the A sector and to the associated economic characteristics.

It is difficult to judge the validity of these assumptions. The 2 to 1 and 3 to 1 ratios used were suggested by the empirical evidence in the two sources referred to in references 2 and 3, above. In my 1971 study the ratios ranged from 4 at the lower income levels to 1.4 at the upper income levels, with the middle of the range at somewhat over 2 (1971, table 31, p. 209). In the much larger sample in the Chenery–Syrquin monograph, the intersectoral ratio (labor force in the primary sector, agriculture and mining, and in the other sectors) of product per worker, at 2.26 in the poorest countries, with the total labor force share in the primary sector of 71.2 percent, rises to a peak of 2.64 at higher income levels with the labor force shares in the primary sector at 49 and 44 percent, respectively; and then declines to 2.10 at the next-to-highest income group, with total labor force share in the primary sector of 25 percent. It is only in the

Notes to Table 3.4 *(cont.)*

is 2:1, the ratio held the same for the groups of countries at different levels of the initial or terminal share (for discussion of this assumption, see text). The entry in parentheses in the vertical stub for each group is the index for the total product for country group, that for MLF in each group being 100.

Panel I, lines 3, 6, 9, 12, 15, 18, 21, 24 and 27: calculated on the assumption of a ratio of product per male worker in the $I+S$ sector to product per male worker in the A sector of 3:1. The entries in parentheses are indexes of the total product for each country group, that for MLF in each group being 100.

Panel II: the disparity measures in columns 1, 4, and 5 are obtained by comparing the percentage shares in male labor force and in product $P_1 P_2$, and adding the differences, signs disregarded (see brief discussion of measure in the text). The needed percentage shares are in panel I (columns 1 and 2, for the measure in column 1 here; columns 1, 3, and 4, for the measure in column 4 here; columns 5 and 6, for the measure in column 5 here).

The proportions in column 2 are those of the share of the RM segment in male labor force (column 3, panel I, lines relating to MLF) to the percentage share in the A sector (column 1 of panel I, lines relating to MLF). The product of this ratio by the TDM in column 1 of panel II should yield the absolute addition to the TDM due to separate treatment of the RM component (see text); and the sum of columns 1 and 3 should yield the TDM in column 4. The slight discrepancies are due to rounding.

The proportions in column 6 are those of the $I+S$ sector in total male labor force in 1970, and appear as percentage shares in column 2 of panel I, lines 1, 4, 7, 10, 13, 16, 19, 22 and 25.

As the discussion in the text indicates, the product of columns 5 and 6 should yield, for the variant P_1, the magnitudes of the decline in the percentage share of the male labor force in agriculture over the decade 1960–70. For variant P_2, the product in column 7 should yield the same magnitudes of the decline, multiplied by the fraction ⅕ (see text).

top income group, with the primary labor force share of 16 percent, that the intersectoral product per worker ratio drops to 1.30 (see Table 3, pp. 20–1). One can, thus, suggest that in the range of the share of the labor force in the *A* sector from 70 to 25 percent, the intersectoral ratio moved within a range from 2.1 to 2.6; and to that extent there is an element of realism in the illustrative assumptions in Table 3.4.

The third important assumption relates to the product differential to be assigned to the recent migrants (RM) segment. For Table 3.4, we assumed that the per worker product of the new migrant segment, at the end of the decade during which the migration occurred, would be the same as the per worker product in the *A* sector at the end of the decade but no larger. This implies that the migrant subgroup sustains a rise in per worker product equal to that of the sector from which it came; but the results would be only partly affected by more favorable assumptions concerning the per worker product of that segment so long as it remains much lower than the product per worker of the 'old-timers' (OT) – a term we use for members of the *I* + *S* labor force who have been attached to that sector for a long time, or descended from the latter. We complete the step by adding the assumption that by the end of the *second* decade after migration, when the length of stay with the *I* + *S* sector extends roughly to a decade and a half, the migrant subgroup would be fully assimilated to the point of generating an average product equal to that of the 'old-timers.' The result is that, say, in 1970 only the migrant segment of the immediately preceding decade is to be considered – there being no separate effect of the migrant subgroups of the decade 1950–60 or of earlier decades. The assumption is clearly unrealistic in implying a rapid rate of rise in per worker product of the migrant segment; but its results are suggestive, if in reality there is a marked movement upward in per worker product of in-migrants a decade to a decade and a half after migration. Table 3.4 applies to the labor and product shares in 1970 and, thus, to the movements from 1960 to 1970; but the results for 1960 and the movements from 1950 to 1960 would be similar. Also the results do not depend on the specific values of the initial shares and changes in them, so long as the general pattern familiar to us now prevails.

The gist of the assumptions stated, and the expediency reasons for adopting them being obvious enough not to require elaboration, we can now note the findings in Table 3.4. With panel I of the table needed largely to derive the disparity measures appearing in panel II, we can concentrate on the latter and attempt to list the findings seriatim. These disparity measures are the sums of differences between two variables in the associated percentage shares, signs disregarded.[4]

1. While our main interest in Table 3.4 is in the effects of *change* in MLF shares in the two main sectors A and $I + S$, that is, essentially of what we designate as recent migrants (the RM segment), it is relevant to begin with the effects of the assumed intersectoral product per worker ratios on the total (or weighted) sectoral disparities at the different levels of the sectoral shares. These measures appear in column 1 of panel II and convey a similar pattern of differences in associated disparities of the two variants P_1 and P_2, despite the wider amplitude of the disparities for P_2. The sectoral disparities widen as we shift from the high shares of sector A countries to about the middle range (87 to 55, or 40 percent) and then narrow appreciably as the share of the labor force in the A sector dwindles rapidly.

This pattern of total disparities in product per worker, with its rise and decline, column 1 of panel II, is of interest, because it is a necessary result of the conditions set – a two-sector model in which the initially high share of the lower income sector in labor force continuously declines, and the ratio of per worker product in the rising sector to that in the declining sector remains at the same level. To illustrate: the TDM of 20.2 in line 28, column 1 can be seen as *double* the difference between 86.8 and 76.7 in column 1, lines 1 and 2 (panel I), with 76.7 derivable as the ratio 86.8:1.132. The *difference* between 86.8 and 86.8:1.132 can be rewritten as the *product* of two components: 86.8 (component A) and (0.132:1.132) or 0.1166 (component B) – the former determined by the movement of the share of labor force in agriculture, the latter being moved by the complementary changes in the share of labor force in the $I + S$ sector. As we shift from one sequence to the next in panel I, component A declines by ever-increasing fractions, which in and of itself would reduce the TDM; while at the same time component B would be rising, but at diminishing

4 For a recent brief discussion of this measure, see chapter 7, below. We use the sum of differences, signs disregarded, as an index of disparity. It would be more comparable to the familiar Gini coefficient if the sum were divided by 200, the maximum limit which the total disparity can approach. Thus, the entry of 20.2 in line 28, column 1 would become 0.101. In that form, the disparity measure is a crude approximation to a Gini coefficient, lower than the latter for cases with more than two classes but yielding comparable differences. For only two classes, the two measures would be identical.

rates, which by itself would raise the TDM. As a consequence, the TDM for this two-sector case would be increasing, so long as the relative rise in the B component exceeds the relative decline in the A component; and would start to decline when, inevitably, the *proportional* rise in the B component, being slowed down by the rise in the $I + S$ share, begins to fall short of the A component.

The comment just made will perhaps be more telling, if illustrated by the data from Table 3.4. In Table 3.5, supplementary to Table 3.4, we calculate the two components, for four pairs of contiguous sequences in panel I of Table 3.4; and demonstrate how the continuously widening drop in the share of the labor force in agriculture (component A) is first more than offset by the rise in component B, and then results in a decline in the total disparity measure.

The illustration also reveals why, with a wider intersectoral disparity in product per worker in the P_2 variant, the point of shift from rising to declining TDMs occurs at a higher level of the A share than for the P_1 variant. And it is easy to infer from the illustration what changing or different levels of the ratio of per worker product in the $I + S$ sector to that in the A sector would mean for the levels and movements of the resulting TDMs. Finally, while both Tables 3.4 and 3.5 use specific data for the decade 1960–70 and for 1970, similar results would be found for any set of sequences in which the share of the labor force in agriculture would be consistently declining over the range from over 90 down to less than 10 percent, while its per worker product would be consistently below that in the $I + S$ sector by a constant or near-constant ratio over the range.

2. When we distinguish the RM segment, and deal with three divisions – the A sector, the RM segment within the $I + S$ sector and the OT group, which we obtain by subtraction – the sectoral product per worker disparity (column 4 of panel II) becomes consistently and significantly larger than that for the two sectors in column 1 of panel II. The reason is that we derive the OT subgroup of the $I + S$ sector as a segment of the labor force with invariably higher per worker product than is true of the total $I + S$ sector – thus, creating necessarily a wider product per worker disparity. This conclusion is inevitable, once we assume that the per worker product for the recent migrants into the $I + S$ sector is below the per worker product for the old-timers while the ratio of per worker product in the total $I + S$ sector to that in the A sector remains the same (whether it be 2:1 or 3:1).

Table 3.5. *Illustration of changes in the two components that determine the total weighted disparity in per worker product for the A and I+S sectors, four pairs of contiguous sequences from Table 3.4*

Successive sequence	Component A (1)	Component B_1 (2)	TDM$_1$ (3)	Component B_2 (4)	TDM$_2$ (5)
1. 5–15	86.8	$\frac{0.132}{1.132}$ 0.1166	20.2	$\frac{0.264}{1.264}$ 0.2089	36.2
2. 25–35	76.7	$\frac{0.233}{1.233}$ 0.1890	29.0	$\frac{0.466}{1.466}$ 0.3179	48.8
3. Line 2/ line 1	0.884	1.621	1.43	1.522	1.35
4. 45–55	65.3	$\frac{0.347}{1.347}$ 0.2576	33.6	$\frac{0.694}{1.694}$ 0.4097	53.5
5. 65–75	54.7	$\frac{0.453}{1.453}$ 0.3118	34.2	$\frac{0.906}{1.906}$ 0.4753	52.0
6. Line 5/ line 4	0.838	1.210	1.02	1.160	0.97
7. 85–95	40.3	$\frac{0.597}{1.597}$ 0.3738	30.2	$\frac{1.194}{2.194}$ 0.5442	43.8
8. 95–105	28.0	$\frac{0.720}{1.720}$ 0.4186	23.4	$\frac{1.440}{2.440}$ 0.5902	33.0
9. Line 8/ line 7	0.695	1.1199	0.78	1.0845	0.75
10. 105–15	20.4	$\frac{0.796}{1.796}$ 0.4432	18.0	$\frac{1.592}{2.592}$ 0.6142	25.0
11. 115–25	12.0	$\frac{0.880}{1.880}$ 0.4681	11.2	$\frac{1.760}{2.760}$ 0.6377	15.3
12. Line 11/ line 10	0.588	1.0562	0.62	1.0383	0.61

Notes: B_1 and TDM$_1$ designate the B component and the total disparity measure for the P_1 variant. B_2 and TDM$_2$ are the B component and the total disparity measure for the P_2 variant.

The A component relating to male labor force alone is the same for the P_1 and P_2 variants. All the data on the components are from Table 3.4, panel I.

Column 3 is derivable as the product of entries in columns 1 and 2. Column 5 is derivable as the product of entries in columns 1 and 4. Entries in columns 3 and 5, lines 3, 6, 9, and 12 are also the ratios of the TDMs in lines 2, 5, 8, and 11 to those in lines 1, 4, 7, and 10.

In line with the distinction of the two components that determine the magnitude of the TDM for two sectors, particularly as illustrated in Table 3.5, there is an alternative way of deriving and viewing the absolute addition of the TDM resulting from the separation of the RM segment within the $I + S$ sector. This can be viewed as *adding* a fraction to the A component, while retaining all other terms, a fraction that is formed by the proportion of the RM segment to the terminal share of the labor force in the *A* sector. These proportions, which appear in column 2 of panel II, can then be applied to the product of the two components (which multiplied by 2 constitute the TDM for the two-sector case) – and this would yield, as indicated in column 3 of panel II, the correct addition to the TDM in column 1 to derive that in column 4. One interesting aspect of this demonstration is the emphasis on the continuous rise in the *proportion* of the agricultural labor force that is lost in the decline, as we shift from the highly agricultural to the highly industrialized countries.

However derived, the absolute addition to the TDMs in column 1 of panel II of Table 3.4, due to the separation of the RM segment within the *I + S* sector, is naturally a function of the magnitude of the absolute magnitude of that segment. Consequently, the pattern of movements of this absolute addition in column 3 of panel II is a faithful reproduction, in timing, of that in the absolute declines of the labor share in the *A* sector rising from low magnitude in the 5–15 sequence, reaching a peak in the 95–105 sequence and then declining sharply. Thus, in absolute terms, the disparity measure is widened by the inclusion of the RM segment most in those countries in which this migration component is absolutely greater.

3. In turning now to the effect of the RM segment on inequality in product per worker *within* the *I + S* sector we find that the disparity so contributed diminishes fairly steadily (except in the movement from the 25–35 to the 45–55 sequences) as we shift from the countries with very low *I + S* shares to the more industrialized countries (see column 5 of panel II). The result is one that could be expected, since a shift of 3.3 percentage points to the *I + S* sector in a country group in which the *total* share of this sector is 13.2 percentage points, means an RM segment equal to a *third* of the OT group; whereas even a major shift of 9.3 percentage points for the 95–105 sequence is about one-seventh of the much larger OT group of 62.7 (see lines 1 and 16 of panel I). Indeed, the large relative magnitude of the influx into the *I + S* sector of the least industrialized countries may, in itself, suggest reasons why the *absolute* magnitude of the influx is so limited.

Still, the introduction of the migrant segment into the *I + S* sector does result in a significant widening of intrasector disparities in product per worker. In viewing the latter as part of total disparities within the countrywide labor force this intra–*I + S* sector disparity should be weighted by the share of that sector in total labor force. When we do this in columns 6 and 7 of panel II, we find that the *weighted* contribution of the migrant segment to per worker inequalities within the $I + S$ sector reproduces precisely the pattern that we found repeatedly in Table 3.1 and the other tables. This identity of the pattern in column 7 of panel II with those of changes in the shares of labor force in the A sector is a necessary result of the assumptions used in Table 3.4 and the procedure based on them. This can be illustrated by the data in Table 3.4, panel I, for the first sequence, that of 5–15; but the illustration holds also for each of these and similar sequences.

For P_1, the entry of 25.2 in line 28, column 5 is the difference between the entries in column 5 of lines 1 and 2, 12.6 percentage points, multiplied by 2. But the 12.6 points difference is that between 3.3:13.2 and 2.9:23.3, the latter in turn being derived from (3.3:113.2)/(26.4:113.2). The 12.6 difference can then be written as that between 3.3:13.2 and 3.3:26.4. This yields one-half of 3.3, which multiplied by 2 yields 3.3 in column 7 – the value *identical* with the percentage-point decline in the share of the A sector.

For P_2, the entry of 33.4 in line 37, column 5 is the difference between 25.0 and 8.3, lines 1 and 3, column 5, or 16.7 multiplied by 2. But the 16.7 points difference is that between 3.3:13.2 and 3.3:39.6, which is two-thirds of 3.3. If we multiply the result by 2, we secure ⅓ of 3.3, or 4.4 – the entry we find in line 37, column 7. It follows that all entries for P_2 in column 7 would, allowing for rounding errors, approximate ⅓ times the comparable entries in column 7 for the P_1 variant.

IV. Concluding comments

Our discussion dealt with the statistical evidence on the shift of the male labor force from agriculture to the other $I + S$ sectors, for less developed and more developed market economies, for the two decades 1950–70 – utilizing the world-wide estimates of the ILO. This evidence revealed a distinctive pattern, in which the absolute magnitude of the declines in the labor force share in agriculture was quite small for the highly agricultural countries with initial high shares in the A sector; widened appreciably as we moved to the more industrialized countries among the less developed, with the initial shares of labor force in agriculture down to about 40 to 30 percent; and then narrowed again as we considered the industrialized, more developed countries with lower initial shares in the A sector. The different levels of shares of the labor force in agriculture were significantly and negatively associated with levels of product per capita or per worker; and among the less developed market economies, differences among the subgroups in the magnitude of the shift of labor force from agriculture were significantly and positively associated with differences in growth rates of per capita product. It follows that among the less developed countries, the poorer and more agricultural countries showed a smaller shift out of agriculture and a lower growth rate of per capita product than the middle- and upper-middle-income, less developed countries, which showed a greater shift of labor force out of agriculture and higher rates of growth of per capita product.

We also explored, with the help of simple but roughly realistic assumptions, the total disparity in per worker product between the A and $I + S$ sectors in countries at different levels of industrialization (as indicated by shares of labor force in the two sectors). The findings can be briefly stated. First, for the two-sector model, without considering the changes in the share over the decade, total (weighted) disparity in product per worker was narrow for countries with very high shares of the A and very low shares of the $I + S$ sectors; widened as the shares of labor force in the A sector approached the middle levels; and then narrowed again as the shares of the A sector declined to low levels (and those of the $I + S$ sector rose to high levels). Secondly, the segregation of the decline in the share of the labor force in the A sector, viewed as a recent migration (RM) segment within the $I + S$ sector, widened the total disparity measure (TDM) for the $A - I + S$ comparison, the absolute additions to this measure following faithfully the pattern of absolute declines in the share of labor force in agriculture, associated with the different initial levels of these shares. And the separation of the RM segment within the $I + S$ sector, contributed also to intrasectoral differences in product per worker within that sector, which when weighted by the share of $I + S$ sector in the total labor force, again followed the pattern of declines in the shares of labor force in agriculture associated with different initial levels of these shares. It follows that the widening of disparity in product per worker among the major sectors, and within the $I + S$ sector, was greater for groups of middle- and higher-income LDCs than either among the low-income LDCs, or among the more developed market economies. But it should be stressed that these findings relate to only a part of the total inequalities in product per worker: the two other components of overall differences in product per worker, those within the A sector and those within the $I + S$

sector were not considered, except for the distinction of the RM segment within the latter.

An acceptable explanation of the findings just summarized would require a critical appraisal of the ILO estimates, particularly for the poorer LDCs, in which the statistical bases are weak and the concept of attachment of the labor force to a sector may be much more ambiguous than in higher-income LDCs or in more developed countries in which the labor force is more distinctly specialized. It would also call for tested analysis of aspects of structural change and growth that were either dealt with here by assumption, or were not considered at all (for instance, the effect of the movement of labor from agriculture on the inequality in per worker product within the A sector). These and other lines of further exploration cannot be pursued here; and the discussion remains an exploratory probing of a limited aspect of recent economic growth experience.

References

Chenery, H. and Syrquin, M., *Patterns of Development, 1950–1970*. London: Oxford University Press, 1975.

Kuznets, S., *Economic Growth of Nations: Total Output and Production Structure*. Cambridge, Mass.: Harvard University Press, 1971.

United Nations, *Patterns of Urban and Rural Population Growth*. New York: United Nations, 1980.

World Bank, *World Development Report, 1979*. Washington, DC: World Bank, 1979.

4. Modern economic growth and the less developed countries (LDCs)

In thinking of the impressive record of Taiwan's economic growth over the last three decades, to be documented and discussed in the papers for this Conference, I was tempted to reflect on the conditions that permit and induce such a performance in an LDC. One such condition is indicated by the existence of the more developed countries, with their demonstrated contribution of modern economic growth to the great increase in product per capita or per worker – for it indicates the existence of a technological backlog, the exploitation of which could generate accelerated advance elsewhere. The characteristics of modern economic growth are thus important in both helping us to identify the LDCs, and in enabling us to infer, if only tentatively, the kinds of breakthrough that can initiate and sustain a high rate of growth in an LDC – after a long period of stagnation or of moderate advance.

I. Distinctive characteristics of modern economic growth[1]

1. The basic feature of modern economic growth, as it has been observed in the more developed countries since the late 18th century, is that the rise in per capita or per worker product was associated largely with extended application of a growing stock of useful knowledge, via technological innovations in production. The high pace of such a rise was increasingly due to advance of science, i.e., of organized systematic knowledge of the processes of nature (including man as a biologi-

In *Experiences and Lessons of Economic Development in Taiwan*, Conference, Dec. 18–20, 1981, edited by Kwoh-ting Li and Tzong-shian Yu, Academia Sinica, Taipei, Taiwan, 1982, pp. 11–20.

1 For a more detailed discussion of the points covered in this section, see Chapter 1, above.

cal species); and to continuous interaction between scientific discovery and advance, technological invention, its application as an innovation, substantial accretion of science-stimulating knowledge as result of the innovation, more knowledge and discovery, and so on.

While generalizations about the characteristics of advance in production-relevant knowledge are risky, two observations may be suggested. One is that the growing stock of useful knowledge reduces the dependence of increased productivity on any single set of natural resources – whatever short-term constraints on specific resource supplies may have arisen in transient historical maladjustments. The second is that the growing scale of production, associated with the increased volumes of fixed capital investment required by advancing technology, could, for a small country, be attained with increased international division of labor, i.e., with larger volumes of international trade and other movements, otherwise facilitated by improved means of transport and communication. It follows that there could be a significant pace of advance and high levels of productivity in countries that were relatively poor in natural resources, as the cases of such countries as Denmark and Switzerland, or among the latecomers that of Japan, demonstrate; and also that the size of a small country's economy was no barrier to accelerated growth and high per worker productivity, assuming an adequate sharing of wider markets through international trade. Given the power of modern technology and effectiveness of modern trade ties, the potential growth of an LDC should only moderately be constrained by scarcity of natural resources, or by scale problems because of smallness of the internal markets.

2. The high rate of growth in per capita and per worker product in the developed countries required, and was accompanied by, rapid shifts in production and social structure – usually referred to as industrialization, urbanization, movement of labor force to employee status, and the like. The high pace of these shifts, and their disjunction with the natural processes of population growth, involved substantial internal (and, at times, external) migration. It also meant a growing difference between parental and children's generations in their economic and social attachment; an increasing input into human capital via formal education as basic orientation for the younger, incoming generation; and reduction in the role of the wider family unit in the provision of important services.

The points to be emphasized here bear on the capacity of the population to respond to changing economic opportunities by education, by migration, and by shifts in both demographic patterns and in sets of values toward greater consonance with the opportunities and requirements associated with modern technology.

3. While the production-related stock of useful knowledge is transnational, in that it is valid in production processes anywhere in this world and in that it is accessible regardless of national boundaries, the organization of mankind that seems most prevalent and conspicuous in modern economic growth is that by sovereign, national, states. Indeed, the spread of modern economic growth placed greater emphasis on the importance and need for organization in national sovereign units – as is evident in the increasing pressure toward formation of such units in the 19th century (either by unification, as in the case of Germany and Italy, or by separation, as in the case of Netherlands and Belgium); and more recently toward the removal of colonial or similarly subordinate status, reaching out to population groups that would earlier have been considered too small to constitute a viable, independent, sovereign unit.

The increased importance of the state lay in the greater service that it could perform in organizing the human element more effectively for realizing the economic growth potential. The sovereign state unit was of critical importance as the formulator of the rules under which economic activity was to be carried on; as a referee in a variety of institutional innovations needed to channel economic growth effectively; as the protector of social consensus needed to assure unity in diversity, the latter reflecting the differential impact of growth on the different groups within the country's population; and as provider of infrastructure that was needed by all but may have been beyond the specific interest of any one group.

Given the disruptive effects of modern economic growth in reducing through obsolescence or slow increase some economic pursuits and in rapidly expanding other, thus upsetting the relative standing of various groups within the economic society; and given the adjustment requirements that became manifest when the new and more productive technology called for new social institutions (new type of plant or economic firm, new relation between the worker and enterprise, etc.), there was even pressing need for the sovereign state that could serve in the guiding, unifying, and monitoring fashion indicated above. While there are recent trends toward a wider than national perspective (in addition to the increasing ties of international trade and other flows), one must still recognize the national sovereign state as the dominant unit, the carrier of the national community's long-term common interests, based usually on heritage of past and shared experience.

4. Modern economic growth was a drawn out, sequential process, originating in one country and spreading slowly to others. Without considering the difficult question of *dating* the time of entry into modern economic growth of the small number of countries now considered developed, one may observe that the spread was slow – in that half a century elapsed between the origin in Great Britain and the beginnings in such European countries as France and Belgium, and still another half century passed before the entry of Russia and Japan – the last major joiners before the post–World War II decades. And we may also note that there were substantial and time-consuming institutional changes within these countries before their sustained entry into modern economic growth could take place.

Meanwhile, the reaching out by the increasing number of developed countries for trade and markets in the rest of the world continued and intensified, contributing to a great deal in the heritage of the present LDCs. The result was a prevalence of colonial and dependent status in much of what we now classify as the less developed part of the world. And there was, and still is, wide diversity among the less developed countries and regions, because of differences among what, until the recent century to two centuries, were relatively isolated parts of the world.

II. Implications for LDCs

The first implication of the comments above on the technological power underlying modern economic growth is that, given the technology, all LDCs may be considered *developable*.[2] In other words, it should be technologically feasible, given other necessary, presumably social, conditions, for these countries and regions to reach a level that would qualify them as "developed" – at some projected time in the future. This level may be thought of as some magnitude of per capita or per worker product; or as some share of nonagricultural, nonnatural resource, sectors or as some level of overall technology, in terms of use of nonhuman energy and of sophistication of the human resources involved; or as a combination of all these, and possibly other, criteria of economic development.

Another, and perhaps more telling, way to formulate this implication is to argue that, at any given time, the worldwide, transnational stock of

2 Excepting small populations at climatic extremes, such as the Eskimoes in the Arctic and nomads in the desert areas – a tiny and diminishing proportion of world population.

available technology sets a potential of full economic development – a level of per capita or per worker product, or of other plausible criteria of economic development – possible with that technology and yet *not* dependent on specific, nonreproducible natural resources in any single country. This long-term or secular, technologically feasible, potential is, in principle, accessible to both developed and less developed countries, and is thus the same for both. It could perhaps be suggested by the current, long-term level of the developed countries taken as a group – not by that for the one or two most advanced, best practice, countries. If so, the secular level of the group of developed countries as a whole might be seen as reflecting full exploitation of the secular technological potential.

But the LDCs are characterized by major social and institutional constraints that make it impossible for them to exploit the technological potential adequately. Patterns of behavior, social institutions, priorities of values – all surviving from the premodern past, are translated into systems of organization of land ownership and tenure that inhibit productive agriculture; into scarcity of skilled labor and of entrepreneurship that make it impossible to adopt modern, nonagricultural technology. Weakness of existing material and human infrastructure, and instability and weakness of the political system, unable to count on effective consensus relating to values that would encourage economic modernization, deserve a special note. In short, it would not be difficult to list a range of social and institutional weaknesses in LDCs that can be blamed for their inability to use much of the current long-term technological potential, and for their continuing to use, perforce, the older and less productive techniques. The result is a shortfall from the potential that would vary widely among the LDCs, depending on their historical heritage and degree of past success in reducing social obstacles; and particularly important, low rates of economic growth and modernization.

The juxtaposition of the long-term technological potential, which has continuously advanced in the course of modern economic growth, with the social and institutional obstacles in LDCs surviving from the past, suggests a second important implication. It is that while, in principle, all LDCs may be considered developable, it does not follow that they will become developed at some future date sufficiently proximate to matter (possibilities that may be expected only after lapse of centuries are of little analytical or practical interest, given man's short lifetime, limited generational linkages, and the multiplication of uncertainties with the lengthening of the span of the projection). While advance to absolutely higher levels of per capita economic performance is likely to be fairly general, LDCs, i.e., countries with major shortfalls relative to the secular levels of the growing technological potential, are likely to remain with us for the very long future.

Nor does it follow that the lower the economic level of an LDC, and hence the greater the implicit technological backlog relative to current product, the greater the effective spur towards higher growth rates. For it may well be that the greater backlog is accompanied by even greater inhibiting effects of the social and institutional obstacles surviving from the past – so that the positive balance and the induced growth rates may be *lower* for the poorer LDCs than for those at middle income levels. No simple and rigid association between the magnitude of the technological backlog and the likelihood of high rates of per capita or per worker growth of individual LDCs can be claimed.

If then we observe, after decades of low growth rates or stagnation, a shift toward high growth rates sustained over a long time span, and find that it was *not* due to sudden acquisition of an internationally valuable natural resource (as was the case, e.g., in Saudi Arabia and Kuwait), our discussion suggests that favorable changes must have occurred in the LDC's capacity to reduce social and institutional obstacles to the use of modern technology; and/or major improvements in the international framework of trade and other ties within which the given LDC could operate. The implication is of radical shifts in the internal institutional structure of the LDC and possibly also in its external conditions – for only radical shifts can account for a sharp break toward much higher growth rates sustained over a substantial time span.

But radical shifts in internal structure and external conditions of a country have long historical roots, and are not easily treated by economic analysis; and yet, as suggested, they may have profound economic growth consequences. Even if we were to accept the shifts as given, the difficulty of distinguishing between the necessary and sufficient conditions of accelerated growth, and of appraising the economic contribution of noneconomic factors, makes meaningful generalization almost impossible. Let me illustrate these points by reference to Taiwan – with some caution since, with limited knowledge, the questions raised will be more in the nature of groping for the light than shedding it.

Consider first the initial radical break that made the high growth rates possible (although far from certain) – the establishment in the early 1950s of a sovereign state that could provide both unity and the basis of a long series of internal policy decisions, while capable of taking advantage of favorable trade and other external ties. Whatever the legal form of that state, effectively it was that of the population inhabiting the Taiwan area. The shift to this state involved the larger Taiwan Island community, who lived for five decades under colonial occupation by Japan and for half a decade as a necessarily neglected province of greater China, the latter enfeebled by the then current civil war. It also involved a smaller but still substantial group of Mainlanders, including much of the political and social elite displaced by the loss of that war. The subsequent high growth rate of Taiwan clearly depended upon the break just described – the formation a small and selected offshoot state, separate from the much larger community on the mainland. Yet it is difficult to view this change in size and status as a response to *economic* factors (granted that the latter may have played a part in the long chain of historical events that led to the change).

But even if we accept the break just noted as given, it was a necessary, not a sufficient condition. For it was quite possible for the new Taiwan entity to commit errors in choosing among various policy alternatives, errors that could have reduced growth to levels much below the average of over 6 percent per year in total product per capita that in fact were realized between 1951–53 and 1978–80.[3] Consider in this connection the long list of headings that identify groups of policy issues to be covered in the papers at the second and third sessions of this Conference: they range from land reform and strategies of technical progress in agriculture, to industrial policy and policy related to development of trade and exports, to monetary policy, to fiscal policy, to financial institutions, to social policies bearing on welfare. And consider also the variety of social frictions that could have been generated by rapid structural changes that usually accompany high growth rates in per capita product – with the possible wearing away of the needed social consensus.

If the possibilities of growth-reducing errors and resistance were minimized (if not totally avoided), the explanation would lie in the effect of favorable internal factors, in *addition* to the two major permissive factors already noted (technological backlog and a viable, modern sovereign state). These factors could be found in the human skills of the largely agricultural Island population, acquired over the decades under Japa-

---

3 See Directorate-General of Budget, Accounting and Statistics, *National Income of the Republic of China*, Taipei, December 1980, Table 5, p. 20.

nese rule; in the valuable experience of the incoming Mainlander group that assumed leadership, and in its detachment from Taiwan's past institutions and established group interests; in the community of purpose between the two groups, aimed at economic growth; and in the strong tradition of family organization that could, combined with a stable modern government, result in a sustained response to the unfolding growth opportunities.

The restriction of choices that contributed to reducing the possible policy errors stemmed also from the external circumstances in which Taiwan found itself. In the aftermath of World War II, the former ties of alliance and mutual assistance between the United States and China were effectively continued – this time between the United States and Taiwan. Again, in the aftermath of the victory of the United States over Japan and of U.S. occupation policy in that country, a restructured Japan was in a position to resume rapid economic growth – in response to the accumulated technological backlog and by taking advantage of radical changes in many of the political and institutional conditions that, in earlier times, constituted severe obstacles to effective exploitation of modern technology. The United States participated directly in the policies designed to advance Taiwan's agriculture, and provided substantial aid in the initial decade. But we need no prolonged discussion here to argue that the clear possibility of drawing upon major sources of accelerated growth in trade and other ties with the United States and Japan (and a number of other trade and investment partners) slanted the policy choices toward reliance on the advantages of an outward-looking economy – with whatever this implied in a variety of relevant policies.

III. Concluding comments

The observations on the breakthrough of an LDC to higher rates of economic growth were illustrated above by reference to Taiwan, because it is of obvious interest here, and because, given the competence within this Conference, my errors in this case would be corrected most speedily. But one should note that there have been, within recent decades (and earlier) breakthroughs among LDCs to higher growth rates, of different origin and orientation from that in Taiwan. Most conspicuous were the cases of LDCs that profited from suddenly acquired control of a highly valuable, internationally sought, natural resource (such as oil), large enough relative to the current economic level of the LDC to become a source of long-term rise in product per capita. The concentration of this resource in a few hands, combined with the difficulty of involving the country's population in effective modernization, created potentially dangerous consequences – alongside the control over large capital flows that permitted rapid acceleration of growth of product. Or we can think of political breakthroughs of a Communist type, that resulted in a totalitarian, centralized economic and social structure, with whatever costs were implied in the intensive mobilization of human resources – in a transformation that tended to limit the growth potential, particularly in productivity per unit of input, to a level much below one that could have been secured with a free market economy and a more outward-looking orientation of the country.

These are necessarily casual observations, and a closer look at more evidence might reveal other types of breakthrough to sustained, high growth performance. The point here is that the case of Taiwan, while not unique, represents a distinctive type of a breakthrough – one in a small, less developed market economy in which the main comparative advantage lay in human capital (not in natural resources), with orientation to rapidly increasing participation in international trade and international division of labor.

Returning now to Taiwan proper, I must admit that the list above of internal and external factors favorable to high growth rates over the last three decades is neither complete, nor adequately tested. In particular, the discussion attempted to suggest how the period of high growth rates was made possible, was initiated as response to a large technological growth potential, given the historical heritage of efficient human capital, and the formation of a stable, sovereign state, capable of leadership in a rapid transformation of internal institutions and in choosing the outward-looking orientation favored by the external historical circumstances. But this model tells us little about the *sequential* development within the span of three decades – except to remind us that, with high rates of growth per capita, there were rapid changes in conditions of life and work, rapid shifts in the structure of production and of use of product, calling for shifts in policy focus to deal with new strains and problems. Nor, for obvious reasons, can our general approach encompass the effects of changes in historical conjuncture, exogenous to Taiwan's economy – changes in the 1970s such as the world oil crises and stagflation in the developed market economies, and the shifts in international relations and alliances.

A substantive discussion of these changes in internal structure and in external circumstances, whether they be expected corrollaries of economic development proceeding at a high rate or shifts in historical conjuncture that are exogenous to the economy, is not feasible here. Much of that substantive treatment may be provided in the papers and discussions at the Conference sessions to follow. Even if a number of difficult questions may remain unanswered, and thus limit our ability to draw firm lessons from the recent growth experience of Taiwan, partial answers should still be useful for orientation in a changing world.

5. Notes on demographic change

These notes raise questions about the economic consequences of demographic trends, consequences in terms of what the trends imply for the rate of economic advance and for the distributive aspects of economic growth. These are questions rather than answers, for lack of firm basis for the latter; and even the questions are selective. The two trends chosen for comment are: the long-term decline in birthrates, associated largely with increasing control of intramarital fertility; and the long-term rise in the proportion of population in advanced ages (65 and over), associated largely with the recent impact of health technology in reducing mortality at the higher ages.

The natural concentration in Professor Easterlin's paper on the recent, forty-year swing in fertility, left little room for noting the underlying downtrend. Yet it is conspicuous in Easterlin's table 4.A.1, from the 1870s to World War II; and even within the swing itself, the average birthrate declined, from 22.3 per thousand in the four quinquennia of 1935–55 to 19.5 per thousand in the twenty-three years from 1955 to 1978. The consensus of the present projections suggests further decline. According to the latest, 1978, assessment (medium variant) by the United Nations, the average for 1955–60 to 1975–80 (the latter weighted by half) of 19.8 per thousand will drop to an average of 15.8 for 1975–80 (weighted by half) through 1995–2000.[1] Two comments should be added. First, the

"Notes on Demographic Change," in *The American Economy in Transition*, edited by Martin Feldstein, Chicago: University of Chicago Press, 1980, pp. 334–341. This chapter consists of comments on and extensions to a paper by Richard A. Easterlin, contained in the cited volume.

1 See United Nations, *World Population Trends and Prospects by Country, 1950–2000: Summary Report of the 1978 Assessment* (New York: United Nations, 1979), tables 2–A and 2–B, pp. 47–56.

marked decline in fertility was observed in, and projected for, many other countries, in some of which it dropped to much lower levels than in the United States (e.g., the United Kingdom, France, Germany, and Sweden). Second, with the age composition moving toward the older, and higher mortality ages, the crude rate of natural increase dropped more relatively than the crude birthrate. Thus, for the United States, the birthrate drops from an average of 37.9 per thousand for 1870–75/1885–90, to the projected rate of 14.2 in 1995–2000, a decline of 62 percent; the rate of natural increase drops from 16.3 to 4.4 per thousand, by 73 percent.

The other trend to be noted is the sustained rise in the proportion of population 65 years old and older. To go back just to 1930, we find a steady rise in the proportion from census to census, from 5.4 percent in 1930 to 9.9 percent in 1970; and the recent projections move the proportion from 10.5 percent in 1975 to 12.7 in the year 2000.[2] The relative rise is far greater than would be produced as a secondary effect of the fall in the birthrates, and hence of the proportions of the very young. This is shown clearly when we observe the share of the next to the oldest group, 55–64, which rises from over 6.8 percent in 1930 to 9.1 in 1970, and is projected to only a slightly higher share in the year 2000.

In turning now to economic consequences of the long-term decline in fertility, one may note first that, given the limited universe in which we live, and the marked decline in mortality due to scientific advance and economic progress, a reduction of fertility was to be expected. And one could view it as a free and rational response of would-be parents to higher survival rates of children and to the value of greater investment of human capital in a smaller number of offspring. But this does not mean that some of the consequences of the downtrend in fertility and of the associated decline in the rate of natural increase may not be problematic. The decline in the proportion of new entrants into, and of the younger groups in, the labor force may result in sluggish mobility, in an inadequate response to new employment and growth opportunities afforded by technological

2 These and other data in the paragraph are: for 1930–70, from U.S. Bureau of the Census, *Historical Statistics of the United States, Colonial Times to 1970, Bicentennial Edition, Part 1* (Washington, D.C.: Government Printing Office, 1975), Series A–119–34, pp. 15–18; for 1975–2000, U.S. Bureau of the Census, "Illustrative Projections of World Population to the 21st Century," *Current Population Reports*, Series P–23, no. 79 (Washington, D.C.: Government Printing Office, 1979), table 2, part U, p. 39.

innovations. And the reduced growth rate in total product may have a damping effect on entrepreneurial capital formation because of lowered growth horizons.

A more interesting aspect of birthrates, and – for posttraditional societies, of the associated rates of natural increase – is their negative correlation, within a country, with the income level of the parental pair (or more strictly, of the family or household – income on a per capita or per consuming unit basis). That the poor tend to have more children, and with the death rates at lower secular levels, more *surviving* children, has been observed repeatedly; and there is some evidence for it for recent decades in the United States. If so, the contribution of the lower income groups, the poorer classes in the population, to new additions to the population and eventually to the labor force, is appreciably greater than their weight in the parental population. Several consequences follow. First, if we assume that the growth rate (G) for product per worker, from one generation to the next, is the same for the offspring of the lower and the higher income groups, say 3 percent per year or 81 percent over a span of two decades, the growth rate for the total body of workers would be *below* this assumed rate – because of the rise in the proportion of the low income groups. Second, if, retaining the assumed overall rate of 3 percent per year for the initial, parental population, we modify the growth rate to make it higher for the lower income offspring and lower for the higher income offspring, thus reducing the initial income inequality, the shortfall in the growth rate of per worker product for the total labor force would be even greater. Thus, other conditions being equal, the negative association between income levels and rate of natural increase makes either for lower rates of growth of product per worker, or for widening income inequality, or for both.[3]

The data easily at hand refer to racial or ethnic groups, characterized by substantially lower than average income per capita. Thus, the 1970 census shows the proportion of the black population to total of 11.1 percent;

3 See Simon Kuznets, "Income-Related Differences in Natural Increase: Bearing on Growth and Distribution of Income," in *Nations and Households in Economic Growth: Essays in Honor of Moses Abramovitz*, ed. Paul A. David and Melvin W. Reder (New York: Academic Press, 1974), pp. 127–46.

The illustrative data used in this earlier paper are not available over a long time span; and I am using here data on racial and ethnic minorities, with lower average incomes, in comparison with the white majority with its higher average income. The comparisons are rough and cannot be pursued here with adequate attention to the limitations of the data.

but the ratio of the black group aged 0–4 to total population aged 0–4 was 14.2 percent (see the series in the *Historical Statistics* volume cited in note 2). In March 1978 the average family comprised 3.33 persons, of whom 1.10 were related children under 18 years of age. But the average white family averaged 3.28 persons, of whom 1.04 were related children, while the average for a black family was 3.77 persons of whom 1.59 were related children under 18. The black family population accounted for 11.5 percent of total family population, and for 14.7 percent of related children under 18. But the money income per person was $3.2 thousand in black families and $5.7 thousand in white. A similar case of higher propensity to have children is found for families with head of Spanish origin: the average number of persons per family was 3.88, of whom 1.66 were related children, and the per capita income of $3.4 thousand was 40 percent below that for all families.[4]

The economic and social class differences in birth and fertility rates just suggested are an important subject for further study; and so are the economic and social class differences in mortality, which are negatively correlated with the per capita income level of the families or households involved. Such further analysis would make it possible to deal more insightfully with the problems raised by concentration of births and of eventually resulting additions to the working population in the lower income levels. But in the present connection one might push speculation further and ask whether the combination of declining fertility and mortality, in the typical pattern associated with economic growth and the demographic transition, is not likely to make, in some phases, even greater concentration of new population and new labor force in the lower income families; and thus aggravate the task of integrating the additions, without limiting effect on growth of product per worker or without worsening inequality in the income distribution.

This possibility can again be illustrated by using crude birth and death rates for a racial group, viewed as a proxy for the lower income and social components in the population. Comparing whites and nonwhites (the latter including races other than black, but greatly dominated by the latter), we find that for 1921–30, the crude vital rates (per 1,000) were: for births – 23.6 for the white population, and 31.9 for nonwhite; for deaths – 11.1 for white and 16.6 for nonwhite; for rates of natural increase – 12.5

4 The data are from U.S. Bureau of the Census, *Current Population Reports*, Series P-60, no. 118 (Washington, D.C.: Government Printing Office, 1979), table 2, pp. 14–19.

and 15.3 respectively, a spread of 2.8 points per thousand. The death rates used here are for total population, and the differential mortality for the younger groups could be different; but the general bearing of the illustration may be valid. By 1961–70, the rates were: births at 18.8 and 27.3 per thousand for the white and nonwhite populations; death rates at 9.5 and 9.7 per thousand, for the two groups; and the rates of natural increase were 9.3 and 17.6, respectively, a spread of 8.3 points per 1,000.[5] The spread in the rates of natural increase, the rates most relevant here, widened partly because the birthrates for the nonwhites declined somewhat less than for the white population; but largely because in the diffusion of lower mortality, the drop in the death rates for the nonwhite group was so much larger and mortality rates for the two groups converged to almost equality. With the ratio of nonwhite population to total in 1930 at 10.2 percent, and rising to 13.0 percent by 1970, the proportion of the nonwhite population aged 0–4 to total population of that age class rose from 11.4 percent in 1930 to 15.9 percent in 1970. The eventual effect would obviously be to raise substantially the proportion of nonwhites in the additions to the labor force.

All of the parameters above need revision, and the suggested inferences are illustrative. They are intended to stress that during the long-term decline of the birth and death rates, the higher proportion of offspring of the lower income groups surviving to join the country's labor force, higher than in the parental population, means pressure making for a more limited growth of product per worker or for widening inequality of income. In some phases of this process, the pressure may be greater, either because the income-origin mix in the addition to working population becomes more biased toward the lower income groups; or because the initial income inequality has widened; or for other reasons (e.g., changes in requirements for labor force participation, raising the levels of education and skill required to levels not easily accessible to children of the poor).

The reduction in fertility obviously had a variety of other consequences, among them the recent and increasing rise in the rate of participation of women in the labor force. And there are also the obvious effects on the age and sex structure of the population viewed as groups of consumers, with the resulting shifts in the structure of total consumer

5 The data here and in the rest of the paragraph are from *Historical Statistics* (Washington, D.C.: Government Printing Office, 1976), Series A–119–34, pp. 16–18; Series B–5–10, p. 49; and Series B–160–80, p. 59.

demand – decline in the relative importance of some consumer goods and rise in that of other goods. But let me turn now to the second trend selected for comment, the long-term rise in the proportion of population in the advanced ages.

Three aspects of this rise were noted in Professor Easterlin's paper. First, within the group of 65 and over, the older subgroups rose proportionately more than the younger. Thus, the share of the 65–74 age group in total population rose from 5.58 percent in 1950 to 6.50 percent in 1975, and is then projected to rise to 6.91 percent in the year 2000; the share of the 75 and over group rose from 2.56 percent in 1950 to 3.99 percent in 1975, and is projected to rise to 5.75 percent in 2000. The share of the younger group rises by less than two-tenths; that of the older group more than doubles.[6] Second, the widening difference in favor of women in life expectation at advanced ages means that, within the total group of 65 and over, the share of women and their excess over men has increased. Thus, the ratio of women to men, within the 65 and over group, rose from 1.02 in 1950 to 1.44 in 1975, and is projected to 1.50 in the year 2000. Third, the excess of women over men grew conspicuously more within the older subgroups. Thus, the ratio of women to men in the 65–74 age class rose from 1.02 in 1950 to 1.30 in 1975, and drops somewhat to 1.27 in the projection to year 2000; the ratio of women to men within the 75 and over age class rises from 1.21 in 1950 to 1.71 in 1975, and is projected to 1.85 by the year 2000.

Partly because of the progressive aging within the 65 and over group, but largely because of factors on the demand side, the labor force participation rates for the male group declined sharply since 1950, and are projected to decline further. Those rates (based on census data) were as high as 68 percent in 1890, declined to 41 percent by 1950, and dropped, in just two decades, to 25 percent in 1970 (see *Historical Statistics, 1976,* Series D29–41, p. 132). The International Labor Office (ILO) data indicate a movement of the labor force participation rates for males 65 and

6 In addition to the Census Bureau projection referred to in note 2, and covering the span from 1975 to 2000, we used for 1950–75 the United Nations' age and sex distribution of population according to the 1973 assessment (this involves projections to 1970 and 1975, but these are close to the Bureau of Census later date). The source is United Nations, Population Division, "Population by Sex and Age for Regions and Countries, 1950–2000, as Assessed in 1973: Medium Variant," ESA/P/WP.60 (mimeographed), (New York: United Nations, 1976), p. 97.

over from 45 percent in 1950 to 26 percent in 1970, and then project a further decline to 19 percent in the year 2000.[7] Both sources show very low rates of participation for women aged 65 and over, ranging from 7 to 10 percent in the census data, hovering below 10 percent in the ILO data, and projected to about 9 percent in the year 2000. Given the differences in the level of participation rates between the two sexes, and rising proportions of females, the combination of the two sexes yields (in the ILO data) a decline for the total participation rate from 26 percent in 1950 to 16 percent in 1970, and a projection to 12 percent in the year 2000.

The reduction of mortality at the advanced ages might have meant also reduction of morbidity; and, at a given age, say in the 65–74 age class, better health and greater productive capacity than before. If so, one may ask why the drastic fall in the labor force participation rates for the older males, and why the failure of the very low rates for older females to rise. Was it because of increasing obsolescence of the knowledge and skill of the older groups, induced by changes in the requirements for effective employment on the demand side? Or, less likely, was it due to favorable changes in the asset position of the aged (or in welfare policies) that made a shift to earlier retirement from the labor force feasible and preferable? The substantial rise in the proportions of the aged in the total population, and further projections of it (which may turn out to be understatements because of breakthroughs in health technology), assign to the question of working capacity and propensity of the aged, indeed of their role in society, large and increasing weight.

Another question relates to the two problems implied in a rising proportion of aged. The first is the likely increase in the share of the aged with shortages of income or wealth relative to needs. While it is not feasible to document this possible trend, several groups of factors appear to have been made for it. One is connected with the unforeseen character of the relevant mortality trends and of other economic circumstances – which could have rendered earlier rational plans for financing retirement seriously deficient (because of extension of life, but not of work; and of the effects of inflation particularly on the nonworking aged). Another is implied in the convergence of death rates for poorer and richer groups in society, with the result that the proportions of lower income groups

7 See International Labour Office, *Labour Force Estimates and Projections, 1950–2000*, 2d ed. (Geneva, 1977), vol. 4, tables 2, 5, pp. 9, 76.

within the total group of 65 and over might have increased.[8] The third is suggested by the recently marked trend on the part of the aged to live separately, in single or two-person households, implying a weakening of the family ties between the active generations and their aged parents; and reduction in the possibly ameliorative effects of intra-larger-family sharing. It is hardly surprising that in the greater concern in recent decades over consumption deficiencies among the lower income groups, particular attention had to be paid to the aged among them.

Even assuming adequate provision for consumption needs of the aged, the other possible problem – increased excess of their consumption over the contribution of their labor and capital to total product – remains. Indeed, the real dissaving involved in such excess may only be increased by transfer and other policies properly oriented to sustain consumption by the aged. The concern here is not with the intricacies of the estimate of such excess. If, simply, one assumes the realistic possibility of a discrepancy, positive or negative, between a given human unit's consumption and the contribution of its labor and capital to total product, it is possible to argue that the rising proportion of the aged in total population – with their limited labor force participation and the likely growth of the poorer subgroups among them – means an increasing weight of the real dissaving, at least in absolute magnitude. The question then arises as to the weight of such dissaving relative to national product; or, better, relative to the net positive savings that may be generated in the economy by groups and institutions other than those represented by the aged.

The notes above stressed the consequences of selected demographic trends; and the need, in considering them, to distinguish the differing incidence among the several socioeconomic groups within the country. Demographic trends are long, so that changes are gradual and are likely to be overshadowed by the shorter term economic and political changes and their reflections. Yet one must emphasize that demographic trends, because of their biological bases, imply substantial constraints within

8 The share of black population in the total, for all ages, rose from 9.7 percent in 1930 to 11.6 percent in 1977; the share within the 65 and over group rose from 5.6 percent in 1930 to 8.2 percent in 1977 (see *Historical Statistics, 1976*, the series referred to in note 2); and *Statistical Abstract of the United States, 1978*, Washington, D.C.: Government Printing Office, 1978, table 29, p. 29). The sharper rise of the share of the lower income, black, population in the aged group is striking.

which people must act. Thus, only women in childbearing ages can produce children (at least until another method is devised); breakthroughs in
health technology are not predictable responses to economic investment,
and some mortality differentials (e.g., between women and men) are not
yet subject to human control; and various age and sex groups differ widely
as producers and as consumers. To be sure, the constraints of the long
biological cycle, from birth to death, are partly modified by society's institutions and dominant views. But this makes it all the more important
to be able to appraise the economic consequences of these *changing* constraints, in their impact on economic advance, on the distribution of this
advance among the several socioeconomic groups, and on the institutional
adjustments that may be called for.

6. Recent population trends in less developed countries and implications for internal income inequality

In a recent paper (chapter 7, below) I explored the effects on the conventional measures of distribution of income among households of demographic elements such as the size and changing composition of households through their life cycle. The exploration emphasized the need to take explicit account of these demographic elements in any attempt to observe trends in the long-term levels of income differentials – particularly those associated with economic growth, since the latter is usually accompanied by marked shifts in the size and age-of-head distributions of households. Of particular interest was the negative association between per capita income and size of the household or family, found also within the age-of-head classes and thus persisting through the household's lifespan. If this cross-sectional association is translated into comparisons of per capita income for households of differing average size over the lifespan, the result is a negative association between the per capita income and size variables. Since, in turn, size of households or families is largely a function of the number of children, the negative association just noted is also one between lifetime per capita income and fertility – *provided* that the differentials in fertility dominate differentials in mortality, as they did in the small sample of countries for recent years used in the cross section in my recent paper.

The present paper deals with a different, though related, question. Given the major population trends observable in recent decades in the

This research was supported in part by AID contract otr-1432 and aided by the Rockefeller Foundation grant RF 70051 to Yale's Economic Demography program. The author is indebted to Yoram Ben-Porath of the Hebrew University of Jerusalem for helpful comments on an earlier draft of this paper.
Reprinted from: *Population and Economic Change in Developing Countries*, edited by Richard A. Easterlin, Chicago: University of Chicago Press, 1980.

economically less developed countries (LDCs), what can one infer about the possible effects on long-term levels or changes in them in the internal distribution of income? For obvious reasons of scarcity of relevant data, and even more of the complex interactions between the population trends and the concurrent structural changes in the economy and society of the countries involved, any answer to the question just raised is bound to be speculative. But there may be value in at least trying to formulate the question unambiguously and in attempting some explicit, relevant speculation.

I. The major population trends

One must begin by stressing that the acceleration in the population growth rate in the LDCs, and their markedly higher rate of natural increase than in the economically more developed countries (MDCs), are recent historical trends – as is clearly indicated in Table 6.1. Such recency, and the brevity of the period over which these trends have prevailed, compared with the preceding centuries of quite different demographic patterns, are basic to the understanding and evaluation of both the trends and their implications.

Table 6.1 shows that from the mid-eighteenth century through 1920, the rate of increase (overwhelmingly, of *natural* increase) in the LDCs was at relatively low level, varying from less than a 0.1% to about 0.5% per year (see col. 5, lines 12–24).[1] Throughout this long period of some seventeen to eighteen decades, the population growth rate in the MDCs was substantially higher – ranging from over 0.4% to well over 1% per year; and showed a marked acceleration already in the first half of the nineteenth century. It is only since the 1920s that the rates of natural increase in the LDCs rose to approach those in the MDCs; they began to exceed the latter in the 1930s and 1940s, when severe economic recession and then World War II reduced population growth in the developed countries; and only since the 1950s have the annual growth rates of the LDCs climbed to well over 2%, while those in the MDCs declined by the early 1970s to less than 1%. Thus, the acceleration and growth excess of population movements in the LDCs were within a relatively short span of

1 We prefer to emphasize the total for LDCs, excluding China. The estimates for the latter before the 1950s were always subject to debate; and there has been ever greater scarcity of data for China since the 1950s. Yet the estimated population for the country accounted for 0.2 of world population for 1975, and about 0.3 of the population total for the LDCs.

Table 6.1. *Growth of population, economically less developed (LDC) and more developed (MDC) countries, 1750–1975*

Dates		World (1)	MDCs (2)	LDCs (3)	China (4)	Other LDCs (5)
		A. Absolute totals (in millions)				
1.	1750	791	201	590	200	390
2.	1800	978	248	730	323	407
3.	1850	1,262	347	915	430	485
4.	1900	1,650	573	1,077	436	641
5.	1920	1,860	673	1,187	476	711
6.	1930	2,069	758	1,311	502	809
7.	1940	2,295	821	1,474	533	941
8a.	1950a	2,515	858	1,658	563	1,095
9a.	1960a	2,998	976	2,022	654	1,368
8b.	1950b	2,501	857	1,644	558	1,086
9b.	1960b	2,986	976	2,010	654	1,356
10.	1970	3,610	1,084	2,526	772	1,754
11.	1975 (proj. med. var.)	3,967	1,132	2,835	838	1,997
		B. Rates of increase (per year, per 1,000)				
12.	1750–1800	4.3	4.2	4.3	9.6	0.9
13.	1800–50	5.1	6.7	4.5	5.2	3.5
14.	1850–1900	5.4	10.6	3.3	0.3	5.6
15.	1900–50	8.4	8.1	8.3	4.9	10.7
16.	1950–75	18.6	11.2	22.0	16.4	24.7
17.	1900–20	6.0	8.1	4.9	4.4	5.2
18.	1920–30	10.8	12.0	10.0	5.3	13.0
19.	1930–40	10.4	8.0	11.8	6.0	15.2
20.	1940–50	9.2	4.4	11.8	5.5	15.3
21.	1950–60	17.7	13.0	20.0	15.1	22.5
22.	1950–60	17.9	13.1	20.3	16.0	22.5
23.	1960–70	19.2	10.6	23.1	16.7	26.1
24.	1970–75	19.0	8.7	23.3	16.5	26.3

Notes: MDCs include Europe, the USSR, North America, temperate South America (Argentina, Uruguay, Chile), Australia, and New Zealand. LDCs include all others.
Lines 1–4: from United Nations, *The Population Debate: Dimensions and Perspectives*, vol. 1 (New York 1975), table 1, pp. 3–4, and the original paper by John Durand cited there. The estimates for China used here are from the Durand paper.
Lines 5–9a: United Nations, *World Population Prospects* (New York, 1966), table A.3.1, p. 133.
Lines 8b–11: United Nations, *Selected World Demographic Indicators, 1950–2000*, mimeographed working paper ESA/P/WP.55, May 1975.
Lines 12–16: Calculated from lines 1–4, 8b, and 11.
Lines 17–21: Calculated from lines 5–9a.
Lines 22–24: Calculated from lines 8b–11.

Table 6.2. *Growth trends and vital rates (per 1,000), observed 1937–75 and projected 1975–2000*

		A. *Absolute totals and growth rates*			
	1937 (1)	1955 (2)	1975 (3)	1985 (4)	2000 (5)
Total (in millions)					
1. World	2,225	2,722	3,967	4,816	6,253
2. MDCs	802	915	1,132	1,231	1,361
3. LDCs	1,423	1,808	2,835	3,585	4,893
4. LDCs, except China	899	1,203	1,997	2,612	3,745
Rates of increase (per year, per 1,000, successive intervals)					
5. World	—	11.3	19.0	18.6	17.6
6. MDCs	—	7.4	10.7	8.4	6.7
7. LDCs	—	13.4	22.7	23.8	21.4
8. LDCs except China	—	16.3	25.7	27.2	24.3

				B. *Vital rates, levels, and changes*				
	1937 (1)	Change to 1950–55 (2)	1950– 55 (3)	Change to 1970–75 (4)	1970– 75 (5)	Change to 1995– 2000 (6)	1995– 2000 (7)	Total Change (8)
World								
9. CBR	35.8	−0.2	35.6	−4.1	31.5	−6.4	25.1	−10.7
10. CDR	25.7	−6.9	18.8	−6.0	12.8	−3.9	8.9	−16.8
11. CRNI	10.1	+6.7	16.8	+1.9	18.7	−2.5	16.2	+6.1
MDCs								
12. CBR	24.1	−1.2	22.9	−5.7	17.2	−1.6	15.6	−8.5
13. CDR	15.5	−5.4	10.1	−0.9	9.2	+0.7	9.9	−5.6
14. CRNI	8.6	+4.2	12.8	−4.8	8.0	−2.3	5.7	−2.9
LDCs								
15. CBR	42.5	−0.4	42.1	−4.6	37.5	−9.7	27.8	−14.7
16. CDR	31.6	−8.3	23.3	−9.0	14.3	−5.7	8.6	−23.0
17. CRNI	10.9	+7.9	18.8	+4.4	23.2	−4.0	19.2	+8.3
LDCs except China								
18. CBR	42.5	+2.0	44.5	−2.4	42.1	−11.3	30.8	−11.7
19. CDR	30.8	−6.4	24.4	−8.4	16.0	−7.1	8.9	−21.9
20. CRNI	11.7	+8.4	20.1	+6.0	26.1	−4.2	21.9	+10.2

Notes: Panel A: The estimates for 1937, lines 1–4, col. 1, are logarithmic interpolations between the totals for 1930 and 1940 shown in lines 6–7 of Table 6.1. The other entries in lines 1–4 are from the source used for Table 6.1, lines 8b–11, with the use of the medium variant projection throughout.

The rates of increase in lines 5–8 are from lines 1–4, with due allowance for the varying durations of the intervals (which are 18, 20, 10, and 15 years respectively).

Panel B: Col. 1: Data from United Nations, *World Population Trends, 1920–1947* (New York, about five decades, following centuries of growth at low rates that would look like stagnation by modern standards.

The second important aspect of these recent trends is that the acceleration, and the resulting excess in the rates of natural increase in the LDCs over those in the MDCs, was due wholly, or almost wholly, to the decline in the death rates – rather than to any movements in the birthrates. A summary of the trends of these vital rates taken separately, but unfortunately limited to the years since 1937, is presented in Table 6.2. Part of this table refers to observed changes, to 1970–75;[2] the other part refers to projections to the year 2000. We deal with the observed changes first.

Between 1937 and 1970–75, a span of about 35 to 36 years, the rise in the rate of natural increase for LDCs (excluding China) from 11.7 to 26.1, some 14.4 points, resulted from a combination of a decline in the crude death rate from 30.8 to 16.0, 14.8 points, and a drop in the birthrate of only 0.4 points. A similar dominance of the drop in the death rate as the overwhelming factor in the rise in the rate of natural increase over the period from 1937 to 1970–75 is also true of LDCs including China (for both comparisons see lines 15–20, cols. 2 and 5). By contrast, whatever movements occurred in the rate of natural increase in the MDCs have been due at least as much to declines in birthrates as to declines in death rates (see lines 12–14, cols. 2 and 5).

It is interesting to estimate the trend were we to extend the view to 1920, the date that is the dividing line before the acceleration in the growth rate of LDC populations. In line 17 of Table 6.1 we observe that the growth rate for LDCs for 1900–1920 was about 0.5% per year, meaning a rate of natural increase of 5.0 per 1,000. Assuming that the

2 The quinquennium 1970–75 and the estimate for 1975 are described as a projection even in the more recent United Nations sources; and we used the medium variant. But since estimates for this recent period could not deviate substantially from the actual, at least with respect to change from the preceding two decades, we felt justified in including them to form an observed 25-year span, 1950–75.

Notes to Table 6.2 (cont.)

1949); table 2, p. 10, shows the vital rates, and we took the mid-value of the ranges shown. MDCs here include North America, Japan, Europe, and Oceania (but exclude temperate South America, a minor omission here and a minor inclusion under the LDCs). China is identified with "Remaining Far East" (after exclusion of Japan). The population weights used to combine the rates are in the source, Table 1, p. 3.

Cols. 2–8: Based on data from the United Nations working paper used for lines 8b–11 of Table 6.1 (on *Selected World Demographic Indicators by Countries, 1950–2000*).

crude birthrate in 1900–1920 averaged about the same as in 1937 (42.5 per 1,000), we would obtain an implicit crude death rate (CDR) for 1900–1920 of 37.5 per thousand – compared with a CDR in 1937 between 31 and 32 per 1,000. If we assume that the recent downward trend in the crude death rate for the LDCs did not begin until the 1920s, the conclusion is that over a decade to a decade and a half before 1937, the drop in the CDR for LDCs was about 6 to 7 points per 1,000 – of the same order of magnitude found in the somewhat longer periods from 1937 to 1950–55, and from 1950–55 to 1970–75 (see line 19, cols. 2 and 4). And while the calculation is obviously approximate, it is reasonable to conclude that the estimated decline in the crude death rates was most likely much greater over that period than any reasonably assumed change in birthrates.[3]

Using the evidence in Table 6.2, and the approximate calculations in the text, one may summarize by saying that over the fifty years terminating in 1970–75, that is, between 1920–25 and 1970–75, crude death rates in the LDCs must have declined from more than 37.5 to between 14 and 16 per 1,000 (see Table 6.2, lines 16 and 19, col. 5); whereas the crude birthrates may have moved from 42.5 per 1,000 to either 42.1 (LDCs excluding China) or 37.5 (LDCs including China). The drop over the five decades was thus about 22.5 points in the crude death rate, and between 0.4 and 5 points in the crude birthrate – the rise in the rate of natural increase almost completely dominated by the downtrend in the death rate.

Several aspects of this recent decline in death rates in the LDCs should be noted. These and other aspects of what appeared to be the major demographic revolution in world population have been widely discussed in the literature;[4] but they deserve at least brief explicit mention here.

3 Kingsley Davis (1951) estimated the death rate for India by decades from 1881–91 to 1931–41, showing a level of about 43 per 1,000 in the first three decades, a bulge in 1911–21 (associated with the influenza pandemic of 1918) to 48.6, and a decline to 36.3 in 1921–31 and to 31.3 in 1931–41 (p. 37). The estimated crude birthrates were set at between 46 and 49 in the first four of the six decades, and then at 46 in 1921–31 and 45 in 1931–41 (p. 69). This combination of relative constancy of the birthrate between 1920 and 1940, with a substantial decline in the death rate, is what we are assuming in the tentative calculation in the text.

4 See particularly the paper in [the original] volume by Samuel H. Preston (chap. 5), "Causes and Consequences of Mortality Declines in Less Developed Countries during the Twentieth Century," for a wide-ranging summary and bibliography. I also found a wealth of data and interpretation in the articles by George H. Stolnitz, beginning with the two-part paper "A Century of International Mortality Trends" (Stolnitz 1955, 1956), reviewing the evidence to 1950, and concluding with the latest, "International Mortality Trends: Some Main Facts and Implications" (Stolnitz 1975).

Table 6.3. *Long-term trends in crude vital rates (per 1,000), currently developed countries (for comparison with recent trends in the LDCs)*

	Levels of vital rates				Changes in rates		
	1800 (1)	1850 (2)	1895 (3)	1925 (4)	1800–1850 (5)	1850–95 (6)	1895–1925 (7)
Five Northern European countries							
1. CBR	34.0	32.8	29.8	20.6	−1.2	−3.0	−9.2
2. CDR	25.2	21.4	17.6	12.2	−3.8	−3.8	−5.4
3. CRNI	8.8	11.4	12.2	8.4	+2.6	+0.8	−3.8
Four other European countries							
4. CBR	n.a.	31.5	30.0	21.2	n.a.	−1.5	−8.8
5. CDR	n.a.	25.0	20.0	13.7	n.a.	−5.0	−6.3
6. CRNI	n.a.	6.5	10.0	7.5	n.a.	+3.5	−2.5

Notes: The averages in lines 1–6 are calculated from the vital rates summarized in Simon Kuznets, *Modern Economic Growth* (New Haven: Yale University Press, 1966), table 2.3, pp. 42–44. Lines 1–3 include England and Wales, Denmark, Finland, Norway and Sweden; lines 4–6 include Belgium, France, Germany, and the Netherlands. For all countries the year indicated represents the midpoint of a long interval over which the crude rates were averaged, the interval varying between sixty, forty, and ten years. The entries represent unweighted arithmetic means of the values for the individual countries included.
The changes in columns 5–7 are derived directly from the averages in columns 1–4.

The first aspect of the recent declines in death rates in the LDCs is that they proceeded at a rate far exceeding that of the past declines in death rates in the currently developed countries. Table 6.3 illustrates the contrast with the older European countries. A drop of 22.5 points in the rates in the LDCs over five decades meant a decline per decade of 4.5 points. For the five northern European countries, the rates of decline per decade were, for the successive intervals in columns 5–7, 0.76, 0.84, and 1.80. For the other four European countries, the declines per decade in the death rates were 1.11 points for the interval 1850–95, and 2.10 for the interval 1895–1925. If the initial position of the LDCs in 1920–25 is compared with that of the European countries either in 1800 or in 1850, the rate of decline in the LDCs over the first five decades of their demographic transition was from four to five times as high as that for the older, settled, currently developed European countries.

One should also note that, in the *earlier* phases of the shift in demographic patterns, the movements of the birthrates in the currently developed countries were also at rates much lower than those in the death rates – so that the initial rises in the crude rates of natural increase were, as in the case of the recent trends for the LDCs, due predominantly to the declines in mortality.

The second distinctive feature of the recent major drop in death rates in the LDCs is that it occurred in regions where the basic economic and institutional structures were little affected by industrialization and modernization – whereas the trends in death rates that we observed for the currently developed countries in Table 6.3 occurred largely in association with marked upward movements in per capita product and, more important, advances of the countries in the economic and institutional transformation associated with modern economic growth. This was certainly true beginning with the mid-nineteenth century. And, one should add, both the rapidity of the recent decline in death rates in the LDCs and its occurrence without association, in many of the regions involved, with any significant economic and institutional changes, can be credited to the nature of the technological revolution in dealing with infectious diseases and with the major health problems of the LDCs, which apparently began after World War I and attained its most striking successes shortly after World War II.

Third, granted the importance of major innovations in the technology related to control of diseases and of mortality, and the pervasive spread of declines in mortality to LDC regions and countries differing widely in institutional and economic structure, complementary effects of other technologies were required and differences in exposure to modernizing influences continued to affect death rates. After all, the new medical and public health tools had to be made accessible to all population groups in the LDCs to produce the wide effects observed (see comment below); here the technological revolution in transport and communication played an important role. And differences in extent and duration of exposure to modernizing influences are reflected even now in death rate differentials among major groups of LDCs (and would be even more prominent in single-country comparisons). Thus, Table 6.4 below shows that, even by 1970–75, crude death rates in sub-Saharan Africa (excluding the southern region) were, at 22 per 1,000, more than twice as high as those for Latin America (excluding the Temperate Zone) at somewhat over 9 per 1,000.

Finally, one should note that declines in death rates (as in other vital rates) of the magnitude suggested for the LDCs over the last fifty years – and perhaps even for each of the quarter-century subperiods separately – mean that the demographic trends involved must have necessarily affected large proportions of the total population involved. For each of these vital rates is a weighted average of group-specific rates, weighted by

Table 6.4. *Vital rates (per 1,000), observed (to 1970–75) and projected (to 1995–2000, medium variant), LDC regions*

	1950– 55 (1)	Change to 1970–75 (2)	1970– 75 (3)	Change to 1980–85 (4)	1980– 85 (5)	Change to 1995– 2000 (6)	1995– 2000 (7)	Total Change (8)
East and middle South Asia (1,162; 2,093)								
1. CBR	44.1	−2.2	41.9	−3.5	38.4	−10.2	28.2	−15.9
2. CDR	25.2	−8.7	16.5	−3.8	12.7	−3.9	8.8	−16.4
3. CRNI	18.9	+6.5	25.4	+0.3	25.7	−6.3	19.4	+0.5
Middle East (186; 366)								
4. CBR	47.1	−4.0	43.1	−2.4	40.7	−9.1	31.6	−15.5
5. CDR	22.4	−7.6	14.8	−3.1	11.7	−3.8	7.9	−14.5
6. CRNI	24.7	+3.6	28.3	+0.7	29.0	−5.3	23.7	−1.0
Sub-Saharan Africa (275; 566)								
7. CBR	48.7	−1.1	47.6	−1.0	46.6	−4.7	41.9	−6.8
8. CDR	28.6	−6.8	21.8	−3.6	18.2	−5.4	12.8	−15.8
9. CRNI	20.1	+5.7	25.8	+2.6	28.4	+0.7	29.1	+9.0
Latin America, except temperate zone (285; 567)								
10. CBR	43.7	−4.8	38.9	−2.3	36.6	−6.0	30.6	−13.1
11. CDR	15.2	−6.0	9.2	−2.0	7.2	−1.9	5.3	−9.9
12. CRNI	28.5	+1.2	29.7	−0.3	29.4	−4.1	25.3	−3.2
LDCs, four regions above (1,908; 3,592)								
13. CBR	45.0	−2.6	42.4	−2.8	39.6	−8.7	30.9	−14.1
14. CDR	23.9	−7.9	16.0	−3.4	12.6	−3.8	8.8	−15.1
15. CRNI	21.1	+5.3	26.4	+0.6	27.0	−4.9	22.1	+1.0

Notes: The underlying data are all from the United Nations working paper cited in the notes to Tables 6.1 and 6.2.

The totals entered in parentheses following the designation of regions are the 1975 and year 2000 populations of the region, in millions.

East and middle South Asia is a combination of east South Asia and middle South Asia. The internal weights, based on the 1975 population, are 3 and 7 for the two subregions respectively.

Middle East comprises western South Asia and North Africa, with approximately equal weights.

Sub-Saharan Africa includes three subregions – eastern Africa, middle Africa, and western Africa (with approximate weights of 4, 2, and 4). Southern Africa was omitted because of the weight in it of the Union of South Africa and the mixed composition of its population with different levels of economic development.

Latin America comprises the Caribbean, Middle America, and Tropical South America, with approximate weights of 1, 3, and 6. The Temperate Zone (Argentina, Uruguay, and Chile) was omitted.

The total of LDCs is a weighted average of the four regions (with weights of 60, 10, 15, and 15, for the regions in the order listed).

For more detail concerning inclusion of individual countries, see the source. China and East Asia, in general, are omitted, and so are some LDCs in Oceania.

the groups' proportions in the total. Thus, a decline in the crude death rate of a few points, say from 32 to 30 per 1,000, could well be accounted for by a decline of 6 points for a group whose mortality declined from 32 to 26 per 1,000 while that of the remaining group stayed constant – the two groups accounting for one-third and two-thirds of the total population respectively. But a much larger decline, and conditions in which the death rate of a small group in the total population cannot be sharply reduced while mortality remains high in the rest of the population, mean that the impact of the decline must necessarily have been widespread. This point is of analytical importance, considering the contrast between the sharp downtrends in the death rates and the minor declines in birthrates – with implications for the possible differential effects of the two sets of trends on the various groups in the population, particularly the smaller economic and social groups at the top and the much larger proportions of the population at middle and below-average economic and social levels.

In turning now to the sections of Table 6.2 that relate to population and vital rate *projections* to the year 2000, we may view the latter as informed judgments of the likely demographic trends – on the assumption that no great catastrophes or miraculous boons introduce major discontinuities, and the more interesting assumption that economic and social progress will take place at a feasible pace to warrant expectation that the growing populations will be sustained at acceptable levels.[5] From our standpoint, the major interest in these projections is their indication that while the growth rates and the vital rates in the developed countries will move slowly downward over the last quarter of this century – and show no declines in the death rates – for LDCs (excluding China) death rates will still decline substantially (see line 19, col. 6). And while the birthrates for the LDCs are assumed to drop even more (see line 18, col. 6), the projections for the last quinquennium still show a rate of natural increase over 2% per year and well above the initial rates either in 1937 or even in 1950–55.

But given the large magnitudes of, and some significant disparities within, the total of LDCs, it is useful to consider the magnitudes and projections separately for the major LDC regions – and with some time break from 1950–75 to 1995–2000 (Table 6.4). The total LDC population for 1975 accounted for in this table can be compared with that in

---

5 A useful *brief* description of the assumptions underlying the projections, and the criteria of plausibility used in selecting them, is in United Nations (1966, chap. 2, pp. 6–7). A wider review of the field is in United Nations (1973, 1:558–88).

Table 6.2, for LDCs excluding China – and it is 1,918 million compared with 1,997 in line 4, column 3 of Table 6.2.

One should begin by noting the dominance of the South Asian region in the 1975 total, and the Asian contribution would become all the larger were we to include China. In 1975, the population for China implicit in Table 6.2 is 838 million. Of the total for South Asia, the contribution of what might be called the clearly Hindic group (Bangladesh, Pakistan, and India) was 758 million. Thus, of the total in 1975 of the four regions shown in Table 6.3 plus China – 2,746 million – as much as 1,596 million was accounted for by the two areas that could be designated centers of the centuries-old Sinic and Hindic civilizations. Of the total additions over the twenty-five year period from 1975 onward – some 1,984 million – 310 million are projected for China (see Table 6.2) and another 593 million for the three Indian countries listed above. Thus, by the year 2000, the areas that are the centers of these two old civilizations would still account for 1,148 plus 1,351 million, or a total of some 2.5 billion out of an aggregate of 4.74 billion for all LDCs in the four regions plus China. The emphasis on this large contribution of these two old civilizations to the population bulk, and to current and projected excess growth of the LDCs, points to a consideration of the past economic and social innovations that permitted the sustained growth of this population mass on an area far smaller than that occupied by the other LDCs – innovations in agriculture and institutional devices. These would presumably affect the responses of the relevant populations to the declines in the death rates and to the changing role of the next generation in the adjustment to widening economic opportunities associated with industrialization and modernization.[6]

6 It is possible to secure from United Nations, *Demographic Yearbook 1957*, the distribution of population among continents and subcontinents in 1920, as well as of the land area (including internal waters); and we find in Clark (1957) a distribution of land among major parts of the world, the land evaluated with respect to rainfall, temperature, and other climatic factors that affect suitability for intensive cultivation (table 33, inset before p. 309). Comparing the large areas within the group that comprises the LDCs we find the following percentage distributions (LDCs, comprising the regions distinguished = 100):

	Population (1920)	Total land	Land in standard units
East and Southeast Asia	77.0	24.8	29.4
Southwest Asia	3.7	8.2	1.3
Africa	11.7	39.4	31.8
Latin America	7.6	27.6	37.5

continued on p. 98

There were marked differences among the regions in the levels of death rates in 1950–55, the earliest quinquennium for which the comparison is easily made. In Latin America, these death rates were as low as 15.2, as result of preceding declines that proceeded at a slow pace to the 1930s and accelerated thereafter (Arriaga and Davis 1969). In the same quinquennium, the crude death rates ranged from 22.5 to 28.5 per 1,000 in the three other LDC regions. With the crude birthrates at roughly similar levels, the result was a substantial range in rates of natural increase, from 19 to 28.5 per 1,000.

Over the twenty-five-year period to 1975, there were substantial declines in the crude death rates in all four LDC regions, leaving the differentials in death rates in 1975 even wider, at least proportionally, than they were in 1950–55 (see col. 3, which shows a range from 9.3 for Latin America to 21.8 for sub-Saharan Africa), and the declines in death rates were substantially larger than the declines in birthrates, leading to a rise in the rate of natural increase in all four regions. Yet for Latin America, the region furthest along in the demographic transition, the decline in birthrates was more substantial and the rise in rates of natural increase rather minor. The result was that by 1975 the regional differentials in rates of natural increase were narrow (from 25.5 to 29.5) – the rates being at relatively high levels in all four regions.

But the most interesting part of Table 6.4 is the indication that for three of the four regions, excluding Latin America, the next decade, to the mid-1980s, will again show greater declines in death rates than in birthrates – with consequent further rises, even though minor, in the rates of natural increase. It is only in the period after the mid-1980s that the birthrates are expected to decline substantially enough to exceed the still-expected further declines in the death rates. Even so, one region – sub-Saharan Africa – is, according to the present projections, to show rising rates of natural increase practically to the end of the century.

Further subdivisions within the regions would reveal even further differences among various groups of the LDCs in the levels of their vital rates, and distinction of narrower time periods would more clearly reveal differences in past and projected changes in these basic demographic trends. Thus, the differences among the currently distinguished four re-

East and Southeast Asia in the first line is dominated by the Sinic and Hindic group; and the capacity shown to sustain enormous populations with a land endowment that is less than a third of that in the rest of the less developed world is striking.

gions with respect to the timing in the demographic transition – from Latin America as the most advanced to sub-Saharan Africa as the least – would be refined further; and so would the difference in timing in reaching the peak rate of natural increase, and the peaks and troughs in the underlying birthrates and death rates. But the distinctions in Table 6.4 are sufficient to indicate both the similarities and the major differences in the movements of the death rates, in their relation to the levels and changes in the birthrates; and to remind us of the diversity of the demographic, and implicitly economic and institutional, patterns among the major groups within the LDC universe. The recognition of this diversity is particularly important, as we shift now to an exploration of the possible implications these movements in death rates, in their relation to those in birthrates, have for the internal economic distributions in the countries affected.

II. Some implications

What were the likely effects of the recent population trends in the LDCs, summarized in the preceding section? In attempting to formulate some speculative but plausible answers to this question, it seemed best to start with (a) the effects of the rapid and striking declines in the death rates; and then turn to (b) the possible reasons for the lag in the declines of the birthrates. The separation between the two trends may seem artificial; and yet I will argue below that the choices with respect to the downward movement of death rates were more limited than those with respect to the adaptive movement of birthrates. If only for this reason, one is warranted in considering the two sets of trends separately before attempting to combine their possible effects.

II.1. Declines in death rates

In dealing with the effects of the recent major declines in mortality in the LDCs, we may ask first what kind of demographic patterns prevailed in these countries before, when high death rates and birthrates yielded low rates of natural increase. Were there substantial *within-country* differences among the various economic and social groups, in demographic structure and in the rates of natural increase?

No adequate direct evidence on this question is available to me, although a long search in the literature and greater familiarity with the sources might have provided it. But some plausible conjectures can be suggested. First, in these pre-1920 decades, as Table 6.1 indicated, the MDCs were characterized by markedly lower death rates than the LDCs, so that the rate of natural increase in the former was substantially higher – *despite* the fact that their birthrates were substantially lower. This suggests that, with death rates in the LDCs at these high levels, even a moderate proportional lowering of the death rate could allow for a moderate decrease in the birthrate and still result in a substantial rise in the rate of natural increase. With CDR at, say, 40 and a CBR at 45, a drop in the former to 36 and in the latter to 42 would mean a rise in the rate of natural increase to 6 per 1,000 – by a full fifth. One may reasonably assume that also *within* the LDC country or region there could have been differences among economic and social groups, where greater wealth and easier access to means of subsistence could have resulted in appreciably lower death rates – and, even if these led to somewhat lower fertility, the more favored economic or social groups might have attained a higher rate of natural increase – just as the MDCs did in the comparison with the LDCs. This would be particularly likely so long as higher economic and social status was not connected with greater health risks in urban conditions (if urban living was a prerequisite of higher income). But in the countries and times of which we are speaking, urban populations constituted a minor fraction of total population.[7]

The implication is that in the earlier decades of high levels of both mortality and fertility, before 1920, differences within the LDCs in economic and social status may have been associated with reductions in mortality that were substantial and larger than the likely restraints on fertility (if any) – thus yielding a higher rate of natural increase among the upper social and economic groups than among the lower ones. If this implication is valid, the resulting contrast with the conditions in times and countries in which the overall level of death rates has been reduced sufficiently so that large *relative* mortality differentials could not convert even minor birthrate excesses into equality or shortage of the rates of natural increase is of major analytical importance.

7 In 1920, of some 1,187 million population estimated in the less developed regions (defined as countries outside of Europe, North America, Japan, the Soviet Union, Australia and New Zealand, and temperate South America), only 69 million were living in places with populations of 20,000 or more. While this low percentage – less than 6% – was largely due to the dominance of Asia, a level of slightly over 10% was the highest shown for any subregion. See United Nations (1969, tables 47–49, pp. 115–17).

Unfortunately, I can find only illustrative evidence, relating primarily to differentials in death rates in one or two less developed countries by economic or social status (directly given, or associated with some ethnic group distinctions), or separate evidence on birthrates by social status or ethnic grouping – but not the two bodies of evidence together. Thus, to cite an example for India, in 1931 the expectation of life at birth for Parsis was (combined with equal weight for men and women) as high as 53 years – compared with 32 years for total population – and the difference is "attributed in large measure to the relatively advantageous position of the Parsis" (United Nations 1953, p. 63). If we apply crude conversion ratios to expectation of life at birth to derive crude death rates as used by Kingsley Davis (that is, setting the latter to 1,000 divided by expectation of life),[8] the corresponding CDRs are 19 per 1,000 for the Parsis (a small group in the large total) compared with more than 31 per 1,000 for total population – a difference that may or may not have been fully compensated by the difference in crude birthrates. Similar evidence of substantial differences in death rates appear in the summary of a sample survey of rural families in Punjab in 1931. One may note that in the 1973 edition of United Nations, *The Determinants* . . . , the relevant section on mortality differentials in less developed countries (par. 132, p. 139) begins with a statement that information on these "differentials by occupation, income, and education is . . . sparse" and quotes only a few cases, mostly for the late 1950s or early 1960s.

A related illustration of interest can be derived from the vital rates for the United States when the distinction is made between the white population and the nonwhite (the latter predominantly Negro). For 1905–10 (the earliest period for which the comparison is given) the *gross* reproduction rate was shown at 1,740 for the white population and 2,240 for the nonwhite – an excess of the latter of some 30%; but the *net* reproduction rate, that is, the one that takes account of mortality, was 1,339 for the white population and 1,329, somewhat lower, for the nonwhite population. This is an illustration of greater mortality in the economically and socially disadvantaged group more than offsetting a much higher fertility; and it is shown for a period when crude death rates averaged (for 1900–1904) 16 per 1,000 for the white population and about 26 per 1,000 for

8 See Davis (1951); the conversion ratio used in the text is described on p. 36. The data on children born and surviving to rural families in Punjab in 1939 for various occupational class groups are in table 26, p. 78, with discussion in the text (p. 76) stressing some limitations of the data.

the nonwhite.[9] It is plausible to assume that further back in time, when the level of death rates was appreciably higher, their excess may have produced an even greater differential in rate of natural increase in favor of the white population. By contrast, in the later period, when death rates declined for both white and nonwhite populations, the *net* reproduction rate of the nonwhite population began to exceed that of the white by a large margin. Thus, by 1957 (the peak year in the United States reproduction rates in recent times) the gross rate of the nonwhite population, at 2,371, exceeded that of the white, at 1,764, by almost 40%; the net rates were 2,206 and 1,701 respectively, an excess of almost 30%.

Finally, one should note briefly the data on demography of peasant communities.[10] They deal largely with fertility, strongly suggesting, though with some exceptions, that fertility is higher among the richer (in terms of land) peasants than among the poorer; with mortality, at least in children, also being distinctly lower among the rich. The result, then, is a positive association within the peasantry between higher economic position and rate of natural increase. But the findings are qualified by sparsity of coverage, particularly for LDCs in the premodern periods of high mortality; the limitation of the data largely to fertility; the absence of data on per capita income of the peasant families classified by size over the life cycle; and the difficulty of assigning weights to the peasant population (distinctly smaller than the rural) within the total. A further exploration of the field, not feasible here, may yield significant findings.

If we assume that the rate of natural increase *within* the LDCs, before the recent sharp decline in death rates, was greater among the upper economic and social groups, the situation would have been in sharp contrast to that in the MDCs for a number of decades and that in the LDCs once overall death rate levels have been substantially reduced. The more familiar finding is that the birthrates *and* the rates of natural increase have been greater among the lower income groups – associated with the greater lag in the declines of birthrates among the former, in conditions under which a generally lower level of death rates reduced the weight of the death variable in offsetting births. This also meant that in the earlier times in the LDCs, the number of *surviving* children per family – once it

9 The data are from U.S. Bureau of the Census (1975). The series on gross and net reproduction rates are series B36–41, p. 53; those on crude birthrates are series B5–10, p. 49; and those on crude death rates are series B167–80, p. 59.

10 See, e.g., a recent paper by Ajami (1976, pp. 453–63), and the literature cited therein, particularly the early paper by Stys (1957, pp. 136–48).

reached a decade or more beyond the marriage date – was greater among the upper economic and social groups than among the lower, with the necessary qualification concerning the urban death rate excess over the rural. Since the number of surviving children is in turn a major factor in determining the size of the family (the other being the degree of "joint-ness"), it is possible that the average size of the family was larger among the upper than among the lower economic and social groups; and that the average income of this larger family, even on a *per capita* basis, was signifi-cantly greater than that of the smaller family among the lower economic and social groups. Such *positive* association between the size of family and *per capita* income is not found in recent cross-sectional studies, which are naturally limited either to MDCs or to LDCs with death rates already substantially reduced by recent advances in health technology. On the contrary, the negative association between size of family or household and its per capita income is a common finding; and while qualified by changes in income levels over the life cycle, still remained a major result in the analysis in a recent paper (Chapter 7, below, section III, on the size of family or household effects).

But more important here is the implication that this situation of higher death rates and lower rates of natural increase among the lower economic and social groups meant a serious aggravation of already existing in-equalities, in that shorter life-spans, greater morbidity, and fewer children surviving to productive ages were both cause and effect of lower economic returns over the family's productive lifespan. This association of lower economic position with higher rates of death and morbidity persisted, of course, beyond the transition in the population patterns from premodern to modern times; and it is still found in the MDCs in recent decades. But the effects of this association must have been far greater when death and morbidity rates were so high, and when substantial reductions in them could be attained by more food, better clothing and shelter, and greater mobility for protection against epidemics or famines. Of course, we cannot now gauge these differentials in death rate and rate of natu-ral increase or test their persistence in conditions of frequent short-term rises in death rates that might have swept over rich and poor alike. But one may assume that if there were these death and natural increase differ-entials in the pre-modern LDCs, they served only to aggravate long-term economic inequalities rather than to temper them.

In this connection, the exploratory illustration of economic losses rep-resented by the deaths of children and young adults in the Appendix to this paper is of interest. These explorations compare the losses of past inputs into children and young adults (the latter dying before their net contribution might have fully covered the past inputs into their consumption), in a less developed and a developed country in the 1930s – relating these annual losses to the total annual product of each of the two countries. The results of the comparison, indicating that relative losses involved in such deaths are more than five times as great in the less developed as in the developed country, only suggest what might be found by comparing similar losses from deaths for the richer (lower mortality) and poorer (higher mortality) groups *within* a premodern LDC. Clearly, the burden of such losses was proportionally much greater among the lower income groups, representing a greater relative drain on their long-term economic capacity and resources.

The comments above are meant to provide a tentative base for evaluating the effects of the striking declines in death rates that we find in the tables in section I. Given their magnitude and the character of the major causal factors involved, it is reasonable to infer that these reductions in death rates were widespread; that their absolute magnitude was greater among those groups in the population for whom the initial levels were higher; and that consequently their effects on the rates of natural increase were far greater for those groups in the population for whom these rates were initially lower – the larger groups at the lower economic and social levels. If the death rates for the upper and lower groups could differ by as much as 10 points (e.g., 30 to 40), it could be expected that a major step forward in health care and medical technology applicable without a major input of scarce resources and without requiring major changes in patterns of life would affect the higher death rates absolutely more than it would affect the lower death rates already reduced by more favorable economic conditions in the past. And one could also argue that the benefit would be greater to those who have sustained the losses caused by higher death rates in the past. The immediate implication, subject to a major qualification noted below, is that the differential reduction in death rates plausibly assumed above, the resulting convergence of internal death rates among various economic and social groups, meant the reduction of an important aspect of persisting inequality that loomed large in the premodern LDC societies.

Before we consider the possible qualification on the equalizing effects of the internal differentials in reduction of death rates in the LDCs once the major declines began, we should stress two aspects of the trends under discussion. The first, already noted, is that little choice was possible, or wanted, in incurring these declines. If they came, largely as effects of developments in the MDCs brought into the LDCs from the outside, as it were, relieving sickness and death without incurring perceptible economic and social costs, there was no incentive for resisting the much-desired opportunity for longer and healthier life. In that sense the situation was quite different from the choices relating to birthrates: reducing these involved a variety of alternatives within limits that could spell substantial differences in population growth rates, for countries or for groups within them. Second, and more important, once contacts with the developed parts of the world were increasingly numerous, it became obvious that the reduction in death rates (and associated reduction in rates of morbidity) was a *necessary* if not sufficient requirement for a healthier, long-lived, population – with the possibility of longer investment in the training and education of the younger generation preserved from demographic calamities, with the chances of developing a forward spirit in a population justifiably believing in man's control over his destiny, and with a family structure in which smaller size and fewer children would make possible a better adjustment to widening economic and social opportunities. Rejecting the contacts that reduced the death rates would thus mean also rejecting the possibility of shifting to a modern demographic pattern and modernization of society that could also mean better use of the potentials of economic growth.[11]

The conclusion is that the reduction of the death rates in the LDCs from their initial high levels in the 1920s was an indispensable condition for eventual modernization and participation in modern economic growth – while the rapidity and magnitudes of the declines were unavoidable (were anybody willing to avoid it) effects of the new technology in situations of a backlog of high mortality and high morbidity problems. Whatever the immediate, or shorter term, consequences of these trends, particularly those when the failure of birthrates to decline resulted in a rapid acceleration of the rates of natural increase, in the longer run the

11 For a brief discussion of the relation between the health revolution and economic development, see the paper by the World Health Organization, "Health Trends and Prospects in Relation to Population and Development," in United Nations (1975). The same paper contains some discussion of the relation between the decline in infant mortality and the birthrate.

major declines in death rates were a precondition of the declines in birth-rates and of other adjustments to the modern demographic patterns of population growth.

The major qualification alluded to above is, of course, the consequence of lag of the decline in birthrates – in conditions where the basic inno-vation introduced by the reduction in death rates was not accompanied by sufficient changes in other aspects of social and material technology. In such conditions, and provided there was – as there was likely to be with stagnant social structure and production technology – scarcity of the traditional resources (whether land or reproducible capital), a rapid acceleration of rates of natural increase among the groups hitherto below the upper economic and social levels may have meant suddenly increased pressures of augmented labor supplies on scarce complementary re-sources. Whether under these conditions a longer and healthier working life of the members of a family compensated, over the life cycle, for the greater pressure of labor on resources is a question that does not ad-mit of an easy answer; and the answer would vary among various groups of LDCs, depending upon the initial resource endowments and the de-gree to which further advances in traditional technology were possible with augmented labor. Here the added knowledge concerning the demo-graphic and economic structures of LDCs before the recent declines in death rates would be required to provide even tentative answers. But one cannot exclude the possibility that in some cases the longer productive life span and greater increase of the lower economic and social groups may still have resulted in some widening of internal income inequality because upper groups took advantage of the greater pressure of labor on land or on other capital, while in other cases the inequality-reducing in-ternal convergence of rates of mortality and morbidity among the several economic groups might have reduced internal income inequality – even if the crude birthrates continued at high levels and failed for some time to respond to the declines in death rates.

On this uncertain conclusion, I end the discussion of the effects of declines in mortality in the LDCs. One should emphasize to the end the indispensable – and in the longer run beneficial – effects of the declines in the death rates, regardless of whether their immediate and direct effect was to widen or to narrow internal income inequalities. This emphasis might have been superfluous except that much recent discussion of the problems created by rapid population growth tends to neglect the source of the latter in the declines in mortality and morbidity – and thus to understate, by omission, their vitally important and beneficial long-term effects.[12]

II.2. Lags in the decline of birthrates

The long lag in fertility decline behind the downtrend in mortality is illustrated in Professor Lindert's paper for this conference, on "Child Costs and Economic Development" and is strongly suggested for the LDCs in the initial section of this paper, with its emphasis on the dominance of declines in mortality in contribution to a rising rate of natural increase in the face of constant or only slightly dropping birthrates. This section deals with a few aspects of the response of birthrates to the major declines in death rates in the LDCs.

Even though the would-be parental pair is the immediate decision unit in this response, one must allow for the wider, blood-related groups (an extended family, a tribe, an ethnic group, a caste) that may set the norms for the would-be parents. In addition, there are the large non-blood collectives, particularly the government, that may react to declining death rates and accelerating population growth in a variety of ways, all of which involve modifications of conditions under which the family unit would make decisions concerning more or fewer children – whether the steps are limited to exhortation and to providing cheaper methods of birth control or extend to drastic policy measures affecting the costs of more children. On the other hand, the effects of declining deaths include more than just increase in numbers of surviving children. The underlying innovation in health and medical technology may reduce involuntary sterility formerly

12 In this connection one may refer to two papers on population growth and income distribution in the United Nations volume, *Population Debate* (1975, vol. 1). The first, by Dharam P. Ghai, "Population Growth, Labour Absorption, and Income Distribution" (pp. 502–9), summarizes the conclusions by listing in table 2 (p. 509) the effects of population growth on income distribution – under two major headings of "high fertility" and "reduced fertility" – with the levels and trends of mortality not mentioned. In the other paper, by H. W. Singer, "Income Distribution and Population Growth" (pp. 510–17), there is explicit mention of lower mortality as "a necessary first step towards achieving the more desirable low birth rate/low death rate type of equilibrium" (p. 516). But the author follows this statement by considering effects of a more equal distribution on death rates, with no discussion of the reverse, the possible effects of declines in mortality on the income distribution in the LDCs. Yet, with all the interest in the latter, the possible effects of the trends in mortality rather than in fertility that dominated the demographic changes in the LDCs in the last few decades seem to be neglected.

associated with widely prevalent debilitating diseases; it may raise intra-marital fertility by prolonging the duration of marriage (within the child-bearing span of the wife) through the reduction of mortality (particularly male) in the procreative ages – just as it may eventually, by reducing un-controllable and unpredictable diseases, introduce changes in would-be parents' outlook on the future and the role of the next generation. Given the diversity of possible sources of decisions in response to declining death rates, the variety of direct and indirect effects of the latter on the birthrate response, and finally our inadequate knowledge of the parame-ters of demographic processes and of economic and institutional patterns in various LDC regions, we can attempt only a limited probing.

This is true even if we eliminate from consideration the communist societies, in which the power of the single-party, ideologically motivated government is such that *its* responses to declining death rates and accel-erating population growth may dominate whatever free responses could have originated within the population masses of the country. Such domi-nation is suggested by the power of intensive propaganda, control over location and migration of the population, disposition of the basic con-sumer goods, particularly housing, needed for a growing population, and the like. I would find it difficult, for lack of adequate knowledge of soci-eties so organized, to formulate a rational basis for evaluating the planned response that the governmental decision centers of these countries would make to declining death rates and rising rates of natural increase. The same criterion might also lead to exclusion of noncommunist, dictatori-ally organized LDCs, in which a similar domination of the state over the free responses of the population might be expected; but there are no clear relevant measures for drawing the line. The purpose of the comment is to call attention to the possible policy interventions of groups not related by blood, particularly those endowed with internal sovereignty. They may be important in both dictatorially and democratically organized societies; but their weight seems more dominant in the former – sufficiently so to warrant limiting further discussion by concentrating on the societies with relative freedom of decision by families and related blood groups.

The importance of the wider, blood-related groups that encompass the individual families is clearly great in LDCs, whether they be the tribal groupings in much of Africa, the racial-ethnic divisions within many Latin American countries, or the groupings in Asian countries where lim-ited intermarriage among groups (say, among castes in India) is still the norm. In conditions of relative weakness and instability of the country's collective institutions, particularly the state, such wider blood-related groups serve an important function in providing long-term security to individual families in conditions of group competition. The response of a family to declining death rates and more surviving children would, with reference to the wider group norms, differ from that of an individual family within a stable political framework, relying securely on the protection and stability of a strong government representing the interests of the community and of all its parts. An adequate analysis would require taking specific account of these various blood-related subgroups within the populations of the several LDC regions in the process of their reaction to declines in death rates. But for obvious reasons our discussion can take only general cognizance of these sources of influence on the decisions of would-be parents.

We may now face a limited question. Assume that the individual families, the pairs of would-be parents, either experience or observe a perceptible reduction in death rates, both through the reduction of infant and child mortality and through declines in deaths of adults. Under what conditions would we expect a relatively prompt and full response of birthrates such as would prevent the rate of natural increase from rising substantially over a relatively long period? These conditions would presumably bear on (1) firmness of judgment with respect to continuity (irreversibility) of the observed declines in mortality; (2) the relation of the resulting numbers of surviving children to the desired numbers; and (3) the identity of the population group in a position to realize an effective birthrate response and the limits of their possible perception of mortality declines.[13]

13 Much of the literature on the response of fertility to mortality declines concentrates on the response of families to the actually incurred death of a child (or children) and the observed reaction. See in this connection Preston's chapter in [the original] volume and the paper for this conference by Yoram Ben-Porath on "Fertility and Child Mortality – Issues in the Demographic Transition of a Migrant Population." Of particular interest also are Preston (1975, pp. 189–200); and his summary introduction to the volume of proceedings of the CICRED seminar on Infant Mortality in Relation to the Level of Fertility (the proceedings were not available to me at the time of writing). For lack of familiarity with the details of most of the sample studies involved, one cannot judge whether the failure to completely "replace" children who die can be translated into an effective absence of a desired number of children as a target firm enough to explain the failure to reduce the birthrate in response to a perceived decline in mortality. There is an apparent lack of symmetry between a situation in which birth frequency has to be raised in an active response to the loss of a child and a situation in which births have to be reduced in response to an increased number of surviving children.

At any rate, it seemed of interest to stress in the brief discussion here aspects of lag, of perception of mortality declines, and of persistence of an excess in

1. Given the emergence of a marked downturn in death rates as a novel phenomenon for populations and countries that for centuries have experienced a much higher average mortality, and, most important, with instability characterized by sharp short-term declines and equally short-term larger rises, a fairly long period of observation and experience at lower and stable death rates would be required before a response could be expected. This is particularly true at the later stages of the woman's childbearing span, when a decision to forgo another child, in reliance on the persistence of low death rates for children, may be beyond repair if the expectation proves false. How long a period of waiting to test the persistence of the mortality trend one should reasonably assume would have to be estimated from an analytical case in which all other factors affecting the decision (except the decline in mortality itself) have been removed (i.e., held constant) – not an easy task. A span of well over a decade seems a minimum, and one could perhaps argue that, ruling out downward revisions in numbers of desired surviving children, a whole generation might have to pass before the next parental generation could react significantly. Yet, given the declines in crude death rates averaging between 4 and 5 points per 1,000 per decade over the last half-century (in the LDCs from the mid-1920s to the mid-1970s), a lag of only one decade would mean a substantial addition to the rate of natural increase – which would continue so long as the death rates continued to decline, even though persistence of the latter would, as time goes on, raise confidence and reduce the lag.

The judgment of confidence in the continuity and irreversibility of a new social trend is hardly susceptible of tests for either ex ante or post facto validity, and one hesitates to assign a large weight to it. Yet complete neglect of it implies a neglect of a possibly major problem of the channels by which effective perception of, and response to, new social processes is attained within the traditional, and later transitional, framework of LDCs. It may well be that a long delay in response to new trends is a rational reaction, due partly to limitation of information, partly to lack of resources for taking chances on uncertain trends and for overcoming the fear of the unknown.

2. The conjecture under (1) becomes less relevant if we can assume that over a long initial period of the decline in mortality in the LDCs, the desired number of surviving children remains higher than, or in the

the possible number of desired surviving children over that actually resulting through much of the early phase of the downtrend in mortality in the LDCs.

neighborhood of, the actual number (as perceived by the family). Given targets or norms, whether individually elaborated or more realistically set as norms in the form of socially approved patterns; whether hard or, more realistically, with soft margins, it is not difficult to see that *beginning* at the premodern levels of death rates and birthrates, there might be a long period of sustained mortality declines – and yet the resulting number of surviving children would remain short of or close to the desired target, thus providing no incentive for a response decline in birthrates.

To begin with, the declines in mortality and morbidity permit those groups in the population that formerly could not reach their fertility targets – either because of involuntary sterility or because of institutional constraints on remarriage of widows or because of other similar consequences of past mortality and morbidity – to start approximating them. Far more important, quantitatively, is the condition of the large economic and social groups below the narrowly defined top. Given the rather low rate of natural increase of LDCs just before the initiation of the recent downtrends in mortality (of about 0.5% in the 1920s), it is reasonable to suggest that for the majority of the population the number of surviving children was below the desired number. This suggestion is strengthened if we assume the earlier conjecture (discussed in section II.1 above) that at the top economic and social levels in the premodern LDCs death rates and rates of natural increase were substantially lower and greater respectively than at the lower levels. For this would mean a long-persisting pattern of association of a much larger number of surviving children with the higher economic and social status, which would most likely be carried over into the initial decades of the declines of death rates in the LDCs – unless there are prompt and major changes in the desired numbers, a possibility that largely depends on underlying major changes in the economy and institutions of the country, a shift at high gear into modernization that is likely to be the exception rather than the rule.

If so, a substantial phase of the long-term decline in death rates in the LDCs would also be a phase of catching up with formerly unavailable potentials of desired number of surviving children. The length of this catching-up phase, representing lack of incentive for a response of birthrates, is a matter for conjecture. It might differ from one group of LDCs to another; and it would certainly differ in its historical chronology, with disparities in the dates when the major mortality declines began among the different groups of LDCs. But if the natural-increase differences in premodern LDCs were as large as they seem from the scattered data on mortality (and some on fertility, particularly for the peasant communities), being at a minimum 10 points per 1,000, it might take at least two decades for the catching-up phase to be completed; nor should the possibility of a longer period be ruled out. If so, this phase would largely overlap with any lag due to lack of confidence in the persistence and irreversibility of the mortality trends, discussed under (1) above.

3. The perception of a trend like that in the death rates in the LDCs in recent decades may be limited to that of major *absolute* declines – which were concentrated in the early childhood ages, at one end, and in the age brackets beyond the early 50s at the other. Following the comment made above, we may ask how the population groups who are in a position to affect birthrates, either because they are of childbearing age or because they exercise influence on those who are, perceive the demographic trends. In the LDCs, in the transition period, and outside the limited upper circles of government, this is hardly done by scrutinizing aggregative statistics or observing graphs. But the answer to how families and the blood-related groups to which they may belong attain their perception of major demographic trends would have to come from greater familiarity with the LDC societies and their mechanisms for ascertaining and diffusing major social data than is possessed here.

One part of the answer is that reduction in the mortality of children, sizable only in the very early ages (below 5), is surely observed by those families in procreative phases of their life cycle that enjoy the benefits of such decreased mortality. And it may be legitimately argued that the knowledge of, and reaction to, this part of the downtrend in mortality could be expected to be more direct and potentially effective (other conditions being favorable) than the knowledge of, and reaction to, the decline in mortality at the advanced adult ages. It also follows that if the knowledge of trends is extrapolated into the future, in the process of formulating birth decisions, the reduction in early childhood mortality would be far more likely to form the basis for such an extrapolation than the changes at the advanced adult ages – which would relate to the role of children four or five decades after their birth. To be sure, neglecting these latter, as we do in the statistical illustration that follows, means neglecting the insurance motive of assuring survival of children to ages when they could support their aged parents. But, granted this limitation, it is of interest to explore what an instantaneous and complete response to declines in early child mortality would mean for the movements of the rates of natural increase.

The estimates of what we may designate the offset response of birthrates to declines in death rates, presented in Table 6.5, are based on two

Table 6.5. *Estimated offset response of birthrates to declines in death rates of children 0–4, 1950–55 to 1970–75, for the four LDC regions of Table 6.4*

	East and Middle South Asia (1)	Middle East (2)	Sub-Saharan Africa (3)	Latin America (4)	All four (5)
A. The relevant demographic parameters (per 1,000 of underlying population)					
Data for 1950–55					
1. Proportion of 0–4 to total population, 1950	153	164	170	169	160
2. Proportion of 0–4 to total population, 1955	162	169	180	178	168
3. CRNI, 1950–55	18.9	24.7	20.1	28.5	21.1
4. 0–4 population in 1955 as proportion of total in 1950 (per 1,000)	178.3	190.9	198.8	204.9	186.5
5. CBR, 1950–55	44.1	47.1	48.7	43.7	45.0
6. CBR in line 5, shifted to the base of 1950	46.26	50.06	51.18	46.88	47.41
7. Cumulative births, 1950–55, as proportion of 1950 population	247.8	276.6	283.5	257.5	260.5
8. Attrition (death rate) per 1,000 of 0–4 population in 1950–55, per year (from lines 4 and 7)	63.0	71.4	68.0	42.5	64.1
9. CDR, total population, 1950–55	25.2	22.4	28.6	15.2	23.9
Data for 1970–75					
10. Proportion of 0–4 to total population, 1970	169	173	178	171	171
11. Proportion of 0–4 to total population, 1975	167	171	181	167	170
12. CRNI, 1970–75	25.4	28.3	25.8	29.7	26.4
13. 0–4 population in 1975 as proportion of total in 1970	190.3	196.8	205.6	193.3	193.7
14. CBR, 1970–75	41.9	43.1	47.6	38.9	42.4
15. CBR, to the base of 1970 population	44.51	46.19	50.73	41.85	45.25
16. Cumulative births, 1970–75, as proportion of 1970 population	240.8	252.9	280.7	230.0	247.7
17. Attrition (death rate) of population 0–4, in 1970–75	45.4	48.1	59.8	33.3	47.4
18. CDR, 1970–75	16.5	14.8	21.8	9.2	16.0

Table 6.5 *(cont.)*

	East and Middle South Asia (1)	Middle East (2)	Sub-Saharan Africa (3)	Latin America (4)	All four (5)
	B. Derivation of offset response in birthrates to decline in death rates of 0–4 population (all entries per 1,000 of relevant population)				
19. Decline in death rates of 0–4 population from 1950–55 to 1970–75	17.6	23.3	8.2	9.2	16.7
20. Proportion of 0–4 population to total at initial date	0.17	0.17	0.18	0.18	0.17
21. Decline in death rates of 0–4 population related to total population (line 19 × line 20) = full offset response	3.0	4.0	1.5	1.7	2.8
22. Observed decline in CBR	2.2	4.0	1.1	4.8	2.6
23. Observed change in CRNI	+6.5	+3.6	+5.7	+1.2	+5.3
24. Derived change in CRNI with full offset response	+5.7	+3.6	+5.3	+4.3	+5.1

Notes: All the underlying data are from the United Nations working paper cited and used in connection with Table 6.4.

Panel A, lines 4 and 13 – The estimates are the proportions in lines 2 and 11, raised by the cumulative growth of population (cumulative natural increase) over the quinquennium, using the entries in lines 3 and 12 respectively.

Panel A, lines 6 and 15 – The estimates use the rise of the base (total) population, but over half rather than the full quinquennium (as it was used for lines 4 and 13)

Panel A, lines 8 and 17 – The entries in lines 4 and 7, and 13 and 16 respectively, were used first to derive attrition (deaths) as the difference between lines 7 and 4, and 13 and 6, related to the initial base (1950 and 1970 respectively) and representing the proportion over the quinquennium. Then the proportion was adjusted for a shift from the 1950 or 1970 base to the 1950–55 and 1970–75, using the entries for 0–4 population in lines 1 and 4, and 10 and 13 respectively. The adjusted proportions, now to the base of 1950–55 and 1970–75 respectively, were then converted into death rates per year.

Panel B – for the rationale, see discussion in the text. Line 19 is the difference between lines 8 and 17 of panel A. Line 20 is based on the shares as shown in lines 1 and 4, and 10 and 13, of panel A. Line 22 was derived from the observed CBRs in lines 3 and 14 of panel A. Line 23 was derived from the observed CRNIs in lines 3 and 12 of panel A. Line 24 equals line 23 reduced by the excess of line 21 over line 22 (or raised by the shortage of line 21 relative to line 22).

assumptions: that the response is to reduction in death rates at ages under 5; that the response is prompt and full, allowing for no lag in the process. Both assumptions are unrealistic, the second far more so than the first. But the result is an extreme version of a full major response of birthrates; and it is of interest, in deriving it, to compare it with the actual movement of the birthrates and the trend in the rates of natural increase.

Given these assumptions, we need measures not only of the decline in crude death rates for total population, but also of the decline in the death rates of the population 0–4. Panel A of Table 6.5 summarizes the results of utilizing the rich data in the United Nations Working Paper repeatedly used here, which shows for individual countries and for regions not only crude birthrates and death rates and total population at quinquennial intervals beginning with 1950, but also the proportions, in total population, of the 0–4 group (as well as of other age groups – 5–14, etc.). On the reasonable premise that all these demographic parameters are consistent with each other, it is possible to derive, by comparing the cumulated crude birthrates over the quinquennium (related to total population at midpoint of the period) with the surviving 0–4 population at the end of the quinquennium (related to the population at the end of the quinquennium) the proportional attrition (per 1,000). If the population is closed, with no emigration or immigration, this attrition rate is identical with the crude death rate for the 0–4 group. Given the size of the regions we deal with, and the demonstrated closeness between the growth rates in total population and the rates of natural increase, it seemed justifiable to identify the attrition rates thus calculated with death rates relating to the 0–4 population. The estimates are clearly approximate, but the resulting orders of magnitude are plausible.[14]

With the results in panel A, which show the declines in death rates of 0–4 population between 1950–55 and 1970–75 and the proportions of that population in the total at the start of each quinquennium, we can estimate the offset response of birthrates – on the assumption that birthrates

14 The death rates derived for 0–4 population in lines 8 and 17 exceed the crude death rates for total population by factors of 2.4 to 3.2 in 1950–55 and 2.7 to 3.6 in 1970–75. Multiplying these ratios by the proportion of 0–4 to total population, averaged over each of the two quinquennia, we can derive the proportions of deaths of children 0–4 to all deaths, which would range from well over 40% to 50% or more. The direct data on distribution of deaths by age for various countries in the United Nations *Demographic Yearbook* (various years) suggest proportions for recent years, back to the 1950s, of between 40% and somewhat over 50%. The agreement cannot be checked fully because of scarcity of data on distribution of deaths by age and the indication that in many countries the deaths of infants are particularly underreported (a bias that would affect death rates for 0–4 population much more than total crude death rates). For the present illustrative purposes, further effort at assembling data on deaths by age, or at using direct information on age-specific death rates for LDCs, did not seem worthwhile. A more intensive study of the effects of declines in death rates would warrant such further effort.

would decline, without any lag, to offset fully the experienced reduction in childhood deaths (panel B). It will be noted that the derived response was only somewhat larger than the actual decline in birthrates in three of the four LDC regions – a rough agreement that, however, cannot be interpreted to mean that the observed drop in the birthrates *did* represent the assumed offset response. It could well have been due to a substantial decline in birthrates of the top economic and social groups, only partly offset by the constancy or slight rise in birthrates among the lower economic groups. In Latin America, the observed decline in birthrates, almost 5 points, greatly exceeded the derived offset of 1.7 points; and this finding is plausible, considering the much longer period over which declines in mortality occurred in Latin America and the greater movement toward the demographic transition that began to affect the birthrates.

But the major aspect of the finding in panel B is that even if we assume full and instantaneous response to declines in child mortality, such a response will not be sufficient to prevent a major rise in the rate of natural increase. As line 24 shows, the *derived* rate of natural increase shows a substantial rise over the two-decade span in *all* of the four LDC regions.

The results are as one would expect. If the birthrates respond to declines in child mortality alone, the rates of natural increase will be raised by the declines in mortality in ages *above* those of childhood – and largely by reduced mortality in the advanced adult ages. If we were to allow for effects of deaths also of children 5 years of age and over, there would be a somewhat larger, but not much larger, offset response. If, as partial data indicate, total deaths of children under 15 were only about 60% of total deaths, while the share of the 0–14 group ranged about 42% of total population, the implicitly more moderate level and decline of death rates for ages 5–14 than for the 0–4 populations might, if taken into account, raise the estimated offset decline in line 21 by about a tenth, but not more than that.

The major conclusion is that if it is largely childhood deaths that affect the birthrate response, then even a full and prompt response (neither likely) would be insufficient to prevent a substantial rise in the rates of natural increase. Under the assumed conditions, the latter will cease rising only when the death rates above the childhood ages cease declining. Or, to put the conclusion in its converse form, while death rates are declining – sharply and with the usual concentration in early and advanced ages – the possibility of avoiding large rises in the rates of natural increase would lie not so much in a response of birthrates to child mortality (a most likely response, yet even so not promptly or fully) as in changing conditions that would affect the total number of surviving children desired. Such changes in conditions are not automatically provided by declines in death rates and by those factors behind them that appeared to operate in the LDCs in recent decades. On the contrary, the conjectures under (2) suggest a long initial period in the decline of death rates when the desired number of surviving children may continue to remain above that yielded by declining child mortality levels.

But what are the implications of our discussion of the responses of birth-rates to the declines in death rates? At the end of the preceding subsection, which dealt with the declines in death rates, we came to a rather uncertain conclusion on the effects of the greater declines in death rates among the lower economic and social groups than among the upper groups, for whom death rates were already appreciably lower because of better nutrition, housing, and so on. We argued that prolongation of life, and closer convergence of death rates among various economic and social groups, removed one major aspect of long-term inequality. This reduction could be offset by greater pressure of higher rates of population growth on scarce traditional resources, unless such pressure was relieved by economic and social innovations associated with modern economic growth. We now add the conclusion that even with full and prompt offset response of birthrates to declines in death rates of 0–4 population, there will be acceleration of rates of natural increase; and such acceleration will be greater among those groups for whom the declines in death rates were greater, that is, among the lower economic and social strata. And this should mean that instead of a positive association between economic and social levels and group rates of natural increase, the trends discussed will produce an inverse association between economic and social levels and rates of natural increase. But this does not imply a necessary widening of per capita income inequalities if we deal with long-term levels of life-cycle income – which will be sustained by the longer span over which life and productivity can now be maintained among the lower income groups, as they could not be so maintained in the pretransition past. The conclusion is still uncertain; but one may argue that both the trends in the birthrates and the trends in income inequality depend heavily on economic and social transformations that relieve the pressure of growing population on the scarcity of traditional resources and that induce downtrends in the birthrates beyond those derivable as offset responses to declines in child mortality.

This latter argument could be developed further by indicating that the technological innovations associated with modern economic growth, which are the main source of the economic advance, depend heavily upon new knowledge; and that they and the associated social innovations require a much greater emphasis on higher levels of education and training of the younger generation that would be carrying the innovational process further. Once this connection between investment in the younger generation and further economic and social advance is established, there will be a shift toward greater investment by the older generation in the young (away from the earlier pattern of the younger generation contributing to their elders within the wider family),[15] with a resulting change in the number of desired surviving children, having major effects on birthrates. The important link in this argument is between the *sources* of economic advance and the contribution needed from the younger generation if these sources are to be maintained – a contribution that demands greater investment in education and training. And it is in this connection that a decline in death rates of the type that has occurred in LDCs in recent decades looms as an indispensable condition. How the eventual declines in birthrates develop, whether they begin at the top, and how rapidly they spread through the wider groups in the population are questions and possibilities with obvious bearing upon income distribution while the transition process is taking place. But these arguments take us well beyond the immediate effects of the death rate trends in the LDCs, the major movement so far observed. And it would require more analysis of the differential death rate movements and of the related movements in birthrates to permit adequate discussion of the wider interconnections just suggested.

Appendix. Economic losses represented by deaths: exploratory illustrations

In this appendix we discuss economic losses represented by deaths, with special attention to the differences between the high death rates of the LDCs and the much lower mortality of the MDCs. The discussion is directly relevant to the effects of the major declines of the death rates in the LDCs emphasized in the text. But, in view of the complexity and

15 See a recent paper by Caldwell (1976), which stresses the "flow from the younger generation to the older" in pretransition society and the reverse flow in the posttransition, nucleated families.

the difficulty of arriving at defensible approximations even of the order of magnitudes, it seemed best to shift the exploration to a separate appendix.

The discussion is limited to direct *economic* costs or losses. No attempt is, or can be, made to attach magnitudes to the psychological and emotional effects of death upon members of the family. Nor can we deal with indirect negative effects – for example, the greater unpredictability and variability over time of mortality in conditions of limited control over disease.

An even more important exclusion is the neglect of the association between high death rates and high levels of morbidity – that is, incidence of disease apart from higher mortality. Given this association, the level of death rates clearly suggests the level of morbidity; and higher incidence of disease either in childhood or in adulthood would presumably have negative effects on productivity, either because of the lasting debilitating effects of an earlier disease (even if incurred in childhood) or because of direct consequences of such diseases affecting adults of working age. Any attempt to measure the losses so involved in LDCs, in comparison with those in the MDCs, would run into the difficulty of separating the effects of health conditions from those of nutrition and other components of the standard of living. But it is reasonable to assume that these losses from higher morbidity associated with higher death rates in the LDCs are significantly greater than similar relative losses in the MDCs. If so, the comparison of economic losses suggested by deaths in the discussion that follows underestimates the excess relative loss in the less developed countries.

In dealing here with direct economic losses debited to deaths, we use for illustration the relevant demographic data for 1937 for two countries, Egypt and the Netherlands (see Table 6.A.1, panel A). With further search, we probably could have found the data for a wider contrast with respect to death rates, both crude and age-specific. But the contrast observed in panel A in the crude death rates, between 27.3 per 1,000 for Egypt and fewer than 9 per 1,000 for the Netherlands, is wide enough for our purposes. The intention is to suggest the wider ramifications of the comparison with respect to the economic losses involved – rather than attempt a full estimate of the orders of magnitude.

A glance at the age-specific death rates in columns 3 and 6 of panel A reveals that these rates are higher in Egypt than in the Netherlands for *each* age class distinguished; that the ratios of the age-specific death rates in Egypt to those in the Netherlands tend to be higher in the early ages

Table 6.A.1. *Economic losses implicit in death rates: an illustrative calculation, Egypt and the Netherlands, 1937*

	A. *Distributions of population and deaths by age classes, and the age-specific death rates*					
	Egypt			The Netherlands		
Age Class	% Share population by age (1)	% share deaths by age (2)	ASDR per 1,000 (3)	% share population by age (4)	% share deaths by age (5)	ASDR per 1,000 (6)
1. Below 1	3.1	26.5	234.4	2.2	8.6	34.3
2. 1–4	10.2	29.5	78.9	8.1	2.6	2.8
3. 5–9	14.0	3.9	7.6	9.8	1.2	1.1
4. 10–14	12.1	2.0	4.5	9.2	0.9	0.9
5. 0–14	39.4	61.9	—	29.3	13.3	—
6. 15–24	15.4	3.2	5.6	17.8	3.1	1.5
7. 25–34	15.7	4.4	7.7	15.4	3.6	2.1
8. 35–44	13.1	4.9	10.1	13.0	4.8	3.2
9. 45–54	8.3	4.5	14.7	10.3	7.7	6.6
10. 55–64	4.5	4.1	24.8	7.5	14.4	16.9
11. 15–64	57.0	21.1	—	64.0	33.6	—
12. 65 and over	3.6	17.0	127.2	6.7	53.1	69.6
13. Total	100.0	100.0	27.27	100.0	100.0	8.78

	B-1. *Economic losses from child mortality*					
	Egypt			The Netherlands		
Age class	Deaths, % of total population (1)	Loss multiple (2)	Loss, % of 100 CU (3)	Deaths, % of total population (4)	Loss multiple (5)	Loss, % of 100 CU (6)
14. Below 1	0.7266	0.25	0.1817	0.0755	0.25	0.0189
15. 1–4	0.8048	1.50	1.2072	0.0227	1.50	0.0340
16. 5–9	0.1064	3.75	0.3990	0.0108	3.75	0.0405
17. 10–14	0.0545	6.25	0.3406	0.0083	6.25	0.0519
18. 0–14	1.6923	—	2.1205	0.1173	—	0.1453
			(2.681)			(0.174)

Table 6.A.1 *(cont.)*

	B-2. *Residual economic losses, adult mortality*							
	Egypt				The Netherlands			
Class Age	Deaths, % of total popula- tion (1)	Assumed output per person (CU) (2)	Residual Cost beginning of age class CU's (3)	Resid- ual loss, % of 100 CU (4)	Deaths (5)	Output (6)	Resid- ual cost (7)	Resid- ual loss (8)
19. 15–24	0.0862	1.000	7.50	0.6465	0.0267	1.000	7.50	0.2002
20. 25–34	0.1209	1.322	7.50	0.7121	0.0327	1.224	7.50	0.2061
21. 35–44	0.1323	1.644	4.28	0.1402	0.0416	1.449	5.26	0.1256
22. 45–54	—	1.644	−2.16	—	—	1.449	0.77	—
23. Total				1.4988				0.5319
				(1.888)				(0.636)
24. Total, for panels B-1 and B-2, % of total product				4.57				0.81

Notes: Panel A – The data used here are taken, or calculated, from United Nations, *Demographic Yearbooks, 1949–1950, and 1951* (New York, 1950, 1951). The distribution of the population by age for Egypt is for late March 1937, and is from the *1949–50 Yearbook*, table 4, pp. 104 ff.; that for the Netherlands is the average of the percentage shares for 1930 and 1945, from the same table. The small fraction of age-unknown is allocated proportionately. The distribution of deaths by age is from United Nations, *Demographic Yearbook, 1951* (New York 1951), table 16, pp. 216 ff., and relates to the deaths in 1937 for both countries.
The age-specific death rates in column 3 are derived by relating the absolute numbers of deaths to the relevant population; but the multiplication of the ratio of column 2 to column 1 by the crude death rate (line 13, col. 3) yields identical results, except for errors of rounding. The age-specific death rates in col. 6 were derived by multiplying the ratio of col. 5 to col. 4, by the crude death rate in line 13, col. 6 (8.78).
Panel B-1, cols. 1 and 4 – The entries were derived by multiplying the age-specific death rates (see panel A, cols. 3 and 6), expressed as proper fractions, by the percentage share of the age-class in total population (see panel A, cols. 1 and 4).
Panel B-1, cols. 2 and 5 – Entries were calculated on three assumptions: (a) Consumption per child is 0.5 of that for the adult in working ages (15–64). (b) Total income of the country is the sum of all consumption units, the latter being 0.5 per child; 1.00 per adult in working ages; 0.75 per adult aged 65 and over. (c) The number of years within the life span of the children dying is 0.5, 3.0, 7.5, and 12.5 respectively for each successive age class under 15 – representing linear interpolation and cumulation of the age-class limits. The entries in cols. 2 and 5 are then the products of 0.5 by the number of years.
Panel B-1, cols. 3 and 6 – The entries are the products of those in cols. 1–2, and 4–5 – for lines 14–17; and direct sums in line 18. The entries in parentheses in line 8, cols. 3 and 6, are the total loss related to the total number of consuming units. Based on the assumptions stated above, the latter total for Egypt is: (39.4%) (0.5) + (57.0%) (1.0) + (3.6%) (0.75) = 79.4; and for the Netherlands, using a similar equation – 83.675. Division by these totals used as proper fractions (to 100) yields the percentages in the parentheses.
Panel B-2, cols. 1 and 5 – These again are the products of the age-specific death rates by the proportion of the age class in total population, both being taken from panel A (see notes to panel A).
Panel B-2, cols. 2 and 6 – The life-cycle pattern of product per capita in the working ages (and also for age 65 and over) is based on the following assumptions: (a) The product per capita in age 65 and over is 0.75 CU, just sufficient to cover consumption. It follows that the product per capita for ages 15–64 must cover more than the per capita CU, to

than at later ages, the decline in these ratios being interrupted only by the extremely high ratio for the 1–4 age class; and that the greater share of the younger age groups – particularly those below 15 – in the total population, in Egypt than in the Netherlands, tends to accentuate the disparity in the crude death rates. Whatever losses are represented by deaths are bound to be much greater in a high death rate country like Egypt, at least in relation to its total economic magnitude, than in a low death rate country like the Netherlands. It also follows that if the recent major declines in the LDCs proceeded on the path suggested in the text, with larger declines among the lower economic and social groups with initially much higher mortality than among the more favored, upper economic groups, the resulting convergence within the country among group death rates would also mean convergence in the relative burden of losses represented by deaths. But how do we estimate, as a first approximation, the direct economic losses that deaths represent?

Two approaches may be followed. In the first, the losses represented by deaths would be defined as inputs into past consumption of children and young adults offset by productive contributions that the deceased might have made. The question being answered, then, is What unoffset consumption inputs might have been avoided if the children and young adults whose deaths we are considering had never been born? In the other approach, the losses represented by deaths are viewed as the *projected* net productive contribution of the deceased that could have been expected but for the irreversible loss. This is the lost opportunities, rather

Notes to Table 6.A.1 *(cont.)*

compensate for the consumption of children under 15. The average excess in per capita product in ages 15–64 is given by the ratio of all consumption units for people under 65 to the number of people of working age (i.e., for Egypt [(39.4 × 0.5) + 57.0 × 1.0)] divided by 57.0; for the Netherlands [(29.3 × 0.5) + (64.0 × 1.0)] divided by 64.0. (b) It is assumed that in the age class 15–24 product per capita just equals consumption, i.e., 1.0; that there is a peaking plateau in ages 35–44 and 45–54, per capita product being equally high in the two age classes; and that in the intermediate age classes (25–34 and 55–64), the per capita product is a simple average of the preceding and following class means. Given assumptions (a) and (b), it is possible to solve a one-variable equation to find the value of the peak level (which proves to be 1.644 in Egypt and 1.449 in the Netherlands), and thus of all the lower-class product per capita.
Panel B-2, cols. 3 and 7 – The initial value here is the product of 0.5 CU (consumption per person per year) by 15, the number of years elapsing to the beginning of the 15–24 age class. From then on the cumulated past costs are affected by the surplus of product over assumed consumption in the successive age classes of adults of working age – the surplus being the difference between the entries in cols. 2 and 6, and 1.00.
Panel B-2, cols. 4 and 8 – The entries are product of the entries in cols. 1 and 4, by the *average* of those in cols. 3 and 7 (e.g., for line 20, it would be the average of 7.50 and 4.28, in col. 4; and of 7.50 and 5.26 in col. 8) – all of this for lines 19 through 22.
For entries in lines 23 and 24, whether the sums are in top lines or in the parentheses, see notes to the relevant part of panel B-1.

than the lost costs, approach; but both deal only with economic costs, opportunities, and returns, not with the psychic. We follow here the first approach, carried through more easily and dealing with historical facts and incurred burdens, rather than with extrapolated possibilities and lost future opportunities.[16]

Panel B-1, columns 1 and 3, reveals that total childhood deaths in a year account for 1.7% of total population in Egypt, but only 0.117% in the Netherlands (line 18) – a ratio of more than 14 to 1. To estimate the input into these children to whose death we are trying to assign an economic weight, we are assuming that the annual consumption per child amounted to 0.5 of the consumption of an adult of working age; that the productive contribution of children was negligible and that no offset to the input of past costs is thus to be entered; that with stable prices, there was no rise over time in per capita consumption of the adults of working age; and that with savings minimal (and disregarded for simplicity), total income (or net product of the nation) was the sum of all consumption (calculated by assigning 1.0 per adult of working age, 0.50 to those below 15, and 0.75 to those 65 and over). Given these assumptions, and cumulation of inputs into children who died after year 0, we can calculate the cost as a percentage of total current product. It works out to 2.68% for Egypt and 0.17% for the Netherlands (see line 18, cols. 3 and 6, in parentheses).

It is of interest to compare the results in Table 6.A.1 with those in Hansen's note (Hansen 1957), which reports measures for India similar to those for the United Kingdom and the United States, for 1931 and 1951 (see Table 6.A.2).

The comparison with the results here confirms the general orders of magnitude and indicates how differences in the assumed child–adult comsumption ratios affect the cost of childhood mortality expressed as a percentage of total product. While we have assumed here the child–adult consumption ratio of 0.5, adults defined as people of working age (and

---

16 This choice follows the approach in an earlier brief paper by W. Lee Hansen (1957). This paper was stimulated by a desire to correct an exaggerated and erroneous estimate of the proportional cost of child mortality made rather casually for India by D. Ghosh, who set this cost as high as 22.5% of national income (compared with Hansen's medium estimate of less than 3%). Hansen's note employed somewhat more elaborate assumptions than are followed here and used data for other countries and dates. But, as will be seen below, the general order of conclusions, when limited to child mortality, is about the same.

The topic here is clearly a part of the wider theme of the economics of family formation in the demographic transition, subject of a brief and illuminating paper by Frank Lorimer (1967).

Table 6.A.2. *Major results of Hansen's*
calculations of costs of childhood deaths

	India (1)	United Kingdom (2)	United States (3)
Deaths before age 15 as *% of total population*			
1. 1931	1.58	0.17	0.18
2. 1951	1.31	0.07	0.08
Costs of childhood deaths, *child–adult consumption* *ratio set at 0.5*			
3. 1931	2.81	0.26	0.32
4. 1951	2.83	0.07	0.09
Costs of childhood deaths, *child–adult consumption* *ratio variable*			
5. 1931	2.78	0.35	0.40
6. 1951	2.82	0.09	0.12

Notes: Taken or calculated from tables 2 and 3, pp. 259–60, of the paper cited in note 19.
The costs of childhood deaths are expressed in percentages of the country's total product, equated to aggregate consumption.
The variable child–adult consumption ratios in lines 5 and 6 were as follows. For India, the ratio was set at 0.5 through age class 5–9, and at 0.8 for age class 10–14. For the United Kingdom and the United States, the ratios for the four successive age classes (the same as used here) were 0.6, 0.7, 0.8, and 0.9.

with the consumption level per person of 65 and over set at 0.75), the resulting cost estimate for Egypt, at 2.7%, is close to that for India, either in 1931 or 1951 (see lines 3–4, col. 1). And the introduction of a somewhat greater consumption allowance for the age group 10–14 in India does not change the cost estimate significantly (see lines 5–6, col. 1). In contrast, introducing higher child–adult consumption ratios for the United Kingdom and the United States raises the cost estimates by a substantial proportion (from 0.26 to 0.35 in the United Kingdom in 1931, and from 0.32 to 0.40 for the United States in the same year; the proportional changes in 1951 are almost as great, see cols. 2 and 3, lines 3–6). Yet, even with the allowance for much higher consumption levels (relative to adults) of children in the United Kingdom and the United States, the relative costs of childhood deaths for India are still much greater in 1931 and 1951.

But if deaths of children represent an economic loss because of past input of resources that cannot be recovered, the same is true of the deaths of adults of working age – so long as the surplus of their contribution to product beyond their own consumption fails to cover past historical costs incurred in raising them to productive ages. This is the rationale for panel B-2 of Table 6.A.1, in which the cumulative input in past consumption (at 0.5 units until age 15, and at 1.0 through the successive ages until age 65) is compared with the cumulative total output credited to the adults. The latter output is estimated on two assumptions: (a) that it is the adult population of working age, 15–64, who produce the goods sufficient for their consumption *and* that of children under 15; (b) that within the working life span, output per person age 15–24 just equals per capita consumption (i.e., 1.0); that the peak per capita output is a plateau at ages 35–44 and 45–54; and that per capita product in the intermediate age classes (25–34 and 55–64) is at an arithmetic mean of the per capita products in the preceding and following age classes. This is clearly only a rough approximation to the life cycle of product per adult; but some such pattern is needed for a proper view of the time span within which the accumulated excess of output over consumption begins to match the accumulated past input into consumption – for the proportion of population that dies and for whom full recovery of past costs cannot be attained.

The results of the estimates in panel B-2 (for details of the procedure see the notes to the table) suggest that for Egypt the costs of mortality in the adult ages when past costs are recovered adds an item equivalent to 2% of product, raising the total past costs of child and early adult mortality to 4.6% (see lines 23–24, col. 4). For the Netherlands, the addition, while smaller absolutely (0.64%), is far greater relative to cost of child mortality. This is due to the much greater weight of costs in column 7, lines 19–22, than in column 5, lines 14–17; whereas total mortality (as percentage of total population) in ages 15–44, of 0.1010 (see col. 5, lines 19–21) is not much lower than the corresponding total of 0.1173 for ages 0–14 (see line 18, col. 4).

Only further exploration, involving many more countries, would reveal whether the approximation to unrequited past costs represented by child and early adult mortality (introduced by the estimates in panel B-2) is typical of less developed and developed countries respectively. But there is one aspect of the estimates underlying panel B-2 that is likely to be typical and deserves explicit note. If the adult population of working age is assumed to produce sufficiently to cover both its own consumption *and* that of the population ages 0–14, the average per capita output for the adult working-age population of Egypt would have to be $76.7/57.0 = 1.346$; whereas that for the Netherlands would have to be $78.65/64.0 = 1.229$. In other words, the excess output demanded from adults of working age in Egypt is proportionately greater than that demanded from the adults of working age in the Netherlands. This reflects a dependency ratio that, whether or not we exclude dependency in ages of 65 and over (it was excluded by our assumption), is significantly greater in LDCs than in MDCs. The source lies in the higher ratio of children to adults of working age – which, for Egypt, amounted to $39.4/57.0 = 0.69$; whereas in the Netherlands it was $29.3/64.0 = 0.46$. It is the difference in these two ratios, combined with assumptions concerning the life-cycle pattern of product per capita within the working ages, that results in a contrast, at the peak plateau, between an output index of 1.664 for Egypt and one of 1.449 for the Netherlands. The implicit question is whether, given average levels of productivity, it is possible to muster such a high excess ratio, or whether, in order to achieve the latter, the whole average level of output in the productive ages would have to be lowered. If both the child–adult consumption ratios and the proportions of children to working-age adults are fixed, the adjustment may be either in the average level of the product or in the pattern; and if the pattern is fixed, the adjustment is limited to the average level – implicitly involving the lowering of consumption for both children and adults.

Assuming for purposes of argument that the results in both panel B-1 and panel B-2 can be viewed as typical, what importance can be assigned to the indicated differences in the economic costs of child and early adult mortality between a less developed and a more developed country? The answer can be suggested only after we take a brief account of the major omissions in the calculations, even allowing (as Hansen did) for a higher child–adult consumption ratio in a developed than in a less developed country.

The first major omission is neglect of the contribution of the mother's engagement in pregnancy, birth, and the immediate burdens of care in infancy – the cost estimates here relating only to the consumption of goods and services by children. The weight of such omission would vary even among less developed countries, depending on institutional practices and the role of women in productive activity; and it is not clear that differences in the weight of this particular cost component can be surmised in comparisons between less developed and developed countries (such costs always viewed as proportions of some overall economic product magnitude). It clearly adds to the absolute costs of child mortality in both groups of countries and thus adds to the accumulated costs that would have to be debited against the output in the early working ages (in estimating the costs of deaths at those age levels); but we have no basis here for any plausible comparisons.

The second omission is of a possible allowance for effects of growth in per capita product on the estimate of past costs embodied in economic loss from childhood (or young adult) mortality. If such growth does occur, the current burden is lessened, since past consumption of children and younger adults is lower in proportion to *current* per capita consumption, and hence in relation to current product. Here the difference in this respect between LDCs, with their much lower growth rates in per capita product (or even absence of growth in many cases in premodern periods), and the MDCs, with their higher and steadier rates of growth in per capita product, is clearly in favor of the latter – reducing more appreciably the ratio of past costs to current output. The magnitudes, and their differences as between LDCs and MDCs, could be calculated using assumptions now used in Table 6.A.1 and introducing illustrative rates of past growth in per capita product.

The third omission, of potentially large magnitude, is that of forgone yields on past costs. These yields are possible even if we retain the oversimplified assumption that equates total product with total consumption and thus completely neglects savings and capital. Even under such conditions, were it have been possible to dispense with past consumption of children or young adults whose deaths we are evaluating, the consumption of surviving adults would have been greater – with effects on productivity, which would be likely to have been greater in LDCs than in MDCs. This greater consumption forgone would also have meant greater productivity in the past – a loss that presumably would be, in terms of current product, proportionately greater in LDCs than in MDCs. An alternative way to evaluate this omission is to allow for interest yield on past costs, and for the presence of capital returns in the economy. If, for the sake of an illustration, we allow for an addition of returns on capital equal to a quarter of total consumption, and use a 5% return rate on past consumption in children viewed as an investment, the application of these rates to panel B-1, columns 2–3 and 5–6, lines 14–17 would yield an estimate of accumulated losses (to age 15) of 3.5014 in column 3 for Egypt and of 0.2165 in column 6 for the Netherlands, which – with rough allowance for the rise in the total product denominators by 25% – would work out to percentages of 3.528 and 0.207 respectively, a wider contrast than between the entries in parentheses in line 8, columns 3 and 6. This would also affect estimates of losses in the younger adult age classes in panel B-2.

Finally, there is a question similar to that discussed in the text in connection with the focus of decision in the response of birthrates to the declines in death rates. Here the question is who bears the costs of childhood mortality or the residual losses involved in the death of adults in the younger working ages. The question may not be relevant for the economy as a whole. But if we are concerned with differential effects of these losses on different economic and social groups within the population, the question of who bears them becomes relevant. Thus in many developed countries the state, in various ways, assumes part of the costs of children and young adults – that is, part of their consumption – even though it may finance the activity from taxes on the income of adults and families, with the burden perhaps falling more heavily on the higher-income families. In many less developed countries, there may also be sharing of such costs within the larger blood group, rather than the full cost falling on the individual family unit. These comments suggest that the question of how the economic losses of mortality have been shared involves complicated effects of benefits and incidence of taxes in those developed societies where the state assumes increasing responsibility; of separation or jointness between the parental family and that of the next generation (bearing particularly on the locus of mortality costs for the younger age classes within the working life span); and of the relation between the single family, no matter how widely defined, and the wider blood-related group of which it may be a member.

It is not feasible here to explore the variety of omissions just indicated and to probe the interrelated and intricate questions they suggest. The discussion of differential costs of mortality, like that of the offset response of birthrates to declines in death rates, emphasizes that the analysis must take account of the wide variety of institutional, economic, and social groupings that condition the impact of losses involved in deaths at different ages or that shape the response of birthrates to declines in mortality.

With inadequate data to indicate the differences in the framework among various groups of LDCs and MDCs, and with limited command over the monographic literature, the probing had to be limited and constrained by oversimplifying assumptions.

Despite these limitations, the discussion above is, I believe, sufficient to suggest the minimum relative magnitudes of the losses represented by deaths of children and younger adults – and the large differences in these losses between MDCs and LDCs on the eve of the recent major down-trends of the death rates in LDCs. The proportionate losses represented by the death rates in the LDCs relating to children and younger adults approximate at least 5% of the current product, compared with probably less than a fifth of that proportion in the developed countries; and reasonable adjustments of these shares, to take account of the omissions, could easily raise these minimal ratios to twice their indicated levels.

Comparisons of LDCs and MDCs are only suggestive of comparisons *within* a less developed country between the mortality experience of the lower economic and social groups and that of the higher, more favorably situated. Yet given the possibility of substantial differences in mortality within the LDCs, associated before the 1920s largely with disparities in economic and social status, one can reasonably assume that in those earlier decades the burden of economic losses of mortality were much heavier relative to the consumption and income levels of the lower income groups than they were for the upper economic and social groups; and that the convergence in death rates, and reduction in overall levels associated with the recent technological breakthroughs in control of death and of public health, also meant reduction in the inequality of the burden of relative losses of mortality at these different economic and social levels. And one must repeat, in conclusion, the comment made at the outset – that death rates are significant as indexes of morbidity and that declining and converging morbidity rates may have direct effects on related disparities in productivity among the various economic and social groups within a less developed country as it benefits from declining mortality.

References

Ajami, I., Differential fertility in peasant communities: A study of six Iranian villages. *Population Studies* 30, no. 3 (November 1976): 453–63.

Arriaga, Eduardo E., and Davis, Kingsley, The pattern of mortality change in Latin America. *Demography* 6, no. 3 (August 1969): 223–42.

Caldwell, John C., Toward a restatement of demographic transition theory. *Population and Development Review* 2, nos. 3–4 (September, December 1976): 321–66.

Clark, Colin, *Conditions of economic progress*. 3d ed. London, 1957.

Davis, Kingsley, *Population of India and Pakistan*. Princeton: Princeton University Press, 1951.

Hansen, W. Lee, A note on the cost of children's mortality. *Journal of Political Economy* 65, no. 3 (June 1957): 257–62.

Lorimer, Frank, The economics of family formation under different conditions. In *World population conference, 1965*, 2:92–95. New York: United Nations, 1967.

Preston, Samuel H., Health programs and population growth. *Population and Development Review* 1, no. 2 (December 1975): 189–200.

Stolnitz, George H., A century of international mortality trends. Part 1. *Population Studies*, vol. 9 (July 1955).

A century of international mortality trends. Part 2. *Population Studies*, vol. 10 (July 1956).

International mortality trends: Some main facts and implications. In *The population debate*, 1:220–36. New York: United Nations, 1975.

Stys, W., The influence of economic conditions on the fertility of peasant women. *Population Studies* 11, no. 2 (November 1957): 136–48.

United Nations, *The determinants and consequences of population trends*. 1st ed. New York: United Nations, 1953.

United Nations, *World population prospects as assessed in 1963*. New York: United Nations, 1966.

Growth of the world's urban and rural population, 1920–2000. New York: United Nations, 1969.

The determinants and consequences of population trends. New York: United Nations, 1973.

U.S. Bureau of the Census, *Historical statistics of the United States, colonial times to 1970, bicentennial edition, part 1*. Washington, D.C., 1975.

7. Demographic aspects of the size distribution of income: an exploratory essay

I. Introduction

This essay is a substantial revision of a paper written in 1974 for a seminar dealing with income distribution, employment, and economic development in Southeast and East Asia.[1] The issues raised in the original paper, while seriously complicating the analysis of income inequalities and of their connection with economic growth, seemed to me sufficiently important and illuminating to merit restatement for better understanding and wider consideration.

The issues, to put them briefly, are that in a meaningful distribution of income by size the recipient unit has to be a family or household and cannot be a person; that families or households differ substantially in size, as judged by the number of members, either in productive or younger and older ages; that, consequently, the conventional distributions of income among families or households by income per family or household make little sense, since they are affected by changing or different inequalities among families or households by size; that, even after size distributions by income per family or household are converted into distributions of persons by family or household income per person, they still reflect differences in the age of the household head (hereafter "age of head"), in the phases in the lifetime span of a family's income, which obscure our

Economic Development and Cultural Change, Volume 25, Number 1, 1976, pp. 1–94.

1 Simon Kuznets, "Demographic Components in Size Distribution of Income," in *Income Distribution, Employment, and Economic Development in Southeast and East Asia*, papers and proceedings of the seminar sponsored and published jointly by the Japan Economic Research Center (Tokyo) and the Council for Asian Manpower Studies (Manila), ed. Harry T. Oshima and Shigeru Ishikawa, 2 vols. (Tokyo, 1975), 2:389–472 (hereafter cited as Tokyo Seminar paper and Tokyo Seminar Proceedings).

view of the differences in the longer, or lifetime, level of income. These characteristics of size and age of the family or household unit, changing in a systematic way through the lifetime span of the unit, are what we mean by the demographic aspects of the size distribution of income. They bear partly on the problem of the recipient unit (size) and partly on the time span over which income and its inequalities are to be considered (age of head, or age phases in general). And though we touch on some of the problems of income definition (scope, continuity, etc.) in their effect on the conventional size distributions, the fuller range of these problems is comparatively neglected. Despite this omission, the issues raised are major in that the conventional distributions of income among families or households by size of income per family or household are found to be affected significantly by the differing sizes of the families or households within the population and by the different phases of the life cycle of size and income by age of head. Comparisons of longer-term levels of income related to some meaningful denominator (e.g., the number of consumer equivalents within the family) are thus obscured; and trends observed in the conventional distributions may well be associated with trends in size differences among families, not in income per person or per consumer.[2] Likewise, comparisons of conventional size distributions between developed and less developed countries are seriously affected by differences in size differentials among households and in time patterns of income with age of head in the two groups of countries.

The discussion in this essay follows the order of topics in the preceding paragraph. In Section II we take up the definition of the recipient unit, dealing largely with the choice between the individual income recipient and a family or household, using general criteria of choice that seem relevant. Having concluded that the family or household is the proper basic recipient unit, we consider in Section III the problems raised by

2 See the discussion of effects of increasing proportions of families with young and old heads on the trends in the size distribution of income among families in the United States from 1947 to 1969 in my paper, "Demographic Aspects of the Distribution of Income among Families: Recent Trends in the United States," in *Econometric and Economic Theory: Essays in Honor of Jan Tinbergen*, ed. Willy Sellekaerts (London: Macmillan Co., 1974), pp. 223–47. When writing that paper and one published in 1962 that touched on the same topic, I was not yet aware of the full implications of the problem. But it was clear then that family structure by size shifts rapidly over time and that such shifts produce trends in conventional size distributions that are *not* movements in inequality in income per person or per consumer.

differences in size, and experiment with conversions of the distributions of income among families or households by size of income per family or household into distributions of income among persons by size of family income per person. In Section IV we observe the connection between size of family or household and the age of the head, that is, the association between the two demographic characteristics whose effects on the size distribution of income concern us. This connection is an aspect of the life cycle of the family or household and of the lifetime income span. Section V presents data on the age-of-head differentials in income per household or per person and concludes the review of the limited body of empirical data that we found feasible to cover. In Section VI we experiment, in a purely illustrative fashion, with the conversion of cross-section differentials in income per family or per person among age-of-head classes of families into life-time spans of gross income for families, either of the same size or of differing size (average over the life span), and with the important implications of the conversion of the negative cross-section association between size of family and per person income into a negative association between lifetime family income per person and the average size of that family as determined by the number of children. Section VII presents a summary of the findings and some reflections on the directions of further work on income inequality, particularly on the analysis of the connections between trends and differences in the latter and trends in economic growth and differences in levels of economic development.

This paper is described in the title as an exploratory essay, and the description is meant to emphasize the limited coverage both in terms of the number and variety of countries and, particularly, in the large obvious and potential deficiencies in the income data – which could be eliminated only by dint of intensive and difficult effort. Most of our discussion is based on data for the United States for 1969, a year selected because of the availability of *Census of Population* detail and a country chosen for emphasis because the necessary detailed data were at hand. Other countries included are Germany (Federal Republic, 1970), Israel (urban households, 1968–69), Taiwan (1964 and 1972, but with different coverage), and the Philippines (1970–71). The choice is clearly limited, and, more important, no adjustments were made in the deficient income data. Even in developed countries, size distributions of income are subject to deficiency errors (as they are in the United States, apart from the limitation of the data used here to money income). In the less developed countries the errors must be quite substantial, in view of the complexity of the data that must be collected, the task of securing reliable quantities for products of processes difficult to measure adequately, and the scarcity of analytical resources for converting defective raw materials into acceptably accurate, and consistent, estimates.

The problems generated by deficiencies of income distribution data (and even of aggregative economic data) have been magnified by the extension of international statistics to a large number of less developed countries. The pressure for aggregative or disaggregated estimates has been fed partly by the spread of political independence and the belief that the production of such data is a privilege and perquisite of national sovereignty, partly by a feeling of obligation to the international community in the way of quantitative evidence on the economic state and performance of the country, and, in the case of income distribution data, by the recently emerged search for evidence on the effects of economic growth on internal income inequalities, particularly in the less developed countries. The result has been a rapid proliferation of economic accounts and income distribution estimates for a number of countries for which adequate results are unlikely, considering the deficiencies of the results in developed countries despite a long-standing recognition of these deficiencies, even relative to the conventional (and inadequate) definitions of recipient units and of income.[3]

3 A recent publication by the World Bank (Shail Jain, *Size Distribution of Income: A Compilation of Data* [Washington, D.C.: World Bank, 1975]) gives the size distribution of income data for as many as 81 countries, six of which are Communist (Bulgaria, Czechoslovakia, Germany DR, Hungary, Poland, and Yugoslavia), with about two-thirds of the remainder among the less developed countries. An adequate estimate of the size distribution of income in a Communist country, given the compulsions and limitations on economic decisions of families and persons, obviously requires some thought concerning the institutional conditions of income distribution and their comparability between Communist and market economies. But more relevant here is the high probability that for many less developed countries the estimates rest on extremely flimsy foundations. The possibility of securing a defensible estimate for a country like Sudan, or Libya, or Dahomey, seems to me quite low. The author of the publication presents it as a compilation of data, without claiming responsibility for quality. But one wonders whether a compilation *excluding* obviously deficient estimates would not have been more useful, even allowing for the difficulties of exercising judgment. In an international compilation that I attempted in the early 1960s (see "Quantitative Aspects of the Economic Growth of Nations. VIII. Distribution of Income by Size," *Economic Development and Cultural Change*, vol. 11, pt. 2 [January 1963]) I remarked that "we deal here not with *data* on the distribution of income by size but with estimates or judgments by courageous and ingenious scholars relating

One implication of designating this essay as exploratory is that, with proliferation of both economic accounts and size distribution estimates of uncertain reliability and quality, and with international publications bulging with data for some countries (like Ethiopia) that have never had a census of population, the better research strategy today in comparative analysis of size distributions of income (and perhaps even of national aggregates and components) may be an intensive analysis for selected countries, of specific analytical value as well as with adequate data bases that warrant the hope of securing acceptable estimates. But this and other implications will become more meaningful in the course of the discussion that follows.

II. The recipient unit

If we are to measure and analyze levels and trends in the size distribution of income among a country's population, the income-recipient unit must be not only easily identifiable but also inclusive and distinctly independent. It must include total population, in order to link income flow (and disposition) to the totals of earners and users. It must be independent, in the sense that decisions made by recipient unit A on income getting and income spending are not so dependent on unit B, so closely allied with A, that the income share of each is meaningful only if combined with the other. In observational data and estimates based on them, the criteria of identifiability, inclusiveness, and independence cannot be, and never are, fully met. That relating to distinctiveness and independence, in particular, involves difficult decisions on the various ties that warrant pooling otherwise separate entities into a single recipient unit; and such decisions must be based on necessarily limited knowledge of internal and external relations among persons within and without the recipient units – if they include, as we shall see they must, more than one person. But the fact that empirical measurement and estimation involve compromises and judgments is all the more reason for discussing the underlying problems

to size distribution of income in the country of their concern" (p. 12). This statement can be applied as well to the greatly multiplied number of estimates and countries to which they relate. And while use has to be made of them, as it was in the past, progress over the last 1½ decades in our knowledge of the various aspects of the size distribution and of economic growth and the extension of coverage to an increasing number of countries with inadequate data bases call for greater discretion.

explicitly, so that we can be fully aware of the nature (and eventually perhaps of the magnitude) of the differences between the measure and the analytical desideratum.

The recipient unit illustrated in Table 7.1 for the United States distribution of money income in 1969, a person 14 years of age or over who received money income in that year, is deficient with respect to all three criteria. A brief list of the shortfalls may help toward a better understanding of the nature of these criteria.

1. The identification even of money income recipients raises problems in the case of small-scale family enterprises and in that of property income from jointly held assets. In a convenience retail store, a handicraft shop, or a family farm, the allocation even of the firm's money income among husband, wife, and other working members of the family is a difficult, and almost arbitrary, matter. Yet in the United States income other than wages and salaries, classified as earnings and representing largely mixed income from self-employment, is received by a substantial proportion of individual recipients – either by itself or in combination with wages and salaries (see lines 13 and 16, cols. 2 and 3). Were income to cover non-money receipts, the question would assume greater dimensions. And in the less developed countries, with much larger proportions of family enterprises, the problem of identifying incomes of individuals (as distinct from families) would loom large indeed.

A similar problem of identification may arise with respect to property income, since assets are often held jointly by husband and wife. Such joint holding is widespread in the industrialized countries and is, in a sense, a counterpart to the joint claims on the family firm's income by family members in the less developed countries.

2. In the light of the comment just made, the exclusion of persons less than 14 years of age raises a question as to the property incomes that may accrue to them. But a more important problem is how, with a distribution among persons 14 and older, the bearing of income flows on the needs and prospects of the country's younger population is to be measured. Since the allocation of these children among the older income recipients is not indicated, we cannot gauge the effect of the size distribution of income on the economic position of this large young population group – a group of great importance in analyzing the *long-term* economic trends. This deficiency would become all the greater if we were to limit the coverage of personal income recipients to the full-time, more continuously employed major earners in order to impart more meaningfulness by ex-

Table 7.1. *Recipients of 1969 money income, 14 years of age and over, by sex, age, and source of income, United States, March 1970*

	A. *Recipients by sex and age*					
	Age (years)					
Group	14–19 (1)	20–24 (2)	25–44 (3)	45–64 (4)	65 and over (5)	Total (6)
Male						
1. All persons (millions)	11.1	7.1	23.1	19.6	8.1	69.0
2. Recipients (%)	60.9	95.1	99.4	99.0	98.7	92.6
3. Recipients (millions)	6.8	6.7	23.0	19.4	8.0	63.9
4. % of recipients full-time workers	6.2	40.8	81.3	76.0	14.2	59.0
5. Average income for line 3 ($ thousands)	1.10	4.15	9.18	9.23	4.31	7.20
6. Average income for line 4 ($ thousands)	3.35	6.16	9.96	10.37	8.36	9.74
Female						
7. All persons (millions)	11.2	8.4	24.3	21.6	10.8	76.3
8. Recipients (%)	49.9	77.5	61.0	66.2	83.7	65.9
9. Recipients (millions)	5.6	6.5	14.8	14.3	9.1	50.2
10. % of recipients full-time workers	6.4	34.6	40.0	45.1	5.1	39.9
11. Average income for line 9 ($ thousands)	0.87	1.03	3.44	3.79	2.17	2.95
12. Average income for line 10 ($ thousands)	3.31	4.59	5.51	5.71	5.42	5.41

	B. *Income recipients by source of income*					
Group	Wages or salaries (1)	Other earnings (2)	Wages, salaries, and other income (3)	Other earnings and other income (4)	Other income only (5)	Total (6)
Male						
13. Income recipients (%)	45.5	6.2	30.4	7.0	10.9	100.0
14. Average income ($ thousands)	6.05	6.86	9.65	10.43	2.95	7.20
15. Income (%)	38.3	6.0	40.8	10.3	4.6	100.0
Female						
16. Income recipients (%)	53.9	2.5	17.5	1.7	24.4	100.0
17. Average income ($ thousands)	2.96	2.60	4.39	4.88	1.78	2.94
18. Income (%)	54.2	2.2	26.1	2.8	14.7	100.0

Table 7.1 *(cont.)*

Group	Wages or salaries (1)	Other earnings (2)	Wages, salaries, and other income (3)	Other earnings and other income (4)	Other income only (5)	Total (6)
Male and female						
19. Income recipients (%)	49.2	4.6	24.7	4.7	16.8	100.0
20. Income (%)	42.2	5.1	37.2	8.5	7.0	100.0

Notes: Taken, or calculated, from U.S. Bureau of the Census, *Current Population Reports,* Series P-60, no. 75, *Income in 1969 of Families and Persons in the United States* (Washington, D.C.: Government Printing Office, 1970), pp. 97 and 129, tables 45 and 58 (hereafter cited as source 1). The income data relate to 1969 and the demographic data to March 1970. "A year-round full-time worker is one who worked primarily at full-time civilian jobs (35 hours or more per week) for 50 weeks or more during the preceding calendar year" (p. 11). Money income comprises wages and salaries, other earnings (from self-employment, farm and nonfarm), and other income (property income, private and public pensions, etc.) (for detailed description see text.

cluding persons with minor and clearly "supplementary" income. This would mean excluding more of the younger, largely nonworking, individuals; the groups in advanced ages and largely retired; and the large proportions of women, who, for various reasons, are not engaged in money income activities.

The more we narrow the population of income-recipient persons to reduce heterogeneity, the more we lose in terms of populations whose needs the income flows must satisfy and whose contributions to income are still to be credited. But the less we omit from the population of individual income recipients, the greater the interdependence among them – and thus the greater the deviation from the criterion of independence.

3. Even if we limited the group of personal income recipients to ages 25–65, most of them would still be members of family units, in which the earning activity of one member would not be independent from that of other members or of the number and ages of children and other dependent members. If we extended the coverage to younger and older groups, such dependence of the income receipts on the role of the persons within the family and on the position of the latter would be even greater. The choice between income-earning and other (e.g., education) activity for the young is largely set by family position and decision. The income levels

of the old, given the wide disparities in their role among societies at different levels of development and family structure, depend upon whether they remain at the head of the larger family until death or form much smaller nuclear units – separate from those of their children and other younger relations.

The shortfalls of the single person as the recipient unit in the size distribution of income among a country's population all point to the dominant position of the family or the household (the terms are discussed in detail below): in the identification of incomes not clearly assignable to individual persons, in the inclusion within families of both economically active and dependent members of the population, and in being the locus of decisions on income getting and income spending of the individual members. Although, despite some limitations to be noted below, the family seems to be the basic recipient unit, it is not an indivisible whole. On the contrary, its internal structure – the economic and other relations among its individual members partly revealed in the usual demographic and economic characteristics of families – constitutes an important datum. But it does mean that in the analysis of the size distribution of income the smaller entities, such as individual persons, are to be viewed not in themselves but as members of the family in its life cycle; and that the larger aggregates, such as the country's total population or socioeconomic groups within it, are to be derived as congeries of families or households.

This emphasis on the family is particularly appropriate to a consideration of the *long-term* levels in the size distribution, since the family is, and has been, a basic institution in the life cycle of individuals and in the transmission of the social and economic heritage from generation to generation. But if the emphasis is on the family and its internal structure, some aspects of the evidence in Table 7.1 should be explicitly noted – for they raise major questions about the meaningfulness of the conventional income concept taken from the accepted national accounting framework, even when extended beyond money income to include the minor (in a developed country like the United States) components of income in kind. Table 7.1 indicates that in the ages 25–64, while the proportion of full-time workers to all persons for *men* averages close to 80 percent (see the product of lines 2 and 4, cols. 3 and 4), it averages between a quarter and three-tenths for *women* (see the product of lines 8 and 10, cols. 3 and 4). Does this mean that seven-tenths to three-quarters of women aged

25–64 engage in only part-time economic activities and contribute only a minor flow of goods? The income per woman not engaged full time can be calculated to average about $1,000 for the age group 25–44 and about $1,100 for the age group 45–64. Obviously these averages would not be affected much by inclusion of the types of income in kind that are recognized in the conventional income concept of standard national accounting. Is it reasonable to assume that for this overwhelming proportion of women aged 25–64 the effective product and real income contributed is reflected by these income averages?

The answer, of course, is that the married women in these ages (a high proportion of all women), perhaps excluding the tiny group of the "idle" rich, are engaged in various productive activities, the product of which is not included under personal income in the accepted economic accounting. Most of these activities would be in the maintenance of the internal family functions, although some may involve nonpaid services outside the family; and the former may represent a substantial proportional addition to the real income of the family. If so, it is likely that in the *poorer* families (i.e., those in which the income of the husband does not meet the family's requirements) the greater engagement of the wife in money or other types of income-earning activity limits the intrafamily services of making a home and providing training and guidance to the children, limits them more than in the case of the more affluent families. Thus, while the engagement of the wife in money-earning activities outside the family may *narrow* the differentials in family income shown in the conventional size distribution of income, the inclusion of the intrafamily activities of the wife in a wider income concept would tend to *widen* the differentials in the size distribution of this wider income total. The matter is of particular importance for the bearing of income inequality on the economic condition of the younger, children's generation, for it may mean that the full real income per child is more unequally distributed when the income concept includes intrafamily services than when it is limited to the conventional definition of personal income.

In this connection Table 7.2 provides additional detail relevant to the implications of Table 7.1. These data distinguish white male and female income recipients from Negro, the two groups that differ in economic levels as well as associated family characteristics. The distinction emphasizes the fact that larger proportions of Negro than of white women are engaged in paid employment and that they are also a far more important source of income supplementary to that of the male (lines 15–18).

Table 7.2. *1969 Money income recipients, persons aged 14 and over, by age classes 20–65, comparisons of ratios between white and Negro, male and female*

Group	Age (years) 20–24 (1)	25–34 (2)	35–44 (3)	45–54 (4)	55–64 (5)
Males					
Income recipients to all persons (%)					
1. White	95.5	99.3	99.6	99.2	98.9
2. Negro	93.0	98.0	99.0	99.2	97.4
Full-time workers to all persons (%)					
3. White	38.2	79.7	85.1	81.4	69.8
4. Negro	45.3	67.6	70.9	66.4	58.7
Income per income recipient (average, $ thousands)					
5. White	4.21	8.71	10.47	10.32	8.73
6. Negro	3.75	5.59	5.96	5.25	4.91
7. Negro/white ratio (line 6/line 5)	0.89	0.64	0.57	0.51	0.56
Females					
Income recipients to all persons (%)					
8. White	77.5	56.6	60.5	63.5	66.8
9. Negro	78.0	80.4	82.7	77.6	77.5
Full-time workers to all persons (%)					
10. White	27.4	20.8	25.7	32.2	27.4
11. Negro	22.2	32.4	35.7	31.5	23.2
Income per recipient (average, $ thousands)					
12. White	2.87	3.31	3.65	4.10	3.75
13. Negro	2.34	3.19	3.26	2.87	2.22
14. Negro/white ratio (line 13/line 12)	0.82	0.96	0.89	0.70	0.59
Males and females					
Average income of female to male recipient (ratio)					
15. White	0.68	0.37	0.35	0.40	0.43
16. Negro	0.63	0.57	0.55	0.55	0.45
Wives in paid labor force, husband – wife families (%)					
17. White	47.8	37.2	40.7	46.4	39.5
18. Negro	53.0	56.5	61.1	57.6	50.2

Note: Taken, or calculated, from source 1. Lines 1–16 are based on table 45 (pp. 97–98); lines 17–18 on table 17 (pp. 35–41).

One should also note that for the same year the average income of the Negro family, about $7.0 thousand, was less than seven-tenths of that of the white family, about $11 thousand;[4] that according to the *Census of Population* the average Negro family comprised 4.16 members, compared with 3.51 members for the average white family; and that the number of members under 18 years of age was 1.90 per Negro family and 1.30 per white family, this larger number of children in the Negro family fully accounting for the excess in its average size in terms of persons. Obviously, the greater engagement of Negro women in paid occupations is associated with the lower income of the male members of the family and is at the same time occurring in a population in which the number of children (who might require more rather than less service within the family) per family is larger. The data thus illustrate the hypothesis suggested above that while supplementary earnings of wives (or other adult female members of the family) may *reduce* income inequality among families in a distribution based on the conventional concept of personal income, they may also *widen* inequality in the distribution of income inclusive of intra-family services. Of course, this is a conjecture, to be tested by empirical data on the use of time within the family by married women and older children, whether or not engaged in gainful (or other) occupation outside the home. But the conjecture is sufficiently plausible and important to merit explicit formulation and use for preliminary exploration.

Because persons receiving income include such a wide and heterogeneous population of primary and supplementary earners, with main and secondary income streams, and also reflect the variables that make for income differentials among families, the distribution of income among individual income recipients tends to be markedly unequal. Average inequality yielded by such distributions is likely to be much wider than for distributions of the same income total for the same year among families or households. Table 7.3 provides the measures for the distributions for the populations already shown in panel A of Table 7.1; and introduces a simple measure of inequality, one that will be used throughout the paper.

This measure is based on differences in the percentage shares of given groups within the population in total number and in total income. These groups may be male and female recipients classified by size of their in-

---

4 U.S. Bureau of the Census, *Current Population Reports*, Series P-60, no. 75, *Income in 1969 of Families and Persons in the United States* (Washington, D.C.: Government Printing Office, 1970), table 17 (hereafter cited as source 1).

Table 7.3. *Distribution of 1969 money income among recipients, 14 years of age and over, by sex*

A. *Shares in number and in income (%)*

Income classes ($ thousands)	Male Number (1)	Male Income (2)	Female Number (3)	Female Income (4)	Both sexes Number (5)	Both sexes Income (6)
1. Less than 0.5	6.1	0.2	15.8	1.3	10.4	0.5
2. 0.5–0.99	4.8	0.5	13.4	3.4	8.6	1.2
3. 1.0–1.49	4.6	0.8	11.3	4.7	7.5	1.7
4. 1.5–1.99	4.0	1.0	7.7	4.5	5.6	1.9
5. 2.0–2.49	4.1	1.3	7.0	5.3	5.4	2.3
6. 2.5–2.99	3.4	1.3	5.0	4.6	3.9	2.1
7. 3.0–3.99	6.6	3.2	10.9	12.7	8.5	5.5
8. 4.0–4.99	6.2	3.9	8.9	13.4	7.5	6.2
9. 5.0–5.99	7.0	5.3	6.9	12.6	7.0	7.1
10. 6.0–6.99	7.6	6.9	4.8	10.4	6.4	7.8
11. 7.0–7.99	8.3	8.7	3.1	7.7	6.0	8.5
12. 8.0–9.99	13.3	16.6	2.8	8.4	8.7	14.5
13. 10.0–14.99	16.1	26.8	1.9	7.6	9.9	22.3
14. 15.0–24.99	6.1	16.1	0.4	2.5	3.6	12.8
15. 25.0 and over	1.8	7.4	0.1	0.9	1.0	5.6
16. Total (N in millions; income in $ billions)	63.9	460.1	50.2	147.9	114.1	608.0

B. *Measures of inequality*

	Male (1)	Female (2)	Both sexes (3)
Total disparity measures (TDM)			
17. Excluding nonrecipients	60.0	72.8	72.0
18. Including nonrecipients	66.6	104.0	90.2
Gini coefficients			
19. Excluding nonrecipients	0.416	0.484	0.489
20. Including nonrecipients	0.447	0.664	0.601

Notes: Calculated from source 1, table 45 (p. 97). The shares in number were given directly in the source, and slight adjustments were made to have the total equal 100.0. The shares in income were calculated by assigning to each income class, except the top, the arithmetic mean of the class limits, with slight allowance for the shape of the distribution in that a mean of 12 was assigned to the class 10.0–14.99 and a mean of 19 to the class 15.0–24.99. The estimate for the top, open-end class was derived from the comparison of the cumulated income total for the classes below 25.0 as the lower limit and the total product of mean income by number of recipients. If this comparison yielded an average income above $25.0 for the open-end class, it was used. If the comparison yielded an average income for the top class of less than $25.0 a mean value of $27.5 was assigned, and an income total slightly larger than that obtained as the product of mean income and number of recipients was used to calculate the TDMs and the Gini coefficients.
The TDM is the sum of the differences, signs disregarded, between the percentage shares

come receipts (as they are in panel A of Table 7.3); or they may be groups of families distinguished by size, or by age of head, or by any other characteristic deemed of interest as possibly contributing to income inequality within the country. These differences in shares are then added, signs disregarded.[5]

> 5 The measure was introduced earlier, to gauge intersectoral inequalities in product per worker, in my paper on the industrial distribution of national product and labor force (see *Economic Development and Cultural Change* 5, no. 4, suppl. [July 1957]: 45). I used it most recently in the Tokyo Seminar paper.
>
> Two technical features of the measure should be noted. First, the sum of the differences could be related to the maximum possible sum (extreme inequality) and thus be converted into an index ranging from 0 (complete equality) to 1.0 (complete inequality). The denominator of this ratio is set by the fact that the measure is quite insensitive to the width of the frequency class, except in the neighborhood of the arithmetic mean per unit. Thus, whether the top-class or the bottom-class interval covers 20 percent or 0.001 percent of the units has no effect on the measure – so long as that class does not include the mean of the distribution. Consequently, it is legitimate to assume the smallest possible frequency, i.e., one close to 0, and set the denominator of the ratio uniformly at 200 – regardless of variations in the detail of the size and frequency distribution. This means that the values in line 17, for example, could be converted to 0.300, 0.364, and 0.360, respectively. Since the *comparative* value of the TDM is not affected, we did not bother to convert to such ratios – particularly since, as indicated in the text, the negative and positive disparities for the classes distinguished and their relative weights within the TDM are interesting in themselves.
>
> Second, as just indicated, the measure is sensitive to the size of the class interval that includes the mean of the distribution (i.e., the unit with an income, relative to the mean, of 1.00). Thus, if the mean income per recipient is $3,000 and the distribution contains an income class from $2,000 to $4,000 with a frequency of 20 percent of all recipients, and within it 10 percent have an average income of $2,400 whereas the other 10 percent have an average income of $3,600, the TDM is lower than it should be by $(-0.2 \times 10.0) + (+0.2 \times 10.0)$, with the signs within the parentheses disregarded, or by 4.0. Such effects are, however, moderated by the fact that in the vicinity of the arithmetic mean (in a unimodal distribution) the income distribution changes its slope rather gently, and the

Notes to Table 7.3 *(cont.)*

in number and the percentage shares in total income for the classes distinguished. Technical and other properties of this measure are discussed in the text.
The measures for the distributions excluding nonrecipients (in the same sex and age categories) are based on lines 1–15. The nonrecipients can be derived from the appropriate lines in Table 7.1; and, with the inclusion of the share of nonrecipients in number (7.5 percent of the larger total for males, 34.2 percent for females, and 21.5 percent for the two sexes combined), all other percentage shares in number are reduced proportionately. The shares in income shown in lines 1–15 remain unchanged. The measures in lines 18 and 20 are based on these new distributions. The Gini coefficients are calculated by the usual procedure from the shares in number and income arrayed in increasing order of income per recipient unit – using the 15 (or 16, including nonrecipients) income classes distinguished here.

In addition to its simplicity, the measure has several advantages. First, the difference for each class, between its percentage shares in number and in total income, can be viewed as the *relative* deviation of per unit income of that class from the per unit income for the whole population, *weighted* by the size of that class. Thus, the difference in percentages in line 1, columns 1 and 2, of −5.9 (col. 2 − col. 1) may be seen as the product of the relative deviation of per unit income (0.2/6.1) −1.00, *weighted* by 6.1 percent, or −5.9 percent. The sum of differences, signs disregarded, is then the total of deviations in relative income per recipient (or family, or whatever unit is used) in the successive classes, weighted by the proportion of each class to the countrywide total of number.

Second, it is based on shares in number and in income for classes distinguished by whatever criteria are of interest (size of income, or age of head of family, or occupational attachment, etc.); and the differences in shares for the classes can be observed in their original form, without being obscured in cumulative arrays, partition values, etc. Thus, it helps to reveal those parts of the distribution in which the share differentials are particularly large and contribute heavily to the magnitude of the summary measures – a practice that we shall follow in the analytical sections below.

The measure is, of course, subject to several limitations. First, like other aggregative measures (e.g., the Gini or Gibrat coefficients), it is a summary that may conceal as much as it reveals. It says nothing about the extremes of the distribution, or about any particular segment of it; but the retention of the original classes in the distribution, and the emphasis in the TDM (total disparity measure) on the identity of these classes, helps. Second, the measure is not as sensitive as the Gini coefficient to income inequalities within the long span in the Lorenz curves or within the spans that constitute, in the measure here, the negative as contrasted with the positive disparities. Third, and in many ways most important, the TDM, like the Gini coefficient, lacks the property of additivity of variance found only in normal and near normal distributions. But for the present purposes it suffices to have a simple gauge like TDM, which, by

marked change in slope used in the illustration above is rather unlikely. Thus, even with fairly wide class intervals in the neighborhood of the arithmetic mean, relative effects on the TDM, in the usual size distribution, are likely to be negligible. This is fortunate, since when a classification is based on a discrete series and published, already classified data must be used, the latter must be taken as given – barring the unlikely opportunity to go back to the unclassified, detailed income data. These technical comments are clearly relevant to the more general observations on TDM made in the text.

large, behaves very much like the somewhat more familiar, and more
positive, Gini coefficient (which we use in places as a supplementary
measure).

The inequality measures in Table 7.3 can be compared with those for
the distributions among families, or among households of two persons
or more, for the same year, distributions that may be considered most
suitable for analysis (see Table 7.5 below). Both the family and household
distributions account for over 90 percent of the total population of the
country and over 90 percent of total income (both excluding the minor
segment of institutional population and its income). The TDM for both
distributions is about 50, and the relevant Gini coefficient is less than
0.35. The inequality measures in Table 7.3, for the combined population
of male and female income recipients, are a TDM of 72.00 excluding
nonrecipients and of 90.00 including them; the relevant Gini coefficients
are 0.49 and 0.60. The excess in the measures in Table 7.3 is substantial,
considering that the full range of Gini coefficients in international comparisons for distributions among households is between somewhat above
0.3 and somewhat above 0.5.[6]

But in view of the grave limitations on cross-section size distributions
of income, even among families or households, to be discussed below, one
need not attribute too much significance to the comparisons of the TDMs
and Gini coefficients in the paragraph above – except as an illustration
of the wide differences in inequality measures for the same population
and income but with different recipient units. These disparities in measured inequality could obviously be reduced by limiting the distribution
of income recipients to men and omitting the younger ages in which education is an alternative to gainful employment. But this would only mean
using the distribution among individual recipients as an approximation to
those among families or households. We turn now to the latter distributions and consider their characteristics and the questions that they raise
(Table 7.4).

First, we comment on the coverage here as contrasted with that for
individual income recipients. In Table 7.4, column 2 of panel A shows that
total population of members of households is close to 200 million (line 3),

6 See Felix Pauker, "Income Distribution at Different Levels of Development:
A Survey of Evidence," *International Labour Review* 108, nos. 2–3 (September
1973): 97–125, and much of the literature cited in it. The statement in the text
refers to distributions among households and families and is intended to exclude
distributions among persons or individual recipients.

Table 7.4. *Households, families, and unrelated individuals, number, average 1969 income, and distribution by age of head, United States, March 1970*

A. Number and average 1969 income

Group	Units (millions) (1)	Persons (millions) (2)	Persons per unit (3)	Av. per unit ($ thousands) (4)	Av. income person ($ thousands) (5)
Households					
1. 2 or more persons	52.2	188.7	3.62	10.61	2.93
2. 1 person	10.7	10.7	1.00	4.33	4.33
3. Total	62.9	199.4	3.17	9.54	3.01
Families					
4. All	51.2	185.4	3.62	10.58	2.92
5. Husband and wife	44.4	163.5	3.67	11.19	3.05
6. Other male head	1.2	3.6	2.95	9.66	3.27
7. Female head	5.6	18.3	3.29	5.91	1.80
Unrelated individuals					
8. Both sexes	14.45	14.45	1.00	4.25	4.25
9. Male	5.44	5.44	1.00	5.36	5.36
10. Female	9.01	9.01	1.00	3.57	3.57

B. Distribution by age of head

	2-person households (1)	Families (2)	1-person households (3)	Unrelated individuals All (4)	Male (5)	Female (6)
11. Total (millions)	52.18	51.24	10.69	14.45	5.44	9.01
Percentage by age						
12. Below 25	7.2	7.0	5.1	12.0	15.1	10.1
13. 25–34	20.6	20.7	8.3	10.6	17.4	6.6
14. 35–44	21.1	21.2	6.6	7.6	12.2	4.8
15. 45–54	20.9	21.1	12.3	12.1	14.3	10.6
16. 55–64	16.2	16.2	21.4	18.8	14.8	21.3
17. 65 and over	14.0	13.8	46.3	38.9	26.2	46.6
18. Sum of lines 12, 16, and 17	37.4	37.0	72.8	69.7	56.1	78.0
19. Sum of lines 13–15	62.6	63.0	27.2	30.3	43.9	22.0

Notes: The data on households, in lines 1–3 of panel A and cols. 1 and 3 of panel B, are from the U.S. Bureau of the Census, *Current Population Reports*, Series P-60, no. 72. *Household Income in 1969 and Selected Social and Economic Characteristics of Households* (Washington, D.C.: Government Printing Office, August 1970), (hereafter cited as source 2). The number of households by size, their population, and the distribution by age of as is the member population of families and unrelated individuals (lines 4 and 8). The total population of the United States, in March 1970, yielded by the census (either the complete count or the various samples) was roughly 203 million. The difference was accounted for by population in group quarters, about 2 million inmates in institutions (prisons, nursing homes, and the like) and 1 million males in military barracks.[7]

While the coverage of population in Table 7.4 is relatively complete, the small segment of institutional population is excluded from the size distribution of income, and such exclusion is generally true for all countries. But this slight deficiency is the tip of a huge analytical problem that must be made explicit. The rationale for excluding much of the institutional population, for example, that in military service or prisons or nursing homes, is presumably that these groups do not exercise normal freedom in decisions on their economic and social actions, either because of legal restraints or because of physical compulsions and disabilities. Assume now that in a dictatorially managed society a substantial proportion, say 15 percent, of the population, particularly of working age, is in prisons, concentration camps, and labor camps, whereas in a more freely organized society only 1 percent is thus deprived of freedom of decision.

7 See U.S. Bureau of the Census, *1970 Population Census*, Subject Reports PC (2)-4B, *Persons by Family Characteristics* (Washington, D.C.: Government Printing Office, 1973), p. xi, table 1. The discrepancies between the totals in this table and in the two reports by the *Current Population Survey* (see notes to Tables 7.1 and 7.4 above) relating to households and to families plus unrelated individuals, respectively, are small, and the rough figures used in the text are consistent.

Notes to Table 7.4 *(cont.)*

head, are given in table 5 (p. 15). Average income is given in tables 1 and 2 (pp. 11–12). The data on families and unrelated individuals are from source 1, tables 17 (pp. 35–41) and 19 (pp. 45–49).
The following quotations are from source 1:
"A household consists of all the persons who occupy a housing unit. A house, an apartment or other group of rooms, or a single room, is regarded as a housing unit when it is occupied or intended for occupancy as separate living quarters. . . . A household includes the related family members and all the unrelated persons, if any, such as lodgers, foster children . . . who share the housing unit. A person living alone in a housing unit, or a group of unrelated persons sharing a housing unit as partners, is also counted as a household. The count of households excludes group quarters [e.g., military barracks, prisons, etc.]" (p. 8).
"The term 'family' as used in this report, refers to a group of two or more persons related by blood, marriage, or adoption and residing together; all such persons are considered members of the same family" (p. 8).
"The term 'unrelated individual' refers to persons 14 years old and over (other than inmates of institutions) who are not living with any relatives. An unrelated individual may constitute a one-person household by himself, or he may be part of a household including one or more other families or unrelated individuals, or he may reside in group quarters such as a rooming house" (p. 9).

Can the size distributions of income for the two countries, both excluding the institutional population, be reasonably compared? And if institutional populations are included, how do we measure the relative position of their income, considering the other limitations to which they are subject? There is no easy answer except to stress that meaningful comparisons of even relatively complete size distributions of income imply assumptions as to comparability of underlying institutional structures – implications that are relevant both to current international comparisons and, for some countries in which the institutional structures have undergone marked historical changes, to intertemporal comparisons.

Second, the difference between households, on the one hand, and families plus unrelated individuals, on the other, should be explored. Households are groups of individuals who occupy the same housing unit (an apartment, a house, or a segregated part of the latter) and who share in housekeeping. The group may include unrelated individuals, such as lodgers, employees, and the like. The family is distinguished in the data by two characteristics: the existence of blood, marriage, or adoption ties among the members, and residence in the same housing unit (with one exception, in that the *Current Population Survey* includes persons in college dormitories, enumerated at their parental homes; see source in n. 7). An unrelated individual is one who either lives alone or with others not related to him or her by blood, marriage, or adoption ties. The individuals who live alone would be classified as one-person households.

If the recipient unit is to be the decision unit with respect to long-term income plans and goals of its members and of the disposition of such incomes, a multiperson household is not fully appropriate; it may include unrelated persons who have no long-term ties to the other members of the household and do not share in its income-getting or income-disposal decisions and plans. To be sure, the overwhelming majority of households, at least in the United States, are families; and the share of unrelated individuals within multiperson households is quite limited (the size of this group is suggested by the difference between 10.7 million one-person households, line 2, col. 2, and the 14.5 million unrelated individuals, line 8, col. 2 – a difference of less than 4 million, compared with a total population in families of over 185 million, line 4, col. 2). But the family is still the more relevant unit, if we are interested in long-term ties among its members and a locus of decision on income getting and income spending.

Yet, if blood or legal ties are the base for identifying the family as the locus of major decisions on income, the concept of the family used in the data, with common residence one criterion, is too narrow. This limitation is considered, first, with explicit reference to the unrelated individuals and, second, in a broader framework for all families.

Table 7.4 indicates that, in terms of number, unrelated individuals account for over 20 percent of all units (i.e., individuals and families), even though they are only 7 percent of the total number of persons. In general, such individuals or one-person households are sizable proportions of total units and households in the developed countries – but form much smaller proportions in the less developed countries.[8]

The age distributions of these individuals show that for the males substantial proportions are younger than 35 or are 65 and over; whereas for the much larger group of women the concentration (about two-thirds) is largely in the ages of 55 and over, reflecting in good part the incidence of widowhood. One may ask whether a young man or woman living separately from the family, either alone in a single-person household or as a boarder in a multiperson household, is not still, for most purposes, a member of his or her family, participating in and affected by that family's decisions. And a similar question may be asked with respect to an older man or woman living alone, in relation to the children's family or families.

This problem also arises in judging the independence even of families of two or more members, recorded as separate units because they occupy different dwellings. If we consider two families, one representing the parental and the other the younger generation, can we assume that for certain major purposes the two units are completely independent of each other and never involved in some pooling of income or resources? The question may be particularly relevant in the case of an advanced country like the United States, where changes in conditions of life and various old age security payments induced a greater residential separation of the parental pairs from their children's families. Although separate residence became more common, it did not necessarily represent a significantly greater independence of decisions than in the past when the two generations shared a residence. To the extent that this question is valid in its application to the family structure of the developed countries, so significantly different from that in the less developed regions, it warrants an inference that the available data (whether on families or households) show too much diffusion among presumably independent families or households in the

8 See, e.g., p. 385, table 10, in my paper, "Fertility Differentials between Less Developed and Developed Regions: Components and Implications," *Proceedings of the American Philosophical Society* 119, no. 5 (October 1975): 363–96.

developed countries – with effects on income inequality dependent upon the basis of the measures adopted.

This difficulty with the family-unrelated individual as the recipient unit, the limitation with regard to the criterion of independence, is almost irremediable. Any attempt, at least in adequate statistical coverage, to identify the family, including its members living apart from and yet participating in and affected by the family's decisions, would run into insuperable difficulties – and we would have to face up to the criterion of identifiability. But it is important to recognize the problem and, as an expedient response, to select procedures for analyzing the data that would tend to reveal changes in the possible effects of this difference between the family, defined both by blood and other ties and residence and as a group of related persons engaged in common decisions affecting all members. This would mean continuous attention to the structure of families, as defined in the data, by size and by age of head to detect trends toward greater separation of residence; the use of inequality measures that, while no less meaningful in other respects, would not be too sensitive to changing or differing structures of families by size; and, in the particular case of unrelated individuals in the United States data, adopting two variants of the total distribution including (all units) and excluding them (families alone).

Some of these comments are illustrated in Table 7.5 below, which provides measures of the size distribution of income among households or families; and others may become clearer when we deal with the problem of differing size of families or units in the next section. But before turning to Table 7.5, we comment on the differences among families by type (Table 7.4, lines 5–7).

The definition of head of family is appropriate here: "One person in each family was designated as head. The head of a family is usually the person regarded as the head by members of the family. Women are not classified as heads if their husbands are resident members of the family at the time of the survey."[9] Disregarding the inherent ambiguity of the concept "head of family" so defined, we stress only that the data cannot show a female head in any husband–wife family, that is, when both wife and husband are present – a group that dominates the population – and that female headship is shown *only* when no husband, no male head, is present.

9 Source 1, p. 9.

The absence of a wife, in the case of "other male heads of families," is not associated with a lower family income when related to the number of persons (see line 6, col. 5, compared with, say, husband–wife families in line 5). But for families with female heads, income per person is only about six-tenths of that of husband–wife families (compare col. 5, lines 7 and 5). These wide differentials in income between female- and male-headed families are found for both white and Negro. The ratios, on a per family basis, are 0.57 for white families and 0.51 for Negro families, but female-head families are 28 percent of all Negro families, only 9 percent of all white families.[10]

Evidence on the male–female headship distinction among families or households is also available for Taiwan for 1972 (excluding Taipei City). In table 22 (pp. 402–3) of the source cited for Table 7.12 below, we find that households with female heads accounted for 7 percent among the nonfarmers and for 4.3 percent among farmers – both distinctly lower than the 11 percent proportion for all families in Table 7.4 (line 7, col. 1, related to line 4, col. 1), and below the 9 percent share for the whites. The income per family with a female head for Taiwan was about 0.8 of the average with a male head among the nonfarmers and as high as 0.86 among the farmers. Apparently, the absence of a male head had a much more moderate effect on family income in Taiwan than in the United States. One would have to know more about the structure of the family and the definition of head in Taiwan to interpret the difference properly.

At any rate, it is impracticable to pursue the distinction among families or units by sex of head further in this paper, since comparative data are not easily available and difficulties would arise in analyzing properly the differential behavior. We note it here primarily to record the possible prevalence of breakdowns in the normal life cycle of families, which are largely husband–wife units but may shift to a female headship in a significant proportion of cases, with marked effects on family income.

Table 7.5 shows the distribution of money income in 1969 among households, families, and unrelated individuals by size of income per household, per family, or per unrelated individual; as well as the two sets of inequality measures, the TDMs and the Gini coefficients. The findings can be briefly summarized.

First, the size distributions of income and measures of inequality are similar for households of two and more persons and families – not a sur-

10 *Ibid.*, table 17.

Table 7.5. *Distribution of 1969 money income among households (HH), families, and unrelated individuals, by income per unit, United States, March 1970*

A. *Shares in number and total income (%)*						
Classes by income per household ($ thousands)	HHs of 2 and more		1-person HH		All HHs	
	Number (1)	Income (2)	Number (3)	Income (4)	Number (5)	Income (6)
1. Below 2.0	4.8	0.5	36.7	8.5	10.2	1.1
2. 2.0–3.99	9.9	2.8	24.6	17.0	12.4	3.9
3. 4.0–5.99	11.3	5.3	13.9	15.9	11.7	6.1
4. 6.0–7.99	13.7	9.0	11.0	17.8	13.2	9.7
5. 8.0–9.99	14.4	12.1	5.5	11.4	12.9	12.1
6. 10.0–14.99	26.5	30.0	5.8	16.0	23.0	28.9
7. 15.0–24.99	15.7	28.2	2.0	8.8	13.4	26.7
8. 25.0 and over	3.7	12.1	0.6	4.6	3.2	11.5
9. Total (*N* in millions; income in $ billions)	52.2	553.7	10.7	46.3	62.9	600.0
Inequality measures						
10. TDM	48.8		71.6		55.0	
11. Gini coefficient	0.344		0.473		0.382	

B. *Shares in number and total income, families and unrelated individuals (%)*						
Classes by income per family, individual, or unit ($ thousands)	Families		Unrelated individuals		All units	
	Number (1)	Income (2)	Number (3)	Income (4)	Number (5)	Income (6)
12. Below 2.0	4.7	0.5	37.1	8.7	11.8	1.3
13. 2.0–3.99	9.9	2.8	23.9	16.9	13.0	4.2
14. 4.0–5.99	11.3	5.3	14.4	17.0	12.0	6.5
15. 6.0–7.99	13.7	9.1	11.1	18.3	13.1	10.0
16. 8.0–9.99	14.4	12.2	5.5	11.6	12.4	12.2
17. 10.0–14.99	26.7	30.6	5.6	15.8	22.1	29.1
18. 15.0–24.99	15.6	27.0	1.8	8.0	12.6	25.1
19. 25.0 and over	3.7	12.5	0.6	3.7	3.0	11.6
20. Total (*N* in millions; income in $ billions)	51.24	541.9	14.45	61.4	65.69	603.3
Inequality Measures						
21. TDM	48.2		70.8		56.2	
22. Gini coefficient	0.337		0.465		0.390	

Notes: The data on households in panel A are from source 2. The size distribution by income per household is shown in table 1 (p. 11), and we computed the income totals for prising result since the two populations differ only slightly in the inclusion of a small group of unrelated individuals within the households. Even the average income per household of two and more persons is close to that per family, as shown in Table 7.4 (col. 4, lines 1 and 4).

Second, the distribution among unrelated individuals and that among households of one person are also quite similar, despite the fact that unrelated individuals, a larger group than one-person households by almost 40 percent, include many who belong to multiperson households. Even the average incomes of the two groups, $4.33 thousand and $4.25 thousand, respectively, are close (see Table 7.4, col. 4, lines 2 and 8). Apparently the unrelated individuals who are members of multiperson households are similar in a number of respects to those living alone (or the differences between the two cancel out in the averages and in the distribution).

Third, the size distribution of income among either one-person households or among unrelated individuals is far more unequal than among households of two and more persons and among families. This is not what one would expect, since differences in size of the unit and in other characteristics may be assumed to be far wider among households of two and more persons or among families. After all, unrelated individuals are single persons and should show less heterogeneity than the more complex family or multiperson household units. That the TDMs and the Gini coefficients are so large suggests that unrelated individuals, or single-person households, contain significantly different components – just like the individual income recipients discussed in connection with Tables 7.1–7.3. The unrelated individuals apparently include, in addition to truly inde-

Notes to Table 7.5 *(cont.)*

the successive income brackets by assigning the mid-value between the class limits to each bracket (but assigned 12 and 19 to brackets 10–15 and 15–25) and calculated the value for the top open-end class either from the mean for the whole distribution or by assuming a value of $27.5 (see notes to Table 7.3 above). The data in panel B are from source 1. We derived income shares for families from the cumulated distributions of families and aggregate family income for successive brackets of income per family shown in table 2 (p. 19). The income shares for the unrelated individuals were estimated from table 17 (p. 35), from income totals obtained by multiplication of frequencies by mid-values of income class intervals, along the lines followed for households (see immediately above) or individual income recipients, as described in the notes to Table 7.3.
The income aggregates, which should be identical for the two populations (of households, on the one hand, and of the combination of families and unrelated individuals, on the other), do not check absolutely because of the calculation of the income totals for households from averages for income brackets and the use for families of the more precise basis of the cumulative distribution of families and aggregate income. The discrepancy, however, between $600.0 billion for the households (line 9, col. 6) and $603.3 billion for families and unrelated individuals combined (line 20, col. 6) is only about 0.5 percent.

pendent mature and substantial income earners in prime working ages, large groups of supplementary income recipients still dependent on their families and of older widowers and widows well beyond the peak of earning capacity. It is this mixture of primary and supplementary, major and minor, income positions among the unrelated individuals that probably contributes to the wide inequality – as was the case with the distribution among persons.

Finally, the inclusion of unrelated individuals or of single-person households with families and with households of two and more persons results in income inequality significantly wider than that for families alone (see lines 10–11 and 21–22, cols. 1 and 3). With such sensitivity to inclusion or exclusion of unrelated individuals and single-person households and the wide differences in the proportion of this group between the developed and less developed countries, the comparison of the customary size distributions of income among households is significantly affected. Moreover, in view of the possible interdependence among the single-person households or unrelated individuals and the larger households with which they may have blood and other ties, the comparison is likely to be misleading in other ways. It follows that if these single-person households or unrelated individuals are to be included their excessive effects, due largely to their small size, must be moderated in an alternative approach to the size distribution.

This brings us to the major question of differences in size among families, unrelated individuals, or households – the problem of relating the differences in income per family or per household to differences in the size of this recipient unit.

III. Differences in size of family or household

Given the wide differences in size among families, or among total units, and the expectation that the larger families or units would have larger incomes per family or per unit, we may ask to what extent the size distribution by income per family is affected. The question is whether the families or units with larger income also tend to be larger, thus representing either more mature households with more members and higher incomes of the heads associated with greater age and maturity within the occupation, or represent families with larger numbers of earners. Table 7.6 is designed to answer one part of this question; the other part will be dealt with later.

Lines 4 and 13 indicate that the number of persons per unit or per

Table 7.6. *Distribution of families and unrelated individuals by 1969 money income, United States, March 1970*

Group	Less than 2.0 (1)	2.0–3.99 (2)	4.0–5.99 (3)	6.0–7.99 (4)	8.0–9.99 (5)	10.0–14.99 (6)	15.0–24.99 (7)	25.0 and over (8)	Total (9)
Families and unrelated individuals									
1. Total income (%)	1.3	4.2	6.5	10.0	12.2	29.1	25.1	11.6	100.0 (603.3)
2. Total families and individuals (%)	11.8	13.0	12.0	13.1	12.4	22.1	12.6	3.0	100.0 (65.69)
3. Income relative (line 1/line 2)	0.11	0.32	0.54	0.76	0.98	1.32	2.00	3.87	1.00 (56.2)
4. Persons per unit	1.57	2.21	2.74	3.08	3.41	3.64	3.90	3.96	3.04
5. Total persons (%)	6.1	9.4	10.8	13.3	14.0	26.4	16.1	3.9	100.0 (199.94)
6. Income relative (line 1/line 5)	0.21	0.44	0.60	0.75	0.87	1.10	1.56	2.97	1.00 (38.8)
7. Consumers per unit	1.41	1.90	2.29	2.51	2.76	2.94	3.23	3.36	2.51
8. Total consumers (%)	6.6	9.8	10.8	13.1	13.7	25.8	16.1	4.1	100.0 (165.20)
9. Income relative (line 1/line 8)	0.20	0.43	0.60	0.76	0.89	1.12	1.56	2.83	1.00 (39.6)

Classes by income per family or unrelated individual ($ thousands)

Families only

10. Income (%)	0.5	2.8	5.3	9.1	12.2	30.6	27.0	12.5	100.0 (541.9)
11. Total families (%)	4.7	9.9	11.3	13.7	14.4	26.7	15.6	3.7	100.0 (51.24)
12. Income relative (line 10/line 11)	0.11	0.28	0.47	0.66	0.85	1.15	1.73	3.98	1.00 (48.2)
13. Persons per family	2.85	3.03	3.36	3.57	3.67	3.80	3.99	4.11	3.62
14. Total persons (%)	3.7	8.3	10.5	13.5	14.6	28.0	17.2	4.2	100.0 (185.49)
15. Income relative (line 10/line 14)	0.14	0.34	0.50	0.67	0.84	1.09	1.57	2.98	1.00 (41.4)
16. Consumers per family	2.32	2.51	2.72	2.86	2.95	3.06	3.30	3.48	2.94
17. Total consumers (%)	3.7	8.4	10.5	13.3	14.4	27.8	17.5	4.4	100.0 (150.8)
18. Income relative (line 10/line 17)	0.14	0.33	0.50	0.68	0.85	1.10	1.54	2.84	1.00 (40.8)

Notes: Calculated from the data in source 1, in which tables 1 and 2 (p. 19) show, for families, the cumulative distributions for the successive income classes per family; the number of all families, of total persons in families, and of total related children in families; and the averages (arithmetic means) of persons and related children per family. These were supplemented by the distribution for unrelated individuals by similar income classes in table 17 (p. 37). The number of consumers was calculated by assuming that a related child (under 18 years of age) is equivalent to one-half of a full consumer unit (see discussion in the text).

In col. 9, the entries in parentheses in lines 1 and 10 refer to total income ($ billions); those in lines 2 and 11 are the number of units (families plus unrelated individuals) and of families (both in millions); those in lines 5 and 14 are the number of persons (in millions); those in lines 8 and 17 refer to number of consumers (in millions); and those in lines 3, 6, 9, 12, 15, and 18 are the TDMs for the relevant distributions, calculated as indicated in the notes to Table 7.3.

family rises as we move from the lower to the higher income per unit or family class. The same is true of the number of consumers per unit or family, approximated by assigning a weight of one-half to children under 18 years of age (an approximation tested below in connection with a more detailed estimate, in Tables 7.8 and 7.9). This positive association between income per unit or family and its size, in terms of persons or consumer units, was to be expected, and other data not given here indicate that the average number of earners per unit or per family is also positively associated with income per unit or per family. More interesting is that the income *per person* or *per consumer* rises as we move from the lower to the higher class of income per unit or per family, and thus from smaller to larger units or families (lines 6, 9, 15, and 18). This positive association between the increasing size of the unit or family and the rising income per person or per consumer cannot, as we shall see below, be taken as an indication of a positive correlation between *size* of family or unit and *per person* or *per consumer* income – for it is not based on a clear distinction of the size variable at the base of the classification. The latter, in Table 7.6, is based on size of income per unit or per family, not on the size of the unit or family in terms of persons or consumers.

With positive association between size of unit or family and total income per unit or family, the adjustment for size of the type carried through in Table 7.6 naturally reduces income inequality. This is reflected in the reduction of the TDM from over 56 for the unadjusted distribution among all units to less than 40 when adjusted for the number of persons and consumers, and in the distribution among families alone from a TDM of over 48 to about 41 (see entries in parentheses in col. 9, lines 3, 6, 9, 12, 15, and 18). But the meaning of this adjustment and its results should be clearly perceived: if in the classification of units or families by income per unit or family we divide by the average number of persons (or consumers) in the successive income classes, the spread in the distribution is reduced. This will *always* be the case if we adjust a size distribution by a positively associated variable, so long as the amplitude (or variance) of that variable is not greater than that of the size distribution itself. This condition is clearly met in Table 7.6, for the range in the income relative in line 3 (from col. 1 to col. 8) is as high as 1 to 35; whereas those in lines 4 and 7 are 1 to over 2. The major point is that the size variable here is not in its full range, as it would be (and is in Table 7.8) in the spread from one to seven and more persons (and a related range for consumers).

One implication of Table 7.6 is brought out explicitly in Table 7.7 –

Table 7.7. *Internal structure of income classes in Table 7.6, distribution among units or families of differing size*

Classes by number of persons in unit or family	Income classes (of Table 7.6)								
	I (1)	II (2)	III (3)	IV (4)	V (5)	VI (6)	VII (7)	VIII (8)	Total (9)
Shares of units (%) (families and unrelated individuals)									
1. 1	69	40	26	19	10	6	3	5	22
2. 2	19	35	33	28	28	25	22	24	27
3. 3	5	11	15	19	19	21	20	17	16
4. 4	3	6	10	14	20	21	24	21	15
5. 5	2	3	7	10	12	14	16	15	10
6. 6	1	2	4	5	6	7	9	9	5
7. 7 and more	1	3	5	5	5	6	6	9	5
8. Total	100	100	100	100	100	100	100	100	100
Shares of families (%)									
9. 2	61	58	45	35	31	26	22	25	34
10. 3	16	18	20	23	21	22	21	18	21
11. 4	10	10	14	18	22	23	24	22	19
12. 5	6	6	9	12	13	15	17	16	13
13. 6	4	3	6	6	7	8	9	10	7
14. 7 and more	3	5	6	6	6	6	7	9	6
15. Total	100	100	100	100	100	100	100	100	100

Notes: Calculated from the source used for Table 7.6. The average number of persons in the group of seven and more persons works out to 8.2.

the structure of units or families, *within* the successive classes by income per unit or family, by size (number of persons). Two conclusions are indicated.

First, as we would expect, in the size classes where income per unit or per family is low there is an unusual concentration of small units or families. Thus within income class I, the lowest in Table 7.7, 88 percent of all units are one-or two-person units, whereas for the total distribution the combined share of the one- and two-person units is less than 50 percent (lines 1 and 2, cols. 1 and 9). Conversely, in the top income class, VIII, the share of units of five persons or over is 33 percent, whereas their share in the total distribution is only 20 percent (lines 5–7, cols. 8 and 9). A similar finding can be easily observed in the structure of income classes of families with families distinguished by number of persons (in lines 9–14).

Second, and equally important, concentration of the size groups within the income classes is not complete. With perfect association, income class I would consist entirely of one-person units in line 1, or two-person units in line 9 – with the residues moving to income class II. Yet we find one-person units even in the top income class, and we find units or families with larger numbers of persons in the lower per unit or per family income classes. It is this mixture that accounts for the limited size range of units in Table 7.6, lines 4, 7, 13, and 16. More important, it substantiates the comment made above that the effects of size of units or families on the size distribution of income can be brought out properly only if one *begins* with the classification by size. In this way the full range of the latter is revealed, and the relation between the size and the income of the unit is observed. This is attempted in Table 7.8, which suggests several findings and raises some questions.

First, the larger units or families have a somewhat larger average income than the small units or families. But this association extends only to units of five persons. Thus the income relatives are lowest for the one-person unit, reach a peak of almost three times for the five-person unit, and then drop even though the number of persons rises (line 3); the pattern is similar for families alone (line 15). These findings are based on money income, and it may be that the inclusion of income in kind (within the conventional definition) would raise the income relatives for the very large families, since a majority of them probably live on farms and in rural rather than urban areas. But it is unlikely that the general pattern – the rapid rise in income from the one- or two-person unit to a peak of about five persons, and then a slight decline, or at least no further significant rise – would be changed. The magnitude of inequality associated with differences in size is measured by a TDM of 25.6 (line 4) and a much smaller TDM of 11.6 for families (line 16). Obviously, the inclusion of unrelated individuals raises substantially the inequality contributed by differences in size of units. Presumably, we have here a component in the variance of income per family or per unit as measured in the conventional size distribution of income. Can it be properly compared with the variance or inequality in the total size distribution of income observed for units and families in Table 7.6, lines 1–3 and 10–12? We deal with this question after noting the other findings in Table 7.8.

Second, when we reduce income for each size group to a per person basis, the association between size and per person income is negative – not positive as it seemed to be in Table 7.6. The income relative per

Table 7.8. *Differentials in 1969 money income, all units and families classified by size (number of persons), United States, March 1970*

Group	1 (1)	2 (2)	3 (3)	4 (4)	5 (5)	6 (6)	7 and More (7)	Total (8)
	Number of persons per unit or family							
All units (families and unrelated individuals)								
1. Income (%)	10.3	25.8	18.8	19.4	13.0	7.0	5.7	100.0 (603.3)
2. Number of units (%)	22.0	26.9	16.3	15.0	9.8	5.3	4.7	100.0 (65.69)
3. Income relative (line 1/ line 2)	0.47	0.96	1.15	1.29	1.33	1.32	1.21	1.00
4. Disparities (line 1 − line 2)	−11.7	−1.1	2.5	4.4	3.2	1.7	1.0	25.6 (0.167)
5. Persons per unit	1.0	2.0	3.0	4.0	5.0	6.0	8.2	3.04
6. Number of persons (%)	7.2	17.7	16.1	19.7	16.1	10.5	12.7	100.0 (199.85)
7. Income relative per person (line 1/line 6)	1.43	1.46	1.17	0.98	0.81	0.67	0.45	1.00
8. Disparities (line 1 − line 6)	3.1	8.1	2.7	−0.3	−3.1	−3.5	−7.0	27.8 (0.188)
9. Consumers per unit	1.0	2.0	2.58	3.15	3.72	4.30	5.65	2.51
10. Number of consumers (%)	8.8	21.4	16.8	18.8	14.5	9.1	10.6	100.0 (184.45)
11. Income relative per consumer (line 1/ line 10)	1.17	1.21	1.12	1.03	0.90	0.77	0.54	1.00
12. Disparities (line 1 − line 10)	1.5	4.4	2.0	0.6	−1.5	−2.1	−4.9	17.0
Families								
13. Income (%)	0	28.7	20.8	21.6	14.5	7.8	6.6	100.0 (541.9)
14. Number of families (%)	0	34.4	20.9	19.3	12.5	6.8	6.1	100.0 (51.24)
15. Income relative per family (line 13/ line 14)	0	0.83	1.00	1.12	1.16	1.15	1.09	1.00
16. Disparities (line 13 − line 14)	0	−5.7	−0.1	2.3	2.0	1.0	0.5	11.6 (0.069)
17. Number of persons (%)	0	19.0	17.3	21.3	17.4	11.2	13.8	100.0 (185.40)

Table 7.8 (cont.)

	Number of persons per unit or family							
	1	2	3	4	5	6	7 and More	Total
Group	(1)	(2)	(3)	(4)	(5)	(6)	(7)	(8)
18. Income relative per person (line 13/ line 17)	0	1.51	1.20	1.01	0.83	0.70	0.48	1.00
19. Disparities (line 13 − line 17)	0	9.7	3.5	0.3	−2.9	−3.4	−7.2	27.0 (0.187)
20. Number of consumers (%)	0	23.5	18.4	20.5	16.0	10.0	11.6	100.0 (150.49)
21. Income relative per consumer (line 19/ line 20)	0	1.22	1.13	1.05	0.91	0.78	0.57	1.00
22. Disparities (line 13 − line 20)	0	5.2	2.4	1.1	−1.5	−2.2	−5.0	17.4

Notes: Based on source 1, tables 17 and 18 (pp. 35–42).
In col. 8, entries in parentheses in lines 1 and 13 are total income ($ billions); those in lines 2 and 14 are total number of units or of families (millions); in lines 6 and 17, total number of persons (millions); in lines 10 and 20, total number of consumers, i.e., persons, with related children under 18 given half-weight (millions). Entries in lines 4, 8, 12, 16, 19, and 22 are the TDMs; and in parentheses in lines 4, 8, 16, and 19 are the Gini coefficients.
The calculation of the number of children for families of differing size was as follows. We assumed that the proportion of children in two-person families was negligible and could be taken as 0 (as was clearly the case with unrelated individuals). For the other size units we made a preliminary assumption that the three-person family had one child, the four-person family had two, the five-person family had three, the six-person family had four, and the families with seven and more persons had six. The total number of children under 18 yielded by this procedure exceeded the reported number in the ratio of 1.0:0.848. We then modified the assumption by multiplying 1, 2, 3, 4, and 6 by 0.848, thus deriving the number of children per family of 3, 4, 5, 6, and 7 and more persons. We estimated the number of adults per family in each of these size classes by subtraction, this number ranging from 2.15 adults per family of three to 3.11 per family of seven and more.
Consumer equivalents for each size class are then the sum of the number of adults and of children under 18, the latter taken at half-weight.

person declines steadily from the high for one- or two-person units to the deep trough for units of seven and more persons. And whereas on a per unit or per family basis the very small units or families contribute a large *negative* disparity to the TDM (lines 4 and 16), on a per person basis these one-or two-person units contribute a substantial *positive* disparity (lines 8 and 19).

Third, the association between size of unit or family and income per *consumer* is also negative (lines 11 and 21). The basis for the approximation used here (and in Table 7.6), one of the questions that Table 7.8 raises, will be discussed below.

Finally, whereas there is a wide spread between the TDMs for all units and for families (25.6 and 11.6) on a per unit or per family basis, this spread almost disappears when we shift to a per person basis (27.8 and 27.0) or to a per consumer basis (17.0 and 17.4). The difference between the TDMs on the per person and per consumer basis persists. This is due to the fact that the reduced allowance for children affects only slightly the smaller units or families (particularly those of one or two persons), but it affects markedly the larger units of five or more. It thus tends to reduce the variance created by the *negative* association between per *person* income and the size of the unit or family.

(a) We now turn to the first question raised above, namely, whether we can compare the income inequality associated with size as shown for families in line 16 (with a TDM of 11.6) with the full income inequality in the size distribution by income per family in Table 7.6, line 12 (with a TDM of 48.2). And the question applies equally to the Gini coefficients. Does the comparison suggest that the differentials in income per family produced by size differences account for over two-tenths of total differences in income per family?

The answer is in the negative, and the comparison is inappropriate for two, quite different, reasons. First, the classification of families by size of income per family in 1969 (used in Table 7.6) presumably reflects fully the short-term, transitory elements in that year's income, whether it is near stochastic in the sense of random selection of families affected negatively or positively or is conjunctural in affecting, if only for that year, large groups (farmers by poor harvest, exporters by blockage of foreign trade, and the like). And a family, of whatever size, if adversely affected will fall into a low income bracket, much lower than its long-term level, while a family favorably affected will be in a higher than usual bracket. But when we put families into large groups by size – two persons, three persons, etc. – we cannot but assume that the stochastic disturbances of the income levels for individual families would largely cancel out within the groups of two-person families, three-person families, etc., since these disturbances are not related to size of family in any meaningful way; and this could be said even of short-term conjunctural effects. Unless further search reveals factors to the contrary, one should assume that for comparison with the income differentials in per family income among families of different size we need measures of inequality in the size distribution by income per family that are relatively *free* from short-term effects peculiar to a given year. This might mean a substantially smaller TDM than the 48.2 shown in Table 7.6, but how much smaller we cannot tell.

The second element of incomparability is the lack of additivity in such measures of income inequality as the TDMs and Gini coefficients. For lack of such additivity we cannot assume that the TDM of 11.6 in Table 7.8 can be compared with that of 48.2 in Table 7.6, in the sense that elimination of the income differences per family among the different size groups of families from the distribution would result in a TDM of 36.6 (i.e., 48.2 − 11.6) for the distribution so adjusted. Indeed, the inter-correlation among the *within*-size group differentials and the *between*-size group differentials may be so large that the removal of the differentials in average income among size groups may have a near negligible effect.[11]

Under the circumstances, we had to forgo the attempt to weigh the relative contribution of a variable like size of unit or family to the total income variance of a size distribution among units or families. In any case, the question will assume a different shape in the discussion below of the difference between the cross-section distribution of annual incomes and the distribution of lifetime or long-period incomes.

(b) The shift from a per person to a per consumer basis is in recognition of the fact that persons of different age and sex differ markedly in many respects relating to income getting and spending. With disparity in age

11 An example is but an illustration, but it may lend realism to the general state-ments in the text. Utilizing the already calculated Gini coefficients in U.S. Bu-reau of the Census, *Trends in the Income of Families and Persons in the United States, 1947–1964*, Technical Paper no. 17, prepared by Mary H. Henson (Washington, D.C.: Government Printing Office, 1967), we can illustrate by using the data for nonfarm families, grouped by size (from two to seven and more persons) for 1964 money income. Tables 4 (p. 63) and 26 (p. 188) show the Gini coefficients for the distribution of *all* families and for the distributions of families *within* each of the six size-of-family groups. The overall Gini coefficient is 0.347, and the within-group Gini coefficients vary from 0.302 to 0.400. If we weight these intragroup Gini coefficients by the share of each size group in all nonfarm fami-lies, the weighted average Gini is 0.347, the same as that for the total distribution, although the weighting *excludes* the effect of differences in average income among the six size groups (which range, in terms of income relatives, from 0.85 to 1.13). A similar weighting of the intragroup Ginis by the shares of the size groups in total income yields a weighted Gini of 0.341, slightly lower than that for the full distribution – but the difference is negligible. Yet the Gini calculated from the average incomes for the six groups of families classified by size is 0.062, and the subtraction from the overall Gini should yield a residual Gini of 0.285. The illustration can be repeated for other years, and other component factors, with similar results.

and in sex, persons range from zero levels of capacity to engage in organized, economically oriented activity to high levels of such capacity and
also differ substantially in the volume of goods required to fulfill whatever
may be considered acceptable or warranted needs. We chose the consumption or need approach on the premise that in the size distribution of
income the use of household or family as the basic recipient unit emphasizes, as it should, relevance of income to needs. Of course, alternative
emphases would also be valuable, for example, viewing the persons in the
family as workers not only in the market but also within the family, along
lines already discussed, and thus converting to a per worker–equivalent
basis, with the broadest relevant definition of work that would necessarily
call for a more inclusive income concept.

At this point, however, we are concerned with the rough approximation to the number of consumers, which involves here merely assigning a
weight of one-half to related children under 18. This omits possible differences in consumption requirements among age classes above the age
of 18 and by sex. But we are interested here only in illustrative orders
of magnitude. Our test, in Table 7.9, is limited to a comparison of the
results secured in Table 7.8, line 9, with two other, readily available scales
of consumer needs or patterns. For Table 7.8 we estimated the average
number of consumers per unit of different size (in persons) by distributing the known number of related children under 18 among units or
families of differing size and weighting the resulting number of children
(for each size group for families of three persons, four persons, etc.) by
half. One of the other scales is that implied in the thresholds of poverty
levels estimated for the United States in terms of money incomes, in connection with the data that we have used for the United States throughout
this paper. The other scale is that used in the study of the size distribution of income in Israel and is based on the analysis of consumption in
the 1968–69 family expenditure study, associated with size of households
and presumably standardized for income differentials.

The comparison shows that within the range of two- to six-person
units, the pattern estimated for Table 7.8 agrees well with those in the
two other attempts at a consumption equivalence scale (compare lines 2,
5, and 7, cols. 2–6). The ratios of consumers to persons in line 2 are
slightly higher than those in line 5; and this could be expected, since we
are trying to approximate general consumer equivalents rather than those
for the poverty-level thresholds. In the former, the ratios of consumption
of children to that of adults should be higher. The comparison with line 7

Table 7.9. *Comparison of consumer equivalents per person for families of differing size, used in Table 7.8, with those implied in the poverty-level thresholds for the United States, 1969, and in standard equivalent adults in Israel, 1968–69*

	Number of persons in family or household						
	1 (1)	2 (2)	3 (3)	4 (4)	5 (5)	6 (6)	7 and More (8.2) (7)
In Table 7.8							
1. Consumers per family	1.0	2.0	2.58	3.15	3.72	4.30	5.65
2. Consumers per person	1.0	1.0	0.86	0.79	0.74	0.72	0.69
U.S. poverty-level thresholds							
3. Income($)	1,888	2,441	2,905	3,721	4,386	4,921	6,034
4. Implied consumers per family	1.55	2.00	2.36	3.05	3.59	4.03	4.94
5. Implied consumers per person	1.55	1.00	0.79	0.76	0.72	0.67	0.60
Israel standard equivalent adults, 1968–69							
6. Per family	1.25	2.00	2.65	3.20	3.75	4.25	5.28
7. Per person	1.25	1.00	0.88	0.80	0.75	0.71	0.64

Notes: Lines 1–2: from Table 7.8, line 9.
Lines 3–5: line 3 from U.S. Bureau of the Census, *Current Population Reports*, Series P-60, no. 76, *Poverty in the United States: 1969* (Washington, D.C.: Government Printing Office, December 1970), table L, p. 18. For lines 4 and 5 we calculated the income per person for the family of two (for it and for a family of one we used the levels for head under 65 years, obtaining an average of $1,220.5, and then divided all entries in line 3 by 1,220.5, to estimate the number of consumer equivalents, at the poverty-level threshold, implicit in the dollar figure shown.
In describing the poverty index used (first elaborated by the Social Security Administration in 1964), *Poverty in the United States* states: "This index provided a range of poverty income cut-offs adjusted to such factors as family size, sex of the family head, number of children under 18 years old, and farm-nonfarm residence. At the core of the definition of poverty was a nutritionally adequate food plan ('economy' plan) designed by the Department of Agriculture for 'emergency or temporary use when funds are low.' The SSA poverty cut-offs also took into account differences in the cost of living between farm and nonfarm families" (p. 18). In an earlier source (*Current Population Reports*, Series P-60, no. 68 [December 1969]) there is an explanation of the conversion of a food plan into a total budget. "In determining the proportion of total family income that should be consumed by food requirements, the SSA observed that the percentage of income expended for necessities, particularly food, reflects the relative well being of both individuals and the society in which they live. In general, families that need to use about the same proportion of their income for a given level of food expenditure are considered to share the same level of living. For families of three or more persons the poverty level was set at three times the cost of the economy food plan [based on a Department of Agriculture study of food consumption which showed this "average food cost-to-family income relationship"]. For smaller families and persons residing alone the cost of the economy food plan was multiplied by factors that were slightly larger to compensate for the relatively higher fixed expenses of these smaller households" (p. 10).
Lines 6–7: taken or calculated from *Report of the Committee on Income Distribution and Social Inequality* (Tel Aviv: N.p., 1971), pp. 38–39. Line 6 represents the "standard equivalent

is with another country, and still the levels and patterns of movement are close. One of the two marked departures is for the one-person unit (col. 1) which we set at 1.0 – not allowing for the possible diseconomies of scale which yield a value of 1.55 in the case of the poverty-level thresholds and of 1.25 in the case of Israel. The other is for the largest family-size class, seven persons and over, in which the ratio in line 2 is distinctly higher than that in either line 5 or line 7 (see col. 7). These two extreme groups are relatively small in the total population of persons in units or families, and it is possible that for the very large units we tend to overestimate the number of consumers slightly and thus underestimate the level of income per consumer.

But the order of magnitudes is plausible, and any revision of the crude assumptions would be warranted only if it were feasible to examine more carefully the bases of the estimates of the poverty-level thresholds – as well as the evidence for Israel or for other countries for which similar attempts have been made. The poverty-level thresholds are particularly intriguing in their assumption that at such levels the expenditures on a minimum food budget should be multiplied by three, to secure total budgets for all families or households of three and more persons (and by a higher multiple for smaller units). This implies, at the poverty level, a proportion of expenditures on food lower than 33 percent – a share no higher than that observed for the *average* volume of consumer expenditures in post–World War II years among many developed countries. To be sure, in the same source the average for the United States is lower, but the question as to the meaning of such "poverty" levels in their dependence on the society's institutional structure remains.[12]

12 See my paper, "Quantitative Aspects of the Economic Growth of Nations. VII. The Share and Structure of Consumption," *Economic Development and Cultural Change*, vol. 10, no. 2, pt. 2 (January 1962). Table 10 (p. 24) shows that the share of food (average for 1950–59) was 27 percent for the top group of developed countries, close to 36 percent for the next group, and as high as 48.4 percent for the poorest group of countries. Appendix table 5 (p. 76) shows for 1950–59 average proportions of close to 30 percent for Belgium, Sweden, and Canada, and well over 30 percent for Finland, France, and the Netherlands.

Notes to Table 7.9 *(cont.)*

adults" per family of different size, the weights based on "consumption patterns obtained from the Family Expenditure Survey," presumably 1968–69. The *Report* shows the weights separately for families of seven, eight, and nine persons, and we estimated that for 8.2 persons by simple arithmetic interpolation between the weights for the eight- and nine-person families.

But since an intensive study of needs and consumption patterns is not feasible here, we accept the rough estimates of consumer equivalents per person for the families of varying size and proceed with the attempt to trace properly the effect of size of unit on the size distribution of income. Ideally this would be done by beginning with the individual unit or family then calculating for each the number of persons or consumer equivalents, dividing the unit or family income by that number, and classifying these units or families by income *per person* or *per consumer*. Such a detailed conversion is not feasible, short of access to the original reports for individual persons or families. But we do have distributions by size of income per family for each family-size group, of two persons, three persons, etc., to the seven and more persons, and can form cells in a cross-classification of families by both size and income per family. We can then calculate for each cell the income per person, knowing that in the group of two-person families two is the proper denominator for dividing each cell, that is, each income class; calculate for each cell income per consuming unit, assuming that the average number of children per adult in the given size-of-family class is the same for each within-size group income level; and then rearray the cells into distributions among the population of persons by family income *per person*, or among the population of consumers by family income *per consumer*. This procedure was used to derive the distributions by income per person and by income per consumer in lines 1–9 of Table 7.10. Given these distributions and their origin in the cells of the type described above, it was possible to trace the structure among various size-of-family groups *within* the successive income classes of the distributions of persons or consumers by family income per person or per consumer (lines 10–31).

The interest in lines 1–9 lies in the magnitude of income inequality shown by the new distributions, particularly in comparison with similar measures for the distributions in Tables 7.6 and 7.8. A brief summary of the TDMs in these three tables is useful in guiding the discussion (Table 7.11).

Several findings can be listed. First, whereas the distributions in column 2, involving the adjustment merely for the *average* size of unit or family by size-of-family income brackets, show markedly lower TDMs than those in column 1, the *complete* shift to a per person basis in column 3 yields a distribution with an inequality measure that is as large as that for the distribution of total units by income per unit in column 1. For families, the distribution of persons by family income per person yields a

Table 7.10. *Distribution of 1969 money income among all units or families: classes by income per person or per consumer, United States, March 1970 ($ thousands)*

Group	Less than 0.70 (1)	0.70–1.39 (2)	1.40–1.99 (3)	2.00–2.99 (4)	3.00–3.99 (5)	4.00–5.99 (6)	6.00–7.99 (7)	8.0 and over (8)	Total (9)
			Shares in number and in income (%)						
All units (per person)									
1. Total income (%)	1.0	4.7	8.8	14.2	19.5	19.3	16.1	16.4	100.0 (602.7)
2. Number of persons (%)	7.1	13.8	16.9	18.6	18.3	13.0	7.7	4.6	100.0 (199.7)
3. Disparities (line 1 − line 2)	−6.1	−9.1	−8.1	−4.4	1.2	6.3	8.4	11.8	55.4 (0.384)
Families (per person)									
4. Total income (%)	1.2	4.3	9.8	15.7	19.9	19.5	15.8	13.8	100.0 (541.4)
5. Number of persons (%)	7.7	12.0	18.2	20.0	17.9	12.9	7.4	3.9	100.0 (185.2)
6. Disparities (line 4 − line 5)	−6.5	−7.7	−8.4	−4.3	2.0	6.6	8.4	9.9	53.8 (0.371)
Families (per consumer)									
7. Total income (%)	0.6	2.8	5.8	15.5	19.0	18.7	20.7	16.9	100.0 (541.4)
8. Number of consumers (%)	4.9	9.0	12.5	22.4	19.4	14.2	11.8	5.8	100.0 (150.3)
9. Disparities (line 7 − line 8)	−4.3	−6.2	−6.7	−6.9	−0.4	4.5	8.9	11.1	49.0 (0.313)

Table 7.10 (cont.)

Group	Less than 0.70 (1)	0.70–1.39 (2)	1.40–1.99 (3)	2.00–2.99 (4)	3.00–3.99 (5)	4.00–5.99 (6)	6.00–7.99 (7)	8.0 and over (8)	Total (9)
	Structure within income classes, shares within each class of persons or consumers in units of different size (%)								
All units (persons)									
10. 1	0	19	0	0	9	8	10	21	19
11. 2	21	0	17	14	13	18	47	49	15
12. 3	8	10	10	13	13	35	33	11	14
13. 4	6	20	14	17	35	30	0	19	17
14. 5	15	9	28	27	18	0	10	0	15
15. 6	11	17	9	17	12	4	0	0	9
16. 7 and more	39	25	22	12	0	5	0	0	11
17. Total	100	100	100	100	100	100	100	100	100
Families (persons)									
18. 2	21	0	17	14	15	19	53	63	19
19. 3	8	12	10	13	14	38	36	14	17
20. 4	6	24	14	17	38	33	0	23	21
21. 5	15	12	28	27	20	0	11	0	18
22. 6	11	21	9	17	13	4	0	0	11
23. 7 and more	39	31	22	12	0	6	0	0	14
24. Total	100	100	100	100	100	100	100	100	100

Families (consumers)

25. 2	40	0	31	15	17	22	41	52	23
26. 3	14	17	15	13	14	36	24	10	18
27. 4	10	12	14	26	33	0	35	16	21
28. 5	7	22	17	11	26	23	0	13	16
29. 6	5	16	10	20	0	14	0	9	10
30. 7 and more	24	33	13	15	10	5	0	0	12
31. Total	100	100	100	100	100	100	100	100	100

Notes: The underlying data are from source 1, in particular table 18 (p. 42), which shows the distribution of income per family, *within* each of the six size-of-family groups (from 2 to 7 and more persons), and table 17 (p. 35), which shows the distribution of income per unit for unrelated individuals (treated here as units of 1 person).

From the cross classifications above, using the eight size-of-income classes (income per family, see our Table 7.6 above), and the classes by size (either seven, including one-person units, or six, when limited to families), we formed 48 or 56 cells. For each cell we derived total income, total persons or consumers (available for each size-of-unit group in Table 7.8), and income per person or per consumer. We then arrayed the cells by rising level of income per person or per consumer and derived a grouping into classes of income per person or per consumer (lines 1–9).

With the identity of the cells shown in the array it was then possible to calculate the structure of distribution within each income per person or income per consumer class, distribution among persons (or consumers) covered by the different size classes among units or families. The percentage shares shown in lines 10–31 are comparable with those calculated for the distribution by income per unit or per family in Table 7.6 above.

In col. 9, entries in parentheses in lines 1, 4, and 7 refer to total income ($ billions); those in lines 2, 5, and 8 refer to total numbers of persons or consumers (millions); those in lines 3, 6, and 9 are the TDMs, with the Gini coefficients in parentheses.

Table 7.11. *TDMs for the distributions in Tables 7.6, 7.8, and 7.10*

	By income per unit or per family (Table 7.6)		By income per person (Table 7.10)	By income per consumer (Table 7.10)	Disparities among size groups of units or families (Table 7.8)	
	As given (1)	Adjusted for average number of persons in income class (2)	(3)	(4)	Income per family (5)	Income per person (6)
1. Total units (families + unrelated individuals	56.2	38.8	55.4	n.c.[a]	25.6	27.8
2. Families	48.2	41.4	53.8	49.0	11.6	27.0

[a] Not calculated.

TDM in column 3 of 53.8, distinctly larger than that for the distribution of families by income per family.

Second, the measures of aggregate inequality, the TDMs, whether for a distribution of families by income per family, or for a distribution of persons by family income per person, or for a distribution of consumers by family income per consumer, do not differ much. The differences are within about one-tenth of the TDM values. This limited range is due to the fact that the TDMs reflect much more than variance associated with differences in size of unit or family. They are affected by many short-term or long-term inequality factors that are unrelated to the size element. This effect is shown in the *intrasize* group distributions by size of income (per family, or per person, or per consumer). Hence one should have expected at the outset that any changes in aggregate inequality with the shift in classification from the income per family to the income per person basis would be relatively limited – so long as the size factor in itself had moderate weight compared with other factors in the kind of distribution (of annual, short-term affected income) used.

Third, despite the comment just made, the relative magnitude of the disparities associated with the size factor, reflected in the TDMs in columns 5 and 6, does suggest the possible direction and extent of change in inequality as we shift from one classification of unit or family income to another. In the conversion from income per unit or per family to unit or family income per person we are, in a sense, *subtracting* the variance represented by the TDM in column 5 (i.e., that associated with disparities among size groups of units or families by income per unit or family) and *adding* the TDM in column 6 (that associated with disparities among size groups of units or families, by income per person). Substantial differences between the TDMs in columns 5 and 6 should, therefore, be reflected in relevant differences between those in columns 1 and 3. And, indeed, for families, in which the "subtracted" TDM in column 5, 11.6, is appreciably smaller than the "added" TDM in column 6, 27.0, the TDM in column 3, 53.8, is larger than that in column 1, 48.2, although the latter difference is only 5.6 points whereas the former is 15.4 points. For total units, with the TDMs in columns 5 and 6 almost the same, the change from the TDM in column 1 to that in column 3 is slight. We shall observe a similar association for other countries covered in Tables 7.12 and 7.13 below.

But it is the shift in the structure of units or families *within* the income classes indicated in lines 10–31 of Table 7.10 (to be compared with that for the distribution by income per unit or family in Table 7.7) that is of most interest. Since the association between income per person (or per consumer) and the size of the unit or family is *negative*, it follows that in the distribution of persons (or consumers) by unit or family income per person (or per consumer) the *smaller* units or families would dominate the upper per person or per consumer income brackets, and the *larger* families would be more concentrated in the lower income per person or per consumer brackets – opposite to the structure shown in Table 7.7 above. And this is, indeed, what we find. In the distribution among all units (lines 10–17), the lower brackets of income per person are dominated by the larger units of six and seven and more persons, which account for 50 percent of all persons in the lowest income bracket and 42 percent in the next lowest – although the proportion of persons in these two size groups in the total distribution is only 20 percent (col. 9, lines 15 and 16). By contrast, in the two top per person income brackets, the two smallest groups of units (one or two persons) account for 57 percent of the next to the top and 70 percent of the top bracket – although the share of these two size groups in the total distribution of persons is only 34 percent (col. 9, lines 10 and 11).

Similar findings may be observed for the distribution of persons in families by family income per person (lines 18–24); and what is also significant, in the distribution of consumers in families by family income per consumer (lines 25–31). The observed concentration in the upper income brackets of persons or consumers in the smaller families, and in the lower income brackets of persons or consumers in the larger families, is far from perfect; but the general association between small size and high per person or per consumer income is clear – and the contrast with the association between small size and lower income per family in Table 7.7 is marked.

The implication of this finding is obvious: the high income units in the conventional size distribution of families or households by income per family or household may, when reduced to a per person or per consumer basis, prove to be low income units. And all characteristics that we tend to associate with low or high family income may be displaced, unless some proper adjustment for the size differentials is made. To be sure, as we shall see below, both sets of distributions, by income per family or by income per person, are greatly affected, by both short-term random and other variables and the phase in the life cycle of the family, which would influence both its size and its total income. But whenever cross-section income distributions are used, the difference produced by the shift just illustrated is clearly important.

The remainder of this section is devoted to a brief summary of the evidence for four other countries, to see whether the findings established for the U.S. distributions of 1969 money income among families and unrelated individuals can be confirmed.[13] These countries are Germany (FR), with a distribution of households for 1970; Israel, with a distribution of urban households for 1968–69; Taiwan, with a distribution of households for 1972; and the Philippines, with a distribution of families for 1970–71. The choice was governed largely by the easy availability of the data, but some effort was made to include less developed countries.

13 At this point it may be useful to refer to the similar calculations for the United States for 1972 which appeared in the Tokyo Seminar paper. Table 9 (pp. 426–29) yields TDMs for the various distributions, classified by per unit or family income, unadjusted and adjusted, and by income per person, with findings similar to those stated here. Likewise, table 10 (p. 433) shows explicitly the structure of the distribution among units of varying size *within* classes of income by person, which demonstrates the relative preponderance of small (large) units in the high (low) brackets of income per person. As indicated, the data for 1969 were used here in order to take advantage of the *Census of Population* data which refer to March 1970 and thus relate to income for 1969. The various parameters in the tables here and in those for the United States in 1972 are quite similar.

Table 7.12 parallels Table 7.6 for the United States. It shows the distribution of households or families by six or seven classes of income per household or family, as well as the average number of persons within these income classes (and in the case of the Philippines where data are shown for the total number of related children under 18, also consumers) per household or family. It should be stressed that intercountry comparisons of income averages and inequality measures, within Table 7.12 or between Table 7.12 and Table 7.6, are not warranted – not only because the income concept differs, but also because the income data are deficient and have not been subjected to critical scrutiny and adequate revision. Thus, the distribution we have used for the United States was limited to money income, and even with the inclusion of income in kind it would fall somewhat short of the personal income totals in the national economic accounts (particularly with respect to property income). The distribution for Taiwan, according to Mrs. Wan-yong Kuo, is understated at the upper income levels, and for lack of detail we could not use the special adjustment that she made for this deficiency.[14] The distribution for the Philippines is based on what may be underestimates of the income totals, since in the source used for Table 7.12, lines 19–27 (and below) average income per family falls short of average expenditure per family for all but the top four income classes, the latter accounting for less than 10 percent of all families (see table 2, p. 1 of the source). We can only compare the results of analysis and conversions for each country taken separately and observe whether they tend to be the same. We should not compare the measures of inequality of the income distribution, whatever base, among countries, but we can compare changes in them introduced by methodological modifications.

In all four countries, the average number of persons per household or family rises as we move from the low to the higher brackets of income per family – in Germany from 1.40 to 4.09 (line 4); in Israel from 2.1 to 3.9, although the peak of 4.3 is reached at the fifth income bracket (line 10); in Taiwan from 3.22 to 7.28 (line 16); and in the Philippines from 4.81 to 6.84 (line 22). The relative range, among classes by income per household or family, differs substantially among the countries – being widest in Germany, with a range from 1 to almost 3, and narrowest in

14 See Wan-yong Kuo, "Income Distribution by Size in Taiwan Area – Changes and Causes," in Tokyo Seminar Proceedings, 1:80–153, particularly the discussion of the adjustment, pp. 85 ff.

Table 7.12. *Distribution of households by rising order of income per household, selected countries*

	Classes of income per household							
	I (1)	II (2)	III (3)	IV (4)	V (5)	VI (6)	VII (7)	Total (8)
Germany (FR), 1970								
1. Total income (%)	3.0	12.7	17.5	16.5	20.2	30.1	—	100.0
2. Number of households (%)	11.9	27.0	22.4	15.1	13.1	10.5	—	100.0
3. Income relative per household (line 1/line 2)	0.24	0.47	0.78	1.09	1.54	2.87	—	1.00 (56.2)
4. Persons per household	1.40	2.08	2.80	3.18	3.82	4.09	—	2.76
5. Number of persons (%)	6.0	20.3	22.7	17.4	18.1	15.5	—	100.0
6. Income relative per person (line 1/line 5)	0.50	0.63	0.77	0.95	1.12	1.94	—	1.00 (33.4)
Israel (urban), 1968–69								
7. Total income (%)	2.7	9.6	14.1	15.8	13.7	17.1	27.0	100.0
8. Number of households (%)	12.6	22.2	17.9	15.3	10.7	10.5	10.8	100.0
9. Income relative per household (line 7/line 8)	0.21	0.43	0.79	1.03	1.28	1.63	2.50	1.00 (52.6)
10. Persons per household	2.1	3.6	3.9	4.0	4.3	3.7	3.9	3.7
11. Number of persons (%)	7.3	21.9	19.2	16.8	12.6	10.7	11.5	100.0
12. Income relative per person (line 7/line 11)	0.37	0.44	0.73	0.94	1.09	1.60	2.35	1.00 (46.0)
Taiwan, 1972								
13. Total income (%)	2.4	6.8	12.0	19.7	28.0	21.8	9.3	100.0
14. Number of households (%)	7.5	13.5	18.1	22.9	23.4	11.8	2.8	100.0
15. Income relative per household (line 13/line 14)	0.32	0.50	0.66	0.86	1.20	1.84	3.64	1.00 (42.2)
16. Persons per household	3.22	4.68	5.30	5.68	6.20	6.73	7.28	5.58
17. Number of persons (%)	4.4	11.3	17.2	23.3	26.0	14.2	3.6	100.0
18. Income relative per person (line 13/line 17)	0.55	0.60	0.70	0.85	1.08	1.54	2.58	1.00 (30.6)
Philippines, 1970–71								
19. Total income (%)	2.9	9.6	11.8	20.4	19.1	20.3	15.9	100.0
20. Number of households (%)	17.3	23.9	17.7	20.0	11.4	7.3	2.4	100.0
21. Income relative per household (line 19/line 20)	0.17	0.40	0.67	1.02	1.68	2.78	6.62	1.00 (69.2)
22. Persons per household	4.81	5.41	5.72	6.13	6.69	6.61	6.84	5.77
23. Number of persons (%)	14.4	22.5	17.6	21.2	13.1	8.3	2.9	100.0
24. Income relative per person (line 19/line 23)	0.20	0.43	0.67	0.96	1.46	2.45	5.48	1.00 (62.0)
25. Consumers per household	3.55	3.91	4.11	4.48	5.03	5.06	5.25	4.24
26. Number of consumers (%)	14.5	22.0	17.2	21.1	13.5	8.7	3.0	100.0
27. Income relative per consumer (line 19/line 26)	0.20	0.44	0.69	0.97	1.42	2.33	5.30	1.00 (60.2)

Table 7.12 *(cont.)*

Notes: Entries in parentheses in col. 8, lines 3, 6, 9, 12, 15, 18, 21, 24, and 27 refer to the TDMs calculated from the percentage shares in the preceding lines.

Lines 1–6: source is Gerhard Göseke and Klaus-Dietrich Bedau, *Verteilung und Schichtung der Einkommen der privaten Haushalte in der Bundesrepublik Deutschland 1950 bis 1975*, Deutsches Institut für Wirtschaftsforschung, Beiträge sur Strukturforschung, Heft 31 (Berlin: Duncker & Humblot, 1974). The table on p. 77 was used to calculate the number of persons in the group of households with seven and more persons; and the more detailed tables for 1970 on pp. 164, 166–69, showing distribution of all households, and then separately for households of from one to seven and more persons, were used to compute the entries in line 4.

Households here follow the "household keeping unit concept" involving living in the same housing unit and having common provisions for essential living needs, particularly food (see United Nations, manual 7, *Methods of Projecting Households and Families* [New York: United Nations, 1973], p. 6). The income distributed is defined in accordance with the personal income concept in national economic accounting, and the estimates are derived on the basis of both labor force and family expenditure surveys and the national economic accounts. The sources of income are, thus, earnings, property incomes, and transfers of various kinds (pensions, social security, veterans' compensation, etc.).

Lines 7–12: data taken or calculated from Israel Central Bureau of Statistics, *Family Expenditure Survey 1968/69, Part IV, Family Income*, Special Series no. 388 (Jerusalem: CBS, 1972). The classes by income per household are from table 5 (p. 8), which shows the distribution of households by monthly *net* income (i.e., gross, excluding direct taxes) but the income amounts given are for *gross* income. The same table also shows average number of persons per household in the several income classes.

Total income includes all money income, except nonrecurrent receipts (e.g., inheritance or severance pay), plus receipts in kind and imputed income on private dwellings and vehicles (p. xxii). Net income is gross income minus direct taxes.

The urban population of Israel accounts for "82 percent of all the families in the country" (p. xi). The investigation unit of household is defined as "a family of consumers," i.e., a group of persons living in the same dwelling most of the week and partaking of at least one common meal a day together. "In the majority of cases, this unit is identical with the family in the accepted sense of the word, but there are also exceptional cases" (e.g., subtenant living and sharing meals with the family, or a group of students living together and sharing meals) (p. xi).

Lines 13–18: data taken or calculated from two sources – (1) excluding Taipei City, Department of Budget, Accounting, and Statistics, Taiwan Provincial Government, *Report on the Survey of Family Income and Expenditure, Taiwan Province, Republic of China, 1972* (Taipei: DGBAS, 1973) (in Chinese but with English titles to the tables); (2) for Taipei City in the same year (kindly provided by Mrs. Wan-yong Kuo of the Economic Planning Council of Taiwan) taken from *Report on the Survey of Family Income and Expenditures of Individual Income in Taipei City, 1972* (Taipei: N.p., 1973) (in Chinese).

Family income, or "total current receipts," comprises total wages and salaries, total property income (interest, actual and imputed rent, and investment income), mixed incomes (net agricultural income including that from forestry and fishing; net operation surplus, presumably from nonagricultural individual firms; and net professional income), gifts and other transfer receipts, and miscellaneous receipts.

The entries in line 16 were calculated from the table showing number of households by size, ranging from one person to more than 10. To derive the number of persons in the 10 and more class we used the 10-person group given in the source, assigned a mean of 12 to the group of 11–14 and a mean of 17 to the 16 and more group (the top open-end class in the source).

Lines 19–27: data taken or calculated from Bureau of the Census and Statistics, *Family Income and Expenditures: 1971*, Series no. 34, *BCS Survey of Households* (Manila: BCS, 1974), pp. 3–6, table 6; p. 20, table 19; p. 138, table 50.

The period of coverage is the "past twelve months . . . from May 1970 to April 1971" (p. ix). The data relate to the distribution among families rather than households: "a family is defined as a group of persons usually living together and related to the head by blood, marriage or adoption excluding those who are mere boarders, guests, or domestic help. A person living alone was considered as a separate family" (p. xi). Family income covers all the Philippines, with a range from 1 to less than 1.5. But the positive association between size of unit and income per unit is generally observed.

Hence, as in the case of the United States, two inferences follow. The first, brought out in Table 7.12, is that the adjustment for differences in *average* number of persons per household or family necessarily reduces the income inequality. Thus, for Germany, the adjustment reduces the TDM from 56.2 to 33.4 (col. 8, lines 3 and 6); for Israel from 52.6 to 46.0 (col. 8, lines 9 and 12); for Taiwan from 42.2 to 30.6 (col. 8, lines 15 and 18); and for the Philippines from 69.2 to 62.0, in adjustment for the average number of persons, and to 60.2 in adjustment for the average number of consumers (col. 8, lines 21, 24, and 27).

The second inference is that the larger units, the larger households or families, must be overrepresented in the upper income classes by income per household or per family and underrepresented in the lower, while the smaller households or families must be underrepresented in the upper income classes and overrepresented in the lower. We have not shown the actual figures because this consequence *inevitably* follows from Table 7.12. If the average size of households or families is higher in the higher income per unit class, this can occur only because the distribution of households or families within that income bracket *favors* the larger households or families in the sense that their proportion within that higher income bracket is greater than their proportion in the total population. If the average size of the household or family in the lower class of income per household or family is small, this can happen only because in the distribution within that low income bracket the smaller households or families are favored, in that their proportion there is higher than in the total population. The automatic nature of this connection between the movements of the averages of persons (or consumers) per family among

Notes to Table 7.12 *(cont.)*

money and income in kind, including gifts, transfers, and inheritance if received within the last 12 months (p. xi).
The number of persons per family (line 22) was calculated from the data on families by size (in tables 3 and 19 of the source), with the 10 and more (the top open-end class) being assigned a mean of 11 persons. (This is a revision of the 12-person mean assigned in the calculations for the Tokyo Seminar paper and was made for better reconciliation with an estimate of the total number of persons derived from the *BCS Survey:* it shows a per capita income of 647 pesos, in table C-3 [p. xviii], and a total of family income of 23,714 million pesos in table 2 [p. 1].)
The average number of children for families, in different classes by income per family, are shown in table 50; and we calculated the relevant means for the income classes used in the table (the group is defined as "children under 18 years of age living with the family").

the successive classes of income per family and the implicit structure within those income classes, that is, the distribution within them of families by size, must be stressed. It is also present when we observe the movement of per person (or per consumer) income from high to low as we shift from the smaller to the larger families or households. This negative association *must* result in a structure within classes of income per person or per consumer that favors small households or families in the upper brackets of income per person and favors larger households or families in the lower brackets of income per person.

Table 7.13 presents, for the same four countries, distributions that distinguish households or families of differing size, show the average income per household or family and the relative frequency of the various size groups, and then, after a simple calculation, show the pattern of income *per person* or *per consumer* (the latter for the Philippines alone) for the several size groups of households or families. It is thus parallel to Table 7.8 for the United States, except that it lacks the distinction between all units (families and unrelated individuals) and families (of two or more persons) alone and that it distinguishes the per consumer basis for only one of the four countries.

The first finding to be noted is that income inequality generated by differences in size of household or family, in the distribution by income per household or family, is narrower in the two less developed countries, Taiwan and the Philippines, than in Germany or Israel, or than in the distribution for all units in the United States in Table 7.8. The TDM for Taiwan and the Philippines is only 12.8 and 16.2, respectively, whereas it is 32.0 for Germany, 20.2 for Israel, and was 25.6 for the U.S. distribution among all units (see col. 3, lines 8, 15, 26, and 37, entries in parentheses; and Table 7.8, col. 8, line 4). This, however, seems to be due largely to the large weight of the single-person units, at least in the distributions for the United States and Germany, and less so for Israel. The TDM for the U.S. distribution of families alone is only 11.6 (see Table 7.8, col. 8, line 16). It may be seen that the proportion of single-person units in the total is as high as 22 percent in the United States (Table 7.8, col. 1, line 2) and somewhat higher than this in Germany (col. 2, line 1), but is appreciably lower, 11 percent, in Israel (col. 2, line 9), and very much lower in Taiwan and the Philippines, with proportions of about 3 percent or less (col. 2, lines 16 and 27). This confirms the earlier comment on the large contribution to income inequality in the conventional size

Table 7.13. *Income differentials, households classified by size (number of persons), selected countries*

Persons in household	Income (%) (1)	Number of households (%) (2)	Income relative per household (3)	Number of persons (%) (4)	Income relative per person (5)	Consumers per household (6)	Number of consumers (%) (7)	Income relative per consumers (8)
Germany (FR), 1970								
1. 1	11.6	22.6	0.51	8.2	1.41	—	—	—
2. 2	22.8	27.8	0.82	20.1	1.13	—	—	—
3. 3	24.6	22.2	1.11	24.2	1.02	—	—	—
4. 4	20.1	15.4	1.31	22.5	0.89	—	—	—
5. 5	11.3	7.2	1.57	13.2	0.86	—	—	—
6. 6	5.4	2.9	1.86	6.4	0.84	—	—	—
7. 7 and more (7.71)	4.2	1.9	2.21	5.4	0.80	—	—	—
8. Total	100.0	100.0	1.00 (32.0)	100.0 (2.75)	1.00 (13.0)	—	—	—
Israel (urban), 1968–69								
9. 1	4.8	10.9	0.44	3.0	1.60	—	—	—
10. 2	19.8	23.0	0.86	12.6	1.57	—	—	—
11. 3	21.4	19.0	1.13	15.6	1.37	—	—	—
12. 4	27.9	21.4	1.30	23.4	1.19	—	—	—
13. 5	12.6	11.4	1.10	15.6	0.81	—	—	—
14. 6 and more (7.2)	13.5	14.3	0.94	29.8	0.47	—	—	—
15. Total	100.0	100.0	1.00 (20.2)	100.0 (3.7)	1.00 (38.6)	—	—	—

Taiwan, 1972

16. 1	1.4	3.3	0.42	0.6	2.33	—	—	—
17. 2	2.8	4.1	0.68	1.5	1.87	—	—	—
18. 3	7.7	9.3	0.83	5.0	1.54	—	—	—
19. 4	12.5	13.8	0.91	9.9	1.26	—	—	—
20. 5	20.9	21.2	0.99	19.1	1.09	—	—	—
21. 6	19.6	19.3	1.02	20.8	0.94	—	—	—
22. 7	13.7	12.6	1.08	15.7	0.87	—	—	—
23. 8	9.0	7.6	1.18	11.0	0.82	—	—	—
24. 9	4.8	3.9	1.23	6.3	0.76	—	—	—
25. 10 and more (11.35)	7.6	4.9	1.55	10.1	0.75	—	—	—
26. Total	100.0	100.0	1.00 (12.8)	100.0 (5.58)	1.00 (18.4)	—	—	—

Philippines, 1970–71

27. 1	1.1	1.8	0.61	0.3	3.67	1.0	0.4	2.75
28. 2	4.6	6.9	0.67	2.4	1.92	2.0	3.3	1.39
29. 3	8.8	11.6	0.76	6.0	1.47	2.58	7.1	1.24
30. 4	13.6	14.9	0.92	10.3	1.32	3.17	11.1	1.23
31. 5	13.9	14.6	0.95	12.7	1.09	3.76	13.0	1.07
32. 6	13.2	13.5	0.98	14.0	0.94	4.35	13.8	0.96
33. 7	12.3	11.6	1.06	14.0	0.88	4.93	13.5	0.91
34. 8	13.1	11.0	1.19	15.4	0.85	5.51	14.3	0.92
35. 9	6.4	5.6	1.15	8.7	0.74	6.10	8.1	0.79
36. 10 and more (11)	13.0	8.5	1.53	16.2	0.80	7.69	15.4	0.84
37. Total	100.0	100.0	1.00 (16.2)	100.0 (5.77)	1.00 (20.6)	4.24	100.0	1.00 (14.2)

Table 7.13. (cont.)

Notes: For sources see notes to Table 7.12. In calculating the number of children per family, in groups of families of differing size (for Philippines lines 27–37), we followed the procedure used for the United States (see notes to Table 7.7 above). The result of the first step, i.e., the assumption of no children in the one- and two-person groups, of one child per family in the group with three persons, two children in the group with four persons, and so on to eight in the group of 10 and more persons, yielded a total number of children that exceeded the actual in the ratio of 1.00 to 0.828. We then multiplied the assumed number of children per family in the size groups of families from three through 10 and more persons by this factor, securing the estimated number of children per family. Subtracting it from the total number of persons, and adding the number of children weighted by one-half, yielded the estimated number of consumers per family in lines 27–37, col. 6.

The entries in parentheses are: col. 3, lines 8, 15, 26, and 37, the TDMs for the distributions among households or families by income per household or family; col. 4, same lines, the average number of persons per household or family; col. 5, same lines, the TDMs for the distributions among households or families of differing size by income per household or family; col. 8, line 37, the TDM for the distribution among families of differing size by income per consumer.

distributions made by the large proportion of single-person units in the developed countries, compared with their low proportion in those less developed.

Second, in every country, except Israel, the income per household or family rises steadily as we move from the smaller to the larger household or family units (col. 3). In Israel the peak is reached at the four-person unit, and the average income declines in the classes of five and six and more persons. This may be because of the concentration of the larger households among Jews of Asian-African origin, groups that for other reasons have lower incomes than the families with heads of Israeli birth or of European-American origin. The rise in average income per unit with a rise in size of unit is the pattern we found for the United States and are likely to find in general.

Third, in all four countries, Israel included, income *per person* declines steadily and markedly as we move from the smaller to the larger households or families (col. 5). The same is true of per consumer income for the Philippines, with minor breaks among the larger units (col. 8, lines 27–36). This negative association between per person income and the size of the family or household, also observed for the United States, necessarily means, as already indicated, that in the distribution of persons by family income *per person*, the internal structure of the successive classes by income per person would be distinguished by the relative preponderance of persons in the *smaller* households or families in the *upper* brackets, and that of persons in the *larger* households or families in the *lower* per person income brackets.

It did not seem worthwhile to show the distributions among persons by family income per person calculated for the four countries from the cross classifications of families or households by both size of unit and income classes *within* size groups by a procedure similar to that used for Table 7.10 for the United States (we had 42 cells for Germany, direct data for Israel, 70 cells for Taiwan, and 70 cells for the Philippines).[15] But we do give in Table 7.14 the TDMs derived, for comparison with those in Tables 7.12 and 7.13.

15 The source for Israel provides a reclassification of households by income per person within the household. The results are summarized, with a fair amount of detail and showing the structure of families by size within classes of income per person, in table 12 (pp. 436–38) of my Tokyo Seminar paper. Table 15 of the same paper (pp. 446–47) shows the classification for Taiwan (1972) of persons by classes of income per person, derived from the cross-classification.

Table 7.14. *TDMs for distributions shown or implicit in Tables 7.12 and 7.13*

Country	Distribution by income per household or family (Table 7.12)		Distri- bution by income per person (3)	Disparities among size groups (Table 7.13)	
	Un- adjusted (1)	Adjusted for average size by income class (2)		Income per family (4)	Income per person (5)
1. Germany	56.2	33.4	47.4	32.0	13.0
2. Israel	52.6	46.0	59.4	20.2	38.6
3. Taiwan	42.2	30.6	41.6	12.8	18.4
4. Philippines	69.2	62.0	70.4	16.2	20.6

Three comments are appropriate. First, the inequality in the distribution by income per person (col. 3) is distinctly wider than that in the distribution of income per family or household merely adjusted for averages of persons per unit in the successive income classes (col. 2). Second, the changes in aggregate inequality, in the conversion from income per family to income per person, while not too large can be in different directions – and result in a different comparative picture as between two countries. Thus, while in column 1 the TDM for Germany is somewhat higher than that for Israel, in column 3 it is appreciably lower. Finally, the comparison confirms, as it must, the association between the differences in the aggregate inequality in columns 4 and 5 and those between the TDMs in columns 1 and 3. For Germany, the disparities in income per household among size-of-household groups were quite wide, with a TDM of 32.0, whereas the TDM for disparities in income per person among size-of-household groups was appreciably lower, 13.0; hence "subtraction" of the former and "addition" of the latter in the conversion from a distribution by income per household to that among persons by household income per person reduced the TDM from 56.2 to 47.4, about 9 points (not the 19-point differential between cols. 4 and 5). Conversely, in the case of Israel, the TDM for the disparities in income per person in column 5, at 38.6, was much larger than that for disparities in income per household in column 4, of 20.2; and the subtraction of the latter and the addition of the former meant a rise in the TDM from column 1 (52.6) to column 3

(59.4). The much narrower differences between columns 4 and 5 for Taiwan and the Philippines meant that the TDMs changed only slightly in the conversion from distributions by income per household or family in column 1 to those by income per person in column 3.

IV. Size of family and the life cycle

The size of a household or family unit changes with its life cycle, with changes in the age of its head, and with the change in the period since its formation. Children are born and added to the family for a number of years, and its size may also increase with addition of other blood- or marriage-related members as the age of the head and his economic position generally advances. Then, as children mature and leave the family, it tends to shrink. Thus, size differences among families or households may be closely associated with the age of head – the small units predominating either when the head is young and before the birth of children or when the head is old enough for the children to have reached adulthood and left the family, while the larger families are concentrated in the age-of-head classes that are in the time spans of bearing and rearing children.

Table 7.15 illustrates this association for households for which the cross-classification by size and age of head is directly available. Single-person households are heavily concentrated in the advanced age-of-head classes, with the share in households with head aged 55 and over as high as two-thirds. The two-person households also tend to be largely in the advanced age-of-head classes, the shares of heads 55 and over being almost six-tenths. By contrast, the larger households are concentrated in the middle age-of-head classes: the three-, four-, and five-person household shares in the age of head from 25 to 55 years old are 60, 80, and 90 percent, respectively. For the still larger households, those of six or seven and more (average number of persons, 8.27) the concentration is within a narrower range of age of head, from 35 to 55, with shares of 67 and 73 percent, respectively.

This association between the size of unit and the age of head within the life cycle means that whatever differences we observe among families or units by size – whether in income per family, per person, or per consumer – may reflect, in substantial part, the differences in such income within the life cycle of a given family or household rather than differences among families or households in total lifetime income. If we are interested in long-term levels of income, whether in the full life cycle or in long spans

Table 7.15. *Distribution of households by size (number of persons) and age of head, United States, March 1970*

Classes of households by number of persons	Age of head (%)						
	Total (millions) (1)	Below 25 (2)	25- 34.9 (3)	35- 44.9 (4)	45- 54.9 (5)	55- 64.9 (6)	65 and over (7)
1. 1	10.69	5.1	8.3	6.5	12.3	21.4	46.4
2. 2	18.13	9.3	10.1	6.4	16.2	27.0	31.0
3. 3	10.90	12.0	21.5	14.3	24.3	17.6	10.3
4. 4	9.94	5.6	32.1	26.8	23.9	8.6	3.0
5. 5	6.53	2.1	30.2	37.6	22.1	6.3	1.7
6. 6	3.50	1.4	24.0	45.4	21.7	5.5	2.0
7. 7 and more (8.27)	3.18	0.5	18.1	49.0	24.0	6.1	2.3
8. All households	62.87	6.8	18.5	18.6	19.5	17.1	19.5
9. Average income per household ($ thousands)	9.54	6.69	9.86	11.73	12.18	9.92	5.20

Note: Taken or calculated from source 2, tables 2 and 5 (pp. 12 and 15).

within it, the conventional cross-section distribution in income among families or units, by income per family, per person, or per consumer, is unrevealing. It is affected by income disparities among units of differing size and/or among families with different ages of head, disparities that reflect different phases within the life cycle that are easily compatible with perfect equality in total lifetime income. Two questions immediately arise. The first is more general. Should we, with our interest in the relation between economic growth and income inequalities, concern ourselves primarily with the distribution of lifetime family incomes? The second relates to the association between size of family and age of head, a more specific question but clearly important for the analysis of the observable size distributions of income and for the inferences from such analysis, particularly with respect to the demographic factors involved.

1. The first question bears upon the time span over which income ought to be covered and forces our attention to the general range of problems in the definition of income within the size distribution to be analyzed, problems that we have neglected so far. The discussion above did touch upon one problem – that of intrafamily and other services of the wife, a matter of some importance if the low income capacity of the husband forces full-time earning employment by the wife. It also touched

on the time-aspect problem in pointing out that measures of inequality for families grouped by characteristics (like size of family) that imply substantial offsetting within the classes of short-term transient elements in income should be compared with those for size distributions in which income has been appropriately adjusted to exclude such elements. But these comments were peripheral, and we completely ignored a third group of problems of income definition (in addition to those of inclusiveness and continuity over time) – that of establishing the net magnitude, net of all inputs *required* for production of income and not contributing to welfare or net consumption (with a particularly relevant task of adjusting income differentials among family groups for differentials in the cost of living, imposed by job location requirements).

But we return to the particular problem – the possibility of concentrating on lifetime incomes and neglecting the short-term changes, whether a single year's random disturbance, a cyclical deviation affecting large groups within the population of families but cancellable over a long period, or even long phases within the life span, longer than economic and related cycles. If no long-term continuous studies of identical groups or cohorts through their life cycles are available, and the few that may be at hand are unlikely to provide an adequate base for an inclusive size distribution of lifetime incomes of a population, one could try to derive such a distribution from the available cross-section studies. This could be done, at least approximately, by identifying cross-section differentials with phase of life-cycle differentials, adjusting for the time trend within the income record of relevant average family or household units and allowing for the effect of acceptable social discount rates on the present value of lifetime income, given the observed time patterns within the life span.[16]

The comment above implies a serious objection to, and criticism of, rather common attempts to derive long-term changes in the size distribution of income from cross-section distributions of families or households by income of a given year, or a series of years. Each of these cross-section distributions is affected by transitory income elements as well as by income disparities among size-of-family, age-of-head, and type-of-family

---

16 This technique is widely used in estimating the present value of lifetime earnings (see, e.g., U.S. Bureau of the Census, *Present Value of Estimated Lifetime Earnings*, Technical Paper no. 16 [Washington, D.C.: Government Printing Office, 1967], which applies it to earnings data available by age, sex, and race in the *Population Census of 1960*, covering incomes for 1959).

groupings that reflect demographic processes, the phases within the life span of a family. These may differ among countries or change over time without affecting the comparative distributions of lifetime family incomes. We shall argue toward the end of this paper that, given these elements in a cross-section size distribution, it may be far more enlightening to study income differentials among families characterized by the occupational or industrial attachment of their heads, with allowance for possible differences among them in family size, than to try to derive an approximation to long-term income levels from cross-section distributions in which the base of classification is the *current year's* income per family or household, or per person, or per consumer.

Still, one aspect of short-term changes in income must be recognized and kept in mind, even though only reasonable conjectures rather than empirical study may be feasible for some time to come. Assume that two families experience the same pattern of income over time and have the same lifetime income as well as the same present value of that income. Assume further that in the case of one family marked short-term disturbances, positive and negative, have occurred that cancel out in averages over successive phases of the lifetime income, whereas in the case of the other family the time path of the income is free from such ups and downs. The assumptions are clearly unrealistic, since the prevalence of disturbances usually makes for a lower *average* time path of lifetime incomes. But the point of these comments is that short-term changes in income have a significant welfare implication. To use a reasonable illustration, one of the positive aspects of rising productivity and more advanced technology in the agricultural sectors of the less developed countries lies in greater protection against the vagaries of the weather and short-term crop failures. When the average income per person or per consumer is low, the negative impact of short-term failures may be far greater than the positive impact of quantitatively compensating short-term successes. Moreover, short-term breakdowns have often been the cause of major economic and social displacements that have had major long-term effects. Concentration on long-term or lifetime incomes may lead to a neglect of short-term income differentials and changes that may have lasting effects. But, in the present connection, one can only note the point and concentrate on the effects of demographic variables on the income differentials within the customary size distribution cross sections as a basis for caution in assuming that the latter reveal long-term or lifetime income differentials.

2. The second question, whether the association between the size of

family or household and age of head is so close that the two demographic characteristics are really one, was already answered in Table 7.15. While the table illustrated the existence of a significant association, it also indicated that the association was not so close as to bar substantial variation – cases where small units were substantially represented among age-of-head groups of, say, 45 through 54 years of age which otherwise were fairly heavily dominated by larger households. But a more detailed answer is provided in Table 7.16, which presents a cross-classification of families or units by the two characteristics – size of unit and age of head – permitting more effective observation of the extent to which each variable is independent and providing a basis for further analysis of some implications. The table involves a fair amount of estimation described in the notes.

The evidence in lines 1–8 repeats that for households in Table 7.15, except that here we deal with families and unrelated individuals. The larger units, as already indicated, are found mostly in the childbearing and child-rearing phases of a family life span (i.e., with heads of ages ranging from the mid-20s to the mid-50s or mid-60s). The smaller units are largely in the upper age-of-head classes, particularly marked for the two-person families, which suggests the addition of a child in the early years of marriage shifting the family into the three-person or larger size.

Data on the distribution of the number of *persons* in the different size groups of units (lines 9–14), rather than on the distribution of units, suggest the same results, as they must if we consider the distribution of size-of-unit groups by age of head rather than that of age of head by size-of-unit groups. The latter will be taken up when we deal directly with the age-of-head characteristics in the next section.

The new evidence in Table 7.16 relates to income, per unit or per person, in the cross classification by size of unit and age of head. The average income levels on a per unit basis for size-of-unit groups (cols. 1–7, lines 19–24 reading down each column) reveals a general pattern of income differentials per unit: the per unit income rises from the low at the one-person group to a peak, usually in the five-person group, and then declines slightly to the group of six and more persons. (The deviations from this movement in the larger unit groups in col. 1, below 25 years of age, and col. 6, 65 and over, are due to the lack of a basis for detailed estimation.) In short, the general rise per unit or per family income from lows for the small units to highs for the large units is confirmed *within* age-of-head groups.

However, for income per person, the movement for size-of-unit groups

Table 7.16. *1969 money income, per family (or unit) and per person, age of head, and size of unit cross classified, United States, March 1970*

Class of units by number of persons	Under 25 (1)	25–34 (2)	35–44 (3)	45–54 (4)	55–64 (5)	65 and over (6)	Total (7)
Age of head (family and unrelated individuals)							
Units (millions)							
1. 1	1.74	1.54	1.09	1.74	2.72	5.62	14.45
2. 2	1.55	1.75	1.11	2.91	4.82	5.52	17.65
3. 3	1.24	2.32	1.54	2.64	1.91	1.04	10.69
4. 4	0.53	3.20	2.67	2.35	0.84	0.28	9.88
5. 5	0.13	1.96	2.44	1.39	0.40	0.11	6.44
6. 6 and more	0.07	1.40	3.10	1.49	0.38	0.13	6.58
7. Families (lines 2–6)	3.52	10.64	10.85	10.78	8.36	7.08	51.24
8. All units (lines 1–6)	5.26	12.18	11.94	12.52	11.08	12.70	65.69
Persons (millions)							
9. 1	1.74	1.54	1.09	1.74	2.72	5.62	14.45
10. 2	3.10	3.50	2.21	5.81	9.65	11.03	35.31
11. 3	3.74	6.97	4.61	7.91	5.73	3.11	32.06
12. 4	2.12	12.80	10.68	9.41	3.38	1.14	39.52
13. 5	0.65	9.82	12.20	6.98	2.00	0.53	32.18
14. 6 and more	0.46	9.83	21.69	10.46	2.67	1.37	46.48
15. Families	10.07	42.92	51.39	40.57	23.42	17.17	185.54
16. Persons per family	2.86	4.03	4.74	3.76	2.80	2.43	3.62
17. All units	11.81	44.46	52.48	42.31	26.14	22.79	199.99
18. Persons per unit	2.24	3.65	4.40	3.40	2.36	1.79	3.04
Money income per unit ($ thousands)							
19. 1	3.16	6.74	6.48	5.56	4.61	2.88	4.25
20. 2	7.03	9.75	11.74	11.35	9.97	6.00	8.79
21. 3	6.54	9.26	11.15	13.22	11.60	8.72	10.56
22. 4	6.97	10.25	12.34	14.42	12.66	10.30	11.86
23. 5	6.97	10.36	12.47	14.80	12.99	10.30	12.27
24. 6 and more	6.97	9.85	11.86	14.11	12.39	10.30	11.89
25. Families	6.84	9.94	11.97	12.93	11.35	6.72	10.58
26. All units	5.62	9.54	11.47	11.91	9.71	5.02	9.19
Money income per person ($ thousands)							
27. 1	3.16	6.74	6.48	5.56	4.61	2.88	4.25
28. 2	3.51	4.87	5.87	5.68	4.98	3.00	4.39
29. 3	2.18	3.09	3.72	4.40	3.87	2.91	3.52
30. 4	1.74	2.56	3.08	3.61	3.17	2.58	2.96
31. 5	1.39	2.07	2.49	2.96	2.60	2.06	2.45

Table 7.16 *(cont.)*

Class of units by number of persons	Age of head (family and unrelated individuals)						
	Under 25 (1)	25–34 (2)	35–44 (3)	45–54 (4)	55–64 (5)	65 and over (6)	Total (7)
32. 6 and more	1.00	1.41	1.69	2.02	1.77	1.03	1.68
33. Families	2.39	2.47	2.53	3.44	4.05	2.77	2.92
34. All units	2.50	2.61	2.61	3.50	4.12	2.80	3.02

Notes: Data are taken, calculated, or estimated from sources 1 and 2. For one-person units, i.e., unrelated individuals, in lines 1, 9, 19, and 27, the data were given directly in table 17 (pp. 35–41) of source 1.

For families the basic source is table 20 (pp. 49–51) of source 1, which shows a cross classification of age of head, type of family (husband–wife, male head, female head), and the families by number of persons. But the age-of-head classification does not distinguish between the 25–34 and 35–44 age classes and between the 45–54 and 55–64 age classes, thus losing important detail on age movement during the life cycle. Detail is also lacking on the number-of-persons classes, because for age of head below 25 years of age, and 65 years and over, source 1 shows, as the top size category, that of four persons and more (rather than of six persons and more). We had to estimate the number of families and persons, and average income per family, for age-of-head classes *within* the 25–44 and 45–64-year spans, and for size classes above three persons for the young and old age-of-head groups.

For estimating the details on the number of families and persons, the base was provided by source 2, table 5 (p. 15). The cross-classification of households of two and more persons by the more detailed classification by age of head was used to estimate, first, the breakdown between the two age classes of families of different size within the 25–44 and 45–64 age-of-head categories in source 1 and, second, to approximate the number of families of four, five, and six and more persons within the under 25 and 65 and over age-of-head classes. The latter was possible because table 5 in source 2 shows the average number of persons for each age-of-head class. In general, the allocation of families into more detailed age-of-head or number-of-person classes followed the plausible assumption that the relative differentials shown among size classes of households of two and more would apply to the same size classes of families.

The estimation of income per family for the additional classes by age of head, or by number of persons, began with those shown for the wider classes in table 20 of source 1. We then assumed that the income per family of, say, two persons in the 25–34 and 35–44 age-of-head classes could be derived by applying to the income for the two-person family in the 25–44 age class interpolating ratios based on the relationship of income per family in the 25–34 and 35–44 age-of-head classes for *all* families (available in table 17 of source 1). There may be some errors in this assumption, but they are likely to be minor, relative to the information secured on the movement of family income over time. For the final estimation, of income per family in the additional size classes in the under 25 and 65 and over age-of-head groups, the same average income (derived from table 20 of source 1) was assigned to the groups of four, five, and six and more persons within the under 25 age-of-head group. This assumption seemed justified because for the 25–44 and 45–64 age-of-head groups, table 20 in source 1 showed only minor differences in the income per family among the classes of four, five, and six and more persons. These means, for the 25–44 age-of-head group, were (in $ thousands) 11.21, 11.52, and 11.23; for the 45–64 age-of-head group, 13.99, 14.39, and 13.76.

The average number of persons per family of six persons and more (line 14), derived in the estimation, was roughly seven persons for all the age-of-head groups except that with head aged 65 and over, which averaged 10 persons. The latter group is numerically quite small, and even a major error in the estimate of number of persons would not weigh much in the total. The average number of persons for all families of six persons and more came out to 7.06.

within age-of-head classes is downward from small to large units, confirming the negative association between size of unit and per person income. In every column, the peak of per person income is either at the one- or two-person unit, followed by quite a steady decline to the lowest per person level in the six and more size-of-unit class (lines 27–32). And the decline within every column is quite marked, to a third or less than a third of the peak. The repetition of the income patterns, observed above for size-of-unit groups without any distinction of age of head, within age-of-head category here is clear evidence that, while the two demographic characteristics are correlated, the association is not close enough to remove the effects of one by standardizing for the other.

Still, one should note some effects of the association, and for simplicity we concentrate on the families, setting the one-person, unrelated-individuals group aside. We then find that while income per family (lines 20–24) tends to rise from smaller to larger units within the age-of-head columns, in the below 25 age-of-head column per family income shows little change with the rise in size, and similar variations from the trough at two persons to the peak at five persons are in a range from 1.0 to 1.06 in the 25–34 and 35–44 age groups, from 1.0 to 1.30 in the 45–54 and 55–64 age groups, and as high as 1.0 to 1.72 in the 65 and over age group. The weighted average of these ranges (using the shares of families in the successive age-of-head groups in the total) is 1.0–1.14, whereas in column 7 the range is from 1.0 to 1.40 (lines 20–23). Thus the overall range in income per family from the two-person to the five-person level, which *includes* the effect of association with age-of-head variable, is wider than the range in per family income when the age-of-head variable is removed.

In the case of income per person, and observing the *decline* from the peak at the two-person family to the trough at the family of six and more persons, we find that this decline is 72 percent of the peak for the under 25 age group, 71 percent for the 25–34 and 35–44 groups, 64 percent for the 45–54 and 55–64 groups, and 66 percent for the 65 and over group. The weighted average of these declines, using the proportions of persons in the age-of-head classes in total persons in families (line 14), works out to 67 percent, whereas that in column 7 is only 62 percent (lines 28–32). Here the effect of the association is to *damp* the decline in per person income from the two-person family to that of six and more persons observed within each age-of-head class separately.

V. Family or unit size and income differentials
by age of head

In turning to the differentials introduced into the size distribution of income by distinction of age of head (already revealed in Table 7.16), we begin by noting some ambiguity in that characteristic. As already indicated, the one person in the family recognized in the U.S. data as head of the family is usually the person so regarded by the members of the family – with the important proviso that in husband–wife families the husband is automatically classified as the head so long as he is resident with the family at the time of the survey. And "married couples related to the head of a family (and residing with him) are included in the head's family and are not classified as separate families."[17] If the head of the family is thus identified either as the husband of the couple (older couple if two related couples reside together) or as another person so recognized by members of the family, what does such headship or the age of the head mean? Does it mean that he or she is the earner of the major part of the family income, or the one who plays the major role in the family's economic decisions or plans, or the one whose age is a most important datum for expecting associated differentials in family size or income or both?

The answer, for the family structure prevalent in an economically developed country like the United States, is that the head as identified in husband–wife families (by far the dominant type) reflects all three elements. But these three elements may be only partially or obscurely represented by the head as identified. The husband in the husband–wife family is not always the major earner; he may not be the main decision maker on some aspects of the family's long- or short-term economic actions, for example, with respect to allocation of consumption or educational plans for the children. And for gauging the age of the family, particularly its size as affected by the number of children, the age of the wife may be a better index than that of the husband. In less industrialized countries, with a different structure of the family and less separation between the older and the middle-age generation, the husband of the oldest couple may be designated the head, although he is neither the major earner nor the main decision maker, and his age is not a good indication of the size of the combined family unit.

17 Source 1, p. 8.

Detailed data on the size and structure of families and units, combined with age of head, are at hand only for the United States, and it would be a rewarding task of further research to look for and organize similar data for other countries, particularly for a few less developed. For the present we examine the data for the United States, even though some important details on the type of family, distinguishing husband–wife, male-head, and particularly female-head families, are lacking.

Table 7.17 shows that the average size of the family varies substantially with differences in the age of head – from less than three persons per family for the under 25 group to a peak of almost five persons per family in the group with heads 35–44 years old, and then down to about 2.5 persons per family in the class with heads 65 and over (line 16). With the unrelated individuals added primarily at the extreme age-of-head groups, under 25 and 65 and over (line 4), the size differences in persons per unit amplify the swing shown by the age differences in persons per family; the movement is from 2.2 persons per unit in the under 25 age-of-head class to a peak of about 4.5 in the 35–44 age-of-head class, and then a drop to 1.8 persons per unit in the 65 and over age-of-head class (line 21). Such size differences in family or unit, with changes in age of head, are obviously relevant to the income differentials in per family or per unit income associated with age-of-head classes, in terms of either a larger number of earners and/or a larger number of consumers.

Lines 1–15 reveal the age structure of members of families for different age-of-head classes. As might have been expected, the rise in the size of the family to a peak at the 35–44 class is due largely to children under 18. Of the 1.88 rise in persons per family (line 16, cols. 1–3), the rise in children per family accounts for as much as 1.58, or eight-tenths (line 19, cols. 1–3); and, in the decline in the number of persons per family from the peak to a trough for the age-of-head group of 65 and over, or 2.31 persons per family, the drop in the number of children, 2.41, more than balances it. Yet there is a slight movement in the size of the family in terms of number of adults, from somewhat less than two persons per family in the under 25 age-of-head class (reflecting the presence of non–husband-wife families with children) to a peak of almost 2.5 adults per family in the 45–54 age-of-head class, and a decline to about 2.25 adults per family in the 65 and over class (line 18). The addition of unrelated individuals accentuates somewhat the swing in number of adults per unit when observed for the successive age-of-head classes (line 23).

With these size differences among families or units by age of head

Table 7.17. *Internal structure by age and size differentials, families and all units by age of head, United States, March 1970*

	Age of head						
	Under 25 (1)	25–34 (2)	35–44 (3)	45–54 (4)	55–64 (5)	65 and over (6)	Total (7)
Internal structure by age							
1. Families (millions)	3.57	10.46	10.88	10.85	8.35	7.03	51.14
2. Persons in line 1 (millions)	10.25	41.46	50.84	40.25	23.28	16.72	182.80
3. Unrelated individuals (millions)	1.75	1.54	1.09	1.74	2.72	5.62	14.45
4. Line 3 as % of line 2	17	4	2	4	12	34	8
Shares in line 2, age classes of persons (members) (%)							
5. Under 6	28	26	10	4	2	1	10
6. 6–13	3	23	30	16	6	3	17
7. 14–17	3	2	14	14	7	2	8
8. 18–24	62	6	4	12	9	3	10
9. 25–34	2	42	6	2	5	3	12
10. 35–44	1	1	33	8	2	4	12
11. 45–54	1	0	1	41	12	5	11
12. 55–64	0	0	1	1	53	13	10
13. 65 and over	0	0	1	2	4	66	10
14. Classes younger than head	34	57	64	56	43	34	—
15. Classes older than head	4	1	3	3	4	0	—
Size differentials, families							
16. Persons per family (from Table 7.16)	2.86	4.03	4.74	3.76	2.80	2.43	3.62
17. Members under 18 (%)	34.1	50.5	54.0	33.8	14.7	6.0	38.3
18. Adults per family	1.88	1.99	2.18	2.49	2.39	2.28	2.23
19. Children per family	0.98	2.04	2.56	1.27	0.41	0.15	1.39
20. Consumers per family	2.37	3.01	3.46	3.12	2.60	2.36	2.93
Size differentials, all units							
21. Persons per unit (from Table 7.16)	2.24	3.65	4.40	3.46	2.36	1.79	3.04

Table 7.17 *(cont.)*

| | Age of head | | | | | | |
	Under 25 (1)	25–34 (2)	35–44 (3)	45–54 (4)	55–64 (5)	65 and over (6)	Total (7)
22. Members under 18 (%)	29.2	48.7	52.9	32.4	13.2	4.5	35.5
23. Adults per unit	1.59	1.87	2.08	2.34	2.05	1.71	1.96
24. Children per unit	0.65	1.78	2.32	1.12	0.31	0.08	1.08
25. Consumers per unit	1.92	2.76	3.24	2.90	2.20	1.75	2.50

Notes: Lines 1, 2, 5–15 from Bureau of the Census, *1970 Census of Population, Subject Reports, Family Composition,* PC (2) 4A (Washington, D.C.: Government Printing Office, 1973), p. 55, table 7. Lines 3, 16, and 21 are either from Table 7.16 above or from source 1, table 17. Lines 17 and 33 are by more detailed calculation from the data underlying lines 1–15. Lines 18–20 and 23–25 are by computation from the lines above.

Although the numbers of families and persons in the 1970 census source differ from those taken from source 1 and used in Table 7.16, the differences are slight, and it seemed warranted to apply age proportions derived for age-of-head classes of families in the census to the estimates of families (or units) by age of head from source 1.

Also, in source 1 the youngest age group (for heads of families and for unrelated individuals, table 17 [p. 35]) is designated 14–24. We identified it with the age group 18–24 in the *Census of Population* data on the assumption that the proportion of heads of families or of unrelated individuals in ages 14–17 within the total 14–24 age class must be minute.

established, we turn to the income differentials (Table 7.18). The findings can be briefly summarized.

First, income per family or per unit shows a marked rise from the low for the under 25 age-of-head class to a peak for the 45–54 class, and then down to a trough in the 65 and over class (lines 1 and 14). The swing is from a trough to a peak about twice the initial level and then down to a terminal trough about half or less than half of the peak. Given this movement of per family or per unit income and the distributions of families and units in lines 5 and 18, the resulting aggregate inequalities are quite substantial, measured by TDMs of 17.4 and 23.6 and Gini coefficients of 0.112 and 0.152 – for the family and unit distributions, respectively, the inclusion of unrelated individuals widening as usual the inequality in the distribution by income *per unit* (lines 10 and 23).

It should be stressed that in the distribution of income per family or per unit the age-of-head variable contributes most inequality at the extreme age classes – under 25 and 65 and over. Thus, in line 10 for families, 7.5

Table 7.18. *Income differentials, families and all units by age of head, United States (Money income in 1969)*

| | Age of head | | | | | | |
	Under 25 (1)	25–34 (2)	35–44 (3)	45–54 (4)	55–64 (5)	65 and over (6)	Total (7)
			Families				
Income relatives							
1. Per family	0.64	0.95	1.13	1.24	1.07	0.64	10.58
2. Per person	0.83	0.85	0.87	1.18	1.38	0.95	2.92
3. Per adult	0.74	1.05	1.16	1.09	1.01	0.62	4.74
4. Per consumer	0.82	0.91	0.96	1.15	1.21	0.79	3.61
% in number of							
5. Families	7.0	20.7	21.2	21.1	16.2	13.8	51.2
6. Persons	5.4	23.1	27.7	21.9	12.6	9.3	185.5
7. Adults	5.8	18.5	20.6	23.5	17.4	14.2	114.5
8. Children	4.8	30.5	39.1	19.3	4.8	1.5	71.0
9. Consumers	5.5	21.4	25.1	22.5	14.4	11.1	150.0
Disparities in shares, distributions, among							
10. Families	−2.5	−1.2	2.8	4.7	1.2	−5.0	17.4 (0.112)
11. Persons	−0.9	−3.6	−3.7	3.9	4.8	−0.5	17.4 (0.101)
12. Adults	−1.3	1.0	3.4	2.3	0	−5.4	13.4 (0.079)
13. Consumers	−1.0	−1.9	−1.1	3.3	3.0	−2.3	12.6 (0.077)
			All units				
Income relatives							
14. Per unit	0.62	1.04	1.25	1.30	1.06	0.54	9.19
15. Per person	0.85	0.86	0.87	1.17	1.37	0.92	3.02
16. Per adult	0.77	1.08	1.19	1.12	1.01	0.63	4.68
17. Per consumer	0.82	0.94	0.97	1.15	1.20	0.77	3.68
% in number of							
18. Units	8.1	18.4	18.2	19.1	16.9	19.3	65.7
19. Persons	5.9	22.2	26.2	21.2	13.1	11.4	200.0
20. Adults	6.5	17.7	19.1	22.2	17.6	16.9	129.0
21. Children	4.8	30.5	39.1	19.3	4.8	1.5	71.0
22. Consumers	6.1	20.4	23.4	21.6	14.9	13.6	164.5
Disparities in shares, distributions among							
23. Units	−3.1	0.7	4.5	5.7	0.9	−8.7	23.6 (0.152)

Table 7.18 *(cont.)*

| | Age of head | | | | | | |
	Under 25 (1)	25–34 (2)	35–44 (3)	45–54 (4)	55–64 (5)	65 and over (6)	Total (7)
24. Persons	−0.9	−3.1	−3.5	3.6	4.8	−0.9	16.8 (0.092)
25. Adults	−1.5	1.4	3.6	2.6	0.2	−6.3	15.6 (0.100)
26. Consumers	−1.1	−1.3	−0.7	3.2	3.0	−3.1	12.4 (0.078)

Notes: Taken or calculated from Tables 7.16 and 7.17.
The entries in col. 7 are as follows: lines 1 and 14 – income per family or per unit ($ thousands); lines 2 and 15 – income per person ($ thousands); lines 3 and 16 – income per adult member of family or unit ($ thousands); lines 4 and 14 – income per consumer (i.e., with children under 18 at half-weight, $ thousands); lines 5 and 18 – total number of families or units (millions); lines 6 and 19 – total number of persons in all families or all units (millions); lines 7 and 20 – total number of adults (i.e., aged 18 and over) in families or units (millions); lines 8 and 21 – total years of age (millions); lines 9 and 22 – total number of consumers, families, or all units (millions); lines 10–13 and 23–26 – TDMs and Gini coefficients in parentheses.

negative points, of a total sum of disparities of 17.4 points, come from these two age classes (cols. 1 and 6); in lines 23, for all units, the two classes contribute all of the negative disparities to the large TDM (see cols. 1, 6, and 7). Were we to eliminate these two classes (i.e., set their frequency at 0) and recalculate the shares in numbers of families or units and in total income, the TDM for families (line 10) would decline to 8.0, or less than half; and that for all units (line 23) would drop to 9.8, again less than half. It follows that, all other conditions being equal, *changes* or *differences* in the proportions of families or units in these extreme age-of-head classes have a major effect on aggregate inequality in the size distribution by income per family or unit: so long as the income relatives for the under 25 and over 65 age-of-head classes are low, their increasing or larger weight makes for wider inequality. Thus, trends in the structure of families or households by age-of-head classes would produce trends in the inequality in the size distribution, even though *lifetime* income of a cohort and the distribution of lifetime incomes would remain unaffected.

Second, the number of persons per family or unit changes with shifts in age of head, in a time pattern similar to that of income per family or per unit (compare lines 16 and 21 of Table 7.17 with lines 1 and 14 of Table 7.18). Hence, when we shift to income per person, both the pattern and amplitude of the movement with age of head are affected. Both among families and among units income per person is below the average and almost constant through the first three age-of-head classes, rises significantly only upon reaching the 45–54 age-of-head class when the number of children in the family declines, attains a peak in the 55–64 age class, and then declines again in the 65 and over age class (lines 2 and 15). Inequality is slightly lower than that contributed by income differentials among age-of-head classes in income per family or per unit; but the interesting change is in the *sources* of inequality. The major contributions to aggregate inequality in per person income differentials are in the 25–34 and 35–44 age-of-head classes, which account, in the case of families, for 7.3 negative points out of a TDM of 17.4 (line 11) and, in the case of all units, for 6.6 negative points out of a TDM of 16.8 (line 24).

It should be stressed that we deal here with effects of the *average* number of persons per family or per unit in the different age-of-head classes. Ideally we should be dealing with variations in the size of family or unit *within* the age-of-head classes as we did for Table 7.16 above. Yet no such data are at hand for countries other than the United States, and we need some basis for observing the results of measurement of the type presented in Table 7.18 and commonly used in this and other countries. But it should be stressed that not all of a single cohort of families will necessarily move from having almost three members per family in the age-of-head class under 25 to four persons per family for the next age-of-head class, and so on. Some families may stay at the two-person level throughout their lifetime span, others may move from two to four and six persons and down again. We shall come back in the next section to an illustrative discussion of the effects of changes in number of persons (or consumers) for different cohorts in their lifetime income and its time pattern, but it is useful to stress at this point that the lifetime span of income per person suggested in Table 7.18 is in essence an *average* of different lifetime spans for families (or units) comprising cohorts with differing patterns of changes in number of persons through the successive phases by age of head.

Third, relatives of income per adult (lines 3 and 16) rise markedly from the low age-of-head classes to a peak in the 35–44 age class and drop to a particularly low level in the 65 and over class. The early peaking is also suggested by the average income per *male income recipient*.[18] The

18 See *ibid.*, table 45 (p. 97) and Table 7.2 above.

sharp reduction to the low levels of the 65 and over age class is associated largely with the withdrawal of a large proportion of the adults in these ages from active employment and partly with a marked decline in per adult income even when employed. Unlike any of the other classifications, that by income per adult shows the major source of inequality to lie in the oldest age-of-head bracket of 65 and over – which accounts for 5.4 negative points out of a TDM of 13.4 for families (line 12) and for 6.3 negative points out of a TDM of 15.6 for all units (line 25).

Fourth, and finally, we find that the income relatives per consumer are quite similar to the income relatives per person, with low but rising levels in the first three age-of-head classes, a peaking in the 55–64 age class when the responsibility for children has been much reduced but earning power still remains high, and a final trough in the 65 and over class (see lines 4 and 17). And, clearly, what has been said about the *average* nature of the movements shown in Table 7.18 (as compared with the more disaggregated picture in Table 7.16) would apply to the age-of-head differentials of income per consumer as they did to those of income per person.

An interesting aspect of the distinction between adults and children under 18 is their different distributions among families or units with different ages of head. Lines 8 and 21 indicate that children are heavily concentrated in two classes, age of head 25–34 and 35–44, accounting for almost seven-tenths, with the third age class, 45–54, accounting for almost 20 percent more. The implication is that the younger children, say under 6 or under 13 (see Table 7.17) are concentrated in the early age-of-head classes, probably *not* including the 45–54 class. But these three early age-of-head classes are all characterized by lower than countrywide income per consumer. By contrast, the adults are more evenly distributed among all age-of-head classes and are thus represented at both relatively high and relatively low income per consumer levels. If we were to limit adults to age-of-head classes below 65 years of age and compare them with children below their teens, the average income per consumer derived for children would be significantly below that of average income per consumer derived for adults.[19] This is another aspect of the negative

19 See discussion in my paper, "Income-related Differences in Natural Increase: Bearing on Growth and Distribution of Income," in *Nations and Households in Economic Growth: Essays in Honor of Moses Abramovitz*, ed. Paul David and Melvin Reder (New York: Academic Press, 1974), pp. 127–46, particularly, p. 133, table 2.

association between the size of family or unit and per consumer income, given the fact that the size of the family or unit is heavily determined by the number of children in it.

Table 7.18 presents measures of inequality generated by the age-of-head component, comparable to the measures generated by the size-of-family or unit component discussed in the preceding sections. In Table 7.16 we have a cross-classification of age of head and size of family or unit, which permits us to calculate the *joint* contribution of the two components to inequality in the distribution of income, either by income per family or unit, or by income per person. Table 7.19 presents a summary of the inequality measures for the total size distribution, for that associated with each of the two demographic components and for that of the two combined.

The 30 or 36 cells of Table 7.16 constituted the raw materials for the computation of the joint effect of the size-of-family or unit and age-of-head components, which, when arrayed either by income per family or unit, or per person, yielded the classification in Table 7.19, lines 1–6 and 11–16. These may be compared with similar classifications by either income per family or unit, or per person, available for the total size distribution (Tables 7.5 and 7.10), or with classifications by size of family or unit and age of head separately, in Tables 7.8 and 7.18.

Three observations may be made concerning the measures of inequality brought together in lines 7–10 and 17–20.

To begin with income per family or per unit, we find that the inclusion of unrelated individuals inflates the contribution of the size component, but in that for units the inequality introduced by the size and the age-of-head components is about the same (see Table 7.19, lines 8 and 9, cols. 2 and 4). Second, when we shift to income per person, differences between results for families and all units are much reduced, and the inequality contribution of the size component is distinctly greater than that of the age-of-head component (see Table 7.19, lines 18 and 19, cols. 1–4). Finally, because of the significant positive correlation between size of family or unit and age of head, the combined measures of inequality are much smaller than the sums of the separate measures. Thus in panel A, the TDMs in line 10, columns 1 and 2, are short of the combined totals in lines 8 and 9 by 10.4 out of 29.0 points and 16.6 out of 49.2 points, roughly a third; for the Gini coefficients, those in line 10 fall short of the sums in lines 8 and 9 by 0.049 out of 0.181 and 0.111 out of 0.319, somewhat over a third. In panel B, the combined TDMs fall short of the

Table 7.19. *Income differentials by size of unit or family and age of head combined, 1969 money income in the United States*

A. *In income per family or per unit ($ thousands)*

	Below 6.0 (1)	6.00–6.99 (2)	7.00–9.49 (3)	9.50–9.99 (4)	10.00–10.99 (5)	11.00–11.99 (6)	12.00–12.99 (7)	13.0 and over (8)	Total (9)
Families									
1. Number of families (%)	0	14.6	9.6	15.6	11.1	20.6	13.1	15.4	100.0 (51.2)
2. Total income (%)	0	8.5	7.7	14.6	10.8	22.5	15.5	20.4	100.0 (541.7)
3. Disparities (line 2 – line 1)	0	–6.1	–1.9	–1.0	–0.3	1.9	2.4	5.0	18.6 (0.132)
All Units									
4. Number of units (%)	18.0	15.4	7.5	12.1	8.6	16.1	10.3	12.0	100.0 (65.7)
5. Total income (%)	7.3	10.6	6.9	13.1	9.7	20.2	13.9	18.3	100.0 (603.6)
6. Disparities (line 5 – line 4)	–10.7	–4.8	–0.6	1.0	1.1	4.1	3.6	6.3	32.6 (0.208)

Comparison of TDMs and Gini coefficients, distributions by income per family or per unit

	TDMs		Gini coefficients	
	Families (1)	Units (2)	Families (3)	Units (4)
7. Total size distribution, Table 7.5, lines 21 and 22	48.2	56.2	0.337	0.390
8. Size of family or unit component, Table 7.8, lines 4 and 16	11.6	25.6	0.069	0.167
9. Age-of-head component, Table 7.18, lines 10 and 23	17.4	23.6	0.112	0.152
10. Both components combined, lines 3 and 6 above	18.6	32.6	0.132	0.208

B. In income per person ($ thousands)

	1.0–1.49 (1)	1.50–1.99 (2)	2.0–2.49 (3)	2.50–2.94 (4)	2.95–3.49 (5)	3.50–4.49 (6)	4.50 and over (7)	Total (8)
Families								
11. Number of persons (%)	6.6	14.3	19.8	10.3	21.0	16.6	11.4	100.0 (185.6)
12. Total income (%)	3.1	8.3	14.9	9.3	21.9	22.0	20.5	100.0 (541.8)
13. Disparities (line 12 − line 11)	−3.5	−6.0	−4.9	−1.0	0.9	5.4	9.1	30.8 (0.210)
All units								
14. Number of persons (%)	6.2	13.2	18.4	12.3	20.4	15.4	14.1	100.0 (200.0)
15. Total income (%)	2.8	7.5	13.4	10.9	20.7	19.7	25.0	100.0 (603.0)
16. Disparities (line 15 − line 14)	−3.4	−5.7	−5.0	−1.4	3.0	4.3	10.9	31.0 (0.205)

Table 7.19 (cont.)

Comparison of TDMs and Gini coefficients, distributions of persons by family or unit income per person

	TDMs		Gini coefficients	
	Families (1)	Units (2)	Families (3)	Units (4)
17. Total distribution, Table 7.10, lines 3 and 6	53.8	55.4	0.371	0.384
18. Size of family or unit component, Table 7.8, lines 8 and 19	27.0	27.8	0.187	0.188
19. Age of head component, Table 7.18, lines 11 and 24	17.4	16.8	0.101	0.092
20. Both components combined, lines 13 and 16 above	30.8	31.0	0.210	0.205

Notes: The distributions in lines 1–6 and 11–16 were calculated from cells in the cross-classification of families and units by size (number of persons) and age of head, given in Table 7.16. For each of 36 cells (in the cross-classification for units) or 30 cells (in that for families), the table shows number of units or families, number of persons, income per unit or family, and income per person. Arraying the cells in increasing order of income per family or unit, or of income per person, we classify the cells by the income classes shown and summarize the frequencies and the income totals for the seven or six income classes distinguished. The income classes were defined in such a way as not to lose much variance in the calculation of the TDMs.
Entries in parentheses in col. 9 of A and col. 8 of B are as follows: *lines 1, 4, 11, and 14*: totals of families or units and totals of persons (millions); *lines 2, 5, 12, and 15*: totals of income ($ billions); *lines 3, 6, 13, and 16*: the Gini coefficients.

sums of the separate measures in lines 18 and 19, by 13.6 points out of a sum of 44.4 and 13.4 points out of a sum of 44.6 – somewhat less than a third; and the combined Gini coefficients fall short of the sum of separate coefficients by 0.078 out of 0.288 and 0.075 out of 0.280, somewhat less and somewhat more than a third.

While this evidence on the significance of the inequality contribution of the size and age-of-head factors, and of their intercorrelation, is convincing and interesting, a proper gauge of the magnitudes involved – in comparison with the total size distribution – requires additive measures of variance and more elaborate calculations than are feasible here.

In turning to the evidence on effects of age of head on the size distribution of income in other countries (Table 7.20), we repeat the warning as to the exploratory and illustrative character of this effort, the limitations imposed by lack of data that could perhaps be assembled with further search, and the biases in the present data that could perhaps be corrected with further effort. Despite the constraints, we may still discern relevant differences and formulate questions that will help to guide later work.

Of the three countries covered in Table 7.20, we have data on the size of family or household, by age of head, for Israel alone. The income per household differentials by age of head are not unlike those in the United States, but with a deeper trough in the advanced age-of-head group of 65 and over (line 3, col. 6). The distribution of households by age of head is also similar to that in the United States, except for a smaller share of young households and a larger share of the old (line 2). These differences in income relatives and in the distribution of households by age of head account for the major contribution of the old age-of-head class to the fairly substantial TDM, over 8 negative points out of a TDM of 18 (line 4, cols. 6 and 7).

But because of the swing in the number of persons with changes in age of head that is familiar from the evidence for the United States, the conversion to per person income reduces the age-of-head differentials substantially, with the TDM dropping from 18.0 to 10.8, and changes the time pattern. Curiously, the negative deviation is largest in the 35–44 age-of-head class (in the United States it was in the 25–34 and 35–44 classes; see Table 7.18, lines 11 and 24). Most intriguing, the low relative of income per person in that age class suggests that the large size of the household, implying many children, produces a substantial decline in per person income. But, generally, with allowance for the specific age and country-of-origin composition of the Israel urban population, the pattern

Table 7.20. *Income differentials, families or households by age of head, selected countries*

	A. *Israel, 1968–69, urban households*						
	Age						
	18–24 (1)	25–34 (2)	35–44 (3)	45–54 (4)	55–64 (5)	65 and over (6)	Total (7)
1. Total income (%)	2.1	17.5	26.1	25.3	19.8	9.2	100.0
2. Number of households (%)	3.0	16.4	22.8	21.1	19.4	17.3	100.0
3. Income relative per household	0.70	1.07	1.15	1.20	1.02	0.53	1.00
4. Disparities (line 1 − line 2)	−0.9	1.1	3.3	4.2	0.4	−8.1	18.0
5. Persons per household	2.7	3.8	4.8	4.3	2.8	2.2	3.7
6. Number of persons (%)	2.2	17.1	30.1	25.0	15.1	10.5	100.0
7. Income relative per person	0.95	1.02	0.87	1.01	1.27	0.88	1.00
8. Income disparities line 1 − line 6	−0.1	0.4	−4.0	0.3	4.7	−1.3	10.8

	B. *Taiwan*						
	Age						
	Under 25 (1)	25–34 (2)	35–44 (3)	45–54 (4)	55–60 (5)	60 and over (6)	Total (7)
Total, 1964							
9. Total income (%)	2.0	22.9	33.1	28.0	7.5	6.5	100.0
10. Number of households (%)	2.8	25.2	34.1	25.5	6.4	6.0	100.0
11. Income relative per household	0.71	0.91	0.97	1.10	1.17	1.08	1.00
12. Disparities (line 9 − line 10)	−0.8	−2.3	−1.0	2.5	1.1	0.5	8.2
Excluding Taipei City, 1972							
13. Total income (%)	2.6	18.4	35.0	30.3	7.4	6.3	100.0 (134.8)
14. Number of households (%)	2.9	20.2	35.8	27.8	6.9	6.4	100.0 (2,371)
15. Income relative per household	0.83	0.91	0.98	1.09	1.07	0.98	1.00 (5.69)

Table 7.20 *(cont.)*

	Age						
	Under 25 (1)	25–34 (2)	35–44 (3)	45–54 (4)	55–60 (5)	60 and over (6)	Total (7)
16. Disparities (line 13 − line 14)	−0.3	−1.8	−0.8	2.5	0.5	−0.1	6.0
Nonfarmer households (excluding Taipei City), 1972							
17. Total income (%)	2.8	20.7	36.2	30.1	6.0	4.2	100.0 (99.3)
18. Number of households (%)	3.2	22.6	36.4	27.5	5.7	4.6	100.0 (1,655)
19. Income relative per household	0.86	0.91	0.99	1.09	1.05	0.91	1.00 (60.0)
20. Disparities (line 17 − line 18)	−0.4	−1.9	−0.2	2.6	0.3	−0.4	5.8
Farmer households, 1972							
21. Total income (%)	1.9	11.9	31.6	31.0	11.3	12.3	100.0 (35.1)
22. Number of households (%)	2.3	14.5	34.2	28.5	9.8	10.7	100.0 (716)
23. Income relative per household	0.83	0.82	0.92	1.09	1.15	1.15	1.00 (49.0)
24. Disparities (line 21 − line 22	−0.4	−2.6	−2.6	2.5	1.5	1.6	11.2

C. *Philippines, 1970–71*

	Age						
	Under 25 (1)	25–34 (2)	35–44 (3)	45–54 (4)	55–64 (5)	65 and over (6)	Total (7)
Total							
25. Total income (%)	3.1	20.6	26.1	24.6	17.6	8.0	100.0 (24.08)
26. Number of families (%)	5.0	24.8	26.9	21.0	14.5	7.8	100.0 (6,347)
27. Income relative per family	0.62	0.83	0.97	1.18	1.21	1.03	1.00 (3.79)

Table 7.20 *(cont.)*

	Age						
	Under 25 (1)	25–34 (2)	35–44 (3)	45–54 (4)	55–64 (5)	65 and over (6)	Total (7)
28. Disparities (line 25 − line 26)	−1.9	−4.2	−0.8	3.6	3.1	0.2	13.8
Manila and suburbs							
29. Total income (%)	3.1	18.7	21.4	25.1	20.9	10.8	100.0 (4.29)
30. Number of families (%)	5.6	27.0	26.5	19.2	15.0	6.7	100.0 (525)
31. Income relative per family	0.55	0.69	0.81	1.31	1.39	1.60	1.00 (8.18)
32. Disparities (line 29 − line 30)	−2.5	−8.3	−5.1	5.9	5.9	4.1	31.8
Other urban areas							
33. Total income (%)	2.0	20.9	26.4	25.3	17.4	8.0	100.0 (7.16)
34. Number of families (%)	3.3	24.5	26.4	22.5	15.1	8.2	100.0 (1,388)
35. Income relative per family	0.61	0.85	1.00	1.12	1.15	0.98	1.00 (5.16)
36. Disparities (line 33 − line 34)	−1.3	−3.6	0	2.8	2.3	−0.2	10.2
Rural areas							
37. Total income (%)	3.7	21.0	27.7	24.0	16.6	7.0	100.0 (12.62)
38. Number of families (%)	5.5	24.6	27.1	20.8	14.2	7.8	100.0 (4,434)
39. Income relative per family	0.67	0.85	1.03	1.15	1.17	0.90	1.00 (2.85)
40. Disparities (line 37 − line 38)	−1.8	−3.6	0.6	3.2	2.4	−0.8	12.4

Notes: Israel: lines 1–8, from table 13 (p. 16) of source cited for Tables 7.12 and 7.13. The number of persons per household is given directly in the source.
Taiwan, 1964: lines 8–12, taken or calculated from Directorate General of Budgets, Accounts, and Statistics, *Report on the Survey of Family Income and Expenditure and Study of Per-*

of its age-of-head differentials is similar to that for the United States and, one may assume, similar to that of other developed, industrialized countries.

The other two countries in Table 7.20 are among the less developed and display rather different patterns – both in the distribution of households or families by age of head and in the movement of the income relatives with shifts in the age of head. The difficulty is that we do not have for either Taiwan or the Philippines data on size of household or family by age of head, and we can only conjecture as to the differentials in income per *person* by age of head. In view of the interest of the data, Table 7.20 provides the available breakdowns between rural and urban, or between farmer and nonfarmer households.

We begin by noting the distributions of households or families by age

Notes to Table 7.20 *(cont.)*

sonal Income Distribution in Taiwan, 1964 (Taipei: DGBAS, December 1966), pp. 278–81, table 18. The sample was drawn from the registered ordinary households, thus excluding military and institutional population, combined households (such as factory dormitories), registered household members living away from home, and servants and employees registered as part of another household (uncommon). Personal and family income includes actual and imputed income, cash or kind, from all sources, except undistributed profits in "enterprises with five or more employees operated at a separate site from the family dwelling" (p. 122).

Taiwan Province, 1972: lines 13–24, from table 23 (pp. 404–11) of source cited for Tables 7.12 and 7.13 (the separation of farmer households from nonfarmer is given in the source). Entries in parentheses in col. 7, lines 13, 17, and 21, are total income ($NT billions); lines 14, 18, and 22, number of households (thousands); lines 15, 19, and 23, income per household ($NT thousands).

Philippines, 1970–71: lines 25–40, from table 47 (pp. 128–29) of source cited for Tables 7.12 and 7.13. This table shows the size distribution of income for each age-of-head class, for the country and the three major subdivisions (Manila and suburbs, other urban, rural). But only median incomes for each age-of-head category are shown. We set the arithmetic mean income at the mid-values of each class interval, except for the classes 10–15, 15–25, and the open ended 25 and over, for which we used 12, 15, and the mean income shown for the last class for Manila and suburbs, other urban, and rural, respectively (in table 2 [pp. 1–2] of the source). The resulting estimates of arithmetic mean income per family were slightly higher than those shown in the source, table 2. For Manila and suburbs the mean in thousands of pesos (line 31, col. 7, in parentheses) is 8.18, whereas the directly observed mean in the source is 7.79; the means for "other urban" are 5.16 in line 35 and 5.14 in the source; for the rural areas they are 2.85 and 2.82, respectively. The totals for the Philippines were derived by addition of the income and family totals for the three major subdivisions.

The entries in parentheses in col. 7, lines 25, 29, 33, and 37, are total income (P billions); lines 26, 30, 34, and 38, number of families (thousands); lines 27, 31, 35, and 39, income per family (P thousands).

Urban areas are defined largely by density of population, presence of a minimum number of business establishments, existence of a marketplace, and the like. It should be stressed that the classification is by nature of the area of residence, not the major occupation or industry. Thus, the number of families shown as residing in rural areas is appreciably larger than the number of families concentrating on farming and related industries; and some of the latter are shown to reside in urban areas (see table 17, [pp. 18–19] of the source).

of head, for Taiwan and the Philippines compared with the United States and Israel. To improve comparability, we estimated roughly the shares for the 55–64 and 65 and over age-of-head classes for Taiwan by assuming that two-thirds of the share of the total 55 and over class would be assignable to the 55–64 class and one-third to the 65 and over class. This apportionment is suggested by the distribution in Taiwan for 1966 (the year of the population census) of total males 55 and over between the two age groups,[20] and it is also similar to the distribution of families in the Philippines in Table 7.20 (Table 7.21).

While the share of the youngest age-of-head class, under 25, is somewhat larger in the United States (but not in Israel) than in Taiwan and in the Philippines, the striking and consistent difference lies in the much greater share of the oldest age-of-head class, that of 65 and over. In Taiwan, the latter is estimated at 7 percent or lower, whether for the country or for the farmer and nonfarmer household subdivisions; in the Philippines the share is somewhat higher, between 7 and 8 percent; whereas in the United States the share is almost 20 percent for units or households, 14 percent even for families; and in Israel it is almost 18 percent.

These differences in patterns are probably due to the age structure of the population, particularly male – from whom the heads of families or households are recruited. The source cited in footnote 20 shows the following shares of males aged 65 and over in all males aged 25 and over: United States, 1970, 16 percent; Israel, urban population, 1961, 10 percent; Taiwan, 1966, 5 percent; and the Philippines, estimate for 1968, 7 percent. Except for Israel, where for ethnic reasons headship among males 65 and over is overrepresented, these percentages check fairly well with the differences in the proportions of households with heads aged 65 and over in Table 7.21. The obvious implication is that the higher birth rate and higher rate of natural increase in such less developed countries as Taiwan and the Philippines swell the proportions of households at the younger age brackets, and, in particular, reduce the shares of the very old age-of-head classes. A recent UN source indicates that for all economically developed countries (DCs) the share in 1970 of population aged 65 and over in total population was 9.6 percent and that of the population 20 years of age and over was 64.6 percent, so that the share of the former in the latter was about 15 percent; for the economically

20 See United Nations, *Demographic Yearbook, 1970* (New York: United Nations, 1971), pp. 270–71, table 6.

Table 7.21. *Comparison of the shares of extreme age-of-head classes, selected areas*

Country or area	Percentage among families, households, or units of those in extreme age-of-head classes			Persons per family or household (4)
	Under 25 (1)	65 and over (2)	Cols. 1 and 2 (3)	
1. U.S. units	8.1	19.3	27.4	3.04
2. U.S. households	6.8	19.5	26.3	3.17
3. U.S. families	7.0	13.8	20.8	3.62
4. Israel	3.0	17.7	20.7	3.7
5. Taiwan, 1964	2.8	4.1	6.9	No data
6. Taiwan, 1972 (excluding Taipei City)	2.9	4.6	7.5	5.65
7. Taiwan, nonfarmer households	3.2	2.4	5.6	5.29
8. Taiwan, farmer households	2.3	6.8	9.1	6.50
9. Philippines, total	5.0	7.8	12.8	5.85
10. Philippines, Manila and suburbs	5.6	6.7	12.3	5.98
11. Philippines, other urban	3.3	8.2	11.5	5.88
12. Philippines, rural	5.5	7.8	13.3	5.83

Note: Based on Table 7.16 above for the United States and Table 7.20 above for the other countries and areas.

less developed countries (LDCs) the corresponding percentages were 3.7, 48.9, and about 7.5.[21] Thus even with the population of 20 and over as base, and the inclusion of women, the relative shares of the 65 and over group in the DCs was about twice that for the LDCs.

As in the United States and Israel, the relative of income per household for the youngest age group, under 25, in Taiwan and the Philippines is low. For Taiwan it is 0.71 in 1964 or slightly over 0.8 in 1972, whether for nonfarmer or farmer households. For the Philippines the relevant income relative varies from a low of 0.55 for Manila and suburbs to a high of 0.67 in rural areas, with an average for the country of 0.62 (Table 7.20, col. 1, lines 11, 15, 19, 23, 27, 31, 35, and 39). But the income relatives for the oldest age-of-head class, 65 and over, for Taiwan and subdivisions and the Philippines and subdivisions, unlike those for the United States

21 See *Selected World Demographic Indicators by Countries, 1950–2000*, Working Paper ESA/P/WP 55, mimeographed (New York: United Nations, May 1975), pp. 2–3.

and Israel, are relatively high. Thus, for Taiwan in 1964, the relative for the 60 and over class was well above 1.0 (Table 7.20, col. 6, line 11); for 1972, excluding Taipei, it was 0.98, close to the countrywide mean (col. 6, line 15); for the Philippines in 1970–71 the relative for the 65 and over class was 1.03 (col. 6, line 27). All of these are to be compared with a relative of 0.53 for the 65 and over class in Israel (col. 6, line 3), or 0.64 and 0.54 for the income per family or per unit for that age group in the United States (see Table 7.18, col. 6, lines 1 and 14).

Clearly, the pattern of movement in per family or per household income for the successive age-of-head classes observed for Taiwan and the Philippines (and probably also for other LDCs) differs substantially from that for the United States (and probably other DCs). There are also intriguing differences in this pattern for the subdivisions within Taiwan and the Philippines. Thus, in Taiwan in 1972 the movement in per household income for the farmer households shows a steady climb from a low in the 25–34 age class (at 0.83) to a peak in the 55–60 and 60 and over classes (at 1.15), whereas for the nonfarmer households there is a steady climb from a low in the age class under 25 to a peak in the 45–54 age class (see lines 19 and 23). In the Philippines, the average income for Manila and suburbs rises sharply and continuously from a low of 0.55 in the age class under 25 to a peak of 1.60 in the oldest age class, 65 and over – with a wide amplitude of the resulting income differentials, yielding a TDM of 31.8 (line 31); whereas for the other urban areas and the rural areas the swing is of narrower amplitude, and the movement is to a peak in the 55–64 age class (lines 35 and 39). These differences must be due to some demographic and economic factors which may also explain the puzzling finding that the average family in Manila and suburbs is somewhat larger than in the rural areas (see Table 7.21). But the search for such evidence is not feasible here.

The combination, in Taiwan and the Philippines, of smaller shares of households or families in the extreme age-of-head classes, with an income relative for the oldest age-of-head class that does not deviate much from the countrywide average, means that inequality in income per family or household introduced by the age-of-head variable is much narrower than in the United States or Israel. The TDMs for the two less developed countries, well below 10 for Taiwan and 13.8 for the Philippines (total), are to be compared with 18.0 for Israel (Table 7.20, col. 7, lines 4, 12, 16, and 28), and either 17.4 for families or 23.6 for households in the United States (Table 7.18). If, for the demographic reasons indicated above, the LDCs, in general, show lower proportions of the oldest age-of-head class, then even if the income relatives in these countries moved with age, as they do in the developed countries, the inequality contributed by the age-of-head factor in the LDCs would be distinctly narrower. The implication is that in the customary comparisons between the DCs and the LDCs of size distributions by income per family or per household the demographic structure would contribute, in cross-section comparisons, a larger element of inequality in the distributions in the DCs than in the LDCs – an element that would be absent from similar comparisons of the distributions of *lifetime* incomes.

The findings just suggested for comparisons of the age-of-head effects on the distributions of income per family or per household may not hold for effects on the distributions by per person income, but the conjectures cannot yield clear results until our empirical data are far richer. We know that the larger family or household in the LDCs than in the DCs is due to more children and that it is associated with the longer period of childbearing and child rearing – which continues to older ages of the father (and thus the family or household head) in the less than in the more developed countries (see the paper cited in footnote 7). This means that whereas the peak size of family or household in the United States and Israel is reached in the 35–44 age class, the peak size in the LDCs may be in the 45–54 age-of-head class (less probably in the 55–64 class). It also means that some children may enter even the 65 and over age-of-head class – so that the share in that class of *persons* in families or households may be somewhat higher than its share of families or households. But such an outcome is far from certain or even highly probable. And it is difficult at present to conjecture the movement of per person income relatives in the successive age-of-head classes in the less developed countries. Given the growing supply of the requisite data in the censuses of population, and in the studies of family incomes in several less developed countries, further exploration of these questions seems both feasible and promising.

VI. Cross-section differentials by age of head and lifetime income

The differences observed in the size and income of families or households at different ages of head contribute significantly to inequalities in the con-ventional, cross-section size distributions of income. Yet they represent *phases* in the lifetime span of a family or household, marked by changes in size, income, and income per person or per consumer. It follows that the inequality component contributed by these cross-section differentials in size and income of families, by age of head, may have no impact on the distribution of *lifetime* incomes. And this component may vary over time, or from one country's cross-section size distribution to another – so that the shift from a comparison of the conventional size distributions to that of distributions of lifetime incomes (or of incomes over long time spans) may require difficult, differential adjustments.

This relation between the cross-section differentials and inequality in lifetime incomes is explored somewhat further in the present section, with the help of illustrative cases but using realistic data based on the discussion above for the United States. The key datum is the cross-classification by both size and age of head (Table 7.16), available for families and for all units (i.e., families and unrelated individuals). To simplify matters, we limit our discussion to families alone and deal essentially with two questions: (a) What is the relation between the cross-section differentials and lifetime income, assuming a cohort of families within which no differences in size are assumed? (b) What is the effect on inequality in lifetime incomes of assumed differences in size within the family cohorts?

(a) Table 7.22 is designed to deal with the first question. In lines 1–6 we derive a lifetime series of income per person for an illustrative family, with a time span extending over 50 years – implying that the family is formed when its head is 20 years old and is dissolved when he is 70. For this 50-year life span of the family, it is assumed that within each interval, marked off by our classification by age of head, the income *per person* is that shown by the cross section for 1969 in Table 7.16, and entered in line 2 here. Given the two assumptions, one relating to the duration and intervals in the lifetime span and the other to the per person income in each interval of that span, the calculation of the gross income for that life span is set, and so are the other calculations in lines 1–6.

The series on income per person in line 2 is taken from Table 7.16, line 33, which is the *average* for the successive age-of-head classes. The underlying averages of persons per family (in line 16 of Table 7.16) ranged from less than three in the under 25 age-of-head class to a peak of 4.74 in the 35–44 class and down to 2.43 in the 65 and over class. But our assumption of the per person income series in line 2 does not mean that the resulting gross lifetime income, which averages $3.014 thousand per year, is dependent on that particular series of average size of family associated with the successive classes by age of head. As we shall see

Table 7.22. *Illustrative relations between lifetime family income per person and cross-section differentials in income per person among age-of-head classes (based on U.S. data)*

	Age-of-head classes, within a family's lifetime span and in cross section						
	Under 25 (1)	25–34 (2)	35–44 (3)	45–54 (4)	55–64 (5)	65 and over (6)	Total (7)
Derivation of lifetime gross income from the cross section in Table 7.3							
1. Years in interval (N)	5	10	10	10	10	5	50
2. Income per person per year (Table 7.16, line 33, $ thousands).	2.39	2.47	2.53	3.44	4.05	2.77	3.014
3. Total income in interval ($ thousands)	11.95	24.70	25.30	34.40	40.50	13.85	150.70
4. Interval in total time span (%)	10	20	20	20	20	10	100
5. Income in interval in total income (%)	7.9	16.4	16.8	22.8	26.9	9.2	100.0
6. Instability over time in gross income per person (line 5 − line 4)	−2.1	−3.6	−3.2	2.8	6.9	−0.8	19.4
Relation of different cross sections to lifetime gross income per person							
7. Alternative cross-section income per person ($ thousands)	2.71	2.74	2.77	3.23	3.53	2.89	3.014
8. Income in interval in total income (%)	9.0	18.2	18.4	21.4	23.4	9.6	100.0 (150.70)
9. Instability over time (line 8 − line 4)	−1.0	−1.8	−1.6	1.4	3.4	−0.4	9.6
Underlying changes in cross section – accommodation through changing income per family by age-of-head class							
10. Persons per family (Table 7.16, line 16)	2.86	4.03	4.74	3.76	2.80	2.43	—
11. Derived income per family (line 10 × line 7)	7.75	11.04	13.13	12.14	9.88	7.02	—
12. Number of families (%) (Table 7.18, line 5).	7.0	20.7	21.2	21.1	16.2	13.8	100.0
13. Total income, derived from lines 11 and 12 (%)	5.1	21.3	25.9	23.8	14.9	9.0	100.0
14. Disparities (line 13 − line 12)	−1.9	0.6	4.7	2.7	−1.3	−4.8	16.0

Table 7.22 *(cont.)*

| | Age-of-head classes, within a family's lifetime span and in cross section | | | | | | |
	Under 25 (1)	25–34 (2)	35–44 (3)	45–54 (4)	55–64 (5)	65 and over (6)	Total (7)
15. Number of persons (%) (Table 7.18, line 6).	5.4	23.1	27.7	21.9	12.6	9.3	100.0
16. Total income, derived from lines 7 and 15 (%)	4.9	21.3	25.9	23.8	15.0	9.1	100.0
17. Disparities (line 16 − line 15)	−0.5	−1.8	−1.8	1.9	2.4	−0.2	8.6

Underlying changes in cross section – accommodation through changing number of persons per family by age-of-head class

18. Income per family (Table 7.16, line 25, $ thousands)	6.84	9.94	11.97	12.93	11.35	6.72	—
19. Derived number of persons per family (line 18 ÷ line 7)	2.52	3.63	4.32	4.00	3.22	2.33	—
20. Persons (%) (lines 19 and 12)	5.0	21.3	25.9	23.9	14.8	9.1	100.0
21. Income (%) (Tables 7.17, 7.18)	4.5	19.4	23.9	25.8	17.4	9.0	100.0
22. Disparities (line 21 − line 20)	−0.5	−1.9	−2.0	1.9	2.6	−0.1	9.0

Notes: For basis of derivation see text. The averages in lines 2 and 7, col. 7, are obtained by weighting the entries in cols. 1–6 by the number of years in each interval.
Averages were not entered in col. 7 of lines 10, 11, 18, and 19 because they were not used in the other calculations in the table or in the discussion.

in lines 7–22, it is easy to modify both the *size-of-family* series and the *income per family* so as to obtain the same lifetime gross income *per person*. However, line 2 does not allow for any differences by size *within* the age-of-head classes, which must be allowed for if we are to observe effects of differences in size of family for different cohorts on their lifetime incomes. Nor does it allow for any variation in age of head within different size-of-family groups.

To return to lines 1–6, we may ask whether there is justification for assuming that a cross-section series of family income per person by age of head in 1969 suggests the time series within the lifetime span of an average family in 1969 – disregarding for the moment the trend and discount elements to be noted presently. The answer to this question depends on our view of the stability over time in the effects of family size and age of head on a countrywide distribution like that for the United States. Consider an occupational or industrial sector, with a specific time pattern of size of family and income per family by age of head, and hence of income per person, for families whose heads are attached to this sector, and envisage the combination of n such sectors with different time patterns of the type indicated. The countrywide distribution used in Table 7.16 is a weighted composite of cohorts of families, some formed in the 1920s, others formed in the 1930s, 1940s, 1950s, and 1960s, each cohort composed of a different mix of occupational and sectoral subgroups, with the lifetime pattern of income per person, by age-of-head classes, possibly changing over time through the 5 decades before 1969. The complexity of the picture is not necessarily evidence against the plausibility of relative stability in the past, with some offsets within the various changes that may have occurred. The purpose of the comment is to emphasize that the inference of lifetime patterns from a cross section depends on the relative stability over time in the *average* pattern derived from the cross section. One should also stress that if there is such stability it is likely to be associated with temporal changes in the time pattern of family income per capita *within* the sectors and in the weights *among* the sectors.

The other difference between cross-section differentials and the span of lifetime income is that a time trend present in the latter is concealed in the former. The 1920–24 cohort of families, represented in 1969 by the 65 and over age-of-head class, must have experienced, in common with the economy at large, a substantial rise in income per person over the 4½ decades since the formation of the family; and the 1965 cohort, represented in 1969 by the under 25 age-of-head class, may be expected to experience a similar growth trend over the long remainder of its life span. In order to have fully comparable phases in the lifetime span of family income, the per person income averages in the cross-section age-of-head classes must be modified by the additions of a trend that would impart a substantial upward tilt to the time profile. The past experience, at least in the developed countries, suggests growth rates in per person income of 2 percent per year – which means a rise of close to 150 percent over the 45 years that elapse from the midpoint of the youngest to the midpoint of the oldest age class in Table 7.22.

We made no effort to introduce this adjustment; nor did we allow for a related factor, discount for the future, required in comparisons of lifetime incomes in the current valuation that may be attached to them (see in this connection the discussion and empirical evidence, on both the time trend and the discount rate, in the paper cited in n. 16 above). The discount rate is likely to be higher than the rate of growth in income per capita. Moreover, it may vary appreciably among economic groups within the population, presumably being higher among the lower than among the upper income levels, at least under normal conditions of peace and continuity. But it would take us too far afield to attempt to explore the possibilities in the way of diverse growth and discount rates, since our aim is merely to indicate a few analytical implications of the relation between the cross-section size and age-of-head differentials in the conventional size distributions. For this purpose, lifetime gross income, unadjusted for the time trend and discount rate, is sufficient.

With this simplification, the cross-section differentials are translated into movements *over time* in the per person income of an illustrative family – which means instability in per person income within the lifetime span. This instability, for a given family unit assumed to survive through the 50-year span, can be measured by tools analogous to those used for the tables relating to the cross section. Lines 4–6 provide the calculation, and yield a TDM for instability over time as high as 19.4 (corresponding to a TDM of 17.4 for the cross section, in Table 7.18, line 11, weighted differently).

Lines 7–22 of Table 7.22 are designed to indicate that the time pattern and amplitude of the cross-section differentials in income per person among the several age-of-head classes can be modified without affecting the total of average lifetime income per person. Assume that we want to reduce substantially the amplitude of the cross-section differentials and thus make for a more stable income pattern over time within the life span of the family. We then introduce in line 7 an alternative cross section of income per person, such that the deviations of the income relative from the countrywide are halved for each age-of-head class. The new TDM for the life span is then about a half of the original (compare lines 6 and 9).

Given this desired change in income per person in the different age-of-head classes, the underlying cross section can be modified either by retaining the original pattern of persons per family in the age-of-head classes and changing the *per family* income (lines 10–17) or by retaining the original pattern of income per family by age-of-head class and modifying the *persons per family* pattern (lines 18–22). Of course, partial modifications in income per family and in persons per family are also possible. The point here is that assuming a different cross-section pattern of income per person by age-of-head classes may mean modifications in cross-section patterns of income per family, or of persons per family, or of both.

The results are obvious. With lifetime income remaining the same, all or some of the underlying cross-section differentials in income per person for age-of-head classes, or in income per family by these classes, or in persons per family by the age classes, have been modified. In our illustration the amplitude has been reduced; but it could also be raised, again without affecting the gross lifetime income per person. What has been affected is instability over time in income per person within the life span; and this would affect the current *value* (i.e., discounted) of the lifetime income were we to introduce this factor.

It should be noted that, while in line 19 the modification affected the number of persons per family in the several age-of-head classes, we are still assuming that this pattern is the same for all families in the cohort for which we estimate lifetime gross income. On this assumption, with the omission of the time trend of growth in per person income and of the discounting factor, the lifetime income per person for a family will be the same – regardless of variations in the cross-section differentials in family income per person in the several age-of-head classes. The introduction of the time trend and of the discounting factor is likely to invalidate this conclusion of compatibility of the same lifetime family income per person with diverse cross-section differentials in income per person in the age-of-head classes. The removal of the assumption that implies the same average number of persons per family by age-of-head classes for all families immediately results in a demonstration of the major effects that differences in the number of persons per family will have on lifetime income per person – the second topic of the present section.

(b) Table 7.23 provides a simple illustration. Rather than assume that each family follows the pattern in Table 7.16, in which the number of persons per family rises from 2.84 in the under 25 age class to 4.74 in the 35–44 class and then drops to 2.43 in the 65 and over class, we now allow different number-of-person patterns for different groups of families. The four cases distinguished in Table 7.23 (A–D) are simple and extreme, and could be made more realistic. But the differences among these make the conclusion obvious. In case A the number of persons is held at two throughout the age-of-head classes. In each of the other three cases, the

Table 7.23. *Effects of differing number of persons per family on lifetime family gross income per person, illustrative cases*

A. *Deriving lifetime gross income per person for differing changes in numbers per family at successive age-of-head classes*

	Age of head						Total or average (7)
	Under 25 (1)	25–34 (2)	35–44 (3)	45–54 (4)	55–64 (5)	65 and over (6)	
1. Years in interval	5	10	10	10	10	5	50
Case A							
2. Persons per family	2	2	2	2	2	2	2.0
3. Income per family per year (Table 7.16, line 20, $ thousands)	7.03	9.75	11.74	11.35	9.97	6.00	9.87
4. Income per person per year ($ thousands)	3.51	4.87	5.87	5.68	4.98	3.00	4.93
Case B							
5. Persons per family	2	3	4	4	3	2	3.20
6. Income per family per year (Table 7.16, $ thousands)	7.03	9.26	12.34	14.42	11.60	6.00	10.83
7. Income per person per year ($ thousands)	3.51	3.09	3.08	3.61	3.87	3.00	3.38
Case C							
8. Persons per family	2	4	6	6	4	2	4.40
9. Income per family per year (Table 7.16, $ thousands)	7.03	10.25	10.14	12.12	12.66	6.00	10.34
10. Income per person per year ($ thousands)	3.51	2.56	1.69	2.02	3.17	3.00	2.54
Case D							
11. Persons per family	3	5	7	7	5	3	5.40
12. Income per family per year (Table 7.16, $ thousands)	6.54	10.36	11.83	14.14	12.99	8.72	11.39
13. Income per person per year ($ thousands)	2.18	2.07	1.69	2.02	2.60	2.91	2.18

B. *Effects of adjustments in cross-section changes made in lines 7–23 of Table 7.22*

	Age of head							Size group of families (number of persons)					
	Under 25 (1)	25–34 (2)	35–44 (3)	45–54 (4)	55–64 (5)	65 and over (6)	Total or average (7)	2 (8)	3 (9)	4 (10)	5 (11)	6 and over (12)	Total (13)
14. Ratios of adjusted income per family to unadjusted (Table 7.22, lines 11 and 18)	1.133	1.111	1.097	0.939	0.870	1.045	—	—	—	—	—	—	—
Adjusted Case A													
15. Adjusted income per person (line 4 × line 14)	3.98	5.41	6.44	5.33	4.33	3.13	5.01	—	—	—	—	—	—
Adjusted Case D													
16. Adjusted income per person (line 13 × line 14)	2.47	2.30	1.85	1.90	2.26	3.04	2.21	—	—	—	—	—	—
Eliminating decline in per person income with rise in number of persons per family													
17. Income per person (Table 7.16, $ thousands)								4.39	3.52	2.96	2.45	1.68	2.92
18. Adjusted income per person ($ thousands)								2.92	2.92	2.92	2.92	2.92	—
19. Adjustment coefficient (line 18/ line 17)								0.665	0.830	0.986	1.192	1.738	—
Case A													
20. Unadjusted income per person (line 4 above)	3.51	4.87	5.87	5.68	4.98	3.00	4.93	—	—	—	—	—	—

Table 7.23 (cont.)

	Age of head							Size group of families (number of persons)					
	Under 25 (1)	25–34 (2)	35–44 (3)	45–54 (4)	55–64 (5)	65 and over (6)	Total or average (7)	2 (8)	3 (9)	4 (10)	5 (11)	6 and over (12)	Total (13)
21. Adjustment coefficient	0.665	0.665	0.665	0.665	0.665	0.665	—	—	—	—	—	—	—
22. Adjusted income per person ($ thousands)	2.33	3.24	3.90	3.78	3.31	2.00	3.28	—	—	—	—	—	—
Case D													
23. Unadjusted income per person (line 13 above)	2.18	2.07	1.69	2.02	2.60	2.91	2.18	—	—	—	—	—	—
24. Adjustment coefficient	0.830	1.192	1.738	1.738	1.192	0.830	—	—	—	—	—	—	—
25. Adjusted income per person ($ thousands)	1.81	2.47	2.94	3.82	3.10	2.42	2.93	—	—	—	—	—	—

Notes: For the rationale of the derivation see discussion in the text. Income for families of six or seven persons (cols. 3 and 4, cases C and D) was estimated from Table 7.16 by using the per person income for the group of families of six persons and over and multiplying it by the persons per family in the case. The averages in col. 7 (lines 2–13, 15, 16, 20, 22, 23, and 25) are weighted by the duration of intervals shown in line 1. The average in col. 7, line 17, is from Table 7.16 and was weighted by the number of persons in the age-of-head cols. in that table.

time pattern is similar to that in Table 7.16 – a rise from the youngest age-of-head class to a peak in the 35–44 and 45–54 classes, and a decline to another trough in the 65 and over class. But the number and average size of family differ markedly, and the lifetime incomes, on either a per family or per person basis, reflect these differences.

With the rise in the average number of persons per family, gross income *per family* also rises – from $9.87 thousand per year for case A to $11.39 thousand per family in case D (with an average of 5.4 persons per family, see col. 7, lines 3, 6, 9, and 12). But with the rise in persons per family, *per person* lifetime income declines sharply – from a high of $4.93 thousand in case A to $2.18 thousand in case D (col. 7, lines 4, 7, 10, and 13).

These findings are the obvious result of the positive correlation in the cross section between income per family and the size of family, and of the more striking negative correlation between family income per person and family size. So long as these correlations are valid and used, the larger family will yield larger lifetime income *per family* and lower lifetime income per *person*.

Of additional interest is the difference in the time patterns of income per person in cases A–D in Table 7.23, which for the larger families are so different from those for the smaller. In case A, both income per family and income per person describe the inverted-U pattern associated with the peaking of per family income in the 35–44 and 45–54 age brackets. But as we move progressively to the larger families in cases B–D, *per family* income continues to peak in the age-of-head classes just mentioned, but the time pattern for *per person* income is reversed. It now assumes a U shape (i.e., per person income is relatively high at the younger and older age classes). In case D, in particular, and even in case C, the trough in per person income is in the 35–44 and 45–54 age-of-head classes. And these low levels of income suggest a period within the lifetime span of family income when, if the illustrative magnitudes are realistic, the pressure of larger numbers within the family creates a phase of income shortage (relative to the long term) that is of obvious implication even for longer term income levels. Thus, if the general economic level of a family is low, a prolonged period of pressure of numbers on income – combined with possible transient disturbances which may be negative – can produce a crisis that may affect the remainder of the family's life span. The pattern shown is, of course, the result of the changes we assigned to number by age of head; but this is just as realistic a pattern as that of income per family in the successive age-of-head classes.

Table 7.24. *Comparison of differences in lifetime incomes in cases A–D in Table 7.23 with those in cross section in Table 7.8*

	A (1)	B (2)	C (3)	D (4)
1. Average size of family (persons)	2.0	3.2	4.4	4.4
Income per family, indexes, col. 1 − 100				
2. Lifetime, Table 7.23	100	110	105	115+
3. Cross section, Table 7.8, line 15, linear interpolation	100	123	137	139
Income per person, indexes, col. 1 − 100				
4. Lifetime, table 23	100	69	52	44
5. Cross section, Table 7.8, line 18, linear interpolation	100	77	62	52

In order to remove these effects, particularly the striking drop in life-time income per person with assumed number-of-person patterns that yield a larger adverse size of family over its life span, we must remove the negative correlation between size of family and income per person. Changes such as were made in Table 7.22 in the pattern of per person income by age of head have no effect – as may be seen from lines 14–16, in which the ratio of per person lifetime income in case D, with this adjustment, remains at somewhat over four-tenths of per person lifetime income in case A (col. 7, lines 15 and 16). It is only when we assume that income per person in the cross section is the same for all sizes of families (line 18) and apply the resulting adjustment coefficients to the income per person series for case A and case D that the wide differential in the lifetime income per person between the two cases is reduced to a narrow spread (of some 10 percent). The spread in lifetime income still remains, even though income per person differentials among groups by size of family have been eliminated because of size differences *within* age-of-head classes. If, using Table 7.16, we had eliminated size-of-family differences in per person income for each *cell* of the cross-classification, the spread in per person income over the lifetime of the family in cases A–D would have also been completely removed.

One final aspect of Table 7.23 is to be noted: the extent to which the resulting differentials in lifetime income in the four cases reflect the magnitude of differentials in income per family or per person associated in the cross section with differences in the size of the family. The summary of interest is shown in Table 7.24.

It will be observed that the cross-section differentials by size of family predict the *direction* of the effect of size on lifetime income per family or lifetime income per person. But whereas for income *per family*, the cross section implies a larger effect than we find in the estimate of lifetime income, for family income *per person* the differentials in lifetime income are wider than in the cross section. The explanation lies in the intervention of the age-of-head variable, which assumed different weights: proportion of families or persons by age-of-head classes, in the cross section, and proportions of the intervals in the total life span, in lifetime income.

The four cases in Table 7.23 are merely illustrative, and their realism lies in the generally inverted U-shaped time pattern, which resembles (for cases B–D) that of the empirical cross sections by age of head. But we have observed repeatedly that differences in size of families, for different age-of-head classes, are largely determined by differences in the number of children, and the evidence in Table 7.17, lines 1–15, on the age structure of family members by age of head was illuminating. It, therefore, seemed of interest to supplement the illustrative examples of Table 7.23 by more realistic simulation, in which again for different cases we assume movements over time in the size of a family, but this time with variations due only to changing number and ages of children – the ages being indicated in order to allow us to assign a half-weight to consumers under 18 and set an assumed age at which a child leaves a family (Table 7.25).

The derivation of the lifetime income from the cross section in Table 7.25, again by means of Table 7.16, is subject not only to all the limitations already discussed in connection with Tables 7.22 and 7.23, but also to an additional one. We assume that the per family income for a specific cell in Table 7.16, say a family of three persons in the 35–44 age-of-head class, is for a husband and wife and one related child (with the family until the age of 20) and would remain the same whether the husband is between 35 and 39 or between 40 and 44 years of age. While the latter caveat applies also to Tables 7.22 and 7.23, the former – specifying husband and wife – does not. Yet that cell in Table 7.16 covers families with female as well as male heads, families with only a male parent and two children, and families of three adults. There is thus disparity in the definition of the cell for Table 7.16 and that for Table 7.25. But the additional realism gained by further breakdown of Table 7.16 most likely would have been moderate.

The results in Table 7.25 might have been expected from Table 7.23: with differences among the three cases in the size of the family determined exclusively by differences in number of children, lifetime income

Table 7.25. *Lifetime gross income, families with differing number of children, illustrative cases*

Age of head (1)	Years in interval (2)	Persons per family (3)	Income per family ($ thousands) (4)	Income per person ($ thousands) (5)	Consumers per family (6)	Income per consumer ($ thousands) (7)
Case 1 – Husband – wife family, no children, no relations
1. Under 25	5	2	7.03	3.51	2.0	3.51
2. 25–34.9	10	2	9.75	4.87	2.0	4.87
3. 35–44.9	10	2	11.74	5.87	2.0	5.87
4. 45–54.9	10	2	11.35	5.68	2.0	5.68
5. 55–64.9	10	2	9.97	4.48	2.0	4.48
6. 65 and over	5	2	6.00	3.00	2.0	3.00
7. Total or average	50	2.0	9.87	4.93	2.0	4.93
Case 2 – Husband – wife, two children born at age of head 25 and 30, no other relations
8. Under 25	5	2	7.03	3.51	2.0	3.51
9. 25–29.9	5	3	9.26	3.09	2.5	3.70
10. 30.0–34.9	5	4	10.25	2.56	3.0	3.42
11. 35.0–42.9	8	4	12.34	3.08	3.0	4.11
12. 43.0–44.9	2	4	12.34	3.08	3.5	3.53
13. 45.0–47.9	3	3	13.22	4.41	2.5	5.29
14. 48.0–49.9	2	3	13.22	4.41	3.0	4.41
15. 50.0–54.9	5	2	11.35	5.68	2.0	5.68
16. 55.0–64.9	10	2	9.97	4.98	2.0	4.98
17. 65 and over	5	2	6.00	3.00	2.0	3.00
18. Total or average	50	2.80	10.17	3.84	2.44	4.22
Case 3 – husband – wife, four children, born at age of head 25, 30, 35, 40, no other relations
19. Under 25	5	2	7.03	3.51	2.0	3.51
20. 25.0–29.9	5	3	9.26	3.09	2.5	3.70
21. 30.0–34.9	5	4	10.25	2.56	3.0	3.42
22. 35.0–39.9	5	5	12.47	2.49	3.5	3.56
23. 40.0–42.9	3	6	10.14	1.69	4.0	2.54
24. 43.0–44.9	2	6	10.14	1.69	4.5	2.25
25. 45.0–47.9	3	5	14.80	2.96	3.5	4.23
26. 48.0–49.9	2	5	14.80	2.96	4.0	3.70
27. 50.0–52.9	3	4	14.42	3.61	3.0	4.81
28. 53.0–54.9	2	4	14.42	3.61	3.5	4.12
29. 55.0–57.9	3	3	11.60	3.87	2.5	4.64
30. 58.0–59.9	2	3	11.60	3.87	3.0	3.87
31. 60–64.9	5	2	9.97	4.98	2.0	4.98
32. 65 and over	5	2	6.00	3.00	2.0	3.00
33. Total or average	50	3.60	10.59	3.18	2.88	3.74

per family for the larger families is greater, but lifetime family income either per person or per consumer varies inversely with average size. The conclusion is the same as in Table 7.23, but it is now in terms of a negative association between per person or per consumer lifetime income and the number of children, that is, fertility – given the reasonable assumption of low death rates or of no significant differentials in relevant mortality among families with differing numbers of children.

The differences in lifetime income even per consumer are substantial in Table 7.25, although the three cases differ within a range from 2.0 to 2.88 consumers per family (col. 6, lines 7, 18, and 33). The relevant lifetime income per consumer, at 100 for the family of two, without children, drops to 75 for a family with four children, a reduction of one-quarter. The movement toward the U pattern, as we allow for a larger number of children, can be seen in case 3 with an average income per consumer below $3.5 thousand per year for the 15 years from age of head 30 to age of head 45 (lines 21–24, averaging). And if we were to compare the lifetime income per family, per person, or per consumer with those derivable from Table 7.8 (in association with size of family differentials), the results would be the same as for cases A–D in Table 7.23. The response of a lifetime income *per family* (whether in terms of persons or consumers) would be more moderate than is implicit in Table 7.8, and the negative response of lifetime income *per person* or *per consumer* would be appreciably greater.

But these details are of secondary importance. The main purpose of Table 7.25 is to stress that the differences in size of family illustrated in Table 7.23 and implicit in Table 7.22 are associated largely with differences in number of children. Hence, there is a line of connection running

Notes to Table 7.25 *(cont.)*

Notes: Common assumptions: (1) age of head of family at marriage is 20 years; (2) dissolution of family occurs when head is 70; (3) related children withdraw from family at 20; (4) related children under 18 are consumers at half-weight. The divisions within the total age span of head of family in col. 1 are determined by the breaks necessary to distinguish periods with differing number of persons, differing number of related children under 18, and differing income per family of a given size (in terms of number of persons) and of a given age of head, as distinguished in Table 7.16.

The entries in col. 4, for income per family, are taken from the appropriate cells in Table 7.16. No allowance is made for possible differences in income per family of a given size, but with the age of head changing *within* the class shown in Table 7.16. For families of six, the income per family was obtained from Table 7.16 by multiplying the income per person for that cell in the group of six-and-over persons by six.

The averages in lines 7, 18, and 33, cols. 3–7, are obtained by multiplying the entries in the lines above by the number of years in the interval and dividing the sum of products by 50. The entries in the same lines in col. 2 are the total number of years in the assumed lifetime of the family, 50 years for each case.

from differential fertility to different size of families or households in the cross section to lower per person or per consumer income for the larger families or households to lower lifetime incomes per person or per consumer for families with larger numbers of children; and to the U pattern for families with larger numbers of children – which implies a phase of stress in the middle age-of-head classes in which the families include the larger number of children.

VII. Concluding comments

In ending our exploratory discussion of the demographic aspects of the size distribution of income, we summarize our conclusions *seriatim*.

1. Since demographic processes directly affect a country's population and the recipients and users of income, we had to begin with the choice of the basic recipient unit within that population. We found the *personal* income recipient, defined for the United States as any person 14 years of age and over who received some income during the year (and presumably defined with a similar lower age limit in other countries), deficient in several major respects. First, that recipient is not clearly identifiable when we deal with income from family enterprises so widely prevalent in agriculture, handicrafts, trade, and transport in the less developed countries, and important even in the industrialized countries. Nor is the individual recipient easily identifiable in the flow of property income from jointly held assets. Second, the definition omits all children, and distribution among personal income recipients cannot reveal how children, a most important segment of the population viewed in the longer term perspective, fare in the distribution and use of income. Third, for most personal income recipients decisions and actions on getting and spending income are not independent of those by other, closely related persons, usually members of their families or households. The personal recipient unit is thus deficient because its actions cannot be analyzed unless combined with those of others – presumably forming an alternative recipient unit, namely, the family or household.

2. Because it includes major and supplementary income recipients, and persons with widely differing capacities or drives for earning income, the distribution of a country's personal income among persons tends to show much wider inequality than the distribution of the same total income among the country's families or households. Measures for these two types of distributions cannot, therefore, be used without adjustment

in intertemporal or interspatial comparisons. Income inequality among the population of persons would be particularly wide if we were also to include nonrecipients (with an income of zero) – those who may be conceived as potential income earners but who are involuntarily prevented from being earners.

3. In the United States, well below half of women aged 25–65 work full time (as compared with 80 percent of men of the same ages), and about a third of all women in these ages are shown to earn or receive no income. The plausible implication of this situation, possibly found in other economically developed countries, is that, given an adequate economic level of the husband's income, women in these ages, most of whom are married, engage in other productive activities, but with results not included in the conventional definition of income. These activities may be largely within the household (in providing care for the family, particularly children), although they may also be outside. This finding naturally raises questions about the exclusion from national product of the returns from these important activities of women as housewives and in other productive roles and about the possible effect of including such income on inequalities in the distribution of income, more widely conceived, among families or households.

4. In the available data, households are defined as groups of persons pooling their income and sharing arrangements for food and other essentials of living, usually residing in the same housing unit. A family differs from a household in that the members of the group residing together and sharing arrangements for living are all related by blood, adoption, or marriage, whereas a household may include nonrelated members (boarders, employees living with the employer, and the like). In fact, at least in the developed countries, the difference between families and households is minor, in that the overwhelming majority of households are family households and the overwhelming majority of families form separate households.

5. We adopted the family or household as the basic recipient unit in the distribution of personal income among a country's population because it is more clearly identifiable, more inclusive, more independent (from others), than the individual recipient unit. But it, too, is subject to some important limitations. One such limitation relates to the institutional population (in military barracks, in prisons, in nursing homes, etc.) which is usually excluded in the size distributions of income, presumably because the persons involved are not members of groups that make their

own decisions about income getting and income spending. This omitted group forms a small proportion of total population in most countries, but there may be cases of dictatorially run societies in which the prison or labor-camp population, or the military forces, accounts for a much greater share.

6. A different problem is raised by possible ties existing among families (and unrelated individuals, treated separately in the U.S. data) or among households. Clearly, a household of one person and another household may be related in that the one person is a member of a family but living separately from it; and an older generation family of two may enjoy ties to another family of four, the head of which is the older couple's son. But we have no data on such ties and can only conjecture their impact on pooling income and economic decisions – which may well differ among societies with different structures of families and family relations.

7. In dealing with the distribution of income among families (and unrelated individuals) or households, we encountered the first major obstacle to meaningful comparisons – the differences among families or households in size, in the number of members. Families can vary from two to well over 10 members; and households can vary from one person to much larger units. These differences in size are a reflection partly of the basic demographic processes of family formation and dissolution, partly of the diverse institutional conditions under which families tend to live separately or jointly. Thus, even the nuclear family of the developed countries grows in size as the parental pair is joined by a limited number of children who remain within the fold until maturity, and then shrinks back to a size of two. In the larger families in the less developed countries, the absolute differences in size through the family's life span are greater. This disparity in size of families or households, in association with the life span of the family units and their differing patterns of separation and joining, is a crucial demographic characteristic of the unit – but it introduces incomparability unless the income total for the unit is related to the size.

8. It makes little sense to talk about inequality in the distribution of income among families or households by income per family or household when the underlying units differ so much in size. A large income for a large family may turn out to be small on a per person or per consumer equivalent basis, and a small income for a small family may turn out to be large with the allowance for size of the family. Size distributions of income among families or households by income per family or household,

reflecting as they do differences in size, are unrevealing – unless the per family or household income differences are so large as to overshadow any reasonably assumed differences in size of units, or unless the latter differences are minor. Neither of these conditions is realistic. It follows that, before any analysis can be undertaken, size distributions of families or households by income per family or household must be converted to distributions of *persons* (or consumer equivalents) by size of family or *household income per person* (or per *consumer*).

9. This requirement is particularly important in view of the widespread use of size distributions of family or household income in intertemporal or international comparisons. The smaller family or household usually receives a smaller income than the larger units, so that the family or household income for a one- or two-person unit is well below the countrywide mean. The proportion of such smaller units among all families or households is far greater in the developed than in the less developed countries – which contributes a much greater inequality component in the size distribution of family or household income in the developed than in the less developed countries. Likewise, the proportion of smaller size units can change rapidly over time, usually rising in the course of population growth and of the shift to modern demographic patterns, again contributing a rising inequality component to the conventional distribution of families or households by income per family or household. The conversion to a per person basis helps to remove this obscuring and often misleading component in the size distribution of income per family or household.

10. Such conversion to a per person (or some variant, depending on the aim of the analysis) basis should, ideally, begin with the individual family or household, its income, and the number of persons in it – deriving the per person income for each family or household separately and then using this per person income as the basis for a size distribution of income among persons. Published results of such a procedure are available only for Israel, but even there with only partial cross-classification detail. We had, therefore, to resort to a conversion based not on identification of per person income of *individual* families or households but of *cells* formed by a cross-classification of the units by size and by income per unit classes. The results, however, were sufficient to indicate what the major results of a detailed conversion would be. It should be stressed that the conversion adopted required that we *begin* with units or cells classified by income per *person*. The task is *not* accomplished by beginning with classes by income

per household (or family), calculating average size of household in these income classes, and then dividing the mean income for each income class by the average size of households in it.

11. The first major finding of the proper conversion is that whereas larger families or households tended to have larger incomes per family or household – a positive correlation that was found in all five countries (United States, Germany, Israel, Taiwan, and the Philippines) covered in the discussion – the larger units showed *lower per person* income than the smaller units. This *negative* correlation between size of family or household and per *person* (or per consumer) income was quite striking and was found in all five countries covered. In other words, the rise in income per household (or family) with the increase in its size does not compensate fully for the latter, with the result that income per person (or per consumer, roughly calculated by assigning half-weight to children under 18) declines as size of unit rises.

12. The second result, partly associated with the first, is the shift in the structure within income classes of households (or families) by size. In the size distribution by income per household, the higher income classes are dominated by the larger households and the lower income classes by the smaller households. In the size distribution among *persons* (or consumers) in households, by household income per person (or per consumer), the upper income classes are dominated by the population in the smaller households, and the lower income classes show an overrepresentation of persons or consumers in the larger households. Thus, the very identity of the lower and upper groups on the income scale shifts as we convert from a size distribution of households by income per household to a size distribution of persons (or consumers) by income per person (or consumer).

13. The third result of the conversion is that the aggregate inequality of the distribution of income among persons (or consumers) in households (or families) by income per person or per consumer may differ from that of the more conventional size distribution among households (or families) by income per family or household. And the differences are not necessarily of the same magnitude and in the same direction for the various countries in our sample and may not be the same even for the same country at different times. While the changes are not proportionately large, since the size component is only one factor in the variance of either per household or per person income, they can affect comparisons in that among distributions for two countries one will show more inequality in a distribution

by income per household and the other will show more inequality, for the same year and income total, in the distribution by income per person (this was found in the comparison between Israel and Germany).

14. Size of family or household and age of head are closely connected. In a developed country like the United States an average family of two members at its formation rises, mostly by addition of children, to a peak of almost five members at age of head 35–44 and then declines to an average of about two and a half at age of head 65 and over. In less developed countries, with more children per family and possibly different family structure, the pattern of family size by age of head may be different, but no data are at hand in our exploration. But age of head, and the implicit duration of family's life, while associated with size, is also a partly independent demographic characteristic and affects income per family and family income per person.

15. In developed countries, like the United States and Israel (and probably others), income per family moves with changes in age of head like an inverted U: It begins with a relatively low level at age of head under 25, rises to a peak about twice the initial trough by age 45–54, and then declines to a terminal trough about half of the peak at age 65 and over. And the developed countries are distinguished by substantial proportions of families or households in young and particularly old age-of-head classes. The combination of this substantial swing in per family income by age of head, with substantial proportions of families at the low income age extremes, introduces a substantial income inequality component into the conventional size distribution of income by income per family or per household in the developed countries. Since time patterns of income per family with age of head can vary in shape and amplitude, while *lifetime* income per family can remain the same, the inequality-of-income component thus introduced has no direct bearing on, and should be excluded from, comparisons of long-term lifetime incomes.

16. For the two less developed countries discussed here, Taiwan and the Philippines, both the distribution of families or households by age of head and the pattern of movement of income per family or household with changes in age of head through the life span differ from those observed for the United States and Israel. The share of the families in the older age brackets, particularly that of 65 and over, is far lower in these less developed countries, a finding explicable in terms of their higher rate of growth and natural increase, which makes for high proportions of the younger age-of-head groups and low shares of the old. The pat-

tern of movement of income per family does not show, as it does in the developed countries, a low level for the group with head aged 65 and over. In Taiwan, in particular, the older age-of-head groups show relatively high income per family, especially among the farmers; and in the Philippines, for Manila and suburbs, the peak income per family is shown among families with head aged 65 and over. Because of the combinations of low shares of families or households at the extreme age classes, particularly the old, and the absence of a second, pronounced trough in per family income at the end of the life span, the inequality component introduced by the age-of-head differentials in income per family in the two less developed countries is appreciably smaller than in the United States and Israel. This suggests that comparisons of size distributions of income among families or households between developed and less developed countries may be significantly biased, if viewed as comparisons of distributions of long-term income levels or lifetime incomes: they may exaggerate inequality in the developed countries compared with that in the less developed.

17. We have no data at hand for the less developed countries to shift from income per family by age of head to family income per person by age of head. A full explanation of the differences between developed and less developed countries with respect to age-of-head differentials in income per family must await further work on the composition of families by age of head in the less developed countries. But the details for the United States show that size of family moves in rough consonance with the movement by age of head of income per family, also revealing an inverted U but with a peak in the size variable at age of head 35–44 and the peak in the income per family variable at age of head 45–54. If we divide average income per family for each age-of-head class by the average number of persons per family for that class, the time pattern of family income per head is quite different from that for income per family, failing to show the marked inverted U. On a per person basis, income in the three youngest age-of-head classes (i.e., under 25, 25–34, and 35–44) slowly rises from about 0.8 to 0.9 of the countrywide mean, rises further to about 1.2 and a peak of 1.4 in the age classes of 45–54 and 55–64, and declines slightly below the mean in the age class 65 and over. The total amplitude of inequality in per person income by age classes is about the same as that for age-of-head differentials in income per *family* – but the pattern is significantly different. When the conversion is to family income per *consumer*, the time pattern is like that in income per person,

but the amplitude of the income inequality among age-of-head classes is substantially reduced.

18. It need not be stressed that the differentials among age-of-head groups of families in family income per person can vary from distribution to distribution but still be compatible with the same *lifetime* income per *person* in all of them. If and when we are in a position to estimate family income per person by age of head in some less developed countries, we may find the time patterns and the amplitudes of the age-of-head differentials in per person income in these countries different from those we found for the United States. We would then have to conclude that comparisons of size distributions by per person income between developed and less developed countries are affected by a component that obscures the differences and similarities in the distributions by size of *lifetime* family income per person, or by size of family income per person within long stretches of the life span of the family.

19. The pattern of income per person (or per consumer) associated with the successive age-of-head classes in the cross section was derived above by using *averages* of family income and of size of family for each of these different age-of-head classes. But for the United States it is possible to distinguish different size groups of families *within* each age-of-head class and to estimate the per family and per person income of each resulting cell. We can then envisage cohorts of families over time that follow paths set by different combinations of these cells. Thus a family of two at age of head under 25 may move to three, four, and five members in the next three age-of-head classes and then down to two by the terminal age class; whereas another family may move from two members in the youngest age-of-head class to four, five, and seven at the peak and then down to two at the terminal age class; and still a third family may be assumed to vary from two to only three at the largest, and then down to two. Given income data for each cell in the cross-classification, it is possible to estimate the movement in per person (or per consumer) income for these cohorts of families with different paths of changes in size. The significant difference between these time patterns of per person income through successive age-of-head classes is that in the *small* families, the pattern, like that of income per family, will be an inverted U. But as the families move to much larger numbers in the central age-of-head classes (i.e., 35–44 and 45–54), the per person income will drop sharply and the per person or per consumer pattern will look like a U, with low income levels in the middle age brackets, and relatively high levels at both ends. A similar

exercise would be of much interest for those other developed countries, for which detail comparable to that for the United States is available, and for at least a few less developed countries, in which the results may be quite different.

20. One implication of the simulation of different time patterns of size of family by age-of-head classes is brought out clearly when we use, as was done in the preceding section of this essay, age-of-head cross-section differences in income per person (for various size classes within age-of-head groups) to derive lifetime gross income per family or per person. If we simplify this task by omitting allowance for both the *time* trend in income per family or per person and the *discount* in deriving current value of lifetime incomes, we can translate the illustrative patterns of movement in the number of persons in the family in the successive age-of-head classes into number and per person income in the corresponding phases of some standard assumed total life span. Using the cross-classification data for the United States in such a translation, we find that the negative correlation between size of family and family income per person is translated into a negative correlation between the average size of family over its lifetime span and lifetime per person (and probably per consumer) gross income. In other words, the larger the family size over the family's lifetime, which usually means the larger number of children, the lower the lifetime income per person or per consumer. The corollary implication is that the time pattern of income per person through the successive phases of a large family's life span is like a U, with the trough in the middle phase of the life span, indicating pressure of number on family income in these middle age-of-head phases. There is thus a line of connection between the impact of higher birth rates on the size of the family, the time pattern of movement of income per family and per person, the cross-section differentials in income per family and per person by age of head, and the differences in gross family income per person and per consumer over the lifetime of the family, as well as a rather unstable time pattern of per person income with a trough in the middle age-of-head brackets. While this finding is a result of illustrative assumptions and will vary with variations in these assumptions, the general connection is not likely to be affected significantly – so long as the negative correlation between size of family and per person income remains.

The explorations that led to the conclusions just summarized were pursued with an interest in the relation between economic growth and income inequalities, either in changes over time in the course of a country's growth or in differences in comparisons among countries at different levels of economic development. Concern with this analytical problem, combined with an interest in the relations between economic growth and population growth, led to an emphasis on the demographic aspects of the size distributions of income used so often for measuring income inequalities, and, I must add, to a relative neglect of the definition-of-income aspects, except those directly raised by a consideration of the recipient unit.

The bearing of the conclusions above on past, current, and future work on the relation between economic growth and income inequality should be tested in further inquiry. But, even as they stand, the conclusions strongly suggest a need for critical reexamination of the mushrooming literature that employs size distributions of income among families or households by income per family or household to gauge income inequalities, in intertemporal and interspatial comparisons. If the aim is to observe and analyze the relation between long-term growth and long-term income levels, it may not be unreasonable to suggest that most of the studies will be found incomplete, and the inferences drawn may turn out to be premature. This is apart from the other characteristics of the size distribution of income data – their reference to a single year's income and the low quality of the underlying basic data, particularly in the less developed countries.

But the empirical basis of our conclusions is narrow. And as one looks ahead it seems clear that an adequate analysis of the demographic aspects of the size distributions of income would have to cover a large sample of countries and periods – for the patterns of the underlying demographic processes change over time and differ among regions. An extensive literature is at hand on the formation and life spans of families, and some studies have been made even of the effects of these life cycles on consumption and savings propensities.[22] But these must be supplemented by analysis of data directly relevant to income differentials associated with size and composition of families through the phases of their life cycle, in different countries, and in different periods. Some time will pass before we attain enough knowledge of the diversity of the structures of the demographic components in their effect on the income level to be able to derive some general, tested findings.

22 A useful summary appears in the United Nations, *The Determinants and Consequences of Population Trends* (New York: United Nations, 1973), 1:335–64, and 434–504. Vol. 2, containing a detailed bibliography, is scheduled to be published shortly.

Meanwhile, it should be helpful to adjust the conventional size distributions of income among families or households by income per family or household. The first and most necessary and obvious adjustment is for size. The other is for age of head or phase in the life cycle of the family. And there may be others as analysis intensifies. A variety of methodological and substantive questions will arise in the course of such adjustments, but these questions could be answered only by specifying the analytical purpose and working with a variety of empirical data. Only by dint of experimentation can we hope to achieve further knowledge of the relevant aspects of the internal structure of families, a subject with which we are not too well acquainted even in the developed countries, let alone in the less developed.

While such further study of the bearing of demographic factors on distribution of income and tentative adjustments of the available conventional size distributions of income among households are both useful and could yield new insights in the longer run, an alternative, not necessarily exclusive, should be noted. This alternative is to emphasize the distribution of income among distinct socioeconomic groups of families or households. Assume that we can define, and distinguish in observational data, socioeconomic groups that play different roles in, and are affected differently by, economic growth, for example, landless agricultural laborers; small, middle-size, and large farmers; handicraft producers; blue-collar employees of factories or modern utilities; small-scale shopkeepers; larger merchants; professional classes. If we can identify the family groups by attachment of the head to one of these socioeconomic classes, we would have analytically meaningful groups, possibly with data on the average size of the family in each. Trends over time and intercountry differentials in income inequality as measured among such groups would be meaningful and revealing. The same can be said even of the division of income among male members of the labor force in their working ages (when they are also likely to be heads of families) by their attachment to the various productive sectors of the economy, assuming that we can make rough adjustments for attachment to more than one sector (particularly for those in agriculture but earning substantial proportions of income in other sectors) and for differing numbers of dependents per male member of the labor force for the several sectors.

This emphasis on group averages and magnitudes would seem to have several advantages, even if we lose the variance among the households within the group. The averaging would remove much of the accidental, one-year effect on the income totals. The differences in the demographic components would probably be much less marked and more easily recognizable if significant among these groups than for individual households. The distribution of families by age of head would differ less between one socioeconomic group and another than, say, among individual households grouped by size of income per household; and the same would be true of the average size of household. And such *inter*group differences of demographic characteristics could be more easily approximated and understood. More important, these socioeconomic groups could be more easily connected to the divisions within the national economic accounts, whether they refer to the production sectors, or to type of income (reflecting status in the labor force), or even to region. This connection cannot be made between national economic accounts and the size distribution of income, however useful the juxtaposition of the aggregate totals from both for rough checking purposes. It is this distribution of income and product among the labor force classified by attachment to the various production sectors, which, on the income side, relies on national economic accounts, that I have found useful on several occasions in my work on economic growth, its antecedents and consequences.

If such a classification by socioeconomic groups could be formulated, and made comparable for countries at different levels of economic development and with different economic structures, the effort to gather information in the censuses and in the field could yield the relevant data, which could then be supplemented occasionally by a detailed size distribution. At least it might influence the way in which households or families are grouped in the field studies on family income and expenditures, and also affect the grouping of data on employment and product as they enter the national economic accounts. To be sure, we would confront here the inadequacy of the standardized international set of economic accounts in its classification of production sectors and definitions of several income items and of labor force. But this confrontation is long overdue, and the delay seems to me to be responsible for many difficulties in international comparisons of economic accounts, and particularly, of measures of economic growth today.

These comments on the possible approach to distribution of income among socioeconomic groups have obviously not been tested by empirical data. They are offered here to point up the need to examine anew our efforts to establish the major connections between economic growth and the income and employment structures of the population.

8. Size and age structure of family households: exploratory comparisons

A family may be defined as a group of persons "related, to a specified degree, through blood, adoption, or marriage."[1] The same source states: "The degree of relationship used in determining the limits of the family is dependent upon the uses to which the data are to be put and so cannot be precisely set for world-wide use."

To the extent that ties of blood, marriage, or adoption are indicative of a community of interest of members, whatever their location, the family, in this broad sense, is an important unit in economic analysis – since it presumably makes joint decisions on the production and disposition of income, either in a continuous and comprehensive fashion, or intermittently and over a limited range. The possibility of such joint action makes the family unit useful in the study of income inequalities, of the supply of labor force, and of the flow of savings and capital formation.

The difficulty is that there are no comparative data on the family in the broad definition of the term. The available statistics relate to households, defined by location and by community of arrangements for providing essentials of living. The data usually cover all households, not limited to family households, although the latter are such a preponderant proportion that the characteristics of the totals can be identified as those of family households.[2] The statistical analysis undertaken here is confined to data

Reprinted from: *Population and Development Review*, Volume 4, Number 2.

1 For this and related definitions, United Nations, *Manual VII. Methods of Projecting Households and Families* (New York, 1973), p. 6.

2 Thus for the United States in March 1976 (used in Table 8.1), only 2.6 out of 72.9 million households had members unrelated to the head; thus, family households comprised 97 percent of the total. (See U.S. Bureau of the Census, *Current Population Reports, Series P-60, no. 104* [Washington: March 1977], Table 3, p. 13). There are no data at hand on this point for other countries, but the large preponderance of family among all households is generally asserted in the source cited in note 1.

on households. But in evaluating the data and the findings that they suggest, we must keep in mind the concept of the family as a group, the relations among whose members are close enough to lead to significant joint decision on economic matters.

Our interest in the size and structure of households is due to the use of households as the main recipient unit in size-distributions of income (and of other associated economic variables). Whatever we learn of the characteristics of household units should promote better understanding, or at least less misunderstanding, of the meaning of the conventional size-distributions of income. In this connection, two earlier papers, to which the present one is a sequel, suggested findings that are relevant here and may be briefly noted.[3] First, in general, the average household in the developing countries and regions has, in recent years, been significantly larger than in the developed countries. One major factor in this difference is the significantly larger proportion of children in the total population of the developing countries than of the developed countries – and children are preponderantly members of family households. Second, the differences in size of households within a country are, as might be expected, positively associated with total income per household. But if we shift to household income per person, or per consumer unit, the smaller households tend to show, quite generally, higher levels of per person, or per consumer unit, income than larger households.

The analysis below deals mainly with comparisons of average size of household – in international cross-section for recent years, in intra-national comparisons of households between the rural and urban populations, and in comparisons over long time spans for a single country. The aim is to allocate the differences in average size between the contribution of the presence of children (reflecting differences in fertility and rates of natural increase) and that of the tendency of adults to live jointly or separately. First the procedure for such an allocation is described in a comparison for the United States (March 1976) and Taiwan (end of 1975) for which we have the requisite detailed data. Then such allocations of differences in average size are illustrated for comparisons among countries and regions at different levels of development; comparisons between

3 The earlier paper, "Fertility differentials between less developed and developed regions: Components and implications," *Proceedings of the American Philosophical Society* 119, no. 5 (October 1975), touches upon the first point (see Table 8.10, and discussion, pp. 385–388). The later paper, Chapter 7, above, explores the second set of findings in Section III, "Differences in size of family or household."

rural and urban households within countries; and comparisons over a long time span within a single country. The distinctive characteristics of the much larger proportion of small households, all adult, in developed regions as compared with those in developing regions are explored in a further comparison between the United States and Taiwan, using the cross-classification of households by size and by age of head (and partly by sex of head). Concluding comments bring us back to the wider concept of the family mentioned above, in an attempt to evaluate the significance of our findings for households in their bearing upon the economic role of the family, widely defined, in countries or regions at different levels of economic development.

I. Allocation of differences in size of average household: an illustration

The comparison of the distributions of households by size (and related variables) in the United States and Taiwan, in Table 8.1, provides an illustration that helps us outline the procedure for distinguishing the differences due to presence of children from those due to presence of related adults. The interest in this distinction stems from the difference in the sources of what might be called the NIC factor (natural increase-children) and the JAA factor (jointness or apartness of adults). In almost all countries, children are the responsibility of their parents or of other related members of the family so that they are naturally members of family households and their proportion in total population is, all other conditions being equal, positively associated with the average size of the household. But in a population with limited emigration and immigration, the proportion of children is a function of fertility and survival; thus there is a direct connection between the population's vital rates and the average size of the household. The forces behind the JAA factor are different, in that they have to do with conditions that affect the degree to which adults related by blood, marriage, or adoption live together or apart. While there is some association between conditions affecting fertility and natural increase and those affecting family togetherness or apartness, the distinction between these two factors is clearly of analytical interest and value.

Table 8.1 uses data for the United States and Taiwan because they are available in revealing detail, and because the two countries differ substantially in the average size of the household. The evidence can be briefly summarized.

Table 8.1. *Structure of households by size, United States, 1970 and 1976, and Taiwan, 1975*

A. *United States, March 1970 and March 1976*

Size–classes of households	March 1976 % shares		Relative money income, 1975 (avg. = 100)		March 1970	Persons per HH	
	HHs (1)	Persons (2)	Per HH (3)	Per person (4)	% shares HHs (5)	Below 18 (6)	18 and over (7)
1. 1 person	20.6	7.1	49	140	17.0	0	1.00
2. 2 persons	30.6	21.4	96	138	28.8	0.06	1.94
3. 3 persons	17.2	18.0	114	109	17.3	0.71	2.29
4. 4 persons	15.7	21.6	127	92	15.8	1.64	2.36
5. 5 persons	8.6	14.7	135	79	10.4	2.54	2.46
6. 6 persons	4.1	8.4	131	64	5.6	3.40	2.60
7. 7 and over	3.2	8.8	124	46	5.1	5.21	3.06
	in millions		US $000s		(mill.)		
8. Total	72.87	210.6	13.78	4.77	62.87	1.12	2.05
9. Persons per household	2.89				3.17		

B. *Taiwan area, end 1975*

Size–classes of households	% shares in		Relative income, 1975 (avg. = 100)		Persons per HH	
	HHs (1)	Persons (2)	Per HH (3)	Per person (4)	Minors (5)	Adults (6)
10. 1 person	3.1	0.6	48	255	0	1.00
11. 2 persons	5.2	2.0	76	202	0.19	1.81
12. 3 persons	10.3	5.9	85	149	0.89	2.11
13. 4 persons	16.9	12.8	95	125	1.75	2.25
14. 5 persons	22.3	21.1	98	104	2.60	2.40
15. 6 persons	18.9	21.6	104	91	3.32	2.68
16. 7 and over	23.3	36.0	128	82	4.45	3.73
17. 7 persons	11.3	14.9	106	80	3.95	3.05
18. 8 persons	6.0	9.1	122	80	4.33	3.67
19. 9 and over	6.0	12.0	144	72	5.50	5.03
	in millions		NT $000s			
20. Total	3.01	15.88	101.81	19.32	2.64	2.63

Notes: Panel A, cols. 1–4 are from U.S. Bureau of the Census, *Current Population Reports*, Series P-60, no. 104 (March 1977), Table 3, p. 13; and Table 15, p. 48.
Panel A, col. 5 was calculated from US Bureau of Census, *Current Population Reports*, Series P-60, no. 72 (August 1970), Table 5, p. 15.
Panel A, cols. 6 and 7: The breakdown between persons under age 18 and 18 and over is given in the source for col. 5 for the total population in households, not for the size-classes

First, the columns relating to average income per household and per person, for households grouped by size, confirm the findings noted above on the consistent negative association between per person income and size of the household, contrasted with the positive association between household total income and household size (columns 3 and 4, Panels A and B).

Second, and more directly relevant here, the difference in average size of household, between 2.89 persons in the United States in March 1976 and 5.27 persons in Taiwan at the end of 1975, is clearly due to a markedly different distribution of households by size in the two countries. In the United States, the proportion of small households (of one and two persons each) was over 50 percent; it was less than 10 percent in Taiwan. In contrast, the proportion of households of six or more persons was well below 10 percent in the United States and 42 percent in Taiwan.

Third, the data for both countries provide a breakdown (directly or indirectly) between the younger population and the older, for each class of households grouped by size. For the United States this breakdown had to be estimated for 1970 (March), the date at which the population census provides more detail than the annual sample survey of family incomes. For Taiwan it was taken directly from the official report on the 1975 family sample survey. The line of division is set at 18 years of age for the United States and that for Taiwan at 21, making direct comparison difficult; but this disparity does not affect what appear to be two main conclusions from the data as given.

The first is that in the one- and two-person households, the proportion of the young population is either zero or so small as to be negligible (see lines 1 and 2, col. 6, Panel A; and lines 10 and 11, col. 5, Panel B); and the

Notes to Table 8.1 *(cont.)*

of households. We estimated the breakdown, for households beginning with the size-class of 2 and through that of 7 and over by using the breakdown given for *families* (of 2 and over) for the same year in U.S. Bureau of the Census, *1970 Census of Population*, Subject Report PC(2) 4A, *Family Composition* (May 1973), Table 3, pp. 7–8; applying the ratios to the size-classes of households; and adjusting to add out to the totals of below 18 and 18 and over given in the source for col. 5.
Panel B: Taken or calculated from Directorate General of Budget, Accounting and Statistics (DGBAS), *Report on the Survey of Personal Income Distribution in Taiwan Area, 1975* (Taipei, 1976), Table 18, pp. 164–169; and text Tables 11, p. 62, and 13, p. 68.
Taiwan Area includes all of the country; Taiwan Province (to be used in later tables) excludes Taipei City.
Minors are defined as persons under 21 years of age; adults as persons 21 years old and over.
The income data refer to "available" income, that is, "distributed factor income plus current transfer receipts less current transfer expenditures" (p. 47).

proportion would be even lower if the line between children and adults were drawn not at 18 or 21 but at a lower age.

The second conclusion is that while the contribution of those under 18 or under 21 is substantial in the shift from two-person households to those in larger size-classes, there is also a rise in the number of adults per household (see cols. 6 and 7 of Panel A, lines 3–8, and cols. 5 and 6 of Panel B, lines 12–19). As the data stand in Table 8.1, direct comparisons of children and adults between the United States and Taiwan cannot be made. Yet with an average of persons aged 18 and over per household in the United States of 2.05 (in 1970), and an average of persons aged 21 and over per household in Taiwan of 2.63 (in 1975), the difference between the two countries in numbers of adults per household must make a substantial contribution to the intercountry differences in average size of the household. And it is particularly at the levels of large households that the difference in contribution of disparities in numbers of adults becomes significant.

Table 8.1 and the comments on the findings that it suggests are preliminary to a full allocation of the differences in average size of the households between Taiwan and the United States – one that would serve as a pattern to be applied to a variety of international and other comparisons.

Before considering the allocation shown in Table 8.2, it may help to state specifically the two assumptions on which it and all following allocations are based, and to indicate the decision with reference to the dividing age-line between children and adults that is followed in the analysis below.

The first assumption is that the proportion of an age group defined as that of children (or that of adults) to total population can be identified with the proportion of the same age group to the total of the population included in individual households. The two sets of ratios are not necessarily identical, because total population includes institutional groups not included under private, individual households, and the proportions of age groups in the institutional population are not usually the same as in the household population. But the data on households in relation to total population, used in the subsequent sections of this article (mostly from the United Nations, *Demographic Yearbooks*, for selected years), show that in the vast majority of countries population in households is close to total population, so that the possible error involved in this assumption is minor to the point of being negligible.

The second assumption is that one- and two-person households in-

Table 8.2. *Allocation of differences in average size of household, Taiwan (end 1975) and United States (March 1976)*

	Children defined as below 18				Children defined as below 15			
	Taiwan (1)	United States (2)	Differ- ence (3)	Per- cent (4)	Taiwan (5)	United States (6)	Differ- ence (7)	Per- cent (8)
A. Allocation between contribution of children and adults								
1. Persons per household	5.27	2.89	2.38	100.0	5.27	2.89	2.38	100.0
2. Percent of children in total	44.1	30.8	—	—	35.3	25.3	—	—
3. Children per household	2.32	0.89	1.43	60.1	1.86	0.73	1.13	47.5
4. Adults per household	2.95	2.00	0.95	39.9	3.41	2.16	1.25	52.5
B. Contribution of different proportions of one-, two-person, and all larger households (of three and over)								
5. Percent of one-person households	3.1	20.6	—	—	3.1	20.6	—	—
6. Deviation from higher average of adults per household	−1.95	−1.95	—	—	−2.41	−2.41	—	—
7. Contribution of one-person households (line 5 × line 6)	−0.060	−0.402	0.342	14.4	−0.075	−0.496	0.421	17.7
8. Percent of two-person households	5.2	30.6	—	—	5.2	30.6	—	—
9. Deviation	−0.95	−0.95	—	—	−1.41	−1.41	—	—
10. Contribution of two-person households (line 8 × line 9)	−0.049	−0.29	0.242	10.1	−0.073	−0.431	0.358	15.0
11. Contribution of households of three and over	+0.109	−0.257	0.366	15.4	0.148	−0.323	0.471	19.8

Notes: All data, with exceptions noted below, are from Table 8.1. The exceptions are the percentages in line 2 for Taiwan, and the percentage in line 2, col. 6 for the United States. The estimates for Taiwan were calculated from the age distribution at the end of 1975, shown in DGBAS, *Statistical Yearbook, 1975* (Taipei, 1976), p. 4. The estimate for the United States was taken from United Nations, "Selected world demographic indicators

clude such negligible proportions of children that they can be assumed
to be limited to adults alone. This was found to be the case for Taiwan
and the United States in Table 8.1 and could be further checked if cross-
classifications by age structure and size-classes of households could be
found for other countries, at different levels of economic development. It
also partly depends on the level of the age-line that distinguishes between
children and adults. This, in turn, raises a question as to the full meaning
of the distinction between children and adults.

The position taken here is that the major attribute of children in this
analysis is their economic and other dependence, which makes it indispensable for them to be members of a family (barring institutional provisions when the family is not available, or community forms of care of the
type involved in some of the Israeli kibbutzim). At the age when, within a
given society, younger members of the family assume a share and responsibility in production, they cease to be effectively dependent and acquire
mobility among households not theretofore feasible. The difficulty is that
this age may differ among societies at different levels of economic and
social development; and yet we need an identical dividing line, if differences arising in the comparison are to be allocated between the NIC and
the JAA factors. In Table 8.2, two such age dividing lines are used – at 18
and 15 years. We adopted the lower dividing line of 15 for our subsequent
analysis, since it appeared more suitable for the developing countries; but
this decision about the age-dividing line can be changed, within the procedure adopted, with results for the allocation that can be easily inferred
from the comparison of the results for the two dividing lines in Table 8.2.

Panel A of the table shows that the proportion of children in the total,

Notes to Table 8.2 *(cont.)*

by countries, 1950–2000," *Working Paper ESA/P/WP, 55* (May 1975) mimeograph, p. 97
(medium variant).
The numbers of children and adults per household are obtained by multiplying the percentages in line 2 by the entries in line 1 (cols. 1–2 and 5–6). The differences in cols. 3
and 7, lines 1, 3, and 4, are obtained by subtraction of the smaller household country from
the larger.
The contributions in Panel B of the one-person, two-person, and three-or-more-person
households, assume that there are *no* children in the two former groups of households. The
contributions are then estimated with reference to the number of adults per household in
the country with the larger average household (measured in terms of total persons).
The residual (line 10) is, for the larger household country, the difference between the sum
of entries in lines 7 and 10 and zero; for the smaller household country, it is the difference
between the sum of entries in lines 7 and 10 and total shortfall in adults per household
(i.e., −0.950 in col. 3 and −1.250 in col. 7).
The percentages in cols. 4 and 8 are to the total difference shown in line 1, cols. 3 and 7.

and thus in the household, population was much larger in Taiwan than in the United States: 44 compared with 31 percent for persons under age 18, and 35 compared with 25 percent for persons under age 15. The contribution of children to the total difference in the average size of the household between the two countries was then 1.43 persons, or 60 percent of the total, when children were defined as under 18; and 1.13 persons, or 47 percent of the total, when children were defined as under 15. In either case, a substantial component in the total difference was the differing number of adults per household. It contributed 40 percent of the total difference when adults were defined as aged 18 years and over, and 53 percent when they were defined as aged 15 years and over. Obviously, the *higher* we set the age-line of division between children and adults, the greater will be the proportional contribution of children to the total difference in size of average household between two countries (or regions) and the smaller the proportional contribution of adults, with *lowering* the age-line of division having the opposite effect.

In Panel B we proceed to distinguish the effects on differing size of households, *in terms of adults*, of the proportions of households containing one, two, and three or more persons (for the last group only the average number of adults per household is involved). In general, the country with the larger average household (in this case Taiwan) will also have a larger number of adults per household; and the contribution to this difference in average number of adults can be traced to the effects of differing proportions of households containing one, two, and three or more persons. It may be observed in Panel B that the greater proportion of one- and two-person households in the United States than in Taiwan makes a marked contribution to the differences in size of average household – 14.4 plus 10.1, or 24.5 percent under one definition of children (see col. 4, lines 7 plus 10); and 17.7 plus 15.0, or 32.7 percent under the other (see col. 8, lines 7 and 10). The greater proportion (and possibly larger size in terms of adults) of households with three or more persons in Taiwan contributes another 15 or 20 percent of the total difference in size of average household between the two countries (see line 11, cols. 4 and 8).

The procedure just outlined could be elaborated were the data for countries or regions involved in the comparison to contain cross-section classifications of households by number of persons as well as age structure of members. Such a cross-classification would permit experimentation with different age levels at which the distinction between children and adults could be made (and with distinguishing ages of adults at which they might become as dependent as children); and the total difference could be allocated among more subgroups of households by number of their adult members. But such data are not at hand and would require a search in basic census or sample sources that is not feasible here.

We now have two procedures for allocating differences in average size of household, for comparisons among and within countries and regions and over long time spans. The procedure for allocating differences between the presence of children factor and the jointness or apartness of adults factor should enable us to observe the differing or changing proportional effects of these two different groups of factors under varying conditions in time and space. The procedure for determining the effects of different or changing proportions of one- and two-person households (assumed to contain only adults) on differences in average size of household should provide some insight into how the jointness or apartness of adults factor operates – whether through a changing proportion of very small (one- or two-person) households, or through a changing or different average number of adults per larger household (three persons or more).

II. Allocation of differences in average size of household: international, rural–urban, and over-time comparisons

International comparisons

Our first set of comparisons (Table 8.3) relates to five countries, selected to cover a wide range in average size of household. The decision to limit the analysis to a few countries, rather than attempt a summary of a larger number of countries in developed and developing regions of the world, was made because of the limitations of the coverage of United Nations data on size and size-distribution of households and the lack of comparability specifically in the definition and distinction of one-person households.[4] This latter limitation is particularly restrictive in its bearing upon

---

4 See on both points the discussion in the United Nations source cited in note 1 (Chapter 2, "Evaluation of data," pp. 12–16). With respect to one-person households, the source comments: "Both lodgers and boarders, and even the single persons living separately in apartments, are marginal groups whose definitions are generally not clear-cut. The distinction between them is sometimes quite arbitrary."

Table 8.3. *Allocations of differences in average size of household, selected countries, recent years*

	A. *Basic data for the individual countries*				
	Sweden, 1970 (1)	Japan, 1970 (2)	Brazil, 1970 (3)	Syria, 1970 (4)	Thailand, 1960 (5)
Average crude vital rates, per 1,000, preceding three (or two, in col. 5) quinquennia					
1. Birth rates	14.7	17.7	39.0	47.3	47.1
2. Death rates	10.0	7.3	10.3	17.0	19.7
3. Rates of natural increase	4.7	10.4	28.7	30.3	27.4
4. Rates of growth of population	6.5	10.0	28.8	30.3	27.7
Data relating to households					
5. Persons per HH	2.59	3.62	4.78	5.91	5.64
6. Percent of total population below 15	20.8	24.0	42.7	45.2	44.7
7. Children per HH	0.54	0.87	2.04	2.67	2.52
8. Adults per HH	2.05	2.75	2.74	3.24	3.12
9. Percent of one-person HHs	25.3	13.2	5.2	5.7	2.5
10. Percent of two-person HHs	29.6	15.0	14.9	9.1	7.3

B. *Allocation of differences between NIC (natural increase-children factor) and JAA (jointness and apartness of adults factor)*

	Japan and Sweden (1)	Brazil and Sweden (2)	Syria and Sweden (3)	Brazil and Japan (4)	Syria and Japan (5)	Syria and Brazil (6)	Thailand and Brazil (7)	Thailand and Sweden (8)
11. Differences in persons per HH	1.03	2.19	3.32	1.16	2.29	1.13	1.06	3.05
12. NIC	0.33	1.50	2.13	1.17	1.80	0.63	0.48	1.98
13. JAA	0.70	0.69	1.19	−0.01	0.49	0.50	0.58	1.07
14. NIC percent	32	68	64	101	79	56	45	65
15. JAA percent	68	32	36	−1	21	44	55	35

C. *Contributions of the proportions of one- and two-person households to differences in average size of households, selected comparisons*

	Larger households (1)	Smaller households (2)	Differential contribution (1 − 2) (3)	Percent of total difference (4)
Japan–Sweden				
16. Contribution of one-person HHs	−0.023	−0.443	0.420	41

Table 8.3 *(cont.)*

	Larger households (1)	Smaller households (2)	Differential contribution (1 − 2) (3)	Percent of total difference (4)
17. Contribution of two-person HHs	−0.011	−0.222	0.211	20
18. Residual (contribution of larger HHs)	0.034	−0.035	0.069	7
Brazil–Sweden				
19. Contribution of one-person HHs	−0.009	−0.440	0.431	20
20. Contribution of two-person HHs	−0.011	−0.219	0.208	10
21. Residual	0.020	−0.031	0.056	2
Syria–Sweden				
22. One-person HHs	−0.013	−0.567	0.554	17
23. Two-person HHs	−0.011	−0.367	0.356	11
24. Residual	0.024	−0.256	0.280	9
Syria–Brazil				
25. One-person HHs	−0.013	−0.012	−0.001	−0.1
26. Two-person HHs	−0.011	−0.018	0.007	0.6
27. Residual	0.024	−0.470	0.494	43.7

Notes: Lines 1–4 and 6: The entries are calculated from the United Nations 1975 working paper cited in the notes to Table 8.2. The entries in lines 1–4 are arithmetic means of the quinquennial (3 or 2) birth, death, natural increase, and growth rates, preceding 1970 or 1960. Those in line 6 are summations of the percentages of total population shown for 0–4 and 5–14 age groups.
Lines 5, 9, and 10 were taken from U.N. summaries of data on distributions of households by size (number of person-classes), in *Demographic Yearbook, 1973* (New York, 1974), Table 24, pp. 396 ff; and *Demographic Yearbook, 1971* (New York, 1972), Table 11, pp. 396 ff.
All other entries by calculation from the basic data in lines 5, 6, 9, and 10. For the procedure see the notes to Table 8.2 above and the discussion in the text.

an allocation of the type outlined in Table 8.2, since it bars reliance on the estimate of effects of the larger proportion of one-person households usually found in the more developed countries with a lower average size of household (but also found in a large number of developing countries).

Table 8.3 includes, for each country, data not only on size of households, but also on the broader demographic characteristics – the relevant rates being averages over the 15-year period preceding the date of line 6 and of the statistics on household size. The rate of population growth (line 4) can differ from the rate of natural increase (line 3), because of a substantial balance of in-and-out migration. But the difference is significant only for Sweden, reflecting a substantial in-migration to the country, which would lower somewhat the percentage proportion of children under age 15 years in the total population.

For the small sample covered here, there is close positive association between rates of natural increase and growth rates of population on one hand, and the proportions of children under age 15 in the total population on the other. Since the differences in birth rates are far more dominant than those in death rates, it is the former that are largely responsible for the differentials in rates of natural increase and growth rates of population, and it is the fertility differentials that largely account for the differences in the proportions of children under age 15 in the total population. The set of connections observed here for the small number of countries would be found also in the larger universe, so long as the birth rate differentials dominated the differences in rate of natural increase in the countries included.

The procedure followed rests on binary comparisons. In Panel B the allocation is between the presence of children factor and the jointness of adults factor; and the dominant impression is of a wide variety of combinations. Thus, in comparing Japan and Sweden, with a difference in average household size of 1.03 persons, we find that the children's proportion contributes only about a third of the total difference, two-thirds being due to the greater jointness of adults in Japan. In the Brazil–Sweden comparison, with a much wider disparity in the average size of households in the two countries, the contribution of children is much larger; the contribution of jointness of adults is absolutely the same, but proportionally much smaller than in the Sweden–Japan comparison. Finally, in the comparison between Syria and Sweden, with a still larger disparity in the average size of the household, the presence of children is dominant; yet the contribution of jointness of adults is also absolutely larger (1.19 persons per household, compared with about 0.7 in the Sweden–Japan and Sweden–Brazil comparisons). Apparently, the international differences in patterns of household and family are substantial not only with respect to differing numbers of children associated with differential fertility, but also in the patterns of joint or separate living of adult members. Some countries, like Japan, Syria, and Thailand, show more of a tendency toward joint residence by adult members than appears to be true of Brazil and Sweden.

There is also considerable variety in the relative contribution of the differing proportions of households of one, two, and three or more persons to the jointness of adults component (Panel C). In the first three of the four binary comparisons shown, the contributions of the one- and two-person households are proportionally high, accounting together for most of the jointness of adults component in the total difference; the relative share of the difference in adults per household among the larger households (of three or more members) is minor. But this is not true of the fourth comparison (Syria–Brazil), in which all of the jointness of adults component is accounted for by the larger number of adults in the Syrian households of three persons and over.

The findings are limited, with the number of countries kept small to obviate too many binary comparisons. But they are varied enough to suggest interesting diversity among countries, not only between the developed and developing groups, but also within the two major divisions, with respect to the relative role of the children and the jointness of adults factors, as well as with respect to the source of contribution to the jointness of adults component of households with differing numbers of persons or adults. There are clearly institutional differences in the structures of households over and above the major effects of fertility and rate of natural increase so clearly associated with levels of economic development. These differences could be brought out more clearly with more intensive analysis of the sex and age structure of households in selected countries, with particular attention to the grouping of households in terms of adult members, for countries otherwise comparable with respect to level of economic development and the magnitude of the presence of children component in the difference in size between average households. Such more intensive study is beyond the limits of the present exploratory essay.

We turn now to data relating to proportions of children under age 15 in total population, which are available for a large number of countries on a worldwide basis, and can be summarized, as of a given date (we use 1955 and 1970), to indicate the possible contribution of this factor to differences in average size of household between developed and developing regions (Table 8.4). The comparison is limited to market economies.

One intriguing finding in Panel A is that in both 1955 and 1970 the percentage proportions of children under 15 differ little among the major

Table 8.4. *Proportions of population under age 15, 1955 and 1970, and approximate allocation of differences in size of average household, 1970, developing and developed market economies*

	Panel A. *Proportions under 15 and growth rates of population, 1955 and 1970*				
	Percent under 15		Population (millions)		Growth rate per 1,000 per year (5)
	1955 (1)	1970 (2)	1955 (3)	1970 (4)	
1. East and Middle South Asia	40.3	43.4	712.1	1,024.7	24.4
2. Middle East	41.9	43.9	108.8	162.2	27.0
3. Sub-Saharan Africa	43.7	44.2	169.2	241.7	24.1
4. Latin America	43.2	44.4	159.6	271.2	36.0
5. All developing countries above	41.4	43.7	1,150	1,700	26.4
6. Developed Europe	23.8	24.2	249.7	282.0	8.1
7. Japan	30.2	24.0	89.8	104.3	10.0
8. United States	29.5	28.3	165.9	204.9	14.2
9. Other overseas	31.0	29.9	27.1	36.8	20.6
10. All developed countries above	27.2	25.8	532.5	628.0	11.0

	Panel B. *Allocation of differences in size of average household between developing and developed countries, 1970*			
	Developing (1)	Developed (2)	Difference (3)	Percent (4)
11. Persons per HH, estimate	5.00	3.00	2.00	100.0
12. Percent under 15	43.7	25.8	—	—
13. Persons under 15 per HH	2.18	0.77	1.41	70.5
14. Adults per HH	2.82	2.23	0.59	29.5
15. Percent of one-person HHs (approximate)	5.0	20.0	—	—
16. Contribution of line 15	−0.091	−0.364	0.273	13.7
17. Percent of two-person HHs (approximate)	10.0	30.0	—	—
18. Contribution of line 17	−0.082	−0.246	0.164	8.2
19. Residual (3+ HHs)	0.173	0.020	0.153	7.6

Notes: The data in Panel A are all from United Nations, *Working Paper, ESA/P/WP 55* (New York, May 1975), mimeograph. Eastern and Middle South Asia is the sum of the two regions so indicated; Middle East is the sum of West South Asia and North Africa; sub-Saharan Africa is the sum of three regions, Eastern, Middle, and Western Africa (omitting Southern); Latin America is the total excluding the temperate region. The growth rates in col. 5 are derived directly from the two population totals in cols. 3 and 4 and therefore reflect net interregional migration. For the developed regions, the composition is developing regions (lines 1–4, col. 2); whereas even the absolute, let alone relative, differences in this proportion among the developed regions are much more marked, between the older countries of developed Europe and Japan, on the one hand, and the United States and other overseas off-shoots of Europe, on the other. This is a reflection of the rather uniformly high fertility and rates of natural increase among the major developing regions (at least at the two dates indicated), despite substantial differences in per capita income between, say, Latin America and Asia. It also reflects the higher fertility and rate of natural increase among the overseas off-shoots of Europe, despite their generally higher per capita income, than in Europe or in Japan.

The other interesting finding is that not only were the proportions of children under 15 substantially higher among the developing regions than among the developed; but also this excess in the proportion of children among the developing regions widened in the 15 years preceding 1970. The proportion rose between 1955 and 1970 for each of the four developing regions, most strikingly among the populous Asian countries, while there were substantial declines in three of the four developed regions. The disparity in the proportions of children under 15 between the developing and developed groups widened from 14.2 percentage points in 1955 to 17.9 percentage points in 1970; and one could assume that with the marked decline in fertility in the developed countries after 1970, the widening has continued to date.

Panel B attempts to translate the evidence in Panel A into a full allocation of the difference between developing and developed market economies in size of the average household, around 1970. Using the 1975 paper cited in note 3 above, which suggested for the early and mid-1960s average household sizes of about 5 and 3.3 respectively, we assumed the average sizes in developing and developed countries to be roughly 5.0

Notes to Table 8.4 *(cont.)*

as follows: developed Europe includes Northern and Western Europe, plus Italy; and the "other overseas" are the sum of Canada, Australia, and New Zealand.

The calculations in Panel B proceed in the manner shown in Tables 8.2 and 8.3 above, but use approximate values in lines 11, 15, and 17. These are based, in part, on the summary distribution of households by size for developing and developed countries in the early and late 1960s (Table 10, p. 385) in my paper, "Fertility differentials between less developed and developed regions: Components and implications," in *Proceedings of the American Philosophical Society* 119, no. 5 (October 1975), and in part on more recent data for individual countries, with crude allowance for the decline in size of households in developed countries and the rise in the proportion of one- and two-person households by 1970.

and 3.0; while on the basis of scattered evidence in the 1971 and 1973 *Demographic Yearbooks* on size-distribution of households in a number of developing and developed market economies, we set the proportions of one- and two-person households at 5 and 10 percent respectively for developing regions compared with 20 and 30 percent respectively for the developed regions. More detailed data might change these assumptions by a couple of percentage points, but not sufficiently to affect the major conclusions, and the same can be said of the effects of more elaborate approximations of the average size of households for the two wide groups of regions.

The allocation for these two groups in 1970 shows about 70 percent of the difference associated with the higher proportion of children under 15 in the developing countries, and 30 percent due to the greater jointness of adults within the developing country households. This is a plausible result, but one must note the possible wide variation in these proportions not only for pairs of individual countries, but also for some pairs of wider regions selected among the regions in Table 8.4. The results relating to contributions of the differing proportions of households of one, two, and three or more persons are clearly dependent upon the differences in proportions *assumed*, but the dominance of the differential contribution of one-person households seems plausible – if there be no incomparability in the definitions of one-person households between the two groups of regions.

Rural–urban comparisons

In turning now to differences in average size of household between rural and urban populations within the same country, we are limited to the small number of countries for which the data are at hand from international compilations (Table 8.5). But there are some intriguing and suggestive findings. They become more striking if we omit the data for Chile from the discussion, because of some peculiarities in the latter that are not easily explicable. Thus, it is puzzling to find the proportion of urban to total households to be higher in Chile than in the three economically more advanced countries in columns 1–3 (see line 1). It is also puzzling to find the average size of households in Chile in 1970, at 5.1, to be as large as the average for Ecuador, a far less developed country, in 1962.

The differences in average size of households illustrated in Table 8.5 are naturally of much narrower range than is true among the major re-

Table 8.5. *Differences in size of average household between rural and urban population, selected countries*

	France 1968 (1)	Finland 1970 (2)	Japan 1970 (3)	Chile 1970 (4)	Ecuador 1962 (5)	Paki- stan 1970 (6)	Philip- pines 1970–71 (7)
A. *Structure by Age*							
1. Percent of urban HHs in total	71.4	56.5	75.1	77.7	34.0	27.2	30.1
Persons per HH							
2. Rural	3.30	3.38	4.09	5.52	5.00	5.77	5.83
3. Urban	3.09	2.69	3.46	4.97	5.36	5.64	5.91
4. Difference (2 − 3)	0.21	0.69	0.63	0.55	−0.36	0.13	−0.08
Percent under 15 in total population							
5. Rural	24.0	25.2	24.9	44.6	45.7	43.8	53.5[a]
6. Urban	23.6	23.4	23.6	39.1	43.9	42.5	49.1[a]
Persons under 15, per HH							
7. Rural	0.79	0.85	1.02	2.46	2.28	2.53	3.12[a]
8. Urban	0.73	0.63	0.81	1.94	2.35	2.40	2.90[a]
9. Difference (7 − 8)	0.06	0.22	0.21	0.52	−0.07	0.13	0.22
10. Line 9 as % of line 4	29	32	33	95	nc	100	nc
Persons, 15 & over, per HH							
11. Rural	2.51	2.53	3.07	3.06	2.72	3.24	2.71[a]
12. Urban	2.36	2.06	2.65	3.03	3.01	3.24	3.01[a]
13. Difference (11 − 12)	0.15	0.47	0.42	0.03	−0.29	0	−0.30
14. Line 13 as % of line 4	71	68	67	5	nc	0	nc
Percent of one-person HHs							
15. Rural	19.4	18.4	7.8	6.0	6.4	5.4	1.9
16. Urban	20.6	28.2	14.9	5.4	7.5	9.3	1.7
Percent of two-person HHs							
17. Rural	27.1	20.6	13.1	8.8	12.1	8.3	7.3
18. Urban	26.2	23.3	15.6	11.8	10.5	8.1	6.0

Table 8.5 *(cont.)*

	B. *Contribution of proportions of one-, two-, and three-or-more-person households (residual)*					
	Rural		Urban		Difference	
	% of HHs (1)	Contri- bution (2)	% of HHs (3)	Contri- bution (4)	Differ- ence (5)	% of total (6)
France						
19. One-person HHs	19.4	−0.293	20.6	−0.311	0.018	9
20. Two-person HHs	27.1	−0.014	26.2	−0.013	−0.001	−1
21. Residual		0.307		0.174	0.133	63
Finland						
22. One-person HHs	18.4	−0.282	28.2	−0.426	0.144	21
23. Two-person HHs	20.6	−0.109	23.3	−0.123	0.014	2
24. Residual		0.391		0.079	0.312	45
Japan						
25. One-person HHs	7.8	−0.016	14.9	−0.031	0.015	2
26. Two-person HHs	13.1	−0.014	15.6	−0.017	0.003	1
27. Residual		0.030		−0.372	0.402	64
Chile						
28. One-person HHs	6.0	−0.012	5.4	−0.011	−0.001	−0.2
29. Two-person HHs	8.8	−0.009	11.8	−0.013	0.004	0.7
30. Residual		0.021		−0.006	0.027	4.9
Pakistan						
31. One-person HHs	5.4	−0.012	9.3	−0.021	0.009	7
32. Two-person HHs	8.3	−0.010	8.1	−0.010	0	0
33. Residual		0.022		0.031	−0.009	−7

nc = not calculated.
[a] Relates to children under 18 and adults aged 18 and over.
Notes: For all countries except the Philippines, the underlying data are from the United Nations, *Demographic Yearbook, 1971* (New York, 1972), Tables 11 and 12, and *Demographic Yearbook, 1973* (New York, 1974), Tables 24 and 26. The data for the Philippines are from Bureau of Census and Statistics, *Family Income and Expenditures: 1971* (Manila, 1975), Tables 3 and 50. The data in this report were utilized fairly intensively in the 1976 paper referred to in note 3, and the earlier paper of which the 1976 paper was a revised version (referred to in the 1976 paper). The notes below refer largely to the six countries, excluding the Philippines.
The distribution of households by size (needed for Panel A) and between rural and urban is limited to the household population. The proportion of population under age 15 to total population may refer to the total including some institutional population.
For the procedure involved in Panel B see the notes to the preceding tables.
For brief definitions of the urban population (defining the rural as a residual) see notes to Table 8.5 in the *1971 Demographic Yearbook*, pp. 154–158. The definitions differ from country to country, but relate either to capitals of country and provinces and to administrative centers; or to agglomerations above a certain population level; or to presence of urban administrations and institutions.

gions in Table 8.4, or the individual selected countries in Table 8.3. After all, the rural and urban populations are parts of the same country, and their demographic and economic patterns are not likely to differ as much as in separate countries that can be at widely different levels within an extensive international range. And yet the rural–urban differences in average size of households and in distribution of households by size are sufficiently large to matter.

As we observe these differences, and exclude Chile from the comparison, we find that among the three developed countries in columns 1–3 rural households exceed urban households in size by substantial margins in Finland and in Japan and by a smaller but still perceptible margin in France. In the three developing countries, in columns 5–7, there is no such consistent excess in size of the average rural household over the urban; indeed, in Ecuador (in 1962) and in the Philippines (in 1970–71), the rural household is smaller than the urban, and in Pakistan the difference in favor of the rural household is slight indeed (less than 3 percent).

This contrasting finding relating to differences in size of rural and urban households in the developed and developing countries in Table 8.5 is *not* due to underlying differences in proportions of children under 15 between the rural and urban populations. These proportions (with one for children under 18 for the Philippines) are uniformly higher in rural than in urban populations, the excess being distinctly narrower for the three developed countries than for the three developing countries (lines 5 and 6). It follows that the failure of the average household in the rural population of the developing countries to exceed that in the urban must be due to the greater contribution of the adults (i.e., persons aged 15 and over) in the urban communities. And it may well be that this result is associated with the greater relative influx of these adults into the urban centers of the developing countries in recent years than would be true of the populations of developed countries, with these migrants becoming members of larger households rather than forming recognizable one-person households.[5] This hypothesis cannot be adequately tested without

5 It is in this connection that incomparability in definitions of one-person households discussed above in citations from the U.N. document (referred to in note 4 above) becomes so relevant. If migrant workers in the cities all tend to be classified as constituting one-person households, the result may be a very high *overall* proportion of one-person households in countries such as Cameroon (46.0 percent in 1957), Sierra Leone (22.7 percent in 1963), Jamaica (19.1 percent in

more data on size and structure of households for the urban and rural populations of a much larger number of countries than we could readily find for Table 8.5.

The other tentative finding is suggested by the data for the three developed countries in Panel B. With differences in average size between rural and urban households fairly substantial, and yet the differences in proportions of children under age 15 in rural and urban populations quite small, it follows that differences in the numbers of *adults* per household, produced by differing proportions of households with different numbers of adult members, must account for a large part of the rural–urban differences in total number of persons per household. And indeed Panel B shows that in France, Finland, and Japan the contribution of the households with three or more persons loomed largest in accounting for the total rural–urban difference. Thus, unlike most of the international comparisons, the intranational comparisons between countryside and city in the developed countries show that the countryside preserves large proportions of the jointness of adults factor that is lost in the urban communities; the countryside is, in this respect, a greater preserver of the older traditions, even though it appears not to retain the tradition with respect to the presence of children factor, or the much lower proportions of one- and two-person households. But again, the hypothesis should be checked with a wider array of countries and data.

Since the few countries used in Table 8.5 all show a higher proportion of children under age 15 in the rural than in the urban population, and since we have data readily available on these proportions for a much larger number of countries, it seemed of interest to consider these data with a greater coverage, and particularly to observe at the same time the proportions of persons 15 through 19, again for the rural and urban population separately, to see whether these proportions are affected by the rural–urban migration. Such migration may affect even children under age 15, but it could hardly have significant effects, particularly compared with those on the older age group (or groups).

Table 8.6 summarizes the relevant information for a large number of

1960) – all of them appreciably higher than many such shares in developed countries (see source cited in note 1, Table 3, pp. 11–15). Whether these be properly defined one-person households or not, their significance in terms of the wider concept of the family is problematic – a question that, as will be seen later in the paper, may be legitimately raised in connection with the one- and even two-person households in the developed countries.

Table 8.6. *Average proportions (%) of groups below 15 and 15–19 years of age in rural and urban populations, developing and developed regions, late 1950s and early 1960s*

	Number of coun- tries (1)	% of rural popu- lation (2)	% of population below age 15			% of population aged 15–19		
			Rural (3)	Urban (4)	No. of agree- ments (5)	Rural (6)	Urban (7)	No. of agree- ments (8)
Developing regions (market economies)								
1. East and Middle South Asia	9	81.7	43.8	40.3	8	8.6	10.2	8
2. Middle East	9	63.4	45.8	43.3	7	7.9	9.1	9
Developing regions (market economies)								
3. Sub-Saharan Africa	13	84.8	42.3	40.8	8	7.0	8.0	10
4. Latin America (ex. temperate)	18	60.9	47.2	41.1	17	9.4	10.3	15
5. All developing countries (cols. 2–4 and 6–7 weighted)	49	77.2	44.3	40.8	40	8.4	9.8	42
Developed regions or countries (market economies)								
6. Developed Europe	8	39.9	25.8	22.8	7	8.3	7.8	8
7. United States (1960)	1	28.5	33.4	30.1	1	8.3	7.0	1
8. Japan (1965)	1	31.9	28.7	24.2	1	10.0	11.6	0
9. Other developed countries	3	26.7	36.6	30.0	2	8.4	8.7	0
10. All developed countries (cols. 2–4 and 6–7 weighted)	13	33.5	29.8	26.3	11	8.6	8.1	9

Notes: The entries in cols. 5 and 8 denote the number of countries in which the sign of relations of cols. 3–4 and 6–7 is in agreement with that shown by the averages for developing and developed regions in the corresponding cols. in lines 5 and 10.

The weights for the developing regions are 60, 10, 15, and 15 for lines 1–4, respectively, and are suggested by cols. 3 and 4 in Panel A of Table 8.4. The weights for the developed regions are 40, 40, 15, and 5 for lines 6–9 respectively, and are suggested by total populations shown in Panel A of Table 8.4.

All data are from the comprehensive Table 6, pp. 166–407 of United Nations, *Demographic Yearbook, 1970* (New York, 1971). The percent proportions were always calculated to the total excluding unallocated by age, whenever the latter were shown. The entries here are unweighted arithmetic means of the proportions for the individual countries within each region.

The following countries (with year for which the data were given) were included. Line 1: Cambodia (1962); Ceylon (1963); India (1961); Indonesia (1961); S. Korea (1966); Nepal (1961); Pakistan (1961); Iran (1966). Line 2: Iraq (1965); Jordan (1961); Syria (1960); Turkey (1960); Algeria (1966); Libya (1964); Morocco (1960); Tunisia (1966); Egypt (1960). Line 3: Central African Republic (1959–60); Congo (1955–7); Ghana (1960); Mali (1960–1); Nigeria (1963); Zambia (1963); Gabon (1961); Namibia (1960); Chad (1964); Congo PR (1960–1); Dahomey (1961); Guinea (1955); Togo (1958–60). Line 4:

countries, at different years but mostly for the early and mid-1960s.[6] The first and obvious conclusion is that the percentage proportions of children under age 15 are consistently higher in the rural than in the urban populations, in both developed and developing countries – although there are some exceptions.

A second, more interesting finding relates to the comparative proportions of persons 15 through 19 years of age (cols. 6–8). For the developing regions, these proportions are higher in the urban population, thus reversing the sign of the difference in the proportions of children under 15; and this excess proportion of the 15–19-year age group among the urban population is found quite consistently (42 out of the 49 countries, three of the exceptions in countries in sub-Saharan Africa and three of them in Latin America). By contrast, developed Europe and the United States show a slight shortage of proportions of the 15–19 group in the urban relative to the rural population (all eight countries in Europe show-

6 The underlying data from U.N. *Demographic Yearbook, 1970*, on distribution of rural and urban populations by age and sex, were utilized intensively, in an analysis aimed at comparing birth rates and fertility between the rural and urban populations, in my earlier paper, "Urban-rural differences in fertility: An international comparison," *Proceedings of the American Philosophical Society* 118, no. 1 (February 1974): 1–29. The paper contains a discussion of a number of aspects of rural–urban differences in proportions of children under age 5; of women in childbearing ages (15–49); and of both men and women in working ages (15–49). It may be consulted on a number of aspects of rural–urban differences relevant to the discussion here. The earlier paper covers a larger number of countries, including communist countries, less developed Europe, and temperate Latin America, all of them excluded from Table 6; and unlike the procedure in Table 8.6, it derives unweighted averages of country proportions for the relevant developed and developing country totals. But for the same coverage, the results in the earlier paper are comparable with those in Table 8.6.

Notes to Table 8.6 *(cont.)*

Costa Rica (1963); Dominican Republic (1960); El Salvador (1961); Guatemala (1964); Honduras (1961); Jamaica (1960); Mexico (1960); Nicaragua (1963); Panama (1960); Brazil (1960); Chile (1960); Colombia (1964); Ecuador (1962); Paraguay (1962); Peru (1961); Venezuela (1961); Trinidad and Tobago (1960); Guyana (1960). In general, we tried to include as many developing countries as possible – excluding only those in which the proportion of urban population was well below 10 percent.
For the developed countries, the following were included. Line 6: Denmark (1965); Finland (average 1960 and 1970, the latter reported in *Demographic Yearbook, 1973* [New York, 1974]); France (1968); Netherlands (1968, semiurban included with rural); Norway (average of 1960 and 1970); Sweden (1965); Switzerland (average for 1960 and 1970); England and Wales (1961). Line 9: Canada (1960); Australia (1966); New Zealand (1961).
For brief definitions of "urban" (and thus of rural as a residual) for a large number of countries see notes to Table 5 of the same *1970 Demographic Yearbook*, pp. 159–165. See also the note on definition of "urban" in Table 8.5 above.

ing this relation). The large weight of developed Europe and the United States, combined with rather limited differentials in the other developed countries, results in a definitely lower proportion of the 15–19 group in the urban population than in the rural in the weighted averages for the developed countries group in line 10.

It should be noted that the proportions shown are ratios to current population, a mixture of different age cohorts, of age groups that are survivals of cohorts originating in different past years. This complicates comparing shares of the age group of say 15–19 with those of 10–14, for the 15–19 group at a given date is part of the cohort born 15 to 20 years ago, whereas the 10–14 group is part of the cohort born 10 to 15 years ago. Assuming constant fertility and mortality (by age groups) and a positive rate of natural increase, we expect the proportions of successive five-year groups in a given population to decline – partly because of different spans of mortality, partly because of the rises in base to which the rate of natural increase is applied in a growing population. And, of course, any changes in vital rates, aggregate and by age, would complicate further the comparison of age-group proportions in current population.

But this does not bar the inference that if we observe, in the case of developing countries, a reversal in the comparative proportions in rural and urban population of the under 15 and 15–19 age groups, the only plausible explanation (barring unsuspected major biases and errors in the basic data) is that there has been sufficient rural–urban migration in the 15–19 group to reverse the urban shortfall in this group that would have otherwise occurred. And the parallel inference for the different finding in the developed countries of Europe and in the United States is that such rural–urban migration in the 15–19 age group was not sufficient there to reverse the disparity in proportions that prevailed in the groups under 15 years of age. It is the evidence concerning the possibly substantial migration among the 15–19 age group from the countryside to the cities, particularly in the developing countries, that led us to set the age-line dividing children from adults at 15.

Finally, we should add that the lack of evidence on the substantial migration from the countryside to the cities of the 15–19 group in the developed countries that was indicated in Table 8.6 is *not* true of the older prime ages in the labor force. In the paper referred to in note 5, Table 10, p. 21, shows proportions to rural and urban population, of men and women (given separately) aged 15–49, these being treated as both childbearing and working ages (prone to migration) for women and working ages (again prone to migration) for men. Combining the percentage shares for men and women, and using the regional averages shown in the table, we obtain the following summary:

Regions[a]	Number of countries (1)	Percent proportions, 15–49	
		Rural (2)	Urban (3)
East and MS Asia	10	44.8	49.1
Middle East	8	41.2	44.2
Sub-Saharan Africa	13	46.5	52.1
Latin America (including temperate)	17	42.4	47.3
Developing countries, weighted (0.60; 0.10; 0.15; 0.15 – succ. lines)		44.3	48.8
Developed Europe	8	46.8	48.2
Japan	1	47.3	55.8
United States and Canada	2	43.5	47.3
Australia–New Zealand	2	45.3	46.6
Developed countries, weighted (0.40; 0.15; 0.425; 0.025 – succ. lines)		46.3	48.9

[a] Comparable to Table 8.6.

The evidence is clear that for the broader span of the working ages the relevant proportions in urban population are greater than in rural population in *both* developing countries and developed countries, reflecting the rural–urban internal migration, which, for obvious reasons, tends to be concentrated in the working ages. The different finding in Table 8.6 for the 15–19 age group suggests that such migration becomes significant at an earlier age in the developing countries than in the developed, a reflection possibly of greater pressures toward early employment and earlier beginning of working life in the developing countries.

Comparisons over time

In turning now to the last type of comparison of size and size-distribution of households, over fairly long periods of the demographic transition and change associated with economic growth, we use data for the United States as an illustration. These cover, with wide gaps, a long period from 1790, with more details relating to the twentieth century; the summary findings are presented in Table 8.7. Over this long period, the area and population of the country grew dramatically; some discontinuity is introduced by inclusion of Hawaii and Alaska in 1960; and there are minor incomparabilities in inclusion and exclusion of institutional households (see the notes in the source cited in Table 8.7).[7] But the broad findings, over the long period, are not likely to be much affected by these statistical inadequacies. However, they are affected by the substantial net immigration inflows that began in the 1830s and continued with some interruptions and changes in volume to recent decades.

Over the almost two-century span, the average size of household declined from 5.8 persons in 1790 to 3.1 in 1970; and as Table 8.1 shows, it declined further to 2.9 in March 1976. But the rate of decline was relatively moderate over the first six decades, and began accelerating only after the Civil War in the 1860s. The decline over the first 60 years was just about 4 percent; over the next 60 years, from 1850 to 1910, almost 20 percent; over the following 60 years, from 1910 to 1970, almost 40 percent.

This acceleration of the rate of decline in the average size of household was accompanied by a marked shift in the relative contribution to this decline of the natural increase-children factor, and of the jointness or apartness of adults factor. Over the first six decades, the decline in the proportion of children under age 15 was sufficient to more than outweigh the decline in total persons per household, with the contribution of the adults serving to *increase* rather than diminish the total of persons per household. The result may be due in part to effect of immigration, the latter being more concentrated in ages above 15. By 1850, the proportion of foreign born (whites and free blacks) to total population was 2.26 million out of a total of 23.2 million, or 9.8 percent. If we were to assume that in both 1790 and 1850, all children under age 15 were native born, and neglect the proportions of adult foreign born in 1790, the percentage under age 15 in 1850 would be raised from 41.5 to 46.0 (i.e., divided by 0.902). On this extreme assumption, the average number of children under age 15 in 1850 would be 2.55 per household, leaving 3.00 adults per household – still a slight rise from the average of 2.90 in 1790. On the other hand, the marked decline in proportion of children under age

---

7 This and later references are to the *Historical Statistics* volume cited in the notes to Table 8.7. The data on foreign born in 1950 are in Series 105–118, p. 14; those on birth rates and children under age 5 per thousand white women of childbearing age are in Series B 5–10, p. 49, and Series B 67–98, p. 54.

Table 8.7. *Allocation of changes in size of average household, United States, selected years, 1790–1970*

	A. *Allocation by age structure (below 15 and 15 and over)*						
Year	Persons per HH (1)	% under 15 in popu- lation (2)	Persons below 15 per HH (3)	Persons 15+ per HH (4)	Changes between successive dates		
					Col. 1 (5)	Col. 3 (6)	Col. 4 (7)
1. 1790	5.79	49.9	2.89	2.90	—	—	—
2. 1850	5.55	41.5	2.30	3.25	−0.24	−0.59	+0.35
3. 1890	4.93	35.5	1.75	3.18	−0.62	−0.55	−0.07
4. 1910	4.54	32.1	1.46	3.08	−0.39	−0.29	−0.10
5. 1930	4.11	29.4	1.21	2.90	−0.43	−0.25	−0.18
6. 1950	3.37	26.9	0.91	2.46	−0.74	−0.30	−0.44
7. 1970	3.14	28.5	0.89	2.25	−0.23	−0.02	−0.21
Wider Intervals							
8. 1790 to 1890	—	—	—	—	−0.86	−1.14	+0.28
9. 1890 to 1930	—	—	—	—	−0.82	−0.54	−0.28
10. 1930 to 1970	—	—	—	—	−0.97	−0.32	−0.65
11. 1890 to 1970	—	—	—	—	−1.79	−0.86	−0.93

	B. *Contributions of 1, 2, and 3+ person households to changes over the wider intervals*							
Year	% in HHs		Contribution to decline in persons per HH (rises marked +)			Columns 3–5 as % of total decline (rises marked −)		
	1 pers. HHs (1)	2 pers. HHs (2)	1 pers. (3)	2 pers. (4)	3+ pers. (5)	1 pers. (6)	2 pers. (7)	3+ pers. (8)
12. 1790	3.7	7.8	—	—	—	—	—	—
13. 1890	3.6	13.2	+0.002	0.049	+0.327	−0.2	5.7	−38.0
14. 1930	7.9	23.4	0.094	0.120	0.066	11.5	14.6	8.0
15. 1970	17.1	28.8	0.255	0.048	0.347	26.3	4.9	35.8
16. 1890–1970	—	—	0.293	0.184	0.453	16.4	10.3	25.3

Notes: All the underlying data are taken, or estimated, from U.S. Bureau of the Census, *Historical Statistics of the United States Colonial Times to 1970, Bicentennial Edition, Part 1* (Washington, D.C., 1975). Persons per household are from Series A-288-319, p. 41. The proportions of one- and two-person households, for the years indicated, are from Series A-335-349, p. 42. The proportions of population below age 15 years, for the years beginning in 1890, are from Series A-119-134, pp. 15ff.

The only entry that had to be estimated was the percent proportion of population below age 15 years in 1790. The earliest date for which this proportion could be calculated for total population was 1850 (when it was 41.5 percent, compared with 35.5 in 1890). The estimation was based on movement of the proportions for the white population (available for the below 15 age group back to 1830 and for the below 16 age group back to 1800).

15 is confirmed by the data on fertility and number of children under age 5 per thousand white women of childbearing age, both available for the span from 1800 to 1850.

This interesting case of the jointness of adults contributing to an *increase* over time in the size of the household is limited to the first six decades (and may have ended earlier). After that date, the declining rate of natural increase continues to contribute to the decline in the average size of the household, but in diminishing proportions, and becomes negligible in the last two decades, between 1950 and 1970; whereas the contribution of the jointness of adults factor, or rather of the growing apartness of adults, is increasingly important in the total reduction in the size of the average household. Thus, over 1930–70, the jointness or apartness of adults factor accounts for two-thirds of the total decline, the children-factor for only one-third.

Panel B, which analyzes the contributions of the different proportions of households with one, two, and three or more persons to the total jointness of adults component, is based on size distributions of households. Although such distributions are not available for any year between 1790 and 1890, the comparison of the percentage proportions of one- and two-person households in 1790 and 1890 (lines 12 and 13, cols. 1 and 2) demonstrates very little change in the shares of the one-person household, and a small absolute (although large relative) rise over the century in the share of two-person households. The analysis indicates that it was the rise in the average number of adults per household of three or more persons that contributed to the positive sign of the jointness of adults factor in the movement from 1790 to 1890 (see line 13, columns 3–5). The further evidence in Panel B on the periods following 1890 indicates that the major contributions to the decline in adult persons per household were made by the rising percentages of the one-person households, and the reduction in average number of adults in households with three or more persons, with the rather moderate share of the contribution of the two-person households. Thus it is the increase in the proportion of households at one extreme, namely, one-person households, and the *decrease* in the proportions at the other extreme, to the right of the size-

Notes to Table 8.7 *(cont.)*

It was done by calculating the relative changes in the percentages of the available younger group and extrapolating back the 1890 proportion of the accumulated relative change. Since the proportion of whites below age 16 years to total white population was as high as 50 percent in 1800, the estimate used in line 1, col. 2, cannot be much off the mark.

distribution well above the three- and four-person household, that may be the major contributors to the decline in numbers of adults per household, particularly after the 1930s.

Table 8.7 covers a range in size of average household that is almost as wide as that found in current cross-sections among developed and developing countries in the selected sample in Table 8.3. And while the record is that for a rapidly growing country affected by immigration, it is likely that the broad findings on the shift from the contribution of declining fertility and natural increase via the declining proportion of children under 15 to the contribution of increasing apartness of adults in the more recent decades would be found in other developed countries. Testing this hypothesis would require comparable long-term data on size and size-structure of households, as well as on age distributions of population, for other developed countries.

Taken together, the findings in this section suggest that the contribution of the factor connected with the jointness or apartness of adults to the total disparity in average size of households is substantial – particularly in rural–urban comparisons within developed countries and in comparisons over time for recent periods for a developed country like the United States. The jointness or apartness of adults factor is also of some weight in the differences in average size of households in international cross-section comparisons. With one- and two-person households comprised predominantly of adults, we should examine their other characteristics for whatever light may be shed on the contributions of these small households to differences in size of households, at least for international comparisons.

III. Small and large households, by age and sex of head: an illustrative comparison

Here we revert to a comparison of the detailed data available for the United States and Taiwan. Unlike our illustration in Tables 8.1 and 8.2, the one here is based at first on data for Taiwan Province (excluding Taipei city): the more detailed cross-classification tables are available, in published form, for the Province alone. But this area accounts for more than 80 percent of all households and an even larger proportion of total population in Taiwan. The analysis illustrates certain significant, hitherto untreated, aspects of the size distribution of households in a developed and developing country.

Table 8.8 shows the distribution of households of differing size by age

Table 8.8. *Distribution of households by size and by age of head, United States, March 1976, and Taiwan Province, end 1975*

		Panel A. *United States*						
	All house-holds	Age of head classes						
Size-classes of households		Below 25	25–34	35–44	45–54	55 & over	55–64	65 & over
	(1)	(2)	(3)	(4)	(5)	(6)	(7)	(8)
% shares in total of all households								
1. All households	100.0	8.1	21.4	16.7	17.5	36.3	15.9	20.4
	(72.87 million)							
2. 1 person	20.6	1.8	2.9	1.4	2.1	12.4	3.5	8.9
3. 2 persons	30.6	3.5	4.6	1.8	4.2	16.5	7.3	9.2
4. 3 persons	17.2	1.8	4.8	2.5	3.9	4.2	2.8	1.4
5. 4 persons	15.7	0.7	5.5	4.4	3.2	1.9	1.4	0.5
6. 5 persons	8.6	0.2	2.3	3.3	2.1	0.7	0.5	0.2
7. 6 persons	4.1	0.1	0.9	1.7	1.1	0.3	0.2	0.1
8. 7 & over	3.2	0	0.4	1.6	0.9	0.3	0.2	0.1
9. Persons per household	2.89	2.30	3.15	4.09	3.43	2.05	2.41	1.77

		Panel B. *Taiwan Province*						
	All house-holds	Age of head classes						
Size-classes of households		Below 25	25–34	35–44	45–54	55 & over	55–59	60 & over
	(1)	(2)	(3)	(4)	(5)	(6)	(7)	(8)
% shares in all households								
10. All households	100.0	3.9	24.1	31.6	28.0	11.8	6.2	5.6
	(2.59 million)							
11. 1 person	2.6	0.1	0.2	0.3	0.9	1.1	0.4	0.7
12. 2 persons	4.8	0.5	1.2	0.5	1.1	1.5	0.4	1.1
13. 3 persons	10.2	0.8	3.5	1.4	2.8	1.7	0.8	0.9
14. 4 persons	16.3	0.8	5.2	3.9	4.7	1.7	1.1	0.6
15. 5 persons	22.3	0.6	6.2	7.9	6.2	1.4	0.9	0.5
16. 6 persons	19.2	0.5	3.9	7.8	5.8	1.2	0.8	0.4
17. 7 & over	24.6	0.6	3.9	9.8	7.1	3.2	1.8	1.4
18. Persons per household, Taiwan Province	5.37	4.63	4.99	5.85	5.39	5.05	5.40	4.67
19. Persons per household, Taiwan area	5.27	4.46	4.89	5.78	5.35	4.86	5.21	4.47

Notes: Panel A was calculated from Table 15, p. 48 of the March 1977 source cited in the notes to Panel A of Table 8.1.
Panel B, lines 10–18 were calculated from Department of Budget, Accounting and Statistics, Taiwan Provincial Government, *Report on the Survey of Family Income & Expenditure,*

of head of household, the cross-classifications being compared for the United States and Taiwan Province for the same size-classes of households and identical age-classes of head ranging from below age 25 years to 55 and over. A number of findings are noteworthy and may not be atypical of other comparisons of the size-distribution of households between developed and developing countries.

First, a dominant proportion of the one- and two-person households, which loom so large in the United States, is accounted for by households with advanced ages of head. Out of the 20.6 percent share of one-person households in all households, 12.4 percentage points are households with head aged 55 years or over; of the 30.6 percentage share of two-person households, 16.5 percentage points are households with heads aged 55 or over. Yet, while the one- and two-person households in the United States are dominated by units at advanced age of head, this is not true of the larger households, of three or more persons. There is a similar, but weaker concentration of the smaller households at the advanced ages of head in Taiwan Province (see lines 9 and 19, cols. 1 and 6), but it is of little weight because the overall proportions of one- and two-person households are so small in that country.

Second, it follows that in the contribution of one- and two-person households to the smaller average size of households in the United States than in Taiwan, the old-age small households play a dominant role. Thus, of the total discrepancy in the shares of one-person households, 18.0 percentage points (i.e., 20.6 minus 2.6), the contribution of the old age group is 11.3 points, or close to two-thirds; of the total differential in the shares of two-person households, 25.8 percentage points (i.e., 30.6 minus 4.8), the contribution of the older age-of-head group is 15.0 points, or somewhat less than six-tenths. The residual discrepancies stem largely from the structure at the *younger* age-of-head levels, below the age of 35. For one- and two-person households combined, the shares of these younger groups under age 35 total 12.8 percentage points for the United States (see lines 2 and 3, cols. 3 and 4), compared with 2.0 percentage points for Taiwan Province (see lines 11 and 12, cols. 3 and 4). A similar

Notes to Table 8.8 *(cont.)*

Taiwan Province, 1975 (June 1976), Table 30, pp. 616 ff. Taiwan Province excludes Taipei City and comprised in 1975 2.59 million households, out of some 3.01 for the Taiwan area (which includes Taipei City). No comparable detailed data for Taipei City are shown in the separate report for the latter.
Panel B, line 19 was calculated from Table 12, pp. 148–49 of the source for Taiwan cited for Panel B of Table 8.1.

comparison for the *intermediate* age classes, from 35 to 55, yields total shares for United States of 9.5 percent compared with 2.8 in Taiwan Province. Thus, the major source of the higher shares of small households in a developed country like the United States is the heavy concentration of these households at advanced ages of head, presumably after children mature and depart; and, secondarily, a greater tendency for apartness at the younger levels of age of head.

Third, the distinctive distribution of small households by age of head in the United States, combined with large proportions of these small households in the total, produces a structure of households by age of head that is necessarily quite different from that in Taiwan Province (and would differ almost as much from that in the Taiwan area as a whole). The shares of both the very young households, under 25 years of age of head and, particularly, the older households are proportionately greater in the United States than in Taiwan Province, the proportions being 8 and 4 percent for the younger age-of-head group and 36 and 12 percent respectively for the old age-of-head group of over 55. Even more interesting are the differences between the two countries in the internal structure by size *within* the extreme age-of-head classes. Thus, in the United States, both the under 25 and the 55 and over age classes are dominated by the one- and two-person households; these account for over six-tenths of the total in the under 25 age class and for almost eight-tenths of the 55 and over age class. In Taiwan Province, one- and two-person households account for less than a fifth of all households at the under 25 age-level of head, and for about a fifth of the total of households with heads aged 55 and over. It is particularly striking to find in Taiwan such a large proportion of young heads (under age 25) in households including five, six, and seven or more members.

Fourth, because of these large effects of small households on the structure of households at the young, and particularly, at the old ages of head in the United States, the movements of the average size of household through the succession of ages of head, or the life-cycle pattern, are markedly different from those in a country like Taiwan. With an overall average of 2.89 persons, the average number per household in the United States rises markedly from 2.3 persons in the under 25 years age-of-head class, to a peak of 4.09 in the 35–44 age-of-head class, and then drops sharply to 2.05 in the 55 and over class (and even more strikingly to 1.77 in the 65 and over class; see line 9). This is a swing to a peak almost double that at the initial and terminal troughs. In Taiwan Province, the range in persons per household through the successive age-of-head classes is from 4.6 persons in the under 25 years of age head class to a peak of 5.9, or only 30 percent higher, and then down to 4.7 in the 60 and over age class. The suggested difference in the life-cycle pattern of a typical household between the two countries is obvious. In the United States, that life cycle begins with a substantial period of life in a one-person household, moves rapidly to a family and a peak size of over four (while the children are still within the family), and then enters a prolonged period of a single-couple and eventually a single-person household. Such patterns, while presumably found also in Taiwan, are far less common than those in which a household varies much less in size over the full span and in which the identity of the head may be shifting, while that of the membership may be only moderately affected. The implications of the difference in the amplitude of the swing in size of household through the successive age-classes of head for the evaluation of distributions of income among households during that life cycle are obviously significant.

The association between size of household and sex of head is illustrated in Panel A of Table 8.9. The proportion of households headed by females in the United States, in early 1976, at 24 percent, was four times as great as the proportion in the Taiwan area. And much of the difference is due to the high proportions of female heads among the one- and two-person households, particularly the former. Thus, of the total disparity of 18.2 percentage points in female head proportions between the two countries, 12.6 points, or about two-thirds, are accounted for by the differing incidence of female headship among the one-person households (i.e., 13.2 minus 0.6). The female head proportions in the United States exceed those in the Taiwan area also for the two-to-four-person households, but it is only for the one-person households that the difference contributes so much to the total disparity in line 1.

Since we observed in Table 8.8 that the large proportion of one-person households in the United States was concentrated in the upper age-of-head class of 55 and over, and we now find in Panel A of Table 8.9 that the large proportion of one-person households in the United States is associated with a large concentration of female headship, it follows that female headship among one-person households in the United States should be concentrated in the advanced age-of-head class of 55 years of age and over. We cannot test this inference with the 1976 data for the United States without much elaborate estimation. But we can use the data for the United States in 1970 (March), when the overall proportion of

Table 8.9. *Distribution of households by size and sex of head, and age and sex of head, United States, 1976 (or 1970) and Taiwan area, 1975*

	Panel A. *By size of household and sex of head*					
	United States, March 1976			Taiwan area, end 1975		
Size-classes of households	All (1)	Male head (2)	Female head (3)	All (4)	Male head (5)	Female head (6)
% shares in all households						
1. All households	100.0 (72.87 million)	75.8	24.2	100.0 (3.01 million)	94.0	6.0
2. 1 person	20.6	7.4	13.2	3.1	2.5	0.6
3. 2 persons	30.6	25.5	5.1	5.2	4.3	0.9
4. 3 persons	17.2	14.3	2.9	10.3	9.4	0.9
5. 4 persons	15.7	14.1	1.6	16.9	15.8	1.1
6. 5 persons	8.6	8.0	0.6	22.3	21.1	1.2
7. 6 persons	4.1	3.7	0.4	18.9	18.3	0.6
8. 7 & over	3.2	2.8	0.4	23.3	22.6	0.7
9. Average number of persons per household	2.89	3.18	1.98	5.27	5.35	4.13

	Panel B. *By age and sex of head*					
Age of head classes	United States, March 1970			Taiwan area, end 1975		
10. All households	100.0 (62.88 million)	78.9	21.1	100.0 (3.01 million)	94.0	6.0
11. Below 25	6.8	5.5	1.3	4.0	2.9	1.1
12. 25–34	18.6	16.5	2.1	24.6	23.3	1.3
13. 35–44	18.5	16.3	2.2	30.8	29.1	1.7
14. 45–54	19.5	16.4	3.1	28.4	27.2	1.2
15. 55 & over	34.6	24.2	12.4	12.2	11.5	0.7
16. Average number of persons per household	3.17	3.48	2.03	5.27	5.35	4.13

Notes: Panel A, cols. 1–3 were calculated from U.S. Bureau of the Census, *Current Population Reports, Series P-60, no. 104* (Washington, March 1977), Table 15, p. 48.
Panel B, cols. 1–3 were calculated from *Historical Statistics,* vol. I source cited for Table 7, Series A-323-334, p. 42. The averages in line 16 are from U.S. Bureau of the Census, *Current Population Reports, Series P-60, no. 72* (Washington, August 1970), Table 5, p. 15.
Panels A and B, cols. 4–6 were calculated from DGBAS, Report on the *Survey of Personal Income Distribution in Taiwan Area, 1975* (Taipei, 1976). Panel A is from Table 33, pp. 220–221 and Table 14, p. 152 (the latter for line 9). Panel B is from Table 32, pp. 218–219.

female-headed households was somewhat lower than in 1976 (21 instead of 24 percent) – but still very much higher than that for Taiwan area in 1975. And the comparison shows a heavy concentration of female-headed households in the advanced age-of-head class of 55 and over – 12.4 out of 21.1 percent, or about six-tenths (3, lines 10 and 15). It is the disparity in female headship incidence for this advanced age-of-head class between the United States and Taiwan that contributes 11.7 percentage points to a total difference of 15.1 percentage points, or well over seven-tenths.

Thus, our finding in Table 8.8, concerning concentration of the large proportions of one- and two-person households in a developed country like the United States predominantly at the older age-of-head classes and secondarily in the very young age-of-head classes, may now be supplemented by the finding that for the one-person households the large proportions in the United States mean concentration on female-headed households in the advanced age-of-head classes. In other words, a substantial proportion of the one-person households in an advanced country like the United States consists of single women in older ages, presumably widows who have survived their husbands. Such a group appears to be quite small in a developing country like Taiwan, small with respect to heading a separate household (see col. 6 of Panels A and B, which fails to show any clear association between female *headship* and either size of household or age of head).

IV. Concluding comments

The statistical evidence on size and size-structure of households surveyed in this paper relates largely to family households – units from one to several persons, distinguished by joint residence and, in case of multiperson units, by ties of blood, marriage, or adoption among the members.

In the comparisons of average size of households in international cross sections of countries at different levels of economic development, between rural and urban households within the same country, and of differences over long spans of time within a developed country, we tried to allocate the differences between two sets of factors. One was the differing number of children under 15 per household, reflecting largely fertility and natural increase (NIC factor). The other was the difference in number of adults per household, reflecting different propensity of adults to live together or apart (the JAA factor). In the various sets of comparisons and findings, we observed wide variations in the relative contribution to differences in average size of households of the two factors, with both being of substantial magnitude in most comparisons. And the jointness or apartness of adults factor could be allocated further among the contributions of different proportions of households with one, two, and three or more persons. These findings relate, of course, to the well-known substantial differences in average size of household: the larger size in the developing countries, with their much lower proportions of one- and two-person households than in the developed countries; similar differences between rural and urban households, particularly in developed countries; and the long-term trends within the developed countries toward smaller households, with increasing proportions of one- and two-person households in the total.

When viewed against the larger concept of the family, noted in the introduction to this paper, as a group of persons sufficiently related by blood, marriage, or adoption to warrant expectation of joint decisions on at least some significant economic matters, size-differences among households due to greater numbers of children under age 15 raise no apparent analytical problems. The children, being dependents, are an important focus of family decisions, but they cannot be viewed as *participants* in such decisions, as is true potentially of all adult members of the wider family group, regardless of whether they live together or apart. Here the major question is: What is the significance of *joint* residence of *adults* for family decisions on economic choices? This question is brought into sharp focus by the finding that in the developed countries in recent years over half of all the households were one- or two-person units, heavily dominated by men and women in advanced ages and secondarily by the young; whereas similar proportions among the developing countries were in the range of 7.5 to 15 percent for the two small household groups.

The question just raised is part of a wider problem bearing upon possible clustering of economic interest and decisions among blood- or marriage-related family households, regardless of their size. Sets of households, differing in location and thus treated as separate units in the available data, may be closely connected by ties of blood or marriage; and in a variety of cases, for example the parental households and those of its offspring, or households of closely related sibling heads, the ties may warrant expectation of common economic interests and decisions. If so, one may ask whether we should consider household-members of such close clusters as separate units. To use an illustration bearing on an often noted connection between economic growth and income distribution: If in the course of economic growth the parental pair stays in agriculture and suffers a decline in relative (if not in absolute) income, while their offspring, having migrated to the city, secures a higher relative economic position, do we view this as emerging inequality among households, or do we combine the two households on the ground of sufficient community of economic interest?

The bearing of blood, marriage, and other family ties among family households differing in location, on their meaning as decision and recipient units in economic processes, for example, in size-distribution of income, poses complex questions. The complexity is not due to inability, on the basis of realistic assumptions on age-specific birth and death rates, to derive the various kinship ties, or to apply the same approach, using plausible marriage rates, to the derivation of size of nuclear or extended families.[8] The difficulty is rather that economic implications of kinship or family ties vary widely among different societies and over time, and will differ in their implications for different types of economic decision. In the present context, one could argue that while, in modern societies, separate location of family households may mean separate decisions on everyday allocation of time or income, this may not be true of some of the larger economic decisions – larger outlays or decisions with long-term consequences as to location or occupation (for example, buying a house, or selecting an occupation for the younger members of the family). Likewise, the blood or marriage ties might become particularly important when one subunit of a related cluster of separate family households suffers a calamitous reverse, or enjoys unusual success. But these are but plausible conjectures that leave the specification of family ties and of the locus of joint decisions necessarily vague. What we need is evidence, data on various types of economic decision within the observable family households, with emphasis on the distinction between decisions made relatively independently and those in which blood and other ties result in jointness of action. As far as one can tell, such data are quite scarce, although this is necessarily a preliminary impression.

Second, if we assume that separate location among related family household units means, by and large, independent economic decisions and that we are warranted in viewing the greatly morsellized households in developed countries as truly separate recipient units, one should note that such morsellization widens the range of income inequalities beyond that afforded within a distribution of households that are relatively larger.

8 See, for example, Leo Goodman, Nathan Keyfitz, and Thomas Pullum, "Family formation and the frequency of various kinship relationships," *Theoretical Population Biology* 5, no. 1, (February 1974): 1–27; and also the papers by T. K. Burch (1970) and A. J. Coale (1965) listed in the references, p. 29, of the above.

All other conditions being equal (including the proportions of dependents, i.e., children below a certain age), a larger number of potentially working adults would allow greater scope for the family household as an income-equalizing mechanism than would a size distribution in which one- and two-person family households would be relatively numerous. And if there is this aspect of widening of income inequality (certainly on a per household, and probably on a per person basis), to what extent would such widening inequality be an integral consequence of economic development, in which the reduction in the number of children, with greater investment in their education and rearing, makes the nuclear family an indispensable social institution? The result is to force, as it were, the separation of the very young, and particularly of the older generation, out of what might be called the standard range of age of head of family households. If such an interpretation is at all plausible, we have the curious case of a secular change in measured income inequality among households originating not at the *production* end, in greater inequality of shares flowing from the production system to a given distribution of individual recipients, but at the *receiving* end, in the way these recipients organize themselves into households as loci of economic decisions and operation.

Finally, we should note that the aspects of clustering of separate households, and of increasing apartness of adults, touched upon in the preceding two paragraphs, are interrelated. The increasing apartness of older adults, reflected in the setting up of two households where hitherto there was only one, is a separation that may still preserve substantial economic ties – and so create a new cluster of two separate households. Likewise, marriage at earlier age, possibly combined with continued dependence of the newly formed household on the parental families, results in forming a new wide cluster (of at least three households, one of the children and two of the two parental couples), while separating the two young adults (newlyweds) from former life as members of the two parental households.

The basic thread of discussion and analysis, only initiated by the data on size and size-structure of family households as conventionally defined in the available statistics, is that the significance of the household as the economic decision and recipient unit is greatly conditioned by different and changing social patterns. The relevant patterns are not only the ones that govern fertility and presence of children, but also those that determine jointness or apartness of adults and the strength of family ties among separate households.

9. Size of households and income disparities

I. The association illustrated

In this paper we explore the relation between differentials in size of households (preponderantly family households including one-person units) and disparities in income per household, per person, or per some version of consuming unit.[1] The relation is important, because, in size distributions of income among the population, the most common unit is the household – a group of persons, usually family members, related by blood, marriage, or adoption, residing together and sharing arrangements for living. Inequality in size of household may "produce" (be associated with) inequality in income per household, in income per person, in income per consuming unit, or in all three. Conversely, if we begin with inequality in income per person or per consuming unit, we shall observe association with size of household and with income per household. In either approach, one would find a connection between differentials in size of household and disparities in income, the latter being substantial components in the observed size distributions of income among the population.

The treatment here can be only illustrative because of scarcity of rele-

Research in Population Economics, Volume 3, pages 1–40. Copyright © 1981 by JAI Press Inc.

1 This paper is a sequel to two earlier papers that touch upon this topic, among others bearing on demographic components in the size distribution of income: Chapter 7 and Chapter 8, above. Two other recent papers bearing on the findings and analysis here should be noted. One is by Pravin Visaria, "Demographic Factors and the Distribution of Income: Some Issues." in International Union for the Scientific Study of Population, *Economic and Demographic Change: Issues for the 1980's*, Helinski (1979), *1*:289–320. The other is by Sheldon Danziger and Michael K. Taussig, "The Income Unit and the Anatomy of Income Distribution." *The Review of Income and Wealth*, Series 25, No. 4, December 1979, pp. 365–375.

vant data and limitations of quality in the data available. Even the demo-graphic data on the distribution of households by size are subject to undercount, differing for population subgroups with different household structure. The scarcer income data for households are far more defective. Most tests and comparisons (with the comprehensive national accounts for relevant totals) show that the available statistics on family income or consumption understate the totals by substantial margins, and margins that differ for different income sources and hence for different economic groups. Furthermore, the data refer to annual income or consumption rather than to longer-term levels, which are of more interest for many analytical purposes. But we had to use demographic and income statistics as they were available and for this reason the findings are at best sug-gestive. This warning, while necessary, does not mitigate the difficulties; these can be significantly overcome only with a large input of work on testing and revision with access to the original, unprocessed data – a task not feasible for an individual scholar.[2]

Table 9.1 provides a summary of data for six countries, bearing on the relation between size differentials among households and disparities in income per household and per person. The sample, while including both developed and less developed market economies, is small. Still, the nature of the association between size differentials among households and income disparities can be explored. We now consider the findings suggested by Table 9.1.

1. Inequalities among households in size, as measured by number of persons, are quite wide. A distribution like that for the United States in which the lower quintile of households (covered by the one-person class) accounts for only 7 percent of the population of persons whereas the top seventh (represented by households of five persons and over) accounts for a third of all persons, is clearly an unequal distribution. The same is suggested by the corresponding Gini coefficient of over 0.3 (see Panel B,

2 The difficulties have grown with the rise in recent decades in the supply of basic socioeconomic statistics, for different population subgroups and for countries at widely different levels of development. In the nature of the relation between the individual scholar and the data producing institutions, the results of scholarly analysis in the preponderant majority of cases are bound to be tentative, subject to revision with the needed improvements in the data base. One can only hope that the explorations by the individual analyst serve to call attention to some important connections, and thus lead to greater attention to the testing and improvement of the supply and quality of the relevant data.

Table 9.1. *Disparity measures and relatives of income per household and per person by size classes of households, six countries*

	A. Percentage shares of size-classes, and size- and income-relatives[a]						
	Percentage in total			Relatives			
Classes of households by number of persons	House-holds (H) (1)	Persons (P) (2)	Income (Y) (3)	Size (P/H) (4)	Income per household (Y/H) (5)	Income per person (Y/P) (6)	
United States, money income, 1975 (2.89)[b]							
1. One-person	20.6	7.1	10.0	0.345	0.49	1.41	
2. Two-person	30.6	21.4	29.5	0.70	0.96	1.38	
3. Three-person	17.2	18.0	19.6	1.05	1.14	1.09	
4. Four-person	15.7	21.6	19.9	1.38	1.27	0.92	
5. Five-person	8.6	14.8	11.6	1.72	1.35	0.78	
6. Six-person	4.1	8.4	5.4	2.05	1.32	0.64	
7. Seven-person-and-over (7.78)	3.2	8.7	4.0	2.72	1.25	0.46	
Germany (FR), total income, 1970 (2.75)[c]							
8. One-person	22.6	8.2	11.6	0.36	0.51	1.41	
9. Two-person	27.8	20.1	22.8	0.72	0.82	1.13	
10. Three-person	22.2	24.2	24.6	1.09	1.11	1.02	
11. Four-person	15.4	22.5	20.1	1.46	1.31	0.89	
12. Five-person	7.2	13.2	11.3	1.83	1.57	0.86	
13. Six-person	2.9	6.4	5.4	2.21	1.86	0.84	
14. Seven-person-and-over (7.71)	1.9	5.4	4.2	2.84	2.21	0.80	

Israel, urban, total gross income, 1968–69 (3.65)[c]

15. One-person	10.9	3.0	4.8	0.28	0.44	1.60
16. Two-person	23.0	12.6	19.8	0.55	0.86	1.57
17. Three-person	19.0	15.6	21.4	0.82	1.13	1.37
18. Four-person	21.4	23.4	27.9	1.09	1.30	1.19
19. Five-person	11.4	15.6	12.6	1.37	1.10	0.81
20. Six-person-and-over (7.2)	14.3	29.8	13.5	2.08	0.94	0.45

Taiwan, total household receipts, 1975 (5.27)[d]

21. One-person	3.2	0.6	1.6	0.19	0.50	2.67
22. Two-person	5.2	2.0	4.1	0.38	0.79	2.05
23. Three-person	10.3	5.8	8.9	0.56	0.86	1.53
24. Four-person	16.8	12.7	16.0	0.76	0.95	1.26
25. Five-person	22.2	21.1	21.9	0.95	0.99	1.04
26. Six-person	19.0	21.6	19.6	1.14	1.03	0.91
27. Seven-person	11.3	15.0	11.9	1.33	1.05	0.79
28. Eight-person	5.9	9.0	7.2	1.53	1.22	0.80
29. Nine-person	2.7	4.7	3.4	1.74	1.26	0.72
30. Ten-person-and-over (11.7)	3.4	7.5	5.4	2.21	1.59	0.72

Philippines, total income, 1970–71 (5.77)[c]

31. One-person	1.8	0.3	1.1	0.17	0.61	3.67
32. Two-person	6.9	2.4	4.6	0.35	0.67	1.92
33. Three-person	11.6	6.0	8.8	0.52	0.76	1.47
34. Four-person	14.9	10.3	13.6	0.69	0.92	1.32
35. Five-person	14.6	12.7	13.9	0.87	0.95	1.09
36. Six-person	13.5	14.0	13.2	1.04	0.98	0.94
37. Seven-person	11.6	14.0	12.3	1.21	1.06	0.88
38. Eight-person	11.0	15.4	13.1	1.40	1.19	0.85
39. Nine-person	5.6	8.7	6.4	1.55	1.15	0.74
40. Ten-person-and-over (11.0)	8.5	16.2	13.0	1.91	1.53	0.80

Table 9.1 (*cont.*)

Classes of households by number of persons	Percentage in total			Relatives		
	Households (H) (1)	Persons (P) (2)	Income (Y) (3)	Size (P/H) (4)	Income per household (Y/H) (5)	Income per person (Y/P) (6)
Thailand, money income, 1962–63 (5.53)ᶜ						
41. One-person	4.0	0.7	2.0	0.18	0.50	2.86
42. Two-to-three-person (2.6)	18.3	8.6	13.3	0.47	0.73	1.55
43. Four-to-five-person (4.5)	29.9	24.3	27.4	0.81	0.92	1.13
44. Six-to-seven-person (6.5)	27.1	31.9	29.4	1.18	1.08	0.94
45. Eight-person-and-over (9.2)	20.7	34.5	27.9	1.67	1.35	0.81

B. *Measures of disparity in size of household and in income per household and per person, among size classes of households*ᶠ

	TDM			Gini Coefficient		
	Size (H–P) (1)	Income per household (H–Y) (2)	Income per person (P–Y) (3)	Size (H–P) (4)	Income per household (H–Y) (5)	Income per person (P–Y) (6)
46. United States, 1975	45.4	23.4	25.2	0.305	0.158	0.165
47. Germany, 1970	44.2	32.0	13.0	0.297	0.213	0.088
48. Israel, 1968/9	43.4	20.2	38.6	0.296	0.135	0.235
49. Taiwan, 1975	31.0	10.4	20.6	0.221	0.082	0.139
50. Philippines, 1970/1	36.2	16.2	20.6	0.251	0.119	0.133
51. Thailand, 1962/3	37.2	19.0	18.2	0.242	0.127	0.118

[a] Entries in parentheses in lines identifying the country refer to the average (arithmetic mean) number of persons per household. Entries in parentheses in the vertical stub of lines 42–45 refer to the average number of persons per household in the given size-class (provided in the source). The relatives in columns 4, 5, and 6 should equal ratios of the relevant percentage shares in columns 1, 2, and 3. The slight discrepancies are due to rounding. The relatives in column 6 should equal the ratio of the relatives in column 5 to those in column 4. The slight discrepancies are again due to rounding.

[b] Lines 1–7: Taken or calculated from U.S. Bureau of the Census, *Current Population Reports, Series P-60, No. 104.* GPO, Washington 1977, Tables 3 and 15, pp. 13–20 and 48–57.

[c] Lines 8–20 and 31–40: Taken or calculated from Table 7.13 of Chapter 7. This chapter provides detailed notes on the sources of data for these three countries (Germany, Israel, and the Philippines) as well as on United States and Taiwan and also provides discussion of related findings (referred to henceforth as Source I).

[d] Lines 21–30: Taken or calculated from two sources, one covering Taipei City and the other covering Taiwan Province (the two comprising Taiwan). The former is by Bureau of Budget, Accounting and Statistics, Taipei City Government, *Report on the Survey of Family Income and Expenditure and Personal Income Distribution of Taipei City 1975,* 1976, Table 16, pp. 108–111. The latter is by Department of Budget, Accounting and Statistics, Taiwan Provincial Government, *Report on the Survey . . . . Taiwan Province 1975,* 1976, Table 25, pp. 538–549. The total and per household number of persons in the open-end, largest size group (line 30) was calculated from the other size groups and the population totals for all households given in other tables.

[e] Lines 41–45: Taken or calculated from National Statistical Office, *Advance Report, Household Expenditure Survey, Whole Kingdom* (Bangkok 1963). Table 9.0, pp. 66–67. Money income was estimated at 81 percent of total income, the latter including value of goods produced and consumed at home (see *Ibid,* Table H, p. 32).

[f] TDM is the sum of differences between percentage shares in the two relevant totals (households and persons, households and income, persons and income): signs are disregarded. They are calculated directly from the percentage shares in columns 1–3 for the six countries in Panel A. The Gini coefficients are calculated directly from the percentage shares arrayed by the order of the relatives in the corresponding columns (col. 4 for households and persons, col. 5 for households and income, and col. 6 for persons and income): all are given in Panel A.

line 46, col. 4) and a total disparity measure, TDM (a simpler measure, but yielding results quite similar to the Gini coefficients) of well over 40.[3] An inspection of the percentage shares in columns 1 and 2 and the resulting size relative in column 4 of Panel A and the disparity measures in columns 1 and 4 in Panel B reveals that the size-of-household differentials are substantial in the other countries also, although they are of somewhat narrower amplitude in the three less developed countries – all of them in East Asia – than for the three more developed countries.

The size differentials just discussed are of interest in so far as they are associated with disparities in income per household, per person, or per consuming unit; and we shall indicate later that the magnitude of the differentials in size is the *minimum* to which the magnitudes of disparities in income per household and income per person add. If so, a wide amplitude of differentials in size of households would mean (with the same associations with disparities in income per household and income per person) a wider amplitude of disparities either in income per household, in income per person, or in both.

We can make one other comment on the differentials in size of households in comparison with those in income. Size of household may be subject to short-term disturbances, whether stochastic or of a different order. Thus a family household may, in a given year, be reduced by the death of a child, to be compensated for by quick response in terms of an additional birth. But it seems plausible to assume that such short-term

3 For a discussion of this measure, see Chapter 7. TDM, as expressed here, is best viewed as the sum of deviations, signs disregarded, in relative size per unit (whether the size is number of persons, or income, or consumption, etc.) in the several classes, from the arithmetic mean, such deviations weighted by the percentage share of each class in the relevant total. Thus, in line 1 of Table 9.1, the entry for the TDM for size differentials among households by number of persons, would read 7.1 percent − 20.6 percent = −13.5 percent, the latter in turn being equal to $(0.345 - 1.00) \times 20.6$ percent, i.e., the relative deviation for the one-person class of households from the countrywide mean, weighted by the percentage share of this class in the total of all households. Expressed as a proper fraction (for United States, size of household inequality, it would then read 0.454), TDM is the ratio of the sum of class deviations, properly weighted, from the arithmetic mean, to the mean.

Both TDM and the slightly more sensitive Gini coefficient tend to understate the full range of differences in the distribution. But there are advantages of simplicity, and, in the case of TDM, ease in identifying the particular classes that are the major sources of inequality. We use the measures on the premise that they are adequate for rough comparisons of order of magnitude – in that substantial differences so revealed would be even greater relatively with more sensitive measures.

changes are of lesser impact on the distribution of households by size than on their distribution by the current year's income. One tends to think of size of household as determined largely by long lasting life cycle and institutional patterns, in which the household unit remains at a given size for a number of years. If so, the amplitude of the size differentials is more clearly reflective of differences in longer-term levels than is the amplitude of income disparities in the conventional grouping of households by the current year's income.

2. The relatives of income per household for the successive size classes of households (col. 5 of Panel A) show for all countries a *positive* association between total income of household and its size. In some cases (e.g., in the United States and particularly in Israel), the rise in the relative income per household reaches a peak at a size class well below the top and then declines. But these can be viewed as only partial limitations of the conspicuous positive association in which the rise in the size of household is, by and large, accompanied by a substantial rise in the household's total income.

The impressive positive association between size of household and its income suggested in Table 9.1 is not an arithmetic necessity or tautology. It is quite possible within a country for some socioeconomic groups, which are characterized by large households, to show an average income per household distinctly lower than that for other groups with a smaller average household (e.g., the households in the United States in 1975 with employed heads who are blue-collar workers compared with those whose employed heads are white-collar workers; or in Taiwan in 1975, farmer households compared with nonfarmer households). In fact, a negative association between average income per household in occupational groups and the size of the average household by occupation is not uncommon; and some of the relevant data will be cited and discussed in a later section. If it is possible for a variety of subgroups within a country to show larger average household size associated with lower average per household income, the positive association for countrywide comparisons cannot be viewed as inevitable and obvious. It is rather the result of a balance of factors that make for a positive association dominating the factors that would otherwise make for a negative association – with outcomes that can differ among countries, or within countries over time, or at different ranges of the size-of-household differentials.

The disparity measures in columns 2 and 5 of Panel B reflect the magnitude of the component that size differentials among households contribute to the distribution of households by size of income per household. Thus within the total inequality among households by income per household in the United States in 1975, there is a component that is measured by a Gini coefficient of 0.158 and that reflects the inequality in the size of household in terms of number of persons – a component that presumably ought to be removed if households are to be used as comparable units in terms of persons. But the Gini coefficient just cited cannot be compared directly with that for the size distribution of income among households by income per household for two reasons. First, Gini coefficients (and the TDMs) are not additive, so the sum of two component measures may add to more or less than that for the total distribution. Second, and even more difficult, the size distribution of income is based on the size of annual income, with the transient and stochastic elements recorded in the income of each single household before it is classified in the size distribution. Such stochastic and other transient elements tend to be much reduced by cancellation for large groups of households that we average under the one-, two-, . . . n-person class. The Gini coefficient for the total distribution of income among households by income per household would be substantially reduced with similar cancellation of stochastic and other transient components, were such cancellation possible. It is not feasible to attempt here a quantitatively meaningful comparison of the effects of size differentials among households on either income per household, per person, or per consuming unit, with the total size distribution of income among households by income per household, per person, or per consuming unit – the latter properly adjusted. We shall have to rely on a rough judgment resting on the absolute values of the disparity measures that we derive.[4]

4 This means, to illustrate, that Gini coefficients of 0.1 and over and TDMs of well over 15, may be viewed as sufficiently large to assume that they contribute significantly to the inequality in the total distribution to whose component the cited disparity measures refer.

The nonadditivity difficulty could be overcome by converting the underlying distribution to near normal shapes (perhaps by taking logs of size or of income) and using variance measures that can then be assumed to be additive. While this requires elaborate calculations, the results will still be affected by inclusion in the measures for the total distribution by size of income of transient disturbances in their full magnitude – let alone the deficiencies in the income data referred to earlier.

Under the circumstances it seemed best to use simple and undemanding measures, applying them to as large a number of countries or subgroups as feasible, and tracing the relations to the specific size or other classes that could be more

3. Whatever factors limit the rise in per household income with increase in household size or even make for negative association between total income and household size, the combination of the two results in the rise in household income falling substantially short of the rise in the number of persons as we move from the smaller to larger households. This can be observed in Panel A by comparing the levels and movements of the size relatives in column 4 with those of income per household in column 5; it can be observed more clearly in the ratio of the two, which represents the relatives of income per person in the successive size classes of households in column 6. This column reveals for each of the six countries a *decline* in per person income as we move from the smaller to the larger households, a decline that is quite substantial and continuous. In some cases (e.g., Taiwan and the Philippines, which are two countries with the most detailed grouping by size at the large levels), the decline in per person income slows down or ceases in the range of large households (above seven persons); but this is a minor qualification of what is an impressive *negative* association between size of household and household income per person.

The corresponding measures of disparity are given in columns 3 and 6 of Panel B. As already indicated, these measures represent the magnitude of the component that the size differentials among households contribute to the total distribution of income among households by income per person. Whereas the magnitudes differ among countries and relative to those for income per household, those in columns 3 and 6 are, on the whole, no less substantial than those in columns 2 and 5.

A more significant finding associated with the one just stated is the difference in *identity* of the households at low and high levels when we compare grouping by income per household with that by income per person.[5] As found in the paper cited, the higher levels of *per household* income are dominated by the larger households whereas the higher levels of *per person* income are dominated by the smaller households; and there is a similar contrast in identity at the lower levels, the latter dominated by smaller households in the distribution by income per household and by larger households in the distribution by income per person. Since for most purposes it is the distribution by income per person (or per consuming

easily observed in these simple measures. The hope is that significant associations will be suggested that then may call for the application of the more elaborate measures to cases where the availability of reliable data warrants it.

5 See Chapter 7, Tables 7.7 and 7.17, and related discussion in the text.

unit) that is the more significant, the use of income per household may lead to misleading identification of the better-off or the worse-off groups within the total population.

4. We come now to the relation between the measure of disparity for the size differentials among households and those for disparities in income per household and income per person. A glance at these measures in Panel B of the table shows that the sum of the two income disparity measures is never smaller than the size disparity measure. In the single case of Taiwan, the sum of the TDMs in columns 2 and 3 (10.4 and 21.6, respectively) equals the TDM in column 1 (31.0); the same is true of the two Gini coefficients in columns 5 and 6 relative to that in column 4. In most other countries, the sum of the disparity measures for income per household and income per person *exceeds* that disparity measure for the size differentials but by relatively small margins (Germany, the Philippines, Thailand). For the United States, the excess in the sum of the disparity measures in columns 2 and 3 relative to 1 is of 48.5 to 45.4, with a similar excess in the sum of the Gini coefficients. This excess becomes striking in the case of Israel: the sum of the TDMs in columns 2 and 3 (58.3) is over a third larger than that for size differentials (43.4). There is a similar showing for the Gini coefficients.

Two comments are relevant. First, our finding that the disparity measure for household size is related to the sum of the measures for disparities in income per household and in income per person is dependent upon the finding of a *positive* response of household income to size but a response that falls short of the rise in household size and thus "leaves room," as it were, for the *negative* association between size and income per person. Were these two findings absent, the relation between the disparity measure for household size and the disparity measures for income per household and for income per person would have been different. Thus, if the association between size and household income remained positive, but the positive response of income were more than proportional to increase in size, the result would have been a measure of disparity in income per household alone greater than that for size, whereas the association between per person income and household size would have been positive. By contrast, were the association between size of household and income per household to become negative, the disparity measure for income per person would become the largest of the three disparity measures, it alone exceeding that for size differentials among households. The summation in these two assumed cases would then be addition of the two smaller disparity measures to yield the *largest* of the three: it being for income per household in the former case and for income per person in the latter case.

Second, given a positive but incomplete response of household income to household size, the finding that the sum of the disparity measures for income per household and for income per person significantly exceeds the disparity for household size is presumably due to some additional factors that introduce elements affecting household income in ways *not associated* with size. In terms of the relatives and percentage shares shown in Panel A and related to TDM, one should view the size and income per household relatives as measures of proportional deviation from the countrywide average, so that 0.345 in line 1, column 4 becomes a proportional deviation of -0.655, whereas that in column 4, line 7 becomes $+1.72$ (being the relatives, as entered, minus 1.00). It will then be noted that, for the United States, the deviations in column 5 (income per household) are for each size class of the same *sign* as in column 4 (size of households) and that, for all size classes, the proportional deviation for household income is of smaller absolute magnitude than that for size, with one important exception. The exception is for the size class of three persons (line 3), for which the positive deviation for income per household ($+0.14$ in col. 5) is much greater than that for size ($+0.05$ in col. 4). If we remove this exception by setting the per household income relative for this size class at 1.025 (thus reducing the income share in column 3 from 19.6 to 17.6 percent) and compensate by adding two percentage points to the income share of one-person class in line 1, column 3 (thus making it 12.0, with resulting shifts in income relatives for this class), the new TDM for income per household becomes 19.4, that for income per person becomes 26.0, and the sum is now identical with TDM for size of 45.4. A different allocation of the two percentage points would yield a different pair of TDMs for income per household and income per person, but so long as the signs of the proportional deviations represented by the relatives in columns 4 and 5 are the same and those in column 5 are all absolutely smaller than those in column 4, the sum of the TDMs for income per household and income per person will be identical with the TDM for size differentials among households.

Even larger disturbances in the association between size and household income are observed for Israel. For the three-person class (line 17) (with a share of 19.0 percent of all households), a negative deviation for size (-0.18) is combined with a positive deviation for income ($+0.13$). For the six-and-over class (line 20) (with a share of 14.3 percent of all households), a positive deviation for size ($+1.08$) is associated with a negative deviation for household income (-0.06). Clearly, there are elements of heterogeneity in the structure of Israel's household population that disturb the positive association between size and household income; and we are aware of them from other sources because of the mixture of Jews and non-Jews, of immigrant and native populations, of the presence of different continent-of-origin stocks among the Jews, and different religious groups among the non-Jews.

II. Some variants

In Section III, we consider some of the factors relevant to the associations between size of household and income disparities of the type observed in Table 9.1. But before doing so we should note, briefly, two other variants of size differentials among households.

The first is suggested by the large proportions in the developed countries today of one-person households, as illustrated in Table 9.1 for Germany and the United States – contrasted with the far more moderate proportions of one-person households in the less developed countries (e.g., Taiwan). This contrast is observed also for the larger number of countries for which we have data on size of households but no data on income. Since the one-person households may be viewed more easily as members of a larger family with which they may be associated than is true of larger households, one may ask what would be the effect on the size differentials and their association with income disparities if one-person households were excluded or transferred to the larger multiperson units.

An illustrative answer to this question is provided in Table 9.2, in which we use the data for the United States and Taiwan to perform the needed calculations. The effect of exclusion of one-person households, thus limiting the distributions to family households of two or more persons, naturally raises the average size of household and reduces both the size differentials and associated disparities in income per household (Panel A and col. 2 and 6 and of Panel C). Since we are eliminating one source of diversity among households with respect to size, the TDMs and the Gini coefficients for the size of household differentials and disparities in income per household should decline – and they do, appreciably more for the United States than for Taiwan. But the more significant finding is that the decline in *per person* income with rise in the size of household

Table 9.2. *Effects of exclusion or transfer of one-person households, United States and Taiwan, 1975*

	A. *Exclusion of one-person households*					
	Percentage in total			Relatives		
Classes of households	H (1)	P (2)	Y (3)	H/P (4)	Y/H (5)	Y/P (6)
United States, 1975 (3.38)						
1. Two-person	38.5	23.0	32.8	0.60	0.85	1.43
2. Three-person	21.7	19.4	21.8	0.89	1.00	1.12
3. Four-person	19.8	23.3	22.1	1.18	1.12	0.95
4. Five-person	10.8	15.9	12.9	1.47	1.19	0.81
5. Six-person	5.2	9.0	6.0	1.73	1.15	0.67
6. Seven-person-and-over	4.0	9.4	4.4	2.35	1.10	0.47
Taiwan (5.41)						
7. Two-person	5.4	2.0	4.2	0.37	0.78	2.10
8. Three-person	10.6	5.8	9.1	0.55	0.86	1.57
9. Four-person	17.3	12.8	16.3	0.74	0.96	1.27
10. Five-person	23.0	21.2	22.2	0.92	0.97	1.05
11. Six-person	19.6	21.8	19.9	1.11	1.02	0.91
12. Seven-person	11.7	15.1	12.1	1.29	1.03	0.80
13. Eight-person	6.1	9.1	7.3	1.49	1.20	0.80
14. Nine-person	2.8	4.7	3.4	1.68	1.21	0.72
15. Ten-person-and-over	3.5	7.5	5.5	2.14	1.57	0.73

	B. *Transfer of one-person households to multiperson households*							
	Assumption 1				Assumption 2			
	Percentage in total			Income relative,	Percentage in total			Income relative,
	H (1)	P (2)	Y (3)	Y/P (4)	H (5)	P (6)	Y (7)	Y/P (8)
United States (3.64)								
16. Two-person	28.6	15.7	21.9	1.39	38.5	21.2	29.5	1.39
17. Three-person	26.0	21.4	25.9	1.21	21.7	17.9	19.6	1.09
18. Four-person	20.2	22.3	22.0	0.99	13.9	15.3	13.9	0.91
19. Five-person	13.2	18.2	15.8	0.87	5.9	8.1	8.3	1.02
20. Six-person	6.6	10.8	8.1	0.75	10.8	17.9	15.8	0.82
21. Seven-person-and-over	5.4	11.6	6.3	0.54	9.2	19.6	12.9	0.66
Taiwan (5.44)								
22. Two-person	5.2	1.9	4.0	2.11	5.4	2.0	4.1	2.05
23. Three-person	10.5	5.8	8.8	1.52	10.6	5.9	8.9	1.51
24. Four-person	17.1	12.5	15.9	1.27	17.3	12.7	16.0	1.26
25. Five-person	22.8	21.0	22.1	1.05	23.0	21.0	21.9	1.04
26. Six-person	19.7	21.7	20.1	0.93	19.6	21.6	19.6	0.91

Table 9.2 *(cont.)*

	Assumption 1				Assumption 2			
	Percentage in total			Income relative,	Percentage in total			Income relative,
	H	P	Y	Y/P	H	P	Y	Y/P
	(1)	(2)	(3)	(4)	(5)	(6)	(7)	(8)
27. Seven-person	11.9	15.3	12.4	0.81	11.7	15.0	11.9	0.79
28. E·ht-person	6.3	9.2	7.6	0.83	6.1	9.0	7.2	0.80
29. Nine-person	2.9	4.8	3.6	0.75	2.8	4.6	3.4	0.74
30. Ten-person-and-over	3.6	7.8	5.5	0.71	3.5	8.2	7.0	0.85

C. *Disparity measures*

	TDM				Gini coefficient			
			Transfer				Transfer	
	Table 1	Excl.	Ass1	Ass2	Table 1	Excl.	Ass1	Ass2
	(1)	(2)	(3)	(4)	(5)	(6)	(7)	(8)
United States								
31. H–P	45.4	35.6	35.0	42.2	0.305	0.230	0.230	0.266
32. H–Y	23.4	11.4	13.6	22.2	0.158	0.073	0.110	0.138
33. P–Y	25.2	24.4	21.4	20.4	0.165	0.166	0.147	0.138
Taiwan								
34. H–P	31.0	29.0	28.8	29.4	0.221	0.203	0.202	0.207
35. H–Y	10.4	9.0	9.6	10.8	0.082	0.067	0.071	0.082
36. P–Y	20.6	20.0	19.2	18.6	0.139	0.136	0.131	0.125

Notes: All calculations use the percentage shares for households (H), person (P), and income (Y) shown for the two countries in Table 9.1.
The entries in parentheses following the name of the country are the arithmetic mean numbers of persons per household associated with the distributions by size given in the panel.
In both assumptions in Panel B, the allocation of the one-person households and their income uses the average income per household. In Assumption 1 (Ass1), the one-person households are allocated by the percentage shares of the size classes in column 1 of Panel A. In Assumption 2 (Ass2), one-person households are allocated to the larger multiperson households, assuming that each of them is assigned one extra person. This allocation, beginning at the top size-end of the distribution, is followed until all of the one-person households have been transferred.

is still quite marked in Table 9.2, Panel A. The exclusion of one-person households leaves the TDMs and the Gini coefficients for the disparities in income per person about the same as they were for the complete size distributions of households in Table 9.1 (see Panel C of Table 9.2, col. 1 and 2, lines 33 and 36, and col. 5 and 6, lines 33 and 36).

If we try to transfer one-person households and their income to multiperson households, we need to have a reasonable scheme for allocating the former among the latter. One cannot claim that the schemes embodied in the two assumptions used for Panel B of Table 9.2 are realistic, but they are of interest as illustrations. Using Assumption 1, we allocate the one-person households to the other size classes proportionately to their relative weight, i.e., to their percentage proportion in the total of all households of two or more. Using Assumption 2, we follow a procedure that allocates the one-person households first to the largest size class in the distribution: one one-person household is assigned to each household of the largest size class; then, of the remaining one-person households, one is assigned to each household of the size class of next-to-largest size, and so on down, until all of the one-person households have been allocated. We should note that in Assumption 1, the additions of one-person households to the two-person size class yields a new group of three-person households, which is subtracted from the former two-person class and added to the former three-person class. In other words, transfer means shifts of the distribution along the full range from the earlier two-person household class to the top size class.

A glance at Panel B and the relevant parts of Panel C of Table 9.2 shows that the assumed transfers have different effects on the size differentials among households and on the disparities in income per household – the latter particularly marked for the United States in Assumption 2. But, while raising the average size of the household even further (to 3.64 in United States and 5.44 in Taiwan), the transfers, in both assumptions, reduce the disparity in income per person. Thus, the TDMs in lines 33 and 36 tend to drift down in columns 3 and 4, and so do the Gini coefficients in columns 7 and 8. The reason is that the high per person income in the one-person household class is transferred to larger sized households, which originally had lower income per person. The effect, however, is limited, and the substantial disparity in income per person, which is negatively associated with size of household, tends to persist even with the experimental transfers of one-person households and their income to larger sized households.

Another variant of size differentials among households (different again from that used in Table 9.1) is suggested by the question whether the unweighted number of persons is a true measure of household size. As already noted, our interest is more in inequalities revealed by the relatives of income per person and not by those in the relatives of income per household since the latter are so dominated by inequalities in size of household. But is the shift from per household to per person bases the proper adjustment for inequalities in size of household? If we are concerned with equivalent *consuming* units, the fact that the proportions of children are greater in the larger sized households suggests the possibility that division by the number of persons *overcorrects* for inequality in size of households. This possibility flows from the realistic hypothesis that the consumption needs of children are, on a per head basis, distinctly lower than those of adults. And there is the additional argument that suggests economies of scale in the larger household, even if all its members are adults.

The issues raised are complex and, indeed, are part of a wider group of issues – of differences in "needs" among members of the household, as distinguished by age and sex (and possibly other demographic and socioeconomic characteristics), and of differences in living – working conditions, which may produce price differentials in the costs of a similar bundle of goods among groups of households. It is not feasible to explore these issues further here, nor do I feel competent to undertake the exploration. But it may suffice here to use whatever limited data on the topic could be assembled in Table 9.3 on an assumption (for three of the four countries) that persons under 18 years should be viewed as half-weight consuming units compared with a full weight for those 18 years of age and over.[6] This crude assumption probably overcorrects for difference in "needs," even including an allowance for economies of scale. For Israel, due to lack of relevant data on age structure by size classes of households, we adopted the conversion coefficients to "standard person" units derived in the Israeli statistics from the country's data on consumption patterns for households of different size. There is no full comparability between the results for Israel and for the three other countries; but the estimates are notional for all four.

Since the larger households usually have a higher proportion of children than the smaller households and since there may be a greater economy of scale in satisfying consumption needs for the former than for the latter, we would expect that the size differentials among households in terms of consuming units or "standard" persons would be narrower than in terms of persons. In addition, since we are not regrouping the households by the consuming unit or standard person equivalent of each

6 See, in this connection, Chapter 7, particularly Table 7.9, and related text discussion.

Table 9.3. *Shift from income per capita to income per consuming unit or per standard person, four countries*

	A. *Shift to income per consuming unit*[a]						
	Person per household				Percentage of shares in		Income relative,
Households by number of persons	Under 18 (1)	18 and over (2)	Cons. units (C) (3)	Ratio (2)/(3) (4)	C (5)	Y (6)	Y/C (7)
United States, 1975[b]							
1. One-person	0	1.00	1.00	1.00	8.4	10.0	1.19
2. Two-person	0.06	1.94	1.97	0.98	24.7	29.5	1.19
3. Three-person	0.70	2.30	2.65	0.87	18.7	19.6	1.05
4. Four-person	1.61	2.39	3.20	0.75	20.6	19.9	0.97
5. Five-person	2.49	2.51	3.76	0.67	13.2	11.6	0.88
6. Six-person	3.34	2.66	4.33	0.61	7.3	5.4	0.74
7. Seven-person	4.81	2.97	5.38	0.55	7.1	4.0	0.56
8. Average	0.89	2.00	2.45	0.82	—	—	—
Taiwan, 1975[c]							
9. One-person	0	1.00	1.00	1.00	0.8	1.6	2.00
10. Two-person	0.16	1.84	1.92	0.96	2.3	4.1	1.78
11. Three-person	0.77	2.23	2.61	0.85	6.5	8.9	1.37
12. Four-person	1.51	2.49	3.24	0.77	13.2	16.0	1.21
13. Five-person	2.24	2.76	3.88	0.71	20.9	21.9	1.05
14. Six-person	2.86	3.14	4.57	0.69	21.0	19.6	0.93
15. Seven-person	3.40	3.60	5.30	0.68	14.5	11.9	0.82
16. Eight-person	3.73	4.27	6.13	0.70	8.8	7.2	0.82
17. Nine-person-and-over	4.74	5.79	8.16	0.71	12.0	8.8	0.73
18. Average	2.27	3.00	4.14	0.73	—	—	—
Philippines, 1970–71[d]							
19. One-person	0	1.00	1.00	1.00	0.4	1.1	2.75
20. Two-person	0.20	1.80	1.90	0.95	3.1	4.6	1.48
21. Three-person	0.95	2.05	2.52	0.81	6.9	8.8	1.28
22. Four-person	1.86	2.14	3.07	0.71	10.8	13.6	1.26
23. Five-person	2.75	2.25	3.63	0.62	12.5	13.9	1.17
24. Six-person	3.51	2.49	4.25	0.59	13.5	13.2	0.98
25. Seven-person	4.18	2.82	4.91	0.57	13.4	12.3	0.92
26. Eight-person	4.58	3.42	5.71	0.60	14.8	13.1	0.89
27. Nine-person-and-over	5.64	4.57	7.39	0.62	24.6	19.4	0.79
28. Average	3.06	2.71	4.24	0.64	—	—	—

Table 9.3 *(cont.)*

B. *Shift to standard person (SP)*			
		Percentage of Shares in		Income relative
Households by number of persons	SP per household (1)	SP (2)	Y (3)	Y/SP (4)
Israel, urban households, 1968–69				
29. One-person	1.25	4.7	4.8	1.02
30. Two-person	2.00	15.9	19.8	1.25
31. Three-person	2.65	17.3	21.4	1.24
32. Four-person	3.20	23.6	27.9	1.18
33. Five-person	3.75	14.7	12.6	0.86
34. Six-person-and-over (7.2)	4.84	23.8	13.5	0.57

C. *Disparity measures*						
	TDM			Gini coefficient		
	Size (H–C or H–SP) (1)	Income per household (H–Y) (2)	Income per C, SP (C, SP–Y) (3)	Size (H–C or H–SP) (4)	Income per household (H–Y) (5)	Income per C, SP (C, SP–Y) (6)
35. United States, 1975	36.2	23.4	14.6	0.244	0.158	0.090
36. Taiwan, 1975	28.0	10.4	17.6	0.200	0.082	0.120
37. Philippines, 1970/1	32.2	16.2	16.6	0.223	0.119	0.108
38. Israel, 1968/69	30.0	20.2	24.8	0.204	0.135	0.146

Sources: For the sources of underlying data, see the notes in Table 9.1 relating to the four countries covered here.

[a] The ratios in column 4, lines 8, 18, and 28 are computed from the arithmetic means in columns 2 and 3 of the same lines.

[b] The estimates in columns 1 and 2 are based on 1970 Census data on proportions of children under 18 in families of two to seven and over (see U.S. Bureau of the Census, 1970 *Census of Population,* Subject Report PC(2) 4A, *Family Composition* (May 1973), Table 3, pp. 7–8. These proportions were applied to size classes of households used in Table 9.1 here (for March 1976, income for 1975). The results were adjusted proportionately so that the totals of under-18 and 18-and-over checked with the totals in the source used for Table 9.1. Numbers in column 3 are calculated from columns 1 and 2 by weighting the numbers aged below 18 by half. For discussion of this weighting see Chapter 7 (Table 7.9 and discussion). Numbers in columns 4–7 are calculated from columns 1–3 or taken directly from sources used for Table 9.1.

[c] The proportions given directly in the source are for persons under 21 and 21 and over (see Kuznets, "Size and Structure of Family Households: Exploratory Comparisons," *Population and Development Review,* Vol. 4, No. 2, June 1978, Table 1, pp. 190–191). For the end of 1974, it is possible to estimate the ratio of total population under 21 to that under 18:

household, but retain size classes by number of persons, we underestimate the full range of size differentials in terms of consuming units (or standard persons): the spread in any variable is reduced if the data are classified by a criterion of size not directly reflecting the given variable. And, indeed, for these reasons, the size disparity measures in Table 9.3 for the four countries are all lower than the corresponding disparity measures in Panel B of Table 9.1. To use the TDMs for illustration: the measure drops from 45.4 to 36.2 for the United States; from 43.4 to 30.0 for Israel; from 31.0 to 28.0 for Taiwan; and from 36.2 to 32.2 for the Philippines.

The conversion to consuming units for the United States reduces the size differentials more sharply than for either Taiwan or the Philippines (the comparison with Taiwan being of most interest). This is despite the fact that for the household population as a whole, the proportion of persons below 18 is about 30 percent in the United States and over 40 percent for Taiwan. The explanation lies in differences in patterns of rise of the proportion of children in the larger households, combined with differences in distributions of household by number of persons. As Table 9.1 shows, in the United States over 51 percent of all households are in the one- and two-person classes, so that the population under 18 years of age is far more concentrated in what for that country are the larger households; whereas in Taiwan, with the shares of one- and two-person households small, no such concentration occurs. This can be seen by comparing the proportions of under 18 in the United States and Taiwan beginning with the class of four persons and more: in the four-person class, the entry for the United States (line 4, col. 1) at 1.61 is already in excess of that for the same class in Taiwan (1.51: line 12, col. 1). This greater proportion of members under 18 years of age in the United States than in Taiwan will be found also for the five-, six-, and seven-and-

Notes to Table 9.3 *(cont.)*

it is 1.161 (see *Taiwan Demographic Fact Book 1974,* Taipei, Dec. 1975, Table 1, pp. 54). We applied this ratio to the total numbers in the successive size classes of households to approximate the distribution in columns 1 and 2.

[d] The averages in line 28 are from the original Chapter 7, Table 7.13. The distribution of members under 18 and of those 18 and over used in columns 1 and 2 follows the pattern established for Taiwan in lines 9–17, columns 1 and 2. This seemed to be a more plausible pattern than the one used in Table 13 of Chapter 7.

[e] For discussion of the scale of standard persons used in Israel for households of increasing size, see Chapter 7, Table 7.9 and discussion. Columns 2–4 are calculated using column 1 and the relevant data in Table 9.1.

[f] See the notes on the measures of disparity, Panel B of Table 9.1.

over size classes. Such differences in pattern and in relative reduction of size differentials among households in the shift from per person to per consuming unit, may be found in other comparisons between the more and the less developed countries.

With the reduction in size differentials among households and the disparities in income per household remaining unaffected, there is a reduction in the disparities in income per consuming unit when we compare them with disparities in income per person. The change, in TDMs, is from 25.2 to 14.6 in the United States (relatively, the largest change); from 38.2 to 24.8 in Israel; from 20.6 to 17.6 in Taiwan; and from 20.6 to 16.6 in the Philippines. Yet the disparities, even in income per consuming unit, remain substantial; and most interestingly, the negative correlation persists: this time between size of household as measured in consuming units and income per consuming unit. A glance at the relevant income relatives in Table 9.3 shows that with the exception of movement from the one- to two-person class in Israel, there is a marked and consistent decline in income per consuming unit as we move from the smaller to the larger households.

III. Factors relevant to the association

We may now ask why income per household increases with rise in household size and why this increase falls short of the rise in numbers (either of persons or consuming units) so as to yield a marked decline in income per capita or per consuming unit when we shift from smaller to larger households.

In considering the answers to the double question just posed, we may start at the beginning of the sequence – size of household, income per household, income per person or consuming unit – or reverse it and proceed from income per person or per consuming unit to size and then to income per household. In the first sequence, we begin with size differences among households (taking them as given) and then attempt to suggest the factors that, given the size differences, yield the observed disparities in income per household and in income per person or per consuming unit. But in this attempt, we must indispensably consider the demographic and socioeconomic characteristics of households of differing size; and so come to view size differentials, in turn, as determined in part by other demographic and socioeconomic groupings within the country (or within any other relevant total). In the second sequence, we begin with, and take as given, disparities among households in income per person or per consuming unit; and then attempt to suggest the factors that, given the income disparities, account for a negative association between the latter and size differentials among households and that do this in such a way as to make for a positive association between size and total income of households. But in this attempt, we must indispensably consider the associated demographic and socioeconomic characteristics of households at low and high levels of income per person or per consuming unit. In this way, we come to view the income disparities, in turn, as determined in part by other demographic and socioeconomic groupings within the relevant total of household population. While the analytical emphases will differ somewhat between the two sequences, the several demographic and socioeconomic groupings whose different responses may account for the association between size-of-household differentials and income disparities will be the same.

The presentation in this section follows the first sequence because the available data center on the household as a unit, whereas those that center on the person or consuming unit are scarce. But it should be possible toward the end of the section to revert briefly to some aspects of the second sequence, referring to the illustrative findings in our discussion relating to those demographic and socioeconomic groupings that we found to be of interest.

(a) The first and obvious reason for the positive association between size and income of household is that the larger number of members will, most likely, mean more members of working age. The latter can participate in earning activity (thus adding to the household's income) and may be induced to do so by the greater needs that a larger number of members represents. And, indeed, we find in Panel A of Table 9.3 that the number of adults per household increases with the rise in size of household, in each of the three countries covered.

Two comments are relevant to the just suggested factor in the positive association between size and income per household. First, for the present purpose the distinction between children and adults should not be with an eye to consumption needs as it was for the conversion in Table 9.3. The distinction should be between those too young or too old to be able to contribute to income as it is defined in the data and those who are of working age, i.e., capable of so contributing. This division line will differ among countries at the several stages of economic development and among socioeconomic groups within a country. The effective application of such a criterion requires data on income earning capabilities at different ages in different situations. No such data are at hand, and as Table 9.3 indicates, data even on age distribution of members of families or households within the size classes of two members and above are extremely scarce. The approximations in Table 9.3 are, for the present purposes, crude indeed.

Second, the activities in which the properly defined working age members are assumed to be able to engage should be among those that are included in the income data. This requirement of consistency between the definition of income recipients within the household and the income covered in the data (or, still better, the income that should be covered) is obvious. Yet it needs to be noted, and the bearing is even wider when we consider the variety of productive activities within the household (by the housewife and other members) that are excluded from the accepted definition of personal income of households in the standard economic accounts. Clearly, a wider definition of productive activity and income can significantly affect the pattern of relatives of income per household, perhaps making the rise with increasing size of household more substantial than it is now in column 5 of Panel A of Table 9.1 and thus moderating the associated decline in the relatives of income per person in column 6.

If we accept the crude approximations in Table 9.3, the rise in number of adults per household with increasing size of household provides one factor that makes for a rise in total income of household as the number of its members increases. But the moderate magnitude of the rise in total income thus attained, relative to increase in persons or consuming units, is also revealed. As already observed, the table shows a rapid rise in the proportion of children in total membership of household, once we pass the two-person level, in both the United States and Taiwan patterns. Hence, in all countries covered, the proportion of persons of working ages to total number of persons or of consuming units declines markedly, beginning with the size class of three persons and reaching a trough in the larger sized households. It follows that unless income per person of working age were to *rise* sharply to offset the decline in the proportion of potential workers to total of persons or consuming units, there would be a drop in household income per person or per consuming unit.

This finding of the rising proportion of children and declining proportion of adults as the size of the household increases beyond two persons is likely to be observed with a lower division line (say of 15 years of age), and the evidence on the importance of the children factor in explaining differentials in size of households (largely countrywide averages in cross-section and time comparisons) in Kuznets (1978; see note 1) supports this inference. But in the present connection, one should stress that marriage and children mean not only a decline in the larger families of the proportions of members of working ages; they mean also the absorption of some of these members of working ages into activities within the household needed to take care of children and of living arrangements, activities the substantial returns on which bypass the markets and are not included in the personal income (or consumption) of the households in the data on size-distributions. If we assume that the absorption of work-time of working age adults is greater the larger the number of children in the household (particularly if the dividing line is set at a young age), the proportion of adults *available* for income securing pursuits in the total membership of the households declines even more sharply with the rise in household size.

(b) Another reason for the positive association between size of household and its income may be that size is associated with other characteristics that bear upon income. Assume that in both the countrywide total of households and within each size class we distinguish two subgroups, A and B, and that the proportions of A are smaller among the smaller households and greater among the larger households, whereas the opposite is true of the proportions of subgroup B. Assume further that, within each size class (or the overwhelming majority of them), the average income per household in subgroup A is significantly above that in subgroup B. This combination of a rising proportion of A households, with a significantly higher income per household for the A households within each or most size classes, would produce a rise in income per household, as we shift from smaller to larger size classes. The result would be a positive association between size and income of household, even if the number of adults of working age per household failed to rise in the shift from smaller to larger households.

An illustration of demographic characteristics associated with size (of the A–B type just conjectured) is provided in Table 9.4: the characteristics being sex of head of household, age of head of household, and a closely related economic characteristic of participation or lack of participation of the head in the labor force. The illustration is limited to the United States even though similar data are available for the same year for Taiwan Province (i.e., Taiwan, excluding Taipei City). But the proportions of households with female heads or with the head not participating in the

Table 9.4. *Effect of differences in structure within size classes of households on income relatives and disparities: structure by sex, age, and labor force participation of heads, United States, 1975*

	Size classes of households (number of persons)							All house-holds (8)
	1 (1)	2 (2)	3 (3)	4 (4)	5 (5)	6 (6)	7 and over (7)	
Countrywide measures as given[a]								
1. Percentage of shares in all households	20.6	30.6	17.2	15.7	8.6	4.1	3.2	45.4 (H–P)
2. Income relative, per household	0.49	0.96	1.14	1.27	1.35	1.32	1.25	23.4 (H–Y)
3. Income relative, per person	1.41	1.38	1.09	0.92	0.78	0.64	0.46	25.2 (P–Y)
Male- and female-headed households								
4. Percentage of male-headed households within size class[b]	36.9	83.4	83.2	90.2	93.8	89.4	86.4	75.8
5. Ratio, income per household, female head to male head[b]	0.64	0.64	0.56	0.49	0.50	0.46	0.49	—
6. Income relative per household, constant percentage in line 4[c]	0.59	0.96	1.13	1.21	1.27	1.24	1.20	19.0 (H–Y)
7. Income relative per person, assumption of line 6[c]	1.72	1.38	1.08	0.88	0.74	0.61	0.44	29.4 (P–Y)
Age of head (35–54 age group versus others)								
8. Percentage of 35–54 year head households within size class[b]	17.0	19.7	37.1	48.7	63.1	69.6	77.7	34.2
9. Ratio, income per household, other age head households to 35–54[b]	0.63	0.79	0.81	0.78	0.74	0.73	0.81	—
10. Income relative per household, constant percentage in line 8[c]	0.53	1.01	1.14	1.24	1.24	1.20	1.13	19.2 (H–Y)

Table 9.4 *(cont.)*

	Size classes of households (number of persons)							All house-holds
	1 (1)	2 (2)	3 (3)	4 (4)	5 (5)	6 (6)	7 and over (7)	(8)
11. Income relative per person, assumption of line 10ᶜ	1.55	1.44	1.09	0.90	0.72	0.58	0.41	29.8 (P–Y)
Head in labor force (L) and not in labor force (N)								
12. Percentage of L within size classᵇ	49.2	64.6	83.3	90.5	91.8	88.0	84.8	72.7
13. Ratio, income per household, N/Lᵇ	0.46	0.54	0.63	0.59	0.54	0.47	0.50	
14. Income relative per household, constant percentage in line 12ᶜ	0.58	1.02	1.10	1.18	1.24	1.22	1.16	17.4 (H–Y)
15. Income relative per person, assumption of line 14ᶜ	1.68	1.45	1.06	0.86	0.72	0.60	0.43	31.0 (P–Y)

ᵃThe entries in columns 1–7 are from Panel A of Table 9.1, lines 1–7, columns 1, 5, and 6. Those in column 8 are the TDMs, from Panel B of Table 9.1, line 46, columns 1–3.
ᵇLines 4–5, 8–9, and 12–13 are calculated from the source for the United States referred to in the notes to Table 9.1 (Table 15, pp. 48–57). Lines 4, 8, and 12 refer to the percentage within each size class and for all households of households with male heads, with heads aged 35–54, and with heads in the labor force. The complementary percentage to 100 is then of households with female heads, with heads aged below 35 and above 54, and with heads not in the labor force. Lines 5, 9, and 13 refer to the ratio, within each size class, of the income per household with female heads to income per household with male heads; of the income per household with heads aged 35–54 to income per household with either younger or older heads; and of the income per household with heads not in the labor force to income per household with heads in the labor force.
ᶜLines 6–7, 10–11, and 14–15 are calculated by assuming (1) that *within* the size classes, percentages of male- and female-headed households are held constant at the countrywide proportions (i.e., 75.8 and 24.2 percent, respectively); (2) that a similar assumption is made with respect to percentages within each size class of households with heads aged 35–54 and of households with heads at younger or older ages (34.2 and 65.8 percent, respectively); and (3) that within each size class, percentages of households with heads in the labor force and with heads not in the labor force are the same (72.7 and 27.3 percent, respectively).
Given these assumptions and the within-size-class averages of income per household for the three comparisons of two groups each, it was possible to compute the average income per household for each size class. Then, having the common distribution in line 1 of households by size classes, we calculated the relatives of income per household in lines 6, 10, and 14 and the relatives of income per person in lines 7, 11, and 15.
The entries in column 8 of lines 6, 10, and 14 are the TDMs for inequality of income per household; those in column 8 of lines 7, 11, and 15 are for inequality in income per person – both sets resulting from size inequalities under the assumptions used.

labor force are quite small in Taiwan Province, and the data would yield only insignificant contributions to the positive association between size of household and its income. Likewise, household income differentials within size classes, by age of head, are far narrower in Taiwan Province than in the United States.

Table 9.4 provides the needed information for each of three sets of characteristics of head of household: (1) differences in percentage proportions of A and B within each size class and (2) the ratio of the lower income per household of the B subgroup to that of the higher income of the A subgroup [see lines 4, 8, and 12 on the percentage shares of the A subgroup (male heads, heads aged from 35 through 54, and heads in the labor force) and lines 5, 9, and 13, on the ratio of average household income of the B group to that of the A group (the B subgroup has female head households, households headed by persons under 35 or over 54 years of age, and households whose heads were not in the labor force)]. A glance at these lines shows that the A–B shares differ substantially among the size classes (the A shares rising markedly from low shares in the one-person class to much higher shares in the larger households), whereas the average household income for the A subgroup substantially exceeds that of the B subgroup within each of the several size classes.

Given the subgroup differentials in income per household, it is the pattern of differences in A–B shares in the successive size classes that are important (by contributing to the rise in income per household and then also in limiting that rise). The contribution of the differing A–B structure can be observed if we assume away these structural differences, i.e., posit the same A–B shares in the successive size classes and then compare with the result for the countrywide picture. The income relatives per household resulting from that assumption are in lines 6, 10, and 14, columns 1–7, and the disparity measures for income per household are in the same lines, column 8. These can be compared with the actual countrywide relatives of income per household, which reflect *variable* structure by size class and are given in line 2. The comparison shows that the differences in structure by A–B subgroups resulted in raising the positive response of income per household to size; this is shown by the finding that the TDM reflecting the differences in structure (23.4) exceeds those based on assumption of the same A–B structure in each of the size classes (19.0 in line 6; 19.2 in line 10; and 17.4 in line 14). The same result is observed when we compare the range of rise in the income per household from the lowest (at the one-person class) to the highest (at the five-person class). For the observed countrywide relative, the range is 0.49 to 1.35 or 2.8; with exclusion of differences in A–B structure, it is reduced to 2.2 for the subgroups by sex of head, to 2.3 for the subgroups by age of head, and to 2.1 for the subgroups by participation and nonparticipation of head in the labor force.

The assumptions used in lines 6, 10, and 14 imply that for the hypothetical distributions, the share of the size classes in total of all households are the same as in line 1, i.e., the one observed with variable structure of A–B subgroups. Hence, the TDM for size differentials among households in line 1 (45.4) is also the one for the hypothetical distributions implied in lines 6, 10, and 14. From what we have learned of the TDM for size differentials as the *minimum* to which the TDMs for income would add, we should infer that lower TDMs for income per household in lines 6, 10, and 14 (compared to line 2) would mean higher TDMs for income per person in lines 7, 11, and 15 (compared to line 3). In other words, the diversity of A–B structure, which made for stronger *positive* response of per household income to size, also made for a *weaker negative* response of per person income to size of household. And, indeed, the TDM in line 3 (25.2) is significantly smaller than those close to 30 in lines 7, 11, and 15.

If the diversity in A–B structure of the type revealed in lines 4, 8, and 12 contributes to the positive response of household income to household size, this contribution is limited if such diversity is reduced once the percentage share of A reaches high levels and leaves less room for further increases. It is therefore of interest that, for the structure by sex of head, a share of male-headed households as high as 83 percent already is reached in the two-persons class (see line 4, col. 2) and that, for the structure by labor force participation, the share of households with heads in the labor force reaches 83 percent already in the three-persons class (see line 12, col. 3). Only for the structure by age of head do we find (in line 8) that the rise in the share of households with heads between the ages of 35 and 54 is fairly continuous through the range of size classes, although even here the rise in the share is moderate beyond the five-persons class. Given variations in the A/B income-per-household ratios among the several size classes of relatively moderate range (see lines 5, 9, and 13), the diversity in A–B structure that diminishes rapidly as we pass to size classes beyond two or three persons can make only a limited contribution to *sustaining* the positive response of income to household size.

Illustrations of the effects of A–B structures similar to those provided in Table 9.4 can probably be found in a number of other countries; and what we know of the effects of sex and age of head on household income (directly and through influence on participation in labor force) would lead us to expect results in the economically developed countries similar to those that we found in the United States. We now turn to another kind of grouping in which the combination of diversity in structure within the successive size classes with per household income differentials between the subgroups within these size classes produces effects which are opposite in direction from those illustrated for the A–B type structure in Table 9.4, on the positive association between size of household and its income and on the negative association between household size and its income per capita.

(c) Assume another pair of subgroups, C and D (with the average income per household of C significantly larger than that of D) in each or most of the size-classes and assume the percentage proportions of C households to be greater among the smaller households and to decline substantially as we move toward the larger size classes. Thus, the major difference between the A–B and C–D structures is that, in the former, the percentage proportions of the higher income households *rise* as we move from the smaller to the larger households, whereas, in the latter, the percentage proportions of the higher income households *decline* as we move from the smaller to the larger households. One implication of this contrast is that in the A–B structure, the higher income households (A) are, on the average, larger in size than the lower income households (B), revealing, for the averages, a *positive* correlation between household income and size. Thus, to refer back to Table 9.4, the higher income households with male heads average 3.2 persons per household, whereas those with female heads average 2.0; those with heads between ages 35 and 54 average 3.8 persons per household, whereas those with heads below 35 or over 54 years average 2.4 persons; those with heads in the labor force average 3.2 persons per household compared with 2.1 persons for households with head not in the labor force. For the C–D structure, we will find the opposite, viz. that the higher income households (C) will, on the average, be smaller than the lower income households (D).

Two illustrations of the C–D structure are presented in Table 9.5: one for the United States and the other for Taiwan. The illustration for the United States (Panel A) distinguishes, among households with employed heads, those with white-collar workers heads from those with blue-collar heads, and treats the sum of the two (which excludes households with heads employed in agriculture or are service workers) as the total

Table 9.5. *Effects of differences in structure within size classes of households on income relatives and disparities, structure by economic subgroups, United States and Taiwan, 1975*

A. *United States, white-collar-worker heads (WW), blue-collar worker heads (BW), and combined total (WBW)[a,b]*

Size classes	WBW Percentage of HH (1)	Income relative per HH (2)	Income relative per P (3)	Percentage of WW in WBW HH (4)	Ratio of Y/H, BW/WW (5)	Income relative derived by assumption Per HH (6)	Per P (7)
1. One-person	13.0	0.58	1.85	70.3	0.77	0.56	1.78
2. Two-person	27.1	0.98	1.57	57.2	0.72	0.97	1.55
3. Three-person	19.9	1.03	1.10	52.7	0.73	1.03	1.10
4. Four-person	20.0	1.10	0.88	52.9	0.71	1.10	0.88
5. Five-person	11.3	1.17	0.75	50.4	0.68	1.16	0.76
6. Six-person	5.1	1.18	0.63	44.5	0.67	1.22	0.65
7. Seven-person-and-over	3.6	1.17	0.51	39.2	0.63	1.25	0.54
8. Total or TDM	40.8 (H–P)	12.0 (H–Y)	29.8 (P–Y)	55.1	—	13.2 (H–Y)	28.6 (P–Y)

B. *Taiwan, nonfarmer (NF), and farmer (F) households[a,c]*

Size classes	Countrywide Percentage of HH (1)	Income relative per HH (2)	Income relative per P (3)	Percentage of NF in total (4)	Ratio of Y/H, F to NF (5)	Income relative derived by assumption Per HH (6)	Per P (7)
9. One-person	3.2	0.50	2.67	79.2	0.75	0.47	2.50
10. Two-person	5.2	0.79	2.05	78.1	0.42	0.79	2.05
11. Three-person	10.3	0.86	1.53	81.9	0.60	0.83	1.48
12. Four-person	16.8	0.95	1.26	82.5	0.59	0.91	1.20
13. Five-person	22.2	0.99	1.04	79.9	0.64	0.96	1.01
14. Six-person	19.0	1.03	0.91	72.3	0.67	1.04	0.92
15. Seven-person	11.3	1.05	0.79	65.0	0.70	1.08	0.81
16. Eight-person	5.9	1.22	0.80	56.9	0.66	1.29	0.84
17. Nine-person	2.7	1.26	0.72	52.4	0.68	1.37	0.79
18. Ten-person-and-over	3.4	1.59	0.72	42.9	0.73	1.74	0.79
19. Total or TDM	31.0 (H–P)	10.4 (H–Y)	20.6 (P–Y)	73.9	—	13.8 (H–Y)	17.2 (P–Y)

[a]For both panels, see the notes on the data and assumptions in Table 9.4. For the nature of the assumptions (constant percentage shares within size classes of the two components, white- and blue-collar worker households for the United States and nonfarmer–farmer

(in cols. 1–3). White-collar households (heads are professionals, administrators, sales, or clerical workers) are characterized by a per household
income that is 30 to 50 percent higher than that of blue-collar households
(heads are craftsmen, operatives, or laborers, excluding those in agriculture; see col. 5). The percentage share of the white-collar households
in the combined total declines from 70 percent in the one-person class
to less than 40 percent in the seven-and-over-person class (col. 4). It
follows also that the average white-collar household is smaller than the
average blue-collar household; the averages being 3.0 and 3.4 persons,
respectively.

With this somewhat negative association between income and size of
household, it is not surprising that our assumption [for cols. 6 and 7 of
Panel A (viz., that the percentage proportions of C and D households
are the same for each size class: 55.1 and 44.9 percent, respectively, as
indicated in line 8, col. 4)] shows that the diversity in the C–D structure among the size classes *reduced* the positive association between size
of household and its total income. Without such diversity, the TDM for
disparity in income per household would have been 13.2; with the diversity, it drops to 12.0 (see line 8, cols. 6 and 2). The effect on disparity
in income per person is opposite: the diversity in structure *magnifies* this
disparity, yielding a TDM of 29.8 compared to one without the diversity
of 28.6 (see line 8, cols. 3 and 7).

The illustration for Taiwan distinguishes farmer households [those
whose heads are substantially engaged in farming or related pursuits
(fishing, hunting, and the like), even though income from agriculture
may not be the dominant source of household income] from nonfarmer
households. The countrywide proportions of nonfarmer households (this
includes a tiny group of farmers in Taipei City) and of farmer households are 74 and 26 percent, respectively. As column 4 of Panel B shows,

Notes to Table 9.5 *(cont.)*

households in Taiwan) used to derive the income relatives in columns 6 and 7 in both
Panels here, see the notes on similar assumptions in Table 9.4.
[b]The data for Panel A are from the source used for Table 9.4. Note that the countrywide
total here (in columns 1–3) includes only households whose heads are employed white-
collar and blue-collar workers, accounting for 49.0 million households out of a total of 72.9
million. The white-collar groups include professional and technical workers; managers
and administrators, except farm; sales workers; and clerical and kindred workers. Blue-
collar workers include craft and kindred workers; operatives, including transport workers
(given separately); and laborers, except farm. All terms used here are from the source.
[c]In Panel B, the entries in columns 1–3 are directly from our Table 9.1 above. The
additional data, needed to secure entries in columns 4 and 5, are from the two sources for
Taiwan cited for Panel A of Table 9.1.

the proportion of nonfarmers is at a high level of about 80 percent in the households of one to five persons, but then declines rapidly in the larger size classes, down to 43 percent among households of ten and over. The countrywide average size of nonfarmer households (5.1 persons) is substantially below that of farmer households (6.0 persons). But, as one might have expected, the income per farmer household within each size class is distinctly below that per nonfarmer household, as is revealed, with some erratic disturbances, in column 5 of Panel B. The relative excess of the income of C-type household (nonfarmer) is between 30 and 60 percent.

The results of diversity here in the C–D structure can again be observed by comparing columns 6 and 7 with columns 2 and 3. The diversity results in moderating the positive response of household income to its size: TDM is reduced from 13.8 to 10.4, which is a relatively substantial reduction. It also results in magnifying the negative response of per person income to increasing size of household, with the TDM rising from 17.2 to 20.6. In terms of what we set out to discuss (viz., why the income per household rose with increasing size and why it rose so moderately as to yield a negative association between size of household and per person income), the C–D illustration for Taiwan (like that for the United States) helps to answer largely the second part of the double question.

The concentration on socioeconomic subgroups in illustrating the C–D structure in Table 9.5, contrasted with the concentration on demographic subgroups of the A–B structure in Table 9.4, is a matter of choice. One could find socioeconomic subgroups that would be of the A–B type and demographic subgroups that would be of the C–D type. And yet there is substance to the contrast. Size differentials among households are, realistically, associated with sex of head, given the concentration of a preponderant majority of households (at least in the statistical reporting) under male headship and given the female headship largely as a result of the "broken" status of the unit or of widowhood. Likewise, the larger households do tend to occur when the head is in the "central" rather than the extreme age phases of the typical life-cycle. It is not easy to find *demographic* characteristics that would distinguish significant subgroups of the C–D type unless one considers some characteristics (like urban versus rural residence) that are greatly affected by associated economic and social groupings.

Likewise, in recent times, when even the less developed countries have substantial modern economic and social components, the major socioeconomic groupings do tend to be of the C–D type. With size differentials among households (preponderantly family households) reflecting differences in proportions of children and in the propensity of adults to live together or apart, it is the more modern components in the society and the economy that tend to reflect first the lower birth rates and the greater tendency to live apart that are the demographic hallmark of modern economic development, particularly under conditions of free markets and effective consumer sovereignty. But it is also the same modern groups that will show higher income per household for comparable size and on the average. The C–D structure is then associated with the contrast between the more modern, economically more advanced groups in society and those that are less "modern" and less advanced in the direction along which economic growth proceeds. This statement clearly applies to the nonfarmer–farmer distinction in the illustration for Taiwan, but, to a lesser degree, also, to the distinction between white-collar and blue-collar households in an economically developed country like the United States. While the bearing of it is particularly relevant to societies in the process of transition from older to more modern modes of production and life, one would argue that *every* society is in transition at the boundaries of *some* of its sectors and classes, even if the phases of major transition may already have been completed.

We are now at the end of a brief, illustrative discussion of the factors relevant to the positive association of size differentials among households with disparities in income per household and to the negative association of the same size differentials with household income per person (and, implicitly, per consuming unit, although we had no adequately cross-classified data at hand). Before we conclude this discussion, two general aspects of the analysis should be noted.

First, while we followed here the first sequence – from size differentials among households to disparities in income per household to those in household income per person – much of what was said of the effects of diversity of structure within size classes for the A–B and C–D subgroups would be relevant also to the second sequence. Were the data available to begin with a distribution of households by income per person (with the associated size and demographic and socioeconomic characteristics), we would first observe the negative association between income per person (or per consuming unit) and size of household. Then, considering the factors relevant to this association, we would argue that low income per person is connected with large household size because of the large proportion of children and because of the propensity of adults to live separately in so far as income and absence of direct obligations to children permit. And we would be illustrating this by the C–D types of socioeconomic groups that were covered in Table 9.5 and briefly discussed earlier. To proceed further, given the combination of disparities in per person or per consuming unit income with size differentials among households (revealed in the negative association between the two), the question would arise why it still allows room for a *positive* association between size and per household income; here the arguments about the greater absolute numbers of members of working ages and the effects of A–B types of largely demographic subgroups within size classes illustrated in Table 9.4 would be brought into play. In short, the second sequence would, in the process of establishing the links, rely also on the characteristics of the several demographic and socioeconomic groups within the population – characteristics that would explain, if illustratively, the ties between size differentials and income disparities.

Second, the illustrations in Tables 9.1–9.5 refer to countrywide measures and to subgroups that comprise the countrywide household population (with the single exception of the white-collar–blue-collar dichotomy for the households in the United States). Yet the factors that are found to be relevant apply not only to countrywide household populations but also to connections between size differentials and income disparities *within* subcountry groups, whether they be distinguished by demographic economic, regional, ethnic, or similar criteria. So long as a subnational group includes households that differ substantially in size, these differences would be associated with differing proportions of children and adults, with differing structures within the size classes by sex and/or age of head, with further subdivisions with different economic and social characteristics that bear on income, and so on. And much of what was said of the factors relevant to the positive association between size differentials and disparities in income per household and to the negative association between size differentials and household income per person (or per consuming unit) could be repeated – changing the identity of some of the subgroups and of findings of such associations for *each* of a wide variety of subnational groupings. This must be the case, since the classifications that we can establish for the countrywide population are never so exhaustive of size differentials among households as to remove such differentials *within* the subnational groups themselves.

This last statement is true even of much finer classifications than the ones we used in Tables 9.4 and 9.5. But we illustrate it for the large subgroups (demographic and other) distinguished in Tables 9.4 and 9.5. In Table 9.6, we provide for each of five dichotomies used (three of the A–B type and two of the C–D type), the minimum of data needed to reveal the size differentials in association with relatives of income per household and income per person and to provide the basis for calculating the TDMs that are analogous to those used for the countrywide totals in Table 9.1 (for the two countries, United States and Taiwan).

Table 9.6 shows size differentials among households of substantial magnitude for all of the ten subgroups; these are revealed by TDMs ranging from about 30 to 54 (which would correspond to Gini coefficients ranging from about 0.2 to somewhat less than 0.4). Most of these measures of size disparities within the subgroups are somewhat below those for the countrywide populations of households (45.4 for the United States and 31.0 for Taiwan), but some (e.g., that for female-headed households in the United States) are substantially greater (see line 9, col. 6). This probably reflects the greater heterogeneity within the female-headed households, with the contrast between the large group of one-person units headed mostly by widows and the various groups of larger households headed by a female in the absence of a resident husband.

In each subgroup, income per household shows positive association with size, as reflected in the relative income indexes in columns 3 and 7. In each subgroup, income per person is negatively correlated with size, as shown in the relative income indexes in columns 4 and 8. The magnitudes of the income disparities, whether in positive or negative correlation with size, are substantial. And one would expect that the negative relation would also be found between size measured in consuming units and income per consuming unit – although the magnitudes of size differentials and of disparities in income per consuming unit would be narrower than those shown now in columns 2 and 6 and in columns 4 and 8, respectively.

There are some interesting differences among the subgroups in the relative magnitudes of the disparities in income per household and in income per person. A good illustration is in the comparison of the non-farmer and farmer households in Taiwan (lines 37–48; particularly the TDMs in line 48). The size differentials (in cols. 2 and 6) are about the same for the two subgroups of households: the TDMs are 29 and 31, respectively. But the magnitude of the positive response of income per household to size of household is much more moderate among the non-farmer households (with a TDM of 11.2) compared with that among the

Table 9.6. *Size differentials and income disparities among households within the demographic and economic subgroups distinguished in Tables 9.4 and 9.5, United States and Taiwan*[a]

Size classes, totals, average TDMs	Higher income per HH subgroup				Lower income per HH subgroup			
	Percentage shares in total HHs (1)	Size relative (2)	Income relative per HH (3)	Income relative per P (4)	Percentage shares in total HHs (5)	Size relative (6)	Income relative per HH (7)	Income relative per P (8)
United States: male head and female head								
1. One-person	9.8	0.32	0.55	1.74	54.3	0.50	0.77	1.56
2. Two-person	33.7	0.63	0.89	1.42	21.1	1.01	1.26	1.25
3. Three-person	18.8	0.94	1.07	1.14	12.0	1.52	1.31	0.86
4. Four-person	18.6	1.26	1.16	0.92	6.3	2.02	1.27	0.63
5. Five-person	10.5	1.57	1.21	0.77	2.6	2.54	1.35	0.53
6. Six-person	4.9	1.90	1.20	0.63	1.8	3.06	1.22	0.41
7. Seven-person-and-over	3.7	2.38	1.16	0.49	1.9	4.37	1.24	0.28
8. Total or average[b]	55.27	3.18	15.87	4.99	17.60	1.98	7.20	3.64
9. TDM[c]	—	40.6 (H–P)	16.2 (H–Y)	27.0 (P–Y)	—	53.8 (H–P)	25.2 (H–Y)	39.2 (P–Y)
United States, HHs with heads aged 35–54 and HHs with heads aged below 35 or over 54								
10. One-person	10.2	0.26	0.55	2.07	26.0	0.41	0.52	1.25
11. Two-person	17.6	0.53	0.90	1.69	37.5	0.82	1.08	1.32
12. Three-person	18.6	0.80	1.01	1.26	16.5	1.23	1.23	1.00
13. Four-person	22.2	1.07	1.12	1.05	12.2	1.64	1.31	0.80
14. Five-person	15.8	1.33	1.16	0.88	4.8	2.04	1.29	0.63
15. Six-person	8.3	1.60	1.11	0.69	1.9	2.47	1.22	0.49
16. Seven-person-and-over	7.3	2.05	1.01	0.49	1.1	3.45	1.23	0.36
17. Total or average[b]	25.05	3.75	17.66	4.71	47.82	2.44	11.74	4.81
18. TDM[c]	—	38.8 (H–P)	12.6 (H–Y)	28.6 (P–Y)	—	44.2 (H–P)	25.2 (H–Y)	24.8 (P–Y)
United States, HHs with heads in and not in the labor force								
19. One-person	13.9	0.31	0.57	1.84	38.2	0.47	0.58	1.23
20. Two-person	27.2	0.63	0.98	1.56	39.6	0.95	1.17	1.23
21. Three-person	19.7	0.94	1.03	1.10	10.5	1.42	1.45	1.02
22. Four-person	19.5	1.26	1.12	0.89	5.5	1.90	1.46	0.77
23. Five-person	10.9	1.57	1.19	0.76	2.6	2.37	1.44	0.61
24. Six-person	5.0	1.88	1.19	0.63	1.8	2.84	1.25	0.44
25. Seven-person-and-over	3.8	2.35	1.14	0.49	1.8	4.29	1.25	0.29

314   Economic development, family, and income distribution

Table 9.6 *(cont.)*

Size classes, totals, average TDMs	Higher income per HH subgroup				Lower income per HH subgroup			
	Percent-age shares in total HHs (1)	Size relative (2)	Income relative per HH (3)	Income relative per P (4)	Percent-age shares in total HHs (5)	Size relative (6)	Income relative per HH (7)	Income relative per P (8)
26. Total or average[b]	52.94	3.18	16.19	5.09	19.92	2.11	7.33	3.46
27. TDM[c]	—	41.6	13.0	29.8	—	44.2	32.0	26.4
		(H–P)	(H–Y)	(P–Y)		(H–P)	(H–Y)	(P–Y)
United States, households of white-collar and blue-collar workers								
28. One-person	16.6	0.33	0.56	1.70	8.6	0.29	0.57	1.97
29. Two-person	28.1	0.66	0.99	1.50	25.8	0.58	0.95	1.64
30. Three-person	19.0	0.99	1.04	1.05	21.0	0.87	1.01	1.16
31. Four-person	19.2	1.32	1.14	0.86	21.0	1.16	1.08	0.93
32. Five-person	10.4	1.66	1.23	0.74	12.4	1.45	1.12	0.77
33. Six-person	4.1	1.99	1.29	0.65	6.3	1.74	1.14	0.66
34. Seven-person-and-over	2.6	2.43	1.31	0.54	4.9	2.20	1.12	0.51
35. Total or average[b]	23.5	3.02	19.66	6.51	19.17	3.44	14.69	4.27
36. TDM[c]	—	41.4	15.4	27.6	—	35.2	10.0	29.4
		(H–P)	(H–Y)	(P–Y)		(H–P)	(H–Y)	(P–Y)
Taiwan, nonfarmer and farmer households								
37. One-person	3.4	0.21	0.47	2.29	2.4	0.17	0.50	3.00
38. Two-person	5.4	0.41	0.85	2.09	4.3	0.33	0.49	1.50
39. Three-person	11.5	0.60	0.86	1.43	7.2	0.50	0.72	1.44
40. Four-person	18.8	0.80	0.95	1.19	11.4	0.67	0.77	1.15
41. Five-person	24.0	1.00	0.98	0.99	17.2	0.83	0.88	1.06
42. Six-person	18.5	1.20	1.05	0.88	20.0	0.99	0.99	1.00
43. Seven-person	9.9	1.39	1.09	0.78	15.1	1.16	1.06	0.91
44. Eight-person	4.6	1.59	1.33	0.84	9.9	1.32	1.21	0.92
45. Nine-person	1.9	1.84	1.37	0.73	4.9	1.49	1.29	0.87
46. Ten-person-and-over	2.0	2.25	1.75	0.78	7.6	1.96	1.78	0.91
47. Total or average[b]	2.25	5.01	119.9	23.9	0.79	6.03	86.1	14.3
48. TDM[c]	—	28.8	11.2	18.2	—	30.6	20.6	10.2
		(H–P)	(H–Y)	(P–Y)		(H–P)	(H–Y)	(P–Y)

[a] All the entries for the United States are taken or calculated from the source for the United States given in the notes to Tables 9.4 and 9.5. All the entries for Taiwan are taken or calculated from the two sources given for that country in the notes to Table 9.5.
[b] The entries in lines 8, 17, 26, and 35 are (1) columns 1 and 5, total of households, in millions; (2) columns 2 and 6, persons per household; (3) columns 3 and 7, income per household, $, U.S. 000s; (4) columns 4 and 8, household income per person, $ U.S., 000s. The entries in line 47 are (1) columns 1 and 5, total of households, in million; (2) columns

farmer households (with a TDM of 20.6; see line 48, cols. 3 and 7). It may well be that the influence of the C–D type of subgroups, which limits the rise in per household income with increase in size of household, is greater for the more heterogeneous population of nonfarmer households than for that of farmer households. But because of this difference in the magnitudes of the *positive* response of income per household, there is an opposite difference in the magnitudes of the *negative* response of income per person. The TDM for disparities in per person income for the non-farmer household (18.2) is almost twice that for the farmer households (10.2; line 48, cols. 4 and 8). The size differentials among households thus contribute a larger component of inequalities in income per person to the population of nonfarmer households than they do to that of farmer households.

The number of such illustrations of different combinations of size differentials among households with disparities in income per house-hold and in income per person (*within* demographic and socioeconomic, intranational groups) could easily be multiplied. But the ones shown in Table 9.6 should suffice to indicate that a fuller study of the associations under discussion requires observing them not only for countrywide popu-lations but for significant subnational groups – in cross section and over time.

IV. Concluding comments

The discussion in the preceding sections of the connection between size differentials among households and disparities in income per household or in household income per person (or consuming unit) was based on data for a small number of countries. The view was focused on size alone, with other characteristics of households (also of bearing on income disparities) considered only as they were reflected in the size aspect. The narrow empirical base and scarcity of data that would reveal cross-relations among household characteristics limited the analysis to crude associations.

Notes to Table 9.6 *(cont.)*

2 and 6, persons per household; (3) columns 3 and 7, income per household, $NT, 000s; columns 4 and 8, household income per person, $NT, 000s.
'The entries for TDM, lines 9, 18, 27, 36, and 48 are (1) in columns 2 and 6, for differentials among households in size (i.e., number of persons); (2) in columns 3 and 7, disparities in income per household among household size classes; (3) in columns 4 and 8, disparities in household income per person, among household size classes.

Yet it would be useful at this juncture, first, to summarize (in general terms unencumbered by qualifications) the major findings illustrated and discussed earlier and, then, to comment on the possible significance of the findings and on feasible directions of further inquiry to which they point.

1. Intracountry differences in size of households, whether size is measured by number of persons or of consuming units, are quite substantial. There is usually a positive association between income per household and size of household, in that larger households are found to secure larger total income. There is usually a negative association between size of household and household income per person or per consuming unit because the rise in per household income with greater size is not sufficiently large to compensate for the increase in persons or in consuming units.

2. Given the associations noted under (1), it follows that size differentials among households contribute to disparities in income per household and in household income per person or per consuming unit. Such income disparities, which are traceable to size differentials among households, may constitute substantial components in the overall inequalities in the countrywide (or other large collective-wide) distributions of income among households by income per household and in the overall inequalities of income among household population by household income per person or per consuming unit.

3. The magnitude of the size differentials among households, the measure of inequality in the size distribution of households, is the *minimum* to which the measures of inequality in associated disparities in income per household and in income per person (or per consuming unit) add. It is the *minimum* because the distribution of income per household or per person by size classes of households may also contain variance *not* associated with household size. Given this relation between, say, the Gini coefficient of the size differentials among households and those for associated disparities in income per household and in income per person (or per consuming unit), the following inference is suggested. With the signs of the association as observed, the larger the Gini coefficient (or a similar measure of inequality) for the distribution of households by size, the larger should be the Gini coefficients either for the associated disparities in income per household, for disparities in income per person (consuming unit), or for both.

4. Since the distributions of households by size differ between developed and less developed market economies by the strikingly larger proportions in the former of one-person households, experimental calculations for the United States and Taiwan dealt with the effects of either omitting one-person households or shifting them under variant assumptions into the larger household size classes. The results, while indicating a reduction in size differentials that is appreciably greater among U.S. households than among Taiwanese households, still reveal a substantial magnitude of associated disparities in income per household and, particularly, in income per person.

5. The positive association of total household income with size of household is due partly to the inclusion of more work-and-earnings-capable adults in the larger households and partly to the greater preponderance among heads of larger households of heads with characteristics that make for higher income [e.g., of male rather than female heads and of heads in the mature, higher earning ages rather than of heads too young (before their prime) or too old (after their prime)]. But the effects of these factors, which tend to raise overall income for the larger households, diminish rapidly as we rise above the small size classes. The larger the household, the lower the proportion of income-earning adults to children and the smaller the rise in the proportion of household with male heads or with heads in the more favorable ages.

6. The resulting shortfall in the increase of household's total income with greater size and the consequent negative association between size and household income per person (or per consuming unit) is sustained by the effect of socioeconomic or ethnic characteristics of heads. In general, in developed, as well as in modernizing and developing countries, the socioeconomic groups that are more advanced, more modern, and hence with a higher per person income tend to show a smaller average size of household (e.g., among professional white-collar employees) than the less modern, lower income groups (e.g., farm workers or lower skilled blue-collar employees). Such negative correlation between average household size and per person household income of the diverse socioeconomic (or ethnic) groups contributes, within a country, to the negative association between size of household and its income per person (or per consuming unit).

7. While the associations between size differentials among households and disparities in income per household and per person were noted for *countrywide* distributions and the relevant factors discussed in terms of

the latter, such associations and the relevant factors would be observed also for subnational units (regions, socioeconomic groups, and the like). So long as we find substantial size differentials among the households of a given group or collective, the effects on disparities in income per household and income per person are also likely to be found and sustained by demographic and socioeconomic subgroupings of households within the given group or collective.

The significance of the findings just summarized depends, primarily, on our view as to the independence of households as they are commonly defined in the available data – independence as units deciding on acquisition and allocation of income or on raising claim to a share in the country's product. It also depends, secondarily, on our interest in income inequalities associated with size of household differentials alone, allowing for other income-affecting characteristics of households only as they are reflected in the size differentials.

If, on the first point (discussed briefly in the first of the four papers listed in note 1), we were to find that separate households form clusters of close common interest that makes for joint economic decisions (as may be the case for a cluster that includes the parental households and those of their children or that comprises households of several siblings), then the approach that yielded these findings would have to be recast. Instead of treating the separate households in the data as independent units, we would have to group them into clusters of common interest (in action and in claims on national product) and only then consider whether size differentials among the clusters are of significant effect on inequalities in income per cluster or in cluster-income per person or per consuming unit. The identification of foci of common interest would, clearly, be difficult and would require a variety of additional data that are not now available on the interrelations of separate households. Still, we must recognize that our findings retain significance only to the extent that independence of interest and claim among the separate households actually prevails, and it may prevail in different degree in different societies and for different levels of economic decision. We followed the approach on the assumption that there is independence among separate households over a wide range of economic decisions. But this is an untested assumption, which, at present, limits the validity of findings for *all* income distributions that utilize households as independent units.

Second, our emphasis on the crude association between size of households and income disparities was initially meant as a warning – as a demonstration that conventional distributions of income by income per household conveyed a misleading impression of the more meaningful distribution of long-term incomes among roughly equivalent (in terms of need) consumer units (or equivalent producer units). For more reliable analysis, adequate data on long-term incomes would be most urgently needed, but it was not feasible to pursue this difficult goal. Even if we take the income data as given and concentrate on the recipient unit, the crude association observed could have been enriched by allowing other characteristics of households to be taken into account (phase of life cycle as reflected by age of head, occupation and industry attachment of head, and the like). But with the scarcity of relevant cross-classified data, this attempt would have reduced coverage below the small number of countries included in the tables in the preceding sections. We chose to limit the discussion to size and related structure of household in its division between children and adults because size differentials are the most obvious and general characteristic of households affecting intranational income disparities; we hoped to use the rather consistent findings as a departure point for further exploration.

The direction suggested for such exploration is that of observing size distributions of households, without the scarce and often more defective income data, for a large number of countries and over long periods for some of them. If inequality in the distribution of households by size contributes to inequality in the distribution of income among households (per household) or among the household population per person (or per consuming unit), differences or trends in inequality in the size distribution of households may contribute to differences and trends in income disparities. Consequently, it would be of interest to observe international or other cross-sectional differences in inequality in the size distributions of households and to observe trends over time in the latter. These cross-sectional and temporal comparisons are the subject of a later paper.

10. Distributions of households by size: differences and trends

This article deals with the distributions of households by size, that is, by number of persons, as they are observed in international comparisons, and for fewer countries, over time.[1] Earlier explorations indicated that, within countries and within significant subnational groups, size differences among households are positively correlated with differences in income *per household* but negatively correlated with differences in household income *per person*.[2] Given this combination, it follows that inequality in the size distribution of households constitutes a minimum to which the *associated* inequalities in income per household and in household income per person should total. Thus, differences and changes in size disparities among households should result in differences or changes in the associated disparities in income per household, or in the associated disparities in household income per person, or in both. These different or changing contributions of the size disparities among households – the major topic of this article – are of interest because they may affect significantly the total distribution of income among the population by income per household, or by household income per person, or both.

I. International comparison for recent years

We begin with an international comparison of the size distributions of households for a large number of countries in recent years. This compari-

Research in Population Economics, Volume 4, pages 1–47. Copyright © 1982 by JAI Press Inc.

1 The data at hand are all on size of household as measured by number of persons. For analytical purposes the conversion of persons to equivalent consuming units is desirable but difficult, with the needed data scarce. However, the findings here are relevant also to comparisons with household size reduced to consuming units, although the magnitudes of the size differentials would be narrower.
2 See Chapter 9, above.

son is feasible because the United Nations has assembled, in its *Demographic Yearbooks* and in some related publications, the distributions of households and of population in households for a large number of countries – in detail that enables us to derive disparity or inequality measures of the simple type used here. We limited them to the TDM (total disparity measure), the sum, signs disregarded, of the differences between percentage shares of the size classes in total households and in total population, because in past work we found their orders of magnitude so closely related to the slightly more sensitive Gini coefficients as to serve our purpose adequately. The main question that we tried to answer was whether there were systematic differences among countries in the inequality in the distributions of their households by size, systematic in the sense of being associated with average size of household and thus also with differences among countries in the level of their economic and demographic development.

The definitions of households differ somewhat among countries; the data are incomplete for some, and we had to resort to adjustments (of no great magnitude) to complete them by estimating the difference between total population and population in households or by deriving distribution of population among size classes of households from the size distributions of households.[3] And, as will be shown, the coverage of the United Nations data is inadequate for some major regions of the world. But the sample is large enough to cover a variety of regions.

A summary of the data on the size of the average household (arithmetic mean number of persons), on the TDM measure of disparities in size and on related measures, for the countries covered by the data, is provided in Table 10.1. A reference to the identity of the countries included (listed in the notes to Table 10.1) reveals that data are lacking for the populous countries of South and East Asia (Mainland China, India, Indonesia, and a number of others) and for sub-Saharan Africa (Nigeria, Ethiopia, and a large number of others). One should also note the omission of such a major Communist country as the USSR, the data for which do not report

3 For definitional problems see United Nations, *Methods of Projecting Households and Families*, Manual VIII, New York, 1973, Chapter I, pp. 5–11; and also the technical notes on Table 42, pp. 51–53, in UN *Demographic Yearbook, 1976*, New York, 1976. We could not use the summary Table 3, pp. 12–15 in the earlier source because the detail by size class of households was insufficient to allow measuring the full range of inequality in size. I am indebted to the Statistical Office of United Nations for providing me with data on the subject received after the last publication in the *Demographic Yearbook* for 1976.

Table 10.1. *Average size of household and associated measures, countries by economic and regional groups, 1960s and 1970s*

	Number of countries (1)	Persons per household (2)	TDM, Size distribution (3)	Percentage in all HHs		Percentage of population below 15 (6)	Persons per HH	
				1-person HH (4)	2-person HH (5)		Below 15 (7)	15 and over (8)
Less developed market economies								
1. East and Southeast Asia	8	5.45	37.6	4.1	8.0	43.2	2.35	3.10
2. Middle East	7	5.33	42.2	6.4	10.9	45.6	2.43	2.90
3. Sub-Saharan Africa	7	4.59	51.4	13.6	15.6	43.0	1.97	2.62
4. Latin America (ex. Caribbean)	12	5.00	43.4	7.4	12.3	42.1	2.10	2.90
5. Caribbean	6	4.46	53.5	16.6	16.1	42.5[a]	1.90	2.56
Developed market economies								
6. Dev. Europe	12	2.96	44.8	20.7	26.8	24.3	0.72	2.24
7. Overseas offshoots	4	3.22	44.45	15.85	27.45	28.5	0.92	2.30
8. Japan	1	3.45	38.8	13.6	16.8	24.5	0.85	2.60
9. DC (lines 6 and 7 weighted 2 each, line 8 weighted 1)	—	3.16	43.5	17.3	25.1	26.0	0.83	2.33
10. Other Europe	4	3.82	43.7	10.9	20.45	29.4	1.12	2.70
11. Israel	1	3.79	46.4	12.2	22.2	33.1	1.25	2.54
Communist countries								
12. All covered by available data	8	3.49	42.7	15.65	20.2	28.4	0.99	2.50

[a] Covers five countries, excludes British Guiana.
Notes: Columns 1–5: Except for entries for United States and Taiwan, the underlying data for all countries are either from the United Nations Demographic

Yearbooks (for 1962, 1963, 1971, 1973, and 1976) or from UN files for more recent years. The data in the UN Demographic Yearbook for 1955 were not used here, because they relate to years well before the 1960s.

The entries for the United States are taken or calculated from U.S. Bureau of the Census, *Current Population Reports, Series P-60, no. 104*, Washington 1977, Table 3 and 15, pp. 13–20 and 48–57.

The entries for Taiwan are taken or calculated from two sources. One, relating to Taipei City, is by the Bureau of Budget, Accounting, and Statistics, Taipei City Government, *Report on the Survey of Family Income and Expenditures . . . Taipei City 1975, 1976*, Table 16, pp. 108–111. The other, relating to Taiwan Province, is by Department of Budget, Accounting, and Statistics, Taiwan Provincial Government, *Report on the Survey of Family Income and . . . , Taiwan Prov., 1975, 1976*, Table 25, pp. 538–548. The total and per household number of persons in the open-end, largest size group was calculated from the other size groups and the population totals for all households given in the other tables in the *Reports*.

For two or three countries we had to estimate the difference between total population and population in private households, on the basis of such ratios for neighboring sets of countries. The related adjustment was also made in the population for the upper, open-end size class.

Column 6: These are ratios of population below 15 to total population. For recent years, these are available at every 0 and 5 year beginning in 1950 in United Nations, *Selected World Demographic Indications by Countries, 1950–2000, Working Paper ESA/P/WP.55*, May 1975. The ratio for that 0 or 5 year was taken for each country that was nearest to the year for which the data on size distribution of households were available for columns 1–5.

The entries for subdivisions of the United Kingdom were obtained for late 1960s from UN *Demographic Yearbook 1970*, New York 1971, Table 6. That for Taiwan was taken from the country's *Statistical Yearbook, 1976*.

In averaging for regional groupings in columns 2–6, we assigned equal weight for each country.

Columns 7 and 8: Obtained by multiplying the averages in column 2 by the percentages in column 6, used as proper fractions, and by the complement of the latter to 1.000.

The following countries and years were covered in the several groupings:

Line 1: South Korea, 1960; Taiwan, 1975; Philippines, 1970; Thailand, 1970; Federation of Malaya, 1957; Khmer (Cambodia), 1962; Pakistan, 1968; Nepal, 1971.

Line 2: Iran, 1966; Kuwait, 1975; Iraq, 1965; United Arab Republic (Egypt), 1960; Libya, 1964; Tunisia, 1966; Morocco, 1971.

Line 3: Lesotho, 1956; Liberia, 1962; Sierra-Leone, 1963; Southern Rhodesia, 1962; Zambia, 1969; Reunion, 1967; Mauritius, 1962.

Line 4: Costa Rica, 1973; Dominican Republic, 1970; Ecuador, 1962; Argentina, 1970; Brazil, 1970; Colombia, 1964; Peru, 1972; Uruguay, 1963; Paraguay, 1962; Venezuela, 1961.

Line 5: Barbados, 1960; Bahamas, 1970; Guadeloupe, 1967; Martinique, 1967; Trinidad and Tobago, 1970; British Guiana, 1960.

Line 6: England and Wales, 1971; Scotland, 1971; France, 1968; West Germany, 1970; Italy, 1971; Switzerland, 1970; Austria, 1971; Netherlands, 1960; Denmark, 1965; Norway, 1975; Sweden, 1975; Finland, 1970.

Line 7: United States, 1975; Canada, 1976; Australia, 1971; New Zealand, 1966.

Line 8: Japan, 1975.

Line 10: North Ireland, 1966; Eire, 1971; Spain, 1970; Portugal, 1960.

Line 11: Israel, 1972.

Line 12: Mongolia, 1969; Cuba, 1970; Bulgaria, 1965; Czechoslovakia, 1970; Hungary, 1970; German Democratic Republic, 1971; Poland, 1970; Yugoslavia, 1971.

the 1-person households. Nevertheless, the coverage is sufficiently varied to suggest some intriguing similarities and differences.

1. The first finding to be observed in Table 10.1 is the familiar difference in size of average household between the less developed and more developed market economies, with the former ranging from 4.5 to 5.5 persons and the latter from 3 to somewhat over 3.5. The rather low average of 3.5 persons per household for the Communist group, which includes such less developed countries as Mongolia, Cuba, and Bulgaria, reflects the effects of Communist organization of society in reducing the birth rates and thus the contribution of children to size of household.

2. A glance at columns 7–8, in conjunction with column 6, reveals that the major source of differences in average size of household is the proportion of children (below 15) in total population and hence within the households. Contrasted with this positive correlation between proportions of children and average size of household is the negative correlation between the latter and the proportions, among all households, of 1- and 2-person units (cols. 4 and 5), the size classes within which the contribution of children to size is minimal.

3. The most striking finding in Table 10.1 is that the average TDM is roughly the same for a number of economic and regional groupings that otherwise differ substantially in their economic development, in the size of their average household, and in their geographical location. A range of TDM from 42 to 45 includes the averages for the 16 countries of Europe (and the two subgroups among them), the 4 overseas offshoots, the 7 countries in the Middle East, the 12 countries of Latin America, and the 8 Communist countries – a total of 47 countries, market and command economies, economically more and less developed, with average size of household ranging from barely above 3 to well above 5. We shall return to a closer examination of this finding after considering briefly the three groups in Table 10.1 for which the level of TDMs differs substantially from that common to most other countries.

4. For one regional group in Table 10.1, the average TDM is distinctly below the range of 42 to 45 observed for so many other groups – that for the eight countries in East and Southeast Asia, with an average TDM of 37.6 (line 1); and one could add to it Japan, with its TDM of 38.8 (line 8). One should also note that for the ESE Asia group and Japan the proportions of 1- and 2-person households are distinctly lower than in other countries at similar levels of development and with the same proportions of children below 15 in column 6.

Inspection of the measures for the eight countries included in line 1 reveals that the TDM for all, except Federation of Malaysia, was either 40 (Pakistan and Nepal) or well below it (the other five countries). We did omit Hong Kong and Singapore, the TDMs for which were 48.4 and 49.0 for 1966 and 1971, respectively, on the argument that these city enclaves were characterized by a structure bound to be different from countries with both urban and rural components. The data thus suggest that the countries in East Asia exhibit a distinctive type of size distribution of households. If this finding is confirmed by additional data and is not due to some aspects of the definition followed in statistical practice, one would have to search for the institutional characteristics that account for a size structure among households so different from that in most other regions.

5. For two regions, sub-Saharan Africa and the Caribbean, inequality in the distribution of households by size is unusually wide, with average TDM above 50 (lines 3 and 5). And, significantly, here the proportions of 1- and 2-person households in all households, in columns 4 and 5, are too high – in comparison with other countries in which the proportions of children below 15 are about the same as in the two regions under discussion.

As already noted, the sample for sub-Saharan Africa is poor, and all we can say is that for the seven countries covered, the TDM ranged from a low of 44.2 for Mauritius in 1972 to a high of 64.2 for Sierra Leone in 1963, with five out of the seven countries characterized by TDMs of 49 or over. The case is strengthened by the finding that for Kenya's urban households in 1962, the TDM is as high as 54.8; but data for many more countries are needed to provide an adequate coverage of this large region.

The difference between the disparity measures for the Caribbean group and those for Latin America suggests the distinctiveness of the former with five out of the six countries showing TDMs well over 50. The distinctiveness is emphasized also by comparison with the measure for five islands in the Pacific (Solomon Island, 1976; Samoa, 1971; Gilbert Islands, 1973; Pacific Islands, 1958; and New Caledonia, 1963), which, with an average household of 5.60 persons, show an average TDM of 44.4. Here again, as in the case of East Asia, specific explanations would be required to account for the different size structure of households.

We return now to the major finding noted earlier: the narrow range within which disparity or inequality measures vary for a large number of countries, the latter differing widely in size of average household, in level of economic development, and even in the system of economic organization. Of the 70 countries covered in Table 10.1, 21 are in the three regions in which inequality in the size distribution of households was either unusually moderate (East and Southeast Asia) or unusually wide (sub-Saharan Africa and the Caribbean). The remaining 49 countries, comprising all the developed market economies, all the Communist countries for which data are available, and the Middle East and Latin America regions among the less developed market economies, can be examined further to observe some correlates of the relative invariance of the inequality measures. We do this by arraying the countries in decreasing size of their average household (the most easily available characteristic of the level of their economic development) and studying the association between household size, disparities in the size distribution of households, and related measures on proportions of population below 15 and the percentage shares in all households of the 1- and 2-person size classes (Table 10.2).

In the arrays summarized in Table 10.2, the average household declines from 5.69 persons in Group I to 2.75 persons in Group VII, and the identity of countries suggested in the regional designations (line 1) indicates that the movement is from less developed to the more developed countries (with some special bias toward lower average size among the Communist countries). But the TDM measures of disparity or inequality remain at levels between 42 and 46, without systematic movement associated with declining size of households. Within the limits of the universe covered by these 49 countries, the absence of a significant association between size of household and extent of inequality in the size distribution of households would suggest the absence of trends in inequality in this size distribution over time as the average size of household declines – if cross-section comparisons can be used as a guide to trends over time.

The downward movement of the size of average household and the relative constancy of the TDM as a gauge of inequality in the size distribution of households are accompanied by a substantial decline of the proportion of children below 15 years of age in total, and hence in household, population (line 4), and an increasing proportion of 1- and 2-person households, both in all households and in total household population (lines 9 and 12). As usual, the difference in average size of household is largely due to differences in number of children below 15 rather than to those in adult members: the decline in average size from Group I to Group VII, of 2.94 persons, is accounted for by a drop in the average of

Table 10.2. *Grouping of 49 countries in decreasing order of size of household*

	Groups in decreasing order of HH size (7 countries each)						
	I (1)	II (2)	III (3)	IV (4)	V (5)	VI (6)	VII (7)
1. Regional affiliation	ME-2 LA-5	ME-4 LA-3	ME-1 LA-2 OD-2 CM-2	LA-2 OD-3 CM-1 DC-1	CM-2 DC-5	CM-2 DC-5	CM-1 DC-6
2. Persons per household	5.69	5.09	4.43	3.76	3.34	3.01	2.75
3. TDM, distribution of HHs by size	43.4	42.3	44.3	43.2	42.2	43.8	46.0
Breakdown by age							
4. Percentage of population below 15	46.1	44.0	39.5	29.4	26.9	23.8	23.3
5. Persons below 15 per HH	2.62	2.24	1.75	1.11	0.90	0.72	0.64
6. Persons 15 and over per HH	3.07	2.85	2.68	2.65	2.44	2.29	2.11
(%) of 1- and 2-person households in all households							
7. 1-person HHs	5.9	6.7	9.2	11.3	14.6	19.8	23.8
8. 2-person HHs	9.3	11.4	15.5	20.5	22.5	25.8	28.9
9. 1- and 2-person HHs combined	15.2	18.1	24.7	31.8	37.1	45.6	52.7
(%) of members of 1- and 2-person households in total population in households							
10. 1-person HHs	1.1	1.3	2.1	3.0	4.4	6.6	8.7
11. 2-person HHs	3.3	4.5	7.1	11.0	13.5	17.2	21.2
12. 1- and 2-person HHs combined	4.4	5.8	9.2	14.0	17.9	23.8	29.9
Excluding the 1- and 2-person households							
13. Persons per HH	6.41	5.86	5.34	4.71	4.36	4.19	4.07
14. TDM	34.0	32.1	31.6	29.4	24.6	23.7	22.2
Breakdown by age							
15. Percentage of population below 15	48.3	46.7	43.3	34.3	32.9	31.7	33.3
16. Persons below 15 per HH	3.10	2.74	2.31	1.62	1.43	1.33	1.36
17. Persons 15 and over per HH	3.31	3.12	3.03	3.09	2.93	2.86	2.71

Notes: The regional affiliation designations in line 1 are as follows (see Table 10.1): ME, Middle East (7 countries); LA, Latin America (12 countries); OD, other developed countries (5 countries, lines 10 and 11 of Table 10.1); CM, Communist countries (8 countries); DC, developed countries (17 altogether, see lines 6–8 of Table 10.1).
For lines 2–12 the individual countries were arrayed in decreasing order of size of average household and then divided into seven groups of 7 countries each. For each group we calculated unweighted arithmetic means of the measures in lines 2, 3, 4, 7–9, and 10–12. The sources of these data were indicated in the notes to Table 10.1.
Lines 5 and 6 were derived by multiplying the percentages in line 4, taken as proper fractions, by the average number of persons per household in line 2.

children per household of 1.98 (line 5) and of adults of 0.96 (line 6), with proportion of two-thirds for the former and one-third for the latter. And there is a sharp rise in the share of 1- and 2-person households in all households, from 15 percent in Group I to over 50 percent in Group VII (line 9); the shares in total household population of the members of these two size classes rise from less than 5 percent to almost 30 (line 12).

We proceed on the hypothesis that the combination of relatively invariant measures of inequality in the size distribution of households with wide differences in size of average household, of the type shown in lines 2 and 3 of Table 10.2 (and would be shown for Gini coefficients or other measures of inequality) is due to the associated changes in the proportions of children (below 15 or with other realistic dividing lines) and in the shares of 1- and 2-person households (the ones from which children are almost totally absent); and that these differences in the children proportions and in the shares of 1- and 2-person households are interrelated in that the factors that make for fewer children also make for a much greater "separateness" in the ways adults live. We shall try to follow this hypothesis, with whatever scant data are at hand; but one test bearing on it can be made in close connection with Table 10.2, using the same bodies of data that were used for lines 1–12.

Keeping the composition of Groups I–VII as they were determined by the size of the average household in the total of all households, one can, for each country, exclude the 1- and 2-person households and recalculate – securing a new average number of persons per household, a new TDM, and a new proportion of children below 15 for total and hence household population – the latter on the realistic assumption that the number of children in the 1- and 2-person households combined is so small proportionately that it can be set at 0. The results of this recalculation, which eliminates the possible influence of differing proportions of 1- and 2-person households on the TDM, are shown in lines 13–17 of Table 10.2.

Exclusion of the 1- and 2-person households naturally raises the aver-

Notes to Table 10.2 *(cont.)*

For lines 13–17 the grouping of the countries was identical with that for lines 2–12, that is, based on decreasing size of the average household for the *total* size distribution of households. Then, for each of the 49 countries, we recalculated the distribution of households by size, omitting the 1- and 2-person households, and computed the unweighted arithmetic means of the measures appearing in lines 13, 14, and 15.
Lines 16 and 17 were again derived by multiplying the percentages in line 15, taken as proper fractions, by the average number of persons per household in line 13.

age size of the households, the increase being particularly large proportionately as one moves toward the lower end of the range from Group I
to Group VII. The decline in average size is reduced: it was from 5.69 to
2.75 in the full distribution, a drop to less than ½ (line 2) and it becomes
one from 6.41 to 4.07 (line 13), a drop to over ⁶/₁₀. Again, the exclusion
reduces the TDMs, which now range from 22 to 34, rather than around
the levels of 42 to 46. But the most interesting result is the *downward*
movement of the TDMs, from Group I to Group VII, which is systematic
and of significant magnitude, being a reduction from 34 to 22, or over ⅓.
In other words, with a still substantial decline in average size of household in line 13 and also a still substantial decline of the share of children
below 15 (from 48 to about 33 percent, see line 15), the omission of the
1- and 2-person household results in a significant decline of the TDMs
as one moves from the larger to the smaller household countries. The
inference is then that the *rise* in the proportion of these 1- and 2-person
households in line 2 is what sustained the TDMs at near constant levels
in line 3.

But the rise in the proportion of 1- and 2-person households may be
partly a function of the decline in the proportion of children, rather than
an independent trend; and we consider in the next section the possible
contribution of the two variables (proportion of children and shares of 1-
and 2-person households) to the total disparity, or inequality, in the size
distribution of households.

II. Allocation of total inequality in the size distribution of households

We begin the analysis by using the two bodies of data that distinguish, for
the usual size classes of households by number of persons, the proportions within each size class of children or minors from those of adults.
With this distinction given, one can observe *separately* the inequality in
the distribution, among the size classes, of the two age groups among
household members; and one can derive total inequality in the size distribution of households as a combination of inequalities in the distribution
of the two, significantly different, age groups.

Table 10.3 presents such data for the United States, taken from the
census of 1970, with the line of division between children below 18 years
of age and adults aged 18 years and over. The table also includes similar
data for Taiwan for end of 1975, with the line of division between minors

Table 10.3. *Allocation of size differentials among households between those for below 18 or minors and those for over 18 or adults, United States, March 1970, and Taiwan, end 1975*

A. Size differentials and related measures

Classes of households by size	Percentage in all HHs (1)	Persons per HH		Percentage shares in relevant totals			Disparities		
		Below 18 or minor (2)	18 and over or adult (3)	Persons (4)	Below 18 or minor (5)	18 and over or adult (6)	Col. 4 minus col. 1 (7)	Col. 5 minus col. 1 (8)	Col. 6 minus col. 1 (9)
United States, March 1970									
1. 1 person	19.6	0	1.00	6.4	0	9.9	−13.2	−19.6	−9.7
2. 2 persons	28.5	0.06	1.94	18.6	1.4	28.1	−9.9	−27.1	−0.4
3. 3 persons	16.7	0.74	2.26	16.3	11.3	19.1	−0.4	−5.4	2.4
4. 4 persons	15.2	1.70	2.30	19.8	23.6	17.8	4.6	8.4	2.6
5. 5 persons	9.7	2.63	2.37	15.8	23.2	11.6	6.1	13.5	1.9
6. 6 persons	5.3	3.52	2.48	10.4	17.2	6.7	5.1	11.9	1.4
7. 7 and over	5.0	5.12	2.72	12.7	23.3	6.8	7.7	18.3	1.8
8. Totals, averages, and TDMs	63.57	1.09	1.98	195.2	69.6	125.6	47.0	104.2	20.2
Taiwan, end of 1975									
9. 1 person	3.1	0	1.00	0.6	0	1.2	−2.5	−3.1	−1.9
10. 2 persons	5.2	0.19	1.81	2.0	0.4	3.6	−3.2	−4.8	−1.6
11. 3 persons	10.3	0.89	2.11	5.9	3.5	8.3	−4.4	−6.8	−2.0
12. 4 persons	16.9	1.75	2.25	12.8	11.2	14.4	−4.1	−5.7	−2.5

	(1)	(2)	(3)	(4)	(5)	(6)	(7)	(8)	(9)
13. 5 persons	22.3	2.60	2.40	21.1	21.9	20.3	-1.2	-0.4	-2.0
14. 6 persons	18.9	3.32	2.68	21.6	23.8	19.2	2.7	4.9	0.3
15. 7 persons	11.3	3.95	3.05	14.9	16.9	13.1	3.6	5.6	1.8
16. 8 persons	6.0	4.33	3.67	9.1	9.8	8.4	3.1	3.8	2.4
17. 9 and over	6.0	5.50	5.03	12.0	12.5	11.5	6.0	6.5	5.5
18. Totals, averages, and TDMs	3.01	2.64	2.63	15.88	7.95	7.92	30.8	41.6	20.0

B. Allocations

	TDMs, persons below 18 or minor (1)	Weight, col. 1 (2)	Col. 1 × col. 2 (3)	TDM, persons 18 and over or adult (4)	Weight, col. 4 (5)	Col. 4 × col. 5 (6)	Cancellation component (7)	Sum, columns 3, 6, and 7 (8)
19. United States, line 8	104.2	0.357	37.2	20.2	0.643	13.0	-3.2	47.0
20. Taiwan, line 18	41.6	0.501	20.8	20.0	0.499	10.0	0	30.8

Notes: *Panel A*: The data for the United States are for the sum of principal individuals (i.e., 1-person households) and family households, from the Bureau of the Census, *1970 Census of Population*. Subject Report PC(2)4A, *Family Composition*, Washington, May 1973, largely Table 3, pp. 7–8. Data needed on members (persons) in family households are from the same source, Table 7, pp. 138ff. For the data on Taiwan, see Kuznets, "Size and Structure of Family Households: Exploratory Comparisons," *Population and Development Review*, vol. 4, no. 2, June 1978, Table 1, pp. 190–191.

Lines 8 and 18: entries in column 1 are the totals of all households, in million; in columns 2 and 3, average number of persons in the two age classes; columns 4–6, totals of persons in million; columns 7–9, the TDMs for the three distributions.

Panel B: The TDM entries in columns 1 and 4 are from Panel A, columns 8 and 9, lines 8 and 18. The weights, in columns 2 and 5 are calculated from columns 2 and 3, lines 8 and 18.

The cancellation component in column 7 is due to divergence in the signs of the deviations in columns 8 and 9 of Panel A (e.g., for the 3-person size class in line 3). It is derived here as the difference between the sums of columns 3 and 6 (Panel B) and the TDM for the distribution by the number of persons (Panel A, column 7, lines 8 and 18). For discussion see text.

aged below 21 years of age and adults aged 21 years and over. Both sets of distributions are used as given, without any interpolation or adjustment. The sample is tiny; Taiwan is atypical with respect to inequality in the size distribution of households; and the division lines between children and adults are not optimal. Yet the data are helpful in suggesting relations between significant age groups and household composition, by size classes of households by number of persons.

The first observation to be noted is that the inequality in the size distribution of households by number of persons can be viewed as the sum of inequalities in the distribution of children–minors and of adults within the *same* size classes, weighted by the proportions of the two age groups in total population within households. Thus, the TDM for distribution of Taiwan households by number of persons, 30.8, equals the sum of the TDM for minors (in the same size classes by number of persons) of 41.6 weighted by 0.501 and of the TDM for adults of 20.9 weighted by 0.499 (see line 20).

Second, this identity between the TDM for distribution by the number of persons and the sum of weighted TDMs for children–minors and adults requires that there be identity of the signs of deviations for the two age groups in columns 8 and 9 of Panel A. This requirement is fulfilled for Taiwan, but not for the United States (see divergence in signs in cols. 8 and 9, line 3). Yet, in general, there is likely to be agreement in signs, because size classes for which children–minors per household are below (or above) the countrywide average are the size classes in which adults per household are also below (or above) their countrywide average. Thus, the effect of disparity in signs, the cancellation component, tends to be small.

Third, the TDM for the children–minor distribution is much larger than that for the adult distribution, in both the United States and Taiwan (see lines 8 and 18, cols. 8 and 9). This should have been expected, because we know that there are practically no children in the 1- and 2-person households, and that the rise of the former cumulates rapidly toward the larger size classes of households – whereas the number of adults per household rises slowly beyond the 2-person class.

But the wider amplitude of disparities in the size distribution of children does not mean that the TDM for that distribution dominates *differences* among countries (or *changes* over time) in the TDM for the total distribution of households by number of persons. As the equations represented by lines 19 and 20 indicate, in addition to the minor cancellation

component, four variables are involved: the TDM for children–minors
and its weight, and the TDM for adults and its weight. Differences or
changes in the two TDMs can be offset, partly or more than offset, by differences and changes in the weights – as may be observed in Table 10.4.
We shift now from the comparison of the United States and Taiwan in
Table 10.3, which is too narrow and too limited for our purposes, to a
comparison of the groups in Table 10.2, each of which includes seven
countries, and which were derived from an array that ranged the countries in decreasing size of the average household (number of persons per
household).

Column 1 in Panel A of Table 10.4 (excluding the modifications to be
discussed later) comprises the arithmetic mean (unweighted) percentage
distributions of households by size classes (number of persons), taken
from the data for the individual countries included in the largest size
group (I) and the smallest (VII). The identity of the countries is shown
in the notes to Table 10.4. With these at hand, and the average size of
household in each of the two groups given in Table 10.2, one can calculate
the percentage shares of persons in the several size classes (col. 4) and the
TDMs for the two size distributions (43.4 and 46.0, respectively, lines 10
and 18, col. 7).

The allocation of the household averages between members below 15
years of age and 15 years old and over (cols. 2 and 3, lines 1–9 and
14–19) is an approximation based on applying the pattern for Taiwan to
Group I and that for the United States to Group VII – but constraining
the approximations so as to yield the averages of children and adults per
households already established in Table 10.2 (see lines 4–6). The approximations are rough and rounded, but there is no reason for assuming
that significant error was introduced into the allocation between the two
age groups, within the several size classes of households (the relevant
classes range from 3 to 7-and-over persons).

We can now observe the allocation of the total TDM for the two size
groups between those generated by the size distributions of children
below 15 and of adults of 15 and over (see lines 10 and 20, cols. 8 and 9;
and particularly the allocations in lines 23 and 24). The average size of
household declines from 5.69 persons in Group I to 2.75 in Group VII;
but the inequality in distribution of households by number of persons
barely changes, with the TDM moving from 43.4 to 46.0. This relative
stability is the result of sizable but compensating movements in the TDMs
for persons below 15 and for adults 15 and over, and their respective

Table 10.4. *Size distributions of households for largest and smallest average household groups (I and VII in Table 10.2), and illustrative modifications*

		A. Size-distributions and related measures								
		Persons per HH		Percentage shares in persons			Disparities			
Size of HH class	Percentage shares in all HHs (1)	Below 15 of age (2)	15 and over (3)	All (4)	Below 15 (5)	15 and over (6)	Col. 4 minus col. 1 (7)	Col. 5 minus col. 1 (8)	Col. 6 minus col. 1 (9)	
Group I										
1. 1 person	5.9	0	1.00	1.0	0	1.9	−4.9	−5.9	−4.0	
2. 2 persons	9.3	0	2.00	3.3	0	6.1	−6.0	−9.3	−3.2	
3. 3 persons	11.5	0.70	2.30	6.1	3.1	8.6	−5.4	−8.4	−2.9	
4. 4 persons	12.7	1.50	2.50	8.9	7.3	10.3	−3.8	−5.4	−2.4	
5. 5 persons	12.9	2.30	2.70	11.3	11.3	11.4	−1.6	−1.6	−1.5	
6. 6 persons	12.2	3.10	2.90	12.9	14.4	11.5	0.7	2.2	−0.7	
7. 7 persons	10.1	3.70	3.30	12.4	14.3	10.9	2.3	4.2	0.8	
8. 8 persons	8.3	4.20	3.80	11.7	13.3	10.3	3.4	5.0	2.0	
9. 9 and over	17.1	5.57	5.21	32.4	36.3	29.0	15.3	19.2	11.9	
9a. 7 and over	35.5	4.72	4.33	56.5	63.9	50.2	21.0	28.4	14.7	
10. Averages, TDMs	5.69	2.62	3.07	—	—	—	43.4	61.2	29.4	
Modification 1 (see notes)										
11. Averages, TDMs	5.69	2.21	3.48	—	—	—	43.4	60.0	34.0	
Modification 2 (see notes)										
12. Averages, TDMs	3.85	1.46	2.39	—	—	—	65.8	112.0	37.4	

Group VII

	Persons per HH (1)	TDM, below 15 (2)	Weight, col. 2 (3)	Col. 2 × col. 3 (4)	TDM, 15 and over (5)	Weight, col. 5 (6)	Col. 5 × col. 6 (7)	Cancellation component (8)	Sum, columns 4, 7, 8 (9)
13. 1 person	23.8	0	1.00	8.7	0	11.3	−15.1	−23.8	−12.5
14. 2 persons	28.9	0	2.00	21.0	0	27.4	−7.9	−28.9	−1.5
15. 3 persons	18.7	0.60	2.40	20.4	17.5	21.3	1.7	−1.2	2.6
16. 4 persons	15.7	1.30	2.70	22.8	31.9	20.1	7.1	16.2	4.4
17. 5 persons	7.4	2.00	3.00	13.4	23.1	10.5	6.0	15.7	3.1
18. 6 persons	3.2	2.70	3.30	7.0	13.5	5.0	3.8	10.3	1.8
19. 7 and over	2.3	3.90	4.06	6.7	14.0	4.4	4.4	11.7	2.1
20. Averages, TDMs	2.75	0.64	2.11	—	—	—	46.0	107.8	28.0
Modification 1 (see notes)									
21. Averages, TDMs	2.75	0.87	1.88	—	—	—	46.0	105.4	22.2
Modification 2 (see notes)									
22. Averages, TDMs	3.71	1.15	2.56	—	—	—	30.0	62.4	19.3

B. Allocations, Panel A as given, and as changed by illustrative modifications

	Persons per HH (1)	TDM, below 15 (2)	Weight, col. 2 (3)	Col. 2 × col. 3 (4)	TDM, 15 and over (5)	Weight, col. 5 (6)	Col. 5 × col. 6 (7)	Cancellation component (8)	Sum, columns 4, 7, 8 (9)
Panel A as given									
23. Group I	5.69	61.2	0.460	28.2	29.4	0.540	15.9	−0.7	43.4
24. Group VII	2.75	107.8	0.233	25.1	28.0	0.767	21.5	−0.6	46.0
Modification 1: Interchanging Group I and VII averages of persons under 15 per household, by size classes (see col. 2 of Panel A)									
25. Group I	5.69	60.0	0.388	23.3	34.0	0.612	20.8	−0.7	43.4
26. Group VII	2.75	105.4	0.316	33.3	22.2	0.684	15.2	−2.5	46.0
Modification 2: Interchanging Group I and VII percentage proportions of 1- and 2-person households									
27. Group I	3.85	112.0	0.380	42.6	37.4	0.620	23.2	0	65.8
28. Group VII	3.71	62.4	0.309	19.3	15.6	0.691	10.7	0	30.0

Table 10.4 (cont.)

C. Comparison of size-distributions, Groups I and VII as given, and as changed by Modification 2

	Group I				Group VII			
Size classes	Percentage HH as given (1)	Percentage HH mod. 2 (2)	Ratio col. 2/col. 1 (3)	Ratio col. 5/col. 1 (4)	Percentage HH as given (5)	Percentage HH mod. 2 (6)	Ratio col. 6/col. 5 (7)	Ratio col. 1/col. 5 (8)
29. 1 person	5.9	23.8	4.03	4.03	23.8	5.9	0.25	0.25
30. 2 person	9.3	28.9	3.11	3.11	28.9	9.3	0.32	0.32
31. 3 person	11.5	6.4	0.56	1.63	18.7	33.5	1.79	0.61
32. 4 person	12.7	7.1	0.56	1.24	15.7	28.2	1.79	0.81
33. 5 person	12.9	7.2	0.56	0.57	7.4	13.3	1.79	1.74
34. 6 person	12.2	6.8	0.56	0.26	3.2	5.7	1.79	3.84
35. 7 and over	35.5	19.8	0.56	0.06	2.3	4.1	1.79	15.43

Notes: Panel A: Columns a and 4, lines 1–9 and 13–19: Derived from data for the seven countries included in groups I and VII in Table 10.2. In order of decreasing average of persons per household, they were: for Group I – Kuwait; Colombia; Iraq; Costa Rica; Paraguay; Venezuela; Dominican Republic; for Group VII – Austria; USA; England and Wales; Denmark; West Germany; German Democratic Republic; Sweden (for year of coverage see notes to Table 10.1). The data for the two groups of seven countries each yielded the unweighted average of shares of the nine or seven size classes of households. Knowing from Table 10.2 the average size of households for Groups I and VII (5.69 and 2.75 persons, respectively), we could calculate the average share in total number of persons in column 4.

Columns 2 and 3, lines 1–9 and 13–19: The allocation in columns 2 and 3 between household members below 15 years of age, and 15 and over is an approximation using the general pattern in Table 10.3, for Taiwan (Group I) and United States (Group VII). This pattern suggests negligible proportions of children below 15 in the 2-person households, and a rapid rise in the ratios of children to adults in the larger size classes. The approximations in columns 2 and 3 were constrained to yield the averages per household under 15 and 15 years of age and over estimated for Groups I and VII in Table 10.2 (i.e., 2.62 and 3.07 for Group I, and 0.64 and 2.11 for Group VII). With columns 2 and 3 given, in addition to entries in columns 1 and 4, all other entries in lines 1–9 and 13–19 could be calculated.

Lines 10 and 20: The entries in columns 1–3 are the averages of persons per household, total and in the two age groups; those in columns 7–9 are the TDMs for the three distributions.

Lines 11 and 20: Modification (1) involves assigning to Group I the averages of persons under 15 per household of Group VII (i.e., those in column 2, lines 13–19); and assigning to Group VII the averages of persons under 15 per household of Group I (i.e., those in column 2, lines 1–6 and 7a). The averages per household of persons 15 years of age and over are then obtained by subtraction from the total number of persons in each of the seven size classes. The averages in columns 2 and 3, and the TDMs in columns 8 and 9 are then calculated for the new distributions. The averages in column 1 and the TDMs in column 7 remain as they were in lines 10 and 20, respectively.

Lines 12 and 21: The modification here involves assigning to Group I the percentage shares of 1- and 2-person households of Group VII (i.e., those in column 1, lines 13 and 14); and assigning to Group VII the percentage shares of 1- and 2-person households of Group I (i.e., those in column 1, lines 1 and 2). The new distributions are then adjusted so that the total of shares in households and persons (in the two age groups) add out to 100 – the adjustments made proportional to the original shares in the remaining size classes (see Panel C). We calculate the averages in columns 1–3 and the TDMs in columns 7–9 from the new distributions (these size distributions are shown in Panel C).

Panel B: All entries calculated from Panel A. For brief notes on the procedure, see the notes to Panel B of Table 10.3.

Panel C: Based entirely on Panel A and showing explicitly the new size distributions yielded by Modification 2, and the unrealistic component in them (see discussion in the text).

weights. Thus, with the marked decline in children per household and the sharp rise in proportions of 1- and 2-person (i.e., virtually childless) households, the TDM in the distribution of children (Table 10.4) rises from 61.2 for Group I to 107.8 for Group VII. But this is more than offset by the decline in the weight of children in total household population, so that the contribution of the children component to total inequality, which amounts to 28.2 in Group I, declines to 25.1 in Group VII (see Table 10.4, lines 23 and 24, col. 4). In contrast, the TDM for the adult component, 29.4 for Group I, declines somewhat to 28.0 in Group VII – but the substantial increase in the weight, from 0.540 to 0.767, yields a substantial rise in the weighted contribution to total inequality, from 15.9 in Group I to 21.5 in Group VII. It is the rise in the contribution to inequality of the adult component that more than offsets the decline in the contribution of the children component – and results in a minor rise in the TDM for the total size distribution from 43.4 to 46.0.

It is not easy to judge whether the differentials of the type and combination shown in lines 23 and 24 are typical and could be expected in other similar comparisons among size distributions of households, for groups with substantially different average household size. In general, in the movement from larger to smaller households that is associated with the decrease in the proportion of children within the household population and rise in the proportions of 1- and 2-person households, one would expect the TDM for the children component to rise substantially and its weight in total population to decline substantially – but the *net* effects on the weighted contribution to total inequality can be either to reduce it (as was the case here) or to raise it. The TDM for the adult component is not likely to move as sensitively as that for the children component in the shift from larger to smaller households; but its weight will be rising, and a rise in the weighted contribution is not unlikely. Any generalizations would have to await far more data on composition of households according to distribution between children and adults in the successive size classes by number of persons, data that would provide such information on a much larger number of countries differing substantially in the size of the average household.

Modification 1 is introduced to illustrate cases where the proportions of children in the composition of households is lowered or raised without affecting the distribution of households by the total number of persons (which means that the lowering or raising of the children component is offset, within each size class of households, by the corresponding raising or lowering of the adult component). This modification was accomplished in Table 10.4 by replacing the entries in column 2, lines 1–7a, by the persons below 15 per household in column 2, lines 13–19 – thus lowering appreciably the proportion of children in Group I (from an average of 2.62 to one of 2.21, see lines 10 and 11, col. 2). By contrast, the shift of the entries of Group I to replace those in Group VII resulted in raising the average number of children below 15 per household from 0.64 to 0.87 (see lines 20 and 21, col. 2). There were complementary changes in the averages of adults of 15 and over per household in the corresponding size classes, and in the averages (the latter rose for Group I from 3.07 to 3.48, and declined for Group VII from 2.11 to 1.88 – see lines 10–11 and 20–21, col. 3).

The TDMs for the total distribution of households by number of persons were not affected by Modification 1; but it is interesting to observe the large effects on the TDMs for the adult components, the weights, and the weight contributions (see lines 25–26). Although the TDM for the children components changed only slightly (from 61.2 to 60.0 in Group I and 107.8 to 105.4 in Group VII), the weights were materially affected, and the net contributions show now a substantial rise as far as the children component is concerned (from 23.3 to 33.3, lines 25 and 26, col. 4) instead of the decline shown in lines 23 and 24. The TDM for the adult component is quite changed by the modification and shows a marked decline from Group I to Group VII (from 34.0 to 22.2), which is only partly offset by the rise in weights, so that the weighted contribution of the adult component now *declines* between Groups I and VII, rather than rise as it did for the unmodified distributions in lines 23 and 24. The sensitivity of the TDMs and weights of the children and adult components, in response to changes that are compatible with maintaining the same size distribution of households by number of persons, suggests that these responses are interrelated so that they can easily offset each other.

Modification 2 assigns the *high* proportions of 1- and 2-person households found in Group VII to Group I and then adjusts the percentage shares of the size classes of 3 persons and larger so that the total adds to 100. The same procedure is then repeated with the shares of 1- and 2-person households in children below 15, in adults of 15 and over, and in total income. In all four adjustments, the shares of the size classes above that of 2 persons are reduced in proportion to the original distribution (see lines 12, 27, and for the resulting distributions of households by number of persons, col. 2 of Panel C). Modification 2 in Group VII assigns to it the *low* proportions of 1- and 2-person households found in Group I, and then the shares of the remaining size classes (3 persons through 7 and over) are adjusted upward, so that the sum of shares for all the size classes equals 100.0. The same procedure is repeated for the distribution by size classes of children below 15, adults 15 and over, and total income (see lines 22, 28, and col. 6 of Panel C).

The effect of Modification 2 is to reduce the average household in Group I from 5.69 persons to 3.85 and to raise the average household in Group VII from 2.75 to 3.71. It also serves to reduce the proportion of children below 15 in Group I, from 0.460 to 0.380, with a comple- mentary rise in the proportion of adults 15 years old and over; whereas the effect on Group VII is to raise the proportion of children below 15, from 0.233 to 0.309, with the complementary decline in the proportion of adults 15 years old and over. Such changes in the proportions of children and adults, a decrease of the shares of the former for Group I, was to be expected because of the decline in size of average household; whereas the rise in the proportion of children in Group VII was associated with a rise in the size of the average household. But the major effect is on the TDMs, for the distributions of children and adults, and also for the total distribution of households by number of persons (see lines 27 and 28, in comparison with lines 23 and 24). The most interesting result is the divergence in the TDMs for the distribution by number of persons (col. 9): for the modified Group I, this TDM is as large as 65.8; for the modified Group VII, it is as small as 30.0. Both values represent substan- tial deviations from the range of TDMs observed for the seven groups in Table 10.2, from that for unmodified Group I and Group VII, and that for Group IV (which is 43.2), a group the average household for which is 3.76 persons, quite close to the averages shown for Modification 2 of Groups I and VII (see Tables 10.2 and 10.4, lines 2 and 3). Comparison of lines 27 and 28 shows that the wide difference in the TDMs between modified Groups I and VII is accounted for by wide differences in the TDMs for both children below 15 (col. 2) and adults 15 and over (col. 5).

Panel C reveals that the marked effects of Modification 2 on the TDMs for the distribution of households by number of persons are due to the procedure by which the modified percentage distributions are adjusted to add to 100. Thus, for Group I, the comparison of columns 2 and 1 (the original distribution of households by size classes and the modified one) shows a *uniform* reduction of shares in column 1 beginning with the 3-person class – by a factor of 0.56 (see col. 3). But it is highly improbable that, with the 1-person and 2-person shares raised by factors of 4.03 and 3.11, respectively, the share of the 3-person class would be reduced as much as that of the higher size classes, say the 6-person and the 7-and-over classes. The failure of the procedure to use the reasonable assumption that the increase in the share of the smaller size classes is diffused and shifts *gradually* to a decline in the shares of the larger size classes is what yields, in the case of Group I, the impression of more than one peak in the distribution in column 2 and the large jump in the size of the TDM. This is shown by the ratios in column 4, which compare the percentage shares of the comparable size classes in the unmodified Group VII with the unmodified Group I and which yield a *gradual* decline of the ratios from a high of 4.03 for 1-person households to a low of 0.06 for the 7-and-over size class.

A similar observation can be made on the effect of Modification 2 in lowering so strikingly the TDM for modified Group VII. Here the *reduction* in the shares of 1- and 2-person households was followed by a uniform proportional rise by a factor of 1.79 of the original share of each size class, from that of 3 persons to that of 7 and over (see col. 7 of Panel C). It is highly unrealistic to assume that if there be a tendency for the smaller size classes of households to diminish in importance, this tendency would be sharply limited to the 1- and 2-person households and be reversed abruptly with the 3-person class – rather than diffuse gradually and raise more the shares of very large size classes. The procedure that followed yielded an unusual concentration of frequencies in just two size classes (3- and 4-person, see col. 6), which accounted for over 9/10 of total frequencies. The comparison of the ratios in column 7 of Panel B with those in column 8 indicates how, in the comparison of Group VII percentage distribution with that of Group I, the ratios rise gradually from that for the 1-person size class and concentrate the compensating increase in the three top size classes.

This, of course, is a single illustration. But the conclusion that it yields may have some validity. The suggestion is that the key to stability or narrow range of the TDMs (or other measures of relative disparity) with substantial changes in the size of average household lies in the interconnectedness of the larger and smaller households within a country's (or a region's, or a similar large entity's) size distribution of households. It is this interconnectedness that is fractured by the procedure used in Modification 2. For Group I we assumed an increase in proportions of smaller households and thus reductions in the shares of larger households; but the procedure drew a sharp line between 1- and 2-person households, and all the size classes above 2 persons, rather than allow for interconnectedness among the several size classes. The latter would imply a gradual diffusion of the process of decline in average size, whether it be associated with reduction of the proportion of children or with the tendency of adults to live separately, or usually with both.

This answer or hypothesis is not specific and is insufficient to explain why for such a large group of countries the TDM in the size distribution by number of households of persons ranges from 41 to 48, rather than from 43 to 46 or from 38 to 50. Specifying the explanation further would require the additional data on the distributions of households by size, and of the age composition within the size classes, for the larger number of countries data for which we still lack.

III. Implications and conjectures

The discussion in the preceding section suggested that for the large group of countries for which the inequality in the distribution of households by number of persons varied within a narrow range (despite substantial differences in size of average household), implications of interest can be drawn from the allocation of total inequality between that contributed by the children and by the adult components. As one moves from the larger to the smaller average household countries, the TDM for the distribution of the adults (within total person size classes) tends to change moderately – as is indicated by the relevant measures of 29.4 for Group I and 28.0 for Group VII (see Table 10.4, lines 23 and 24, col. 5). If this is a general pattern, the rise in the weight of the adult component as one moves from larger to smaller household countries would lead to a substantial rise of the weighted contribution of this component to total inequality in the size distribution of households by number of persons. Because this latter is about the same for the groups of countries ranging from large average household to small, and because the cancellation component may be assumed to be negligible, the weighted contribution of the children component to total inequality must *decline* as one moves from the larger average household to the smaller average household countries. Because the weights of the children component also *decline* as one moves from the large to the smaller household countries, the TDM for the children component, derived as the ratio of the weighted contribution to the weight, may move either way. As shall be seen presently, whether (under the assumptions stated) the TDM for the children component rises or declines as one moves from larger to smaller household countries will depend on the magnitude of the TDM assumed for the adult component, *relative* to the TDM for the total size distribution of households by number of persons.

In Table 10.5 we assume a constant TDM for the size distribution of households in the seven groups distinguished in Table 10.2 (for which the average household declines from 5.69 in Group I to 2.75 in Group VII). This average TDM (in line 1 of Table 10.5) is the arithmetic mean of the slightly divergent TDMs in line 2 of Table 10.2. We then introduce the changing proportions of children below 15 and of adults 15 and over, using the data in line 3 of Table 10.2.

The rest of the table demonstrates the differences in the movement of the derived TDMs for the children component as one varies the level of the constant TDM assumed for the adult component, from a low of 20.00 for lines 4–6 to a high of 50.00 for lines 13–15. It can be observed that in the movement from Group I to Group VII, the derived TDMs for the children component will rise as long as the TDM assumed for the adult component is *below* the level of the TDM for the total size distribution of households (i.e., below 43.74); that when the TDM of 50.00 is assumed for the adult component, the derived TDMs for the children component *decline* (see line 15); and that the rises in the derived TDMs for the children component are the greater, the lower the assumed level of the TDM for the adult component. Thus, when the latter is 20.00, the rise of the derived TDMs (in line 6) is from 71.50 to 121.89, or 70 percent; in line 9 it is from 59.80 to 88.97, or about 49 percent; in line 12, it is from 48.11 to 56.05, or 17 percent. And it is clear that, under the assumptions used, the derived TDMs for the children component will be *constant* over the range of the seven groups if the assumed TDM for the adult component is set at 43.74, that is, at the value of the TDM for the total size distribution of households by number of persons.

The explanation of these findings, if it be needed, lies in the implication of the procedure in which the *movement* or changes in the derived TDMs for the children component depends on the ratio of the link-relative of the *weighted* contribution of the children component (lines 5, 8, 11, and 14) to the link-relative of the proportion of children below 15 (line 2). Thus, in line 5, the relative (cols. 1 and 2) is that of 32.54 to 32.96, or 0.9873, whereas that in line 2 is 0.440 to 0.461, or 0.9544. The ratio of 0.9873 to 0.9544 is 1.0345; multiplying by the entry in line 6, column 1, of

Table 10.5. *Derived TDM for distribution of children below 15 by household size classes, groups by size of average household from Table 10.2*

	Groups from Table 10.2						
	I (1)	II (2)	III (3)	IV (4)	V (5)	VI (6)	VII (7)
1. Average TDM, distribution by number of persons	43.74	43.74	43.74	43.74	43.74	43.74	43.74
2. Proportion of children below 15	0.461	0.440	0.395	0.294	0.269	0.238	0.233
3. Proportion of adults, 15 & over	0.539	0.560	0.605	0.706	0.731	0.762	0.767
TDM for adults assumed at 20.00							
4. Contribution of adults (20.00 × line 3)	10.78	11.20	12.10	14.12	14.62	15.24	15.34
5. Contribution of children (line 1 − line 4)	32.96	32.54	31.64	29.62	29.12	28.50	28.40
6. Derived TDM, children (line 5/line 2)	71.50	73.95	80.10	100.75	108.23	119.75	121.89
TDM for adults assumed at 30.00							
7. Contribution of adults (30.00 × line 3)	16.17	16.80	18.15	21.18	21.93	22.86	23.01
8. Contribution of children (line 1 − line 7)	27.57	26.94	25.59	22.56	21.81	20.88	20.73
9. Derived TDM, children (line 8/line 2)	59.80	61.23	64.78	76.73	81.08	87.73	88.97
TDM for adults assumed at 40.00							
10. Contribution of adults (40.00 × line 3)	21.56	22.40	24.20	28.24	29.24	30.48	30.68
11. Contribution of children (line 1 − line 10)	22.18	21.34	19.54	15.50	14.50	13.26	13.06
12. Derived TDM, children (line 11/line 2)	48.11	48.50	49.47	52.72	53.90	55.71	56.05
TDM for adults assumed at 50.00							
13. Contribution of adults (50.00 × line 3)	26.95	28.00	30.25	35.30	36.55	38.10	38.35
14. Contribution of children (line 1 − line 13)	16.79	15.74	13.49	8.44	7.19	5.64	5.39
15. Derived TDM, children (line 14/line 2)	36.42	35.77	34.15	28.71	26.73	23.70	23.13

Notes: The entry in line 1 is the average TDM for all seven groups in Table 10.2, line 3 – an unweighted arithmetic mean.
Line 2 is taken from Table 10.2, line 4. Line 3 is the complement to 1, that is, 1.0 minus the proportion shown in line 2.
The calculations that follow for the different assumed values of the TDM for adults (held constant for the several groups) assume also that the cancellation component in the allocation identity is 0.

71.50, by 1.0345, we obtain 73.95, or the derived TDM for the children component of Group II. In short, so long as the relative decline in the weighted contribution of the children component is not as great as the relative decline in the weights, the derived TDM for that component will rise. And a *shortfall* of the assumed TDM for the adult component relative to the total TDM in line 1 will tend to reduce the proportional decline in the weighted contribution of the children component, compared to the proportional decline in the share of children in total population.

Given the values of 29.4 and 28.0 for the TDM of the adult components in Groups I and VII, respectively, in Table 10.4 (see lines 23 and 24, col. 5), one may argue that a reasonable level for an assumed TDM of the adult component is about 30; and that it is likely to vary among the groups within a relatively narrow range, so that the assumption of constancy is not unrealistic. If so, Table 10.5 implies that, in the movement from the larger to the smaller average household countries, the derived TDM for the children component will rise, from roughly 60 in Group I to about 90 in Group VII and that, accordingly, the inequality in the distribution (within size classes by number of persons) of the children below 15 will exceed that in the distribution of adults by an increasing margin. But does this inference bear on the income disparities between children and adults? The conjecture here is that under realistic conditions, the larger TDM of the children component inferred for the smaller average household countries is also likely to mean an average per person income for children below 15 that is *short* of the average per person income for the adults – by a *greater* margin than would be true for the per person income of children versus adults in the larger household countries.

Because the conditions for such an inference cannot be made clear without an illustrative demonstration, we use Table 10.6, which presents it for Groups I and VII identified in Table 10.4. Almost all the evidence here is taken directly from Table 10.4. The major new item is in lines 3 and 11, which determine the inequality, the income disparity between the shares of size classes of households in the total of persons and the shares of these size classes in the total of income. The data introduced are thus on the component of income inequality in the distribution among persons that is *associated* with the usual negative relation between size of household and per person income of household. These new data are patterned after the measures observed in an earlier article (see note 2) for Taiwan (for Group I) and for the United States (for Group VII). The illustration is subject to the constraint that the inequality in per person income, associated with the negative correlation between size of

Table 10.6. *Illustrative differentials in income per person between children and adults, Groups I and VII*

| | Size classes of households | | | | | | | Sums, TDMs, and averages |
	1 person (1)	2 persons (2)	3 persons (3)	4 persons (4)	5 persons (5)	6 persons (6)	7 and over (7)	(8)
Group I								
1. Percentage shares in households	5.9	9.3	11.5	12.7	12.9	12.2	35.5	100.0
2. Percentage shares in persons	1.0	3.3	6.1	8.9	11.3	12.9	56.5	100.0
3. Differences, percentage shares in income minus percentage shares in persons	1.0	2.0	3.0	3.0	2.0	−0.3	−10.7	22.0
4. Percentage shares in income (line 2 + line 3)	2.0	5.3	9.1	11.9	13.3	12.6	45.8	100.0
5. Income relative, per HH (line 4/line 1)	0.34	0.57	0.79	0.94	1.03	1.03	1.29	22.2
6. Income relative, per P (line 4/line 2)	2.00	1.61	1.49	1.34	1.18	0.98	0.81	22.0
7. Percentage shares of children below 15	0	0	3.1	7.3	11.3	14.4	63.9	(39.8)0.936
8. Percentage shares of adults, 15+	1.9	6.1	8.6	10.3	11.4	11.5	50.2	(10.4)1.056

Group VII

9. Percentage shares in households	23.8	28.9	18.7	15.7	7.4	3.2	2.3	100.0
10. Percentage shares in persons	8.7	21.0	20.4	22.8	13.4	7.0	6.7	100.0
11. Differences, percentage shares in income minus percentage shares in persons	3.0	7.0	1.0	-3.0	-3.0	-2.0	-3.0	22.0
12. Percentage shares in income (line 10 + line 11)	11.7	28.0	21.4	19.8	10.4	5.0	3.7	100.0
13. IR, per HH	0.49	0.97	1.14	1.26	1.41	1.29	2.04	26.0
14. IR, per P	1.35	1.33	1.05	0.87	0.78	0.71	0.55	22.0
15. Percentage shares in children below 15	0	0	17.5	31.9	23.1	13.5	14.0	(87.2)0.814
16. Percentage shares in adults, 15 & over	11.3	27.4	21.3	20.1	10.5	5.0	4.4	(2.2)1.057

Notes: The entries in column 8, except the sums of percentages (in lines 1, 2, 4, 9, 10, and 12) are as follows: Lines 3, 6, 11, and 14 – all at 22.0, the TDM for the disparities between shares in total persons and shares in total income. Lines 5 and 13 – the TDM for the disparities between the shares in households and in total income. Lines 7 and 15 – the first entry, in parentheses, is the TDM for the children under 15 (obtained by multiplying the percentage of shares in lines 7 and 15, respectively, by the relatives of income per person in lines 6 and 14, and dividing the sums of products by 100). Lines 8 and 16 – the first entry, in parentheses, is the TDM for the disparities between the shares in adults 15 years old and older and the shares in total income, whereas the second entry is the average relative per person income for adults 15 and over (obtained by multiplying the percentage shares in lines 8 and 16, respectively, by the income relative per person in lines 6 and 14, and dividing the sums of products by 100).

Lines 1, 2, 7, 8, 9, 10, 15, and 16, columns 1–7, are taken directly from Table 10.4.

The entries in lines 3 and 11, columns 1–7, are illustrative differences between shares in persons and shares in total income following roughly the patterns observed for Taiwan (in 1975) and United States (in 1975) and constrained so as to yield the same TDM of 22.0 for both Group I and Group VII.

household and household income per person, is set at the *same* magnitude, with a TDM of 22.0, for Group I and Group VII. In the article referred to earlier, the corresponding TDMs were 20.6 for Taiwan and 25.2 for the United States (see Table 10.1).

Because children are more concentrated in the larger size households than adults and because the per person income in the larger households tend to be lower than the per person income in the smaller households, the weighted per person income for children is bound to be lower than per person income of the adults. And, indeed, Table 10.6 shows that for both Groups I and VII the derived income relative for per person income of children, at 0.936 and 0.814 is significantly lower than the derived income relative of per person income for adults (see second entry, col. 8, lines 7–8 and 15–16). What is more significant is that for the small household Group VII, with a lower proportion of children and greater inequality in the distribution of the children component (as inferred from Table 10.5), the shortfall of the per person income of children, at 0.77 of the income of adults, is significantly greater than the shortfall of per person income of children in Group I, at 0.89 of income of adults. If one may generalize, the finding would mean that, in the smaller household (and thus economically more developed) countries, the relative gap between the weighted per person income of children and adults would be wider than that between the weighted per person income of children and adults in the larger household (and thus economically less developed) countries. The greater shortfall of per person income of children in the more developed countries would, however, apply to a much higher countrywide per capita income. And it must be emphasized that the inference depends on the assumption that inequality in household income per person, associated with the differences among households, is not narrower in developed than in less developed countries.

If this finding is broadly valid, its significance is enhanced by the observation that the procedure used in Tables 10.5 and 10.6 *understates* the possible income disparity between children and adults, because the distribution yielding the size classes of households is by number of all persons. If the distribution were in size classes by the number of children (or the number of adults, deriving that by the number of children as a residual), the contrast between the weighted per person income of children and that of adults would be greater. This follows from the general principle that variance in a variable is greater when the classification is by the size of that variable, not by any other characteristic. On the other hand, an allowance for lower per unit consumption for children than for adults and conversion of household classes by number of persons to household classes by number of consuming units would reduce the gap between children and adults. But the analysis of this particular aspect of size differentials among households and associated income disparities deserves more extended treatment than is feasible here.[4]

Because the main interest in the size differentials among households is in the contribution of these differentials to inequality in the income distribution among persons, it is only a partial digression to consider the comparison in Table 10.7. It presents, for each of several groups of households by occupation of employed head for the United States for 1975, and for each of several roughly comparable groups by occupation of head for Taiwan for 1977, the size differentials among households (col. 3) – and, particularly important, the contribution of these differentials to inequality in distribution of income among households (col. 7) and of household income per person among persons (col. 8). The United States data cover money income only, one of the reasons for not including service and farm workers that receive substantial income in kind (lines 9 and 10); whereas the data for Taiwan include income (and some transfers) in both money and kind. The occupational classifications for the two countries are only roughly comparable. And as in the rest of the paper, no attempt is made to convert household size in terms of numbers of persons to size in terms of consuming units. But the comparison is of value for suggesting the kind of findings that are of sufficient interest to warrant exploration with more and better data.

The eight occupational groups used for the United States were arrayed in declining order of income per person, and so were the 10 occupational groups used for Taiwan (col. 1). The reason for such an array, chosen

4 For earlier discussion see my paper on "Income-Related Differences in Natural Increase: Bearing on Growth and Distribution of Income," in Paul A. David and Melvin W. Reder (eds.), *Nations and Households in Economic Growth: Essays in Honor of Moses Abramovitz*, New York and London, 1974, pp. 127–146.

Table 2, p. 133, of this paper shows differences in per person incomes (expressed as relatives of countrywide average) of children and adults, for 1971, of 0.75 to 1.13 for white families, a ratio of 0.67; and of 0.77 and 1.25 for black families, a ratio of 0.61. Similar relatives to countrywide income per consuming unit (allowing 0.5 weight to a child under 18 and 1.0 to an adult 18 and over) are 0.83 and 1.04 for white families, a ratio of 0.80; and 0.79 and 1.11 for black families, a ratio of 0.71.

These income relatives were derived for groups of families (2 persons and over) classified by number of children, not by the number of persons.

Table 10.7. Inequality in the size distribution of households, and contribution to disparities in income per household and in household income per person, occupational groups, United States, 1975, and Taiwan, 1977

A. United States (demographic data, March 1976; money income, 1975)

Occupational groups, employed heads (1)	Money income per person, $000s (2)	No. of HHs, (millions) (3)	Persons per HH (4)	TDM (H-P) (5)	Sum, TDM (H-Y, P-Y) (6)	TDM (H-Y) (7)	TDM (P-Y) (8)
1. Professional, technical	6.99	8.33	3.04	42.6	43.4	14.8	28.6
2. Managers, administrat., ex. farm	6.86	7.34	3.27	38.8	40.4	10.2	30.2
3. Sales workers	6.19	2.92	3.04	39.0	40.8	13.0	27.8
4. Clerical and kindred workers	5.15	4.92	2.59	46.2	49.4	18.2	31.2
5. Craft and kindred workers	4.58	9.20	3.51	37.2	38.0	7.4	30.6
6. Transport equipment operators	4.11	2.50	3.57	38.0	38.0	9.6	28.4
7. Other operatives	4.01	5.27	3.31	42.6	42.6	13.2	29.4
8. Laborers, ex. farm	3.78	2.20	3.27	41.8	41.8	11.6	30.2
9. Service workers	3.87	4.62	2.91	47.0	51.2	22.4	28.8
10. Farm workers	3.39	1.75	3.47	42.0	44.8	15.0	29.8

B. Taiwan, 1977 (demographic data, end of 1977, available income for 1977)

Occupation of head (1)	Income per person ($NT,000s) (2)	No. of HH (000s) (3)	Persons per HH (4)	TDM (H-P) (5)	Sum, TDM (H-Y, P-Y) (6)	TDM (H-Y) (7)	TDM (P-Y) (8)
11. Professional, technical and related workers	37.7	240	4.53	30.0	30.4	8.2	22.2
12. Managers and administrative workers	33.0	170	5.14	28.2	31.8	11.4	20.4

13. Clerical workers	32.9	441	4.72	28.8	28.8	28.8	8.4	20.4
14. Sales workers	27.8	426	5.15	29.2	29.2	29.2	14.0	15.2
15. Service workers	25.1	191	4.68	34.0	34.2	34.2	15.0	19.2
16. Transport operators	24.1	168	5.17	26.0	27.8	27.8	13.0	14.8
17. Laborers	23.1	112	5.18	31.8	33.8	33.8	17.6	16.2
18. Other industrial workers	21.4	628	5.25	29.9	31.0	31.0	16.0	15.0
19. Farmers (incl. hunters)	17.2	608	5.70	32.2	32.8	32.8	19.6	13.2
20. Loggers and fishermen	16.2	87	5.37	29.6	33.6	33.6	21.6	12.0

Notes: The entries in column 5 are the TDMs, derived from comparing shares within each occupational group, of size classes in the number of households and of the same size classes in the number of persons. The entries in column 6 are the sums of the TDMs, in the relevant line, in columns 7 and 8. The entries in column 7 are the TDMs derived from comparing shares, within each occupational group, of size classes in the number of households and in total income. The entries in column 8 are the TDMs, derived from comparing shares, within each occupational group, of size classes in total persons and in total income.
Panel A: Taken or calculated from US Bureau of the Census, *Current Population Reports*, Series P-60, no. 104, "Household Money Income in 1975 and Selected Social and Economic Characteristics of Households," (Washington, 1977), Table 15, pp. 48ff. Occupational groups, lines 1–8 are arrayed in decreasing order of money income per person. The 10 groups covered comprise households with *civilian* employed heads (49.0 million out of a total of 72.9 million, the latter including households with heads not in the labor force, in the labor force but unemployed, and employed in military services).
Panel B: Taken or calculated from Directorate General of Budget, Accounting and Statistics, *Report on the Survey of Personal Income Distribution in Taiwan Area, Republic of China, 1977* (Taipei, 1978). Table 15, pp. 236ff and Table 59, pp. 400ff. The 10 occupational groups covered exclude two groups shown in the source, service men (military) plus workers not classified, and nonworking. These two groups together account for 175 thousand households, out of a total of 3,247 thousand.
Available income is defined as distributed factor income, plus current transfer receipts by households, minus current transfer payments by households. Factor incomes and transfers include flows in both money and kind.

after experimenting with alternative ordering (e.g., by average size of household or the value of the TDM in col. 5), is that the corollaries for average household income per person were substantially and interestingly different in the United States and in Taiwan.

For the eight occupational groups in the United States, the size differentials among households, measured directly by the TDMs in column 5, lines 1–8, differ, in range from 37.2 to 46.2; but there appears to be no association with either average size of household in column 3 or with income per person in the occupation in column 1. The approximations to these size differentials among households in the eight occupational groups, obtained by adding the TDMs in columns 7 and 8, fluctuate in a similar fashion, ranging from 38.0 and 49.4, with no correlation either with size of average household or with occupational income per person.

What is observed for the United States is that for an occupational group with a large size differential among households, the contribution to inequality in distribution of income by *per household* income is also large (compare col. 5 or 6 with col. 7). For craft and kindred workers, and transport equipment operators (lines 5 and 6) – the groups with the lowest TDMs in columns 5 and 6 – the TDMs for the differences in shares of households and shares in total income (in col. 7) are also among the lowest. By contrast, for the professional–technical group, the clerical group, and other industrial operatives, for which the TDMs for size differentials among households are the highest (lines 1, 4, and 7, cols. 5 and 6), the TDMs for the contribution to disparity in income per household, in column 7, are also among the highest. The result of this strong positive response of the contribution of income disparities among households, the contribution to disparities in household income *per person*, reflected by TDMs in column 8, differs relatively little among the eight occupational groups. These TDMs in column 8 range from 27.8 to 31.2, without obvious correlation either with per person income differences, or with average size of household differences, or with total size differentials among households (compare entries in col. 8 with those in col. 1, 3, 5, or 6). The same finding would remain even if we were to include the service and farm occupational groups, in lines 9 and 10.

For Taiwan and the 10 occupational groups distinguished, the range in per person income from the highest to the lowest (in column 1) is as great as in the United States; and there is a weak association (negative) with average size of household (in column 3), which tends to be somewhat higher in lower income ranges. The inequality in the size distribution within the occupational groups ranges in column 5 from 26.0 to 34.0, and in column 6 from 27.8 to 34.2 – but there is no apparent association with either size of average household or per person income (in cols. 3 and 1, respectively).

The significant difference emerges in the contribution of the size differentials to the inequality in distribution of households by income per household (see the TDMs in col. 7). Here there is a clear tendency for this contribution to inequality in income per household to rise, as one moves from higher to lower income per person occupations – even though inequality in distribution of households by size (i.e., number of persons) does not change with income per person. This rise in the TDM in column 7 indicates that the positive association of household income with size of household becomes *stronger* as one moves toward the low-income occupations: in the latter, unlike the case of the higher income occupations, a larger household means more effectively a larger than average household income.

As a consequence of this rise of the TDMs in column 7, as one moves from the higher to the lower income occupations, there is a *downward* movement of the TDMs in column 8, that is, in the contribution of size differentials among households to inequality in the distribution of household income *per person*. Thus, in the four higher income occupational groups (lines 11–14), the average TDM for contribution to inequality in income per household averages (unweighted mean) 10.5; and it then rises, in the four lower income occupational groups (lines 17–20), to a mean of 18.7. By contrast, the TDM in column 8, measuring contribution of size differentials in households by number of persons to inequality in distribution of household income per person, averages for the four highest income occupational group 22.05 and then declines to an average for the four lowest income occupational groups of 14.1.

This difference between Taiwan and the United States, in the effects of size differentials among households within different occupational groups on contributions to inequality in per household income and in household income per person, may be due to the differences in per person income levels in the two countries. If so, it might be found in similar comparisons between other pairs of high and moderate income countries; but this is still to be explored. One should also test how much of this difference in response would remain were one to measure size and per unit income not in persons but in consuming units. Yet, given the various qualifications, the results are sufficiently intriguing to be of interest; and they particularly suggest that, at generally lower levels of economic product per capita, pressures of larger numbers in larger households would result in a stronger positive response in greater attempts to raise total household income than would be the case at higher levels of economic product and performance per capita, where a lower response to greater numbers within a larger household might be permitted to result in a somewhat lower, but still adequate, income per person. Another contributory explanation may lie in differences among countries in the availability of ways to raise income in larger households within some occupational groups (e.g., in farm or rural occupations, compared with industrial or urban occupations). But further elaboration and testing of hypotheses requires a wider and richer empirical base.

IV. Trends over time

We turn now to consider changes over time in the inequality in the distribution of households by number of persons, and in particular, to observe whether the limited range of differences in the inequality in size distributions of households in cross-sectional comparisons means also a relative stability of such inequality in the temporal changes that usually accompany economic growth – decline in average size of households and the reduction in the proportion in total population of children below a working age. An adequate study of the time trends requires combing through the census volumes for the countries for which an historical series of censuses exists and through sample studies covering different points of time for countries without a long history of censuses. Such an undertaking is not feasible here; and this exploratory effort is based largely on the data assembled and published by the United Nations, supplemented by data for two or three countries from sources at hand.

We begin with a summary of the evidence for the two and a half to three decades since World War II, for countries for which the coverage permits the observation of changes extending, in most cases, over a two-decade period and, in a few, over a decade and a half (Table 10.8). The table shows the size of the average household for two or more dates since World War II, the TDM for the total size distribution and various associated measures that suggest some aspects of the time changes in the structure of households in the country. Despite the substantial number of countries in the table, 25 in all, the coverage is deficient – particularly for the Communist and the less developed market economies. Of the latter, no countries in Asia except a few in the southeast and in Africa

Table 10.8. *Post–World War II changes, size of average household and associated characteristics, selected developed and less developed market economies*

Country and years of coverage	Persons per HH (1)	Percentage of persons below 15 (2)	TDM, size distribution (3)	Percentage in HHs		Excluding 1-person HHs	
				1-person HHs (4)	2-person HHs (5)	Persons per HH (6)	TDM (7)
Developed market economies							
England and Wales							
1. 1951	3.19	22.1	38.2	10.7	27.6	3.45	33.4
2. 1971	2.86	23.6	43.0	18.2	31.9	3.28	34.4
West Germany							
3. 1950 (ex. Saar and W. Berlin)	3.04	23.3	42.4	18.5	24.8	3.52	34.0
4. 1970	2.74	23.1	46.4	25.1	27.1	3.32	33.8
France							
5. 1946	3.07	21.6	44.6	18.6	26.7	3.54	36.8
6. 1968	3.06	24.8	46.6	20.3	26.9	3.59	37.4
Netherlands							
7. 1947	3.79	29.3	43.2	9.2	22.6	4.07	37.8
8. 1960	3.58	30.0	44.8	11.9	24.3	3.93	37.4
Denmark							
9. 1950	3.15	26.3	40.8	13.8	27.0	3.49	34.4
10. 1965	2.80	23.7	44.0	21.9	27.4	3.31	32.6
Norway							
11. 1950	3.25	24.5	41.4	14.9	22.2	3.64	33.4
12. 1975	2.94	24.1	44.2	21.1	25.4	3.46	33.8
Sweden							
13. 1950	2.90	23.4	42.6	20.7	24.8	3.40	32.8
14. 1975	2.41	21.0	45.6	30.0	30.8	3.02	29.6
Finland							
15. 1950	3.57	30.0	48.2	18.5	18.0	4.15	36.8
16. 1970	2.99	24.6	46.4	23.9	22.1	3.61	34.4
Austria							
17. 1951	3.11	22.8	44.8	17.5	27.2	3.56	37.4
18. 1971	2.90	24.5	48.8	24.6	26.5	3.52	37.4
Eire							
19. 1946	4.16	27.8	45.4	10.4	17.9	4.53	39.6
20. 1971	3.94	31.1	48.8	14.2	20.5	4.43	41.2

Table 10.8 *(cont.)*

Country and years of coverage	Persons per HH (1)	Percentage of persons below 15 (2)	TDM, size distribution (3)	Percentage in HHs		Excluding 1-person HHs	
				1-person HHs (4)	2-person HHs (5)	Persons per HH (6)	TDM (7)
United States							
21. 1950	3.37	26.9	43.8	10.9	28.8	3.63	36.4
22. 1977	2.86	25.3	45.6	20.9	30.7	3.35	36.0
Canada							
23. 1956	3.94	32.1	42.4	7.9	21.9	4.24	38.6
24. 1976	3.13	27.2	44.2	16.8	27.8	3.56	35.6
Australia							
25. 1947	3.75	25.1	39.4	8.1	20.3	3.99	33.8
26. 1971	3.31	28.8	43.2	13.5	26.6	3.67	35.6
New Zealand							
27. 1951	3.61	29.1	41.0	9.1	23.4	3.87	35.2
28. 1966	3.56	32.6	45.0	12.5	24.8	3.93	36.8
Japan							
29. 1950	4.97	35.5	38.8	5.4	10.2	5.20	35.6
30. 1975	3.45	24.5	38.8	13.6	16.8	3.84	28.8
Less developed market economies							
Taiwan							
31. 1956	5.60	44.2	41.2	7.7	7.2	5.98	35.0
32. 1966	5.86	43.3	37.4	6.6	5.4	6.21	32.4
33. 1970	5.85	40.5	32.0	2.5	4.8	5.98	29.8
34. 1977	5.06	34.7	30.8	3.4	6.2	5.20	29.0
Philippines							
35. 1957	5.70	44.2	35.2	1.6	6.7	5.78	34.0
36. 1970	5.94	45.5	36.8	2.3	7.2	6.06	35.4
Thailand							
37. 1960	5.64	44.7	37.0	2.5	7.3	5.76	35.2
38. 1970	5.71	46.2	36.8	3.2	6.9	5.88	34.2
Mexico							
39. 1940	4.08	42.4	46.4	12.7	17.4	4.53	39.0
40. 1950	4.47	42.9	47.0	11.5	14.6	4.92	39.0
41. 1970	4.85	46.5	45.2	7.8	14.2	5.18	40.0
Costa Rica							
42. 1950	5.52	44.0	43.0	4.8	10.6	5.75	39.6
43. 1973	5.60	42.2	43.0	4.7	9.6	5.83	39.4

Table 10.8 (cont.)

Country and years of coverage	Persons per HH (1)	Percentage of persons below 15 (2)	TDM, size distribution (3)	Percentage in HHs		Excluding 1-person HHs	
				1-person HHs (4)	2-person HHs (5)	Persons per HH (6)	TDM (7)
Dominican Republic							
44. 1950	4.93	44.2	48.0	13.7	20.9	5.37	41.8
45. 1970	5.29	48.3	45.8	8.1	11.5	5.67	40.4
Ecuador							
46. 1950	5.12	43.3	43.4	6.8	11.0	5.43	39.0
47. 1962	5.13	45.4	43.8	6.8	11.5	5.43	39.6
Venezuela							
48. 1950	5.34	42.3	44.6	7.0	10.8	5.65	40.0
49. 1961	5.33	46.0	45.6	8.8	10.0	5.74	39.4
Paraguay							
50. 1950	5.32	42.4	41.8	5.0	10.4	5.54	38.8
51. 1962	5.43	45.9	43.2	6.1	9.9	5.72	38.8
Trinidad and Tobago							
52. 1946	4.02	36.8	54.4	16.9	20.8	4.63	45.6
53. 1970	4.78	42.8	52.2	14.6	13.7	5.42	42.6

Notes: Columns 1, 3, 4, 5: Except for United States, 1977 (line 22); Taiwan, 1966, 1970, and 1977 (lines 32–34); and Mexico, 1940, 1950 (lines 39–40), the entries are from United Nations *Demographic Yearbooks* cited for the data in Table 10.1 (including the *Demographic Yearbook* for 1955 covering the early postwar years).

The US data for 1977 are taken or calculated from Bureau of Census, *Current Population Reports*, Series P-60, no. 109 (Washington, D.C., 1978) showing data for March 1977, Table 17, pp. 47ff.

The Taiwan data for 1966 and later years are from the usual sources on distribution of income and expenditures of households in Taiwan cited for Tables 10.1 and 10.3.

The data for Mexico for 1940 and 1950 are from Julio Duran Ochoa, "XX. La Explosion Demografica," in Fondo de Cultura Economica *Mexico: 50 anos de revolucion*, vol. II, *La Vida Social* (Mexico City, 1961). The classification of families by size and the number of single persons not forming families are in Table 9, p. 17. The classification of total population by age, for the 2 years, is in Table 8, p. 16 (used in column 2, lines 33–40).

Column 2: Except for Taiwan and Mexico (1940 and 1950), the entries are either from the United Nations working paper cited for the same data (percentage of population below 15 years of age) used for Table 10.1; or, for some earlier years, from the early issues (1949–1950, 1951, etc.), of United Nations *Demographic Yearbooks*, and B.R. Mitchell, *European Historical Statistics 1790–1970*, London 1975, Tables B1 and B2, pp. 19ff.

For Taiwan we used the *Statistical Yearbook, 1976* (see notes to Table 10.1). The entry for 1977 relates to end of 1976.

For Mexico see the source cited for columns 1, 3, 4, 5, above.

Columns 6 and 7: Calculated from the distributions underlying the entries in columns 1, 3, 4, and 5.

For a few entries approximations had to be made to the average of persons per household are represented; and the coverage for Latin America omits some of the major units. Even for the developed market economies with a much better coverage, major countries, particularly in southern Europe, are missing. Still, the recurrence of similar findings for a number of countries yields results that are of some interest and generality; and they can be listed briefly.

1. In all 15 developed countries, excepting France, size of the average household declined: in several cases, quite strikingly, considering the brevity of the period. Thus, in Finland, the decline was close to a fifth (lines 15–16, col. 1); in Canada, about the same (lines 23–24, col. 1), and in Japan, the drop was by almost a third (lines 29–30). In contrast, for the 10 less developed market economies (with the exception of Taiwan for the period 1970–1977), the size of the average household was either relatively constant or tended to rise (lines 31–33, 35–53, col. 1). It is likely that this contrast between the changes over the last two to three decades, the decline of the size of average household in the developed countries and the stability or rise in the less developed countries, would be confirmed by a larger and more adequate sample.

2. One would expect the downward trend in the size of average household in the developed countries to be associated with decline in the proportion of children below 15 years of age, in column 2. But this is not generally true, even disregarding France (in which the average household changed little in size). The proportion of children below 15 *rose* in Netherlands, Austria, Eire, Australia, and New Zealand; and barely changed in West Germany and Norway. With seven exceptions out of the 14 countries that showed a significant decline in average size of household, one may argue that this decline is only *partly* explained by reduction in proportions of children. As shall be seen presently, it was due more to a rising proportion of 1-person households in the distribution of households by size.

In contrast, there was greater uniformity among the 10 less developed countries in the tendency of the proportion of children under 15 years of age to rise. The exceptions were Taiwan, which proved to be an ex-

Notes to Table 10.8 *(cont.)*

in the upper, open-end, size class (with the number of private households given, and a full distribution of households by the adequate range of size classes). We used in these few cases approximations for the same country for another year, or for neighboring countries. Because this usually involved a class of 10 persons and over, with small shares in the totals, the relative resulting error could be assumed to be moderate.

ceptional case in other respects, and Costa Rica. It is of some interest that this rise in the proportion of children was observed even in countries in which the average size of household barely changed, for example, in Ecuador and Venezuela (lines 46–49, cols. 1 and 2).

3. Except for Finland and Japan, the inequality in the size distribution of households in the other 13 developed economies widened perceptibly over the last one and a half to three decades (col. 3). The rises were moderate, but it is their prevalence in so many countries that is significant. No such common tendency toward a rise is observed among the less developed countries. In Taiwan, the finding is of a sharp reduction in the inequality, the TDM declining from 41.2 in 1956 to 32.0 in 1970 and hovering around 31 by 1977 (col. 3, lines 32–34), a trend not found in any of the other less developed countries. Some of these show moderate rises (Philippines, Venezuela, and Paraguay); others show stability or moderate declines. There is, thus, a contrast for the post–World War II decades between the widening inequality in the size distribution of households in almost all developed countries and the absence of a common tendency in the TDM for the size distribution to change in the same direction, with the exception of the significant decline for Taiwan.

4. The almost general widening of the inequality in the size distributions of households in the more developed economies is associated with the rise in the proportions of 1-person households (col. 3), which was far greater than the rise in the proportions of 2-person households in a number of countries (compare the changes in col. 4 with those in col. 5 for England and Wales, West Germany, Denmark, Norway, Sweden, Austria, and the United States). It is also interesting to note that this rise in the proportion of 1-person households occurred even in Japan, in which the TDM for the size distribution of households in column 3 was stable over the period.[5]

Such rises in proportions of 1-person households can be found in some of the less developed countries in Table 10.8 (e.g., Philippines, Thailand, Paraguay), but they are small; whereas in a number of other less developed countries, even excluding the unique case of Taiwan, the shares of the 1-person households in the total were either constant or declined. There is

---

5 The trend toward living alone was commented upon in the United States, in reference to the evidence for that country (see Frances E. Kobrin, "The Fall of Household Size and the Rise of the Primary Individual in the United States," *Demography*, Vol. 13, no. 1, February 1976; and Robert T. Michael, Victor R. Fuchs, and Sharon R. Scott, "Changes in the Propensity to Live Alone: 1950–1976," *Demography*, Vol. 17, no. 1, February 1980).

thus conformity between the prevalence of rises in the TDMs in column 3 and the rises in proportions of 1-person households in column 4 for the developed countries and between the absence of consistent movements in the TDMs in column 3 and in the movements of the proportions of 1-person households in column 4 for the less developed countries.

5. The contribution of the rise in the shares of 1-person households to the widening in the inequality in the size distribution of households in the developed countries is demonstrated when we exclude these households and deal with the distributions of households of 2 persons and more (cols. 6 and 7). In all countries except France, this exclusion of 1-person households still leaves a downward trend in the size of average household but naturally a more moderate trend in column 6 than in column 1. But the significant change is in the TDMs, the measures of inequality in the size distribution of households. In column 7, which should be compared with column 3, the TDMs are naturally lower; but the more important change is the disappearance of the tendency in the TDMs, observed in column 3, to rise. Of the 15 developed countries in Table 10.8, one still finds some rise in the TDMs in column 7, in England and Wales, France, Eire, Australia, and New Zealand; for the remaining 10 countries, one finds either stability (Austria) or declines – some quite substantial. The broad conclusion is that the prevalence of some widening in inequality in the size distributions of households among the developed economies in the post–World War II period was largely due to the rise in proportions of 1-person households – so that the exclusion of the latter removes any significant trend, with some weight of evidence toward narrower inequality in the size distributions of what might be called family households.

With the shares of 1-person households in the less developed countries generally low and with the trends in these shares over the post–World War II decades rather diverse, the exclusion of these 1-person households does not change much the conclusions established on the basis of the rather small sample for the distributions of all households. This conclusion relates to the absence of movements in the same direction, either of the TDMs in column 3 or of those in column 7. Perhaps with a wider sample, a more perceptible order in the post–World War II changes in the size distributions of households in the less developed economies might be observed.

In Table 10.9 we present measures of size distributions of households for four countries for which the data at hand extend over a long span before the 1950s. Two countries are in Southeast Asia (Japan and Taiwan), and

Table 10.9. *Long-term trends to 1950, measures of size distributions of households, four countries*

Country and year	Persons per HH (1)	Percentage of population below 15 (2)	TDM, size distribution (3)	Percentage in HHs		Excluding 1-person HHs	
				1-person HH (4)	2-person HH (5)	Persons per HH (6)	TDM (7)
Sweden							
1. 1860	4.28	33.5	49.8	15.5	14.4	4.88	39.6
2. 1870	4.07	34.1	49.6	17.9	14.5	4.74	38.4
3. 1880	3.94	32.6	51.6	20.0	15.1	4.67	39.8
4. 1900	3.72	32.4	54.6	23.6	15.8	4.56	40.2
5. 1910	3.72	31.7	53.4	22.6	15.7	4.51	39.8
6. 1920	3.64	29.3	52.2	21.9	16.0	4.38	39.0
7. 1930	3.46	24.8	48.8	20.0	18.0	4.07	36.6
8. 1950	2.90	23.4	42.6	20.7	24.8	3.40	32.8
United States							
9. 1790	5.79	49.9	40.0	3.7	7.8	5.98	37.0
10. 1900	4.76	34.4	43.8	5.1	15.0	4.96	40.2
11. 1930	4.11	29.2	48.2	7.9	23.4	4.38	45.2
12. 1940	3.67	24.9	41.0	7.1	24.8	3.87	36.6
13. 1950	3.37	26.9	43.8	10.9	28.8	3.63	36.4
Japan							
14. 1920	4.99	36.5	41.2	18.3		n.a.[a]	n.a.
15. 1930	5.00	36.6	40.4	17.3		n.a.	n.a.
16. 1950	4.97	35.4	38.8	5.4	10.2	5.20	35.6
Taiwan							
17. 1930	5.82	41.0	46.4	7.6	7.5	6.22	41.8
18. 1956	5.60	44.2	41.2	7.7	7.2	5.98	35.0

[a] n.a., Not available.

Notes: Entries in lines 8, 13, 16, and 18 are from Table 10.8.

Sweden: Taken or calculated from Central Bureau of Statistics of Sweden, *Historical Statistics of Sweden, I. Population,* Stockholm, 1955. Distribution of households by size for the years shown from 1860 through 1930 is from Table A-24, p. 34, which also shows population not included in households; and indicates that there is no full comparability between the size-distributions of households before 1920, and those for 1920 and later dates. The data on total population, and by age, in Table 16, p. 22, when combined with the data in Table A-24, permit calculation of population of each size-of-household class, the proportions of population aged under 15, and all the entries in lines 1–7.

United States: Taken or calculated from Bureau of the Census, *Historical Statistics of the United States, Colonial Times to 1970, Bicentennial Edition, Part I* (Washington, D.C., 1976). We used Series A335–349, p. 42, showing distribution of households by size classes; Series A288–319, p. 41, showing average size of household; and Series A119–134, pp. 15ff, showing distribution of total population by age, with a special estimate for 1790. The data for this early year, referring to free population alone, are not fully comparable with those for later years.

Japan: Lines 14–15 taken or calculated from Irene B. Taeuber, *The Population of Japan* for both one finds a downward trend in the TDM for the size distribution of all households or of households excluding the 1-person class – with the indication that for the 1920s and the 1930s the inequality in the size distribution in these two countries was *not* narrow compared with the ranges above 40 that were found in so many countries in the post–World War II decades. Whether such long-term declines in the inequality measures for the size distributions of households – striking for Taiwan, but substantial even for Japan, particularly when we exclude the 1-person households – are due to some specific aspects of the changing statistical definition of households or represents a really greater clustering of the distribution around its mean is a question that could be answered only with a detailed examination of the underlying basic census and other data.

No such downward trend in the inequality in the size distribution of households is found for Sweden and the United States with the exception of the more recent decades (covered in Table 10.8) for the distribution of households *excluding* the 1-person size class. With this exclusion the TDMs for Sweden of 32.8 in 1950 and of 29.6 for 1975 are distinctly lower than the comparable TDMs for 1860–1930 in column 7 of Table 10.9. Likewise for the United States, the TDM for 1950 of 36.4 and for 1977 of 36.0 are lower than those for 1900 and 1930 in column 7 of Table 10.9. But the trends in the *complete* distribution show for Sweden a long swing, with the TDM measures of inequality in the size distribution first rising from about 50 in 1860 and 1870 to a peak of almost 55 in 1900, and then declining to 42.6 in 1950, to rise to 45.6 in 1975. The significant finding suggested here is that despite the marked decline in the size of the average household, from 4.3 in 1860 to 2.4 in 1975, the underlying long-term trend in the inequality in the size distribution from 1860 to 1930 has been constant. In the United States, if we disregard the entry for the earliest year, 1790, the measure of inequality in the size distribution in column 3 fluctuates, but again the underlying trend from about 44 in 1900 to about 46 in 1977 is one of long-term stability, despite the marked decline in the size of the average household from about 4.8 persons in 1900 to 2.9 in 1977.

Notes to Table 10.9 *(cont.)*

(Princeton, N.J., 1958), Table 35, p. 108 for distribution of private households by size classes (with 1- and 2-person classes combined); and Table 21, p. 73, for the age distribution of total population.
Taiwan: Derived from George W. Barclay, *Colonial Development and Population in Taiwan* (Princeton, N.J., 1954). Table 45, p. 178, on average size of households (Taiwanese population alone) and Figure 30, p. 179, for distribution of households by size classes (Taiwanese population); and Table 18, p. 99, showing the age distribution of the Taiwanese about 1930.

One should also note that for both Sweden and the United States, the long-term stability of the inequality measures of the size distribution of all households was accompanied by both a substantial decline in the proportion in total population of children below 15 and a substantial rise in the proportions of 1-person households. Including the most recent year from Table 10.8, the decline in the proportion of children aged below 15 in Sweden was from 34 percent in 1860 and 1870 to 21 percent in 1975; in the United States from 34 percent in 1900 to 24 percent in 1977. The rises in the share of 1-person households were from 15.5 to 30.0 percent in Sweden, and from 5.1 to 20.9 percent in the United States.

The general bearing of the findings in Table 10.9 is to confirm the exceptional character of the inequality measures and trends for the two countries in Southeast Asia; and the broad conformity of the long-term trends in inequality in the size distribution of all households in Sweden and in the United States to what we would expect from the cross-sectional data for the post–World War II years.

V. Summary

Our interest in the size distribution of households by number of persons stems from earlier findings, which indicate that size differentials among households contributed to inequality in the distribution of income among household by income per household; or to inequality in distribution of household income among persons (or consuming units); or to both. The *positive* association between per household income and household size means that, in the conventional income distribution among households, there is a substantial component due merely to differences in size among small and large households. The *negative* association between household size and household income per person (or per consuming unit) means that in the distribution of household income among persons or consuming units, there is a substantial component due merely to effect of household size on per person income.

Given these associations, it follows that the inequality in the size distribution of households is the *minimum* to which the *associated* inequalities in the distribution of income among households by per household income and in the distribution of household income among persons (or consuming units) should total. It also follows that, other conditions being equal, a wider inequality in the size distribution of households must mean wider inequality in the associated distributions of income among households by income per household, or a wider inequality in the associated distributions of household income among persons, or both. Thus, differences or changes in size distributions of households may spell differences in the associated distributions of income per household, or in the associated distributions of household income per person, or in both.

With these connections in mind, we may now summarize the findings of this exploratory survey of international differences and of trends over time in the size differentials among households by number of persons. The survey was exploratory because we had to rely largely on the assembly of data by the United Nations, rather than search for the relevant data through the country censuses and sample studies.

1. The international comparison for recent years covered data from 70 countries: developed and less developed market economies, and a few Communist countries. Excepting a few special regions – Eastern Asia with quite low disparity measures, and sub-Saharan Africa (small sample) and the Caribbean, with high disparity measures – the measures of disparity in the size distribution of households tend to vary within a fairly narrow range (TDMs from about 40 to 48). What is even more significant, for the group of 49 countries for which inequality in the size distribution of households varies within a narrow range, there is no correlation between the inequality measures and the size of the average household – which ranges from well over 5 persons to well below 3 persons per household; yet the group includes not only developed and less developed market economies but also eight Communist countries. This means that the inequality in size distribution of households is about the same for developed and less developed market economies and for more and less developed Communist countries. The exceptions being largely in circumscribed regions may, unless they are results of statistically different treatment of the data, be due to some specific institutional characteristics of household structure in the limited groups of countries involved.

2. The relative invariance of inequality measures for the size distribution of households by number of persons is strikingly clear when one arrays the 49 countries into seven groups in declining order of size of average household and then averages the TDM measures. In the same grouping, as one moves from the largest household group (Group I, 5.69 persons per household) to the smallest household group (Group VII, 2.75 persons per household), there is a systematic decline in the proportion in total population of children below 15 years of age and a systematic rise in the percentage in total households of 1- and 2-person households, the

two size classes in which the share of children is minuscule. The stability of the TDM measures is thus maintained not only with a marked decline in average household size but also with a marked shift in the age structure within the households.

3. Total disparity or inequality in the size distribution of households can be allocated between the disparity within the size classes by the number of children below 15 (TDMc), *weighted* by their proportion in household population (Wc), the disparity within the same size classes of adults aged 15 and over (TDMa), weighted by the proportion of adults in total household population (Wa), the sum of (TDMc.Wc) + (TDMa.Wa) reduced by a possible cancellation component due to disagreement in the disparity signs for the children and adults, respectively. Because the size classes where children and adults are above (or below) their average size for the country tend to be the same, the cancellation component is small and can be disregarded. The allocation of total disparity in the size distribution of households thus contains two components: the weighted disparity for the distribution of children below 15 and the weighted disparity for the distribution of adults 15 years of age and over – both disparities being for size classes by number of persons.

4. TDMc, the disparity for the children's distribution, is greater than TDMa, that for the adults' distribution, even in the larger household group of countries, in which the weight, Wc, is well over 0.4. As one moves, in the cross-section, from the larger to the smaller household countries, TDMc rises, largely because the proportion of 1- and 2-person households rises; but the drop in the weight, Wc, may largely offset or more than offset the rise in TDMc, so that the product, the *weighted* contribution to total inequality, may remain constant or even decline slightly. In the absence of a marked shift toward smaller size households, of a diffused movement that would raise the proportions of 1- and 2-person households substantially, those of 3- and 4-person households less markedly, and reduce the proportions of the larger size households substantially, the change in size of average household and proportions of children below 15 might yield either a marked rise or a marked decline in total inequality in the size distribution, the TDM. Experimental modifications, which show the alternative results as one makes different assumptions concerning the concentrated (rather than diffused) changes in the shares of the 1- and 2-person households, illustrate the point. The suggestion is that it is the interconnectedness within the structure of household distribution by size that makes for controlled variations in the

weighted contributions of the children and adult components. Of course, no complete stability can be assumed; but it is true that whereas average size of households vary by a factor of 2 or 2.5 to 1, and proportions of children can decline from over 0.4 to barely over 0.2, the TDM for the size distribution varies within a range of about a tenth about a mean of about 44 (corresponding to a Gini coefficient of about 0.3).

5. It was noted earlier that TDM (H-P), the disparity in the size distribution of households by number of persons, is the *minimum* to which TDM (H-Y), disparity in distribution of income by income per household, and TDM (P-Y), disparity in the distribution of household income per person, should total. It is a minimum since TDM (H-Y) + TDM (P-Y) can be larger than TDM (H-P) because there may be some special factors, *unrelated to size*, that affect the income disparities among size classes. If one assumes that no such unrelated-to-size factors affect the disparity among size classes, two sets of inferences can be suggested.

6. The first emerges if one holds TDM (H-P) constant for the several groups of countries in descending order of size of average household, assume relative constancy in the TDMa (the disparity for the adult component at plausible levels), and, then, knowing the changing weights Wc and Wa, derive the TDMc as a residual. This derived TDMc will show a marked rise, as one moves from the larger to the smaller average household groups in the array. In other words, the disparity in the distribution of children will widen as one moves from countries with large families, many children, and few 1- and 2-person households, to countries with small families, few children, and large proportions of 1- and 2-person families. If one then assumes that TDM (P-Y), the disparity in distribution of household income per person (associated with size distribution of households) is about the same in the large and small household countries, the higher TDMc in the smaller household countries will be translated into wider difference between the weighted per person income for children and weighted per person income of adults, a *wider* shortfall of per person income of children relative to that of adults. In other words, under the assumptions stated, and they are plausible, the relative shortfall in the per person income of children in the more developed countries (with overall higher per person income) will be greater than that in per person income of children in the less developed, larger household countries (with overall lower per person income).

7. The second conjecture is suggested by a comparison of the relation between disparities in the size distributions of households and the associated disparities in income per household and in household income per

person, for groups of households distinguished by occupation of head, in the United States (in 1975) and in Taiwan (in 1977). The eight occupational groups in the United States excluded service and farm occupations, because the United States data exclude income in kind (likely to be large in these two occupations), and covered employed civilian workers alone. The 10 groups in Taiwan exclude armed services, unclassified, and retired, and the data covered all income, money and kind. The TDM (H-P) varied among occupational groups somewhat more than they would differ among countries, but the variance was not large and not associated either with size of average household or with occupational income per person.

The significant finding was in the difference in the responses of TDM (H-Y) and TDM (P-Y) to the level of per person income of the occupational groups among households in the United States and Taiwan. For the United States, differences in TDM (H-P) among occupations, uncorrelated with income levels, were reflected in similar differences in TDM (H-Y), so that wide (or narrow) disparity in size of households resulted in wide (or narrow) disparity in associated distributions of per household income. Consequently, the differences in TDM (P-Y) among occupations, in the associated distributions of household income per person were negligible, the relevant measures being almost the same in all occupational groups, high income and low income. In Taiwan, the array of occupational groups by declining level of per person income yielded a definite trend in the TDM (H-Y), a rise in the level of this disparity in income per household. Because TDM (H-P) (the disparity in size distribution of households) did not vary with the per person income level of the occupational groups, the TDM (P-Y), the disparity in the associated distribution of household income per person, showed a marked decline as one moved from the higher to the lower income occupations. In other words, in Taiwan, the lower the per person income of the occupational group, the greater was the *positive* response of per household income to household size and the weaker was the *negative* response of per person income to household size. The economic rationale of the lower income country response of the type shown in Taiwan is clear, although the explanatory factors may also lie in the greater ease of augmenting income in households in rural or small town occupations in a country like Taiwan than in a more urbanized country like the United States.

8. The data base for the study of trends over time in the size distribution of households was far narrower here than that for international comparisons for recent years. Even the evidence on trends in the two to three decades span following World War II was limited to 25 countries, of

which as many as 15 were developed market economies and only 10 were less developed market economies. A wider coverage would have required search in the censuses and sample studies of single countries, a task not feasible in the exploratory comparisons here.

9. The general finding of the post-World War II decades was a prevalent decline in the size of average household in the developed market economies, accompanied by significant rises in the proportions of 1-person households but not as generally by a decline in the proportions of population below 15 years of age. There was also a fairly prevalent rise, if moderate, in the TDM for the size distributions, largely due to the increase in the proportions of 1-person households. Exclusion of the latter and recalculation of the measures indicate that the prevalent, if limited, rise in the TDMs for the size distribution disappears.

In the few less developed market economies, no such general trends can be observed in the post–World War II decades. Excepting the marked decline in the TDM (H-P) for Taiwan, there were no major movements in the inequality in the size distribution of households for the less developed countries nor was there much movement in the average size of households. The low size disparity that is shown in Table 10.1 for the distinct group of countries in East–Southeast Asia (Japan, Korea, Taiwan, Philippines, Thailand) appeared to be true not only for recent years but also in the 1960s.

10. For periods further back, stretching into the past prior to World War II, adequate evidence was available for only two countries, Sweden and the United States. For Sweden, the complete distribution, including 1-person households, shows a long swing in inequality of the size distribution, rising from 1860 to a peak by 1900 and then declining to 1950 to rise slightly again by 1975. But if one excludes the 1-person households, the TDM for the size distribution of households in Sweden appears to be constant over the period and then declines after 1950. For the United States, the record back to 1900 suggests relative constancy of the TDM for the total size distribution, and a recent decline if one excludes the 1-person households. Because the decline in the size of the average household in both Sweden and United States was quite marked over the period, for either the total distribution or excluding the 1-person household, the absence of any distinct trends over the long-term, in the TDM for the size distributions in the two countries, is in conformity to what one should have expected from the cross-sectional comparison for recent years.

11. The limited range of differences in inequality in size distributions of households in cross-sectional comparisons, and the relative stability of such inequality over long periods, mean invariance and stability in the *sum of effects* of size differences among households (size effects) on disparities in income per household (such income positively correlated with size) and on disparities in income per person or per consuming unit (such income negatively associated with household size). Hence, the greater the size effects on disparities in income per household, the smaller would be the size effects on disparities in income per person or per consuming unit and vice versa. If we have grounds to assume that the size effects on disparities in income per household are greater in the less developed than in the developed countries and were greater in the earlier than in the later stages of economic growth in the developed countries, it would follow that the size effects on disparities on income per person or per consuming unit would be smaller among the LDCs than among the DCs and would rise from the earlier to the later stages of economic growth. An opposite assumption would yield an inference of greater contribution of the size effects to disparities in income per person or per consuming unit among the LDCs than among the DCs and a decline in these size effects in the course of long-term growth. It is thus important to view the invariance or constancy over time in the inequality in the size distributions of households as compatible with marked differences and significant trends in the size effects on the income disparities of most interest, those by income per person or per consuming unit.

There is no need to extend the discussion here by emphasizing the limitations of the findings, and of the suggested conjectures, due to the narrowness of the empirical base and due to the failure to pursue a variety of alternative measures, having to do with conversion to consuming units, alternative measures of disparity, and the like.

The main aim of the analysis and discussion was to illustrate the otherwise obvious point that differences in size differentials and structure of households have important effects on inequality in the income distributions among the most relevant recipient units, persons or consumer equivalents. Whatever findings were suggested in the tables and discussion are details on the theme just indicated and one that so far has not been considered adequately in the conventional income distributions among households by income per household.

11. Children and adults in the income distribution

I. Introduction

If families or households are grouped by their size, as measured by number of persons, the common finding is that the larger families or households show a larger income per unit. But if the family or household income is divided by the number of members, per person income is larger in the smaller families or households and smaller in the larger units. An illustration of the positive association between the size of family and income per family, and of the negative association between size of family and family income per person, is provided in Table 11.1 below for the United States in 1969–70 (money income is for calendar 1969 and size of family is shown for March 1970). Income per family ranged from a low of $8.8 thousand for a family of two persons to $12.2 thousand for a family of five or six persons and $11.5 thousand for a family of seven persons or more. Family income per person declined sharply from $4.4 thousand for families of two persons to $1.4 thousand for families of seven or more.[1]

Larger families or households usually contain a higher proportion of children among the members and a smaller proportion of adults than the smaller families or households. It follows that children are more concentrated than adults in larger families or households and, consequently, in families or households with lower per person income. It also follows that there will be a disparity between the lower average income per person in families or households with children and the higher average income per person in families or households without children (or with low proportions of children to adults). Discussion in this paper explores the differences in per person income between children and adults in the income distribution.

© 1982 by The University of Chicago. All rights reserved.
1 For a detailed discussion of these two associations, see Chapter 9, above.

370

Statistics for the United States, and for families rather than for households, are used here because of the requirements of the data needed to measure fully the gap between average per capita income levels of children and adults. As will be shown in the second section of the paper, a complete measure of the gap requires that the multiperson units (whether families or households) be classified by the number of children – and such classifications are at hand only for this country (except for incomplete data for the Philippines for 1970–71) and for families rather than households.[2]

Following the second section, which deals with a shift from distribution of families by number of persons to the distribution by number of children, the third section considers the effect of inclusion of unrelated individuals. This introduces substantial inequality in the number of *adults* per unit among units (families and unrelated individuals) grouped by number of children. But the effect on inequality in per person income between children and adults, the main finding in this paper, is moderate: it widens such inequality, but by a narrow margin.

The fourth section explores the question whether differences among families by number of children persist within the several age-of-head groups. The finding that these differences are found also within the several age-of-head groups indicates that the associated disparities in income per person among families with differing numbers of children will probably persist even when cumulated over the full lifetime span of the families.

In the fifth section, the cross section per person income patterns illustrated in the preceding sections are used to suggest time patterns of per person income for imaginary types of households, assuming substantial differences among them in the number of children born and surviving during the life-cycle span of each household type. While the illustrative

2 Further search, not feasible here, might reveal similar data for other countries. In absence of such a search, the data used here are illustrative. Families in the available U.S. data are defined as units the members of which are related by blood, marriage, or adoption; and residing in the same quarters (with some exceptions for members away at colleges or other schools). Households are units that share quarters and living arrangements, with the members not necessarily related by blood, marriage, or adoption (although the dominant proportion of households are family households). Families exclude individuals not related to the head, such unrelated individuals either residing alone and forming one-person households or living within multiperson households with other members to whom they are not related. In the size-of-unit classification, the family groupings begin at two persons; the household groups begin at one person.

cases are necessarily oversimplified, and to that extent unrealistic, they help to visualize more clearly the implications of the lower levels of per person income among children and adults in larger families, in the shares of both groups in the current income, and of the children, when adults, in the prospective income.

The concluding comments emphasize the main and somewhat puzzling finding relating to the income disparities among children and adults associated with differences in number of children in the family, and consider briefly the dependence of this finding on assumptions embodied in the definitions of child, adult, family, consumer unit, and income underlying the data used here and of possible bearing on identical or roughly similar data elsewhere.

II. Distribution of families by number of persons and by number of children

Table 11.1 relates to 1969–70 because the demographic data for March 1970 are available not only from the Bureau of the Census *Current Population Survey* (which also provides the data on money income in calendar 1969), but also from the *1970 Census of Population.*[3] The purpose of the table is to demonstrate how important is the presence of children for size differences among families by the number of persons, and hence also for differences in per capita income among the large and the small families. Furthermore, in permitting a comparison with the distribution of the same families by number of children (in Table 11.3 below), Table 11.1 demonstrates that the distribution by number of persons fails to provide a full measure of the relative income levels of children, and hence of the income disparity between children and adults.

The percentage shares in panel A provide the basis for measuring inequality in the distribution of families by number of persons, and separately by number of children and adults within the same size-of-family classes. Two measures of inequality are used. The first, total disparity measure (TDM), is the sum of differences, signs disregarded, between the percentage shares of the same classes in two related variables (e.g., in number of families and in number of persons, or in number of families

3 A major source of data in this paper is Bureau of the Census, *Income in 1969 of Families and Persons in the United States*, Current Population Reports, Series P-60, no. 75 (Washington, D.C., December 1970) (hereafter cited as *Income in 1969*).

and in total income). Each difference in percentages can be viewed as the relative deviation of the class mean from the overall mean, weighted by the percentage share of the class in total frequency. Thus, the difference in line 1 between the share of the two-person class in total families and in total persons, columns 1 and 2, or −15.4%, can be derived as relative deviation of the class mean from the overall mean, that is, (2.00 − 3.62)/ 3.62, or −0.447, multiplied by the weight of the two-person class in all families, that is, by 34.4%. The measure is simple and makes for easy identification of the frequency classes that are responsible for most inequality. It is also a simplified form of the Gini coefficient of concentration, if converted to a proper fraction by relating total disparity to 200, the maximum possible. This proper fraction then represents one minus the ratio of two areas. In the denominator is the total area between the diagonal of perfect equality in the Lorenz curve and the two coordinates at 0-0 and 1.0-1.0 points. In the numerator is the area between the equality diagonal and a broken line, the first segment of which is a straight line from the 0-0 point to the point where the arithmetic mean value of the Y variable is reached on the Y-axis and the corresponding cumulative frequency proportion is reached on the X-axis, and the second segment is the line from the latter point to the 1.0-1.0 point in the upper corner.[4]

The other measure is the familiar Gini coefficient, calculated here from the simple formula in which it equals one minus the sum of all classes or products $(f_{i+1} - f_i)(y_i + y_{i+1})$, where f represents the cumulated fractions of total frequencies and y represents the cumulated fractions of total magnitude, the cumulations being from the lowest to the highest magnitude classes. It will be noted that the TDMs, when expressed as proper fractions and divided by 200 (or some reasonable approximation to it), are consistently lower than the Ginis, as they should be; but the differences between the two measures are in the same direction and of roughly the same magnitudes.

The first finding in Table 11.1 to be noted is the relation between the inequality in the size of families observed in the comparison of columns 1 and 2 of panel A, and in the inequality of income per family and of per person income for the same family size classes in columns 1 and 2 of panel B. The size differences among families are measured by a TDM of 38.0 and a Gini coefficient of 0.248 (lines 15 and 16, col. 1), fairly

4 This interpretation of the TDM as a simplified Gini coefficient was suggested to me by Dr. Shirley W. Y. Kuo of the National Taiwan University.

Table 11.1. Children and adults, distribution of families by number of persons per family, United States, 1969–70

A. Shares of families (F), persons (P), children under 18 (Pc), adults 18 and over (Pa), by size classes of families

Size of family	% of all F (1)	% of all P (2)	Pc per F (3)	Pa per F (4)	% of all Pc (5)	% of all Pa (6)	% of all P — Pc (7)	% of all P — Pa (8)
1. Two persons	34.4	19.0	.06	1.94	1.5	29.7	.5	18.5
2. Three persons	20.9	17.3	.72	2.28	11.0	21.1	4.1	13.2
3. Four persons	19.3	21.4	1.66	2.34	23.5	20.0	8.9	12.5
4. Five persons	12.5	17.3	2.56	2.44	23.6	13.5	8.9	8.4
5. Six persons	6.8	11.2	3.43	2.57	17.1	7.7	6.4	4.8
6. Seven and over	6.1	13.8	5.24	2.98	23.3	8.0	8.8	5.0
7. Averages and totals[a]	51.24	185.40	1.36	2.26	69.79	115.61	37.6	62.4

B. Money income (Y) per person (all persons, children and adults)

	Y/F ($) (1)	Y/P ($) (2)	Y/P multiplied by proportion in total P of: P (3)	Pc (4)	Pa (5)	% in total Y/P of: Col. 3 (6)	Col. 4 (7)	Col. 5 (8)
8. Two persons	8,788	4,394	835	22	813	28.6	.8	27.8
9. Three persons	10,557	3,519	609	144	465	20.8	4.9	15.9
10. Four persons	11,855	2,964	634	264	370	21.7	9.0	12.7
11. Five persons	12,222	2,444	423	218	204	14.5	7.5	7.0

12. Six persons	12,180	2,030	227	130	97	7.8	4.5	3.3
13. Seven and over	11,544	1,404	194	124	70	6.6	4.2	2.4
14. Averages and totals[b]	10,577	2,922	2,922	902	2,020	100.0	30.9	69.1

C. Measures of disparity among families[c]

	Families by number of persons (F−P) (1)	Families by number of children (F−Pc) (2)	Families by number of adults (F−Pa) (3)	Col. 2 by proportion of Pc (4)	Col. 3 by proportion of Pa (5)	Families by Y/F (F−Y) (6)	Persons by Y/P (P−Y) (7)
15. TDMs	38.0	85.6	9.4	32.3	5.9	11.6	26.8
16. Ginis	.248	.551	.064	.207	.040	.074	.175

D. Derivation of income disparities among three groups: children (Pc), adults with children (Pca), and adults without children (Paa)[d]

	% in total P (1)	% in total Y (2)	Difference (3)	Per person Income (relative) (4)	Income ($) (5)
17. Pc	37.6	30.9	−6.7	.822	2,402
18. Pca	43.9	41.3	−2.6	.941	2,750
19. Paa	18.5	27.8	9.3	1.503	4,392
20. Total, TDM, average	100.0	100.0	18.6	1.000	2,922

Sources: The major source of the data, except for the breakdown in panel A between children and adults in cols. 3 and 4, is Bureau of the Census, Income in 1969 of Families and Persons in the United States, Current Population Reports, Series P-60, no. 75 (Washington, D.C., December 1970), referred to henceforth as Income in 1969. The

Notes to Table 11.1 (cont.)

distributions in panel A, cols. 1 and 2, are from table 18, p. 42, and so are the average incomes per family in col. 1, lines 8–14. The allocation between children and adults within each size class of families is estimated on the basis of the distribution shown in Bureau of the Census, *Census of Population 1970, Subject Reports, Final Report PC(2)-4A, Family Composition* (Washington, D.C., 1973), table 3, pp. 7 ff., and table 7, pp. 55 ff. (henceforth cited as *Census of Population 1970*). The census data yield a somewhat higher proportion of children to total population in the families than is indicated in the *Income in 1969* data, and we adjusted the ratios proportionately. The discrepancy just noted is due largely to the inclusion of persons in college dormitories in their parental homes in the coverage in *Income in 1969*, whereas the census totals place this group among those in group quarters, i.e., outside the family and household population; see Bureau of the Census, *Census of Population 1970, Subject Reports, Final Report PC(2)-4B, Persons by Family Characteristics* (Washington, D.C., 1973), table 1, p. xi. The needed adjustment was, however, quite small, involving a reduction of the total of children and their ratios to all persons within each size class by about 2.5%.

[a] The entries are as follows: Columns 1, 2, 5, and 6 – total number of families and persons, all in million. The data, and all other demographic data, refer to March 1970; the income data refer to the calendar year 1969. The entries in cols. 3 and 4 are the average (arithmetic mean) number of children and of adults per family. The entries in cols. 7 and 8 are the percentages of children and of adults in the total population within the families.

[b] The entries in cols. 1 and 2 are the arithmetic mean income (in $) per family and per person, for the country as a whole. Those in cols. 3–5 are the sums of entries in the corresponding columns, lines 8–13; and so are the entries in cols. 6–8.

[c] The entries here are the measures of disparity or inequality, derivable from the distributions of families by number of persons, by number of children, and by number of adults (all in panel A); and of families by income per family and of persons by family income per person (derivable from panels A and B). As indicated in the discussion of these measures in the text, we expect to find an additive relation between the measures for distribution of families by children and adults and by total persons, when the measures for *F-Pc* and *F-Pa* are weighted by the proportions of children and adults in the total population within families. We also expect to find an additive relation between the measures for distribution of families by the number of persons, and the two measures for *F-Y* and *P-Y*, respectively.

[d] Given the tiny share of children in the population of persons in two person families, the latter group is identified here as that of adults without children. With this identification, the percentage shares in cols. 1 and 2 of panel D are derivable directly from cols. 7 and 8, lines 1–7 and 8–14. The entry in line 20, col. 3 is the TDM for the disparity between *P* and *Y* of the three broad groups. It can be compared with the TDM for *P-Y*, in line 15, col. 7.

substantial magnitudes. As the discussion in the paper cited in footnote 1 indicates, given the *positive* correlation between per family income and family size and the *negative* correlation between per person income and family size (see cols. 1 and 2 of panel B), the TDM (or Ginis) for size differences among families is the *minimum* to which the TDMs (or Ginis) for income per family and per person income, for the same size classes, should add. And, indeed, we find in Table 11.1 that the TDMs for *F-Y* and *P-Y*, 11.6 and 26.8, add to 38.4, slightly larger than the 38.0 shown for *F-P* (line 15); and that the relevant Gini coefficients, 0.074 and 0.175, add to 0.249, compared with 0.248 (line 16).

If size differentials among families were of magnitudes smaller or larger than those shown in Table 11.1, and the associations between income and family size remained in the directions indicated, the TDMs (or Ginis) for *F-Y*, or for *P-Y*, or for both would have to differ from those in Table 11.1. The income disparity of particular interest here is that among size classes of families by per person income – for it may be viewed as a direct contribution to the overall distribution of income among the population by per capita income, a far more significant distribution than the usual one among families by income per family.

If the size differentials among families are the dominant factor that produces the associated disparities in family income per family and in family income per person, the sum of TDM (or Ginis) of *F-Y* and *P-Y* will roughly equal TDM or Gini for *F-P* (but never fall short of it). Consequently, the larger the *F-Y* disparity, the smaller will be the *P-Y* income disparity. The *F-Y* disparity will be larger if the upward movement of per family income is greater with a rise in family size, and it will be smaller the less the family income rises as the number of persons in the family rises. If then the distribution is like the one shown in Table 11.1, with TDM (or Gini) for *F-Y*, at 11.6 (or 0.074), being less than a third of the *F-P* measures (or of the sum of the measures for *F-Y* and *P-Y*), and the TDM (or Gini) for *P-Y* is over two-thirds, the finding is due to the very limited rise in income per family (in col. 1 of panel B) with the marked rise in the size of family. The movement is only from $8.8 thousand for the two-person family to a peak of $12.2 thousand for the five- and six-person family – a rise of only about 40% – while the number of persons rises by a factor of 2.5–3. No wonder per person income, in column 2 of panel B, drops so precipitously, from $4.4 thousand in the two-person group to $1.4 thousand in the largest size group (with an average of 8.2 persons per family) – a drop to less than a third.

One clue to an explanation of the limited magnitude of the rise in per family income in column 1 of panel B is provided by the movement of number of *adults* per family, for the size classes of families, in column 4 of panel A. While the number of adults per family rises as family size increases, the rise in the former is quite limited as compared with the rise in the number of children, with the result that the ratio of adults to children declines sharply as size of family rises (compare cols. 3 and 4 of panel A). If it can be assumed that children, as defined in Table 11.1, contribute little to the income of the family,[5] and hence that the adults are by far the major contributors to family income, the limited rise in the number of adults per family is one factor in the limited rise of family income in column 1 of panel B.

But it is not the only factor, since income per family *declines* from a peak in the five-person family, while the number of adults per family *rises* in families larger than five persons each. Such a result may be due to the existence of socioeconomic groups, some of which are characterized by a lower income per family, and yet a larger number of both children and adults per family, than other groups. To use an illustration at hand relating to households, including one-person households in the United States for 1969–70:[6] in the 6.95 million households with head among professional, technical, and kindred workers, children under 18 averaged 1.283 per household and adults averaged 2.073 – whereas for 8.68 million households with head among craftsmen, foremen, and kindred workers the averages per household were 1.493 children under 18 and 2.276 adults. Yet the average annual income per household for the professional group was $14.7 thousand, and that per household for the craftsmen group was $11.1 thousand. Obviously, as we moved up the size classes of household by number of persons, in the larger size classes there was

5   This would certainly be true of income from labor service, but may also be true of pure property incomes. The labor force participation ratio for the United States in 1970 is shown as 0.6% for population age 0–14, 42.5% for population age 15–19, and 51.4% for population 20–24 years of age (see International Labour Office, *Labour Force 1950–2000, Estimates and Projections* [Geneva, 1977], vol. 4, table 2, p. 9). If we assume that the total population age 15–17 is 70% of that for the 5-year class 15–19, and that the labor force participation ratio for the 15–17 age class is 33% (which implies a participation ratio of 65% for the 18–19 subclass), the overall labor force participation ratio for the population of children under 18 works out to 6.5%. In terms of possible labor *income* the fraction would be much smaller.

6   See Bureau of the Census, *Current Population Reports*, Series P-60, no. 72 (Washington, D.C., August 1970), table 5, p. 15 (hereafter cited as *CPR*).

likely to have been a greater proportion of craftsmen households, which would have depressed the average income per household and yet raised the average number of both children and adults per household.

The reasons for the limited rise in adults per family as the average size of family rises to over eight persons can be explored, even if tentatively, at a later junction – in connection with Table 11.2, where families are classified by number of children (not of persons) and then the level of adults per family with zero, one, two, etc., children is determined. Here the comparison of the movements of the number of adults and children per family, in columns 4 and 3 of panel A, may be seen to bear on the second major finding suggested by Table 11.1 – the role of children in making for the wide size differentials among families by number of persons – and consequently also making for larger inequality in the distribution of per person income among the size classes in panel B (i.e., the inequality measured by a TDM of 26.8 and a Gini coefficient of 0.175).

Panel A shows that the size differentials among families by number of persons can be decomposed into inequalities among families in terms of children per family and in terms of adults per family – both for the common size classes by the number of persons. This decomposition is provided in line 15, in which the TDM for F-Pc, 85.6, weighted by the proportion of children in total population (0.376), or 32.2, plus the TDM for F-Pa, 9.4, weighted by the proportion of adults in total population (0.624), or 5.9, add to 38.1 (as compared with 38.0, for F-P). Thus, while children account for only 37.6% of total population, they contribute over 80% of the disparity among families by size as measured by the number of persons. The decomposition in terms of Ginis yields the same results. In other words, given the wide disparity between families by number of persons and the distribution of children within these size classes, it is the presence of children that is largely responsible for the wide inequality in size of families. Were the children eliminated, and only adults allocated among the families in the manner observed in panel A, TDM (F-P) would have been only 9.4, compared with that of 38.0, and the Gini coefficient would have been only 0.064 instead of 0.248.[7]

---

7 This is literally true only if, while omitting all children, we retain the size classes by number of persons now shown in panels A and B. If, combined with omission of children, we were to allow a reclassification of families by number of adults, the distribution would show a greater range in number of adults per family. But the point is that we are interested here in the contribution of children (and adults) to size differentials among families by the *total* number of persons per family

If the same assumption of omitting all children is applied, while retaining the size classes and the series of income per family now in column 1 of panel B, the income per person in column 2 of panel B becomes, for successive size classes, $4,530; $4,630; $5,066; $5,009; $4,739; and $3,890. The pattern, then, is not a sustained and marked decline in per person income, but a rise from the two-person to the four-person families and then a moderate decline except in the top size class. With this change, TDM, $P\text{-}Y$, becomes 5.2, instead of the 26.8 TDM now shown in line 15. In other words, just as with the omission of all children the TDM, $H\text{-}P$, dropped to less than a quarter of its value, so did the associated TDM, $P\text{-}Y$, drop to less than a fifth of its value.

Finally, to complete the notes on the findings in Table 11.1, we observe the classification, in panel D, of population into three large groups: one comprises all children in the families, the second comprises all adults in families without children (here approximated by adults in two-person families, although, as panel A shows, these units do include a tiny proportion of children); and the third consists of adults in families with children.

The aspect of this classification that is of interest and worth noting is that the average income of adults in families with children is higher than the average income of children, although these adults and children are members of the identical group of families. The reason for this result is that, within the same group of families, children are more concentrated in the larger families, and hence in the low-income-per-person families, than are the adults – their cohabiting relations. This difference will be even more important in dealing with distributions of families by number of children rather than of persons.

These latter distributions show the number of families with no children, one child, and so on up to six or more children, and also reveal the per family income for each of these number-of-children classes. But in order to derive from these distributions measures of the type shown in Table 11.1, it is necessary to estimate the number of adults per family in each class by the number of children per family. Fortunately, data are available to make such an estimate possible, abundantly for March 1970 and adequately for a few other years. The data in Table 11.2 relate to

– for it is the latter that are given to us by the data, and result in the income disparities per person with which we are concerned. This comment applies also to the inferences in the next paragraph, concerning the contribution of children to the $P\text{-}Y$ disparity.

Table 11.2. *Adults (Pa) per family (F) for groups of families by number of children under 18 (Pc), Census and Current Population Reports (CPR) data, United States, March 1970*

Groups by number of children	Families (million) (1)	Persons (million) (2)	Pc (million) (3)	Pa (million) (4)	P/F (5)	Pc/F (6)	Pa/F (7)
Census data, all families							
1. No children	21.66	49.14	0	49.14	2.27	0	2.27
2. One child	9.70	31.19	9.70	21.49	3.22	1.0	2.22
3. Two children	9.00	37.43	18.00	19.43	4.16	2.0	2.16
4. Three and more	10.79	65.04	41.91	23.13	6.03	3.89	2.14
5. Totals and averages	51.15	182.80	69.61	113.19	3.57	1.36	2.21
CPR data, husband–wife families							
6. No children	18.42	41.94	0	41.94	2.28	0	2.28
7. One child	8.33	28.12	8.33	19.79	3.38	1.0	2.38
8. Two children	8.13	34.66	16.27	18.39	4.26	2.0	2.26
9. Three children	4.99	26.33	14.98	11.35	5.28	3.0	2.28
10. Four children	2.53	16.05	10.12	5.93	6.34	4.0	2.34
11. Five and more	2.04	16.35	11.15	5.20	8.02	5.47	2.55
12. Totals and averages	44.44	163.45	60.85	102.60	3.68	1.37	2.31
CPR data, female-headed families							
13. No children	2.217	5.028	0	5.028	2.27	0	2.27
14. One child	1.212	3.112	1.212	1.900	2.57	1.0	1.57
15. Two children	.959	3.408	1.918	1.490	3.55	2.0	1.55
16. Three children	.545	2.575	1.635	.940	4.73	3.0	1.73
17. Four and more	.647	4.218	3.284	.934	6.52	5.08	1.44
18. Totals and averages	5.580	18.341	8.049	10.292	3.29	1.44	1.84
CPR data, husband–wife and female-headed families							
19. No children	20.63	46.97	0	46.97	2.28	0	2.28
20. One child	9.54	31.24	9.54	21.70	3.27	1.0	2.27
21. Two children	9.09	38.07	18.19	19.88	4.19	2.0	2.19
22. Three children	5.54	28.90	16.61	12.29	5.22	3.0	2.22
23. Four and more	5.21	36.62	24.56	12.06	7.02	4.71	2.31
24. Totals and averages	50.02	181.80	68.90	112.90	3.63	1.38	2.26

Note: The totals may not check because of rounding. Lines 1–5 are calculated from the data in *Census of Population 1970*, tables 3 and 7. Lines 6–24 are calculated from *Income in 1969*, used extensively for table 1. The data are from table 19, pp. 43 ff.

March 1970, but there is no basis for assuming that the results for other years would be much different.

The broad result is that the average number of adults per family is roughly the same for the various classes of families distinguished by the number of children per family. Thus the census data in lines 1–4 show a variation in the number of adults per family between 2.14 and 2.27, while the number of children per family varies from 0 to 3.2; and the number of adults per family declines slightly as the number of children per family increases. The Current Population Reports data, the ones that also provide information on income, show for the husband–wife families, the dominant type-of-family group, a variation in the number of adults per family only from 2.28 to 2.38, while the number of children per family varies from 0 to 5.47; and there is relative stability in the adults per family averages, with no evidence of any correlation with numbers of children per family (see lines 6–11, cols. 7 and 6). In one other sizable type-of-family group, that with female heads (indicating the absence of husband), the average number of adults per family is largest in the family with no children (see line 13, col. 7), and that number is well below two in female-headed families with one or more children. The combination of husband–wife and female-headed families – which, for March 1970, accounts for 50 million out of some 51.3 million families – yields an average of adults per family that is relatively constant, while the number of children per family rises from 0 to 4.7 (see lines 19–23, cols. 7 and 6).

It is now possible to consider the reasons for the findings in Tables 11.1 and 11.2 relating to the movement in the number of adults per family: quite moderate rise as families are classified by increasing number of persons; and, somewhat of a surprise, no rise but a rough constancy in the number of adults per family as families are classified by increasing number of children per family. At first glance, the reasons are statistical, but they imply a number of substantive factors.

The statistical reason is that a family is defined so that it must have a minimum of two persons. If the satisfaction of this minimum in the case of two-person families involves as large a number of *adults* per two-person family as 1.94 (see Table 11.1, line 1, col. 4), and the proportion of two-person families in all families is as high as 34.4% (see Table 11.1, line 1, col. 1), then, given an average of adults per family for all families of only 2.26, the possible rise in the number of adults per family in the more-than-two-person classes is quite limited. The average number of adults per family in families with more than two persons will, therefore, be no higher than [(100.0 × 2.26) − (34.4 × 1.94)]: 65.6, or 2.43. Given the admixture of female-headed families among those in the three-, four-, or even five-person classes, the limited progression now shown in Table 11.1, column 4, in adults per family is almost inevitable. Likewise, in the case of the classes by number of children, it will be noted that in Table 11.2 the proportion of families with no children is as high as 21.66/51.15, or 42.3% (see lines 1 and 5, col. 1); the average number of adults per family with no children is well in excess of two (in fact, it is 2.27, see line 1, col. 7), while the overall average of adults per family is somewhat lower, at 2.21 (see line 5, col. 7). The results obtained in Tables 11.1 and 11.2 for the movement of adults per family with rising number of persons or children per family are largely predetermined by the definition of family, with a minimal number of two persons, and the very low average number of adults per family, low in being close to the two-person minimum. The results, the range in the number of adults per family, might have been quite different if we either defined families with a lower minimum – say, one person – or raised the number of adults per family, either by lowering the age of separation between children and adults (e.g., at below 15 rather than below 18) or by assuming, with a given number of children per family, a larger average number of adults per family unit.

It is clear that the definitions with which we operate – of a family unit, of children versus adults – while contributing to the results obtained in Table 11.1 and to be obtained in Table 11.3, have substantive implications and raise substantive questions. Can it be assumed that the population of what the Bureau of the Census calls "unrelated individuals," persons outside of institutions but living outside their own families, either alone or with nonrelatives, are not tied by community of interest to their families and should not be included with the latter? In defining families not only by blood and other ties but also by identity of residence, can it be assumed that there are no significant economic ties among families related by blood or marriage but living in different locations (perhaps on the same street)? And in dealing with societies at different levels of economic and social development, can it be assumed that the division line of under 18 and 18 and over between children and adults can be applied in all countries, and possibly among various economic and social groups within the same country? These questions about the substantive implications of the definitions used in this paper are noted here, and some will recur in later discussion, but they cannot be answered adequately. Still, awareness of them is useful if only to induce probing the substantive significance of the statistical results.

If the effects of including the "unrelated individuals," to be illustrated directly below, are set aside, and it is assumed that the families as defined in the tables here for the United States represent units largely indepen-

Table 11.3. *Children and adults, distribution of families by number of related children under 18, United States, 1969–70*

A. *Shares of families (F), persons (P), children (Pc), and adults (Pa)*
(families grouped by number of children per family)

Groups by number of children	Numbers (in millions)				% in relevant totals				% in P	
	F (1)	Pc (2)	Pa (3)	P (4)	F (5)	P (6)	Pc (7)	Pa (8)	Pc (9)	Pa (10)
1. No children	21.42	0	48.34	48.34	41.8	26.1	0	41.8	0	26.1
2. One child	9.76	9.76	22.01	31.77	19.0	17.1	13.9	19.0	5.2	11.9
3. Two children	9.20	18.41	20.77	39.18	18.0	21.1	26.4	18.0	9.9	11.2
4. Three children	5.58	16.75	12.60	29.35	10.9	15.8	24.0	10.9	9.0	6.8
5. Four children	2.85	11.39	6.43	17.82	5.6	9.7	16.4	5.6	6.2	3.5
6. Five children	1.29	6.43	2.90	9.33	2.5	5.0	9.2	2.5	3.5	1.5
7. Six and over	1.14	7.05	2.56	9.61	2.2	5.2	10.1	2.2	3.8	1.4
8. Totals and averages[a]	51.24	69.79	115.61	185.40	100.0	3.62	1.36	2.26	37.6	62.4

B. *Money income (Y) per person, all persons, children, and adults*

	Y/F ($) (1)	Y/P[b] ($) (2)	Y/P multiplied by proportion in P of:			% in total Y/P of:		
			P (3)	Pc (4)	Pa (5)	Col. 3 (6)	Col. 4 (7)	Col. 5 (8)
9. No children	10,073	4,464	1,165	0	1,165	39.8	0	39.8
10. One child	10,752	3,302	565	172	393	19.3	5.9	13.4
11. Two children	11,145	2,618	552	259	293	18.9	8.9	13.4
12. Three children	11,242	2,139	338	193	145	11.6	6.6	5.0
13. Four children	11,067	1,769	172	110	62	5.9	3.8	2.1
14. Five children	10,267	1,415	71	50	21	2.4	1.7	.7
15. Six and over	9,806	1,158	60	44	16	2.1	1.5	.6
16. Totals and averages[c]	10,577	2,923	2,923	828	2,095	100.0	28.4	71.6

C. *Measures of disparity among families[d]*

	Families by number of persons (F-P) (1)	Families by number of children (F-Pc) (2)	Families by number of adults (F-Pa) (3)	Col. 2 × proportion of Pc (4)	Col. 3 × proportion of Pa (5)	Families by Y-F (F-Y) (6)	Persons by Y-P (P-Y) (7)
17. TDMs	35.2	93.8	0	35.3	0	4.4	31.8
18. Ginis	.224	.596	0	.224	0	.025	.207

Table 11.3 *(cont.)*

D. *Derivation of income disparity among three groups: children (Pc), adults with children (Pca), and adults without children (Paa)*[e]

	% in total P (1)	% in total Y (2)	Difference (3)	Per person Income relative (4)	Income ($) (5)
19. *Pc*	37.6	28.4	−9.2	.755	2,207
20. *Pca*	36.3	31.8	−4.5	.876	2,561
21. *Paa*	28.1	39.8	13.7	1.525	4,458
22. Total, TDM, average	100.0	100.0	27.4	1.000	2,923

Note: The estimate of the number of adults in the groups distinguished in the vertical stub was based on the assumption that the average number of adults per family was the same in each number-of-children class. The rough average was 2.26, but in my calculations I used the more detailed figure of 2.2564. The data, combined with the assumption, permitted all the calculations the results of which are summarized in Table 11.3.
[a] The entries are: cols. 1–4 – totals of families, children, adults and all persons within families, in million; cols. 6–8 – average number per family, all persons, children, adults.
[b] Calculated by dividing the income per family by the number of persons per family in the classes in the vertical stub. This number per family equals the changing number of children plus a constant average of adult persons per family in the successive children per family classes.
[c] Entries in cols. 1 and 2 are the countrywide averages of money income per family and per person. Those in cols. 3–5 are the sums of entries in the corresponding columns, line 9–15; and so are the entries in cols. 6–8.
[d] See comments on panel C in Table 11.1.
[e] See comments on panel D in Table 11.1. The entry in line 22, col. 3 is the TDM, measuring the per person income disparity among the three broad groups distinguished. It should be compared with the TDM (P-Y) in line 17, col. 7.
Sources: The basic data in panel A, col. 1, the totals of children, all persons, and hence adults (line 8, cols. 2–4), and the average income per family, in lines 10–17, col. 1 of panel B, are all taken directly from *Income in 1969*, table 19. The entries in col. 2, lines 1–7, were then calculated by multiplying the numbers of families by children per family (including the top open-end class of over six children, which worked out to average 6.21).

dent of each other in their decisions on securing and spending of income, the results in Table 11.2 do carry a major significant finding. It is to the effect that in 1970, and probably in other years, families differed widely in the number of children, while the number of associated adults was about the same, whether the family had no children or had as many as four or well over. And the groups of families involved in such a disparate combination of children and adults, with such different "dependency" ratios, were quite large. Thus for the combination of husband–wife and female-headed families, families with four or more children numbered over 5 million, and the 24.6 million children in them were over a third of all children (see lines 23 and 24).

This finding carries two implications. The first is that the cross-section distribution of families by number of children of the type shown in lines 19–23, column 1, of Table 11.2, for the combined total of husband–wife and female-headed families, is not compatible with the assumption that almost all families have, over time, the same number of children over the life-cycle span of the family. In other words, the implication is of substantial differences among families in the number of children, even when cumulated over the lifetime of the family (including or excluding the few years of separate life of the future adult members of the family, past childhood, terminable at age 18, and before forming the family unit). This important implication of the cross section for the long-term characteristics of the family unit and its child and adult members in the movement over time will be treated in a later section of this paper.

The second implication was already suggested in the discussion of Table 11.1. If the number of adults, the major source of income of the family, barely changes with increase in the number of children and hence in the size of the family, one should expect that income per family, in the distribution by the number of children, would show even a milder rise in moving toward the classes with a larger number of children per family. Hence, the TDM or Gini coefficient for the disparity F-Y would be smaller than that found for the distribution by number of persons in Table 11.1. Conversely, the resulting disparity in family income per capita, the TDM or Gini for the disparity in family income per capita, F-Y, would be larger than in Table 11.1.

This is what we find in Table 11.3, which parallels Table 11.1, with the major difference that now the distribution is among families by number of children rather than by the number of persons.

Comparing first the movements of per family income in panel B of Tables 11.1 and 11.3, the rise in the latter table from about $10 thousand for families with no children to $11.2 thousand for families with three children is, at about 12%, much milder than the rise from $8.8 thousand for families of two persons to $12.2 thousand for families of five and six persons. Conversely, the decline in per family income in Table 11.3 from $11.2 thousand for families with three children to $9.8 thousand for families with six children and more is more marked than the drop in Table 11.1 from $12.2 thousand for families with five or six persons to $11.5 thousand for families with seven and more persons.

Because of this milder rise (and sharper decrease) in income per family in panel B of Table 11.3 than in the same panel of Table 11.1, the disparity between families and income, F-Y, is appreciably lower in Table 11.3: the relevant TDM and Gini are 4.4 and 0.025, respectively, compared with 11.6 and 0.074 in Table 11.1. However, the disparities in the distribution of income per person, for classes of families and persons by number of children, are wider in Table 11.3, reflecting more fully the effects of the presence and unequal distribution of the number of children. The relevant measures, for P-Y, are a TDM and Gini in Table 11.3 of 31.8 and 0.207, compared with 26.8 and 0.175 in Table 11.1. Thus, despite the lowering of the spread of size differences in the distribution of families by number of persons in Table 11.3, measured by a TDM of 35.2 and a Gini coefficient of 0.224 (compared with 38.0 and 0.248 in Table 11.1), the fuller reflection of the effects of differences in number of children results in a P-Y disparity, reflecting only differences in number of children and allowing for no variation in number of adults, that is substantially greater than the P-Y disparity revealed by the distribution of families by number of persons in Table 11.1.

To put it briefly: if the effect of differing numbers of children on the per person income of families is allowed for, the P-Y disparity thus contributed to the total distribution of income is measured by a TDM of 31.8 and a Gini coefficient of 0.207. The total disparity in the distribution of household income per person in the total population within families for the United States in that year is approximated by a TDM of 53.8 and a Gini coefficient of 0.371.[8] While the measures are not directly additive, it is difficult to avoid the conclusion that the unequal distribution of children is a major contributor to inequality in the distribution of household income per person among the population.

This conclusion is clear also in the comparison of panel D in Table 11.3 with that in Table 11.1. This panel derives income disparities among three groups of persons: children; adults in families with children; and adults in families without children. In panel D of Table 11.1, the average incomes of these three large subgroups of the total population within families were $2,402, $2,750, and $4,392, respectively, and the TDM (P-Y) for the three groups was 18.6. In panel D of Table 11.3, the average incomes for the children and for adults in families with children are $2,207 and $2,561, about 10% lower than in Table 11.1; while the average income for adults in families without children in Table 11.3, at $4,458, is about 3% higher. The TDM (P-Y) for the three large groups is as high as 27.4

8 The measures are taken from Chapter 7, above, Table 7.10.

in Table 11.3, and there is a more marked excess of the income per person for adults within families with children than for the children in the same families.

It was already noted that the substantive meaning of these findings depends upon the validity of the assumptions implicit in the definition of units such as families or households and in the lines of distinction between children and adults – assumptions as to the relative independence of families from each other in securing and disposing of income, and as to the nature of children as pure dependents and of adults as income providers. Before shifting to the next section, one should add that a similar argument is applicable to our use of money income as it is defined in our data. According to this definition (see *Income in 1969*, p. 6), money income includes receipts, before taxes, of wages, salaries, and related payments; net income from self-employment, farm and nonfarm; a variety of property incomes, such as dividends, interest, net rent, royalties; and a variety of transfers, including "regular contributions from persons not living in the households." If different definitions of income were to have been used, whether expanded to include both income in kind and services of family members within the family, whether extended over periods longer than a year to reduce transitory components, whether adjusted for differences in purchasing power of the money incomes among various socioeconomic groups, the results would most likely be different magnitudes of per person income disparities between children and adults. But the recognition of these possibly preferable, but more difficult, alternatives should not bar the attempt to explore the more narrowly defined available data, so long as we recognize their limitations.

III. Inclusion of unrelated individuals

This discussion has dealt so far with families, groups of at least two persons, each group with two defining characteristics: all members are related by blood, marriage, or adoption ties; and all members live together in the same housing unit.[9] The total of families, so defined, falls short

---

9 A housing unit is defined as "a house, an apartment or other group of rooms, or a single room . . . occupied or intended for occupancy as separate living quarters; that is, when the occupants do not live and eat with any other persons in the structure and there is either (1) direct access from outside or through a common hall or (2) a kitchen or cooking equipment for the exclusive use of the occupants" (see *Income in 1969*, p. 8).

of what might be called household population (i.e., population outside of institutions, such as jails, barracks, etc.), and I shall now account for the omission.

The difference between the population in families and that in households – a household consisting of all persons, related and unrelated, who occupy the same housing unit – is accounted for by unrelated individuals, defined (again in *Income in 1969*, p. 9) as "persons 14 years old and over (other than inmates of institutions) who are not living with any relatives." *Income in 1969* shows that for March 1970, the population of unrelated individuals amounted to 14.45 million persons (see table 17, p. 35), which, added to 185.40 million persons in families (see table 18, p. 42), yields a total of 199.85 million persons. This can be compared with the total number of persons in households of 199.38 million (see *CPR*, table 5, p. 15).

To complete describing the relation between families and unrelated individuals, on the one hand, and households, on the other, it is necessary to introduce the distinction, within families, between primary and secondary families, and that within unrelated individuals between primary and secondary individuals. A primary family is one the head of which is the head of the household, whereas a secondary family is one that lives in the housing quarters of the primary family to which it is not related (e.g., husband and wife who are lodgers in the housing unit inhabited by a primary family, with no blood, marriage, or adoption ties between the two families). *Income in 1969* indicates that out of the total of 51,237 thousand families in March 1970, as many as 51,110 thousand were primary families (for the latter figure, see table 39, p. 83), thus leaving a residual of only 127 thousand secondary families. The latter, by the way, were characterized by a much lower income per family than was true of the primary families.

A primary individual is one who lives in a household, either alone or with other primary individuals to whom he is not related. A secondary individual is a "person, such as a lodger, guest, or resident employee, who is not related to any other person in the household" (*Income in 1969*, p. 9). *Income in 1969* shows that, for March 1970, of the 14.45 million unrelated individuals, 11.76 million were primary individuals and 2.69 million were secondary individuals. The sums of primary families cited above (51.11 million) and of primary unrelated individuals (11.76 million) yield a total that should equal that of all households, the latter being in fact 62.87 million (see *CPR*, table 5, p. 15). It should be noted, however, that the total of primary unrelated individuals, 11.76 million, is larger than the number of one-person households, 10.69 million. The discrepancy is accounted for by the primary unrelated individuals who form households of more than one person; table 1 of *CPR* (p. 11) indicates over a million of two-, three-, and four-person households with members unrelated to each other.

In Table 11.4 all unrelated individuals, viewed as adults, are added to the population in families as classified by the number of related children under 18. Before commenting on the effects of this extension of the covered population on inequality in per person income generated by differences in number of children per family, some relevant characteristics of the population of unrelated individuals should be noted.

Of the 14.45 million unrelated individuals, 5.44 million, or 37.6%, were male and 9.01 million, or 62.4%, were female. But this dominance of females was due to the greater number of unrelated females in the advanced ages. Unrelated individuals aged under 55 years accounted for only 6.10 million, of whom 3.21 million were male and 2.89 million were female. But unrelated individuals 55 years old or older added up to 8.35 million, of whom 2.23 were male and as many as 6.12 million were female. This preponderance of females concentrated in the older ages was due in part to the survival of females to older age than related males (their husbands). But that the surviving widows should have, in the United States, formed independent households with a single person in each must have been due to distinctive institutional patterns of family structure, patterns that have not prevailed in the United States in the earlier past and are not observed in the economically less developed countries in recent years.

Given the dominance among unrelated individuals of the more advanced age groups of 55 and over, and particularly of older women, it is somewhat of a surprise to find that the per person income of all unrelated individuals, at $4.25 thousand, is only slightly below the per person income of families with no children ($4.46 thousand) and greatly in excess of the per person income of all other families with one or more children (see Table 11.4, panel 5, col. 1). It may be that among the older men and women, only those who can afford it establish separate households rather than remain members of a related younger family, so that only older men and women with higher than average per person income enter the group reported in line 9a of Table 11.4.

Comparing Table 11.4 with Table 11.3, we find that the inclusion of

Table 11.4. *Children and adults, Table 11.3 supplemented by inclusion of unrelated individuals (U)*

A. *Shares of families (F) and unrelated individuals (U), persons (P), children (Pc), adults (Pa), groups by number of children per family (F)*[a]

Groups	% in relevant totals			% in P	
	F,U (1)	P (2)	Pa (3)	Pc (4)	Pa (5)
1a. U	22.0	7.2	11.1	0	7.2
1b. F, no children	32.6	24.2	37.2	0	24.2
2. F, one child	14.9	15.9	16.9	4.9	11.0
3. F, two children	14.0	19.6	16.0	9.2	10.4
4. F, three children	8.5	14.7	9.7	8.4	5.3
5. F, four children	4.3	8.9	4.9	5.7	3.2
6. F, five children	2.0	4.7	2.2	3.2	1.5
7. F, six and more children	1.7	4.8	2.0	3.5	1.3
8. Totals	65.69	199.85	130.06	34.9	65.1

B. *Money income per person, all persons, children, and adults*[b]

Groups	Y/P $ (1)	Y/P multiplied by proportion in P of:			% in total Y/P of:		
		P (2)	Pc (3)	Pa (4)	Col. 2 (5)	Col. 3 (6)	Col. 4 (7)
9a. U	4,248	306	0	306	10.1	0	10.1
9b. F, no children	4,464	1,080	0	1,080	35.8	0	35.8
10. F, one child	3,302	525	162	363	17.4	5.4	12.0
11. F, two children	2,618	513	241	272	17.0	8.0	9.0
12. F, three children	2,139	314	179	135	10.4	5.9	4.5
13. F, four children	1,769	157	101	56	5.2	3.3	1.9
14. F, five children	1,415	67	46	21	2.2	1.5	.7
15. F, six and more children	1,158	56	41	15	1.9	1.4	.5
16. Totals and average	3,018	3,018	770	2,248	100.0	25.5	74.5

C. *Measures of disparity among related groups*[b]

	FU by number of persons (FU-P) (1)	FU by number of children (FU-Pc) (2)	FU by number of adults (FU-Pa) (3)	Col. 2 by proportion of Pc (4)	Col. 3 by proportion of Pa (5)	FU by Y/FU (FU-Y) (6)	Persons by Y/P (P-Y) (7)
17. TDMs	46.6	111.2	21.8	38.8	14.3	23.8	32.0

Table 11.4 *(cont.)*

D. *Derivation of income disparities among three groups: children (Pc); adults with children (Pca); and adults without children (Paa)*[b]

	% in P (1)	% in Y (2)	Difference (3)	Per person Income Relative (4)	Income ($) (5)
18. *Pc*	34.9	25.5	−9.4	.731	2,206
19. *Pca*	33.7	28.6	−5.1	.849	2,562
20. *Paa*	31.4	45.9	14.5	1.462	4,412
21. Total, TDM, average	100.0	100.0	29.0	1.000	3,018

Note: Unrelated individuals are "persons 14 years old and over (other than inmates of institutions) who are not living with any relatives. An unrelated individual may constitute a one-person household by himself, or he may be part of a household including one or more families or unrelated individuals, or he may reside in group quarters such as a rooming house" (*Income in 1969*, p. 9). Female, as well as male, unrelated individuals are referred to in the sentence just quoted. The calculation assumes that all unrelated individuals are 18 years of age and over, i.e., adults in the sense the term is used here. This is not correct, since the definition above allows for unrelated individuals down to 14 years of age; but it was impossible to allocate the younger individuals among the number-of-children classes. The error, however, is quite small, as the comparison of the number of children in Tables 11.3 and 11.4, 69.79 million (which does not include any unrelated individuals), with that in the data on households (*CPR*, table 15) of 70.19 million (which includes the younger unrelated individuals), demonstrates. The difference is 0.4 million, out of a total of 14.45 million.
[a] The number of children and their distribution among children-per-family classes remains as given in Table 11.3 (see col. 2, lines 1–8). The *U* units are, by definition, without children. The entries in line 8 are, in millions: total number of families and unrelated individuals (col. 1); total persons in the population of families and unrelated individuals (col. 2); and total of adult persons in that population (col. 3).
[b] See notes to these panels in Tables 11.1 and 11.3 above. The TDM in line 21, col. 3, is to be compared with that in line 17, col. 7.
Sources: All the data, except those relating to number and average money income of unrelated individuals, are from Table 11.3; and hence from *Income in 1969*, which provides the bases for Tables 11.3 and 11.1. The data on unrelated individuals are from the same source, table 17, p. 35.

unrelated individuals results in a wider inequality in the distribution of the units (families and unrelated individuals, or FU) by numbers of adults, and hence also by the number of persons. Thus, the relevant TDMs between *F* and *P* in Table 11.3 were 35.2 for *F-P*, 35.3 for (*F-Pc*) weighted, and 0 for (*F-Pa*) weighted, whereas in Table 11.4 the comparable TDMs become 46.4 for *FU-P*, 36.6 for (*FU-Pc*) weighted, and 14.3 for (*FU-Pa*) weighted (see line 17 in both tables). Also, the inequality in income per unit in Table 11.4 is appreciably wider than that in income per family in Table 11.3, the relevant TDMs being 23.8 for *FU-Y* and only 4.4 for *F-Y* (line 17, both tables).

By contrast, the effects of inclusion of unrelated individuals on income disparities in per person income, of most relevance to this discussion as a measure of contribution to the more meaningful overall distribution of income among the population by income per capita, are quite small. The TDM for P-Y in Table 11.4, at 32.0, is barely above that in Table 11.3, at 31.8 (line 17, both tables). The TDMs for income disparities among the three major population groups in panel D of Tables 11.3 and 11.4 show a somewhat greater rise, from 27.4 to 29.0, but even so the rise is moderate. The limited range of these effects, as compared with those on inequality in size of units and disparities in total income per unit, is due to the fact that the weight of unrelated individuals in total persons, at 7.2%, is so much smaller than their weight in total of all units, at over 22%; and that per person income of unrelated individuals, at $4,248, is not that much higher than the per person income of all adults in families (which could be computed from panel D of Table 11.3 at $3,250 per adult).

This comparison can be concluded by suggesting that the effects just described would be found, on a somewhat reduced scale, in drawing a similar comparison between households of two persons and over (analogous to all families in Table 11.3) and all households including one-person units (analogous to Table 11.4), both sets classified by the number of children in the household. Here also, the effects on the distribution by total income per household, so widely used, would be quite substantial – the more so, the larger the proportion of one-person households in the total. Yet the more significant comparison of income on a per person basis would show only minor differences associated with the inclusion of one-person units.

IV. The life-cycle aspects

The central question here bears on the relation of disparities in the distribution and per person income between children and adults, of the type shown in Tables 11.2, 11.3, and 11.4, to the life cycle of the family. It was suggested, in the comments above on Table 11.2, that the distribution of families by the number of related children, shown in that table (and in Table 11.3), is not compatible with the assumption that all families have a roughly similar pattern of children over the family's life cycle, similar with respect to numbers of children if not fully in respect to their timing within the life span. Were such an assumption valid, it would have meant that for the cumulative numbers and per capita income over the full life span of the family unit there would be *no* substantial differences among families in the average number of children and in the per person income among children and adults – and, therefore, no transferable differentials in lifetime income from one generation to the next – arising out of this particular demographic factor. I shall return to this question here; and, in order to simplify matters, discuss it in application to families. The inclusion of unrelated individuals, while affecting the parameters slightly, would not modify the reasoning.

The lack of validity of the assumption could be demonstrated in two ways. In the first, the families are viewed as continuous units within the assumed life span – from, say, formation at age of head 22, beginning of year, to dissolution at the end of age of head 70, a span of 49 years. This view neglects the limited dissolution within the life span which can be produced by premature death or by divorce. If so, a family with, say, six children could have reached that status only by a succession of preceding births within that family (neglecting shift of related children into the family from elsewhere). And, given the short childbearing life span, the span of the antecedent births should have been limited enough to allow for subsequent reduction in the number of children as they attain the dividing age line of 18 years, well before the dissolution of the family assumed to occur at age of head 70.

With such continuity in the life span of a given family, and limited differences in the timing patterns, the assumption that each family has the same number of total children would imply that the cross-section distribution of families by number of related children under 18 present varies from zero to the largest number of children, the latter the *same* for all families. To illustrate: assume that a cohort of families, all formed at age of head 22, would have the first child at 23 and then proceed to have a maximum of three children, spaced at 6-year intervals (so that the last of the three would be born at age of head 35 and "leave" the family at age of head 52, end of year). Keeping the assumption of continuity to exclude deaths within the span considered (under 18 for children and under 71 for adults), and distributing the family years among years with differing numbers of children in the family, it would be found that, for each family, out of the total of 49 family years, 19 were with zero children; 12 each were with one and two children, respectively; six were with three children; and none were with more than three children. It should be noted that in this illustration the average number of children per family year is as high as 1.10, within range of the average of 1.36 per family found in Table 11.3.[10]

This argument implies that in an overall distribution of families and children by the age-of-head classes, the averaging that takes place is not of families with roughly the same number of children ever born (and, by the conditions of the argument, all assumed to survive, at least until they pass the dividing age of 18) – but of families with widely different numbers of children ever born. Reference to Table 11.3, panel A, shows a range, not from zero to three children, indicated in the illustration in the preceding paragraph, but from one to over six. This means that even when cumulated over the total life span of a family, about 50 years, the average number of children per family, and hence the average per person income of children and of associated adults, would differ substantially.

In this connection, the actual distribution of the same population of families for the United States for March 1970 that was covered in the earlier tables should be noted, but this time the distribution of persons, children, and adults is for classes of families by age of head (Table 11.5). The table parallels Table 11.3 and should be compared with the latter.

One important aspect of the comparison is the sharp reduction in the inequality in the distribution of families by number of children – from a TDM for families and children (F-PC) of 93.8 in Table 11.3 (line 9) to 56.0 in Table 11.5 (line 9). And such a reduction could have been expected from observing that the range in children per family in Table 11.5 is from 0.15 to 2.54, compared with that from zero to well over six in Table 11.3. And whereas the range of the number of children per family in Table 11.5 could easily have been duplicated by assuming all families had about three children within the life span, the juxtaposition of the two tables completes the judgment that the averaging for Table 11.5 was of families with widely divergent numbers of children ever born – which, given the assumption of continuity in family units over their life span, yields the conclusion that numbers of children per family must have differed widely even when cumulated over the total span from formation to dissolution.

With disparities in the distribution of children among family classes by age of head so much narrower than in the distribution among classes

10 For more detailed illustrations of model types of families with different numbers of children assumed for each, see tables and discussion in the next section.

Table 11.5. *Children and adults, distribution of families by age of head, United States, 1969–70*

A. *Shares of families (F), persons (P), children (Pc), and adults (Pa), families grouped by age of head*

Age-of-head classes (years)	% in F (1)	P/F (2)	Pc/F (3)	Pa/F (4)	% share in relevant totals			% in P	
					P (5)	Pc (6)	Pa (7)	Pc (8)	Pa (9)
1. 14–24	6.9	2.85	0.92	1.93	5.4	4.8	5.9	1.8	3.6
2. 25–34	20.7	3.96	2.01	1.95	22.7	30.4	18.0	11.5	11.2
3. 35–44	21.3	4.72	2.54	2.18	27.7	39.6	20.5	14.9	12.8
4. 45–54	21.1	3.79	1.23	2.56	22.2	19.1	24.0	7.2	15.0
5. 55–64	16.2	2.84	0.39	2.45	12.7	4.6	17.6	1.7	11.0
6. 65 and over	13.8	2.44	0.15	2.29	9.3	1.5	14.0	0.5	8.8
7. Totals and averages	51.24	3.62	1.36	2.26	185.40	69.79	115.61	37.6	62.4

B. *Money income (Y) per person, all persons, children, and adults*

Age-of-head classes (years)	Y/F $ (1)	Y/P $ (2)	Y/P multiplied by proportion in P of:			% in total Y/P of:		
			P (3)	Pc (4)	Pa (5)	Col. 3 (6)	Col. 4 (7)	Col. 5 (8)
8. 14–24	6,842	2,401	130	43	87	4.4	1.4	3.0
9. 25–34	9,942	2,511	570	289	281	19.5	9.9	9.6
10. 35–44	11,974	2,537	703	378	325	24.0	12.9	11.1
11. 45–54	12,933	3,412	757	245	512	25.9	8.4	17.5
12. 55–64	11,353	3,998	508	68	440	17.4	2.3	15.1
13. 65 and over	6,722	2,755	256	14	242	8.8	0.5	8.3
14. Totals and averages	10,577	2,923	2,924	1,037	1,887	100.0	35.4	64.6

C. *Measures of disparity among related groups*

	F by number of persons (F-P) (1)	F by number of children (F-Pc) (2)	F by number of adults (F-Pa) (3)	Col. 2 by Proportion of Pc (4)	Col. 3 by Proportion of Pa (5)	F by Y/F (F-Y) (6)	Persons by Y/P (P-Y) (7)
15. TDMs	19.0	56.0	9.0	21.1	5.6	17.4	16.8

Table 11.5 *(cont.)*

D. *Derivation of income disparity among three groups:*
children (Pc); adults in families with children (Pca);
adults in families with no (or few) children (Paa)

	% in P (1)	% in Y (2)	Difference (3)	Per person Income relative (4)	Per person Income ($) (5)
16. Pc	37.6	35.4	−2.2	.941	2,753
17. Pca	42.6	41.2	−1.4	.967	2,828
18. Paa	19.8	23.4	3.6	1.182	3,456
19. Totals, TDM, averages	100.0	100.0	7.2	1.000	2,924

Note: For explanation of entries in lines 7, 14, and 15, see the notes on comparable lines in Tables 11.1 and 11.3. For panel D, the 55–64 and 65 and over age classes were taken to represent adults in families almost without children (*Paa*).
Sources: The basic data on number of families and money income per family by age of head are from *Income in 1969*, table 17, pp. 35 ff. The numbers of persons, children, and adults, per family in the age-of-head classes were estimated from the numbers of persons, children, and adults per household for classes of households by age of head (see *CPR*, p. 15, the data omitting the one-person households). A slight adjustment was required to bring the totals of children and adults to those established for families in Table 11.3 (or Table 11.1). But comparison of panel A here with panel A in Table 11.6 below, which shows the data of children and adults per household for households of two persons or more, reveals the closeness of the two sets of ratios.

by number of children, one would expect the disparities in the distribution of all persons among age-of-head classes in Table 11.5 to be narrower than that of all persons among number-of-children classes in Table 11.3. Indeed, the comparable TDMs are 19.8 in Table 11.5 and 35.2 in Table 11.3, although one should note that the measure in Table 11.5 is reduced by some negative association between children per family and adults per family for the six age-of-head classes (see cols. 3 and 4, panel A of Table 11.5). Likewise, the associated disparities in average income per person between children and adults are appreciably narrower in Table 11.5, with TDM (*P-Y*) being 16.8 and TDM (*Pcca-Y*) being 7.2 (see lines 15 and 19), compared with 31.8 and 27.4, respectively, in Table 11.3 (see lines 17 and 22). But here again the comparison is complicated by the presence in Table 11.5 of the life-cycle component of income in its full strength, combined with the negative correlation between the movements of children per family and adults per family. There is no need here to try to deal with these elements of incomparability. It would suffice to emphasize the conclusion as to the reduction in disparity in the distribution of children per family, first noted, and move to the second way of disproving the assumption advanced at the start of this section.

This second way is by use of data that would permit us to observe differences in the distribution of families by number of children and the disparities in average income per person between children and adults within separate age-of-head classes. Were all families to follow a roughly similar pattern of having children, similar in number and in timing within the total life span, the distribution of families by number of children within the separate age-of-head classes, and particularly within the major age classes, would show only minor differences and so would yield only minor differences between children and adults in the average per person income. If with relevant data we find, within the major age-of-head classes, substantial differences in children per family and resulting major differences in per person income between children and adults, the initial hypothesis would have to be rejected and we would conclude that, even with cumulation of numbers and incomes over the full life span of a family, substantial differences in average numbers per family and substantial disparities in per person income would remain.

Some relevant data are available, but since they are not focused sharply on the question here, they must be arranged to suit the purposes of this inquiry. The following comments on Table 11.6, which summarizes the data, are intended to explain the procedure followed.

Panel A shows disparities among households of two and over in size of households by number of persons, within each of the six age-of-head classes. One would have wished an even more detailed age-of-head classification, but none is at hand. I calculated, for each of the six age classes, a TDM for H-P (i.e., for inequality in the distribution of households by size [col. 4]) and the same measure for the total distribution of households over two by size (col. 4, line 7). The result is that, compared with a TDM of 38.4 for the overall distribution, the TDMs within the age-of-head classes vary from 27.2 to 35.6. When weighted by shares in either number of households or number of persons, the weighted TDM for within-age-of-head groups becomes about 31 – a reduction from the overall of about one-fifth. If only four wider age classes are used, the shift from the overall measure to the intra-age-of-head class measures is somewhat narrower, the weighted measure of 32.7 indicating a reduction of about one-seventh.

But panel A bears only upon inequality in distribution of households or

Table 11.6. *Size of household and income-per-person disparities between families with and without own children (within age-of-head classes), United States, 1969–70*

A. *Size disparities, households of two or more, within age-of-head classes, March 1970*[a]

Age-of-head classes (years)	% of Households (1)	Persons per household (2)	% of persons (3)	TDM (H-P) (4)	TDM weighted by % of households (5)	% of persons (6)
1. Below 25	7.2	2.85	5.7	27.2	1.96	1.55
2. 25–34	20.6	3.97	22.7	27.6	5.69	6.27
3. 35–44	21.1	4.73	27.5	30.4	6.41	8.36
4. 45–54	20.9	3.79	22.0	35.6	7.44	7.83
5. 55–64	16.2	2.84	12.7	34.4	5.57	4.37
6. 65 and over	14.0	2.44	9.4	27.6	3.86	2.59
7. Totals, average, TDM, six classes	52.18	3.62	188.69	38.4	30.9	31.0
8. Line 7, four classes	52.18	3.62	188.69	38.4	32.7	32.7

B. *Disparities in income per person for families without own children (Faa) and families with own children (Fcca), within four age-of-head classes, U.S., 1969–70*[b]

	Age-of-head classes (years)				
	Below 25 (1)	25–44 (2)	45–64 (3)	65 and over (4)	Total (5)
9. *Faa* (million)	1.41	2.93	11.34	6.88	22.57
10. *Fcca* (million)	2.11	18.56	7.80	0.20	28.67
11. All *F* (million)	3.52	21.49	19.14	7.08	51.24
12. Money income (*Y*) per *Faa* ($ thousand)	7.59	11.64	11.90	6.70	10.01
13. Money income (*Y*) per *Fcca* ($ thousand)	6.34	10.87	12.75	7.30	11.02
14. Total Income of *Faa* ($ billion)	10.75	34.11	135.00	46.10	225.96
15. Total income of *Fcaa* ($ billion)	13.36	201.68	99.44	1.48	315.96
16. Total *Y* ($ billion)	24.11	235.79	234.44	47.58	541.92
17. Adults (*Pa*) per family	1.95	2.08	2.50	2.29	3.35
18. Adults in *Faa* (million)	2.75	6.10	28.34	15.76	52.95
19. Own children (*Pc*) per family	0.91	2.24	0.85	0.15	1.34
20. Total children (million)	3.20	48.06	16.35	1.03	68.65
21. Adults in families with own children (million)	4.10	38.61	19.50	0.46	62.67

Table 11.6 *(cont.)*

	Age-of-head classes (years)				
	Below 25 (1)	25–44 (2)	45–64 (3)	65 and over (4)	Total (5)
22. Children and adults in families with children (million)	7.30	86.67	35.85	1.50	131.32
23. All persons, lines 18 and 22 (million)	10.06	92.76	64.19	17.26	184.27
% in Y					
24. *Y* in *Faa*, lines 14 and 16	44.6	14.5	57.6	97.0	41.7
25. *Y* in *Fcca*, lines 15 and 16	55.4	85.5	42.4	3.0	58.3
% in P					
26. *P* in *Faa*, lines 18 and 23	27.4	6.6	44.2	91.3	28.7
27. *P* in *Fcca*, lines 22 and 23	72.6	93.4	55.8	8.7	71.3
28. TDM ($P-Y$)	34.4	15.8	26.8	11.4	26.0
29. *P* weights and *P*-weighted TDM	.055	.503	.348	.094	20.1
30. *Y* weights and *Y*-weighted TDM	.044	.435	.433	.088	21.0

Sources: The underlying data in panel A are from *CPR*, table 5, p. 15. Underlying data in panel B are from *Income in 1969*, table 21, pp. 51 ff.; this table is the source of entries in lines 9–16.
[a]The entries in line 7 are: cols. 1 and 3, total of households of two or more, and of the population in them, in millions; in col. 3, arithmetic mean of persons per household; in col. 4, the TDM for inequality in size of households calculated from cols. 1 and 3, lines 1–6; in cols. 5 and 6, the TDMs for the disparity within each of the six age-of-head classes, weighted by shares in households and in persons, respectively. The entries in line 8, cols. 5 and 6, are averages of the TDMs within four age-of-head classes (below 25, 25–44, 45–64, and 65 and over), again weighted by shares in households and persons, respectively.
[b]Families are classified by the presence or absence of *own* children, not of *related* children referred to in all other tables here. *Income in 1969* defines own children as "sons and daughters, including stepchildren and adopted children, of the family head," while related children in a family "include own children and all other children in the household who are related to the family head by blood, marriage, or adoption" (p. 9). The difference may be seen by comparing the number of families without own children, 22.57 million (line 9, col. 5 above) with that of families without related children, of 21.42 million (in Table 11.3, line 1, col. 1). This comparison led me to assume that the total number of *own* children was smaller than that of related children by the difference between the two totals, namely, 1.15–1.16 million. The additional data underlying lines 17 and 19 are provided in *CPR*, used for panel A here, from which were calculated, for the four age-of-head classes, the averages of adults and children per household (for households of two persons and over). These averages were then adjusted so that when applied to the data in lines 9–11, they would yield the totals of *own* children (from Table 11.3, minus the difference between own and related children derived in the preceding paragraph) and of adults (the latter as used in Table 11.3). The minor adjustments needed were applied only to the very large age-of-head classes, 25–44 and 45–64. With the entries in lines 17 and 19, it was possible to derive all the other entries. Line 18 is the product of lines 9 and 17; line 20 is the product of lines 19 and 11; line 21 is the product of lines 17 and 10. The products and totals will not check precisely, because the original calculations were for figures with three rather

families by number of persons. It has only indirect bearing upon inequality in the distribution of families by number of children and on the associated disparity in income per person. Of more direct relevance are the data summarized in panel B, data that distinguish families with own children from those without own children and make it possible to establish the numbers and per person income of the two groups, not only for the total population of families but also within four broad age-of-head classes.

As distinct from *related* children, the group covered in the preceding tables, *own* children include only the sons and daughters born to or adopted by the head of the family – and thus exclude other relations of the head below the age of 18. As indicated in the notes to Table 11.6, the difference between the totals of own and of related children is not large; out of a total of some 70 million of the latter, perhaps a million and a half are not own, and even a large relative error in the estimate would not affect the results substantially. It can then be seen whether, within the four age-of-head classes, the expected difference in per person income between the two major groups – families without children and families with children – persists.

The findings are summarized in lines 24–28, particularly in the TDMs reflecting the inequality in per person income between the two major groups. For all families, regardless of the age of head (col. 5), the TDM is 26.0, which can be compared with a similar measure in panel D of Table 11.3 of 27.4 (line 22, col. 3). The small difference is due largely to using a constant number of adults per family, for all groups by number of children, in Table 11.3; whereas here the per family numbers of adults in the two major groups are allowed to differ, and they do in that the number of adults for all families works out to 2.35 per family, compared with 2.19 per family for the units with own children (see lines 17 and 21, col. 5). But the difference is small, so that the relation between within-age-of-head TDMs and that for the overall distribution in Table 11.6 can be viewed as roughly applying to the probable findings for the comparison of families with and without related children in Table 11.3.

Notes to Table 11.6 *(cont.)*

than two decimal places. The TDMs in line 28 are calculated directly from lines 24–27 above, and measure the income disparity in per person income between families without own children and families with own children, for each of the four age-of-head groups and for the total in col. 5. The P weights in line 29 are calculated from line 23; the Y weights in line 30 are calculated from line 16.

For the four broad age-of-head groups here, the TDMs vary from 11.4 to 34.4. But there are only two large groups, age of head 25–44 and age of head 45–64, which together account for over 80% of all persons and almost 90% of all income. The weighted TDMs, between 20 and 21, are about one-fifth below the overall measure, and with more detailed age-of-head breakdown, the reduction might be one-third, a weighted average of TDM of about 18. This suggests a substantial disparity in per person income between families with and without children, and hence between children and adults, within age-of-head groups – and hence subject to cumulative differences over the life span of the families.

V. Model type families: analytical illustrations

Two conclusions are suggested by the data summarized and discussed in the preceding sections. The first is that, for the United States in 1969–70 and most probably other years, cross-section differences among families by number of related children under 18 were wide, were associated with wide disparities in per person income between children and adults, and thus contributed substantially to the inequality in the distribution of family income per person among the population. The second is that these differences among families in the number of related children, and the associated disparities in per person income between children and adults, were observed also within the several age-of-head classes, which indicates that differences among families in number of children and per person income would persist even if numbers and incomes were cumulated over the total life span of the families. A third conclusion, so far partly implicit, is that viewed in the time sequence within the life span of the family, a family with large numbers of children would tend to show not only a larger cumulative average number of persons and a lower cumulative per person income but greater variation over time in the numbers of persons and in the income per person within the life span.

In this section, model types of families are used, differing in the number of children (ranging from one to seven) they have over the life span; and, with the help of simplifying assumptions, the effects of this difference on the size and per person income of each type of family are illustrated.[11]

11 The rest of this section is a brief exercise in the derivation, from the data for the United States for 1969–70 discussed in this paper, of various patterns of *lifetime* income per person. A more elaborate discussion of a set of somewhat different derivations was presented in Chapter 7, above.

For Table 11.7 and the data underlying it on the number of children and adults for each year within the life span of family of each of the seven types, the following simplifying assumptions were made for all types. First, the formation of the family was set at year 22 of head (beginning of year) and the dissolution toward the end at age of head 70 (end of year), a total family life span of 49 years. Second, the first child is born at age of head 23 (i.e., a year after formation of family), and other children follow, at time patterns different for the several model types (to be specified below). Third, effects of mortality and of other sources of possible changes in the family within the life span indicated above (divorce, separation, and joining) are excluded. Fourth, the average number of adults per family, for all types and all years within the span, is set at 2.26 – the average shown in Table 11.3.

The seven model types of families are defined as follows: I, one child; II, two children, spaced 7 years apart; III, three children, spaced 6 years apart; IV, four children, spaced 5 years apart; V, five children, spaced 4 years apart; VI, six children, spaced 3 years apart; VII, seven children, spaced 2 years apart. The combination of the general assumptions in the paragraph above, and the specific type definitions just presented, permit us to derive for each of the 49 span years, for each model type, the number of children and adults, and total persons. This set of detailed data is then summarized, in the fashion presented in Table 11.7, which parallels the empirical distribution in panel A of Table 11.3.

The assumptions just listed are quite restrictive. Thus, assuming away mortality, particularly of children, neglects the difference between children ever born and children surviving (my data and examples bear on the latter, not on the former). This difference varies between more developed and less developed countries, and its movement is a key trend in the demographic transition. In addition to mortality, divorce and separation, particularly in a more developed country like the United States, contribute significantly to the incidence of incomplete families, particularly those without a male head – with effects on the income position of children in such family units. The assumption of the same number of adults per family for groups of families classified by differing numbers of children may not be too far-fetched for the U.S. experience, as is suggested by the evidence in Section I; but there is a question whether similar combinations of a relatively invariant number of adults with a wide range in the number of children per family would be found in less developed countries with more widely inclusive family units. One may also

Table 11.7. *Distribution of family-years (Tf) by number of child-years (Tc), adult-years (Ta), and person-years (Tp), life span of model type families*

	Types of families (Tc)							Totals, unweighted (% share)
	I (1)	II (2)	III (3)	IV (4)	V (5)	VI (6)	VII (7)	(8)
Number of children in family-year								
1. No children	31	24	19	16	15	16	19	140 (40.8)
2. One child	18	14	12	10	8	6	4	72 (21.0)
3. Two children	0	11	12	10	8	6	4	51 (14.9)
4. Three children	0	0	6	10	8	6	4	34 (9.9)
5. Four children	0	0	0	3	8	6	4	21 (6.1)
6. Five children	0	0	0	0	2	6	4	12 (3.5)
7. Six children	0	0	0	0	0	3	4	7 —
8. Seven children	0	0	0	0	0	0	6	6 —
9. Six and over	0	0	0	0	0	3	10	13 (3.8)
Totals, averages, and disparity measures								
10. Total family-years (Tf)	49	49	49	49	49	49	49	343
11. Child-years (Tc)	18.00	36.00	54.00	72.00	90.00	108.00	126.00	504.00
12. Adult-years (Ta)	110.74	110.74	110.74	110.74	110.74	110.74	110.74	775.18
13. Persons per family-year (Tp/Tf)	2.63	2.99	3.36	3.73	4.10	4.46	4.83	3.73
14. Proportion of child-years in person-years	.140	.245	.328	.394	.448	.494	.532	.394
15. TDM (Tf-Tp)	17.8	24.0	27.0	31.0	34.0	44.4	44.4	37.6
16. TDM (Tf-Tc)	126.6	98.0	82.2	78.4	76.2	86.6	86.6	95.0

Note: For the definitions and assumptions underlying the illustrative exhibit above, see text. The entries in parentheses in col. 8, lines 1–6 and 9 are the percentage shares of family-years with 0, 1, etc. children, in the total of family-years in line 10, col. 8.

question the spacing of the children in the illustration so that the total periods of childbearing and maturing of children to age 18 do not differ widely among the several model types, making for a greater concentration of the characteristic number of children within a narrower range of age of head than is likely to prevail in reality (although there is some support in Table 11.5). In short, the analytical illustrations explore the cumulative effect on the family life cycle of specific relations between numbers of surviving children and family income per capita found in recent U.S. data – simplified by neglecting effects of mortality and of other causes of family change before completion of the family life cycle.

The results in Table 11.7 indicate that the several model types yield, in the progression of columns from the one-child type to the seven-children type, a steady rise in average size of family (by between 0.36 and 0.37 per child, which is the ratio of 18 to 49; see the differences between successive entries in line 13); that this increase is due solely to the assumption of an increasingly large number of children, so that the ratio of the latter to total persons per family rises steadily. It also follows that disparity, within the life span of the family, between the persons or children per family in the successive years (quinquennia or decades), also widens as we move from the one-child to the multichildren family – as reflected in the rise of the TDM for family years to person years in line 15 of Table 11.7. Finally, the source of instability over time in the size of the family being due exclusively to instability in the number of children, the TDM for inequality in number of children per family, shown in line 16, will, if weighted by the proportion of child years in person years in line 14, yield the TDM in line 15. The reason the latter rises is that the decline in the inequality in distribution of children among the family years is more than offset by the rise in the proportion of children among persons.

Before passing to the next table, note the result of a simple addition for the seven model types in column 8 of Table 11.7 – addition with equal weights. Though such unweighted addition is hardly realistic in approximating a total distribution of families among the model types, the results are not too different from those found in Table 11.3. The percentage shares of groups with zero, one, etc., children, in parentheses in column 8, are similar to those in column 5 of panel A in Table 11.3. The total proportion of children years here is 39.4%, compared with 37.6% of children in total persons in Table 11.3; the TDMs for F-P are 37.6 here and 35.2 in Table 11.3. Such rough agreement may be due to the fact that the distortion of weights implied in unweighted addition is true for both the *low*-children-per-unit groups (such as I and II here) and the *high*-children-per-unit groups (such as V–VII here) – the two sets of distortion almost balancing each other.

In Table 11.8 a per person income is assigned to each family type, for each year within its life span, corresponding to the number of children in that family in that year. These per person incomes are taken from panel B of Table 11.3, shown there for each class of family, with zero, one, etc., and six and over children. The procedure makes it possible to calculate per person income for each family type for each year and then cumulate it into a total over the whole span of 49 years. It is also possible to calculate for each model family type the distribution of person years and income years among three major groups – children, adults in families with children, and adults in families without children – shown in Table 11.8 in lines 2–4 and 6–8; and to compute the relevant measure of disparity, the TDM for $Tcca$-Tp, in line 10. Finally, using also the income cells for the several-children-per-family groups from one to six and over, it is possible to calculate the more inclusive measure of income-per-person disparity contributed by the presence of children component, TDM for Tp-Yp, in line 11.

The use of data from Table 11.3 to estimate the income per person for the model type families naturally transfers to the latter the disparities observed for a particular country for a particular year and disregards the growth factor that would be found in per person income of a cohort of families observed over time. But we are concerned here only with the effects of differing numbers of children over the life cycle among the model families. And the cross-section pattern for another year would be the same, so long as per person income declines perceptibly with increases in the number of children in the family and with relatively narrow variations in the number of adults per family.

Two major conclusions stand out in Table 11.8. First, the cumulative per person income over the life span declines markedly as we move from type I to type VI–VII families, so that lifetime income of the latter is about 60% of the former. Second, the greater variability within the life span in the number of children and total persons per family, observed for the multichildren family types in Table 11.7, is now reflected in the greater variability in per person income, within the life span, in the families with the larger number of children. Thus, the TDMs, in both lines 10 and 11, rise steadily from column 1 to column 6 – the more sensitive measure, when based on more than three divisions, rising more appreciably (com-

Table 11.8. *Income per person, children and adults, family model types by number of children within the life span*

	Family types						Unweighted total
	I (1)	II (2)	III (3)	IV (4)	V (5)	VI+VII (6)	(7)
Person-years (Tp)							
1. Total	128.74	146.74	164.74	182.74	200.74	455.48	1,279.18
% shares in total, line 1							
2. Tc	14.0	24.5	32.8	39.4	44.8	51.4	39.4
3. Tca	31.6	38.5	41.1	40.8	38.3	31.2	35.9
4. Taa	54.4	37.0	26.1	19.8	16.9	17.4	24.7
Total income (Yp)							
5. Total ($ thousand)	506.1	513.5	522.2	526.3	525.8	1,030.0	3,623.8
% shares in total, line 5							
6. Yc	11.7	20.2	27.0	32.5	36.2	37.8	29.2
7. Yca	26.5	32.7	36.3	36.9	35.0	28.0	31.9
8. Yaa	61.8	47.1	36.7	30.6	28.8	34.2	38.9
Averages and disparity measures							
9. Income per person life-cycle span ($ thousand)	3.93	3.50	3.17	2.88	2.62	2.26	2.84
Income instability within life-cycle span							
10. TDM (Tcaa-Yp)	14.8	20.2	21.2	21.6	23.8	33.6	28.4
11. TDM (Tp-Yp)	14.6	20.2	23.2	27.0	30.4	43.6	34.6

Note: The entries in lines 1–4 are based on the distributions of family-years by number of children- and adult-years shown for the seven family types in Table 11.7. To the numbers of children and adult family-years were applied the per person income for groups of families classified by the number of related children under 18 shown in panel B of Table 11.3 for the United States. In $ thousand, they were: no children, 4.46; one child, 3.30; two children, 2.62; three children, 2.14; four children, 1.77; five children, 1.42; six and more children, 1.16. The TDMs in line 10 are analogous to that shown in panel D of Table 11.3; TDMs in line 11 are analogous to that shown in panel C of Table 11.3 (for *P-Y*).

pare line 11 with line 10, for cols. 2 through 6). Incidentally, the measures for the unweighted totals of the seven model types in column 7 are again fairly close to those shown for Table 11.3; the TDM here for three major population groups, in line 10, at 28.4 is only slightly larger than the corresponding measure in Table 11.3, 27.4 (see line 22); and the measure for *P-Y*, in line 11, at 34.6 is somewhat larger than that in Table 11.3, at 31.8 (see line 17).

The variability or instability over time introduces an element different from, and additional to, the disparity in total cumulative income per person over the life span. If two families secure the same total cumulative income per person over their life span, the family with greater instability of income over time would certainly be considered worse off – on the premise that the negative impacts of the sharper trough on welfare, on the possibility of long-term planning, and on vulnerability to short-term disturbances would hardly be offset by a sharper peak. Consequently, the time profile of a family with a larger number of children over the life span is less favorable than that of a family with a smaller number of children. And these differences in the profiles associated with disparities in the number of children would be translated into cross-section differences among families within phases of the total life span – the greater, the wider the range among families in that phase in the number of children.

The illustrative examples used in this section could be explored further in a variety of ways – dealing with the time patterns through successive age-of-head classes for the different model type families; and, in particular, attempting combinations of the several types in cohorts, comprising all types and visualizing these cohorts in their succession over time. But for such exploration, which would permit derivation of both hypothetical cross sections and a series of cohort life spans, to be worthwhile, one would need a variety of data not now at hand, and beyond the feasible here. It seems best to end the illustrative discussion here, emphasizing only that in the case of multichildren families, a lower lifetime income per person is likely to be accompanied by substantial temporal variability in per person income – even allowing for effects of time profiles of income per family or per adult with changing age of head, and for those in growth trends in per person income.

VI. Concluding comments

I have emphasized income disparities among families distinguished by differing numbers of children, because the latter seemed to me a major demographic factor affecting inequality in the distribution among persons of both longer term and shorter term income. One main function of the family may be assumed to be the rearing of the next generation to satisfactory maturity, while providing adequate economic and living conditions for the parent generation. Given the major effects of differences in the number of children, ever born and surviving, on per person income of members of the family, both children and adults, and the substantial contribution that the results as measured here make to inequality in the distribution of income among members of the population, this demographic aspect of the income distribution appears to deserve deeper exploration than was feasible here.

The main finding here, illustrated in Tables 11.2 and 11.3, is that differences in number of children among families are associated with little positive variation in number of adults and in family income; while the number of children per family rises from zero to more than six, the number of adults per family barely changes and the narrow variation is true also of total income per family. No wonder, then, that per person income drops so sharply from the high in no-children families to the low in the family class with most children. If these results are accepted, they are puzzling, for they imply that among families there prevail wide differences in the desire for children[12] – differences that induce some families to have more children despite the depressing effect on per person income, in the long and in the shorter run.

One may, therefore, ask whether the results, as obtained here, are not misleading – in being secured with inappropriate concepts, and implications of such concepts. Thus, it could be argued that children are not equivalent to adults in terms of their consumption needs; and that the appropriate reduction in the conversion of persons to consuming units, combined with the possible economies of scale in larger families, would reduce substantially the disparities now shown on a per person basis between children and adults.[13] If so, the reduction in per unit income, viewable as the cost of having more children, will be substantially smaller. But the difficulty is that the available conversions for a shift from per person to per consuming unit bases are all derived from the empirical

12 An easy alternative explanation might be that the results are due to error, or more realistically to a lag in the response of families to rapidly changing circumstances, which were unforeseen and which introduced a major disparity in per person income associated now (but not in the past) with the differences in numbers of children per family. But this explanation is not warranted by U.S. experience in recent decades, however it might be considered in connection with the rapid declines in mortality in recent decades in the less developed countries. A glance at data, similar to those used in Table 11.3, for both earlier and later years in the United States, in the span from 1950 to 1979, suggests patterns similar to those found for 1969–70 in Table 11.3.

13 See the brief illustration and discussion of these conversions in Chapter 7, above.

data which reflect the effects of adjustments to a reduced income per person – rather than the consumption needs of children viewed as the future members of the next adult generation of producers. Our interest is in the reduced economic base for the children in terms of what this base, and the lower income of associated adults in the family, means for the capacity of the children when they reach adulthood to contribute to social product. One may question whether, beyond the first few years of life, the consumption needs of children, *when viewed from that standpoint*, are significantly lower per child than they are per adult.

Alternatively, one might argue that the assumption of this analysis, that children do not contribute to income, is due to the narrow definition of income, which excludes services rendered within the family household by members to each other. While it is true that market-oriented employment for children under 18 is exceedingly limited in a country like the United States, it is likely that, in families with large numbers of siblings under 18, the older siblings assist in the intrafamily services and chores. If the value of these services, which are bound to be larger in multichildren families than in those with few children, are included, the addition to the per person or per unit income of the multichildren families will be proportionately larger and serve to reduce the income disparity. A similar but distinct argument would be to the effect that the intrafamily household services and products of family members, excluded from the traditional concept of income (even if including market-oriented type of income in kind, in addition to money personal income), even adult members, would be proportionately larger in the multichildren families. But here again the difficulty lies in the possibility of a different result, if the *quality* of intrafamily services is taken into account. To the extent that joint life and close bonds between adults and children in the family prevail, fewer hours devoted to services to family members in a higher income, smaller family may weigh, in their contribution to bringing up the next generation, as heavily proportionately as the greater number of hours devoted to these services in the lower income multichildren families.

A third argument might refer to services in kind provided to the households by the governmental sector, in the way of health care, education, and recreation, not now included in the conventional total personal income (which does include money transfers). Such services, particularly education and health care, are provided at low direct cost to both multichildren and other families, and they would presumably add a larger proportion to the family income of the families with the larger number of children. But here again one may ask whether this is, in fact, true, with reference to, say, the educational services provided by the government (I am not considering the tax components of family income, which bear upon another aspect of the income comparisons). It may be argued that the educational services provided by the government to the children of the families with smaller number and at a higher conventional income level are far greater per child than would be true of those utilized by children in larger families at a lower income level. This distinct possibility is due to the differentiation in quality and level of education provided by the government sector, which permits a range of choice that favors those members of the child population who can take greater advantage of the longer and more advanced type of education. And there are elements of such choice in recreation, and even health, services provided by the government.

All of these are, of course, conjectural arguments. Their purpose is to suggest that some plausible results of allowing for conventional conversions from persons to consuming units, of expanding family income to include intrahousehold services of family members, and of including in family income the value of services in kind provided by the government (or other social institutions) may be only plausible rather than valid. But, due to limitations of knowledge, one can only speculate.

In particular, the data used here are insufficient to determine how the family income or, better, consumption is apportioned among the members, children and adults, young and old. All that the data tell us is that family income – money income here and market-oriented income in general – is lower per member of the family when the latter includes more children. To be able to evaluate the effects of this difference on the growth of the children as future active economic agents, and even on the growth of the productivity of the adult members over the life span of the family unit, we need an insight into the internal economic structure of the family. It is quite possible that different socioeconomic groups among families, at similar levels of per person income and similar proportions of children to adults, have different allocations of consumption between children and adults and different provisions for engagement of the family members, young and old, in intrafamily services.

All that one can do so far is to call attention to the results of the comparisons, even if only for one developed country; speculate on their consequences; and muse on the important question that arises. That question is about the significance of the association of low per person income with more children per family for the long-term trends in economic differentials within the current and later generations.[14]

14 In an earlier paper I tried to explore the question by a different approach, not directly concerned with effects on the distribution of income, with results that were largely conjectural (see "Income-related Differences in Natural Increase: Bearing on Growth and Distribution of Income," in *Nations and Households in Economic Growth: Essays in Honor of Moses Abramovitz*, ed. Paul A. David and Melvin W. Reder [New York: Academic Press, 1974]).

Afterword: Some notes on the scientific methods of Simon Kuznets[1]

"Anyone can start a row in economics; it is much harder to find out what is really happening to the economy." Simon Kuznets made this statement during a conversation he had with Henry Rosovsky and me at Harvard University in the early 1970s. I was startled when he said it, since our profession thrives on controversy. Indeed, to many economists cleverness in debate, rather than the applicability of the debate to any issue of the real world, is what economics is all about. To Kuznets, however, there was a real economic world and the task of the economist was to describe it accurately and to explain it in a way that would be helpful to those who had to make economic policy.

I. Four aspects of Kuznets's approach to economics

If there was any aspect of Kuznets's approach to economics that may be said to have dominated all the other aspects, it was his concern with the great policy issues of his age. My emphasis on this point may surprise those who are familiar with Kuznets's work, since he never became directly involved in those highly politicized disputes over economic policy that often split the profession into partisan camps. Moreover, many of the

1 Since this paper is a highly personal account of Simon Kuznets's methods, based to a large extent on recollections of conversations and seminar discussions, I have kept references and other scholarly paraphernalia to a minimum. For other views of Kuznets's approach to economics, which overlap but may not coincide exactly with mine, see Easterlin's introduction to this volume as well as Abramovitz (1971, 1985); Patinkin (1976); Ben-Porath (1986); Bergson (1986); and Bergson *et al.* (1987). I have benefited from comments and criticisms on an earlier draft by Moses Abramovitz, Abram Bergson, Ansley Coale, Milton Friedman, Robert E. Gallman, Zvi Griliches, Edith Kuznets, David Landes, W. Arthur Lewis, Barbara McCutcheon, Marc Nerlove, Dwight Perkins, Gustav Ranis, Samuel H. Preston, W. W. Rostow, T. W. Schultz, Robert M. Solow, Kenneth Wachter, and Nathaniel Wilcox.

problems on which he worked, such as the relationship between the rate of population growth and of technological innovation, are hardly likely to be resolved or even affected significantly by new legislation, nor did his findings on such issues enter prominently into the shifting partisan alignments of his age. Nevertheless, Kuznets recognized the importance of the points at issue in the political debates over economic policy, and he believed that the development of a reliable body of evidence bearing upon these issues was an urgent task of economists. He saw economics as an empirical science aimed at disclosing the factors which affect economic performance.

It is important to keep in mind how new the issues with which Kuznets grappled during his career were when he first began to address them in the mid 1920s. The proposition that Western Europe and America had undergone an irreversible economic transformation – an industrial revolution – was not effectively enunciated until the end of the 1880s. Although optimism about the economy was widespread during the first three decades of the twentieth century, these years also spawned influential theories that economic progress was grinding to a halt. The notion of a general crisis for capitalism, set forth in the work of such socialist or radical theorists as Hobson, Hilferding, and Lenin, became widely accepted by professional economists during the 1930s, and Hansen's suggestion that a correct fiscal policy could bring an end to secular stagnation, despite a certain optimism, seemed to endorse the view that secular stagnation was the natural condition of free market economies in the twentieth century (Abramovitz 1952).

Kuznets broke new ground in several respects when he set out to describe the phenomenon he called modern economic growth. Such growth was not a lucky accident, the outcome of a fortunate but ephemeral conjunction of circumstances. It was, rather, the central feature of a new historical epoch marked by the application of science to industry and possessing other characteristics that gave it unity and set it apart from the epochs that preceded it (1966, p. 2). Among the primary features of modern economic growth were sustained rises in output per capita or per worker accompanied by increases in population and by sweeping changes in the structure of the economy. When Kuznets first began his work on economic growth in the mid 1920s, not all the processes that he later identified had worked themselves out. Europe and America were still passing through the demographic and epidemiological transitions (U.S. life expectation at birth in 1920 was still under 55 years), and the nature of these phenomena was not yet fully apparent. It would be another two decades before the theory of the demographic transition was formulated, and it would be another three to four decades before it became clear that the economic advances of the last half of the nineteenth century were part of a new epoch of economic growth that was about two centuries old and that was in the process of spreading from its origins in Western Europe and in certain countries of European settlement to the impoverished nations of Africa, Asia, and Latin America.

To Kuznets, accurate description of the characteristics of modern economic growth and of the factors that tended to promote or retard growth were necessary not only for the continued prosperity of the developed nations but also to formulate policies that would close the enormous gap in per capita income that had arisen between the developed and the less developed nations. Much of his work was directed toward measuring and explaining differing patterns in the inequality of the distribution of income, across and within nations, over time. He believed that at low levels of per capita income, economic growth tended to increase inequality of the distribution of income, but at intermediate and higher levels, growth reduced inequality. On this question, as on so many others, Kuznets sought to distinguish factors affecting the income distribution that were more or less inescapable consequences of the dynamics of population or income growth from those that were amenable to current policy.

The last point touches on a second aspect of Kuznets's approach: his concern with the role of long-term factors in the determination of current economic performance. In his view many current economic opportunities and problems were determined by economic conditions and relationships that evolved slowly, often taking many decades to work out. At a time when Keynes declared that "In the long run we are all dead," an aphorism reiterated by many economists not only during the 1930s but during the 1940s and 1950s, Kuznets continued to call attention to the role of long-term factors that had to be taken into account by policymakers, factors which led him to conclude that the opportunities for returning to high employment levels and rapid economic growth were greater than generally believed.

Current social problems, Kuznets emphasized, are often the result of past growth – the consequence of past desirable attainments, which at a later time produce socially undesirable consequences that require remedial policy action. Of his numerous illustrations of this principle, one is particularly cogent: the explosion of population growth in the less developed nations of Asia, Africa, Oceania, and Latin America in the quarter century following World War II. This population explosion threatened to thwart efforts to raise per capita incomes from their dismally low levels because birth rates remained traditionally high, while public health policies and improved nutrition cut death rates in these regions by more than 50 percent in less than a generation. One obvious solution to the problem was to reduce fertility, yet there was a web of traditional patterns of behavior and beliefs that tended to keep fertility high. Nevertheless, Kuznets believed that properly designed public policies could hasten the social and ideological changes required to reduce fertility and to lead these societies to prefer a greater investment in a smaller number of children. Such a program required not only government and private campaigns to disseminate the technology of birth control but a restructuring of social and economic incentives that would provide rewards for families with fewer children.

Kuznets pointed out that this urgently needed program to reduce fertility would have its negative as well as its positive side. Since it was those in upper income brackets who would respond most rapidly to the new incentives, the immediate impact of a campaign to reduce birth rates would be to increase the inequality of the income distribution. This initial impact could be overcome by a determined effort to change the social and economic conditions of the lower classes in a way that would promote their interest in smaller families. Yet as the experience of the United States and other developed nations has shown, the success of the program to curtail fertility is bound, much further down the line, to create a new set of problems, similar to those which are currently at the center of the modern women's movement: the restructuring of society in such a way as to promote equal opportunity for women in all occupational markets.

Economic growth creates social problems because it is profoundly disruptive to traditional values and religious beliefs, to longstanding social and family patterns of organization, and to numerous monopolies of privilege. Despite the fact that modern economic growth has brought with it tremendous increases in longevity and good health, has brought to the lower classes standards of living as well as social and economic opportunities previously available only to a tiny minority, and has greatly reduced the inequality in the income distribution of developed nations, the social restructuring of society required by modern economic growth has been fiercely resisted – sometimes because of an unwillingness to give up traditional values and ways of life, sometimes by entrenched classes determined to protect their ancient privileges. Because of the complex responses to change and because the epoch of modern economic growth was still unfolding, many aspects of the social restructuring that was under way were still obscure and difficult to predict (Kuznets 1966, p. 15). As late as 1972 Kuznets felt compelled to point out that despite the multitude of tentative partial generalizations, cross-sectional studies, and econometric exercises, there was as yet no "tested generalization, significantly specific to permit the quantitative prediction of aggregate growth, or even of changes in the structural parameters in the course of growth" (1972, p. 58).

The difficulty of predicting the future relates to two methodological problems with which Kuznets continually struggled: How long a period of observation is needed to identify the underlying process at work in any specific aspect of economic growth? How can one determine whether such a process, once identified, is sufficiently stable to provide a reliable basis for prediction? These problems are illustrated by an issue on which Kuznets was the preeminent investigator of his age, the interrelationship between demographic processes and modern economic growth.

Kuznets considered the acceleration of population growth during the nineteenth century not only as one of the most important consequences of economic growth, but also a major factor contributing to it. A particularly important aspect of the phenomenon was the concentration of the decline of death rates at early ages, which contributed to the reduction in fertility rates. The reduced fertility rate released a large proportion of the female labor force to gainful occupations, accelerated the transition to modern families, mobile and responsive to economic incentives, and promoted new ideologies conducive to economic growth (1966, pp. 56–62). In this connection Kuznets noted the increase in the share of women in the U.S. labor force from 17 percent in 1890 to 27 percent in 1950, which he attributed to the lower fertility rates, the shift in employment opportunities from manual to service sector positions, and urbanization, which made organized labor markets more accessible to women. He also called attention to the fact that the most rapidly growing occupations – those in the professional, technical, clerical, sales, and other services – were the ones in which women had made the greatest inroads. Nevertheless in the late 1950s and early 1960s, when the new women's movement was still incipient, Kuznets did not anticipate the explosive entry of women into the labor force during the next quarter century, nor the new ideology that would facilitate that development (1966, pp. 193–195).

A third aspect of Kuznets's method was his approach to the establishment of the priorities for empirical research in economics. At any moment there are more issues and problems demanding the attention of economists than there are resources to address them. In Kuznets's view the priorities for research were determined by a complex interaction of three factors: (1) the needs of policymakers inside and outside of the government, particularly the issues that they considered paramount for promoting economic growth, stability, and equity; (2) the beliefs of economists and other social scientists regarding the most effective measures for resolving the problems on this social agenda; and (3) the availability of the data needed to address these issues and the effectiveness of the tools, both analytical and mechanical, required to process and analyze the data (1972, p. 39).

In explaining both the enormous growth of economic research between 1930 and 1970, and the direction that it took, Kuznets emphasized the importance of the interaction between these three factors, rather than the ascendency of any one over the other. This expansion of economic research undoubtedly depended on the social agenda, since it was largely through the government that the training of the scientific personnel, the collection of the primary data, and the financing of individual research projects were directly or indirectly promoted.[2] However, which direction this research took was heavily influenced by developments within the academic community. Thus, while the devastating impact of the great depression of the 1930s promoted greater government intervention in the economy, the direction that the intervention took, as well as the type of research that the government promoted, was greatly affected by Keynesian theory which had gained such dominance in the scholarly community. In the absence of this influential theory, government policy "might have been limited to new provisions for unemployment insurance, new plans for public works, and the like" (1972, p. 42). Since the theory indicated that the depression could recur unless the government was continuously concerned with insuring a sufficiently high level of final demand, government policy moved heavily in a Keynesian direction. This interaction between social priorities and economic theory gave an enormous stimulus to the development of national income accounts, of measures of employment and unemployment, of the size distribution of income, and of other

2 Foundations and other private institutions also played an important role.

macro variables as a means of monitoring economic performance and of guiding government intervention.

Kuznets emphasized the critical role played by academic research on the innovations in economic measurement adopted by government agencies in the free market economies. It was not primarily from the government bureaucracy but from the scholarly community that new approaches to measuring economic performance arose. It was not until they had been advanced and explored within the scholarly community that the national income and product accounts, input–output analysis, flow-of-funds measures, and periodic sample surveys were adopted by government agencies as standard procedures on which they relied.

The increased importance placed on economic measurement was also promoted by the enormous strides made since World War II in methods of collecting and summarizing primary data, as well as in analyzing them. In this connection Kuznets emphasized not only the enormous advances in computer technology and in methods of statistical inference, but also the advances in the mathematical modelling of both simple and complex socioeconomic behavior. Just as he viewed Keynesian theory as a great stimulus to quantitative economic research, he viewed the postwar explosion of economic models as having the potential to promote more well-defined empirical research and eventually to increase the body of empirically tested and confirmed economic theory (1972, pp. 54–58).

This emphasis on the intimate interconnection between measurement and theory was the fourth, and perhaps the most distinctive aspect of Kuznets's method. Although Kuznets was a quintessential empiricist and a standard-bearer for empirical research, his empiricism did not imply hostility to theory. Quite the contrary, he continually emphasized that a sound theory was needed to identify the variables that had to be measured, and theory had to be invoked in order to determine how the raw data thrown up by normal business or governmental activities had to be combined in order to create the desired measures. Since measurement was dependent on theory, he emphasized that as theory advanced, due to either deeper insights or sounder empirical knowledge, past measures would have to be revised. Thus empirical and theoretical knowledge are at any point in time only asymptotically valid, subject to changing knowledge in both areas as well as to changing social goals and values (1972, pp. 18–22). In attempting to pursue his empirical objectives Kuznets frequently encountered theoretical issues that had not yet been addressed adequately. On such occasions he made notable contributions to theory, as in his work on the theory of national income accounting, in which he extended utility theory to issues involved in designing measures of output that reflected economic welfare.

Kuznets did not pit deductive theory against inductive theory but made use of both approaches in his work. Nor did he object to simplifying assumptions that, although a gloss on reality, facilitated an analysis without distorting it. Kuznets was, however, impatient with theorists who knew so little about the institutions or processes about which they theorized that they could not distinguish between metaphors and reality and so failed to consider the logical implications of assumptions that violently distorted the real world. One of Kuznets's repeated contributions was the demonstration that certain so-called pure theories embodied false assumptions about empirical matters, assumptions that critically affected the conclusions derived from the theories. In so doing he helped to counter the view that in theoretical work, cleverness and elegance were all that mattered. Clever economic theories that did not ultimately contribute to the bottom line, curing or keeping the economy healthy and promoting its growth, were no more useful than biomedical theories that did not ultimately contribute to fighting disease or otherwise improving people's health and longevity.

Kuznets not only used theory but sought to extend it by identifying empirical regularities that could provide the basis for new theories or to modify and extend existing ones. In this connection he made notable contributions to the theory of technological change, the theory of industrialization and other aspects of long-term structural changes in modern economies, the theory of economic cycles, the theory of the size distribution of income, the theory of the interrelationship between population change and economic growth, the theory of capital formation (including the role of variations in saving rates over the life cycle), and the theory of changes in vital rates on the socioeconomic characteristics of households.

I am acutely aware that the preceding comments are at best a gloss on the methods that underpinned the work of a scholar as prolific and as broad ranging in issues, and as flexible in methods, as Kuznets was. Others might have emphasized much different aspects of his approach than those that I have singled out. And enough can be written on each of these points to fill a book. Since the editors, although generous in their charge, did not give me that liberty, I have limited my desire to elaborate on Kuznets's methods to two points: his approach to what one might call the art of measurement in economics and his contribution to economic theory.

II. How to measure in economics

To many of those who studied under Kuznets, his demonstrations and discussions of the art of measurement were the most valuable aspect of their training. By the art of measurement I mean not merely statistical and econometric theory, which are important but quite adequately conveyed in papers and books. A far more difficult question in practice is how to apply statistical methods and economic models to the incomplete and biased data with which economists normally work and still produce reliable estimates of key economic variables and parameters. That question cannot be answered by a simple rule because economic data are so variable in quality and because the circumstances under which a given set of defects in the data are tolerable depends on the issues that are being addressed, on the statistical and analytical procedures that are being employed, and on the sensitivity of the results to systematic errors in the data, to the choice of behavioral models, and to the choice of statistical procedures.

Good judgment on these issues is developed with experience, and Kuznets tried to convey his rich experience on these matters in the same way that doctors use rounds to teach medical students the art of diagnosing illnesses. Kuznets conducted his "rounds" in three different ways: first, in his lectures on economic growth where he discussed problems of measurement and gave numerous examples of good and bad attempts to measure key economic variables and relationships; second, in his seminar on the application of quantitative methods to the analysis of time series, which was largely a laboratory course in which students applied various procedures to typical bodies of economic data, and collectively discussed the problems and interpreted the outcomes; third, in his supervision of dissertations, during which Kuznets varied his approach to the degree of independence desired by the student, while always serving as a sympathetic, thorough, and penetrating critic.[3]

3 Because of schedule conflicts, I was not able to take the applications seminar, and so will confine the balance of this section to my experiences in Kuznets's growth course and during his supervision of my dissertation, which lasted for five years. However, fellow students at Johns Hopkins who took the seminar told me how much they had learned about the art of measurement from the course.

At the time I took it, Kuznets's course on economic growth covered four main topics: population, technological change, long-term trends in national product and its components, and cross-sectional analysis of differences in per capita income, industrial structure, and the political and social characteristics of developed and less developed nations. On each of these topics, Kuznets defined the issues to be studied, the types of evidence available to study them, the methodological problems of obtaining from the available data the kinds of information required to resolve the issues, and the results obtained from applying different analytical and statistical procedures to different types of data (including qualitative and anecdotal information). He also interpreted the findings to date, carefully evaluating the conclusions that they could support, pointing up crucial gaps in information revealed by the studies (often suggesting how they might be closed), and carefully evaluating conflicting findings in order to determine whether the conflicts were merely the consequences of poorly conceived or poorly executed studies, or raised new issues that constituted an agenda for the next round of research.

One of the first methodological points that emerged from the course was that while the statistical analysis of quantitative data was a powerful instrument in the study of long-term changes in the economies of nations, it provided no magical solutions. Quite the contrary, it was filled with pitfalls that had entrapped some of the most able investigators (virtually no one was immune), and that even when the data were good, the procedures appropriate, and the results fairly unambiguous, great care had to be exercised in drawing conclusions about the domain to which the findings applied and the predictions that could reliably be based upon them. High on his list of major dangers was the superficial acceptance of primary data without an adequate understanding of the circucumstances under which the data were produced. Adequate understanding involved detailed historical knowledge of the changing institutions, conventions, and practices which affected the production of the primary data but which were difficult to ascertain and to quantify.

Throughout his lectures it was apparent that Kuznets practiced what he preached about the need to know history. He was well versed in the history of economics as a discipline, in the history of censuses and other data sources (not only in the United States and Europe but also in many less developed nations), in the history of science and technology, and in the general economic history of numerous countries. One might think that with such wide reading his grasp of any one of these topics was bound to be superficial. Yet the depth of his knowledge on each of these questions was strikingly evident.

When Kuznets dealt with the development of the Watt steam engine, for example, he not only carefully identified each of its new components but he went into considerable detail about the host of problems that Watt had to overcome. Numerous events preceding the basic design and many that came afterward were set forth, including Watt's education as a mechanic, his exclusion from the guild, the opportunities opened to him when he was hired as the instrument maker for the laboratory at the University of Glasgow, the way in which his scientific cast of mind developed, his difficulty in finding machinists who could mill parts to the tolerances required by his design, the difficulties of financing both the long developmental process and the sales of expensive equipment, the advantages of his partnership with Matthew Boulton, and the persistent search for improvements in the original design, especially for adaptations that transformed the engine from a steam-powered pump into a general power source capable of driving all kinds of machinery. Kuznets did not assume that the search for generalizations about the process of invention and diffusion made details about the personalities, beliefs, and circumstances of inventors and entrepreneurs irrelevant. Quite the contrary, he believed that the mastery of these details was a precondition for valid generalizations.

Another point high on Kuznets's list of major dangers was the easy assumption that a good fit of a mathematical model to the data made it an adequate description of the significant features of the data. Because of the limitations of data, especially in time series, many mathematical models, varying in complexity and structure, may give fairly good fits to a given body of data. Nor can Occam's razor be glibly invoked to settle such issues, since it is possible that the curve which gives the best fit incorrectly leads to the conclusion that the data were generated by a simple process, an elegant "law" of behavior embodied in a single equation, when in fact they were generated by several distinct processes that are badly distorted by the simple function.

Kuznets's comments on methods were always deeply embedded in a more general evaluation of the substantive findings of a particular investigation. Thus, whether a given body of data was good or bad depended not only on the inherent limitations of the data set but on the types of measures that were being constructed from it and the issues to which these measures were addressed. Consequently, his evaluation of the validity of substantive findings tended less to be cast as simply right or wrong, although this was sometimes the judgment, but more often focused on reliability of the results (usually expressed as the probable range of error in the estimates – not just t-values, but a more fundamental assessment which included judgments of the probable influence of systematic errors in the underlying data as well as errors introduced by the selection of the behavioral models and statistical techniques), and on their domain of applicability.

Although he placed great emphasis on the development of data bases of the highest quality (i.e., those least afflicted by sample selection biases, by definitional changes which led to lumping data that are intrinsically different in some important dimension into the same category, etc.), Kuznets was not a purist who insisted on working only with "perfect" data. Since no data set is ever perfect, his emphasis was on how to exploit the data at hand in order to extract from them whatever useful information they might contain. But then the limitations of the data on the resulting analysis had to be specified, with some results treated as conjectural, and still others merely as illustrative computations. Providing that they were carried out with due caution regarding the nature of the results, such preliminary analyses were useful, because they increased the likelihood of upgrading the available data sets or closing gaps in them by demonstrating the social usefulness of such efforts. Indeed, he viewed the preliminary analysis of the available data as an essential part of an asymptotic process of discovery, during which both the underlying data sets and analytical procedures were perfected and made more suitable to the resolution of the substantive issues.

Like many other statisticians, Kuznets worried about imposing so much structure on the data that the a priori assumptions of the investigation overwhelmed whatever information there was in the data. He was skeptical about fitting simple (two or three parameter) curves to data sets with relatively few observations of questionable quality. Consequently, he tended to work with frequency distributions, usually in either one-way or two-way classifications, rather than with regressions. Kuznets did not object to regressions per se (his students frequently used them with his blessings), but only to statistical procedures that were inappropriate (especially too restrictive) for the issues under study and that presumed too much about imperfect data. He considered it misleading to attach too much importance to R^2 and t statistics, when the systematic biases in the data overwhelmed sampling variability.

He had numerous "horror" stories of how very able investigators had been misled by relying too heavily on a priori assumptions of what the world was really like, and on arguments by analogy, as well as by misplaced confidence in formal measures of goodness of fit. The case that impressed me most was his discussion early in the course of Raymond Pearl's contention that a simple logistic curve summarized tendencies so stable in human populations that it represented a law of population growth.[4] Pearl's theory was suggested by experiments with fruit flies raised in closed containers which show that with increasing density and a fixed food supply, the growth of the population was well described by a logistic curve. Using Malthusian types of arguments, he contended that the analogy applied to humans because space is also limited on earth. He then proceeded to fit logistic curves to data for various populations and, with one or two exceptions that he explained as special cases, obtained apparently good fits. Pearl also showed that one of the conditions for a logistic curve to be applicable, a decline in birth rates as population density increases, was supported by cross-sectional regressions on U.S. cities between birth rates and two density measures, after controlling for city size and per capita wealth or income. One implication of Pearl's findings was that population growth moved in long cycles, with population increasing until it came close to its asymptote. It hovered at this asymptote until some exogenous factor caused the asymptote to shift.

Kuznets carefully discussed both the a priori and statistical aspects of the argument, but I focus here on some of his statistical points. Although the data that Pearl gathered to test his theories came from a fairly exhaustive list of the nations for which such data were available at the time, they were mainly Western nations at relatively high levels of economic development. The observations were primarily for the period from the early or mid nineteenth century to 1920, and since they were usually decennial estimates, there were generally about twelve or fewer observations per country; consequently, "good fits" in the sense of a high R^2 did not mean they were significant. Even if the fits were statistically significant, however, they did not necessarily justify the conclusion that the underlying process was well described by a logistic curve, or provide the basis for a "law" invariant to social and cultural conditions. Since the logistic curve has three segments (convex from above, linear, and concave from above),

4 Pearl was a noted biologist and statistician whose theories on population growth are summarized in his 1925 book.

it would give good fit to data sets that were strictly linear, as well as to those that were strictly increasing at a decreasing rate or strictly increasing at an increasing rate. Examination of the underlying data revealed such segmentation to be pretty much the case.

Kuznets's manner of discussing these examples was nearly as important as the substance of his points. There was no attempt to demean Pearl or to puff up his own image. His aim was to demonstrate both the possibilities and limitations of quantitative methods in the social sciences. Valuable as they were, such methods did not provide easy, let alone automatic, solutions to otherwise difficult problems. No matter how high-powered the technique, the results it yielded had to be carefully evaluated not only by looking at such internal evidence as the scatter of observations around the fitted curve, but also by a thorough consideration of such relevant external evidence as the nature of the societies that yielded the data, and of the conventions followed by the agencies that gathered, processed, and published them.

The results, he emphasized time and again, had meaning only if the investigator defined and studied the universe from which the data were drawn, and that required a substantial effort to discover and understand the relevant social institutions of the societies under study as well as how they were changing over time. To be a good quantitative economist, then, required not only logical and technical cleverness, but also a substantial knowledge of recent and more distant history. Although he admired cleverness and technical proficiency, I believe that he considered the capacity to be thorough and to pursue details rigorously as a rarer quality and as a more binding constraint on good work.

In assessing the reliability of particular estimates, Kuznets emphasized the importance of systematically investigating their relationship to other series and other kinds of information that were logically related to them. He was, in this connection, a master of devising algebraic identities that brought other available data to bear on the estimates at issue in a particularly illuminating way. They were also marvelous devices for revealing implicit and unsupported assumptions, and thus contributed to the social research agenda. A dazzling example of this skill is contained in his evaluation of the time series on U.S. national income and its sectoral distribution generated by Robert F. Martin for the period 1799 through 1869 (Kuznets 1952a, 1952b). What puzzled Kuznets about these widely cited figures was that they implied a decline of about 8 percent in per capita income over the 40 years between 1799 and 1839, which witnessed vigorous growth in population, a vast geographic expansion, and the introduction and initial diffusion of the steamboat, the railroad, and the factory system.

To evaluate Martin's series in the light of the available data, Kuznets employed the following identity:

$$(1) \quad \bar{Y} = \rho (\lambda_a W_a + \lambda_n W_n)$$

where

$\bar{Y} =$ per capita income

$\rho =$ the labor force participation rate

$\lambda_a =$ the share of the labor force in agriculture

$\lambda_n =$ the share of the labor force outside agriculture

$W_a =$ output per worker in agriculture

$W_n =$ output per worker outside agriculture

Marshalling the available fragments of data, Kuznets surmised that even if there had been no increase in W_a or W_n over the period 1799 to 1839, the rise in ρ and the rise in λ_n relative to λ_a should jointly have led to about a 19 percent increase in per capita income since W_n/W_a, as indicated by Martin's data, was equal to about 5. He then went on to marshal fragmentary data suggesting that W_a and W_n had both probably risen, contrary to the implication of Martin's series, so that even Kuznets's exercise probably underestimated the total growth of per capita income during 1799–1839.

Kuznets's exercise on Martin's data touched off a major stream of research involving numerous investigators that have greatly illuminated the course of U.S. economic growth prior to 1840 (Engerman and Gallman 1983). It was characteristic of Kuznets that he considered the mathematics underlying his computations so obvious that he never made equation (1) explicit. Although this and other Kuznetsian identities were often used by his students in teaching, the simple equation (or a variant of it) was not put into print until the publication of David's influential paper in 1967, more than a decade after Kuznets's original discussion of it. Subsequently a variety of Kuznetsian and Kuznets-like identities have been set forth as differential equations and effectively exploited.

Did the numerous biases that afflicted the data sets with which economists had to work, the pitfalls of curve fitting, and the sensitivity of results to the presumed underlying behavioral models, as well as to the choice of statistical procedures, doom the usefulness of quantitative methods in the study of economic growth? By no means. Kuznets was neither an optimist nor a pessimist on this question but a realist and an architect of procedures needed to make the most of defective data and imperfect tools. In the most difficult of circumstances, Kuznets pointed out, such as those which confronted Pearl in his attempt to demonstrate that the logistic curve represented the law of human population growth, there was important information to be gleaned. What Pearl had indirectly demonstrated was that all of the advanced nations on which data were available had experienced declines in their percentage rates of natural increase between 1850 and 1920. That finding was robust no matter what segment of the logistic curve Pearl had fitted to his data, since it is a characteristic of the logistic function that the percentage rate of increase is always declining. This was no mean finding. It was one of the early demonstrations of what subsequent research confirmed as a major demographic feature of modern economic growth. Hidden among the oysters was a genuine pearl.

The last point calls attention to what I believe was the most powerful lesson that Kuznets taught about the art of measurement in economics: sensitivity analysis. It was sensitivity analysis, not clever a priori arguments, that separated robust findings from conjectures. Anyone good enough to get a Ph.D. after the mid 1950s could marshal an a priori case for why one procedure should be preferred over another, or why some bias in the data could be ignored. It was much harder to demonstrate that a finding based on such a priori arguments should be taken seriously, since it was equally easy to construct a priori arguments proving that the designated procedure badly biased the result or that the imperfections in the data were fatal. Kuznets's solution to such problems was sensitivity analysis, by which he meant a careful examination of both the procedures and data in order to see if plausible ranges of the systematic errors in the data, or the substitution of reasonable alternative estimation procedures, would make a material difference in the finding. If they did not, the finding was robust; otherwise the data added nothing to the theoretical considerations that preceded the measurement. The original conjecture was still just a conjecture.

I learned about sensitivity analysis during the course of my dissertation. In order to estimate the social savings of railroads in the interregional distribution of grain and meat, it was necessary to know the total amount of each commodity shipped during 1890 from each primary market and the total receipts at each secondary market. The outshipments from the ten Midwestern primary markets could be obtained directly from the annual reports of the boards of trade in each of these cities, but the reports did not list either the specific destinations or the specific quantities assigned to each destination. It occurred to me that I could fill the gap by estimating the required consumption of each commodity in each secondary market and then subtract out local production (using the disappearance procedures of the USDA to convert stocks into net flows available for human consumption) to obtain the import requirements as a residual. Although feasible, it was a laborious task which required information on the boundaries of over a hundred secondary markets; budget studies by regions with considerable detail on consumption by age, sex, and occupation; information on live weights of animals as well as coefficients needed to convert live weights into dressed equivalents, and a host of other details. After many weeks of searching in libraries at Johns Hopkins and the Library of Congress, and of lengthy calculations on old-fashioned mechanical computers, I finally produced a set of estimates, one that I was quite prepared to defend on conceptual grounds. So I proudly presented them to Kuznets. He looked my tables over carefully and said: "Very interesting, Mr. Fogel. What kind of figures do you obtain when you estimate the requirements of secondary markets by another procedure?" "What other procedure?" I asked. "Think about it for a while, Mr. Fogel, and I am sure that something will occur to you. Then let me see the results." With some hard thinking and further searching in the sources, I discovered an alternate way of estimating requirements in two of the major secondary markets. The results in these markets were close enough to the original estimates to satisfy Kuznets. And that, as I have often told my students, is how I learned about sensitivity analysis.

III. Kuznets as a theorist

Kuznets is one of the most important theorists since Keynes. Some measure of his impact on theory in one of the major areas of his research, the interrelationship between population change and economic growth, is provided by the author index of *The Determinants and Consequences of Population Trends: New Summary of Findings on Interaction of Demographic, Economic and Social Factors*. Prepared by a United Nations commission, the study summarizes and interprets the worldwide literature in this field from the earliest times to the 1970s. Among the individuals frequently cited in the author index are Donald J. Bogue, Colin Clark, Ansley J. Coale, Richard A. Easterlin, Phillip M. Houser, Edgar M. Hoover, Charles P. Kindleberger, W. A. Lewis, Thomas R. Malthus, H. Myint, Gunnar Myrdal, Frank W. Notestein, Alfred Sauvey, Joseph J. Spengler, Dorothy S. Thomas, Irene B. Tauber, and B. T. Urlanis. The citations to Kuznets, however, exceed those to any of these specialists, usually by large margins. They even exceed the citations to such collective authors as FAO, ILO, OECD, and WHO. Indeed, only the combined agencies of the United Nations have more citations than Kuznets.

Since the interrelationship between population and economic growth is only one of the major themes on which Kuznets theorized, it is obvious that I cannot comment in detail on the substance of his numerous contributions. So I want only to present some brief comments about his approach to theory. In this connection it is useful to begin with a distinction that Kuznets often made between a partial and a general theory of economic growth. By a partial theory Kuznets meant the in-depth consideration of a few variables torn from the context of the general process of economic growth. In this connection he welcomed the explosion of mathematical growth models that began in the late 1940s and the 1950s as a return to issues that had been so important to Smith, Malthus, and Schumpeter, thus finally overcoming the long neglect of growth theory. Yet he feared that because of the severe aesthetic constraints placed on the issues and on the interrelations of variables by the type of mathematical modeling that was fashionable, this stream of research might rapidly dissipate without making a lasting contribution to what Kuznets considered the principal objective of theoretical work in this field: the development of a tested and confirmed general theory of growth that included a theory of technological change, of population growth, of changes in the economic structure of production, of changes in political and social organization, and of the role of international political relations. A general theory not only needed to encompass each of these major elements but to describe the feedback mechanisms that linked them together in a dynamic context.

Kuznets recognized that such a theory was a tall order and would probably not be accomplished in his lifetime. He not only welcomed partial models as contributions toward that goal, as long as they contributed to the ultimate object of a general theory, but himself contributed numerous partial models. His presidential address to the American Economic Association, in which he considered the impact of economic growth on the inequality of the income distribution (1955), exemplifies his approach to such partial theories. It was in this paper that Kuznets set forth the hypotheses that in early stages of economic growth (i.e., at low levels of per capita income), growth tended to increase the inequality of the income distribution, but that at later stages (high levels of per capita income), growth reduced inequality. That hypothesis, which has come to be known in the literature as the "inverted-U hypothesis," set off a large train of both theoretical and empirical research aimed at elaborating the hypothesis and at testing it empirically. The hypothesis has been put to practical use by the World Bank, which transformed the hypothesis into an econometric model suitable for estimating the share of the world population living in poverty (Anand and Kanbur 1984a, 1984b, 1987; cf. Fei, Ranis, and Kuo 1978).

It is interesting to note that Kuznets's 1955 paper has not only been treated as an important theoretical paper but also as providing empirical support for the inverted-U hypothesis (Fields 1980, pp. 78, 84). This is a rather strange development since Kuznets was at pains to stress its theoretical nature, repeatedly warning that his allusions to fragmentary data were not evidence but little more than "pure guesswork." Most of the paper is devoted to explicating the conflicting factors that arose during the course of growth and that created pressures both to increase and to reduce inequality. The paper also describes processes that influenced the relative strength of the conflicting factors at different stages in the growth process. It would have been easy for Kuznets to set forth his model in a mathematical form (since the computations he presented to illustrate the process implied a set of equations), but Kuznets chose to make the same points with numerical examples. Numerical examples had two advantages over a mathematical presentation. They emphasized the limited range of the changes in the key variables and parameters needed to bring about the postulated curve. Numerical examples also made his argument accessible to a wider range of readers. Since there was nothing in the model which required a long chain of reasoning to reveal some deeply buried implication, there was no reason to restrict his audience.

This example reveals something important both about Kuznets's approach to theory and about certain problems in the profession. Because Kuznets developed a theory consistent with the available fragmentary evidence, because he used numbers rather than algebra to set forth the theory, his paper was widely interpreted as an "empirical paper," despite Kuznets's repeated warnings about the fragility of the data that suggested the theory. He also stressed that even if the data turned out to be valid, they pertained to an extremely limited period of time and to exceptional historical experiences, so that caution had to be exercised in the conclusions that were drawn from his theory. Nevertheless, Kuznets's caveats were jettisoned and his hypothesis was raised to the level of law, becoming the basis for numerous formal models and elaborate econometric exercises, some of which lost touch with the complex reality that Kuznets was trying to uncover and to characterize.

The example calls attention to a shortcoming of current theory. That is the tendency to value a theory according to the type of mathematics it employs. On this criterion the best theory employs the most general mathematics, as free as possible from such empirical or quasi-empirical limitations, as the specification of the form of functions. But that criterion is purely aesthetic – equivalent to constraints that a sonnet imposes on a poet. Aside from aesthetic considerations, such severe limitations are generally unnecessary in economics because the range of most economic variables is fairly constrained. Making use of that knowledge frequently makes it possible to solve models that cannot be solved in a purely analytical (abstract) framework. Ansley Coale, an elegant analyst, has frequently made use of the limited ranges of variation in demographic behavior to close demographic models with empirical relationships, and thereby manipulate models that would otherwise remain intractable. It is this flexibility in demographic modeling that in no small measure accounts for the vastly improved quality of empirical research in this field, in the face of data problems as severe as any encountered in economics proper.

Kuznets was more interested in theories that proposed to describe and generalize on some aspects of the observable behavior of the economy than those that sought the simplest set of a priori assumptions, and the weakest specification of functional relationships, that could produce a particular generalization. Among the theories that he found most fruitful, but not necessarily correct, were Malthus's statements on the relationship between population and economic growth, Schumpeter's theory of the business cycle, Hoffmann's theory of the sequencing of industrialization, Hansen's theory of the effect of population growth on savings rates, theories about the behavior of savings over the life cycle, theories of human capital formation, theories about the factors affecting the size distribution of income, and neoclassical models of economic growth (particularly as developed by Solow, Denison, Griliches, and Jorgenson, since they implied accounting identities that when flexibly approached were useful in arraying data bearing on the growth process).

Kuznets appreciated the advantages of formalizing such generalizations and of demonstrating how they could be deduced from a limited set of a priori assumptions. Such work had shown that downward-sloping demand curves, perhaps the single most important analytical and empirical tool of economics, did not require the dubious, convoluted assumptions about consumer psychology of earlier theorists, but could be generated from a few simple assumptions about preference orderings. The mathematical development of the theory of consumer demand also called attention to the important distinction between income and substitution effects and had a large impact on the development of statistical procedures for the estimation of demand functions.

Yet, without in any way belittling these achievements, Kuznets feared that such formalization of theory was becoming increasingly sterile, partly as the result of an overinvestment in it. Too many papers merely explored the consequence of changing one or another assumption in a given hypothetico-deductive model. Though they pointed up the sensitivity of such models to their assumptions, they rarely served as guides to study of the real economic world. Nevertheless these intellectual exercises acquired a vogue, and those engaged in this work developed a set of standards for judging quality that had little to do with the ultimate bearing of the models on empirical research. To avoid sterility, hypothetico-deductive modeling had to be intimately connected with, and regularly infused by, findings from empirical, experimental, and clinical research, as they normally were in the natural sciences.

Kuznets was impatient with economists who became infatuated with elegance and forgot that the aim of theory was to promote the search for tested knowledge about economic behavior. There was a limit to how far theory in economics could become separated from the product which the patrons of economics – the policymakers – demand of the discipline. Although, as I tried to indicate in the first section of this paper, he placed great emphasis on the importance of specialized research institutions and university graduate programs that were sufficiently free from government and business bureaucracies to explore novel ideas and methods, Kuznets also emphasized that all work, even the purest of theory, had ultimately to be judged by its social payoff. One may quarrel about the proper way to measure the payoff to pure theory, but as a practical matter the resources available for such work are heavily dependent upon the volume and quality of that part of the output of scientific disciplines whose social usefulness is readily apparent to policymakers. It is not the pure theorists but the experimentalists and empiricists whose output is directly keyed to societal demands that have been most effective in convincing policymakers to support those seemingly dainty and irrelevant exercises (the pure theory) that they neither understand nor are inclined to support.

IV. A brief talk by Kuznets

No one understood the social context of the rise of economics better than Kuznets. So it is fitting to close my comments on his scientific methods by presenting a brief autobiographical talk, to my knowledge the only such liberty he allowed himself. The occasion was a dinner in honor of his eightieth birthday, sponsored jointly by the economics department of Harvard University and the National Bureau of Economic Research. It was a remarkable occasion, attended by some two hundred well-wishers, coming from as far away as India, and representing not only economics but other disciplines that Kuznets had influenced. Those present included numerous past presidents of the American Economic Association, the Econometrics Society, and other scholarly associations, seven Nobel prize winners, and economists who had served in government at cabinet and subcabinet levels. It was, as Henry Rosovsky pointed out, one of the most impressive assemblies of scholarly talent ever gathered in a single room. At the end of an hour of accolades showered on Kuznets with deep sincerity, he rose to respond:[5]

> You probably will not be able to hear me, as usual. I am really very grateful to all of you who came here, particularly to those who organized this festivity, and those who were so eloquent on behalf of a person whom I did not recognize. I have an inclination always to think of how much I do not know and how much I have to learn. So it is very difficult for me to recognize in your descriptions the kind of person I think I am. Furthermore, there were certain circumstances that determined my long-term research program that were not of my making and which made it easy to do what I have done. I would like briefly to describe those circumstances.
>
> I came to this country in 1922, at the age of twenty-one, so that most of the first quarter of my life was spent in Russia, primarily in study but also accumulating a fair amount of experience: war, revolution, two years in an institution devoted to economics, two years in the Soviet government. In fact, I ended up as the head of a section of the bureau of

5 What follows is a transcription, which I have edited lightly for publication, of a talk that Kuznets gave at Harvard University on April 25, 1981.

labor statistics of the Ukraine, and my first publication was in Russian at the ripe age of twenty. So when I came to the United States, I came with a peculiar equipment: formal training in a scientific *gymnasium*, a fair amount of experience with statistical research in economics, a fair amount of reading (I knew Schumpeter's work well before I came here), and a liking for orderly quantitative procedures applied to socially oriented topics.

I spent from 1922 to 1927 working toward my Ph.D. degree at Columbia University, where I met Wesley Mitchell, who had a tremendous influence on me. I then wrote my first postdoctoral research monograph on secular movements in production and prices. In 1927 I joined the National Bureau of Economic Research, at which I stayed for three and a half decades. At the National Bureau I also met Edith. We married in 1929 and she has been with me through thick and thin for 50 years now. While at the National Bureau, I was asked to teach in the statistics department at the University of Pennsylvania. I agreed because I felt I should try teaching, although I had earlier turned down an invitation from Columbia college to become an instructor there. I began teaching on a part-time basis in 1930 and became a full-time professor in 1936, while continuing at the Bureau.

From 1936 until 1971, when I retired from Harvard, I continually combined graduate teaching in economics with special research work under the auspices of specialized research institutions. The National Bureau of Economic Research, the Social Science Research Council, and the Economic Growth Center at Yale University all helped to shape my research program and permitted me to pursue it in environments that promoted solid performance. At the same time, I taught at the University of Pennsylvania in both statistics and economics, at Johns Hopkins and at Harvard, which gave me an opportunity to interest the younger generation in some of the problems in which I was interested. Now I submit that the availability of specialized research institutions in this country, which were rare abroad, and the possibility of combining that opportunity with graduate teaching at the university was one, almost indispensable, condition for the kind of sustained research program that I preferred to follow.

A second set of circumstances should be noted. There was an explosion of quantitative economic research in this country beginning with the 1930s. The U.S. government, and later governments of many other countries, began to accept responsibility for economic growth, for adequate employment, and, in general, for shaping the long-term conditions of economic life in ways in which they did not do previously. These new efforts required recourse to macro measures of the kind on which the National Bureau was working. It was within the year that I began preparing to take over the national income work of the Bureau that I was drafted by the Department of Commerce to construct the first of the official government estimates of national income, in fulfillment of a

Senate resolution requesting such estimates. The same sort of pressures continued during World War II because macro measures were needed to check and shape the war production program. If the external circumstances, the concern of the government and the nation with especially urgent economic problems and policies, had not occurred when they did, there would not have been a coincidence between the measures on which I was working and what was needed. Because such measures were needed to carry out national policy, it was possible to secure cooperation and a volume of resources that otherwise would not have been available.

As I look back on the sequence of studies that I was instrumental in completing, they began with a group of related studies of factors – cyclical fluctuations, secular movements, seasonal variations – that affected the development of the American economy. Then they shifted to national income for a single country, the United States. Then they shifted to a wider view, using national income estimates and their components to compare the performance of different countries in many parts of the world on an international scale. That sequence of studies would not have been feasible between 1900 and 1920 or even between 1910 and 1930. It was feasible only between 1930 and 1970.

Let me conclude by thanking you all for participating in this festivity, and I thank you not only for that. In a sense you are all collaborators, who are to be praised for whatever I am praised, and blamed for whatever I am blamed. So let me share the glory and let me share the troubles with you. And perhaps tomorrow we can return to real work.[6]

Robert William Fogel
University of Chicago

References

Abramovitz, Moses. 1985. *Simon Kuznets: An appreciation.* Department of Economics, Stanford University. Photocopy.

1971. Nobel prize for economics: Kuznets and economic growth. *Science*, October 29.

1952. Economics of growth. In *A survey of contemporary economics*, vol. 2. Bernard F. Haley, ed. Homewood, IL: Richard D. Irwin.

Anand, Sudhir, and S. M. Ravi Kanbur. 1987. *International poverty projections.* Paper presented at the UNU/WIDER conference on poverty, undernutrition and living standards, Helsinki, Finland, July 27–31.

1984a. Inequality and development: A reconsideration. In *Towards in-*

6 The last sentence referred to an all-day meeting on April 26 devoted to a discussion of recent developments in the international study of economic growth.

come distribution policies: From income distribution research to income distribution policy in LDC's. H. P. Nissen, ed. EADI-Book Series, No. 3, Tilburg.

1984b. The Kuznets process and the inequality-development relationship. St. Catherine's College, Oxford. Mimeograph. Forthcoming in *Journal of Development Economics*.

Ben-Porath, Yoram. 1986. *Simon Kuznets in person and in writing*. The Maurice Falk Institute for Economic Research in Israel. Discussion Paper No. 86.08.

Bergson, Abram. 1986. Simon Kuznets: 30 April 1901–8 July 1985. *American Philosophical Society Yearbook*: 134–138.

Bergson, Abram, Harvey Leibenstein, Henry Rosovsky, and Zvi Griliches (Chairman). 1987. Faculty of arts and sciences – Memorial minute: Simon Kuznets. Minute placed upon the records at a meeting of the Harvard University faculty, December 16, 1986. *Harvard Gazette*, March 20, 1987.

David, P. A. 1967. The growth of real product in the United States before 1840: New evidence, controlled conjectures. *Journal of Economic History* 27:151–97.

Engerman, S. L., and R. E. Gallman. 1983. U.S. economic growth. *Research in Economic History* 8:1–46.

Fei, J. C. H., Gustav Ranis, and S. W. Y. Kuo. 1978. Growth and the family distribution of income by factor components. *Quarterly Journal of Economics* 92:17–53.

Fields, Gary S. 1980. *Poverty, inequality and development*. Cambridge: Cambridge University Press.

Kuznets, Simon. 1972. *Quantitative economic research: Trends and problems*. Economic research retrospect and prospect, Fiftieth Anniversary Colloquia. General Series 96, vol. 7. New York: National Bureau of Economic Research.

1966. *Modern economic growth: Rate, structure, and spread*. Studies in Comparative Economics 7. New Haven, CT, and London: Yale University Press.

1955. Economic growth and income inequality. *American Economic Review, Papers and Proceedings* 45:1–28. Presidential address. Reprinted in *Economic growth and structure: Selected essays*. New York: Norton.

1952a. National income estimates for the United States prior to 1870. *Journal of Economic History* 12:115–130.

1952b. Long-term changes in the national income of the United States of America since 1870. In *Income and Wealth of the United States: Trends and structure.* Income and Wealth, ser. 2. International Association for Research in Income and Wealth. Cambridge: Bowes and Bowes.

Patinkin, Don. 1976. Keynes and econometrics: On the interaction between macroeconomic revolutions of the interwar period. *Econometrica* 44:1091–1123.

Pearl, Raymond. 1925. *The biology of population growth.* New York: A. A. Knopf.

United Nations. 1978. *The determinants and consequences of population trends,* vol. 2. New York: United Nations Publication.

Bibliography of Simon Kuznets

The basis for this chronological bibliography is a listing compiled in 1981 by Robert W. Fogel, Marilyn Coopersmith, and Kathleen McCauley and published in *Economic Development and Cultural Change* in 1983. The EDCC bibliography has been edited by Edith Kuznets, and various items have been added, including some published pieces and a number of unpublished works, such as memoranda prepared while Kuznets served with the federal government during World War II. The listing remains incomplete, although it contains every important published work. A number of typescripts – articles never published, first drafts, etc. – have been omitted. All of these papers will form part of the Kuznets collection being gathered together by Mrs. Kuznets for the Harvard University Archive. Many of the items have been published in translation, but the translations do not appear in the bibliography.

Books

Cyclical Fluctuations: Retail and Wholesale Trade, United States, 1919–1925. Prefatory note by Wesley C. Mitchell. New York: Adelphi Co., 1926.

Secular Movements in Production and Prices: Their Nature and Their Bearing upon Cyclical Fluctuations. Boston: Houghton Mifflin Co., 1930.

Wesen und Bedeutung des Trends, Zur Theorie der Säkulären Bewegung. Veröffentlichungen der Frankfurter Gesellschaft für Konjunkturforschung, Heft 7. Bonn: Kurt Schroeder, 1930.

Seasonal Variations in Industry and Trade. New York: National Bureau of Economic Research, 1933.

National Income, 1929–1932. Senate Document no. 124, 73d Cong., 2d sess. Washington, D.C.: Government Printing Office, 1934.

National Income and Capital Formation, 1919–1935. New York: National Bureau of Economic Research, 1937.

Commodity Flow and Capital Formation, vol. 1. New York: National Bureau of Economic Research, 1938.

National Income and Its Composition, 1919–1938. Assisted by Lillian Epstein and Elizabeth Jenks. 2 vols. New York: National Bureau of Economic Research, 1941.

With Milton Friedman, *Income from Independent Professional Practice*. New York: National Bureau of Economic Research, 1945.

439

National Product in Wartime. New York: National Bureau of Economic Research, 1945.

National Income: A Summary of Findings. Twenty-fifth Anniversary Series. New York: National Bureau of Economic Research, 1946.

National Product since 1869. Assisted by Lillian Epstein and Elizabeth Jenks. New York: National Bureau of Economic Research, 1946.

With E. D. Burdick, E. P. Hutchinson, and D. T. Rowlands, *Population of Philadelphia and Environs in 1950.* Philadelphia: University of Pennsylvania, Institute of State and Local Government, 1946.

Editor and author of Introduction, *Income and Wealth of the United States: Trends and Structure, Income and Wealth,* Ser. 2. International Association for Research in Income and Wealth. Cambridge: Bowes and Bowes, 1952.

Economic Change: Selected Essays in Business Cycles, National Income, and Economic Growth. New York: W. W. Norton & Co., 1953.

Shares of Upper Income Groups in Income and Savings. Assisted by Elizabeth Jenks. New York: National Bureau of Economic Research, 1953.

Editor (with Wilbert E. Moore and Joseph J. Spengler) and author of Foreword, *Economic Growth: Brazil, India, Japan.* Durham, N.C.: Duke University Press, 1955.

Editor and author of Introduction, *Income and Wealth,* Ser. 5. International Association for Research in Income and Wealth. Cambridge: Bowes & Bowes, 1955.

Six Lectures on Economic Growth. Glencoe, Ill.: Free Press, 1959.

Capital in the American Economy: Its Formation and Financing. Assisted by Elizabeth Jenks. Studies in Capital Formation and Financing 9. National Bureau of Economic Research. Princeton, N.J.: Princeton University Press, 1961.

Editor, with Abram Bergson, *Economic Trends in the Soviet Union.* Cambridge, Mass.: Harvard University Press, 1963.

Postwar Economic Growth: Four Lectures. Cambridge, Mass.: Harvard University Press, Belknap Press, 1964.

Six Lectures on Economic Growth. 1959. (In Spanish.) *Aspectos Cuantitativos del Desarrollo Económico.* 2d ed., rev. and enl. Conferencias. Mexico City: C.E.M.L.A., 1964. Two new papers added.

Economic Growth and Structure: Selected Essays. New York: W. W. Norton & Co., 1965. Translated into French, with a new Preface. *Croissance et Structures Economiques.* Paris: Calmann-Lévy, 1972.

Modern Economic Growth: Rate, Structure, and Spread. Studies in Comparative Economics 7. New Haven, Conn., and London: Yale University Press, 1966.

Toward a Theory of Economic Growth, with Reflections on the Economic Growth of Modern Nations. New York: W. W. Norton & Co., 1968.

Modern Economic Growth: Rate, Structure and Spread, An Adaptation. Prepared by Dr. John Murphy. Current Thought Series, no. 8. Bombay: Vakils, Feffer & Simons, 1970. Translated into a number of foreign languages.

Economic Growth of Nations: Total Output and Production Structure. Cambridge, Mass.: Harvard University Press, Belknap Press, 1971.

Quantitative Economic Research: Trends and Problems. Economic Research Retrospect and Prospect, Fiftieth Anniversary Colloquia. General Series 96, vol. 7. New York: National Bureau of Economic Research, 1972.

Population, Capital, and Growth: Selected Essays. New York: W. W. Norton & Co., 1973.

Growth, Population, and Income Distribution: Selected Essays. New York: W. W. Norton & Co., 1979.

Articles*

"Money Wages of Factory Employees in Kharkov in 1920." (In Russian.) In *Materials on Labor Statistics of Ukraine,* 2d issue. Kharkov: Central Soviet of Trade Unions, Southern Bureau, Division of Statistics, July 1921.

"On Moving Correlation of Time Sequences." *Journal of the American Statistical Association* 23 (1928): 121–36.

"On the Analysis of Time Series." *Journal of the American Statistical Association* 23 (1928): 398–410.

"Random Events and Cyclical Oscillations." *Journal of the American Statistical Association* 24 (1929): 258–75.

"Equilibrium Economics and Business-Cycle Theory." *Quarterly Journal of Economics* 44 (1930): 381–415. Reprinted in *Economic Change: Selected Essays in Business Cycles, National Income, and Economic Growth.* New York: W. W. Norton & Co., 1953.

"Monetary Business Cycle Theory in Germany." *Journal of Political Economy* 38 (1930): 125–63.

"Static and Dynamic Economics." *American Economic Review* 20 (1930): 426–41. Reprinted in *Economic Change: Selected Essays in Business Cycles, National Income, and Economic Growth.* New York: W. W. Norton & Co., 1953.

"Conjuncture." *Encyclopaedia of the Social Sciences* (New York: Macmillan Co., 1931), 4:203–4.

"Curve Fitting." *Encyclopaedia of the Social Sciences* (New York: Macmillan Co., 1931), 4:652–56.

"Seasonal Pattern and Seasonal Amplitude: Measurement of Their Short-Term Variations." *Journal of the American Statistical Association* 27 (1932): 9–20.

"National Income." *Encyclopaedia of the Social Sciences* (New York: Macmillan Co., 1933), 11:205–24.

"Gross Capital Formation, 1919–1933." Bulletin 52. New York: National Bureau of Economic Research, 1934.

"National Income, 1929–1932." Bulletin 49. New York: National Bureau of Economic Research, 1934.

"Relation between Capital Goods and Finished Products in the Business Cycle." In *Economic Essays in Honor of Wesley Clair Mitchell.* New York: Columbia University Press, 1934. Reprinted in *Economic Change: Selected Essays in*

---

* Includes occasional and other papers, comments, introductions, and bulletins and pamphlets.

Business Cycles, National Income, and Economic Growth. New York: W. W. Norton & Co., 1953.

"Time Series." *Encyclopaedia of the Social Sciences* (New York: Macmillan Co., 1934), 14:629–36.

"The Attitudes of Members of the American Statistical Association toward the Question of Calendar Reform." *Journal of the American Statistical Association* 30 (1935): 437–45.

"Changes in National Income in the United States." In *On Economic Planning*. Paper delivered at the Regional Study Conference of the International Industrial Relations Institute, New York, November 23–27, 1934. New York: Covici-Friede, 1935.

With Wesley C. Mitchell, "Current Problems in Measurement of National Income." In *XXII Session de l'Institut de Statistique, Londres*, Sec. 2. Communication The Hague, 1934. Also published in *Bulletin of the International Institute of Statistics* (1935), pp. 281–98.

"Income Originating in Nine Basic Industries, 1919–1934." Bulletin 59. New York: National Bureau of Economic Research, 1936.

"Changing Inventory Valuations and Their Effect on Business Savings and on National Income Produced." In *Studies in Income and Wealth*, vol. 1. Conference on Research in National Income and Wealth. New York: National Bureau of Economic Research, 1937. [Discussion on pp. 165–72.]

Discussion of Morris A. Copeland, "Concepts of National Income." In *Studies in Income and Wealth*, vol. 1. Conference on Research in National Income and Wealth. New York: National Bureau of Economic Research, 1937: 35–48.

Discussion of Gerhard Colm, "Public Revenue and Public Expenditure in National Income." In *Studies in Income and Wealth*, vol. 1. Conference on Research in National Income and Wealth. New York: National Bureau of Economic Research, 1937.

"National Income, 1919–1935." Bulletin 66. New York: National Bureau of Economic Research, 1937: 230–38.

"Dr. Warburton's Review of *National Income and Capital Formation* – a Comment." *Journal of the American Statistical Association* 33 (1938): 714–19.

"On the Measurement of National Wealth." In *Studies in Income and Wealth*, vol. 2. Conference on Research in National Income and Wealth. New York: National Bureau of Economic Research, 1938, pp. 3–61. [Discussion on pp. 78–82.]

Discussion of Roy Blough and W. W. Hewett, "Capital Gains in Income Theory and Taxation Policy." In *Studies in Income and Wealth*, vol. 2. Conference on Research in National Income and Wealth. New York: National Bureau of Economic Research, 1938, pp. 249–51.

Discussion of G. C. Means, Lauchlin Currie, and R. Nathan, "Problems in Estimating National Income Arising from Production by Government." In *Studies in Income and Wealth*, vol. 2. Conference on Research in National Income and Wealth. New York: National Bureau of Economic Research, 1938, pp. 292–306.

"Capital Formation in the United States, 1919–1935." In *Capital Formation and Its Elements*. New York: National Industrial Conference Board, 1939.

"Commodity Flow and Capital Formation in the Recent Recovery and Decline, 1932–1938." Bulletin 74. New York: National Bureau of Economic Research, 1939.

"National Income and Capital Formation." Paper presented in session on "Income and Capital Formation." *American Economic Review, Papers and Proceedings* 29, suppl., pt. 2 (1939): 57–58.

Discussion of C. L. Merwin, Jr., "American Studies of the Distribution of Wealth and Income by Size." In *Studies in Income and Wealth*, vol. 3. Conference on Research in National Income and Wealth. New York: National Bureau of Economic Research, 1939: 85–93.

Discussion of Clark Warburton, "Three Estimates of the Value of the Nation's Output of Commodities and Services: A Comparison." In *Studies in Income and Wealth*, vol. 3. Conference on Research in National Income and Wealth. New York: National Bureau of Economic Research, 1939: 381–90.

Discussion of R. R. Nathan, "Some Problems Involved in Allocating Incomes by States." In *Studies in Income and Wealth*, vol. 3. Conference on Research in National Income and Wealth. New York: National Bureau of Economic Research, 1939: 430–34.

With Milton Friedman, "Incomes from Independent Professional Practice, 1929–1936." Bulletins 72–73. New York: National Bureau of Economic Research, 1939.

"Schumpeter's *Business Cycles*." (Review article.) *American Economic Review* 30 (1940): 257–71. Reprinted in *Economic Change: Selected Essays in Business Cycles, National Income, and Economic Growth*. New York: W. W. Norton & Co., 1953.

"National and Regional Measures of Income." *Southern Economic Journal* 6 (1940): 291–313.

"Capital Formation, 1879–1938." In *Studies in Economics and Industrial Relations*. Philadelphia: University of Pennsylvania Press, 1941.

"National Income, 1919–1938." Occasional Paper 2. New York: National Bureau of Economic Research, 1941.

"Statistics and Economic History." *Journal of Economic History* 1 (1941): 26–41.

"Analysis of the Production Program," U.S. War Production Board Planning Committee, Document 151, August 12, 1942.

"National Income and Taxable Capacity." *American Economic Review, Papers and Proceedings* 32, suppl. (1942): 37–75.

"Uses of National Income in Peace and War." Occasional Paper 6. New York: National Bureau of Economic Research, 1942.

"The Why and How of Distributions of Income by Size." In *Income Size Distributions in the United States*, pt. 1. *Studies in Income and Wealth*, vol. 5. Conference on Research in Income and Wealth. New York: National Bureau of Economic Research, 1943.

"U.S. Production in Two Wars," Memorandum to the U.S. War Production Board Planning Committee, 89 pages, 1943(?).

"National Product, War and Prewar." Occasional Paper 17. New York: National Bureau of Economic Research, 1944.

Reply to Milton Gilbert, Hans Staehle, and W. S. Woytinsky, "National Product, War and Prewar: Some Comments on Professor Kuznets' Study." *Review of Economic Statistics* 26 (1944): 126–35.

"Taxes and National Income." Paper read before the American Philosophical Society in the Symposium on Taxation and the Social Structure, February. *Proceedings of the American Philosophical Society* 88 (1944): 10–21.

"Measurement of Economic Growth." *Journal of Economic History* 7, suppl. (1947): 10–34.

Comment on William Vickrey, "Resource Distribution Patterns and the Classification of Families." In *Studies in Income and Wealth*, vol. 10. Conference on Research in Income and Wealth. New York: National Bureau of Economic Research, 1947.

"Foreign Economic Relations of the United States and Their Impact upon the Domestic Economy." *Proceedings of the American Philosophical Society* 92 (1948): 228–43. Reprinted in *Economic Change: Selected Essays in Business Cycles, National Income, and Economic Growth*. New York: W. W. Norton & Co., 1953.

"National Income: A New Version." *Review of Economics and Statistics* 30 (1948): 151–79.

"National Income and Industrial Structure." *Econometrica* 16 (1948): 86–90. Abstract of paper published in full in 1951.

"On the Valuation of Social Income – Reflections on Professor Hicks' Article." *Economica* 15, pt. 1 (February 1948): 1–16; pt. 2 (May 1948): 116–31.

"Ingreso Nacional y Bienestar Económico." *Boletín del Banco Central de Venezuela* nos. 53 and 54 (July–August 1949), pp. 11–21. Reprinted as "National Income and Economic Welfare." In *Economic Change: Selected Essays in Business Cycles, National Income, and Economic Growth*. New York: W. W. Norton & Co., 1953.

"Programme d'Enquêtes comparatives sur le processus d'industrialization dans le monde actuel" (An outline of a comparative study of industrialization), April 1949, 77 pages (mimeograph).

Introduction and "Suggestions for an Inquiry into the Economic Growth of Nations." In *Problems in the Study of Economic Growth*. Special Conference Series, no. 1. Universities – National Bureau Committee on Economic Research. Mimeographed. New York: National Bureau of Economic Research, July 1949: ii–iii, 1–20.

"Notes on the Quantitative Approach to Economic Growth." In *Problems in the Study of Economic Growth*, Special Conference Series, no. 1. Universities – National Bureau Committee on Economic Research. New York: National Bureau of Economic Research, July 1949: 117–35.

"Wesley Clair Mitchell, 1874–1948: An Appreciation." *Journal of the American Statistical Association* 44 (1949): 126–31.

Comment on Raymond W. Goldsmith, A. G. Hart, and Morris A. Copeland, "Problems in the Measurement of Wealth." In *Studies in Income and*

Wealth, vol. 12. Conference on Research in Income and Wealth. New York: National Bureau of Economic Research, 1950.

"Conditions of Statistical Research." Presidential address, American Statistical Association. *Journal of the American Statistical Association* 45 (1950): 1–14.

"Share of Upper Income Groups in Income and Savings." Occasional Paper 35. New York: National Bureau of Economic Research, 1950.

"Diferencias Internacionales en los Niveles de Ingresos (Reflexiones sobre sus Causas)." *Boletín del Banco Central de Venezuela*, nos. 65 and 66 (July–August 1950), pp. 20–36. Reprinted as "International Differences in Income Levels: Reflections on Their Causes." In *Economic Change: Selected Essays in Business Cycles, National Income, and Economic Growth*. New York: W. W. Norton & Co., 1953.

Comment on Raymond W. Goldsmith, "A Perpetual Inventory of National Wealth." In *Studies in Income and Wealth*, vol. 14. Conference on Research in Income and Wealth. New York: National Bureau of Economic Research, 1951.

Comment on Joseph A. Schumpeter, "Historical Approach to the Analysis of Business Cycles." In *Conference on Business Cycles*. Special Conference Series, no. 2. Universities – National Bureau Committee for Economic Research. New York: National Bureau of Economic Research, 1951.

"Government Product and National Income." In *Income and Wealth*, Ser. 1. International Association for Research in Income and Wealth. Cambridge: Bowes & Bowes, 1951.

"National Income and Industrial Structure." *Proceedings of the International Statistical Conference 5 1947* (Calcutta, 1951): 205–39. A brief abstract in *Econometrica* 16 (January 1948): 86–90. Reprinted in *Economic Change: Selected Essays in Business Cycles, National Income, and Economic Growth*. New York: W. W. Norton & Co., 1953.

"The State as a Unit in the Study of Economic Growth." *Journal of Economic History* 11 (1951): 25–41.

"Statistical Trends and Historical Change." *Economic History Review* 3, 2d. ser. (1951): 265–78.

Comment on Moses Abramovitz, "Economics of Growth." In *A Survey of Contemporary Economics*, vol. 2, edited by Bernard F. Haley for the American Economic Association. Homewood, Ill.: Richard D. Irwin, Inc., 1952.

"Comments on Mr. Ou's Study of the National Income of China." Typewritten, 1946. Listed in *Bibliography on Income and Wealth, 1937–1947*, vol. 1. International Association for Research in Income and Wealth. Cambridge: Bowes and Bowes, 1952.

"Directions of Further Inquiry." In *Studies in Income and Wealth*, vol. 15. Conference on Research in Income and Wealth. New York: National Bureau of Economic Research, 1952.

Foreword to *Conference on Research in Business Finance*. Special Conference Series, no. 3. Universities – National Bureau Committee on Economic Research. New York: National Bureau of Economic Research, 1952.

"National Income." In *Encyclopaedia Britannica*, 1951–57, 16:143–45.

"Wealth, National." In *Encyclopaedia Britannica*, 1953–56, 23:449.

"Wealth, Primitive." In *Encyclopaedia Britannica*, 1953–56, 23:450.

"Wealth and Income, Concepts of." In *Encyclopaedia Britannica*, 1953–56, 23:450–51.

"Wealth and Income, Statistics of." In *Encyclopaedia Britannica*, 1953–56, 23:451–54.

Introduction to Daniel Creamer, ed., *Bibliography on Income and Wealth, 1937–1947*, vol. 1, International Association for Research in Income and Wealth. Cambridge: Bowes & Bowes, 1952.

"Long-Term Changes in the National Income of the United States of America since 1870." In *Income and Wealth of the United States: Trends and Structure*. Income and Wealth, ser. 2. International Association for Research in Income and Wealth. Cambridge: Bowes & Bowes, 1952, pp. 29–241.

"National Income Estimates for the United States Prior to 1870." *Journal of Economic History* 12 (1952): 115–30.

"Proportion of Capital Formation to National Product." *American Economic Review, Papers and Proceedings* 42 (1952): 507–26.

"A Note on Aggregation Problems." In *Savings in the Modern Economy: A Symposium*, edited by Walter W. Heller, Francis M. Boddy, and Carl L. Nelson, Minneapolis: University of Minnesota Press, 1953.

"Retardation of Industrial Growth." *Journal of Economic and Business History* 1 (1929): 534–60. Reprinted in *Economic Change: Selected Essays in Business Cycles, National Income, and Economic Growth*. New York: W. W. Norton & Co., 1953.

"Concepts and Assumptions in Long-Term Projections of National Product." In *Long-Range Economic Projection: Studies in Income and Wealth*, vol. 16. Conference on Research in Income and Wealth, National Bureau of Economic Research. Princeton, N.J.: Princeton University Press, 1954.

With Ernest Rubin, "Immigration and the Foreign Born." Occasional Paper 46. New York: National Bureau of Economic Research, 1954.

"Economic Policy and Its Study" (in Hebrew). *Economic Quarterly* 1 (1954).

"Introductory Notes" in *Papers of the Conference on Strategic Factors in Periods of Rapid Economic Growth*, sponsored by the Committee on Economic Growth of the Social Science Research Council, New York, April 9–10, 1954: 1–6 (mimeograph).

"Underdeveloped Countries and the Pre-Industrial Phase in the Advanced Countries: An Attempt at Comparison." In *Proceedings of the World Population Conference* (Rome, 1954) *Papers* 5:947–69.

"Comparative Study of Long-Term Records of Economic Growth." *Items: Social Science Research Council* 9 (1955): 42–46.

"Economic Growth and Income Inequality." *American Economic Review, Papers and Proceedings* 45 (1955): 1–28. Presidential address. Reprinted in *Economic Growth and Structure: Selected Essays*. New York: W. W. Norton & Co., 1965.

"International Differences in Capital Formation and Financing." In *Capital Formation and Economic Growth*. Special Conference Series, no. 6. Universities – National Bureau Committee for Economic Research. Princeton, N.J.: Princeton University Press, 1955.

"Population, Income and Capital (Statistical Evidence)." In *Economic Progress*. Papers and Proceedings of a Round Table held by the International Economic Association at Sta Margherita Ligure, Italy, August 28–September 2, 1953, edited by Léon H. Dupriez. Louvain: Institut de Recherches Economiques et Sociales, 1955.

"Problems in Comparisons of Economic Trends." In *Economic Growth: Brazil, India, Japan*, edited by Simon Kuznets, Wilbert E. Moore, and Joseph J. Spengler. Durham, N.C.: Duke University Press, 1955.

"Problems in Economic Growth: An Exploratory Memorandum." Mimeographed. Committee for Economic Development, March 1955.

"Toward a Theory of Economic Growth" and "Reply to Discussion." In *National Policy for Economic Welfare at Home and Abroad*, edited by Robert Lekachman. Columbia University Bicentennial Conference Series. Garden City, N.Y.: Doubleday & Co., 1955. Reprinted in *Economic Growth and Structure: Selected Essays*. New York: W. W. Norton & Co., 1965.

"National Income: The Measure and Its Meaning," University Lecture, December 12, 1956, 16 pages (mimeograph).

"Quantitative Aspects of the Economic Growth of Nations. I. Levels and Variability of Rates of Growth." *Economic Development and Cultural Change* 5 (1956): 1–94.

Comment on Edward F. Denison, "Theoretical Aspects of Quality Change, Capital Consumption, and Net Capital Formation." In *Problems of Capital Formation: Concepts, Measurement, and Controlling Factors: Studies in Income and Wealth*, vol. 19. Princeton, N.J.: Princeton University Press, 1957.

Foreword to Leon Grebler, David M. Blank, and Louis Winnick, *Capital Formation in Residential Real Estate: Trends and Prospects*. Studies in Capital Formation and Financing, vol. 1. National Bureau of Economic Research. Princeton, N.J.: Princeton University Press, 1957.

Foreword to Alvin S. Tostlebe, *Capital in Agriculture: Its Formation and Financing since 1870*. Studies in Capital Formation and Financing, no. 2. National Bureau of Economic Research. Princeton, N.J.: Princeton University Press, 1957.

With Dorothy Swaine Thomas, Introduction to Everett S. Lee, Ann Ratner Miller, Carol P. Brainerd, and Richard A. Easterlin, *Population Redistribution and Economic Growth, United States, 1870–1950. I. Methodological Considerations and Reference Tables*. Prepared under the direction of Simon Kuznets and Dorothy Swaine Thomas. *Memoirs of the American Philosophical Society*, vol. 45 (1957).

"Notes on the Economic Growth of Italy," 1957(?), 34 pages (typescript).

"Quantitative Aspects of the Economic Growth of Nations. II. Industrial Distribution of National Product and Labor Force." *Economic Development and Cultural Change* 5, suppl. (1957): 1–111.

Summary of Discussion and Postscript to W. W. Rostow, John R. Meyer, and Alfred H. Conrad, "The Integration of Economic Theory and Economic History," *Journal of Economic History* 17 (1957): 545–53.

"Sur la Croissance Economique des Nations Modernes." *Economie Appliquée* 10 (1957): 211–59. Reprinted in English as "Reflections on the Economic Growth of Modern Nations," in *Economic Growth and Structure: Selected Essays*. New York: W. W. Norton & Co., 1965.

Preface and "Economic Growth of Small Nations." In *The Challenge of Development*. Jerusalem: Hebrew University, Eliezer Kaplan School of Economics and Social Sciences, 1958. Reprinted in *Economic Consequences of the Size of Nations*. International Economic Association. New York: St. Martin's Press, 1960.

Foreword to Raymond W. Goldsmith, *Financial Intermediaries in the American Economy since 1900*. Studies in Capital Formation and Financing, no. 3. National Bureau of Economic Research. Princeton, N.J.: Princeton University Press, 1958.

With Dorothy Swaine Thomas, "Internal Migration and Economic Growth." In *Selected Studies of Migration since World War II. Proceedings of the Thirty-fourth Annual Conference of the Milbank Memorial Fund*, pt. 3 (New York, 1958), pp. 196–211.

"Long Swings in the Growth of Population and in Related Economic Variables." *Proceedings of the American Philosophical Society* 102 (1958): 25–52. Reprinted in *Economic Growth and Structure: Selected Essays*. New York: W. W. Norton & Co., 1965.

Preface to O. J. Firestone, *Canada's Economic Development, 1867–1953: Income and Wealth*, Ser. 7. International Association for Research in Income and Wealth. Cambridge: Bowes & Bowes, 1958.

"The Problem of Measurement." In *Social, Economic and Technological Change: A Theoretical Approach*. Paris: International Social Science Council, 1958.

"Regional Economic Trends and Levels of Living." In *Population and World Politics*, edited by Philip M. Hauser. Glencoe, Ill.: Free Press, 1958. Reprinted in *Economic Growth and Structure: Selected Essays*. New York: W. W. Norton & Co., 1965.

"Quantitative Aspects of the Economic Growth of Nations. III. Industrial Distribution of Income and Labor Force by States, United States, 1919–1921 to 1955." *Economic Development and Cultural Change* 6, no. 4, pt. 2 (1958): 1–128.

"Security and Growth in a Divided and Turbulent World." In *Problems of United States Economic Development*, vol. 1. New York: Committee for Economic Development, 1958.

"Canada's Economic Prospects." (Review article.) *American Economic Review* 49 (1959): 359–85.

"Notes on the Study of Economic Growth." *Items: Social Science Research Council* 13 (1959): 13–17.

"On Comparative Study of Economic Structure and Growth of Nations: An Exploratory Report." In *The Comparative Study of Economic Growth and Structure: Suggestions on Research Objectives and Organization*. New York: National Bureau of Economic Research, 1959.

"Quantitative Aspects of the Economic Growth of Nations. IV. Distribution of National Income by Factor Shares." *Economic Development and Cultural Change* 7, pt. 2 (1959): 1–100.

Foreword to *The State and Economic Growth*, edited by Hugh G. J. Aitken. New York: Social Science Research Council, 1959, pp. v–vi.

"The Changing Distribution and Structure of Economic Activity." In *Population Redistribution and Economic Growth: United States, 1870–1950*, vol. 2: *Analyses of Economic Change. Memoirs of the American Philosophical Society* 51 (1960): 206–87.

"Economic Structure and Life of the Jews." In *The Jews: Their History, Culture, and Religion*, 3d ed., vol. 2, edited by Louis Finkelstein. New York: Harper & Bros., 1960.

Foreword to Melville J. Ulmer, *Capital in Transportation, Communications, and Public Utilities: Its Formation and Financing*. Studies in Capital Formation and Financing, no. 4. National Bureau of Economic Research. Princeton, N.J.: Princeton University Press, 1960.

Introduction to Daniel Creamer, Sergei P. Dobrovolsky, and Israel Borenstein, *Capital in Manufacturing and Mining: Its Formation and Financing*. Studies in Capital Formation and Financing, no. 6. National Bureau of Economic Research. Princeton, N.J.: Princeton University Press, 1960.

Foreword to *The Israeli Economy: The First Decade*, by Don Patinkin. The Falk Project for Economic Research in Israel. Jerusalem: The Jerusalem Post Press, December 1960.

"How to Judge Quality." In *The New Republic*, October 20, 1962, pp. 29–32.

"Problems in Measuring Economic Growth." In *Economic Growth: Some Theories and Concepts*. Symposia Studies Series No. 14. Washington, D.C.: National Institute of Social and Behavioral Science, 1963, pp. 12–18.

"Demographic Aspects of Modern Economic Growth," Background Paper A10/2/E/389, contributed to the U.N. World Population Conference, 1965, Belgrade, Yugoslavia, August 30–September 10, 1965, and moderator's statement (mimeograph).

"Population Change and Aggregate Output." In *Demographic and Economic Change in Developed Countries*. Special Conference Series, no. 11. Universities – National Bureau Committee for Economic Research. Princeton, N.J.: Princeton University Press, 1960; and "Reply" to comments by Richard E. Quandt and Milton Friedman. Reprinted in *Economic Growth and Structure: Selected Essays*. New York: W. W. Norton & Co., 1965.

"Present Underdeveloped Countries and Past Growth Patterns." In *Economic Growth: Rationale, Problems, Cases*, edited by Eastin Nelson. Austin: University of Texas Press, 1960. Reprinted in *Economic Growth and Structure: Selected Essays*. New York: W. W. Norton & Co., 1965.

"Quantitative Aspects of the Economic Growth of Nations. V. Capital Formation Proportions: International Comparisons for Recent Years." *Economic Development and Cultural Change* 8, pt. 2 (1960): 1–96.

"Economic Growth and the Contribution of Agriculture: Notes on Measurement." In *The Role of Agriculture in Economic Development. International Journal of Agrarian Affairs* 3 (1961): 56–75.

Foreword to Morris A. Copeland, *Trends in Government Financing*. Studies in Capital Formation and Financing, no. 7. National Bureau of Economic Research. Princeton, N.J.: Princeton University Press, 1961.

"Quantitative Aspects of the Economic Growth of Nations. VI. Long-Term Trends in Capital Formation Proportions." *Economic Development and Cultural Change* 9, pt. 2 (1961): 1–124.

"Uses of National Income Estimates in Economic Growth Analysis and Policy." International Association for Research in Income and Wealth. Meeting in Rio de Janeiro, June 8–13, 1959. In *Statistical Methods, National Income Accounts, Input-Output Analysis*. Washington, D.C.: Bank for Reconstruction and Development, Economic Development Institute, 1961.

"The Economic Requirements of Modern Industrialization." In *Transactions of the Fifth World Congress of Sociology*, vol. 2. Held in Washington, D.C., September 2–8, 1962. International Sociological Association, 1962. Reprinted in *Economic Growth and Structure: Selected Essays*. New York: W. W. Norton & Co., 1965.

"Income Distribution and Changes in Consumption." In *The Changing American Population*, edited by Hoke S. Simpson. A Report of the Arden House Conference. New York: Institute of Life Insurance, 1962.

"International Aspects of Economic Growth." In *Bulletin of the International House of Japan* 9 (April 1962): 2–8.

"Inventive Activity: Problems of Definition and Measurement." In *The Rate and Direction of Inventive Activity: Economic and Social Factors*. Special Conference Series, no. 13. Universities – National Bureau Committee for Economic Research. Princeton, N.J.: Princeton University Press, 1962.

"Quantitative Aspects of the Economic Growth of Nations. VII. The Share and Structure of Consumption." *Economic Development and Cultural Change*, vol. 10, no. 2, pt. 2 (1962): 1–92.

"A Comparative Appraisal." In *Economic Trends in the Soviet Union*, edited by Abram Bergson and Simon Kuznets. Cambridge, Mass.: Harvard University Press, 1963.

"Consumption, Industrialization and Urbanization." In *Industrialization and Society*, edited by Bert F. Hoselitz and Wilbert E. Moore. *Proceedings of the Chicago Conference on Social Implications of Industrialization and Technical Change*, September 15–22, 1960. Paris: Mouton & Cie., 1963.

"The Contribution of Wesley C. Mitchell." In *Institutional Economics: Veblen, Commons, and Mitchell Reconsidered*. A Series of Lectures, Institute of Industrial Relations, University of California at Los Angeles. Berkeley and Los Angeles: University of California Press, 1963.

"Economic Growth and the Contribution of Agriculture: Notes on Measurement." In *The Role of Agriculture in Economic Development. Proceedings of the Eleventh International Conference of Agricultural Economists*. Held in Cuernavaca, Morelos, Mexico, August 19–30, 1961. London: Oxford University Press, 1963. "Introductory Statement," "Reply to Discussion." See also article in *International Journal of Agrarian Affairs*, vol. 3

(1961), "Economic Growth and the Contribution of Agriculture: Notes on Measurement." Reprinted in *Economic Growth and Structure: Selected Essays*. New York: W. W. Norton & Co., 1965.

"Notes on the Take-Off." In *The Economics of Take-Off into Sustained Growth*, edited by W. W. Rostow. Proceedings of a Conference held by the International Economic Association, Konstanz, Germany, 1960. New York: St. Martin's Press, 1963. Reprinted in *Economic Growth and Structure: Selected Essays*. New York: W. W. Norton & Co., 1965.

"Parts and Wholes in Economics." In *Parts and Wholes. Hayden Colloquium on Scientific Method and Concept*, edited by Daniel Lerner. New York: Free Press of Glencoe, 1963.

"Quantitative Aspects of the Economic Growth of Nations. VIII. Distribution of Income by Size." *Economic Development and Cultural Change* 11, pt. 2 (1963): 1–80.

"Caratteristiche del Progresso Economico Moderno." *La Scuola in Azione*. Scuola Enrico Mattei di Studi Superiori sugli Idrocarburi, San Donato Milanese, no. 8 (1964), pp. 5–20.

Introduction to "Population Redistribution, Migration, and Economic Growth," by Hope T. Eldridge and Dorothy Swaine Thomas, *Population Redistribution and Economic Growth: United States, 1870–1950. III. Demographic Analyses and Interrelations. Memoirs of the American Philosophical Society*, vol. 61 (1964).

"Note sur Certaines Conséquences des Inégalités de la Repartition des Revenus." *Economie Appliquée* 16, no. 4 (1964): 561–78. Reprinted as "Inequalities in the Size Distribution of Income" in *Economic Growth and Structure: Selected Essays*. New York: W. W. Norton & Co., 1965.

"Notes on the Pattern of U.S. Economic Growth." In *The Nation's Economic Objectives*, edited by Edgar O. Edwards. Rice University Semicentennial Publications. Chicago: University of Chicago Press, 1964. Reprinted in *Economic Growth and Structure: Selected Essays*. New York: W. W. Norton & Co., 1965.

"Quantitative Aspects of the Economic Growth of Nations. IX. Level and Structure of Foreign Trade: Comparisons for Recent Years." *Economic Development and Cultural Change* 13, pt. 2 (1964): 1–106.

Comments on E. J. R. Booth, "The Present State of Knowledge about Economic Growth"; W. W. McPherson, "Overview of Southern Economic Growth"; and G. S. Tolley, "Development Differentials," in *Optimizing Institutions for Economic Growth*. Sponsored by the Agricultural Policy Institute, North Carolina State, and the Southern Land Economics Research Committee, 1965.

Contribution to *Agriculture and Economic Growth, a Report by a Group of Experts*. Paris: Organisation for Economic Co-Operation and Development, 1965.

"Growth and Structure of National Product, Countries in the ECAFE Region, 1950–1961." In *Report of the Asian Population Conference*, pt. 2, *Selected Papers*. Held at New Delhi, December 10–20, 1963. New York: United

Nations Economic Commission for Asia and the Far East, E/CN.11/ 670, 1965.

"Learning from the Growth Processes of the Developed States." In *Fiscal and Monetary Problems in Developing States. Proceedings of the Third Rehovot Conference*, edited by David Krivine. Praeger Special Studies in International Economics and Development. New York and London: Frederick A. Praeger, Inc., 1967: 3–18.

"Population and Economic Growth." In *Population Problems*. Paper read at the Autumn General Meeting, November 11, 1966. *Proceedings of the American Philosophical Society* 3 (1967): 170–93. Reprinted in *Population, Capital and Growth: Selected Essays*. New York: W. W. Norton & Co., 1973.

"Quantitative Aspects of the Economic Growth of Nations. X. Level and Structure of Foreign Trade: Long-Term Trends." *Economic Development and Cultural Change* 15, pt. 2 (1967): 1–140.

"Tendencias a Largo Plazo en las Relaciones Proporcionales del Comercio Exterior." *Revista de Economía Latinoamericana*, Publicada bajo los auspicios del Banco Central de Venezuela, nos. 19–20 (1967).

"Capital Formation in Modern Economic Growth (and some implications for the past)." Read at the *Third International Conference of Economic History*. Munich, 1965. Paris: Mouton & Cie., 1968. Reprinted in *Population, Capital, and Growth: Selected Essays*. New York: W. W. Norton & Co., 1973.

"Developed and Underdeveloped Countries: Some Problems of Comparative Analysis." In *Zeitschrift für die Gesamte Staatswissenschaft* 124 (1968): 96–107.

"Economic Capacity and Population Growth." In *World Population: The View Ahead. Proceedings of the Conference on World Problems* held at Indiana University on May 3–6, 1967, edited by Richard N. Farmer, John D. Long, and George J. Stolnitz. International Development Research Center Series no. 1, published by the Bureau of Business Research, Graduate School of Business, Indiana University. Reprinted in *Population, Capital, and Growth: Selected Essays*. New York: W. W. Norton & Co., 1973.

"Notes on Japan's Economic Growth." In *Economic Growth: The Japanese Experience since the Meiji Era*, edited by Lawrence Klein and Kazushi Ohkawa. Publication of the Economic Growth Center, Yale University. Homewood, Ill.: Richard D. Irwin, Inc., 1968.

"Trends in Level and Structure of Consumption." In *Economic Growth: The Japanese Experience since the Meiji Era*, edited by Lawrence Klein and Kazushi Ohkawa. Publication of the Economic Growth Center, Yale University. Homewood, Ill.: Richard D. Irwin, Inc., 1968.

"Economic Aspects of Fertility Trends in the Less Developed Countries." In *Fertility and Family Planning: A World View*, edited by S. J. Behrman, Leslie Corsa, Jr., and Ronald Freedman. Ann Arbor: University of Michigan Press, 1969. Reprinted in *Population, Capital, and Growth: Selected Essays*. New York: W. W. Norton & Co., 1973.

"Methodological Problems in the Study of Economic Growth" and "Functions of Economists in Public Service." In *Economic Papers*. Special English Series, no. 1. Institute of Economics, Academia Sinica, Nankang, Taipei, Taiwan, 1969.

Foreword to *National Income of India: Trends and Structure*, by M. Mukherjee. Calcutta: Statistical Publishing Society, 1969.

"The Penalties of Success." In *Survey of Current Business*, vol. 51, no. 7, pt. II, July 1971, pp. 114–16.

"Economic Implications of Technical Assistance." In *Technical Assistance and Development. Proceedings of the Truman International Conference on Technical Assistance and Development*, held at the Harry S. Truman Research Institute. Hebrew University of Jerusalem, May 1970. Publication no. 6. Jerusalem: Truman Research Institute, 1971.

"Notes on Stage of Economic Growth as a System Determinant." In *Comparison of Economic Systems: Theoretical and Methodological Approaches*, edited by Alexander Eckstein. Berkeley: University of California Press, 1971. Reprinted in *Population, Capital, and Growth: Selected Essays*. New York: W. W. Norton & Co., 1973.

"Data for Quantitative Economic Analysis: Problems of Supply and Demand." Expanded version of a lecture delivered at the Federation of Swedish Industries, December 13, 1971. Stockholm: P. A. Norstedt & Sons, 1972. Reprinted in *Population, Capital, and Growth: Selected Essays*. New York: W. W. Norton & Co., 1973.

"Economic Structure of U.S. Jewry: Recent Trends." Institute of Contemporary Jewry. Jerusalem: Hebrew University of Jerusalem, 1972. (Revised version of "Economic Structure and Life of the Jews," 1960 [above].)

Foreword to Jacob Schmookler, *Patents, Invention, and Economic Change: Data and Selected Essays*, edited by Zvi Griliches and Leonid Hurwicz. Cambridge, Mass.: Harvard University Press, 1972.

"The Gap: Concept, Measurement, Trends." In *The Gap between Rich and Poor Nations. Proceedings of a Conference held by the International Economic Association* at Bled, Yugoslavia, edited by Gustav Ranis. London and Basingstoke: Macmillan Press; New York: St. Martin's Press, 1972. Reprinted in *Population, Capital, and Growth: Selected Essays*. New York: W. W. Norton & Co. 1973.

"Innovations and Adjustments in Economic Growth." *Swedish Journal of Economics* 74 (1972): 431–51. Expanded version of a lecture delivered May 10, 1972, in the Davidson Lecture Series, Whittemore School of Business and Economics, University of New Hampshire, Durham. Reprinted in *Population, Capital, and Growth: Selected Essays*. New York: W. W. Norton & Co., 1973.

"Modern Economic Growth: Findings and Reflections." Nobel Memorial Lecture, December 1971. In *Les Prix Nobel en 1971*. Stockholm, 1972. Reprinted in *American Economic Review* 63 (1973): 247–58. Reprinted in *Population, Capital, and Growth: Selected Essays*. New York: W. W. Norton & Co., 1973.

"Problems in Comparing Recent Growth Rates for Developed and Less De-

454   Economic development, family, and income distribution

veloped Countries." *Economic Development and Cultural Change* 20 (1972): 185–209. Reprinted in *Population, Capital, and Growth: Selected Essays*. New York: W. W. Norton & Co., 1973.

Concluding Remarks to *The Measurement of Economic and Social Performance*, edited by Milton Moss. Studies in Income and Wealth 38. Conference on Research in Income and Wealth, National Bureau of Economic Research. New York: Columbia University Press, 1973.

With Gustav Ranis, Kazushi Ohkawa, Yasukichi Yasuba, and Tsunehiko Watanabe, contribution to Round Table Discussion, "Japan's Economic Growth and Less-Developed Nations," *Oriental Economist* 41 (January 1973): 24–34, and 41 (February 1973): 36–43.

General Remarks in *Economic Growth: The Japanese Experience since the Meiji Era*, edited by Kazushi Ohkawa and Yujiro Hayami. Tokyo: Japan Economic Research Center, 1973.

"Notes on the Economic Development of Israel." (In Hebrew.) *Economic Quarterly* 20 (1973): 189–209.

"Demographic Aspects of the Distribution of Income among Families: Recent Trends in the United States." In *Econometrics and Economic Theory: Essays in Honor of Jan Tinbergen*, edited by Willy Sellekaerts. London: Macmillan Press, 1974. Reprinted in *Growth, Population and Income Distribution: Selected Essays*. New York: W. W. Norton & Co., 1979.

"Income-Related Differences in Natural Increase: Bearing on Growth and Distribution of Income." In *Nations and Households in Economic Growth: Essays in Honor of Moses Abramovitz*, edited by Paul A. David and Melvin W. Reder. New York and London: Academic Press, 1974. Reprinted in *Growth, Population and Income Distribution: Selected Essays*. New York: W. W. Norton & Co., 1979.

"Notes on Theories of Economic Growth." *Academia Economic Papers* 2 (March 1974): 1–12. Institute of Economics, Academia Sinica, Nankang, Taipei, Taiwan. Revised summary of lecture delivered July 1972.

"Rural-Urban Differences in Fertility: An International Comparison." *Proceedings of the American Philosophical Society* 118 (1974): 1–29. Reprinted in *Growth, Population, and Income Distribution: Selected Essays*. New York: W. W. Norton & Co., 1979.

"Sources of Economic Growth in a Less Developed Country." *Academia Economic Papers*, vol. 2 (1974). Institute of Economics, Academia Sinica, Nankang, Taipei, Taiwan. Edited transcript of the public lecture delivered July 4, 1972.

"Reflections on the Symposium Theme" (probably notes on Nobel Symposium 29: *Man, Environment, and Resources in the Perspective of the Past and the Future*, Stockholm, September 16–20, 1974, typescript).

"Demographic Components in Size-Distributions of Income." In *Income Distribution, Employment and Economic Development in Southeast and East Asia*. Papers and Proceedings of the Seminar sponsored jointly by the Japan Economic Research Center and the Council for Asian Manpower Studies, December 16–20, 1974 (with contribution from ILO World

Employment Programme), vol. 2, pp. 389–472, July 1975, the Japan
Economic Research Center, Tokyo, and the Council for Asian Manpower Studies, Manila. See also Introduction, pp. 151–55, and Summary, vol. 2, pp. 789–91.

"Fertility Differentials between Less Developed and Developed Regions: Components and Implications." *Proceedings of the American Philosophical Society* 119 (1975): 363–96. Reprinted in *Growth, Population and Income
Distribution: Selected Essays.* New York: W. W. Norton & Co., 1979.

"Immigration of Russian Jews to the United States: Background and Structure."
Perspectives in American History 9 (1975): 33–124.

"Population Increase, Causes, Consequences, and Remedies: Perspective of the
Past." In *Man, Environment, and Resources in the Perspective of the Past
and the Future*, edited by Torgny Segerstedt and Sam Nilsson. Nobel
Symposium 29, Stockholm, September 16–20, 1974. Stockholm: Nobel
Foundation, 1975.

"Population Trends and Modern Economic Growth: Notes Towards a Histori-
cal Perspective." In *The Population Debate: Dimensions and Perspectives.*
Papers of the World Population Conference, Bucharest, 1974, mimeo-
graph, vol. 1. Department of Economic and Social Affairs. Population
Studies, no. 57. New York: United Nations, 1975. Reprinted in *Growth,
Population and Income Distribution: Selected Essays.* New York: W. W.
Norton & Co., 1979.

"Postwar Growth of Less Developed Countries." In *Economic Growth in Developing Countries – Material and Human Resources: Proceedings of the Seventh
Rehovot Conference*, edited by Yohanan Ramati. Praeger Special Studies
in International Economics and Development. New York: Praeger Publishers, 1975, p. 489.

"Aspects of the Post–World War II Growth in Less Developed Countries." In
*Evolution, Welfare, and Time in Economics: Essays in Honor of Nicholas
Georgescu-Roegen*, edited by Anthony M. Tang, Fred M. Westfield, and
James S. Worley. Lexington, Mass.: Lexington Books, D. C. Health
& Co., 1976. Reprinted in *Growth, Population and Income Distribution:
Selected Essays.* New York: W. W. Norton & Co., 1979.

"Demographic Aspects of the Size Distribution of Income: An Exploratory Essay." *Economic Development and Cultural Change* 25 (1976): 1–94.

"Demographic Implications of Economic Growth." In *Conference on Population
and Economic Development in Taiwan*, sponsored by the Institute of Economics, Academia Sinica, Taipei, Taiwan, December 29, 1975–January
2, 1976.

"Notes on the Study of Economic Growth of Nations." In *Essays on Economic
Development and Cultural Change*, edited by Manning Nash, in honor of
Bert F. Hoselitz. *Economic Development and Cultural Change* 25 (1977):
300–313. Reprinted in *Growth, Population and Income Distribution: Selected Essays.* New York: W. W. Norton & Co., 1979.

"Two Centuries of Economic Growth: Reflections on U.S. Experience." The
Richard T. Ely Lecture in the *American Economic Review, Papers and*

Proceedings 67, no. 1 (1977): 1–14. Reprinted in *Growth, Population, and Income Distribution: Selected Essays*. New York: W. W. Norton & Co., 1979.

"Technological Innovations and Economic Growth." In *Technological Innovation: A Critical Review of Current Knowledge*, edited by Patrick Kelly and Melvin Krantzberg. San Francisco: San Francisco Press, 1978. Reprinted in *Growth, Population, and Income Distribution: Selected Essays*. New York: W. W. Norton & Co., 1979.

"Size and Age Structure of Family Households: Exploratory Comparisons." *Population and Development Review* 4 (1978): 187–223.

"Gaps in the Science-Technology-Development Sequence: A Comment." In *Science, Technology, and Economic Development: A Historical and Comparative Study*, edited by William Beranek, Jr., and Gustav Ranis. New York: Praeger Publishers, 1978.

"Economic Growth and Shifts in Price Structure." In *Hommage à Francois Perroux*. Grenoble: Presses Universitaires de Grenoble, 1978, pp. 247–54.

With Nancy Birdsall, John Fei, Gustav Ranis, and T. Paul Schultz, "Demography and Development in the 1980s." In *World Population and Development: Challenges and Prospects*, edited by Philip M. Hauser. Syracuse, N.Y.: Syracuse University Press, 1979.

"Growth and Structural Shifts." In *Economic Growth and Structural Change in Taiwan – the Postwar Experience of the Republic of China*, edited by Walter Galenson. Ithaca, N.Y., and London: Cornell University Press, 1979.

"Driving Forces of Economic Growth: What Can We Learn from History?" In *Weltwirtschaftliches Archiv* 116 (1980): 409–31. Also printed in *Towards an Explanation of Economic Growth*, edited by Herbert Giersch. Tübingen: J. C. B. Mohr, 1980.

"Modern Economic Growth." In *Views on Global Economic Development*, edited by Valerie Kreutzer. Washington, D.C.: Department of State, International Communication Agency, 1980.

"Notes on Demographic Change." In *American Economy in Transition*, edited by Martin Feldstein. Papers of a Conference held in January 1980 marking the Sixtieth Anniversary of the National Bureau of Economic Research. Chicago: University of Chicago Press, 1980.

"Notes on Income Distribution in Taiwan." In *Quantitative Economics and Development: Essays in Memory of Ta-Chung Liu*, edited by L. R. Klein, M. Nerlove, and S. C. Tsiang. New York and London: Academic Press, 1980.

"Recent Population Trends in Less Developed Countries and Implications for Internal Income Inequality." In *Population and Economic Change in Developing Countries*. A Conference Report, Universities – National Bureau Committee for Economic Research, no. 30, edited by Richard Easterlin. Chicago: University of Chicago Press, 1980.

Comment on Victor R. Fuchs, "Economic Growth and the Rise of Service Employment." In *Towards an Explanation of Economic Growth*, edited by Herbert Giersch. Tübingen: J. C. B. Mohr, 1981.

"A Note on Production Structure and Aggregate Growth." In *Economic Welfare and the Economics of Soviet Socialism: Essays in Honor of Abram Bergson*, edited by Steven Rosefielde. New York: Cambridge University Press, 1981.

"Produttività." In *Enciclopedia del Novecento*, vol. 5. Rome: Istituto dell' Enciclopedia Italiana, 1981.

"Size of Households and Income Disparities." In *Research in Population Economics* 3, edited by Julian L. Simon and Peter H. Lindert. Greenwich, Conn.: JAI Press, 1981.

"The Use of Statistics in Economic Research: Reflections on the Last Half Century," Address at the Colloquium in honor of the Fiftieth Anniversary of the Statistics Department of the Wharton School, University of Pennsylvania, May 8, 1981 (typescript).

"Children and Adults in the Income Distribution." *Economic Development and Cultural Change* 30 (July 1982): 697–738.

"Distributions of Households by Size: Differences and Trends." In *Research in Population Economics* 4, edited by Julian L. Simon and Peter H. Lindert. Greenwich, Conn.: JAI Press, 1982.

"Modern Economic Growth and the Less Developed Countries (LDCs)." In *Experiences and Lessons of Economic Development in Taiwan*, edited by Kwoh-ting Li and Tzong-shian Yu. Taipei: Academia Sinica, 1982, pp. 11–20.

"The Pattern of Shift of Labor Force from Agriculture, 1950–1970." In *The Theory and Experience of Economic Development: Essays in Honor of Sir W. Arthur Lewis*, edited by Mark Gersovitz, Carlos F. Diaz-Alejandro, Gustav Ranis, and Mark R. Rosenzweig. London: George Allen & Unwin, 1982.

"P. C. Mahalanobis: Some Personal Reminiscences." In *Samvadadhvam*, Indian Statistical Institute, vol. 10, no. 1 (December 1974): 33–34.

Book reviews

Alvin H. Hansen, *Business Cycle Theory: Its Development and Present Status*. In *Political Science Quarterly* 43 (1928): 452–54.

Dr. F. Schmidt, *Die Industriekonjunktur – ein Rechenfehler!* In *Journal of the American Statistical Association* 23 (1928): 218–20.

E. D. Mouzon, Jr., *The Determination of Secular Trends*. In *Journal of the American Statistical Association* 24 (1929): 445–46.

S. O. Zagorsky, *State Control of Industry in Russia During the War*. In *Political Science Quarterly* 44 (1929): 267–68.

A. Michelson, P. N. Apostol, and M. W. Bernatzky, *Russian Finance During the War*. In *Political Science Quarterly* 44 (1929): 269–70.

Baron B. E. Nolde, *Russia in the Economic War*. In *Political Science Quarterly* 44 (1929): 271–72.

Lucy D. W. Wilson, *New Schools of Russia*. In *Political Science Quarterly* 44 (1929): 272.

H. N. Brailsford, *How the Soviets Work*. In *Political Science Quarterly* 44 (1929): 272.

Scott Nearing and Jack Hardy, *The Economic Organization of the Soviet Union*. In *Political Science Quarterly* 44 (1929): 273.

Robert W. Dunn, *Soviet Trade Unions*. In *Political Science Quarterly* 44 (1929): 273.

Karl Borders, *Village Life Under the Soviets*. In *Political Science Quarterly* 44 (1929): 273.

Julius Hecker, *Religion Under the Soviets*. In *Political Science Quarterly* 44 (1929): 274.

R. Page Arnot, *Soviet Russia and Her Neighbors*. In *Political Science Quarterly* 44 (1929): 275.

Jessica Smith, *Women in Soviet Russia*. In *Political Science Quarterly* 44 (1929): 276.

Annie J. Haines, *Health Work in Soviet Russia*. In *Political Science Quarterly* 44 (1929): 276.

Walter Hahn, *Die Statistische Analyse der Konjunkturschwingungen, Probleme der Weltwirtschaft*. In *Journal of the American Statistical Association* 25 (1930): 372–73.

L. Hersch, *Seasonal Unemployment in the Building Industry in Certain European Countries*. In *Journal of the American Statistical Association* 25 (1930): 486.

John E. Partington, *Railroad Purchasing and the Business Cycle*. In *Journal of the American Statistical Association* 26 (1931): 231–33.

Horace Secrist, *Banking Ratios*. In *Annals of the American Academy of Political and Social Science* 154 (1931): 174.

Lewis H. Haney, *Business Forecasting*. In *Journal of the American Statistical Association* 27 (1932): 116–18.

Colin Clark, *The National Income, 1924–1931*. In *Journal of the American Statistical Association* 28 (1933): 363–64.

Howard S. Ellis, *German Monetary Theory, 1905–1933*. In *Annals of the American Academy of Political and Social Science* 178 (1935): 206–7.

R. F. Fowler, *The Depreciation of Capital*. In *Annals of the American Academy of Political and Social Science* 179 (1935): 258.

Walter Rautenstrauch, *Who Gets the Money?* In *Journal of the American Statistical Association* 30 (1935): 642–43.

Wilbert G. Fritz, *Contributions to Business Cycle Theory*. In *Annals of the American Academy of Political and Social Science* 184 (1936): 224–25.

John Strachey, *The Nature of the Capitalist Crisis*. In *Annals of the American Academy of Political and Social Science* 184 (1936): 227–29.

Gerhard Tintner, *Prices in the Trade Cycle*. In *Annals of the American Academy of Political and Social Science* 185 (1936): 241–42.

Harold G. Moulton, *The Formation of Capital, and Income and Economic Progress*. In *Political Science Quarterly* 51 (1936): 300–306.

Harold G. Moulton and others, *America's Capacity to Produce, America's Capacity to Consume, the Formation of Capital, and Income and Economic Progress*. For the Brookings Institution. In *Science and Society* 1 (1937): 241–47.

Dan Throop Smith, *Deficits and Depressions*. In *Annals of the American Academy of Political and Social Science* 193 (1937): 200–201.

A. L. Bowley, *Wages and Income in the United Kingdom since 1860*. In *Journal of the American Statistical Association* 33 (1938): 456–58.

Harold F. Clark, assisted by Mervyn Crobaugh, Wilbur I. Gooch, Byrne J. Horton, and Rosemary N. Kurtak, *Life Earnings in Selected Occupations in the United States*. In *American Economic Review* 28 (1938): 374–76.

Maurice Leven, *The Income Structure of the United States*. In *Annals of the American Academy of Political and Social Science* 198 (1938): 228–30.

Erik Lindahl, Einar Dahlgren, and Karin Kock, *National Income of Sweden, 1861–1930, pts. 1 and 2*. In *Journal of Political Economy* 46 (1938): 425–29.

Alvin H. Hansen, *Full Recovery or Stagnation?* In *American Economic Review* 28 (1938): 752–53.

Committee of Statistical Experts, League of Nations, "Statistics Relating to Capital Formation: A Note on Methods." In *Journal of Political Economy* 47 (1939): 738–40.

Michal Kalecki, *Essays in the Theory of Economic Fluctuations*. In *American Economic Review* 29 (1939): 804–6.

Leonard P. Ayres, *Turning Points in Business Cycles*. In *Annals of the American Academy of Political and Social Science* 209 (1940): 232–33.

Colin Clark, *The Conditions of Economic Progress*. In *Manchester School of Economics and Social Studies* 12 (1941): 28–34.

Alvin H. Hansen, *Fiscal Policy and Business Cycles*. In *Annals of the American Academy of Political and Social Science* 217 (1941): 214–15.

Wassily W. Leontief, *The Structure of the American Economy, 1919–1929*. In *Journal of Economic History* 1 (1941): 246.

Alvin H. Hansen, *Fiscal Policy and Business Cycles*. In *Review of Economic Statistics* 24 (1942): 31–36.

Studies in the National Income, 1924–1938, edited by A. L. Bowley. In *Review of Economic Statistics* 26 (1944): 99–100.

Leon H. Dupriez, *Des Mouvements Economiques Généraux*. In *Journal of the American Statistical Association* 42 (1947): 639–41.

Oscar Morgenstern, *On the Accuracy of Economic Observations*. In *Journal of the American Statistical Association* 45 (1950): 576–79.

Alvin H. Hansen, *Business Cycles and National Income*. In *American Economic Review* 41 (1951): 967–71.

Joseph A. Schumpeter, *History of Economic Analysis*. In *Journal of Economic History* 15 (1955): 323–25.

Talcott Parsons and Neil J. Smelser, *Economy and Society: A Study in the Integration of Economic and Social Theory*. In *Annals of the American Academy of Political and Social Science* 312 (1957): 175–76.

Edward F. Denison, "The Sources of Economic Growth in the United States." In *Challenge* (April 1962): 44–45.

Index

Abramovitz, Moses, 436
aged, the, 83; and consumption, 85; and dissaving, 85; and income, 84–5; and work, 83–4
Africa, sub-Saharan, 261, 322–3
Ajami, I, 102n, 129
Anand, Sudhir, 436
Arriaga, Eduardo, E., 118n, 130
Asia: East 261, 322–3; Middle East, 261, 322–3; Middle South, 261; South East, 322–3

Barclay, George W., 362n
Bedau, Klaus-Dietrich, 177n
Ben-Porath, Yoram, 109n, 437
Bergson, Abram, 437
birth rates: of less developed countries (LDC), 87–99, 102–3, 105–6; and social norms, 108–9, 111; of the U.S., 78
Brazil, 250–5
Burch, T. K., 276n

Caldwell, John C., 118n, 130
Caribbean, 322–3
Chenery, H., 53, 59, 67
Chile, 257–60
China, 97
Clark, Colin, 130
Coale, A. J., 276n

Danziger, Sheldon, 278n
David, P. A., 437
Davis, Kingsley, 92n, 101, 130
death rates: of less developed countries (LDC), 87–99, 103–6; of the U.S., 79, 81–2

deflation procedures and rates of growth, 17
developed countries, other, 261

economic costs of death, 118–29
economic growth: acceleration of, 8; diffusion of, 20–1, 71; and diversity, 21; and economies of scale, 11; and education, 16–17, 19, 118; and fixed capital, 11–12; and international flows, 22; measurement of, 8, 17, 19, 25–6, 28; obstacles to, 72–3; and production structure, 15–18, 30–67, 69, 108; and science, 10; and social and institutional changes, 12–13; and the sovereign national state, 18, 20–6, 70, 73–4; and technical innovation, 8–14; unpredictability of, 13–14; and war, 22–3
economic measurement, 5–6, 8, 17, 19, 25–6, 28, 419–29
economies of scale and economic growth, 11
Ecuador, 257–60
education and economic growth, 16–17, 19, 118
Engerman, S. L., 437
Europe: developed, 261, 322–3; other, 322–3; overseas offshoots, 322–3

families, modal, 402–10
family, defined, 371n
family structure, rural and urban areas, 257–68
Fei, J. C. W., 437
Fields, Gary S., 437
Finland, 257–60

461